PASSION AND PRINCIPLE

PASSION AND PRINCIPLE

John and Jessie Frémont, the Couple
Whose Power, Politics, and Love Shaped
Nineteenth-Century America

SALLY DENTON

BLOOMSBURY

Published by Bloomsbury USA, New York
Distributed to the trade by Holtzbrinck Publishers

All papers used by Bloomsbury USA are natural, recyclable products made from wood grown in well-managed forests. The manufacturing processes conform to the environmental regulations of the country of origin.

LIBRARY OF CONGRESS CATALOGING-IN-PUBLICATION DATA

Denton, Sally.
    Passion and principle : John and Jessie Frémont, the couple whose power, politics, and love shaped nineteenth-century america / Sally Denton.—1st U.S. ed.
        p. cm.
    Includes bibliographical references and index.
    ISBN 978-1-59691-019-5 (alk. paper)
    1. Frémont, John Charles, 1813–1890.   2. Frémont, Jessie Benton, 1824–1902.
3. Frémont, John Charles, 1813–1890—Marriage.   4. Explorers—West (U.S.)—
Biography.   5. Pioneers—West (U.S.)—Biography.   6. Generals—United States—
Biography.   7. Politicians—United States—Biography.   8. Women pioneers—
West (U.S.)—Biography.   9. Politicians' spouses—United States—Biography.
10. Married people—United States—Biography.   I. Title.

    E415.9.F8D46   2007
    973.6092'2—dc22
    [B]

                                                                    2007002000

First U.S. Edition 2007

1   3   5   7   9   10   8   6   4   2

Typeset by Westchester Book Group
Printed in the United States of America by Quebecor World Fairfield

For Bob Trapp,
finest newspaperman in the American West
of any century

CONTENTS

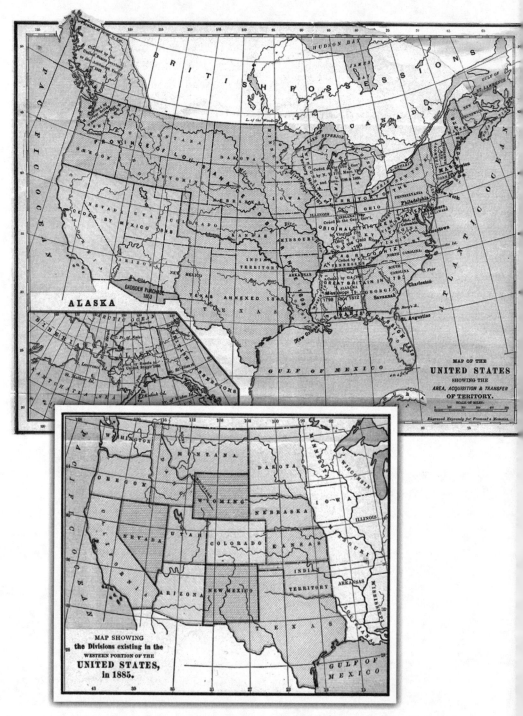

Maps showing the acquisition of American territory and divisions as they evolved between 1840 and 1885. The maps were commissioned by John C. Frémont, to be published in his 1887 memoir. (Author's personal collection.)

PROLOGUE

It is late February 1840. The air is crisp, though not cold. The trees are laden with tiny buds that announce the arrival of Washington's all-too-brief spring, those few weeks of starkly blue skies and fresh foliage before the city begins the inexorable march into its season of heat and humidity. The rudiments of the French urban planner Charles L'Enfant are in place—the radial avenues, emerging from the Capitol—but still just a grand vision, not a reality. The unpaved roads, overgrown fields dotted with shanties, unsightly slave pens, open sewage pits, animals roaming the city of thirty thousand souls, makeshift saloons and gambling halls—the seat of government a far cry from the elegant capital of the future.

Georgetown's elite Miss English's Female Seminary is an oasis of gentility near the still-crude capital of marble edifices and muddy streets. The tree-shaded estate on the heights of the Potomac is surrounded by manicured rose gardens and strawberry fields, and by the mansions of diplomats and bureaucrats whose Thoroughbred horses carry them the three miles into the seat of government. A very proper Danish woman, Miss English, boasts twenty-five teachers and forty-five boarders—the daughters of the South's most cultivated families.

Jessie Ann rushes into the drawing room, breathless with anticipation at seeing her father. She is a raven-haired beauty, he a towering frontiersman. The two have had a legendary bond throughout her sixteen years of life, Jessie acting as Thomas Hart Benton's constant companion and confidante, a surrogate for her invalid mother. They are the talk of the town, traveling in the most rarefied social and political circles of this raucous, dusty capital. Their symbiosis is envied, her devotion to him inspiring. She has missed him dreadfully and can't wait for their reunion. She is known for her magnetism and loveliness—considered by many to be the prettiest girl in Washington—the large, expressive brown eyes, the rich, dark hair parted in the center and pulled back in the fashion of the day, the full lips and slim figure hinted at beneath her rustling silk gowns. He is not just any father, not merely the dominant man in her life, but also the most powerful senator in America.

She is his consort and collaborator, his apprentice and creation. But now she is rebelling at her father's sending her to what she disdainfully calls "a Society School." She has no use for the petty restrictions of the snobbish finishing school. She is determined today to persuade her beloved father to resume her tutoring at his knee.

She is desperate to return to the small desk that sits in the corner of Benton's library next to the fireplace, where a young Jessie has served as her father's secretary, taking his dictation and ultimately helping him research and write his many speeches. It is at this desk that she has seen and heard so much, all that has made Miss English's seem so shallow and irrelevant. It is in this book-lined room where for years she sat patiently and quietly as a string of dignitaries—politicians, explorers, scientists, and diplomats—have come to see her father, a prevailing force for American expansion and what would become Manifest Destiny. Many Washington men covet this role Benton enjoys with Jessie. She has already had two proposals of marriage, including one from President Martin Van Buren, prompting Benton to cloister his daughter in the rural academy.

Benton took her quail hunting, introduced her to bird-watching with his friend John Audubon, taught her five languages, and impressed upon her the importance of disciplining her mind and exercising her body. She was often deposited for hours at the congressional library, where she learned to read from Thomas Jefferson's six-thousand-volume collection of books. From her earliest years, Jessie accompanied Benton to Senate debates and was as comfortable in the White House as in her own home, where Andrew Jackson tangled her child's locks with his fingers while discussing politics with her father, one of Jackson's strongest supporters in fighting the Bank of the United States and building the Democratic Party.

But Jessie has not just learned the classics and accompanied her father as an attractive escort. Her immersion in her father's political world has been complete, giving her a sensibility lacking in other girls of her generation. All that she has heard and imbibed are as much a part of her education as any refinement of arts, literature, and culture. Very much her father's daughter, she is as trained and astute a politician as any young man her age. A later president, James Buchanan, would call Jessie "the square root of Tom Benton." Another observer will refer to her as "a Benton in petticoats."

Lately at the family home on C Street—a massive, ivy-covered structure with thick walls and spacious rooms, gleaming wooden floors and polished banisters—something new is going on, something Jessie cannot bear to be missing. The oak table in the study is piled with colorful maps of the still uncharted American West. She has long been thrilled and intrigued by the constant discussion of expansionism, the girl an armchair adventurer before she was a teen. With all of this new excitement and breadth, Jessie bridles even more at the snooty academy. She feels no rapport with her fellow students—mostly the conceited daughters of senators, congressmen, and army and navy officers. She finds the focus on music and deportment mundane compared to the academic curriculum her father imposed on her. She spends her time fomenting dissent among the adolescent girls, defiantly climbing an immense mulberry tree whose limbs reach up to her second-story window and on whose branches she routinely tears her dresses.

"Miss Jessie, although extremely intelligent, lacks the docility of a model student," a letter from the academy has informed her father. "Moreover, she has the objectionable manner of seeming to take our orders and assignments under consideration, to be accepted or disregarded by some standard of her own." While the missive is designed to compel Benton to rein in his feisty daughter lest she become an embarrassment, Jessie hopes it has had the opposite effect. He hasn't raised her—the unmistakable favorite of his six children—to be a parlor creature, and she instinctively knows he will be both proud and unsurprised by her independent streak.

Today, her sister Eliza, a quiet, unimaginative girl two years older than Jessie, will perform a Bach fugue at the school. After the musicale, Jessie intends to do whatever is necessary to make her father relent and take her home. A hundred guests have gathered in the school's auditorium. Heavy indigo velvet curtains are pulled open, allowing in the last rays of daylight. A row of floor candles illuminates the small stage where an oval grand piano awaits Eliza.

Jessie enters the room where she gets a glimpse of a sultry uniformed officer standing at her father's side. Spellbound by his Gallic good looks, she makes her way slowly toward them. She can't take her eyes off the dusky, blue-eyed young man. His slight stature is oddly imposing, his tanned face and flashing white teeth rarities in this setting. She embraces her father and turns to his companion.

"May I present Lieutenant John Charles Frémont," Benton introduces the gentleman. She extends her hand, and finds that she can barely speak when he brushes it with his lips. He, too, is enchanted, struck by what he later calls her "girlish beauty and perfect health." The moment that passes between the twenty-seven-year-old explorer and sixteen-year-old Washington belle is one of the most fatefully charged in American history. Neither forgets it, and neither will the nation forget the two.

Frémont is fresh from an expedition exploring the plateau country between the Mississippi and Missouri rivers, now in Washington to report his findings to the president—Jessie's disappointed suitor, Martin Van Buren. The young surveyor has been ensconced at a Capitol Hill town house belonging to the Swiss scientist Ferdinand R. Hassler. Frémont's mentor, the distinguished astronomer Joseph Nicolas Nicollet, built an observatory on top of Hassler's house, where the three men chart the night sky and where Frémont has been creating an enormous map of his recent findings. Word spread through the capital, prompting senators and congressmen to drop by the town house. Among the first and most enthusiastic is Missouri's stalwart Senator Benton, who is intoxicated by his desire to probe the American West to open trade with India. He is enamored with this attractive and engaging young man—just the instrument he seeks to fulfill the national destiny he envisions. The men have an instant bond. Frémont sees in this thunderingly potent senator an articulation of the dreams still amorphous in Frémont's own imaginings. They are truly kindred spirits. In only a short while they have come not only to a mutual admiration, but also to a common vision of America's future, though this vision, like much else in their lives, will ultimately diverge. They have talked late into several nights, the avuncular Benton tutoring John in the same way he has mentored his own daughter. These conversations, Frémont later recalls, "gave shape and solidity to my own crude ideas."

Suddenly there is a new ingredient in the dynamic. The senator is noticeably alarmed by the instant attraction Jessie and John have for each other. He knows, as much of Washington does, that Frémont, for all his courage and adventure in the West, is also a poor man of dubious background and breeding. He is not a suitable mate for the senator's exceptional daughter. But what Benton sees now are two young people visibly and beguilingly drawn to one another, and he feels the stirrings of something unsettling. This looming figure is suddenly powerless in the face of something larger, something he recognizes directly. He stares at Jessie, perhaps really sees her for the first time. She is no longer a child, but the strong, decisive woman he has formed. Did he not expect that he would make a woman like this, a woman who would know her own mind?

Brusquely, uneasily, Benton ushers her out. From that moment, this couple is passionately, historically enmeshed—John her "very perfect gentle knight," Jessie his "rose of rare color." The romance and the alliance, the passion and the principle, that begin that Washington day will be entwined with the destiny of a continent. What begins in this room will have an impact on the making of a great nation, from the founding of a new American political party to the country's torment of Civil War and slavery. But for now, they are just two young people completely smitten with each other.

"At last I've met a handsomer man than Cousin Preston," Jessie giddily remarks that evening.

Frémont goes home and confides to his dear friend and patron Nicollet, "I have fallen in love at first sight."

1

JOHN 1813–1840

Before him lies a boundless continent, and he urges forward as if time pressed and he was afraid of finding no room for his exertions.

—Alexis de Tocqueville,
Democracy in America

BORN JANUARY 21, 1813, in Savannah, Georgia, into a scandalous love triangle, John Charles Frémont seemed destined to wander. "About [his] cradle hung as dark clouds as have surrounded the infancy of any notable American," wrote Allan Nevins, one of Frémont's first biographers—"the clouds of illegitimacy, poverty, and total uncertainty of the future." Quiet but proud offspring of Virginia gentility and either French royalty or Canadian merchants—depending on which conflicting histories one credits—John was indisputably the love child of an unlikely match.

His father, Jean Charles Fremon—the *t* and *accent aigu* added to his son's name many years later—had escaped Lyons during the French Revolution on a passenger ship bound for Saint Domingue, according to most biographical versions. After a British man-of-war captured the ship, Fremon was among the many taken prisoner and held on one of the English islands for an unknown number of years. Other historical and genealogical accounts identify Frémont's father as a French-Canadian named Louis-René Frémont—with both the *t* and the accent—born in Québec to Jean Louis and Catherine Reine. This Louis-René filed in 1800 for a seat in Québec's parliament, the Chambre de l'Assemblée, but withdrew his candidacy before the election. He then traveled from

Canada to Saint Domingue—now Haiti—where he intended to join a relative who lived in the colony, which Napoleon had recently restored to French rule, and where slaves and free blacks had overthrown the French elite.

By all accounts, Jean Charles Fremon was imprisoned for several years, making willow baskets and painting frescoes on the ceilings of the Spanish-style mansions of the wealthy landholders, for which he was paid a small prisoner's stipend. He somehow made good his escape, apparently intending to return to either Canada or France, landing first in Norfolk, Virginia, in 1808, with his paltry savings, and where he apparently joined his brother Francis Fremon. Now calling himself Charles Fremon, the slender, dark-skinned immigrant began teaching his native language to Norfolk's privileged society. The Southern states were brimming with French refugees, who were held in high regard by the local Francophiles.

Fluent in English and exceedingly courteous, the charismatic nomad was quickly accepted by the old colonial families of the Tidewater region. His charisma drew people to him—a shock of black hair, impeccable manners, dancing dark eyes, and a pleasant personality. Before long he abandoned his notion of returning to his homeland, finding Virginia pleasant and profitable, and accepted a teaching job at William and Mary College, midway between Norfolk and Richmond. But when a position became available at the desirable Richmond academy run by the scholar Louis H. Girardin, Fremon eagerly moved to the thriving Virginia capital. A longtime friend of Thomas Jefferson, Girardin and his partner, David Doyle, had educated the progeny of Virginia's most prominent families. Fremon's acceptance into this highbrow and reputable establishment gave him entrée into the city's upper-class society.

Both Girardin and Doyle found him a welcome addition to the faculty, but when rumors began circulating that he was cohabiting with an unmarried Richmond woman, they confronted him. Rather than deny the reports of his libertine behavior, Fremon took offense at their interference in his private life, boldly declaring, "I will do as I please." Girardin dismissed the charming rake, charging he was not "a fit person to give instructions to young ladies." The incident had little effect on the teacher's standing in the community—he remained a favorite guest at the best homes—and he was soon back at Girardin's academy. "Richmond people do not care much about these things," Doyle's successor, John Wood, said upon rehiring Fremon.

Fremon ended his affair with the unknown woman and rented a cottage at the Haymarket Gardens, a verdant recreational park that Major John Pryor owned on the banks of the James River. A prominent Revolutionary War veteran who had fought under George Washington, Pryor was a wealthy Richmond businessman, proprietor of the largest livery stable in the capital, and secretary of the influential Jockey Club. The repulsively vulgar seventy-five-year-old was notorious not only for his shady horse racing ventures but also for his arresting thirty-year-old wife. The improbable match was a classically tawdry tale of decayed southern gentry and social expediency. Charles Fremon's emergence as Anne Pryor's French teacher would only add to the drama.

Anne Beverley Whiting was the youngest of fifteen children. Her father, Colonel Thomas Whiting, a Virginia landholder who had been a leading member of the House of Burgesses, had been the king's attorney before the American Revolution. President of the Naval Board during the Revolution—a most dignified position—Whiting's lineage traced a connection through marriage to George Washington, whom he had held as an infant during the future president's baptism. His Elmington estate encompassed all the acreage in Gloucester County between the North and Ware rivers. It was to his third wife, Elizabeth Sewall, that Anne was born.

Whiting died when Anne was six months old. His estate was divided equally among his surviving children, each of whom also received "thirty negroes," according to his will. As a baby, Anne was powerless to protect her inheritance, and when her mother married Samuel Carey, Anne's fortune dwindled as Carey directed the family's finances. The five children from Whiting's first marriage engaged in protracted, and apparently unsuccessful, litigation against Carey in an effort to acquire control of the bequests. With the death of her mother, the orphaned Anne found the Carey home intolerable—"disagreeable from the vexations of lawsuits"—and moved in with her married sister Catherine.

By age seventeen, Anne had blossomed into a graceful belle, and Catherine avidly sought a suitable mate for the dispossessed girl. She settled on John Pryor as Anne's deliverer from what one observer called "the greatest of all calamities, poverty." Anne was repulsed by the gouty and crude man forty-five years her senior, and rebuffed his pursuit despite her sister's ardent efforts. Finally she relented, apparently entering the marriage in 1796 with stoic resignation. Her dowry included "the negroes contained in lot No. 3"—three men, two women, and two children who apparently constituted what was left of her inheritance.

From the start the arrangement was problematic, he a cantankerous and impotent elderly man—"a disabled, stiff-limbed old soldier," the *Richmond Dispatch* later portrayed him—she increasingly desperate in the loveless, childless union. Her bride's nest was a modest, rambling structure on the grounds of Haymarket Gardens, consisting of two long wings and attached servants' quarters. "I was married too young to be sensible of the importance of the state in which I was about to enter," Anne wrote afterward, "and found when too late that I had acted with too much precipitancy, and could never feel that love for him to whom I was united, without which the marriage state of all others is the most wretched."

For twelve years she suffered in silence, eventually refusing to join Pryor in the fast-paced horsy set that was her husband's milieu, and slipping steadily into what was then called melancholia—the nineteenth-century euphemism for depression. Not until the stunningly handsome and wildly romantic Jean Fremon came to Richmond in 1810—taking up lodging on Pryor's estate—did Anne feel the stirrings of love for the first time in her life. Hired by Pryor to teach French to Anne, Fremon lured her smoothly into an affair. Though as discreet as possible, their mutual arousal was impossible to hide, especially for the Byronic Fremon. They planned to wait for Pryor to die—then Anne would inherit his abundant holdings and the two would be free to marry—but their designs were preempted when her husband learned of the illicit liaison.

The hot-tempered Pryor confronted the two lovers on July 9, 1811, threatening first to kill Anne. "You may spare yourself the crime," she railed at him. "I shall leave your house tomorrow morning forever!" The two men exchanged threats, each vowing to kill the other, but by dawn the next day Anne and Charles had left Richmond. "I did not run away, but was turned out of doors at night and in an approaching storm," Anne later claimed. Anne "totally alienated her affections from me by the vile and invidious machinations of an execrable monster of baseness and depravity, with whom I have recently discovered she has for some time past indulged in criminal intercourse," Pryor declared in his divorce petition, published in the *Virginia Patriot*.

On the eve of the War of 1812, Richmond was a flourishing community of some seven thousand, what historian Jay Winik described as "a thriving hybrid of old-fashioned Southern gentility and newfangled

urban enterprise." Such a city was primed to find interest in the couple's
scurrilous conduct, and the scandal was rich fodder for gossip among
Richmond's patrician society. But Anne and Charles embarked on their
own adventure, apparently following Fremon's long-standing, and
mysterious, interest in the character and condition of North American
Indians, touring the Indian regions of the southeastern United States.
Combining their assets, they loaded their belongings onto a stagecoach,
and along with two of her slaves set out for Williamsburg and then Norfolk, where Anne would collect additional possessions in those towns—
property Anne had apparently been granted the previous year as a result
of litigation against her father's estate.

Family lore would have it that they had enough money between them
to "gratify Fremon's wish to tour the South and learn something of the
habits of the Indians, in which he felt a keen interest." His unexplained
anthropological curiosity about American Indians is said to have fostered
an early attachment to the subject in his son, John, the legend of his
ethnographic exploration evolving with John's future fame. Though the
story was no doubt embellished by a succeeding generation, the evidence suggests that the couple did indeed move from town to town, often camping for extended periods with Native Americans.

By October, they were settled in a tiny brick house in Savannah, Georgia, on the property of one of that town's more prominent citizens. Located in what was then known as the Yamacraw section of the small city,
they set up housekeeping while awaiting her final divorce so they could
marry. Their funds nearly exhausted, Charles began advertising his services as a teacher of French and dancing instructor, and Anne sought
boarders to supplement their meager holdings. "We are poor," she wrote
a friend at this time, "but we can be content with little, for I have found
that happiness consists not in riches."

The Virginia House of Delegates declined Pryor's divorce petition on
December 11, 1811, and when Anne's first child, John Charles, was born
January 21, 1813, the birth was possibly out of wedlock. Much would be
made of John's illegitimacy later in his life—by both political rivals and
psychological biographers—his future marred by "the dual heritage of
scandal and the blunt label of bastard." Observers would attribute John's
driving ambition, remote personality, and defiance of authority to this
hapless beginning. Still, his early family life was affectionate and
stimulating—his nanny the bighearted "Black Hannah," inherited by his
mother, had accompanied the family from Richmond. Overall it was a

time that he remembered with fondness despite its many hardships. "A child of love, a child who knew the meaning of discrimination before he knew the word," wrote his biographer Ferol Egan, "Frémont came from a background with all the trappings of a Charles Dickens novel."

Shortly after John's birth, the couple took to wandering again. John later recalled his first memories as those of Indian villages, where his parents and their servants would tether their horses, aromatic smoke permeating their campsite. In an ironic twist of fate the toddler narrowly escaped a bullet fired by his future father-in-law. In September 1813, the Fremons were temporarily lodged at a Nashville hotel—alternatively identified in historical accounts as the City Hotel and Clayton Talbot's Tavern—where Thomas Hart Benton and his brother, Jesse, also were guests. Then an up-and-coming lawyer and Tennessee politician, Benton had come to Nashville to confront General Andrew Jackson, who had acted as a second for Jesse Benton's rival in a recent duel. The town had poured out to greet Jackson, celebrated for his role as a fighter of Indians and for his heroic march from Natchez to Nashville during the War of 1812. Undaunted by Jackson's fame and support, Benton was determined to avenge what he considered Jackson's brutal treatment of Jesse. Such frontier violence was commonplace, the days of Daniel Boone still fresh in the young nation's mind.

"The quarrel was an opera bouffe episode," according to historian Nevins, Jackson widely proclaiming his intention to horsewhip Benton. But after a volley of gunshots and a series of physical blows, it was Jackson who was carried away bleeding—the blood from the injury soaking two mattresses and leaving Jackson perilously close to death. The fracas left a minié ball from Jesse's pistol lodged in the future president's shoulder, and another stray bullet meant for Jackson penetrated the thin wall of the hotel room where John was sleeping with his traveling parents. Out of the duel between Jackson and Benton grew a friendship and political alliance that would benefit them both—and, fatefully, John.

The family would stay at least a year in Nashville, where Anne gave birth to their daughter, Elizabeth. They then moved back to Norfolk, hoping to settle permanently. Now that Pryor had died, Charles and Anne were free to marry—though there is no evidence that they ever did so—and the scandal that had surrounded their elopement had faded, though it was never wholly forgotten. Anne had many family members in Norfolk. Charles's brother, Francis, also still lived there, and the couple's third child, a boy named Horation "Frank" Francis, would be born there in 1817.

It had been seven of the happiest, most adventurous and fun-loving years of her life, Anne was by all accounts unconcerned about their improvident circumstances and passionately in love with her husband. But when Charles died suddenly that same year, she was left in utter poverty, a widow with three small children. Francis Fremon urged her to move to France with him. The recent accidental fatal shooting of Francis's sixteen-year-old son at a Fourth of July celebration had left him mourning and desirous of returning to his native land. There, Francis assured Anne, the Fremon clan would embrace her brood. But Anne felt herself an ingrained American and would not consider relocating.

Instead, she moved into quarters near the Dinwiddie Courthouse, where John received his first formal instruction. Little is known of their time in Norfolk after Charles's death, though Anne had now taken to calling herself "Mrs. Fremont" with the *t*. How she survived, owning no property and at thirty-seven years old facing an unpredictable and precarious future, can be attributed to her fortitude, energy, and devotion to her children. She would focus her hopes and dreams on her firstborn son, and John would gallantly rise to the call. He adored his mother, whom he saw as "a woman of most extraordinary grace and beauty, of gentle, captivating manners, with a sweet but singularly melancholy disposition." From that early bond forged with a romantic and independent woman his own respect and admiration of women would be formed.

In 1823, Anne, now nearly destitute, turned her sights several hundred miles down the coast to Charleston, South Carolina, determined as she was to rear her children in genteel surroundings while also offering them the opportunity that the bustling trade center might afford.

Founded in 1670, and originally called Charles Towne for King Charles II of England—who had granted the Carolina Territory to eight of his cronies—the Charleston the wandering Fremont family embraced was far more sophisticated and refined than the haunts of their early existence. Later known as "the Antebellum City," it stretched languidly on a peninsula between the Ashley and Cooper rivers, or, as proud Charlestonians would say, the site where "the Ashley and Cooper rivers merge to form the Atlantic Ocean." Lush magnolia and cypress gardens graced the city, which boasted the College of Charleston, one of the nation's oldest colleges, as well as the country's first theater building. In the plantation economy of the post-Revolutionary decades, Charleston's port—one of the busiest in the country—was crowded with ships bearing exports of cotton and indigo.

While most of its white settlers had been English, the city of twenty-three thousand had a black majority, a large French population, and was home to a diverse population of varied ethnic and religious backgrounds. Even at its inception, the city exhibited a legendary tolerance, welcoming Sephardic Jews—making it one of the largest Jewish communities in North America—as well as persecuted French Huguenots. The social inclusiveness was a paradox with the slave-ridden ships pouring into the Charleston port at the same moment.

None of the city's complexity or irony would be lost on the young John Charles Frémont. The wealthiest and largest city south of Philadelphia, Charleston would be fertile intellectual, social, and political ground for the brilliant adolescent. Its cobblestone streets and Spanish moss–covered oaks, its ironwork balconies and pastel stucco homes nestled amid colonial brick mansions, the blend of Caribbean whimsy and stately Southern decorum, all served to capture the young man's imagination and sense of adventure. Though not an aristocratic heir, John would find unparalleled access to the old South's bastion of culture and society in this rousing environment. He moved among the slaves whose toil as artisans and domestics, plantation laborers and clerks, drove the city, and listened to their strange dialect—a combination of African, Portuguese, and English—forming the beginnings of a later passion for their cause. "Negroes abounded, for it was a poor planter or merchant who did not keep a half dozen servants in attendance upon his stables, table, and household," wrote a historian about the time and place, "their merry chatter filled the streets, and their songs echoed from the wharves, covered with imported luxuries and West Indian products—barrels of molasses, bags of coffee, cocoanuts [sic], and bananas—as well as Carolina staples."

But above all, it was a city of the mind, a city that prided itself in the intellectual pursuits of its notable families, clans that despite reversals of fortune since the Revolutionary War sought solace and enhancement in books and ideas. There, John would begin his education. By age thirteen he was clerking for John W. Mitchell, an outstanding attorney known for his erudition—with whom Anne hoped her son would learn a profession while earning a living at the same time. So impressed was Mitchell with the young man's acumen and enthusiasm that within a

year Mitchell had made financial arrangements for John to enter a select
academy run by Dr. Charles Roberton. Mitchell thought the stellar lad
more prone to the pulpit than the bar, and expressed his opinion to both
Frémont and Roberton. Educated at the University of Edinburgh, the
Scottish Roberton was a renowned classical scholar who had for years
been grooming the city's sons for entrance to the College of Charleston.
"He lived an inner life among the Greeks and Latins," Frémont later
wrote of his teacher. Roberton took a particular interest in John—"I
could not help loving him, so much did he captivate me"—a youth he
saw as "the very seat of genius." Placed in the most advanced class, John
was immediately earning top grades and attracting the attention of influential Charlestonians who saw something special in the young man with
the intense blue eyes, the inquisitive mind, the elegant manners, and
sculpted features. "I entered upon the study of Greek with genuine
pleasure and excitement. It had a mysterious charm for me as if behind
the strange characters belonging to an ancient world I was to find things
of wonderful interest." Slender and reserved, soft-spoken but forceful, he
was widely regarded as a talented and promising student, proceeding rapidly into the upper grades of the preparatory academy. Within a year he
had read Caesar, Homer, and Virgil, and seemed to retain everything he
saw, read, or heard, "as if he learned by mere intuition," one of his teachers recalled. So advanced were his academics—especially in mathematics—
that he entered college a junior. But he was also restless, facile, and
impetuous, traits that would interfere with his scholastic dedication, and
while learning came effortlessly to him, he was easily bored.

He inherited from both parents a physical beauty, an impulsive passion, the sense of victimized outcast, a roaming spirit, contempt for authority, and a reckless abandon—all of which would combine to form
the historic man he would become. The origins of his innate intelligence and burning ambition would be less apparent. Though confirmed
at St. Philip's Episcopal Church—the first Anglican church built in
Charleston—and considered virtuous and humble enough to pursue the
ministry, his passions lay elsewhere. "When I contemplated his bold,
fearless disposition," his teacher wrote of John, "his powerful inventive
genius, his admiration of warlike exploits, and his love of heroic and adventurous deeds, I did not think it likely he would be a minister of the
Gospel." So taken was he with Herodotus's Battle of Marathon—the
bravery of Miltiades and his ten thousand Greeks in their battle against
tyranny and oppression—and Xenophon's *Anabasis*, that he wrote poetry

inspired by the epics. He excelled in mathematics, "devoured myriad Greek and Latin texts," was fluent in French, having studied the language as well as speaking it at home with his father, proficient in astronomy, and had a photographic memory.

But by 1830 he was forced to drop out of school to help his mother financially, and went to work as a tutor for a wealthy plantation owner. During this time he fell in love with a Creole beauty named Cecilia, whose family had escaped a Dominican massacre. "They were all unusually handsome;" John later wrote, "clear brunette complexions, large dark eyes, and abundant blue-black hair." Her parents became his surrogates, her siblings his best friends, and for the first time in his life John felt a youthful abandon, boating, hunting, and fishing with his French-speaking comrades. It was also the first time he pushed his physical limits, sailing out into a crashing sea, traipsing through dangerous and wild backwoods, ascending precarious outcroppings. Years later he would reminisce about those fleeting moments—the "bit of sunshine that made the glory of my youth . . . days of unreflecting life when I lived in the glow of a passion that now I know extended its refining influence over my whole life."

He returned to college the following year, but the love affair had changed him. Though expected to be present on campus seven hours daily, John took to cutting classes and being ill-prepared when he attended. "Taking counsel of his heart, and not of his head," wrote one of his biographers, "he set college rules at defiance." Expelled for "habitual irregularity and incorrigible negligence," he mocked the seriousness with which the naysayers predicted his doom. "To me this came like summer wind that breathed over something sweeter than the 'bank whereon the wild thyme blows.' I smiled to myself while I listened to words about the disappointment of friends—and the broken career. I was living in a charmed atmosphere and their edict only gave me complete freedom."

Though responding irreverently and insouciantly at his expulsion, the turn of events marked a series of personal setbacks. First, his seventeen-year-old sister, Elizabeth, died. At about the same time, his fifteen-year-old brother, Frank, abruptly left home to seek fame and fortune as a stage actor, leaving a grief-stricken Anne dependent upon her oldest son. It was more necessary than ever to earn a living, his domestic circumstances forcing him into a more prudent and mature approach to life, and his relationship with his mother deepened as his zeal for Cecilia cooled.

He became a math instructor for John A. Wooten's private school, spending many of his hours in Wooten's "Apprentices' Library." It would be these days of independent study that perhaps contributed most to John's future professional choices, for here he found two books of life-changing relevance. Though their titles did not survive his later recollections, they both deeply affected him. One was a Dutch volume filled with astronomical calculations and exquisitely drawn maps of the stars—"by its aid I became well acquainted with the night skies and familiarized myself with the ordinary observations necessary to determine latitude and longitude." The other tome contrasted the acts of men "who had made themselves famous by brave and noble deeds, or infamous by cruel and base acts." While at Wooten's, he attracted the attention of one of Charleston's most famous citizens, and the man who would change his life.

Joel Roberts Poinsett had recently returned from a stint as minister to Mexico under President John Quincy Adams—bringing back the showy scarlet plant he contributed to botany, and that was later named for him—and held Sunday breakfasts with Charleston's promising young men. Poinsett was impressed with Frémont's quick wit and able mind.

Though Frémont's French heritage would later become a lightning rod for scandal and ostracism, it would be pivotal in his rise. He was blessed with a handful of forceful male mentors, the most important of whom would be Poinsett and a brilliant savant, astronomer, and French expatriate, Joseph Nicolas Nicollet. These men alone would win him several appointments and set the young explorer on his future course.

Highly educated and well traveled, the forty-nine-year-old Poinsett spent his boyhood in England, received early schooling at a Connecticut academy, studied medicine in Scotland, received training at Woolrich Military Academy, and studied law in both Great Britain and Charleston. As a young man the Charleston native had spent time in Russia and western Europe in preparation for a diplomatic career. By the time Poinsett met Frémont, Poinsett had observed colonial rebellions in South America, been instrumental in promoting Chile's independence from Spain, and served in both the South Carolina legislature and the U.S. Congress.

Hosted at his columned center-hall colonial on the outskirts of Charleston, Poinsett's famous weekly breakfasts included a revolving retinue of the city's best and brightest, with a stream of visiting dignitaries that included presidents, military commanders, and scientists. Though short and stocky, his comportment exuded an elegance of style; an academic mastery of varied subjects and languages; and, above all, a political sophistication that attracted the most skilled of politicians. Though born and bred a Southerner, he strongly disdained slavery, was an avid Unionist—siding with President Jackson against his own state's rights South Carolina colleagues—and his ministry in Mexico had instilled in him a growing passion for U.S. expansionism. As protégé of such an exceptional man, the twenty-year-old John Frémont would formulate a like-minded philosophy, while witnessing realpolitik from a coveted and intimate position. "When General Jackson's course drew the line in South Carolina," wrote Frémont half a century later, "I had joined the party of Mr. Poinsett and gave unwavering allegiance to the Union."

The South Carolina capital was alive with philosophical debate, with talk of expansionism, slavery, and states' rights permeating Poinsett's salons. Frémont was in the midst of it all, and when he expressed his desire to Poinsett for a civilian appointment from the U.S. Navy—no naval academy yet existed—Poinsett reluctantly intervened on his behalf, arranging for him to teach navigational mathematics on the sloop-of-war *Natchez* during a cruise to South America. The ship had entered the Charleston port to enforce General Jackson's proclamation against John C. Calhoun and the South Carolina nullifiers who were refusing to pay tariffs legislated by Congress. "By his aid but not with his approval," Frémont wrote of his mentor's halfhearted assistance, Poinsett disagreed with Frémont's entry into the navy but was eager to see him expand his horizons. John's affair with Cecilia now at an end, he welcomed the two-year appointment.

In May 1833 Frémont's journey would begin, and though filled with anticipation at the future opening before him, he was distressed at parting from his mother. "We were only two, my mother and I," he wrote of the separation. "Circumstances had more than usually endeared us to each other, and I knew that her life would be solitary without me."

During the voyage he returned to his own application, focusing now on astronomy, with his eye turned toward exploration. He studied Spanish to read Coronado and Cortés, and pored over books by and about General William Ashley and John Jacob Astor. Bored by the tedium of the ship and singularly unimpressed with the captain, Frémont found the highlight of the cruise to be when he was selected as a second in a duel between two young officers. In a bold and conniving move of which he would be proud, he conspired with the other second to replace the lead in the duelists' weapons with gunpowder, thereby possibly saving two lives. Greatly enjoying what he called "our little *ruse de guerre*," they carried the officers back to the ship, "nobody hurt and nobody wiser."

While he was at sea, Congress had authorized funding for several navy professorships in mathematics at an annual salary of $1,200. Shortly after returning with the *Natchez* to Charleston, John applied for the position and was ordered to appear before an examining board scheduled for May 1836. That gave him a month to prepare, a pleasant time back with his mother and friends. "All day long I was at my books, and the earliest dawn found me at an upper window against which stood a tall poplar, where the rustling of the glossy leaves made a soothing accompaniment. The surroundings go for a great deal in intellectual work." But it would be a full year before the appointment finally arrived, and by that time Frémont's life had taken a propitious and pivotal turn. In a stroke of the good fortune that now seemed to embrace him, his benefactor Poinsett had become secretary of war in 1837 in the new Martin Van Buren administration—an apparent quid pro quo for his loyal support of President Jackson against the treasonous nullifiers.

Part of Poinsett's bureaucratic domain, the U.S. Army's Bureau of Topographical Engineers was in the national spotlight as the agency charged with exploring the American frontier in the expansionist fervor of the moment. At the forefront of the public agenda was the forcible relocation of eastern Native American tribes to areas west of the Mississippi River, an application of the Indian Removal Act of 1830—what one historian has called "one of the cruelest acts in our national history"—and a highly unpopular policy among the Cherokees residing in Georgia, North Carolina, and Tennessee. "For the good of the bordering States, and for the welfare of the Indians as well, this was a wise and humane measure," Frémont wrote, indicating his solidarity with Jefferson's vision of an "empire of liberty for whites, with the inclusion of peaceable Indians," as one historian described it. "But the Cherokees were averse to the change."

Meanwhile, violent clashes between the relocated Indians and the indigenous tribes of the western region, as well as hostilities between white settlers and the Indians, prompted Poinsett to advocate building army forts connected by newly built roads and railroads. In the event of necessary military action, and to oversee the peaceful distribution of land, Poinsett ordered a reconnaissance survey for a railway route from Charleston to Cincinnati. Not only did Poinsett believe that such a railroad would open Charleston to commerce with the West, but, perhaps more importantly, "he envisioned it as a conduit by which more free, white laborers might migrate into the South, thus eroding the financial foundation of the region's slavery," according to Frémont biographer Tom Chaffin. Captain W. G. Williams would lead the expedition, and Poinsett arranged for Frémont to act as Williams's assistant.

Traveling on horseback through the wilderness, the twenty-four-year-old Frémont knew he had met his life's calling—"here I found the path which I was 'destined to walk.'" His fascination with the Indians, begun in childhood wanderings with his father, grew now into an absorption that would continue for the rest of his life. "Through many of the years to come the occupation of my prime of life was to be among Indians and its [America's] waste places . . . As it sometimes chanced, I was present at Indian feasts, where all would get wild with excitement and some furious with drink. Bloody frays were a certain accompaniment, slashing with knives, hands badly cut from clutching the blades and ugly body wounds. Their exhibition of brute courage and indifference to pain compelled admiration . . . but these were the exceptional occasion." All in all, he was less impressed with their savagery and far more impressed with their resourcefulness, industriousness, courage, and capability of being civilized, Christianized, and agrarianized. "In their villages and in their ordinary farming life they lived peaceably and comfortably . . . The depreciating and hurtful influence was the proximity of the whites." Ultimately, he would come to see Washington's ever-changing policies—now lax, now brutal, and ever political—as the principal detriment to their well-being.

At the end of the survey, he returned to Charleston, fit and tanned and burning with his newfound ambition. "Handsome as Lord Byron and as adventurous as Sir Richard Burton," as one biographer described him, Frémont was now firmly established on the path of science and exploration that would fix him in the nation's mythology.

Summoned to Washington by Secretary Poinsett, Frémont arrived in the capital in March 1838, just as the War Department finalized plans for an ambitious survey of the upper Mississippi and Missouri River basin. Poinsett secured from President Van Buren an appointment for Frémont as a second lieutenant in the Topographical Corps, an elite army unit of thirty-six officers, and the twenty-five-year-old Frémont anxiously awaited orders to join the historic expedition to map the nation's boundaries and chart routes to the great American West. With Poinsett his only friend in Washington, Frémont was consumed with what he called a "flattened lonesomeness," and was dispirited by the raw, ugly, and unimaginative city. He found the White House and the Capitol to be the only imposing structures, and the poplar-lined Pennsylvania Avenue the only thoroughfare worthy of being called an avenue. He lamented the lack of beauty in his physical surroundings, so immersed had he been in the outdoor life, finding in Washington "no attractive spot . . . where a stranger could go and feel the freedom of both eye and thought." Perhaps inheriting his mother's tendency toward melancholia, he exhibited the same ennui that had overtaken him in college, finding his cerebral and creative prowess stymied or aroused depending upon his environment—a portent of the restiveness that would mark his personal and professional life. "Shut in to narrow limits," he later wrote of the stifling hiatus in Washington, "the mind is driven in upon itself and loses its elasticity; but the breast expands when, upon some hill-top, the eye ranges over a broad expanse of country, or in the face of the ocean." When his much-anticipated orders finally came through, he quickly regained his solid emotional footing as elation replaced his gloom, and set out for St. Louis to prepare for the expedition.

Not only did Frémont receive one of the most coveted assignments in the War Department—a four-dollar-a-day mission his West Point counterparts would envy with a passion that would rise to outright hostility—but he was also granted the once-in-a-lifetime opportunity to work with the eminent and legendary Joseph N. Nicollet. The renowned mathematician, cartographer, and astronomer was at the peak of his career. Having immigrated to the United States from France in 1830, spurred by the exploits of his fellow countrymen La Salle and Champlain, the "Parisian intellectual," as Nicollet was called, had a driving aspiration to create the first geographical and topographical map of the entire country. Such a map had been sought since Thomas Jefferson's earliest forays into expansionist exploration, beginning in 1786 with his encouragement of American John Ledyard—"the Connecticut Marco Polo"—to cross the Bering Strait and explore the North American interior. Ledyard had sailed with Captain James Cook when the Englishman landed at Vancouver Island, buying from the natives furs he sold in China at a 160 percent profit. Ledyard had informed Jefferson, then U.S. minister to France, of the great trade opportunities in the Pacific Northwest. While Ledyard's expedition was cut short at the hands of Siberian police who arrested him as a spy, Jefferson was unfazed, arranging first for the American Philosophical Society to finance an ill-fated journey of the famous French naturalist André Michaux, to ascend the Missouri River, and, after Michaux was recalled on suspicion of being a French spy, planning in the spring of 1804 the "Grand Excursion"—an aborted exploration intended to chart the Red and Arkansas rivers that was halted by a Spanish army four times its size. Though that forgotten expedition—"blocked and forced to retrograde by a foreign power," as twentieth-century historian Dan Flores would describe it—receded into the annals of America's hidden history where failed exploits reside, its fate inextricably linked with the Aaron Burr conspiracy, it was in fact one of the earliest successful episodes of resistance to American imperialism, assuming the status of "an international incident," according to Flores, that came "precipitously close to involving the United States in a war with Imperial Spain." In one of "its last heroic acts of self-preservation in the Southwest," Flores wrote, "Spain mustered the resolve—and the military force—to resist." Still, Jefferson pursued his goal to establish a national presence throughout the continent that "both competing imperial powers and indigenous peoples would acknowledge," and ultimately, as president, was able to secure a secret appropriation from Congress for Meriwether Lewis and William Clark to find the source of the Missouri, locate a water route to the Pacific, and thoroughly document the geographical life along the way. "Their instructions from the President were detailed," according to one historical account, and it was clear that it was but one of several planned scientific probes into the American West. "They were to make observations on the latitude and longitude, temperature, rainfall, mountains, interlocking streams, animals, plants, and Indians."

The exciting reports from Lewis and Clark of mountains crowded with beaver promoted a thriving North American fur trade, but did little for providing accurate geographical information that could be incorporated into a map, and therefore promote westward migration. Their chronometer failed, making it impossible to determine longitude, and they were unable to make precise astronomical calculations necessary to establish latitude. In 1804, Baron Alexander von Humboldt, who had been exploring in Mexico, visited Washington and presumably provided Jefferson with the intelligence information that prompted the president to dispatch Zebulon Pike to the region. In 1806, at Jefferson's behest,

Pike ostensibly sought the source of the Mississippi, but in fact was primarily concerned with spying against the Spanish in New Mexico. Secondarily, Pike had explored the Arkansas and Red rivers, and eventually the Colorado and the upper Rio Grande, and ultimately reported, misleadingly, that the entire region was unfit for habitation. Arrested by Spanish troops, his notes confiscated, Pike was forced to rely solely on his memory in creating a report. U.S. Army major Stephen H. Long perpetuated that mythology after exploring the Platte, Purgatory, and Cimarron rivers, labeling the entire Plains region the Great American Desert—what would turn out to be a false description depicted on maps for the next fifty years. "In regard to this extensive section of country between the Missouri River and the Rocky Mountains," Long wrote, "we do not hesitate in giving the opinion that it is almost wholly unfit for cultivation, and of course uninhabitable by a people depending upon agriculture for their subsistence."

By the winter of 1838, nearly four decades of official exploration had been virtually useless, the Euro-American explorers apparently spending as much time and energy in the wholesale slaughter of animals as in the gathering of scientific specimens. (As historian Flores wrote in his insightful 2001 book *The Natural West,* "absorbing the mounting tension of these [Lewis and Clark] journal entries almost two centuries later, you're almost prompted to shout aloud at Meriwether Lewis, 'Christ Amighty, order them to stop shooting up grizzly bears!'")

The preeminent explorer of his day, and the first in America to use astronomical instruments, Nicollet saw the country as an empty canvas on which to make his final mark. At fifty-two, he was losing a decadelong battle with cancer, and he eagerly welcomed the enthusiastic, gifted, and French-speaking Frémont to assist him in what he sensed would be one of his last expeditions.

For his part, Frémont was delighted to work with a man "in the circles to which [François] Arago and other savants of equal rank belonged. Not only had he been trained in science, but he was habitually schooled to the social observances which make daily intercourse attractive, and become invaluable where hardships are to be mutually borne and difficulties overcome and hazards met. His mind was of the higher order. A musician as well as a mathematician, it was harmonious and complete." Such "social observances" would have a lasting impact on the young Frémont. Nicollet possessed a sophisticated ethnological interest in the plight of Native Americans—he "personally feared for the ultimate destruction of the natives," as one writer described his compassion—reminiscent to John of his own father's sensibilities. The avuncular Nicollet introduced John into his lively St. Louis social circle, a group that included scientists, fur traders, soldiers, and politicians, and the proud Frenchman would insist on adding the accent to John's last name, instilling in his young assistant a reverence for his heritage. Frémont would meet a youthful Robert E. Lee, then a captain with the army's Corps of Engineers, and fraternize with the veteran explorer William Clark—"who was ending his honorable days in St. Louis, where he held superintendency over all the Indians of the West," as Jessie Benton would later write. Here, too, Frémont would have his first memorable encounters with French Roman Catholic priests, forming associations that would come back to haunt him in his later political life.

Ordered to act as disbursing agent for the expedition, as well as to relieve Nicollet of all burdensome tasks, Frémont had the prestigious responsibility of outfitting the party—a sophisticated and meticulous undertaking that required extensive planning and a methodical mind. The necessary provisions ranged from food to scientific instruments, guns and ammunition to cooking paraphernalia, hunting necessities to medical supplies, recreational spirits and tobacco to life-saving remedies, boats and wagons to horses and cattle. The final inventory was staggering in its breadth: ham, bacon, oatmeal, sugar, tea, hung beef, dried fish, flour, potatoes, paper, books, ink, pens, compasses, microscopes, pots and pans, cups and plates, tableware, soap, lanterns, medicine, bandages, knives, rifles, needles. A famed gourmet, Nicollet asked Frémont to acquire a plentiful supply of French chocolates, bouillon, claret, cognac, port, sardines, and fine chicory coffee. Still, Frémont's most daunting and essential mission was the selection of the seasoned mountain men who would serve as guides, scouts, and Indian translators.

In early May 1838, the exploring party set off from St. Louis. Along with Nicollet and Frémont were Charles Geyer, a German botanist, and a group of sixty French Canadian scouts and hunters. Their mission to survey the uncharted territory between the Mississippi and Missouri rivers began with the steamboat journey aboard the *Burlington* five hundred miles upriver to Fort Snelling, at the confluence of the Mississippi and Minnesota rivers. There they spent four weeks provisioning, Nicollet, Frémont, and Geyer the houseguests of Henry Sibley, who commanded a formidable outpost for the American Fur Company. The son of a prominent Detroit lawyer, Sibley had rejected his own legal studies for the dangerous, adventurous, and highly profitable pursuit of fur trading. Overseeing hundreds of clerks, traders, Indians, trappers, and voyageurs, the famously handsome bachelor increasingly resembled the Sioux among whom he lived, wearing buckskin leggings and routinely venturing deep into his wild surroundings. Still, his breeding was palpable, his cultured background evident in the supply of books, cigars, liquor, and furnishings that steamboats regularly brought him from St. Louis. He lived in a large rustic house "filled with Irish wolfhounds, guns, and saddles," as one account described his hunting lodge existence. Roughly the same age as Frémont, the dark-haired, dark-eyed Sibley spent many hours with the nascent explorer. Intrigued by his six-foot-tall host—"he belonged to the men who love dogs and horses"—Frémont was impressed by the vastness of Sibley's library and the richness of his frontier life. Here, too, Frémont became enamored with a young Sioux woman, whose name, Beautiful Day, he would never forget.

On June 9 the journey began in earnest, the party moving up the Minnesota River and exploring the terrain. Frémont would carry the memories of this momentous expedition throughout his life. Protégé to a master, he was awed by Nicollet's breadth of knowledge and depth of experience and felt for the first time his participation in something truly epic. Nicollet and Geyer were at the top of their fields—botany, geography, astronomy, geology—and Frémont found himself not the perpetual outsider of his youth, but a coveted member of an elite and highbrow realm. Fascinated with the tools of their trade—the sextants, barometers, telescopes, and chronometers—he made himself an expert in all of their uses. Geyer collected and cataloged the botanical samples as Nicollet and Frémont measured latitude and longitude, charted the constellations, and made mathematical calculations to determine the altitude. On this journey Frémont acquired the discipline and focus that would distinguish him for the rest of his life.

His surroundings brimmed with evidence of his French origins, traces of what he described as "former travels by early French explorers"— from the *hommes des montagnes*, as they called their French Canadian scouts, to the landmarks of Traverse des Sioux, Lac qui Parle, and the Lesueur River, to Nicollet himself. Frémont would develop lifelong attachments to Alexis Godey, Basil Lajeunesse, and Antoine Robidoux, impressed by their bravery and frontier skills. He listened with awe as Nicollet conversed with a Sioux chief nearly seven feet tall, reminiscing of earlier times when his French predecessors forged potent alliances with the Sioux. Nicollet sought to convince the hopeful chief that the benevolent powers in Washington had dispatched Nicollet to count the lodges of the Sisseton Sioux and to bring them food. The chief gratefully accepted the gifts of gunpowder and rations, and Frémont witnessed for the first time how "consideration, compassion, and tact represented the differences between safety and danger in leading an expedition into tribal territories," as historian Ferol Egan depicted the diplomatic skills of the French explorer.

Romantic by nature, Frémont wrote poetically of the landscape as if a first love, a glorious adventure. He relished observing the night sky and listening to the elevated discussions around the campfire on subjects ranging from politics to science, from military affairs to philosophy. He was humbled and grateful when Nicollet insisted on naming a Minnesota lake for him, not yet dreaming that it would be but the first of hundreds of landmarks that would bear his name over the next century and a half. He found himself looking westward, beyond all boundaries to an unknown land of mythology and allure.

His mentor Nicollet approached the task at hand with an urgency spawned as much by the precariousness of the landscape as his impending death. "It is necessary to make haste in order to take nature by surprise," Nicollet wrote in his journal, "while it is still in a quasi-virgin state and while the consequences of its laws are still open to us." Though Nicollet's Washington benefactors were driven by the dream of an expanded American empire—one that included the brutal Indian removal policies he found appalling—Nicollet was decidedly apolitical. "Nicollet's passions lay in uniformity of measurements, not geopolitics," historian Tom Chaffin wrote of the straightforward scientist, "in natural systems, not man-made boundaries." Still, his obsession with watersheds was actually political in an unconventional way, Nicollet presciently recognizing that the distribution of the West's water and natural resources related directly to the distribution of the nation's wealth.

"In all the course of our campaign, it is not only in science that I have tried to develop the ideas of Mr. Frémont," Nicollet wrote of the young man he was grooming to consummate the surveys his declining health would cut short for him. For his part, Frémont had fully absorbed the pleasures and complexities of outdoor life—playing lacrosse with Indian warriors, hunting deer and elk in the woods, camping under the stars "with bright fires, where fat venison was roasting on sticks . . . stewing with corn or wild rice in pots hanging from tripods; squaws busy over the cooking and children rolling about over the ground. No sleep is better or more restoring than follows such a dinner, earned by such a day."

They would return satisfied and hopeful to St. Louis. A fatigued Nicollet would await the arrival of Geyer's specimens, while Frémont returned to Washington to report verbally to Secretary of War Joel Poinsett, to carry official dispatches to Nicollet's friends, and to lobby Poinsett for support and funding for an immediate expedition to the upper Missouri.

John Charles Frémont arrived in the capital in January 1839. He brought with him a letter from Nicollet to Poinsett, in which Nicollet praised Frémont and pronounced the expedition a scientific success, with the added social and military benefits of making various Indian tribes "friendly to the United States." He also conveyed a stunning bearskin bedspread made by the Indians for Mrs. Poinsett, and a letter from Nicollet introducing Frémont to the scientist Ferdinand Hassler. The acquaintance with Hassler would prove yet another defining and fortunate connection for Frémont. The seventy-year-old mathematician knew the most prominent scientists, government officials, and politicians in Washington. Superintendent of the U.S. Coast Survey, the temperamental Hassler was much revered, possessing "considerable knowledge in such fields as ethnology, astronomy, physics, jurisprudence, and political science," according to one description of the Swiss genius. Frémont's brief stay in Washington during that winter would be punctuated with incursions into Hassler's intellectually and socially stimulating world.

In February, Frémont wrote to his superior, Lieutenant Colonel John James Abert of the Bureau of Topographical Engineers, outlining the proposed expedition for a "Military and Geographical Survey of the Country West of the Mississippi and North of the Missouri." A week later he received a response, ordering him to return to St. Louis immediately to begin preparations for the journey, approving the engagement once again of Geyer, and subtly chastising Frémont for his unsystematic bookkeeping while instructing him in the necessity of maintaining accurate financial records for the army. "The experience which you have had with your accts., will, I hope, prevent the encountering of similar difficulties hereafter, & impress upon your mind the necessity of bills in detail and receipts." Frémont was far more interested in exploration than bureaucratic accounting, and his haphazard attention to business matters would become legendary, ultimately carrying devastating consequences.

But for now, the callow adventurer was consumed with exhilaration at the journey ahead.

With the help of Pierre Chouteau's American Fur Company, the small group was outfitted and ready to begin by early April. In addition to Nicollet, Geyer, and Frémont, five more men joined the expedition, including a dynamic Prussian artilleryman named Louis Zindel, particularly skilled at making rockets, and the most famous mountain man of the day, Étienne Provôt. Boarding the company's steamship, the *Antelope*, which was "taking its customary advantage of the annual rise in the Missouri from the snows of the Rocky Mountains," Frémont wrote, "starting on its regular voyage to the trading-posts on the upper waters of the river," the party "struggled against the currents" for more than two months. Traveling only by day, the small ship, carrying seventy French and mixed-race employees of the fur company, made slow progress through the snags and sawyers of the now bloated, now shallow river. Nicollet, Geyer, and Frémont took turns sketching the stream, rotating in five-hour shifts from dawn to nightfall. When they finally reached Fort Pierre—a wild territory 1,271 miles upriver from St. Louis at the center of what is now South Dakota—they disembarked and began hiring more hunters and scouts. Wary of a large village of Yankton Sioux, Nicollet made his customary offerings of weapons and food with the hopes of securing safe passage. "The village covered some acres of ground," Frémont wrote in his memoir, "and the lodges were pitched in regular lines . . . The girls were noticeably well clothed, wearing finely dressed skins nearly white, much embroidered with beads and porcupine quills dyed many colors . . . These were the best formed and best looking Indians of the plains, having the free bearing belonging with their unrestrained life in sunshine and open air." Grateful for the gifts, one of the chiefs offered Frémont his beautiful eighteen-year-old daughter. Embarrassed and afraid of offending the chief, Frémont uneasily declined the proposal. "I promptly replied that I was going far away and not coming back, and did not like to take the girl away from her people; that it might bring bad luck; but that I was greatly pleased with the offer." He then showered the girl with gifts, producing a package of beads, mirrors, and rich scarlet- and indigo-colored fabrics.

In early July, the party of nineteen men began forging northeast on horseback "toward the British line and the rising sun." Here Frémont acquired the equestrian skills that would serve him well in later years, the men pushing their mounts to top speed; and here, too, he developed what would become his lifelong admiration and respect for horseflesh. These were not the frail-limbed Thoroughbreds of his Southern roots, but stout American-bred, grass-fed animals, sure-footed and fit, capable of traveling dozens of miles at a full gallop. During his first buffalo hunt, he was overwhelmed by the required skill—both as a horseman and as a marksman—and found new reverence for the prairie hunter. "The only things visible to me in our flying course were the buffalo and the dust, and there was tumult in my breast as well as around me. I made repeated ineffectual attempts to steady myself for a shot at a cow after a hard struggle to get up with her, and each time barely escaped a fall. In such work a man must be able to forget his horse, but my horsemanship was not yet equal to such a proof."

The landscape was stunning in its grandeur. One of their guides took them through ravines and oak-wooded hills to a precipice overlooking the impressive basin of the James River, then stopped to remark: "You wanted geography; look—there's geography for you!" Ever mindful of Stephen Long's dismissal of the region as a desert, Nicollet was aghast at the misguided folly in such an analysis. "The fact that the ground is sterile because it is too clayey does not necessarily mean that it cannot be fertilized and improved," he would write in his report.

In late July the party began a nine-day survey of Devil's Lake in present-day northeastern North Dakota. Plagued by mosquitoes, they had no choice but to move on prematurely. "Mosquitoes had infested the camp in such swarms and such pertinacity that the animals would quit feeding and come up to the fires to shelter themselves in the smoke," wrote Frémont. On August 6 they headed south along the Cheyenne River, then east to the dividing line between the Cheyenne and Red rivers. Stopping at a fifteen-hundred-foot plateau, they could see "the wide-spread valley of the Red river, its green wooded line extending far away to the north on its way to British America." The prairie was laden with purple asters and goldenrod, the yellowing aspen and cottonwoods hinting at fall, and the men relaxed in the glow of the temperate Indian summer.

Nicollet felt his life's work had been fulfilled, that he had indeed found the source of the Mississippi River and determined the drainage systems that would dictate the future course of American expansion. Frémont was no longer the green and inexperienced apprentice he had been a mere eighteen months earlier, but had emerged, newly shaped by the hands of a grand master. "He had learned comradeship with scouts, voyageurs, fur-traders, frontier soldiers, and Indians," wrote a historian. "He had mastered the art of camp-management; he had been taught woodcraft and prairie-craft . . . He knew how to find water and firewood where both were scarce, to conciliate Indians, to deal with buffalo, prairie fires, and camp emergencies . . . [He learned] to take accurate astronomical observations at every halt, record topography, observe botany, soils, and minerals." Above all, he had come into his own, no longer Nicollet's young assistant but a proficient American explorer in his own right.

As the expedition drew to a close, Nicollet, Geyer, and Frémont arrived at Prairie du Chien in a bark canoe, where a steamboat was preparing to leave for St. Louis. Nicollet continued to St. Louis by canoe, remembering the inclement weather of the previous year. But desiring to rest for a few days at the site in what is now southwestern Wisconsin, Frémont and Geyer watched a steamer fire up its boiler and begin its glide down the Mississippi. That evening, as they were installed for the first time in six months in comfortable beds, it began to snow. By the next morning, the river was frozen, blocking all steamship traffic from the north. For the next month they waited for a steamer from the south, a frustrating delay that forced patience upon the characteristically impatient Frémont. "I had time enough while there to learn two things," he wrote later: "one, how to skate; the other, the value of a day." When it became clear that a boat would not arrive until the following spring, they embarked on a difficult wagon journey across Illinois to St. Louis, arriving the week before Christmas. By the end of the month, he was on his way to Washington "to assist Mr. Nicollet in working up the material collected in the expeditions."

Already known as a man of talent and promise, an attractive addition to Washington parlors, an eye-catching escort and educated conversationalist, Frémont returned to the capital with the enhanced reputation as heir apparent to the most distinguished explorer in the world. Arriving in December 1839, eager to rendezvous with Nicollet and to begin writing their report and finalizing their maps, Frémont was alarmed to find that Nicollet had not yet surfaced in official circles. Fearing the worst—that he had become too ill to complete his journey to Washington and may be dying in some remote location—Frémont left immediately for Baltimore, where quarters were kept for Nicollet by his Catholic friends at St. Mary's College. "Here, as in St. Louis, Mr. Nicollet's relations with the upper clergy were intimate and friendly . . . they received him as the abbots of old welcomed a congenial traveler into their calm retreats when monasteries were seats of learning." But his mentor was not in Baltimore, and Frémont returned to Washington, disappointed and anxious.

On January 12, 1840, a gaunt and feeble Nicollet arrived in Washington. The two men rented a boardinghouse together and began their work, but were soon established in a comfortable suite of rooms provided them by Ferdinand Hassler. This "bachelor quarters," as Frémont called it, was a fortuitous arrangement, for it brought together two dear friends in Hassler and Nicollet, and afforded the three an opportunity to endlessly discuss the scientific and political results of the expedition.

Frémont marveled at the relationship between the two men, so "opposite in complexion of mind and in manner . . . the one flint and the other steel," and yet so totally devoted to one another. The self-deprecating and understated Nicollet stood in stark contrast to the flamboyant and fiery Hassler. "Mr. Nicollet was urbane, forbearing, rounding off obstructions in intercourse; polished and persuasive, and careful of the feelings of others. Mr. Hassler was abrupt, full of sharp edges and intolerant of pretentious mediocrity," Frémont wrote of his colorful older housemates. Conspicuous for his white flannel suits, Hassler traveled to his Coast Survey operations in an ostentatious foreign-built carriage commonly called "the ark," equipped for sleeping, and fully stocked with the German wines he insisted on imbibing even at dinner parties hosted by others.

Frémont watched with amusement as the two set up housekeeping. "In this arrangement there was some disparity of purse as well as of age. It was interesting to see the manner in which these two proceeded to organize the establishment. Of one thing they were aware, as many otherwise good housekeepers in our country are not, that the essential element in a household for economy and health is the cook." To that end, they hired a French chef whom President Van Buren had just rejected because of his high salary demands. He came with a list of necessary utensils "incomprehensible even to Mr. Nicollet" and written out under the intimidating heading, *Pour un cuisinier Français il faut une batterie de cuisine*. This "made him master of the situation. A man who knew so much about his tools was likely to know how to use them, and he did."

The house overlooked the Potomac River, and the view, combined with the observatory Hassler built on the roof, provided Frémont with the inspiration he found necessary to write. They divided their time between work and chess, their gourmet meals spiced with energetic conversation. It was a time and a place Frémont would never forget, a pivotal moment at the end of the great scientists' lives and the beginning of his own. He had not yet come to see himself as destined to play a major role in America's future, though both Hassler and Nicollet no doubt saw that for him as they gently but forcefully guided him toward his life's mission. He was in what he called "a condition of happy thoughtlessness, relieved from work, and my mind not burdened with a care. The campaign was over and its objects accomplished. What now remained to be done was merely the giving a definite shape to its results, so interesting that it could not be called labor, but pleasure only."

That Nicollet insisted upon Frémont accompanying him to a meeting with Van Buren and Poinsett was momentous, though the young lieutenant did not fully grasp the significance. He naïvely assumed that such inclusion was pro forma and did not recognize that his meeting with the president and secretary of war was portentous, while the powerful men in his presence all knew that his future had been sealed. Nicollet and Poinsett had tacitly passed the torch.

There followed myriad invitations, the city of thirty thousand now a thriving center of social interaction among those at the heart of power, and Frémont was welcomed into the capital's elite circles. A coveted guest at balls, salons, and receptions, he was feted by dignitaries and socialites, welcomed into the mansions of such bastions as the esteemed Dolley Madison. He "was in demand for his vivacity, his handsome if dapper figure, and his ability to talk about South American ports and western wigwams," as one account described Frémont's appeal. It was a heady time for the illegitimate son of a wayward émigré.

He joined Nicollet on a vacation in Baltimore, where the ailing scientist could be cared for by his friends the Catholic priests at the Sulpician seminary. In the rooms they kept for him, Nicollet found the trappings of his past—"the wealth of linen and other luxuries of his former civilized life," as Frémont described the wardrobe—the tailored suits and elegant finery more suitable to high society than life on the trail. Bishop Chance, the president of the college, was their host. The exhausted Nicollet gained strength while Frémont absorbed the intellectual discourse, basking in the serenity and simple comforts of the monks' lives.

The spell was broken when Frémont received word that his only brother was dead.

Horation "Frank" Francis Frémont, a twenty-three-year-old failed thespian, apparently had returned home to Charleston, where he died of an

accidental gunshot wound that a biographer of John would later speculate was a suicide. He left behind an unborn daughter, Nina, who would
eventually become Frémont's ward.

John obtained a leave of absence from the Topographical Corps to attend the funeral. Crushed with grief, and at the sad realization that he
and his mother were all that remained of the Frémont family, he made
arrangements for a family friend to stay a month with his mother. He
then returned to Washington, to the work at hand: to produce the definitive map of the Mississippi and its headwaters. Despondent and reserved, he immersed himself in the project, and when the account was
later published it would be enthusiastically endorsed. *A Report Intended to
Illustrate a Map of the Hydrographical Basin of the Upper Mississippi River*
was the first document of its kind, relying on barometric calculations
and including ninety thousand readings of latitude and longitude.

The results of the expedition were thrilling to Washington insiders obsessed with western expansion, and a string of politicians began visiting
the Hassler town house to watch the maps grow. The cartography was
rigorous and often greeted with impatience by political observers. "It
must be exact," Frémont wrote. "First, the foundations must be laid in
observations made in the field; then the reduction of these observations
to latitude and longitude; afterward the projection of the map, and the
laying down upon it of positions fixed by the observations; then the tracing from the sketch-books of the lines of the rivers, the forms of the
lakes, the contours of the hills."

Texas and Oregon were at the forefront of political discussion, and relations with Mexico and Great Britain were becoming increasingly
strained over boundary disputes. The course of John C. Frémont's life
would be irrevocably determined by a man he met at this time. Thomas
Hart Benton, the senior senator from Missouri, was the single most influential and outspoken advocate for a national empire that stretched to
the Pacific Ocean. A disciple of Thomas Jefferson—"the one man who
had foreseen and planned our ownership of its Pacific port, with the resulting gain of overland commerce from Asia peopling our waste lands
and enriching the whole country," as Benton's daughter Jessie would
later write—Benton had devoted his political life to opening trade with
Asia. The son of a landed widow from Tennessee, he had fantasized as a
child, aroused by the exploits of Clive of India. He felt the struggle for
India "greater than that of Tyre and Sidon." He set his sights on the Pacific, envisioning American ports on the California and Oregon coasts.

To this end, Benton, as chairman of the Senate Military Affairs Committee, was willing to do anything within his power to secure authorization for immediate western surveys. In Frémont, Benton found his Ledyard. In Benton, Frémont found his Jefferson.

Until meeting Benton, Frémont was committed to a profession of engineering, trained as he was by the best in the world. But now such a career paled in comparison to the vision set forth before him, this meeting with Benton "pregnant of results and decisive of my life." Suddenly he saw himself as part of a grand design, a man of destiny in what had not yet been coined "Manifest Destiny," compelled to accomplish a mission of utmost historic importance. "In this interview with Mr. Benton my mind had been quick to see a larger field and differing and greater results. It would be travel over a part of the world which still remained the New—opening up of unknown lands; the making unknown countries known; and the study without books—the learning at first hand from nature herself; the drinking first at her unknown springs—became a source of never-ending delight to me."

The relationship quickly became personal, as the senator regularly invited John to the Benton home on C Street. For the young officer whose own family had been marked by death and poverty, the energetic family life of the Benton household was fresh and sustaining. In the senator and Mrs. Benton he witnessed a warm and devoted marriage of the kind he never knew when he was growing up. While two of their daughters were away at boarding school, he saw the three children at home exhibiting social graces and curious minds. Their manners were flawless, their discourse elevated, and their love and affection for each other infectious. Susan and Sarah performed for the family in their music room, and young Randolph absorbed the incessant talk of exploration. It was with interest and enthusiasm that Frémont agreed to accompany Benton to a concert at Miss English's Academy, where he would finally meet the older girls, Jessie and Eliza.

2

JESSIE 1824–1840

The plan of reading which I have formed [for my daughter Martha] is considerably different from that which I think would be most proper for her sex in any other country than America. I am obliged to extend my views beyond herself, and consider her as the head of a little family of her own. The chance that in marriage she will draw a blockhead I calculate at about fourteen to one, and course that the education of her family will probably rest on her own ideas and directions without assistance.

—Thomas Jefferson, 1783

BORN MARCH 14, 1782, near Hillsborough, North Carolina, Thomas Hart Benton was the son of a scholarly Englishman and his puritanical Virginia wife. Within weeks, two of his great senatorial adversaries—Daniel Webster and John C. Calhoun—also came into the world, all born into the turbulent era after Thomas Jefferson wrote his Declaration of Independence but before the Revolutionary War had ended. Benton's father, Jesse, was a lawyer, land speculator, the onetime heir to a vast slave-driven plantation, and the secretary to the last royal governor of North Carolina.

"Out of his element in the new Republic," Jessie Benton later described her grandfather Jesse, who was known particularly for the extensive personal library he had inherited from his father, the breadth of which gave the three generations of Bentons their reputations as learned men and women. Greek, Latin, French, Spanish, and English volumes were equally represented, and Jesse Benton was fluent in all five languages, reading *Don Quixote*, Shakespeare, and Madame de Sévigné in their original editions. He formed a close friendship with a "man of high character and the same cultivated mind"—a young chaplain brought by Governor Tryon from England, the two men finding solace and mutual support in "the angry agitation of the coming separation from the mother-country." The friendship would last their lifetime.

The intellectual Jesse found a like-minded mate in the slender, blue-eyed Ann Gooch, herself descended from an English line of colonial governors. With the death of her parents, Ann had become the ward of her mother's brother, Thomas Hart—a delegate to the first North Carolina revolutionary convention in 1774. Jesse adored his young wife, who had a mane of ginger hair, was reserved in nature, graceful and dignified, highly educated by the day's standards for women, and whom he affectionately called "my Nancy." She was twenty-four years old when she delivered her first son, a redhead who was quickly spoiled not only by his proud mother but also by two older sisters. Thomas Hart Benton grew into a tall, ruddy, and burly boy, sharp and hot-tempered, yet tender and abidingly kind.

His father died when he was eight, leaving his mother a young widow with eight children and a debt-ridden estate. She collapsed with grief, confining herself in her room. She emerged months later with her long, thick, auburn hair turned completely white, and placed a hand on Thomas's head as she pronounced him head of the family. "When I came out I rushed into the grove, and there, with cries of tears, *I made war on myself* until I could accept that ghost in place of my mother." His father's friend, a chaplain, found him in the orchard, calming the boy as best he could and giving him his first lesson in Greek: The Sermon on the Mount was read from a pocket-size volume of the Greek Testament. "Blessed are those who mourn, for they shall be comforted."

Thomas spent his childhood in Hillsborough, he and his three brothers—Jesse, Nathaniel, and Samuel—encouraged by their mother to live a wholesome and robust outdoor life. Each was given a dog to train but had to share one horse among them. Fixated on consumption, the dread disease that had claimed her husband and threatened her children, Ann instilled in Thomas a daily routine that would be his lifelong antidote to illness. He would rise at dawn, "curry" himself with stiff brushes, conduct several breathing exercises, and then bathe in cold water. Within four years of her husband's death, Ann had managed to pay off Jesse's substantial debts and secure her estate, which included more than a thousand acres of land and six slaves. She then turned her attention to the education of her eldest son, determined to cultivate him as a lawyer. She tutored him in Greek and Latin, and insisted that he spend several hours a day in the family library where, as a ten-year-old, he read the folio editions of the *British State Trials*. From this early reading, according to one of his biographers, he absorbed an "old-Whig intellectual passion for liberty and hatred of tyranny." He took seriously his responsibility as man of the house, and embraced his mother's Puritan warnings against tobacco, gambling, and hard liquor. Raised by a smart, resourceful, courageous, and self-reliant woman, Thomas inherited what his daughter Jessie would later describe as Ann's "active sense of justice . . . for women, even those 'despised of men.'"

For two years, he rode the family horse three miles each way to attend a private academy. Pinning all of her hopes on Thomas, Ann managed to save enough money for him to go to college, and when he turned sixteen, in 1798, he moved twelve miles south to enter the University of North Carolina at Chapel Hill. There he continued a classical education at the tiny school where aristocratic sons of the South made up its forty students. But he only lasted three months, involved first in a brawl in which he produced a loaded weapon, and then, more seriously, he was caught red-handed with cash stolen from his three roommates. Exposed and expelled, a defiant Thomas taunted the crowd of jeering students who had come to bid him good riddance. "I am leaving here now," he shouted at them, "but damn you, you will hear from me again!" Still, the bravado covered a deep humiliation, and the incident fostered within him a lifelong commitment to a path of honor and integrity. He came "home to the family seat of the proud Benton line," as one historian portrayed the devastating situation, "there to face his brothers and sisters, and above all his moralistic, pious mother, and confess his errors in a scene which must have had terrifying overtones." From that moment forward, Thomas would be known as an unwaveringly honest man—a rarity in a rough-and-tumble Washington filled with bribes and political fix-and-favor.

Perhaps out of shame, perhaps due to an economic downturn, Ann set her sights on the new state of Tennessee, where her husband had claimed forty thousand acres in the heart of that territory's Bluegrass Country. With Thomas's long-planned college career at an untimely end, she feared he would follow in the footsteps of his hard-drinking and gambling uncle, William Benton, if they stayed in North Carolina. Only two years after statehood, Tennessee was rumored to offer great opportunities to young men, and Ann hoped the change of scenery would rekindle

Thomas's ambitions to become a lawyer. In 1798, against the objections of William and other family members, she sold the North Carolina property, packed up the extensive library and several generations' worth of Benton family furnishings, and took her four daughters, four sons, and eight slaves to the wild acreage near Nashville. Traveling the four-hundred mile distance across a dangerous landscape inhabited by Creek Indians, she was determined that her sons would develop the land into a profitable plantation. When various title disputes were finally resolved, Ann Benton ended up with 2,560 acres, only 40 of which had been cleared. There, 25 miles from the new state capital of Nashville, her sons and slaves built a stone and wood home with a wide veranda overlooking their stunningly scenic estate.

Thomas superintended the first planting of cotton and corn and assisted the slaves in building the necessary structures. Indomitable and indefatigable, Ann had overseen the expansion of her property from one house and a few ramshackle slave quarters into a tiny community that boasted a general store, a schoolhouse, and several log dwellings she leased to tenants attracted to Widow Benton's Settlement, as it was called. The first year cotton brought fifteen cents a pound—an exorbitant amount driven by the New Orleans export market—and with four hundred pounds per acre, the Benton family reaped a sizable return. But the following year, an unseasonable frost decimated the fields. Thomas determined at that moment that he was not cut out to be a farmer. "You may have this land," he told his brothers. "I am through with a pursuit in which I can't influence results." He then turned his complete attention to studying law, now bringing to his scholastic pursuits the keen intellect and inquiring mind that he had squandered in his younger years. He had matured during the homesteading experience, and though frontier life was crude in comparison to the polish of Hillsborough society, it had a certain excitement. Nashville was a "raw, pretentious place, where horse-racing, cock-fighting, gambling, whiskey-drinking" all thrived, according to one author, and Benton "bore his full share . . . in the excessively unattractive social life of the place and epoch."

But the carefree days came to an end, as one by one the older girls died of tuberculosis—their hilltop "graves of three sisters" becoming a local landmark. His love and admiration for his mother deepened as he determined to make her proud of her oldest son. Her stoicism and fortitude were astonishing to Thomas, who could hardly fathom the grief she had endured. "Ann is still beautiful, though her hair is snow white, and her eyes are the saddest I ever saw," wrote a friend who visited her at this time. "She always dresses in black, with neck- and wrist-bands of white, like a nun, and in truth she is mother confessor to the whole country-side." Indeed, her efforts at helping others became legendary, as she ministered to her slaves and the many neighbors suffering from the epidemic of tuberculosis.

Benton pursued his career with a newfound dedication. He traveled by horseback to Nashville to watch the proceedings of the Superior Court and to various county courthouses to observe legal arguments. When, in 1803, the United States bought almost a million square miles of territory from France, Benton thought it was the most momentous event since the Revolutionary War. The Louisiana Purchase was Thomas Jefferson's most significant act as president—what historian Sean Wilentz called "one of the luckiest strokes in the history of American diplomacy . . . a virtual second Declaration of Independence"—and had far-reaching ramifications for Tennessee settlers who had long been victims of the whims and corruptions of foreign "governors" seated in New Orleans who manipulated trade. Benton thought Jefferson a national visionary, and his bold transaction—extending the nation's boundaries from the Gulf of Mexico to Canada, and from the Mississippi to the Rocky Mountains—would form the beginning of Benton's own expansionist views. Cheap and available land for all who wanted to claim it was the key to Jefferson's utopia. "Give the people land and opportunity," one historian described Benton's emerging philosophy, "and they could build in the great Western expanse an Arcadia of happy, self-respecting, republican freeholders."

Benton was fascinated with the adventurous men of the "West" he found in Tennessee—Davy Crockett, Peter Cartwright, and Sam Houston—and especially by the older, larger-than-life Andrew Jackson, then a State Supreme Court justice, through whom Benton would find his political identity. "They were above all a people of strong, virile character, certain to make their weight felt either for good or for evil," a later president, Theodore Roosevelt, would write of Crockett, Benton, Jackson, and their ilk, and in many ways of himself. "They had narrow, bitter prejudices and dislikes; the hard and dangerous lives they had led had run their character into a stern and almost forbidding mould. They valued personal prowess very highly, and respected no man who did not possess the strongest capacity for self-help, and who could not shift for himself in any danger. They felt an intense, although perhaps ignorant, pride in and love for their country, and looked upon all the lands hemming in the United States as territory which they or their children should some day inherit; for they were a race of masterful spirit, and accustomed to regard with easy toler-ance any but the most flagrant violations of law."

Fifteen years his senior, Jackson tutored the young Benton in the emerging traditions of Southern politics, and the two became close friends. They differed in class and background, but they also were simi-lar: both largely self-educated, both impetuous, both born into families for whom death would be an all too familiar visitor. In 1806, at age twenty-four, Benton was admitted to the bar under Jackson's patronage, and would eventually be considered one of the best constitutional lawyers in America. The two men developed a symbiotic relationship, sharing identical political views and both considering themselves Jeffer-sonians, Westerners, and Unionists. With such a skilled and practiced mentor, Benton's transition into electoral politics was effortless. By 1809 he had distinguished himself in a handful of legal cases as a populist with a passionate commitment to equality before the law. He took up the cause of common people who found the legal system burdensome if not inaccessible, and wrote several newspaper articles about court abuses and other flaws of the judiciary. "He was the first person who ever insisted on giving to the negro the right of counsel, not that he had any senti-ment in favor of the blacks . . . It was their right as a matter of law, and he was a true Saxon champion of the law and the rights of the meanest under it." No political machinery had yet evolved in the region, so Ben-ton's personal charisma alone would carry him into the state legislature. Once in office, he introduced reforms aimed at the poorest class, includ-ing a radically progressive law that gave the slave the same rights to a jury trial as those afforded white men. This legislation, above all else, would presage his future political career as one of the most "enlightened . . . of his class," as Roosevelt would describe him.

When the session adjourned, he rode through the woods to his mother's home, finally believing that he was worthy of that formidable woman's pride. "He could stand a little straighter," wrote a historian, "hold his broad shoulders a little squarer, throw his large head back a lit-tle further. He was Senator Benton, sir, author of the new Tennessee court system."

Called "Western Warhawks," Benton and Jackson advocated war with the United Kingdom—the two Jeffersonian Democrats firmly believing that England's Tory government was not only heaping insults on the young republic, but interfering with U.S. trade as well. In this they shared the views of Speaker of the House Henry Clay and a young congressman from South Carolina, John C. Calhoun, both of whom would be their ardent foes in future political battles. "Who are we? And for what are we going to fight?" Jackson wrote in March 1812. "[A]re we the titled Slaves of George the third? the military conscripts of Napoleon the great? or the frozen peasants of the Russian Czar? No—we are the free born sons of America; the citizens of the only republick now existing in the world."

When President James Madison asked Congress to declare war in the summer of 1812, Benton eagerly volunteered to serve as aide-de-camp to Major General Jackson in the Tennessee Militia. On the eve of battle, Benton suddenly found himself "on the same sad downward road" of pulmonary disease that had taken his three sisters. "Constant fever, the hacking cough, and restless nights and days without energy admonished him that his turn had come," his daughter Jessie would later write. Depressed at what he saw as imminent death, he embraced the coming war as "the occasion to end his life in action rather than in the slow progress of a fatal illness." The inescapability of the disease sent him into despair. "If it had been a battle I would have had a chance, or even in a desperate duel, but for this there was no chance. All was fixed and inevitable." He eschewed the standard treatments of the day—primitive and ineffective measures that included leeches and poultices—and the aggressive idealist took his daily rituals to heightened levels, walking rather than riding during his regiment's long march to New Orleans, exposing his throat and chest to the sun, sleeping naked in the cool night air, swimming in the cold streams along the way. Though disappointed that he never actually engaged in battle, he returned to Tennessee a changed and healed man. He had cured himself and took from the experience a lifelong belief that one could indeed trick fate with "open air, night and day; abundant perspiration from steady exercise; bathing and rubbing, always if possible in sunshine; always all the sunshine possible; simple food regularly taken; and 'to forget yourself in some pursuit.'"

In the culture of violence in the backwoods "west," it was inevitable that the six-foot-tall, hot-headed Benton would partake in his share of the duels that prevailed throughout the country, and particularly in his region. On the frontier, every man of honor was expected to engage in a duel, and Tennessee was known especially for the ubiquitous affrays that involved judges, legislators, and other high state officials. Though the state had outlawed the conduct in 1801—and the practice had received even more opprobrium after Aaron Burr killed Alexander Hamilton in 1804—men of high rank continued to settle their quarrels by the implicit American dueling code, which, unlike in other societies, demanded death rather than wounding. Insults to family or personal honor were the root of most duels, though they were also fought over cheating, property disputes, and any number of other slights. A strict set of rules attended each duel—each duelist chose a friend as his "second" and the challenged selected the weapon to be used—and they were customarily fought at daybreak in a secluded wooded location to avoid the sheriff.

While Benton would eventually kill a man in 1817, it would be the Nashville duel of 1813 for which he would become infamous, a quarrel that took on farcical proportions. The argument began when Thomas's younger brother Jesse was shot in the buttocks during a duel with General William Carroll, whose second was Andrew Jackson. Blaming Jackson for ridiculing Jesse's awkward injury and conducting the duel between Jesse and Carroll in "a savage, unequal, unfair, and base manner," an irate Thomas Hart Benton began to publicly and vociferously insult Jackson. Jackson responded by traveling to Nashville to confront Benton at a popular inn. The details were murky and contradictory—"as many versions were reported as there were participants and spectators"—and all that was known for sure after the notorious three-to-a-side encounter was that Jackson was shot in the shoulder and the Benton brothers strutted through Nashville claiming victory. And in that strange twist of fate, a stray bullet had lodged in adjoining quarters where the infant John Charles Frémont was sleeping. His parents heard "the report of fire-arms . . . and the whistling of balls" through their room.

Thomas Hart Benton's bravado continued even as his onetime friend was fighting for his life, doctors working frantically to stop Jackson's hemorrhaging. Benton and a bevy of supporters taunted Jackson while Jackson's blood soaked through two mattresses. During his agony, Jackson vowed revenge. The next day, Benton returned to the hotel bearing Jackson's sword, which he had taken during the melee. "With great formality," according to one account, ". . . and in a loud voice, [Benton] three times summoned General Jackson to come forth and recover it." When Jackson failed to appear, Benton broke the sword across his knee and threw the pieces onto the ground.

Less than two years later, Benton would leave Tennessee for St. Louis in Missouri Territory, as a direct result of the hostilities. "I see no alternative but to kill or be killed; for I will not crouch to Jackson," Benton wrote a friend after Jackson's popularity mushroomed with his 1815 victory in a battle in New Orleans. Benton could no longer survive professionally in the small state where Jackson wielded so much power. "I am literally in hell here," Benton wrote at the time, ". . . for it is a settled plan to turn out puppy after puppy to bully me, and when I have got into a scrape, to have me killed somehow in the scuffle." Ten years later they would be staunch allies again, Benton supporting Jackson for president, but for now Benton thought prospects for a political career more promising in Missouri than in Jackson's shadow in Tennessee.

His most difficult challenge would be convincing his mother to relocate from Bentontown, as her settlement was now called, to Missouri. He promised her a new home, but she wistfully surveyed the land around her and announced that she could not bear to leave the graves of five of her children. The plantation had prospered, and Ann Gooch Benton felt rooted to the land. Still, she held open the possibility of joining Thomas later, and bade him Godspeed in his striking out toward a new future. Now a fine-looking thirty-three-year-old man, with piercing blue eyes and a shock of reddish-blond hair, he left Tennessee with $400 and a dozen boxes of books and personal belongings. He ferried his small amount of luggage across the Mississippi in a keelboat, arriving in St. Louis on a Sunday. He did not know a soul in the town of two thousand whites and three hundred slaves. Still, he sensed that the tiny community, already known as the gateway to the West, where the expeditions of Lewis and Clark and Zebulon Pike had begun, would play a riveting role in the westward expansion of the United States. The settlement had come under American control with Jefferson's Louisiana Purchase, and as a main port for Mississippi steamboats was destined for growth and prosperity.

As luck would have it, the first person Benton met when he alighted on the western bank of the river was the patriarch of the town. The white-haired old gentleman, Charles Gratiot, saw that the newcomer was asking for directions, and struck up a conversation. A French merchant, Gratiot had immigrated to St. Louis in 1777 and married into the prominent fur-trading Chouteau family, which had settled the community in 1764 and named it for King Louis IX, a Catholic saint. Gratiot kindly installed Benton in a sumptuous room in the family mansion, seeing in him a well-bred young man of promise and talent. The rich and influential of St. Louis visited Gratiot regularly, including the territory's governor, William Clark, and through Gratiot Benton met the city's elite. Within a week of his arrival he had opened a law office on the un-paved Rue de la Tour, and a retinue of clients immediately greeted him. The humiliation of Chapel Hill, the death of his sisters, the volatile tem-per of his youth, the controversy of the Jackson duel, and the struggles of frontier life had molded him into a man of intellectual depth and emo-tional sentiment, of strong personality and enthusiastic optimism, of in-cisive wit and roguish charm. He would quickly distinguish himself as a lawyer and then as a newspaper editor, and before long had earned wide popularity in a blossoming political career.

Good fortune struck Benton again, through a wartime friendship he de-veloped with James Patton Preston of Cherry Grove, Virginia. In 1816, Preston became governor of Virginia and invited his army colleague Benton to visit him in Richmond. While a houseguest at the newly built Federal style governor's mansion, Benton would fall in love for the first time in his life.

Twenty-year-old Elizabeth McDowell, the governor's niece, frequently visited her uncle in the state capital. Daughter of Colonel James Mc-Dowell and Sarah Preston McDowell, the petite brunette was a favorite belle in upper-class Virginia society. Vivacious and well-read, mannered and manicured, she was one of the most popular guests at the many soirees of the day, dancing gracefully at a Richmond ball, "her dark beauty set off by a gown of pink brocade over very small hoops, her tiny feet encased in pearl-silk stockings and buckled slippers." Her many young suitors clamored for her attention, and she politely and whimsi-cally played them against each other. When she first met Thomas Hart Benton—thirteen years her senior—she was singularly unimpressed. She had driven to Richmond in her private London-built coach, a yellow-colored extravagance with scarlet goatskin upholstery, accompanied by a maid and a manservant, because her uncle wanted to introduce her to his much-esteemed friend from St. Louis. She knew that Preston held Benton in high regard, so often did he speak of the man's extraordinary abilities and future prospects, but she was stunned to learn her uncle in-tended to make a match of the two.

Benton, not surprisingly, was instantly smitten. Elizabeth, by contrast, was alarmed. To her, Benton was but one more of numerous suitors, "not particularly good looking and so openly enamored as to seem

tongue-tied and dull among the handsome, eloquent cavaliers of her little court." Indeed, Benton could barely contain himself, and Elizabeth
found his unrestrained fawning unappealing.

Descended from proud and wealthy Scotch-Irish stock, the McDowells
were landed gentry, James's father having been granted thousands of acres
by the English government in exchange for his military service. The considerable plantation in the Blue Ridge foothills was at the confluence of
two streams, and included pasturelands, wild forests, and mountaintops.
They raised tobacco and wheat and were known for possessing the best
imported horses. The plantation was self-sustaining, except for supplemental groceries and fine fabrics brought by wagon from Richmond. It
was their "pleasure and pride . . . that they lived on land which had never
been bought or sold, and that in sixty years no negro had been transferred
to another owner." Elizabeth was the youngest of three children born to
James and Sarah. She was indulged in every way. Her bedroom was elegantly appointed, its mahogany four-poster bed piled high with feather
comforters, the silver candelabra on her dressing table polished to a high
sheen, her wardrobe the most fashionable of all her friends. She had attended the prestigious Ann Smith Academy, where the daughters of the
moneyed aristocracy appeared with their waiting maids and riding horses,
and were taught embroidery, how to care for their complexions and hands,
and how to run a proper household. "No high-born Virginia maiden
would 'spread her hand' by turning a door-knob," as a nineteenth-century
account described Elizabeth's rearing, "or touching the tongs, or handling
a heavy object. Long gloves and deep sun-bonnets were constantly worn,
and they ate little meat or butter."

She divided her time among the palatial Cherry Grove manor near
Lexington, Virginia, the governor's mansion in Richmond, and the fashionable resort at White Sulphur Springs. Her coddled upbringing could
not have been more different from that of Benton's, whose own childhood had been marred by tragedy and uncertainty, privations and conflict.
When he visited Elizabeth at Cherry Grove a few weeks later, her parents
eagerly encouraged the romance. The McDowells thought him distinguished and pedigreed—Benton's grandfather was the younger brother
of Sir William Gooch, who had been deputy governor of Virginia; and
Benton's mother, Ann, was related to Henry Clay—then a rising political
leader in the still-young republic—and tried to sway Elizabeth in favor of
the classically educated Missourian. "Both parents fell under the spell of
this courtly gentleman in high black-silk stock and double-breasted suit,"

wrote a biographer, "whose deferential manner, combined with an aston-ishingly wide knowledge of affairs, made him a welcome visitor indeed." But when he proposed marriage to the standoffish young woman, she quickly rebuffed him and he returned to St. Louis, dejected and disheart-ened, but still determined to make her his wife.

He immersed himself in his legal career, with many of his cases in-volving land-title disputes tracing back to old French and Spanish land grants—his practice earning him what one called a "reputation in some quarters as a lackey for the local French aristocracy." He toured Missouri Territory, visiting the county courthouses where he met judges and other lawyers, and gained his valuable trial experience in the busy St. Louis court, where he tried out his flamboyant antics and polished his oratory. The capital of the "Far West" was growing rapidly, and Benton was at the heart of it—spiritually, intellectually, and politically. He was a popular guest at the best homes in town, a favorite among fellow attor-neys, a friend to the up-and-coming leaders of the community, and a protégé to the elder statesmen of the territory. Satisfied, if not downright happy with the world before him, he turned his attention to his domestic situation. First he must convince his mother to move to St. Louis, and next he must persuade Elizabeth to marry him.

Ann Gooch Benton would be an easier conquest than Elizabeth Mc-Dowell. She had read her son's many letters with interest, and once she realized that he was indeed firmly established in Missouri, Ann finally turned her back on the thriving settlement she had founded nearly twenty years earlier. In June 1817, Ann traveled by carriage and steam-boat to St. Louis, where Thomas had bought them a spacious brick house in a tree-shaded neighborhood. Once Ann and her orphaned grandchild, Sarah, were settled with Thomas in their new home—Ann surrounded by her favorite books and furnishings and cared for by her much-loved servants—Benton returned to Cherry Grove to propose yet again.

Elizabeth refused him a second time, and he departed as baffled as he was hurt. She had rejected him "gently but with a firmness disconcert-ing indeed in one so gentle," he told his mother upon his return to St. Louis. The following year he received a letter from Mrs. McDowell in-dicating that her daughter remained unmarried—a revelation Benton took as encouragement—and he quickly responded with a written pro-posal to Elizabeth. Now, for the third time, she turned him down, adding insult to injury by suggesting he look elsewhere for a wife. "No other woman except my mother has ever fully engaged my affections," he wrote her back. "There is no one else for me, and I shall not lose hope until I learn you are definitely pledged to another."

His emotions were genuine, his determination fixed; he would seek no other spouse but would patiently and resolutely wait for her to change her mind. Meanwhile, he began his political career in earnest.

At age thirty-five, Benton decided to have his portrait painted. The large canvas captured him at the prime of his life, an immense yet elegant man with an aquiline nose, intense eyes, affable countenance, and aristocratic bearing. His wavy hair was brushed back from the high forehead, his thin lips pursed but on the verge of a smile. Destined to become the most powerful senator in America, Benton seemed poised for a future he alone could fully envision.

In August 1818, in response to several letters he had written to the newspaper, Benton was hired as editor of the *St. Louis Enquirer*—a dynamic competitor to the *Missouri Gazette*, the more staid establishment newspaper. He took this new job seriously, feeling that his words were helping to shape the future of the country. The upstart paper gained influence and readership under Benton's mantle, and in his editorials he addressed the controversial political matters of the era. Most of his articles focused on the future of the West, the disputes with Spain, France, and Great Britain over Texas and Oregon, the necessity for migration to the Pacific Northwest, the need to monopolize trade with Asia, and the opening of a "Road to India." One of the earliest, enthusiastic supporters of the nationalist and expansionist politicians, Benton would become the godfather of what would later be called Manifest Destiny. He advocated penetrating and seizing the wilderness, to be "placed forever under the domination of our people."

In 1821 Benton entered the U.S. Senate as Missouri gained admission to the Union. At the moment, slavery was heating up as a national political issue, with Missouri the bellwether—Northerners had demanded the abolition of slavery as a condition for statehood, while Southerners had lobbied for Missouri to enter the Union as a slave state. It would be the first time the question of slavery expansion had entered national politics, and the first time the country's statesmen divided so clearly along geographical lines. As a Southern slaveholder, Benton naturally sympathized with the South, coming down solidly against any restrictions. Still he straddled the fence between extremist views as best he could, describing himself as "equally opposed to slavery agitation and slavery extension."

Like his idol Jefferson, Benton preferred the subject not become a matter of national political debate. "Neither he [Jefferson] nor most other first-rank southern political leaders took up the antislavery cause too publicly or too vociferously," as historian Wilentz put it.

During Benton's senatorial campaign Elizabeth rejected his fifth proposition. "Papa and Mamma admire and respect you," she wrote. "I humbly admire and respect you, but I have decided that I could never marry an Army man, a Democrat, or a man with red hair." It was his response to this most candid, and immature, rejection that finally changed her mind: "I cannot alter the color of my hair," Benton wrote her. "I could not be other than a Democrat without violence to principle, but if you become my wife, I shall resign all connection with the Army and shall arrange that you spend as little time in the West as need be, for I, who love home and to whom family ties are very dear, appreciate your sentiments about Cherry Grove and your parents."

Had she run out of options, and was she now, at twenty-seven, considered a spinster? Was she finally—six years and six proposals later— touched by his unwavering devotion? Had she suddenly fallen in love with him? She had no enthusiasm for frontier Missouri, no interest in the rough-edged political world of Washington, and certainly no desire to leave her father's Eden. Whatever her motives, the ravishing Elizabeth McDowell relented to the persistent Thomas Hart Benton, but only after he had become a U.S. senator. Her legendary reluctance and ambivalence would set the stage for their long, one-sided marriage, during which she stoically endured her increasing unhappiness as he ardently doted on the "one whom I find to be inexpressibly dear to me under every circumstance of my life."

They married on March 21, 1821, at her father's lush, slave-dependent estate. "It is indeed a great day to me, for I consider it the first day of my life and the beginning of the only existence which is worth having," he wrote to Governor Preston, signing the letter "sincerely, truly, and happily yours." The couple exchanged vows at eight that evening in a candlelit drawing room, and went by private coach to Richmond for their honeymoon. Now forty years old, a senator from a new state, finally wed to the love of his life, engaged in exciting historical events, Benton was positively ecstatic. So effervescent and tender was Benton toward Elizabeth, his behavior drew much attention from his colleagues. Initially, Elizabeth would prove to be an extraordinary mate. A woman of discriminating judgment and educated sensibility, she was a welcome addition to official Washington, and at first she flourished in the social and political realms. She joined Thomas's mother as a valuable intellectual partner in the senator's life. A man described as exhibiting "unfailing gentleness to all women," Benton was fortunate to have "both in his mother and his wife friends and sharers in his largest ideas," his daughter, Jessie, would later write, attributing this tenderness to Benton's early devotion to his beloved sisters.

As soon as the congressional session ended, Benton spirited Elizabeth to St. Louis, excited for his wife and mother to meet. Though Ann believed Elizabeth's long delay in accepting Thomas's proposal was inexplicable at best and offensive at worst, she determined to hold her tongue and graciously accept her new daughter-in-law into the family. Still, she could not help expressing a bit of sarcasm to a confidant: "Army man, Westerner, Democrat, red hair—these are in fuller force than ever, after six years."

St. Louis society turned out to welcome the couple, and Elizabeth was ultimately charmed by the warmth and unexpected sophistication of the "West." When they returned to Washington in the fall of 1821, she was pregnant.

The public record is ample on Benton, his political career, and his steadfast affection for Elizabeth. Elizabeth's own feelings were more opaque, her initial ambivalence developing over time into a thinly veiled disapproval of her husband and his enthusiasms. On the surface she was a dutiful and considerate wife, having been well trained in domestic perfection, and in the early years of marriage their image was one of pleasant compatibility. She accompanied him to the requisite social and political functions, always impeccably coiffed, and exhibited a graceful domesticity in her housekeeping, serving as soft-spoken but exceedingly courteous hostess to the steady stream of guests. Delicate and frail, her small figure and white skin were in stark contrast to her muscular, suntanned husband. Though not a religious man, Thomas proudly escorted her on his arm to a prominent pew at a Washington Presbyterian church. He pampered her during her pregnancy, sending her to Cherry Grove for her "confinement," and was delighted beyond measure when Elizabeth, whom they called Eliza, was born on February 20, 1822. He embraced fatherhood with relish, and spent many hours making elaborate arrangements for his wife and baby to travel among Washington, Cherry Grove, and St. Louis.

Benton had often wondered what would happen when he and Andrew Jackson met again, imagining various scenarios, for it was inevitable that the two would cross paths. When the Tennessee legislature elected Jackson to the U.S. Senate in 1823, Benton knew his reunion with the man who still carried Benton's bullet in his shoulder was looming. To his great surprise, as the first days of the new Congress convened, Jackson strode directly toward Benton, who was seated in the third row facing the vice president's dais, and chose the chair next to him. "Several Senators saw our situation and offered mediation," Benton wrote of the incident. "I declined it on the ground that what had happened could neither be explained, resented, nor denied." After a frosty start, the two men gradually warmed up as Benton was assigned to a committee chaired by Jackson. "He asked me how my wife was, and I asked him how his was. When he called and left his card, 'Andrew Jackson, for Colonel Benton and Lady,' forthwith I called and left mine: 'Colonel Benton for General Jackson and Lady.' Since then we have dined together at several places, and yesterday at the President's. I made him the first bow. He held forth his hand and we shook hands. I then introduced him to my wife, and thus civil relations are perfectly established between us." Benton was clearly relieved, and the two men would prove to be the closest of friends for the rest of their lives—a relationship strengthened further by Elizabeth's congenial acceptance of the unsophisticated and much-maligned Rachel Jackson. In time, Benton would be Jackson's most influential advocate, their political futures inextricably linked.

He had wanted a son, but on May 31, 1824, his second daughter was born at his father-in-law's home in Cherry Grove. Ever the gentleman, when he first laid eyes on the dark-haired baby girl swaddled in a pink blanket, he gallantly declared: "Two daughters are a crown to any household." Still he named her "Jessie" after his father, and gave her the middle name "Ann," for his mother—his only child to be doubly named for his side of the family. From that day forward he proceeded to treat her as if she were the prince of his brood, molding and shaping her in an image for which there was no role model. "I think I came into my father's life like a breath of his own compelling nature," Jessie would later reflect, "strong, resolute, but open to all tender and gracious influences, and above all, loving him."

Benton and his well-born wife would eventually have six children, but Jessie Ann was his obvious favorite. Her birth changed the dynamic in the marriage and signaled the beginning of Elizabeth's gradual withdrawal from political life and Washington society. By the time Jessie was a young girl, Elizabeth would be a recluse, lounging on a chaise in her private quarters, silently suffering headaches, and avoiding her husband's heated political discussions, which upset her digestion.

From the start, Benton recognized a kindred spirit in his Jessie, a healthy and spirited little creature who was the polar opposite of her mother in disposition and style. Animated and mischievous, perceptive and playful, willful and curious, she had what she later described as an innate instinct to "go straight to the hidden spot in my father's armor." Her father was alternately intrigued and exasperated by the child's strong personality, and early on took it upon himself to oversee her rearing. She unabashedly preferred him over her mother, and under his careful guidance and tutoring she was a highly responsive student—"his praise acted upon her as a heady stimulant; his displeasure, as an effective check," as one observer put it. He placed a small desk in the corner of his library, where Jessie would spend nearly all of her waking hours. The little girl's presence in Benton's library became a familiar sight to all who visited the important senator, her huge chocolate brown eyes taking in everything around her.

A childhood incident was symbolic of Jessie's impish character, and Benton never tired of telling the story. Jackson's 1828 presidential bid had been especially vicious, with Jackson's campaign accusing President John Quincy Adams of procuring prostitutes for Czar Alexander, and Adams's countering with the "coffin handbills" to remind voters that Jackson had killed several people. There were also charges that Jackson's wife, Rachel, had married him while she was still married to another man—a charge with merit, since it was true, but it was a mistake that resulted from her first husband deserting her and the untrustworthy recordkeeping that existed on the frontier. The four-year-old Jessie and her sister, Eliza, got into a box of chalk in Benton's office and proceeded to scribble over every page of a campaign speech he had just completed, rendering it illegible. Enraged, the senator uncharacteristically shouted at the small girls, demanding to know "Who did this?" Eliza quickly dissolved into tears, but Jessie rose, prepared to take the full blame, and scrambled for an explanation. Benton could not help being amused by her performance, her face smeared with dark blue marker, her velvet dress covered with chalk dust. "A little girl that cries 'Hurrah for Jackson!'" she offered, unaware that she had ruined her father's final speech for Jackson but sensing that political maneuvering could save the day.

Quick on her feet, she had deflected what had begun as a highly un-pleasant scene.

In March 1829, the Bentons hosted a hundred guests at their Capitol Hill boardinghouse to celebrate Jackson's inaugural. The tall, white-haired, deeply lined Jackson had taken the oath of office at noon. Dra-matic in his stature, bereaved by the sudden death of his wife, Rachel, the president-elect spoke briefly to a crowd of twenty thousand. Known as a champion of the people, a founder of the Democratic Party who em-bodied what Benton called "the *demos krateo* principle," Jackson ushered in an age of populism underscored by the inauguration itself, where throngs poured into the small city, "the highest and most polished down to the most vulgar and gross," as a dour New England Federalist put it. The first president born in a log cabin, the self-made Jackson would oversee one of the most tumultuous periods in American history—"the feud between the capitalist and laborer, the house of Have and the house of Want," as George Bancroft described the era of struggle between the country's social and economic classes. It would be a gripping time for the nation, and Jessie Ann Benton would spend her formative years at the heart of it all.

The following year the Benton family moved into a large colonial-style house on Sixteenth Street—"bought by my father from a Boston gentle-man who had lived much in London, and who built it with thick walls and spacious rooms and beautified the ground in the rear, where grass and trees were framed in by high thick growths of ivy and scarlet-trumpet creeper which covered the stables." Jessie considered this her home, though she spent much of her childhood in St. Louis and Cherry Grove as well. By the mid-1830s she had four more siblings: Randolph, Sarah, James, and Susan. They stayed in Washington during the winters, where Benton oversaw the education of the children, assigning a special place to each of them in his library on the second floor. He was gentle and solicitous toward them all, encouraging their individual strengths and aptitudes, rarely raising his voice, and showering them with a heavy dose of parental love. His demonstrative affection was in stark contrast with his blustering, often bullying, manner on the floor of the Senate, prompting colleagues to call him the public lion and the private lamb.

While the lively household was filled with fun and laughter, their daily existence was also highly ordered and disciplined. Benton instilled his own regimen of sunshine, nutrition, and exercise on his progeny. He insisted that the nursery windows remain open in all seasons, directed a diet of milk, fruit, and vegetables, allowed meat only twice a week, and demanded that they play outside, rain or shine, for a requisite amount of time each day. A Polish tutor named John Sobieski lived with them and taught the children music, history, and languages.

Benton returned from the Senate every afternoon at four P.M., went to his bedroom, where he changed for dinner, and joined the family in the drawing room exactly forty-five minutes later. There the group engaged in animated conversation to which every family member was expected to contribute. An ironclad rule existed that prohibited "any vexatious topic," as Jessie recalled the routine. If anyone violated this tenet, he or she lost the privilege of dining with the family the following day. "Banishment, 'putting into Coventry,' was the only and most dreaded punishment." Everyone had a designated place in the drawing room. "In this way the habit of eating in peace and with pleasurable surroundings became a necessity that grew with our growth. It was a time, too, of most charming talk and instruction." After dinner, Elizabeth sat at a table laden with beeswax candles, where she quietly knitted. Thomas had a table on the other side of the room, on which sat the book he was currently reading and the day's mail. The children gathered around a massive square table that held a "high shaded lamp, our work baskets and portfolios, and there *our* little world revolved."

Jessie was the most avid student from the start, and her father began including her more and more frequently in his public life. He took her often to visit the president, who had become deeply attached to the young girl. There they would always find him upstairs, his rocking chair pulled close to the fire, the sun streaming in through the southern exposed windows. Still mourning his beloved Rachel, whom he felt had been "slandered" to death in a character assassination he forever blamed on Henry Clay, Jackson seemed to Jessie achingly sad and lonely. "Among my earliest memories of the White House is the impression that I was to keep still and not fidget, or show pain, even if General Jackson twisted his fingers a little too tightly in my curls; he liked my father to bring me when they had their talks, and would keep me by him, his hand on my head— forgetting me of course in the interest of discussion—so that sometimes his long, bony fingers took an unconscious grip that would make me look at my father, but give no other sign."

She had learned to read by the time she was four years old, and before she was a teen she spoke five languages, read Latin and Greek, and was well versed in history, geography, literature, and science. Eventually Benton placed a chair next to the desk in his library, and there she spent as much time as he would permit. While tutors conducted her formal education, he "did the important part of appointing studies and preparing us for our teachers, making broad and lucid what they might have left as 'parroting,' as he expressed it." He espoused a strict set of intellectual habits: "*First*, to look for every word in the dictionary, the *exact* meaning of which is not known to you; *secondly*, to search for every place on the maps which is mentioned in your studies; *third*, to observe the chronology of all events."

He instilled in her a dedication to Jacksonian democracy and to the egalitarian views of Jefferson—what Jackson himself had called "good old Jeffersonian Democratic republican principles"—and taught her to value logic, to form opinions based upon fact, and to defend her principles with courage and an unwavering ferocity in the face of opposition. He began taking her to the Capitol every morning, leaving her for several hours in the care of the congressional librarian to peruse the collection of more than six thousand books that had belonged to Thomas Jefferson before he donated it to the federal government after the British burned the original Library of Congress during the War of 1812. Eventually he let her observe the debates on the floor of the Senate, and every day they would walk together and discuss her experiences. On one such outing she came across the skeleton of a bird lying exposed in a mass of purple flowers. She turned to her father and said, "When I die, don't bury me in a box. Lay me in a bed of violets, for I want the flowers to grow up through my bones." He vowed that if he was still alive, he would see her wishes fulfilled.

As the Jackson administration progressed, Benton family dinners became more public affairs. Intoxicated by the lure of the American frontier, Benton consorted with explorers and generals, army engineers and political figures, presidents and fellow congressmen, inviting them all to his Washington home, endlessly lobbying for western expansion. His library and dining room became famous for the vigorous and progressive dialogue that regularly occurred, intense discussions on the issues of the day. The mahogany table that seated twenty-four swelled with food and drink as discourse proceeded late into the night. Elizabeth routinely excused herself early, and Jessie naturally slipped into the role of hostess. In what was a relatively small capital of twenty thousand on the banks of the Potomac, Benton was at the center of power, and Jessie basked in the glow, acquiring along the way a political education that would prepare her for anything.

Every other March, when the short congressional session ended, the family took a two-week-long journey by coach and steamboat to their western home in St. Louis, traveling on the National Road—"a broad macadamized turnpike from Washington to Wheeling where it met the Ohio and connected with all river navigation, down to New Orleans, and up to St. Louis," as Jessie described it. During these trips, Benton had the baggage sent ahead and then reserved the best coaches for his family's comfort, arranging for fresh horses every ten miles. A skilled horseman, the senator drove the four animals himself, allowing the children to alternate in the seat next to him. They dined and slept at wayside taverns, and Jessie thought it all a glorious escapade.

Their St. Louis manor, situated at the end of a locust-lined path, hosted its own stream of adventurers, missionary priests, French fur traders, Mexican merchants, army officers, and painted and blanketed Indian guides. "Although St. Louis was not more than a *petite ville* in numbers, yet it had great interests and had a stirring life, much of which revolved about my father, who was the connecting link and powerful friendly intermediary between these interests and the Government," Jessie later wrote. Considered the Far West at the time, St. Louis was the outfitting post for expeditions into the intermountain Rockies and on to the coast. "Thither came buckskin-clad voyageurs, 'all animated with a common purpose,' all with eyes turned westward," as one account described the milieu. Jessie found it thrilling, and preferred the time spent in this frontier town to the more stuffy Washington society. Once, when Washington Irving visited the Benton household, the Indians performed a war dance for him that Jessie as a young child found terrifying. Noticing her fear, a "kind-faced young officer" named Albert Sidney Johnston (who would later die fighting for the Confederacy at Shiloh) picked her up and comforted her. One of the more frequent visitors was General William Clark, who, with Meriwether Lewis, had mapped the road to Oregon. As diverse as their backgrounds were, all were devoted to a single destiny: to explore the rich, uncharted territory of America, and to establish trade routes stretching to the Sea of Cortés and beyond.

Jessie loved St. Louis, charmed by the scenery, its French flavor, and its exotic transients. "The Potomac was a wide and beautifully blue river, but it did nothing, and was nothing more than a feature in the landscape;"

she wrote of the banal waterway that wound through the nation's capital, "while here the tawny swift Mississippi was stirring with busy life,
and the little city itself was animated from its thronged river-bank out
through to the Indian camps on the rolling prairie back of the town."
There, too, her father relaxed from the rigors of life in Washington,
spending much of his time outdoors, teaching his children to hunt and
fish, ride horses, and explore the outlying terrain. Every morning he
held court at an outside settee, where a light breakfast of coffee, pastries,
and fruit was served to all who visited him.

But perhaps the most favorite part of all to Jessie was the time spent
with Grandmother Benton, whom she adored. Ann lived in a separate
wing of her son's house, cared for by her old servants, and spent nearly
every waking hour reading. Jessie was fascinated by her grandmother's
breadth of knowledge—"her extensive reading made all countries familiar to her"—and found her liberal ideas refreshing. "She was more
English than my mother in nearness to the mother-country, but she had a
singularly large unprejudiced view of things . . . Both her father and husband were English—both scholarly men and misfits in a new country."
Jessie was particularly touched by how Thomas Hart Benton "deferred
to her calm wisdom." She had a long, thick braid that reached her knees,
and which she wore in a widow's cap. "It was a pleasure to her and a
privilege to me to let down and brush and smooth out this beautiful
hair, and to hear her talk."

In Washington the Benton children were all tutored at home, but
while in St. Louis they were sent to school, accompanied by a black maid
named Sara. "She had been trained from her youth up for her post—as
was the Southern custom—and understood 'manners.' Erect, silent,
holding a hand of each, she drilled us in manners as we went along." In
the afternoons, Jessie and her father were both tutored in Spanish, Benton declaring it necessary that Jessie become fluent in the language "of
our near neighbor, Mexico, with whom closer relations must come." He
also used the occasion to teach her military strategy, inviting her to join
his regular discussions with two friends. One, a Spanish officer who had
served under the Duke of Wellington in Spain, the other a captain in
the French army during Waterloo, the three men endlessly replayed the
strategic decisions of the Spanish theater of the Napoleonic Wars. Jessie
would gather the maps and pins—"beeswax heads for the Spanish troops,
red wax for the English, and for the French, black"—and the men would
simulate troop movements to prove "what might have been," as Jessie

recalled the sessions that continued "not only day after day, but summer after summer."

Jessie's St. Louis experiences were rich and memorable. The city was bordered by an immense, unexplored wilderness, and the community felt like a foreign country. She was captivated by the many priests and nuns in their strange black attire, the peasant women in "their thick white caps, sabots and full red petticoats with big blue or yellow handkerchiefs crossed over the white bodices." When the old Indian warrior Chief Black Hawk was captured, Jessie watched as he was brought as a prisoner to Jefferson Barracks.

Proficient in French—having learned the language in infancy from a French nurse—she spoke it with her many new friends. "Sallow-faced, tawny-haired, with laughing black eyes, these young French-Americans were delightful gay playmates," Jessie described them, "and a great change from our English-fashioned young friends across the mountains." She envied their Catholic religion, which seemed less dogmatic than the strict Calvinism that Elizabeth imposed upon the Benton children. Jessie's interest in Catholicism ushered in a bitter argument with her mother, who chastised Jessie for neglecting her Sunday school lesson one day. Jessie passionately announced that she planned to "go to mass to learn more about a church that doesn't confine your Sunday reading to one good book. Besides, I hate the Presbyterian church—no flowers, no candle light, no pictures." Aghast, Elizabeth sent her rebellious daughter to her room to await Benton's return. That night, her sister Eliza asked her if their father had punished her. "He scolded me for disrespect to mother," Jessie answered, "but not to the Presbyterians."

The journey to St. Louis was so far—and always dictated by the stage of water in the Ohio River—that the family would make the trek only in alternate years, after the short session of Congress that adjourned in March. Often the family spent March through May in New Orleans, where Benton had several clients who were French and Spanish landholders, though Elizabeth incessantly worried that the French customs, the ubiquitous Catholic churches, the theaters and amusements in this "provincial Paris" were dangerous influences on her children—especially the open-minded Jessie.

Every other year, after a long session, Thomas would go to St. Louis, and Elizabeth would take the children to Cherry Grove for the summer. From Washington, the family traveled by public conveyance to Fredericksburg,

Virginia, where McDowell family slaves met them with saddle horses and "Cinderella's Pumpkin"—an English-built yellow coach. The luggage and younger children were transferred to the carriage, and Elizabeth and the older children continued the journey on horseback.

Though in principle she loved her Virginia relatives, Jessie always felt an outcast among them—"put through the ordeal of examination, comparison, and criticism"—and she never welcomed these sojourns to her mother's family home. She dreaded spending the long summers without her beloved father and felt little affinity with her aristocratic cousins and very proper grandparents. Compared to Washington and St. Louis, it was a sterile and shallow world that epitomized the pretense she felt her mother embodied. "The oak floors were kept so brightly waxed and polished that if carpet had not been laid across the halls you could hardly keep your footing, and you saw the furniture reflected as in smooth water," she wrote. "If any one walked on these shining surfaces, immediately they left there would appear, quickly, like gnomes coming out of the ground, a young servant with waxed brushes and rubbing-cloth, and an older one, grumbling little low orders until the spot was restored to brightness."

Nestled in an idyllic valley of the Blue Ridge Mountains, the property was impeccably manicured—"a double avenue of cherry-trees," Jessie recalled, "which had been arched on the inner boughs and trimmed straight on the outer side"—the decorum in the home stiflingly formal. Her stern grandfather James McDowell, master of the plantation, found Jessie annoyingly rambunctious, precocious, and outspoken, and didn't hesitate to express his contempt. While her grandmother was sweet and affectionate, Jessie thought her diffidence to her husband pathetic and weak. The relatives mocked Jessie's sturdy double-soled walking shoes, which her father had had made for her—calling them "Jefferson shoes," which was a euphemism for "negro shoes"—insisting that she don "little slippers laced to and fro on top of the foot and around the ankle." Just as these Virginia connections hated the "Pope and all his works," they "abhorred Jefferson and his *leveling* doctrines," and "despised" white people who worked for a living. Resentful of their prejudices, Jessie adamantly defied them. "I grew to connect thick shoes and Jefferson with 'Democratic ideas,' and knowing my father was a 'Democrat' and that he respected Jefferson, I took my shoes as a badge of loyalty to him and his beliefs."

Still, she usually managed to enjoy herself at the "home place" where she had been born, where her mother's family had lived for five generations, and where the large house was filled with relatives, music, flowers, and laughter. While her girl cousins "played battledoor and shuttlecock, and graces, and amused themselves with their large doll's house," Jessie stole away alone or with a boy cousin whenever the opportunity arose. She spent as much time as possible outdoors, climbing oak and sycamore trees, picking cherries in the fruit orchard, and often sneaking away to the forbidden cabins to play with the slave children. She called these friends the "cabin children" and delighted in their company, for they knew the secret pleasures of the estate—where to hunt duck eggs and find hornets' nests, how to build a seesaw with nothing more than a plank and a fence, how to gather and dry lavender. The whitewashed slave cottages had large fireplaces, and the smell of roasting potatoes and chestnuts swirled through their little community. Jessie loved the "Baby-Cabin," which was filled with cradles and pallets where many babies were cared for by old women who fed the infants milk and hominy while their mothers worked at the McDowell home and their fathers tilled the family's fields.

She was particularly intrigued by an elderly slave they called "Uncle Primus," who was blind and inseparable from his English mastiff guide dog, and by a tall, powerful banjo player named Big Sam, who led the slaves in song and dance at the end of the day, everything from "shucklin' songs to Buryin' hymns, and, always, 'When Moses,'" as Jessie remembered the pleasant summer evenings. Though she didn't realize it at the time, her opinions of slavery were formed by these experiences.

She received tutoring at Cherry Grove, and, like the rest of her indoor atmosphere, she found it dull and uninspiring. "After the charming way my father taught me, explaining, and reading to me from splendidly illustrated works from the Congressional Library, and loving to have me question him, other teaching was very flat." In this environment, history, which Jessie found fascinating as Benton taught it to her, was reduced to merely memorizing dates and battles—none of the great debate and discussion she was accustomed to in Washington and St. Louis. The day's instruction always ended with a solemn reading of a chapter in the Bible, "to be read in a respectful manner and voice, which made it sound like we were crying." Jessie, along with her sisters and female cousins, were taught sewing and other domestic skills, with a disciplined focus on the rules of housekeeping. "There was a large working force under well-drilled servants," she wrote, "and in Virginia this management of a household was as much a branch of education as it had been in England in Addison's time." The priorities of Jessie's Virginia and Missouri grandmothers could not have been more different. While Grandmother McDowell rebuked Jessie for spending too much time reading, Grandmother Benton encouraged Jessie to abandon all domestic pastimes for intellectual pursuits. "You should never waste your time, doing what an uneducated person can do better for you," was Ann Gooch Benton's credo.

The brightest spot in her Cherry Grove education was the discovery of novels, which her grandmother possessed in abundance but children were prohibited from reading "because they were not true." Exploring the secret places of her grandparents' house, she came upon a garret room with a sloping roof and gables. There she found a treasure trove of novels secreted among storage boxes and chests. Certain that she would not be discovered, for all the slaves thought the room haunted and her cousins had no interest in the concealed alcove, Jessie read her first, and, ironically, lifetime favorite, novel. Hidden in the eaves of a forgotten room, in a mansion on a grand estate, Jessie read *Ivanhoe*, the action and romance classic of Sir Walter Scott—the inventor of the historical novel and creator of aristocratic characters with whom Southern slaveholders identified. A tale of chivalry, love, and adventure, it would be a metaphor for Jessie's future life.

On the rare occasions when her father visited the family at Cherry Grove, Jessie came alive. She was routinely chastised for her disobedience, and her father could always be counted on to defend her. "She will not do so when she is older," he would dismiss his in-laws' complaints about the headstrong girl. "Wait until she begins to think." Then he would take her hunting out into the wheatfields far from the house, letting her carry his game bag, which he filled with freshly killed quail. They would find a serene spot under an apple tree, and Benton would draw out a little book of Homer and read to her. She could never bear to displease him—"no words could so hurt me as to see him turn away his head, lower his eyelids and not look up from his book while I stood by him"—and was on her absolute best behavior whenever he was present. But his presence at Cherry Grove was woefully infrequent, and Jessie was most often left to the disapproving reprimands of her mother and many relatives.

Of all of her homes, it would be Cherry Grove that contributed most to Jessie's views of slavery, for it was there that she would witness the system firsthand in all its complexities. When she was eleven, her grandfather died, leaving an estate that included forty slaves, many of whom were inherited by Jessie's mother. Elizabeth had always been ambivalent on the issue, but by the 1830s her deeply held religious convictions had swayed her firmly against the institution. She promptly set free the slaves bequeathed to her, while maintaining them and their children until they were self-supporting. Elizabeth's brother, Jessie's uncle James McDowell, became an outspoken critic of slavery—unusual for his time and place— and as a Virginia legislator advocated gradual emancipation.

By the mid-1830s, Benton's own views of slavery were changing, and Jessie watched and listened with fascination as each of her parents took a stand at odds with their Southern roots. While Benton had long considered the North responsible for fanning the flames of agitation, he increasingly saw the South as the main culprit. As time went on, Benton's resistance to slavery and Southern demands increased, though preservation of the Union always took precedence in his mind. "He belongs in that group of men to whom our country, in the second great crisis of its existence, owes most," Theodore Roosevelt wrote of the progressive Democrat, "for his name must be numbered among the names of the Southern men who, when the South went wrong, stood by the nation as against their own section."

To Jessie, Washington was "home," and every winter the family returned to the Sixteenth Street residence, though her mother had a "mild contempt for our house in Washington because it was bought not inherited." The capital had developed during the Jackson presidency, as more diplomats and congressmen made the city their permanent residence. Balls and society functions had acquired a sophistication reminiscent of Southern gentility, the coveted invitations drawn from those in and around the presidency, the cabinet, the Supreme Court, the Congress, the diplomatic corps, and the army and navy. Jessie would have her share of Washington society, beginning as a young girl when she was invited to one of Jackson's famous White House dinner parties, where camellia and laurestina lined the entrance, wood fires burned in every room, and the massive horseshoe-shaped table was "covered with every good and glittering thing French skill could devise, and at either end was a monster salmon in waves of meat jelly." As a preteen she attended the new Russian minister's Georgetown mansion, where she received white kid gloves and a lace fan as party favors. Count Alexander de la Bodisco was a flamboyant presence in Washington circles, where his prancing black horses "always made a sort of royal progress of his daily drive to the Capitol from his residence," as Jessie recalled the conspicuous movements of the generous and popular diplomat. Jessie was included in his foreign circle at her young age because of her fluency in Spanish and French. At thirteen she attended her first White House ball, when the newly elected president, Martin Van Buren, hosted a party to introduce his son Smith to the young belles of the capital, and where Jessie attracted great attention for her beautiful face, fit and trim figure, and graceful bearing. During the late 1830s, Benton and Jessie were the talk of the town, as Elizabeth had become increasingly cloistered and Jessie had supplanted her as Benton's escort. As chairman of the Senate Committee on Military Affairs, the Missouri Democrat's company was much sought after, and Jessie's charm and wit made her a favorite in her own right.

In the fall of 1838, Thomas and Elizabeth Benton decided it was time for fourteen-year-old Jessie to attend a private boarding school. Both parents were alarmed by the number of suitors who had asked for Jessie's hand in marriage, including "two members of the official family." The Bentons took Eliza and Jessie the three miles to Miss English's Academy in Georgetown for their personal interviews with the director, and while Jessie balked, the more conventional Eliza enthusiastically welcomed the experience. "You will find Eliza a patient Griselda in study," Elizabeth told the Danish headmistress. "And Miss Jessie?" she asked. Elizabeth laughed and replied: "I fear you will find her a Don Quixote."

While Eliza fit in comfortably, delighted to be with her friends Eleanora Calvert, Georgia Washington, and Mildred Fitzhugh, daughters of prominent Maryland and Virginia families, Jessie was distraught from the beginning, pronouncing it "a great misfortune." She begged and cajoled her father, cried and implored him to let her continue her studies with him. When it was clear he would not relent, that he felt strongly about the need for her to associate with her peers, she fell silent, retreating to her bedroom, where she wept all night. She could not understand the hypocrisy in her father, that after he had raised her as a son he now expected her to waste her eager mind on fanciful pursuits. The next morning she approached her father in his library, her face swollen and her long brown hair cropped short below her ears. "I won't need other groups of girls," she told him. "I mean to have no more society, just to study here and be my father's companion as Madame de Staël was hers." Benton stood his ground, and Jessie was sent against her will to the elite school. "Then I learned," Jessie wrote of her lost innocence, "that men like their womenkind to be pretty, and not of the short-haired variety."

Miserable from the start, Jessie hated the social pretense and intellectual narrowness. "It was a favorite place for the daughters of Senators and members of Congress and army and navy people, and there was no end to the conceit, the assumption, the class distinction there," she wrote. While Eliza was careful to associate only with the best-bred daughters, Jessie irreverently chose friends from a group of less affluent girls. Her favorite, Harriet Beall Williams, was the daughter of a government bureaucrat and was a day student whose family could not afford the cost of room and board. Tall, blonde, and striking, Harriet was every bit as spontaneous and bright as Jessie, and the two found kindred spirits in each other. "Naturally we were in sympathy with other idlers," Jessie wrote. Regularly flaunting the rules, challenging authority, and disregarding their studies, Jessie and Harriet caused much angst among their superiors.

Jessie's tenure at Miss English's reached a climax when she acted as de facto campaign manager for Harriet's election as May Queen. When the vivacious girl won by popular vote, the school's principal intervened to set aside the election in favor of another student the faculty thought "more worthy of the honor." Jessie, along with most of the student body, was outraged, convinced that the vote was nullified based upon Harriet's humble economic origins. While all of her fellow pupils sat silently by, Jessie arose and challenged the principal, leading a mutiny of "we, the commons," as she called her rebellious cohorts. "This decision is most unjust and unfair to everybody. The first choice was honestly made, and besides the new Queen can't even dance." For this outburst, she was sent to the infirmary for a day's solitary confinement and a dose of senna tea. Harriet's mother withdrew her daughter from school, leaving Jessie bereft at the treatment that contradicted everything her father had taught her, everything she thought he stood for. The event led to a new round of appeals from Jessie to Benton, imploring him to rescue her, to let her return home "to study and be his friend and companion."

In a satisfying and ironic twist, Harriet was soon betrothed to the fabulously wealthy Count Bodisco, and the fifteen-year-old Jessie would be the first bridesmaid to her teenage friend. That the groom was sixty years old, short and homely, and with an unfortunate brown wig, spawned titillating chatter throughout the capital. "Fancy the stir when it was known that this dazzling personage was to marry the very young daughter of very quiet people in Georgetown," Jessie recalled. Still, he lavished his young bride with gifts and attention, and the two exhibited an unmistakable affection for each other. The Bodisco wedding was the gossip of

Washington, a sumptuous affair more evocative of Czarist Russia than Jacksonian America. The count insisted that the eight bridesmaids match Harriet in age and beauty, while the groomsmen would be eminent older men, renowned in their careers. The elegant Henry Clay would give the bride away. Jessie was escorted by the most eligible bachelor, Senator James Buchanan of Pennsylvania—a man who, ironically, would be a rival for the presidency against Jessie's future husband. Stunning in a white brocade gown made for her by a famous English dressmaker, Jessie thought this her "first unaided appearance as a chief actor" in her life. "I was in grownup finery and one *does* act up to their dress."

Among all the glittering personages, Jessie thought Harriet the "fairest and tallest. Her dress was fashioned on that of Russian brides and was of rich white satin with much silver lace—soft and flexible as silk lace, but of most rich and luminous effect. On her yellow hair rested a coronet of red velvet covered with diamonds, and from that fell, over the shoulders, and ran down the long train, an exquisite veil of silver lace, light and sparkling as cobwebs on the grass when the first level morning sun lights up the dewdrops on them. Large ear-rings of diamonds trembled against her rose-leaf cheeks and shone on her long white throat."

The event marked the beginning of Jessie's thoughts of her future, of what marriage would and should entail. Initially happy with her friend's good fortune, she gradually came to be distressed by the match, thinking it a convenient arrangement, a gross barter of youth and innocence for wealth and social standing. For the first time she saw with trepidation the constraints on women in pre-Victorian America, and vowed to herself she would not succumb to the petty restrictions.

In 1839, as the rest of the country struggled to emerge from the Panic of 1837, the Benton family moved into a three-story home on C Street in Southeast Washington. Just a few blocks from the Capitol, the house became the central meeting point for expansionist politicians. Brilliant and ambitious, Benton had been the most outspoken advocate for Jacksonian radicalism in the U.S. Senate throughout the decade. A passionate spokesman for western expansion, a scholar who used the ancient Roman senators as his model, he had become a famous orator, called a "walking library" by his peers. Fluent in Spanish and French, so knowledgeable in history and geography that he could draw esoteric details out of thin air, he "could cite with equal facility from the classics, the Bible, the histories of Britain, Europe, and the Orient, and the documents and writings of the Founding Fathers," a biographer described his role as one of the Senate's most learned men. While his blustering speeches had once resulted in an infamous clearing out of the Senate chambers, he had increasingly gained stature, not only through his role as mouthpiece of the administration and close personal friendship with the president, but for his sheer erudition as well.

He fought tirelessly against monopolies and a national bank— "chartered companies, with exclusive and extraordinary privileges, are the legislative evil and opprobrium of the age in which we live," he declared in 1835—both of which he saw as a clash of class. "Democracy implies a government by the people," he exclaimed in a speech; "Aristocracy implies a government of the rich." Drawing on parallels with the fight that British statesmen waged against the Bank of England, Benton, who came to be called "Old Bullion" for his efforts, contended that vesting the Bank of the United States with so much power was in contradiction to a free and democratic society. "To whom is all this power granted?" he thundered on the Senate floor. "To a company of private individuals, many of them foreigners, and the mass of them residing in a remote and narrow corner of the Union . . . It tends to aggravate the inequality of fortunes; to make the rich richer, and the poor poorer; to multiply nabobs and paupers; and to deepen and widen the gulf which separates Dives from Lazarus."

In the battle against the national bank, Benton developed a lifelong and pivotal friendship with Francis Preston Blair—a man whom the Benton children would call "Father Blair" and who would ultimately become the nemesis of Benton's beloved daughter Jessie. Diminutive and hatchet-faced, an honors graduate of Transylvania College, the Kentuckian had come to the capital to edit the *Globe*, the administration newspaper and the forerunner of the *Congressional Record*. Nine years younger than the senator, Blair would eventually consider Benton the greatest living American. Their families would become enmeshed. Blair's two sons would go on to practice law in Missouri under Benton's patronage, and his daughter Elizabeth would be Jessie's closest friend for much of her adult life. Though two decades later there would be a breach of epic and historic dimensions, for now the political and personal bonds were unbreakable.

By the end of the 1830s, Benton's dream of the West had become an outright obsession. A self-proclaimed disciple of Jefferson, Benton differed from the Founding Father in subtle but key areas. "Unlike Jefferson's inward-looking, continental conception of empire, Benton's like Britain's, was outward-looking and maritime—focused more on trade and ports and gold and silver than on agriculture, territory, and settlement," according to historian Tom Chaffin. This fixation on trade rather than territory set him apart from his expansionist colleagues at the time, but made him similar to those who would guide American diplomacy late in the nineteenth century and in the twentieth century. He saw western expansion as a "course of empire," his philosophy based on his knowledge of world history, and his premise rooted in the assumption that historical empires proceeded westward toward trade with Asia. Benton's "resolve," as Jessie would later describe it, was "to carry out Jefferson's plan of overland communication with the Asiatic countries, and to hold for ourselves the port on the Pacific which was its key."

The nation's boundaries remained ill-defined, and the immense and unpopulated region of the West, not yet mapped or explored, put the country in direct conflict with Mexico and Great Britain. Twenty years later, Benton remained deeply opposed to the Treaty of 1818, which gave joint occupation of Oregon to America and Great Britain. "My father became possessed by this Oregon question," Jessie later wrote.

It was against this political backdrop that Lieutenant Colonel John C. Frémont entered the senator's life.

Shortly after the Bodisco wedding, Jessie made yet another impassioned plea to her father. Unlike her previous appeals, she was testy, even confrontational about his acquiescence with such a disingenuous institution. At the wedding she had overheard Miss English herself fawning over Harriet, claiming credit for her pupil's great success. "This conduct is a shameless revulsion of feeling, which makes the thought of going back there most unpleasant," Jessie insisted. Benton listened quietly and then announced that she must return. He agreed that the behavior was deplorable, he told her, but felt that the school's benefits far outweighed its shortcomings. Though perhaps conflicted, Benton ultimately believed that the discipline imposed by the academy was advantageous to his bold and assertive daughter. While such strength of character, such outrage at life's injustices, would be admirable in a son, he had come to fear that such traits would not bode well for Jessie's future.

Jessie considered seeking her mother's intervention, but knew such efforts would be futile. Her relationship with her mother had always been complicated. She disliked her mother for not appreciating her father;

resented her for not understanding and embracing Jessie's spirit; admired her for freeing her slaves; lacked respect for her long-suffering submission; was frustrated by her infirmity; pitied her resignation and unhappiness; feared for her mortality; was enraged at her passivity; and loved her deeply despite it all. To call it a rivalry simplified the depth of emotions, the complexity of the dynamics. In any event, Jessie knew Elizabeth was not reliable as an advocate.

Along the way, Benton requested from Miss English a private report about Jessie's progress, which prompted the famous letter—"Miss Jessie, although extremely intelligent, lacks the docility of a model student. Moreover, she has the objectionable manner of seeming to take our orders and assignments under consideration, to be accepted or disregarded by some standard of her own." He had always relished his daughter's independent spirit, championed the wit and pluck that set her apart, even delighted that others found her unmanageable. Still, it was time that Jessie's impulses be contained.

He filed the letter and left his home for a meeting with Secretary of War Joel Poinsett. Poinsett and the French geographer Joseph Nicollet had arranged to introduce the senator to Nicollet's brilliant and promising protégé John Charles Frémont. Now fifty-eight years old, Benton was more enthusiastic than ever about associating his name with a western map, seeing it as the culmination and legacy for his lifetime of public service. When he arrived at the Hassler, Nicollet, and Frémont boardinghouse he was initially upset that no map of the Mississippi Valley expedition had yet been created. "Mr. Benton had expected to find the map in progress, and was disappointed to see only the blank projection," Frémont recalled of their first interview. "But his disappointment gave way to interest of another kind when he saw spread out on the tables the evidences of the material first to be digested. His visit was not simply one of intelligent curiosity, but there was purpose in it, as indeed, I found when afterward I came to know him, there was in all that he did. The character of his mind was to utilize, and what he could not assimilate he did not touch." Indeed, Benton was consumed with a sense of purpose—to "save" Oregon from the British, to occupy the territory there as soon as practicable, to promote migration and establish a government there under military protection. To him, the situation was urgent and called for immediate action. Before the United States could control Oregon, before settlers could be expected to migrate in necessary numbers, new expeditions must be funded, extensive maps must be produced.

Benton was enthralled by the astronomical tables, sextants, and barometers, and enchanted by the explorers' tales, and an animated discussion continued throughout the afternoon. For their part, the scientists were stunned by Benton's own knowledge of the frontier. Though he had never been west of Missouri, his decades of conversation with the many St. Louis adventurers, the books and maps he had absorbed for years, had made him a veritable expert. His exhilaration was infectious, especially with the young Frémont. "The interview left on me a profound impression and raised excited interest," Frémont wrote. "The thought of penetrating into the recesses of that wilderness region filled me with enthusiasm—I saw visions."

Many lives can be marked by a turning point, a moment at which all the disparate strands of the past come together. At that moment, a person's future seems suddenly fixed and obvious. For the twenty-eight-year-old Frémont, meeting Thomas Hart Benton was the apex of all that had gone before. "From Poinsett, Frémont had acquired an ideology of U.S. nationalism, and, from Nicollet, he had gained a scientific and spatial comprehension of the continent, one in which domains defined by river basins and mountains transcended those etched on maps by distant politicians and their hireling mapmakers," observed one of his biographers. "Now, from Benton, the young man's worldview gained yet another dimension: Frémont embraced a historical and temporal view of America and its politics—learned to view America as a force moving through history and, equally important, as belonging to a long procession of world empires."

There were striking parallels in the backgrounds of Benton and Frémont, though neither recognized them at first. Each lost his father at a young age, and each was raised by a beautiful, formidable, and intelligent woman named Ann. Each would become a scholar, each driven to make their beloved and bereaved mother proud. Each would seek a peer in marriage, and each would marry a much younger woman. For now, what they saw in each other was a symbiotic venue to fulfill their individual dreams.

Benton invited Frémont to the C Street home for dinner, and before long he was a fixture there, joining the family every evening. He was ineffably drawn to the congenial family life, a domestic richness that circumstances had prevented him from knowing in his own childhood. He was touched by the unrelenting gentleness Benton showed toward the frail, ailing, and remote Elizabeth, and impressed by the attention he gave the children. The atmosphere was a rare combination of discipline and frivolity, punctuated always by impeccable manners, intellectual conversation, and musical performances. Three children were living at home— Sarah, Susan, and Randolph. Another child, James, had died not long before, and Eliza and Jessie Ann were away at boarding school. Their warmth and exuberance enveloped him, and from this safe haven he and Benton plotted the future course of America.

3

The Pathfinder
and His Wife 1840–1844

. . . to arrive where we started
And know the place for the first time

—T. S. Eliot, *Little Gidding*

THEY WERE IRRESISTIBLY drawn to each other from the moment they met. Like many classic love affairs, it began with a knowing, an instant recognition that each had met his or her mate, that their lives would be entwined.

He was in uniform—"slender, upright, elastic and tough as fine steel," she later recalled—his dark, curly hair, his ocean blue eyes radiating eloquence and elegance. The twenty-seven-year-old explorer had a reputation as the most handsome man in Washington, and Jessie couldn't help staring. Though they were seated next to each other during the musicale, neither spoke more than a few words. Later that night, with teenage glee, she confided in Eliza: "I'm so glad I wore the pin candy-stripe with the rose sash instead of the dotted muslin with the blue. It made me look much older."

What he saw was a fresh fifteen-year-old "in the bloom of her girlish beauty." She was radiant and energetic—"perfect health effervesced in bright talk," he later recalled. He thought her classically beautiful. Her oval face and flawless complexion, her dainty nose and deep-set brown eyes framed by arched brows, her perfect lips, made him nearly speechless. But even more attractive to him was the quick wit, a playfulness and charm he found refreshing in comparison to the capital's many belles.

"Her beauty had come far enough down from English ancestry to be now in her that American kind which is made up largely of mind expressed in the face," he wrote. "At that time of awakening mind the qualities that made hers could only be seen in flitting shadows across the face, or in the expressions of incipient thought and unused and untried feeling . . . There are features which convey to us a soul so white that they impress with instant pleasure, and of this kind were hers."

They would not see each other for several months. When Jessie returned from Miss English's on vacation, Frémont was invited to the Benton family home for a party, specially requested by the visiting Grandmother McDowell, who thought him "a highly superior young man." Lovestricken since first meeting Jessie, John immediately found upon seeing her that his feelings had not waned. She was equally enthusiastic, and the two talked with each other the entire evening. Alarmed by the budding romance, Senator and Mrs. Benton took steps to keep the two apart, but not before the lovers had arranged for a safe and secret exchange of letters. "She has a delicacy and winsomeness, alluring gayety with a hint of fire underneath," Frémont told Nicollet the next day.

An outcast from birth, John found Jessie equally willing to flout convention, to be ruled by the personal impulses that brought excitement to life. Like his mother, she had the courage to seize love when she found it. From the first, Jessie could not hide her infatuation with John, though it was clear her parents found it distressing. They quickly came to know each another through a fulsome correspondence, like minds who shared a passion for books, exploration, and, not least, Thomas Hart Benton, who completed the triangle and was the inspiration for them both.

From her satin chaise, where she spent her days suffering from some vague and undiagnosed illness that Jessie thought a willful malaise, Elizabeth discouraged her daughter's interest in the army officer. Despite Elizabeth's being only forty-seven years old, her black hair had turned gray. Though her illness was never discussed or defined, she rarely joined the family anymore, dining alone in her room on a tray brought by a servant. Her health deteriorated and she had lost all interest in life, rarely reading or conversing, not even knitting anymore, but rallying now to intervene in Jessie's romantic future. She begged Jessie to abandon her foolish passion for a man who was not up to her breeding, urging her instead to consider the proposal from President Van Buren, who was just finishing his first term and running for reelection. Though he was forty-two years older than Jessie and the father of four grown sons, all older than

Jessie, Elizabeth thought that the widower was a perfect match. The Bodisco marriage fresh in Jessie's mind, she thought the suggestion grotesque.

For his part, Thomas Hart Benton was more direct, appealing to Jessie's ambitious and pragmatic nature. Diplomatic as ever, he first praised the young Frémont, whom he greatly admired. Not sharing his wife's social pretenses, and fearing it would further alienate his spirited daughter, Benton did not mention the disparity in breeding. Instead he pointed out that marriage to an army lieutenant would be one of financial struggle, constant moving, little opportunity for advancement—all in all, a mundane and common lifestyle in great contrast with Jessie's cultivated upbringing. Benton spoke with Frémont as well, making it clear that the courtship must immediately halt. Benton felt he could not exclude Frémont from the regular drawing room salons that occurred every evening, attended as they were by the very men Benton was lobbying for western exploration. Still, he insisted that their emotional attachment be broken, and he kept a watchful eye on them both.

On March 4, 1841, William Henry Harrison was sworn in as the ninth president of the United States. The elderly Whig had defeated the Democrat Van Buren in what had been called the first of the "riproaring campaigns" in American history—an upset attributed to the economic downturn of 1837, for which Van Buren was blamed. The press had portrayed Harrison as a rugged frontiersman, despite his aristocratic Virginia background, and Van Buren as a "silver spoon" aristocrat, despite his upbringing as the son of an upstate New York tavernkeeper. Frémont attended the inauguration ceremonies with the Benton family, where it became obvious that neither John nor Jessie had taken the Bentons' admonitions seriously. That evening, her father openly confronted Jessie. "We all admire Lieutenant Frémont, but with no family, no money, and the prospect of slow promotion in the Army, we think him no proper match for you. And besides, you are too young to think of marriage in any case." He then issued a dictum, which he conveyed to John as well: There could be no thoughts of marriage for one full year while Jessie matured. If, at the end of that period, both found they were still in love, the subject would be reopened. Stunned and upset, the lovers overtly agreed to the ultimatum, though Frémont began plotting for a secret engagement. If anything, the restriction only heightened Jessie's ardor and sense of injustice—her love for John becoming "not only a passionate impulse but a political statement," as one historian described it.

A month later, Harrison was dead of pneumonia, throwing the nation into mourning while offering an opportunity to John and Jessie. An elaborate funeral procession was planned, the cortege scheduled to pass directly in front of the Capitol Hill quarters Frémont shared with Hassler and Nicollet. Frémont graciously invited the Benton family to view the somber event from his second-story balcony. While the senator and Elizabeth could not attend, Benton made an exception for the historic event, assuming that Frémont would be marching with his corps in the procession, and allowed Jessie to go with Grandmother McDowell.

On April 4, 1841—what John would later call his "red letter day"—he filled the suite with roses and potted geraniums. He had transformed the work area, usually brimming with maps, documents, and instruments, into an elegant parlor, serving expensive French bonbons and English teas. "It was for my grandmother's special pleasure that we were there," Jessie wrote, "and only a few of our friends had been added. These wise elders were troubled that their young host should have made such graceful preparations for them—expensive to a 'poor army man.'" After greeting each of his guests individually—and after all were preoccupied with the sad event unfolding on the street below—he removed himself and Jessie to a quiet corner near the fireplace. There he proposed marriage, which Jessie readily accepted, and they entered a pact to keep their plans secret for the time being.

The next day, John arranged for all the flowers to be delivered to Jessie's mother, who was not mollified by the gesture. Learning that John had procured sick leave to see Jessie, that the couple had indiscreetly embraced, and now even more suspicious with the floral delivery, a livid Thomas and Elizabeth Benton met secretly with Secretary of War Poinsett, who reluctantly agreed to help them banish Frémont from Washington. Appealing primarily to her friend Mrs. Poinsett, Elizabeth "frankly stated the case—my extreme youth . . . and the need for gaining time to dispel the impression" the dashing lieutenant had made, Jessie wrote. Poinsett reluctantly agreed to intervene, and on June 4, 1841, John suddenly received orders from Colonel John James Abert "detaching him from his duty on the map, and directing him to proceed without delay to make a survey of the Des Moines River in Iowa." Though the need for the survey was crucial, Frémont and Nicollet both considered the completion of the report and maps of the previous expedition more important. Nicollet was very much opposed to Frémont's leaving. He had long hoped to lead the expedition to the frontier in the

Northwest himself, but his declining health precluded his participation. He was consumed with sadness that he could not complete his earlier work, and disappointed that he was losing his key assistant at a critical moment. Though Nicollet openly protested, the orders stayed.

Shocked, John wrote a heartfelt letter to Jessie, plighting his troth. They were allowed a thirty-minute private farewell meeting in Benton's library, and when Jessie emerged, her face streaked with tears, her head bowed in anguish, Benton faltered briefly, recalling his own sorrow at Elizabeth's numerous rejections. John shook hands with the senator, and with a heavy heart walked down the steps of the C Street home. For Jessie it would be the first of many partings, weeks and months of utter loneliness, punctuated by sheer dread and fear for John's safety.

John proceeded to St. Louis, and though leading the expedition was an advancement for his career, it would not "cure the special complaint for which I had been sent there," as he put it. He outfitted with the help of Chouteau's American Fur Company, and once again hired the botanist Charles Geyer to make drawings. On June 27 the men departed from St. Louis, traveling upriver two hundred miles, to Raccoon Forks. With forty-five thousand settlers in Iowa Territory, the Sauk and Fox tribes were being pushed out of their homeland, creating violent tensions and boundary disputes. From Raccoon Forks they would follow the Des Moines River to its mouth. Driven by an urgent desire to return to Jessie, Frémont pushed his men, working overtime with his own astronomical observations.

Jessie was miserable from the moment John departed. With the hope of distracting her, if not quelling her ardor, Elizabeth took Jessie to Cherry Grove to attend the wedding of her cousin Sally McDowell. Jessie seemed to fully enjoy the Virginia festivities, dancing with the many young groomsmen, even dressing up in her cousin Preston's cadet uniform, which caused a stir in the decorous family. She seemed so genuinely happy that Elizabeth wrote her husband: "I truly believe our Jessie's childish love affair has quite blown over." Little did she know that Jessie was pining for John more feverishly than ever.

As they prepared to leave Cherry Grove, Grandmother McDowell became suddenly ill and died within a few days. That day, Eliza found Jessie weeping violently in the garden, and seeking to comfort her sister, pointed out that their grandmother had lived a long and full life. "I'm not grieving for grandmother," the distraught Jessie replied. "She was happy. My heart is breaking for my own unhappy life."

When she returned to Washington, Jessie placed a small shrine on her desk: a newspaper woodcut of John, a bowl of violets, and a candle she kept lit day and night. "The violet is my friendly flower," she wrote. "She lives in quiet places. She lays no claim to beauty's dower. Nor flaunts her perfumed graces."

When John returned in August, the two were ever more solidly committed, though determined to exercise discretion for fear of inspiring another plot to separate them. It became more and more difficult to find private time under Benton's careful observation, but Nicollet, along with sympathetic friends of Jessie's, provided locations for clandestine love trysts. Empathetic to Jessie's misery, her sister Eliza had become a devoted accomplice, assisting in the subterfuge whenever she could.

In late September Jessie was invited to her first state dinner. President John Tyler, Harrison's vice president who had ascended to the office, hosted the glamorous Prince de Joinville, son of King Louis Philippe of France. Jessie was included not only for her great beauty but also for her fluency in French. She wore her first "real Paris dress," as she put it, the palest pink and made of "fine muslin and valenciennes." One of the more lavish White House events to occur since the founding of the Republic, the dinner was attended by the full diplomatic corps and army and navy officers, all in dress uniform. Secretary of State Daniel Webster gave a toast, and dancing proceeded in the East Room. That the prince most frequently selected Jessie as his partner attracted much attention, and Jessie's parents mistook her effusive joyfulness as evidence that she had outgrown her infatuation with John. The next day Benton finally acquiesced to Jessie's many entreaties, announcing that she need not return to Miss English's Academy. Now, he told her, she could resume her education at home.

In fact, the Bentons' relaxed vigilance was misguided, for Jessie and John were scheming for their elopement with careful precision. Maria Crittenden, the wife of Attorney General John J. Crittenden, was among Jessie's friends who offered her home as a secret meeting place. In mid-October, Frémont and Nicollet visited three Protestant clergymen in one day, hoping that one of them would perform the ceremony. Each refused, citing Benton's notorious temper and broad political power. Discouraged, John approached Washington mayor William Winston Seaton. Speaking in guarded terms about a hypothetical marriage, inciting Seaton's misgivings by refusing to identify the "parties," John sensed the meeting was a mistake. Seaton refused, prompting John and Jessie to advance expeditiously lest the mayor report the meeting to his friend Senator Benton. With this, Mrs. Crittenden stepped in, agreeing to accompany John to St. Peter's Catholic Church, where the two would persuade Father Joseph Van Horseigh to perform the secret ceremony.

On October 19, 1841, Jessie and John were married, apparently at the Crittenden home. Details of the service would remain vague throughout history, becoming even murkier over the decades as their political rivals sought to smear the couple with evidence of their "secret Catholicism." Responding many years later to an inquiry, Jessie would contend it was a civil rather than a religious ceremony. "It was in a drawing room—no altar lights or any such thing—I was asked nothing but my age."

The couple parted separately that evening, and decided that Jessie would tell her father at the first propitious moment. By November, she still had not broken the news, and an extremely ill Nicollet urged Frémont to do so immediately. "The possibility of an accidental discovery is very strong!" a friend warned John. "Why don't you go, manly and open as you are, forward and put things by a single step to the right . . . only act now and you will *soon* get over little disturbances which might arise at first. Nothing very serious *can* happen now more to you—the prize is secured." Perhaps John was thinking of the possible ramifications of marrying an underage girl. In any event, he agreed with his friends that time was of the essence. "Let me go to the Senator and explain at once," he implored Jessie. "This is a matter between men."

Jessie agreed that the truth must be told, but felt they should do it together. "Come to the house tomorrow morning before ten o'clock," she told him. "I will ask for an early interview."

The next day, John arrived at the C Street residence, and the two entered Benton's library, where they found both the senator and his wife. Benton was sullen and angry—it seemed clear that the rumor had reached him; in fact, some reports indicated that the marriage became known the day the certificate was filed with the court. Barely acknowledging them, Benton sat stonily in his chair. He would not meet Jessie's eyes, focusing entirely on John. She watched as her new husband, usually brave and articulate, fumbled and sweated before nervously blurting out the news.

Neither was fully prepared for Benton's reaction. He ignored Jessie altogether, "looking at Frémont as though he were a stray dog." Enraged, he yelled at the young man: "Get out of my house and never cross my door again! Jessie shall stay here." With that, as Jessie would later tell her children and grandchildren, she put her arm through John's and quoted the biblical words of Ruth, "Whither thou goest, I will go. Where thou lodgest, I will lodge; thy people shall be my people, thy God my God." Once proud of his daughter's independence, Benton was now furious at her defiance.

Elizabeth, who hated conflict and could not abide shouting, begged her husband to calm down. She urged him to allow a second, Protestant ceremony, which only further infuriated him. Jessie had never seen her father deny her mother any request, and his gruff dismissal of Elizabeth was a dismal sign.

The couple fled first to Baltimore and eventually took a room at a Washington hotel. On November 27, Benton placed their marriage announcement in the *Globe*, insisting that the long-standing etiquette of listing the groom's name first be reversed. "On the 19th ult., in this city, by the Rev. Mr. Van Horseigh, Miss Jessie Ann Benton, second daughter of Col. Benton, to Mr. J. C. Frémont of the United States Army," it read. When a newspaper editor objected to the terminology, Benton insisted: "Damn it, sir! It will go in that way or not at all! John C. Frémont did not marry my daughter; she married him." In fact, Benton was protecting the reputation of his new son-in-law. Stipulating that Jessie married John preempted any accusations that John had taken a woman not yet of legal age.

Frémont had on his hands a very distraught young bride. Thrilled to be married to the man she loved, Jessie was deeply saddened by the breach with her father, whom she had adored since her earliest memories. Many friends and relatives intervened with the senator, pointing out Frémont's accomplishments and appealing to Benton's gentler nature, to the man for whom family meant more than anything else. "I am told that Col. Benton is very angry with them both," wrote one of Jessie's friends from school. "But I think it must be a mistake for Col. Benton is more devoted to Jessie than any one of his other children." Naturally, the capital rang with vicious gossip, smugly advanced by the senator's many political enemies as well as Jessie's spurned suitors and Frémont's jealous rivals. "To most Washingtonians, Senator Benton's daughter had made a reckless marriage," wrote biographer Pamela Herr, "giving up the wealth and prestige that could so easily have been hers for the mere glint in the eye of a Frenchman's bastard." Her own cousins, long resentful of her pluck and irreverence, besmirched her. "It is a sad & distressing business," her cousin James McDowell III wrote his father. "I anticipated nothing else from her ungovernable passions."

In the end, the hostile Benton could not stay angry at his favorite daughter for long, especially as Frémont's own cachet began to rise in Washington circles with news of his successful survey. Toward the end of the year, Benton summoned John to the family home. "Go collect your belongings and return at once to the house," he ordered the young man. "I will prepare Mrs. Benton."

When the blissfully happy couple arrived, they moved into a sun-filled suite overlooking a garden that the household servants had prepared for them. Benton insisted that it be furnished as a bedroom and a study, his eye toward their future collaboration as instruments of his own political vision. Already Benton was unabashedly using his influence to secure an expedition for his new son-in-law. "The thought of my own endless courtship, coupled with the picture of my daughter's felicity, impels me to final approval of this marriage," Benton confessed to a friend.

Jessie was elated beyond measure. "We three understood each other and acted together—then and later—without question or delay."

Benton's "Road to India" became ever more pressing in the last six months of 1841 as British activity in the Northwest increased. But President Tyler, the Virginia Whig occupying the White House, posed a threat to his plans. Tyler was only nominally a Whig, having joined that party because he objected to Andrew Jackson's use—or, as he saw it, abuse—of presidential power. If any expansion was to take place—and Tyler was unsure of the wisdom of that—he preferred that it be in the South, since he supported the expansion of slavery, which Oregon would do nothing to help. Benton, Nicollet, Poinsett, Senator Lewis F. Linn of Benton's Missouri, Senator Henry Dodge of Wisconsin, and other like-minded politicians decided it was necessary to advance their cause with discretion and diplomacy—neither of which was considered Benton's strong suit. Though Benton and his allies in Congress had already authorized thirty thousand dollars to promote migration to Oregon—a policy endorsed by the deceased President Harrison—they now feared White House opposition. "Mr. Tyler threw the weight of his administration against any measure to encourage and aid the emigration to Oregon," Frémont wrote of the charged political environment. "His Secretary of War, Mr. [John] Spencer, was from the east, and a lawyer. These were the altered circumstances which required prudence and reserve in avoiding any check to the projected movement to settle the Oregon question by emigration."

For two decades Benton had advocated the American occupation of the Northwest up to the forty-ninth parallel. But now Tyler, afraid of conflict with England, and deeply prejudiced by Spencer, Poinsett's replacement in the War Department, was a powerful rival. With a massive British naval force patrolling the Pacific Coast, poised for what many thought would be an invasion of California, then under Mexico's weak and far-flung control, Benton's group thought it was critical to national interests to establish a presence in the territory. Meanwhile, rumors of war with Mexico had reached a frenzy—Texas had declared its independence, Sam Houston had defeated Santa Anna's army at San Jacinto, and the region was in the news every day. All political-minded Americans had their eye on the West.

The expedition Benton and his cronies had in mind, to be led by Nicollet, would go as far as South Pass and result in a thorough mapping of the Oregon Trail. They determined that the much revered Nicollet was the appropriate emissary to advance their cause with the president, and by New Year's Day 1842, Tyler had reluctantly agreed to support a new expedition. When Nicollet finally admitted what all had been thinking—that his health would prohibit him from leading such a crucial and momentous undertaking—the ailing explorer made clear that Frémont was his choice as heir apparent.

Word of Frémont's sudden rise spread quickly through the capital, and when he and Jessie arrived at the White House for a New Year's party—glamorous and cloaked with the fresh hint of romantic scandal—they were greeted like celebrities. Jessie emerged first from Hassler's showy "Ark," which the elderly scientist had loaned the newlyweds for the occasion. She wore an indigo velvet gown trimmed with Mechlin lace, strapped slippers, yellow gloves, and a blue bonnet with three ostrich feathers. Next came John, resplendent in his army uniform, striking and gloriously happy. "His piercing eyes, chiseled features, and lithe body suggested the hero to an era steeped in the poetry of Byron and Shelley and the exploits of Napoleon," wrote one observer. The Marine Band played to the largest crowd since Colonel Thomas Meacham presented his giant cheese to President Jackson, and dozens of people pressed forward to get a glimpse of the radiant couple. In a brief private exchange, President Tyler congratulated them on their marriage and John on his upcoming expedition, warning him not to go any farther west than the Rockies lest he provoke a war with England.

That evening, they returned to a holiday dinner at the Benton home, where the senator announced the long-awaited news. The Senate Committee on Military Affairs, which Benton chaired, had approved a four-month expedition. The ensuing discussion focused on how to conceal from President Tyler the true intent of the mission. They must make its purpose seem banal and minor to the president, not reveal the historic and far-reaching plans they had in mind: to map a route to the Pacific to promote migration; to focus American attention on the Rocky Mountains and the West; to gather intelligence on Mexican movements; and, ultimately, in further expeditions, to plant an American flag on Oregon soil in a direct challenge to Great Britain. "Louisiana, Florida, Texas, all had been acquired in my father's earlier day," Jessie wrote, not entirely accurately, since Texas was not yet part of the United States. "He knew the opposition each had met, and did not intend to have it roused in advance to interfere with what he knew then, and what our whole country to-day knows, was a crowning advantage to our national strength—the holding the best port on the North Pacific."

The original orders from Abert—head of the Corps of Topographical Engineers who now reported to Secretary of War Spencer instead of to Poinsett—called for Frémont to survey a relatively small portion of the migrant route. But Benton thought Abert's orders too vague, and especially believed that a route through South Pass in the Rockies must be thoroughly mapped if the sizable overland migration and military occupation he envisioned was ever going to occur. "I think it would be well for you to name, in the instructions for Mr. Frémont, the great pass through the Rocky Mountains," Benton wrote Abert in response to the first orders. "It is the gate through the mountains from the valley of the Mppi: . . . [It] will be a through fare for nations to the end of time." As chairman of the Senate committee that oversaw the corps' appropriations, Benton's demand could not be ignored by Abert, who found a way to expand Frémont's orders while appearing not to. In typical bureaucratic fashion, he gave the explorer great latitude while declining to specifically include South Pass in the orders. "If you can do what he [Benton] desires this season," Abert wrote Frémont, "without hazarding the work committed to you it is extremely desirable that it be done."

Of course Frémont, as Benton's surrogate, had every intention of carrying the flag into the farthest reaches of the continent, to fulfill his father-in-law's geopolitical dream of an American nation that stretched from ocean to ocean. "The object of the expedition, as 'ordered by the Topographical Bureau with the sanction of the Secretary of War,'" Frémont later wrote, "was simply to explore the country between the Missouri River and the Rocky Mountains; but its real purpose, the objects which were had in view in designing it, were known only to the circle of its friends." It was to this "circle of friends" and their ideology—not to an ever-changing president and bureaucracy—that Frémont's loyalty would be fixed. From this point forward he would accept and obey orders only as he saw fit, and only when they perpetuated the "circle's" larger purpose. Such independence was destined to raise the ire of his more conventional colleagues, and inevitably he would be cast as a renegade.

Benton's interest in the West was political, not scientific. But Frémont, while steeped in the political discourse of Benton and the other architects of expansionism, absorbing the passion of the men who foresaw the occupation of a Pacific port, was first and foremost a scientist. Much would be made later of Frémont's opportune marriage to the daughter of one of America's most powerful political figures, many scholars dismissing Frémont's achievements and crediting Benton for his rise. But the reality was far more complicated. Benton, like the other enlightened and intellectual men who had guided the young Frémont in varying stages of his early education and career, was a fortunate connection for Frémont. But when Benton entered his sphere, Frémont was hardly the swashbuckling neophyte that many historians have caricatured. By 1841 he was a brilliant, disciplined, and rigorously trained scientist—"the product of the training imposed upon him by Poinsett, Nicollet, Hassler; the training of Charleston College's 'scientific department,' of mathematics classes on a Federal warship, of officers of the Topographical Survey, of Nicollet's two campaigns," as biographer Allan Nevins summarized his record. He was far less a novice than Lewis and Clark, Zebulon M. Pike, or Stephen Long, those legendary explorers of early America. When John married Jessie, he was already an expert topographer, a skilled astronomer, a student of botany and geology, an accomplished surveyor, and a proven leader of men. To the list of his important patrons he had merely added his most powerful patron of all.

The Army Corps of Topographical Engineers was but three years old, its mandate to produce maps to determine boundaries and protect American territory from foreign infiltration. The topographer was the key figure in any expedition, for he was trained to meld celestial and terrestrial observations—to determine both longitude and latitude—to create an accurate map. Frémont, from his singular access to the world's most advanced scientists, far surpassed the knowledge and expertise of his colleagues at West Point, whose solid and plodding instructors were, for the most part, years behind the savants of Europe. One of the great ironies of John C. Frémont's life would be the impression that his career was advanced by his favorable political marriage, when, in fact, his life-long rivals the West Point legatees held comfortable political sinecures of their own—and while Frémont received political help, he had risen as much through his brains as he had through his connections. The observations Frémont was expected to make included "distance estimates, angles of elevation, altitudes, magnetic bearings, magnetic declinations . . . triangulations of objects, and the positions of roads, trails, and settlements, along with major topographic features such as mountain peaks, valleys, and the confluence of watercourses," as one author put it— hardly the pursuits of a dilettante.

Ecstatic at the turn of events, Jessie and John threw themselves into preparations, Jessie naturally filling the role of John's assistant, secretary, adviser, and confidante, just as she had so ably done for her father. The immediate task at hand was to finish the report for the Des Moines River survey, which had remained half completed while John waited for Nicollet's health to improve. In what would set a precedent for their future collaborations, John organized the material, created an outline, and wrote the report. Jessie would edit and make suggestions. John was romantic by nature, an erstwhile poet and avid reader, and his writing style was livelier than that usually seen in government documents. For her part, Jessie had helped write so many of her father's political speeches that she instinctively knew how to blend factual accuracy and scientific detail with literary grace. The final report was submitted in Jessie's handwriting and was a first indication of what the two could accomplish together.

By April, Frémont had purchased navigational instruments and other scientific equipment in New York City. He commissioned an unusual flag, with twenty-six stars and an eagle whose talons held an Indian peace pipe along with arrows. He ordered an airtight rubber raft for use in the many water crossings he anticipated. "The first boat of the kind made or used in such work," Frémont proudly proclaimed it. With great fanfare, he had the raft delivered to the Benton home, where it could be displayed to the family and guests in the upper gallery of the dining room. But the stench from the India rubber was so offensive, nauseating the newly pregnant Jessie, that it was quickly removed to the stables.

He also had purchased twenty-five pounds of daguerreotype equipment from a New York chemist, hoping to be the first explorer to capture the American West with the experimental prephotographic process. Nicollet had been one of the earliest proponents of daguerreotypy, invented by the French scientist Louis Jacques Mandé Daguerre and introduced in Paris only three years earlier. Nicollet immediately recognized the value of the nascent art for documenting geographic landforms and watersheds, and had instilled in Frémont his enthusiasm for the radical new technology. The apparatus produced an image on a polished silver surface and was considered "a literal, indisputably accurate mechanical transcription of reality." Its potential in a world of geographical and ethnological research—shifting boundaries, unmapped terrain, and indigenous cultures—was truly revolutionary, its detail one of "unimpeachable veracity."

He hired only one expedition member in Washington—the German-born Charles Preuss, a cartographer and artist recommended to him by Hassler—at the rate of three dollars per day, and asked Pierre Chouteau Jr. in St. Louis to order supplies and hire guides. Benton had hoped to accompany his son-in-law, eager as he was to see the western landscape to which he had devoted most of his political life. But in the end, he decided he was too old, and sent his twelve-year-old son Randolph, despite Elizabeth's objections, "for the development of mind and body which such an expedition would give," as Frémont explained.

For Jessie, the spring had been filled with social engagements, musicales, intimate evenings, and luxurious afternoons. Jessie's friends Nancy Polk and Harriet Bodisco each hosted a ball in the couple's honor. Anne Royall, a serious-minded journalist and early feminist, gave a tea for Jessie, and high-ranking military officials, including Stephen Watts Kearny, entertained John. They dined at the home of Secretary of State Daniel Webster, where they learned that Webster advocated the purchase of northern California.

Jessie eased into the role of John's partner, finding soon that she served naturally as a barrier between him and the many people wishing an audience. Inventors and migrants, job seekers and adventurers made their way to the C Street residence. With a diplomacy and patience she would perfect in the future, she determined who should be granted access into their inner sanctum, and who would waste their precious time.

Though she was glad for her husband, and absolutely dedicated to the secret mission of opening migration to Oregon, Jessie dreaded the coming separation. Their first months of marriage had been supremely happy, beyond all idealistic expectations, and the thought of John leaving filled her with an immobilizing sorrow. John, too, was overcome with mixed emotions. Thrilled to be leading his first major expedition, he hated to leave the warmth and exuberance of the only family home he had ever known. He was passionately in love, and the sight of his teenage, crestfallen wife gave him pause. Still, nothing could dampen his excitement for the journey ahead. "The poor half-orphan of the Charleston streets, the youth brought into the backdoor of the Army by Poinsett's influence, had achieved a position that any West Pointer might envy," a historian wrote of the elevated moment in Frémont's life.

On the morning of May 2, 1842, John dressed in his new blue and gold uniform. Jessie adjusted the braid and buttons, straightened his collar, and declared that after he returned she would give birth to a son, whom they would name John Charles and who would "look exactly like his father." She intended to accompany him to the railway station, to wave good-bye from the platform. But her mother collapsed upon bidding Randolph good-bye, and Jessie stayed behind to care for her. Friends and colleagues crowded the station, excitedly bidding farewell to the twenty-nine-year-old explorer, while Jessie wept alone in her room. Thus began a long and unchanging pattern of a patient but anxious wife awaiting the return of a peripatetic but devoted husband.

Benton watched with alarm as Jessie's loneliness turned to despair. Pregnant and miserable in the heat and humidity, she struggled to keep her spirits elevated. John was "gone into the silence and the unknown," she wrote. "How silent, how unknown it is impossible to make clear." When her father asked for her help in his research—"you are too young to fritter away your life without some useful pursuit"—she readily accepted the task. He invited her to join him in his library, where she found six new pens and a stack of foolscap. Her first assignment was to translate sections of *Conquista de la Nueva España*, a sixteenth-century chronicle written by Spanish conquistador Bernal Díaz del Castillo, who had served under Cortés during his conquest of Mexico. Benton gave her enough work to occupy her mind and concentrate her energies, all with the dual purpose of keeping her engaged with her husband's pursuits. "Be not disturbed about the future," he quoted Marcus Aurelius to her, "for if you ever come to it, you will have the same reason for your guide which preserves you at present." When she had completed the translation, Benton asked her to copy parts of the 1818 treaty with Great Britain that had settled the Oregon boundary, albeit not to Benton's satisfaction.

Quick and thorough, she worked as prodigiously as ever, and her relationship with her father returned to the affectionate partnership it had been before her elopement. "My father gave me early the place a son would have had. I grant I am a woman but . . . think you I am no stronger than my sex, being so father'd and so husbanded?" The two were joined in a common purpose, their eyes more than ever on the West. Perhaps it was her idea, perhaps her father's, but during the hot summer of 1842 Jessie and Thomas Hart Benton arrived at the notion that a lively narrative of John's expedition would do more to arouse public interest in expansionism than any political discourse. With that in mind, they turned their attention to the written reports of earlier explorers. "She no more had a woman's mind than she had a man's," wrote twentieth-century journalist Charles Moody. "It was simply a *great* mind . . . Clear, logical, unhesitant, fearless, it grasped whole whatever matters came before it, digested them promptly, and drew from them sound and certain conclusions."

Typically, Benton insisted that she obey the distinctive family regimen of three hours of solid work followed by exercise, frivolity, and relaxation. She rose every morning at dawn, and after a small breakfast with her father she began her work. From eight until eleven, she immersed herself in the reports of Lewis and Clark, Zebulon Pike, Stephen Long, and Captain Bonneville. Next came the travelogues of Alexander von Humboldt and the thrilling stories of Balboa and Magellan, Astor and De Soto. To the impressionable and romantic young woman, the exploits of her new husband were equivalent to those of the world's greatest adventurers. Her own destiny, she came to believe, was to see his place in history firmly established. Like other Victorian women, Jessie recognized that her dreams and ambitions could be realized only if channeled through her husband. Given her intellect and background, her passions and aspirations, it was only natural that her symbiosis with John would be complete.

As Jessie's baby grew within her, her mother was failing rapidly. Headaches began to plague the forty-nine-year-old woman, and she received regular visits from an elderly doctor who "bled" her. Benton was uncomfortable with the primitive procedure, aware that younger physicians thought it barbaric and ineffective. Elizabeth seemed worse after each visit. Still, she begged her husband to let the treatments continue, and after being bled thirty-three times, she suffered a stroke that left her in a coma for three days.

Benton never left her side, trying to warm her cold hands in his, speaking to her as if she were cognizant, his large frame folded in upon itself in helplessness. To see her powerful father so afflicted and aggrieved was a shock to Jessie. When Elizabeth regained consciousness, it was clear that she had been severely brain damaged, for she could barely speak and could not even feed herself. She expressed her desire for Jessie's company, now finding comfort and entertainment from the independent girl who had always vexed her. Jessie's older sister, Eliza, took over the household duties, while Jessie sat with her mother every day, telling stories of the day's events, reading Elizabeth's favorite passages from the Bible, and encouraging her to take sips of bouillon. In the evenings, Benton would carry her from the couch to her bed, promising her that they would soon go for a drive in the country. He was always cheerful and optimistic in her presence, and would "then bolt to his own room to give way to the strong man's agony at the realization of the ruin that had befallen that now speechless, emaciated woman," Jessie recalled. She would live as an invalid for twelve more years, never fully regaining her faculties. "So good . . . so kind," she said to Benton one day, struggling for the words as he lifted her in his arms. It was the only time Jessie saw her father break down. He fell to his knees right then and wept uncontrollably.

By the end of the summer, Jessie gave way to the anxiety she had kept in check. Her mother's incapacity, her father's sadness, her fears for John, all weighed heavily on her. Just a teenager, she was nervous about childbirth and became increasingly worried that John would not return before the baby was born.

On May 22, John had arrived in St. Louis, where he spent two weeks at the opulent mansion of Thomas Hart Benton's niece Sarah Benton Brant. There he employed frontiersman Lucien B. Maxwell as a hunter, and hired twenty other men, mostly French Creoles and Canadian voyageurs, including Basil Lajeunesse, who would accompany him on many future expeditions and with whom he would develop a deep and lasting camaraderie. After leaving St. Louis, he took on the famous guide Christopher "Kit" Carson, who became his lifelong friend and loyal advocate.

"The friendship begun on the little Missouri steamboat struggling upstream in the June sunshine of 1842 was to last until Carson's death in 1868, and . . . was to be the happiest of partnerships," as historian Allan Nevins described the legendary association that would make Carson a national icon. When they met, the recently widowed Carson was returning to Taos from St. Louis, where he had placed his young half-Indian daughter in a convent school. Carson was considered the most skilled guide in the West, familiar with Indian customs, fluent in French, Spanish, and various Indian dialects, thoughtful and resourceful, unassuming and courageous, and thoroughly knowledgeable about the wild terrain beyond the Continental Divide.

Carson was born in Kentucky on Christmas Eve 1809, the ninth of fourteen children. His father was mortally wounded by a falling tree limb when Carson was nine years old. Uneducated and poverty-stricken, at thirteen he apprenticed to a saddlemaker in Boone's Lick, Missouri. At sixteen he ran away, joining a wagon train destined for Santa Fe. Once there, he moved seventy miles north to Taos, where he worked as a teamster, cook, and interpreter before joining a trapping excursion to California in 1829. He quickly gained a reputation as a fearless and competent scout, hiring out to fur traders trapping in the Colorado Rockies and Sierra Nevada range.

Frémont was impressed with Carson's modesty and quiet demeanor—his "clear steady blue eye and frank speech and address"—and quickly recruited the stocky, muscled, bowlegged thirty-three-year-old mountain man to join the historic journey, paying him $100 a month. It was, by all accounts, a perfect match. "I had been some time in the mountains and thought I could guide him to any point he wished to go," Carson later recalled with understatement.

The *St. Louis Republican* reported Frémont's departure, pronouncing the expedition "important" and editorializing in favor of occupying Oregon. "Since the attention of the country has been directed to the settlement of the Oregon territory by our able senator (Dr. Linn) and by the reports of those who have visited that region in person, the importance of providing ample security for the settlers there, and of opening a safe and easy communication from the western boundary of Missouri to the Columbia River, has been universally admitted."

For two months, Frémont's expedition proceeded according to plan, and to Abert's orders, following the established route along the Platte in what is now Kansas and Nebraska. They had reached South Pass by

August 8 and, finding not a gorge but a miles-wide gap, they ascended the gradual summit effortlessly. Though it was the most important landmark for westward migration—linking Oregon and California with the United States—Frémont and his men found it anticlimactic. With eight more weeks of temperate weather, he decided to push northwest, toward Oregon, and deep into the central Rockies. Whether that was his intention all along or whether he was emboldened by his fortunate meeting with the uniquely qualified Carson, the venture far exceeded official orders. They marched along the western slope of the stunning Wind River Range—the glacier-capped chain of peaks that stretch north to south for a hundred miles in western Wyoming and form a triple divide for the Columbia, Missouri, and Colorado rivers. "A lofty snow-peak of the mountain is glittering in the first rays of the sun," Frémont wrote in his diary. "The whole valley is glowing and bright, and all the mountain peaks are gleaming like silver. Though these snow-mountains are not the Alps, they have their own character of grandeur and magnificence, and will doubtless find pens and pencils to do them justice."

His detractors would point to this detour as evidence that the expedition was not in the first instance scientific, but rather an opportunity to advance Frémont's "growing appetite for glory," as biographer Chaffin put it, though no evidence of such an appetite had surfaced before. If anything, those who knew him best during these years saw him as amiable and self-effacing, confident but not arrogant, forceful but not intimidating. His nature was quiet and determined, and except for Preuss, who despised the wilderness and constantly complained about the food, the camping, the mosquitoes, and even that he was expected to ride a horse instead of being transported in a wagon, Frémont's men uniformly respected and admired him.

On August 13, Frémont and eleven of the men set off with "nothing but our arms and instruments" and each with a mule and a blanket, through mountainous terrain "infested by Blackfeet." He was determined to climb what he thought was the highest peak. The next day they abandoned their mules and continued on foot, and because the day had turned warm, they left their blankets and coats behind at what he called "the Camp of the Mules." Frémont underestimated the distance to the mountain—"the peak appeared so near"—and the men were soon overtaken with altitude sickness. Suffering from headaches and vomiting, he sent Lajeunesse and four other men back to camp with instructions to return with four mules, food, and blankets. He and his men remained ill throughout the day, hungry and cold, but their spirits lifted at sundown as Lajeunesse and four fresh and mounted men returned, carrying food and blankets. They devoured the dried meat, having gone two days without food, drank strong coffee, and retired for the night. "We rolled ourselves up in our blankets, and, with our feet turned to a blazing fire, slept soundly until morning."

At daybreak on August 15, Carson took all but five men Frémont had selected for the final climb, leading the others back to the lower elevation. The rest began the perilous trek through gorges and rock defiles to a meadow above three glacier lakes. There they turned their mules loose to graze, and began climbing slowly toward the mountain's summit. "Hitherto I had worn a pair of thick moccasins, with soles of *parflêche*; but here I put on a light thin pair which I had brought for the purpose, as now the use of our toes became necessary to a further advance." They reached an overhanging buttress that blocked their route and forced them to ascend a vertical precipice of granite, "putting hands and feet in the crevices between the blocks." He managed to leap onto the narrow summit, almost falling over the other side into "an immense snow-field five hundred feet below" surrounded by ice. "Here, on the summit, where the stillness was absolute, unbroken by any sound, and the solitude complete, we thought ourselves beyond the region of animated life." Just then, a solitary bumblebee appeared. "It was a strange place, the icy rock and the highest peak of the Rocky Mountains, for a lover of warm sunshine and flowers; and we pleased ourselves with the idea that he was the first of his species to cross the mountain barrier—a solitary pioneer to foretell the advance of civilization."

The crest measured three feet in width, allowing only one climber at a time. "As soon as I had gratified the first feelings of curiosity I descended, and each man ascended in his turn." They mounted the barometer in the snow, and measured the altitude at 13,500 feet, which they mistakenly believed to be the highest peak in the Rockies. They fired their guns, broke open a bottle of brandy, and Frémont placed a ramrod in a fissure and "unfurled the national flag to wave in the breeze where never flag waved before."

An ebullient John returned to Washington at the end of October, ecstatic over the success of the expedition and desperate to see Jessie. He had raised an American flag on one of the highest peaks in the Rockies, staking it as a gateway to the West. When he walked through the door of the Benton home, she dissolved into tears.

Two weeks later, on November 15, 1842, Jessie gave birth at home to a six-pound daughter. Delighted to have John back with her, she could not hide her disappointment that she had failed to bear him a son. "This is the first hard blow my pride has ever sustained," she confided in her husband. But like his father-in-law upon learning of Jessie's birth, John concealed his own displeasure, if indeed he felt any, assuring her he was thrilled to have a daughter. At Benton's request, they named her Elizabeth after Jessie's mother, and called her Lily.

The next day, John laid the flag across Jessie's bed. "This flag which I raised over the highest peak of the Rocky Mountains I have brought to you." He also presented her with the bumblebee, pressed into a book along with flowers he had collected for her during his mountain ascent. She would cherish them for the rest of her life, among the few material possessions left at the end of her days. The eighteen-year-old mother recovered quickly from childbirth. "Jessie is sitting up and has got through with her sickness very well indeed," John wrote to his friend Nicollet when Lily was eleven days old.

Within days of Lily's birth, Frémont was at work pulling together his documentation in preparation for his eagerly awaited report to Abert. Frémont wrote a letter to Professor John Torrey, the nation's preeminent botanist, asking him to examine and catalog plant specimens from the expedition. At Benton's suggestion, Frémont asked Preuss to hurriedly complete "a series of maps representing each day's journey, a guidebook in atlas form . . . for the use of the emigration," indicating campsites where water, wood, and grass for animals could be found. John, Jessie, and Benton all agreed that his report must combine scientific precision with literary merit, be full of practical information as well as mathematical calculations, and that, above all, it should be exciting and accessible to the general population.

Jessie and John endlessly discussed the content of the report, and when it came time to write, Jessie helped him organize his study. She placed pens and ink on his desk, provided him with a large supply of foolscap, and left him sequestered with his notes carefully laid out on a table. For three days he agonized, starting and stopping, throwing pages into the fireplace. On the fourth day he admitted to Jessie he had writer's block, indicating that headaches and nosebleeds precluded him from going forward. "I write more easily by dictation," he admitted. "Writing myself I have too much time to think and dwell upon words as well as ideas. In dictation there is not time for this and then, too, I see the face of my second mind, and get there at times the slight dissent confirming my own doubt, or the pleased expression which represents the popular impression of a mind new to the subject." Jessie readily accepted the role of his "second mind," to become for John what she had long been for her father. "The horseback life, the sleep in the open air had unfitted him for the indoor work of writing," Jessie explained to her parents as she intervened to be what John called his "amanuensis."

Her father at first objected to the arrangement, feeling that it would jeopardize Jessie's health so soon after childbirth, and, perhaps even more strongly, that a woman's place was with her newborn baby rather than in intellectual pursuits. But true to her nature, Jessie chose the most mentally challenging path. In any case, she rationalized, they could not afford to hire a secretary on John's meager army salary, and time was of the essence to persuade the Senate to immediately fund more expeditions.

They established a disciplined schedule, working from nine until one every day while a wet nurse cared for Lily. Jessie sat at the desk as John paced the room, reviewing his notes and re-creating the four-month journey day by day. She interrupted him when clarification was necessary. Both were lovers of language, and they would often stop the narrative dictation to discuss the exact choice of words. Later critics of Frémont, and there would be many, would create and perpetuate a myth that Jessie actually wrote the report. But any careful comparison of John's correspondence, reports, and memoirs with Jessie's published books and essays reveals a distinct difference in style. "It was a true collaboration of two quick and sympathetic minds," concluded Allan Nevins, "but the content is wholly Frémont's."

They were inseparable and synergetic, and their teamwork turned the expedition into a wonderful adventure and a best-selling book. They brought the characters alive—Kit Carson, Arapaho Indians, mountain men, fur traders, and scouts—and gave drama to the landscape John had mapped and charted. On the page, the unshaven, rough-hewn explorers became heroes on a visionary quest. For the first time in American history, an explorer's report had a gripping narrative. "It was both a keenly observed description of a western journey by a trained scientist and a dramatic adventure story buffed to a high literary polish," wrote one historian.

John submitted the 215-page document to the War Department on

March 1, 1843. The secretary of war, at the request of the Senate, transmitted it to Congress, which published it under the title *A Report of an Exploration of the Country Lying Between the Missouri River and the Rocky Mountains on the Line of the Kansas and Great Platte Rivers*. Within days, the Senate, following a motion made by Senator Linn, ordered a thousand copies of the report printed. Soon it was excerpted in newspapers throughout America, and would be compared by literary critics to *Robinson Crusoe*. "Frémont chasing buffalo, Galahad Carson reclaiming the orphaned boy's horses from the Indians, Odysseus Godey riding charge against hordes of the red butchers—there was here a spectacle that fed the nation's deepest need," wrote historian Bernard de Voto. "They were adventure books, they were charters of Manifest Destiny, they were texts of navigation for the uncharted sea so many dreamed of crossing, they were a pageant of daring, endurance, and high endeavor in the country of peaks and unknown rivers." Frémont was an instant celebrity, his name suddenly synonymous with the lure of the West— currently romanticized by George Catlin's paintings, James Fenimore Cooper's *Leatherstocking Tales*, and Washington Irving's *Adventures of Captain Bonneville*—and the couple became the toast of Washington. Henry Wadsworth Longfellow, fascinated by Frémont's achievement, would find inspiration in the report for his epic poem "Evangeline."

While elevating Frémont and Kit Carson to international fame, it would also serve as a guide for thousands of American migrants. Proving that the Platte River valley had rich soil, the report delineated prime locations where new settlements could be built and crops could be raised to feed the many soldiers and migrants who would now be moving westward. That twelve-year-old Randolph Benton could accompany such a journey was further evidence that it was now safe for families to move west.

The "circle of friends" leaped at the opportunity presented by Frémont's sudden fame and the rousing national enthusiasm. Benton, Linn, and their expansionist colleagues rallied support for the most important nationally sanctioned expedition since Lewis and Clark—a survey of the Oregon Trail from the Rockies west to the Pacific. "Events justified the wisdom of silence until the fast-coming hour," Jessie later wrote of the group's behind-the-scenes machinations. "War with Mexico was nearing, and in that event the ownership of the bay of San Francisco would be open to the chances of war."

President Tyler remained cautious and diffident on the Oregon question, but he far underestimated the support in Congress for Benton's coalition. When Linn introduced a bill in the Senate calling on Tyler to erect as many as five stockade forts from the Missouri and Arkansas rivers to Oregon and providing 640 acres of land to each male settler who would cultivate the land for five consecutive years, the vote passed, twenty-four to twenty-two. That the bill was defeated in the House of Representatives was but a minor setback for the expansionists, who worked behind the scenes with Abert to get funding for the expedition. Though Abert continued to have reservations about Frémont's record-keeping, and though he found Benton overbearing and annoying, he embraced the publicity and attention the Topographical Corps was receiving. Together, toward mutual benefit, Abert and Benton successfully circumvented their opponents in Congress and the White House, and agreed upon a budget for the expedition.

On March 10, 1843, Frémont received the official orders from Abert to cross the Rocky Mountains, explore the headwaters of the streams that flowed to the Gulf of Mexico, proceed northwest to the Columbia River, and on his return explore the eastern slope of the Wind River Range. A detour into California was never mentioned in the orders, nor in any correspondence Frémont had with the men he hired.

He again acquired a daguerreotype apparatus in New York, having failed to use it successfully on the first expedition, and again purchased a rubber boat. By May the preparations were completed and he, Jessie, Elizabeth, and the baby Lily traveled to St. Louis, where Jessie intended to await his return. Accompanying them on the two-week journey by coach and steamboat were Preuss and Jacob Dodson, a free black servant from the Benton household who would act as Frémont's personal assistant on the trek.

Once in St. Louis, Frémont hurriedly bought supplies and hired men, working feverishly for fear that their adversaries would maneuver surreptitiously to halt the expedition. With Congress in recess they had some leeway, and Frémont moved expeditiously to take advantage of the situation. The family stayed at the Benton home and, as before, Chouteau's company served as the outfitting headquarters. Lajeunesse eagerly signed on, along with six others from the previous journey and numerous experienced frontiersmen. Frémont hired Louis Zindel, a Prussian explosives expert he had known from his days with Nicollet, and enlisted a father-and-son team of Delaware Indians as hunters. Carson had returned to

Taos after the last expedition, so Frémont engaged the services of forty-four-year-old Thomas "Broken Hand" Fitzpatrick as a guide, paying him nearly as much as Preuss—a fact that angered an already disaffected Preuss. Frémont also was persuaded to bring a handful of what one historian called "gentlemen-travelers, dreamy-eyed novices," including the twenty-year-old William Gilpin, who had been a West Point cadet and who was now editor of the *St. Louis Argus*; the frail eighteen-year-old Theodore Talbot, who brought Byron's poetry with him and who would keep an informal journal; and a Harvard law student named Frederick Dwight. The core group would number thirty-nine men, with a dozen more supernumeraries, making it the best-outfitted exploring body in American history. It was a tough lot of men, all experienced and capable except for the handful of tenderfoots.

The provisions were extensive, packed expertly into a dozen large mule-drawn carts. Frémont bought a covered wagon to transport his prized scientific instruments—a telescope, two chronometers, two sextants, two barometers, six thermometers, and several compasses—and loaded another cart with the rubber boat and gifts for the Indians. He had arranged, through Benton's close personal friend Colonel Stephen Watts Kearny, to obtain government weapons from the St. Louis Arsenal. Kearny provided him with a letter of requisition for ordnance, to be presented to Captain William H. Bell. Frémont's request included thirty-three Hall breech-loading rifle carbines—an advanced weapon fired by flintlock using fixed cartridges and capable of quick reloading—and five kegs of rifle powder. Then he made a fateful decision that would have far-reaching negative consequences for him. He requested a howitzer and five hundred pounds of artillery ammunition—a move that later critics would claim marked his party as military rather than scientific. "I shall be led into countries inhabited by hostile Indians," Frémont justified the need in a letter to Kearny, "so that it is absolutely necessary to the performance of this service that my party . . . be furnished with every means of defense which may conduce to its safety." While cannons had been taken on expeditions before, most frontiersmen considered them cumbersome and useless. Still, Frémont apparently felt the massive weapon would be intimidating to warrior Indians. Captain Bell balked at releasing the cannon to a second lieutenant leading a scientific exploration, but followed the order of his superior officer. Two days later, Bell documented his objection in a letter to the Ordnance Office in Washington, writing that Kearny had ordered him to comply with Frémont's request against Bell's own better judgment. "In true bureaucratic fashion," historian Ernest Allen Lewis wrote in 1981, "he didn't like the situation because the request had not gone through the proper channels."

Jessie's grandmother Ann Gooch Benton had died five years earlier, leaving the large St. Louis home unoccupied except for Senator Benton's regular visits back to meet with constituents and garner support for his expansionist platform—"his long cherished work for the occupation of Oregon," as Jessie described it. Jessie and John moved into the south bedroom overlooking the orchard and furnished with French antiques. Elizabeth was installed in a comfortable suite, where she would be cared for by Jessie and the servants, and a nursery had been set up for Lily.

The week in St. Louis before John's departure was exhilarating and hectic. Jessie acted as secretary to both her husband and her father, arising at dawn and eating a small breakfast with the two men on the outside portal where Benton always held court. John would then leave for Chouteau's, and she would take notes of her father's meetings. At eleven A.M. John would return, apprise her of the status of the planning, which she methodically wrote down, and the three would have lunch together. Jessie oversaw the constant entertaining, every evening a dinner party with different St. Louis dignitaries and friends.

When John left on May 17, she handled his departure more stoically than the time before. Though she no doubt wept in private, she exhibited a surface calm and optimism in the presence of others. Intensely invested in the thrust of the expedition—what she called the "grand plan ripening and expanding from Jefferson's time"—and occupied with the details of preparation, she saw herself as a thoroughly involved participant in a historic cause long championed by her father and now being fulfilled by her husband. "I . . . had full knowledge of the large scope and national importance of these journeys—a knowledge as yet strictly confined to the few carrying out their aim." Everyone else outside the chosen "few," including the secretary of war and the head of the Topographical Corps, assumed the expedition was merely a "geographical survey[s] to determine lines of travel." The expedition was obviously as much a covert intelligence-gathering and military reconnaissance operation directed by Benton as head of the Senate Military Affairs Committee as a scientific journey, and Jessie was a full accomplice in the grand scheme. "Following out my duty as secretary, I was to open the mail and forward to the camp at Kaw Landing, now Kansas City, all that in my judgment required Mr. Frémont's attention."

On a clear spring day, more than a week after John had left, she took her daily walk in the open country beyond the town. Before returning home, she stopped at a cathedral, seeking a moment of solace and comfort to relieve the loneliness she feared would only grow worse. She had had a mere six months with her husband since his return from the last expedition, and now they were separated again. This was the life of which her father had warned her, the uncertain circumstances of marriage to an explorer, and she sought the inner strength to endure. She returned home to find the mail on her desk, brought by the afternoon boat. On the top of the stack was a long, official-looking envelope dated May 22, from Abert in Washington. She quickly ripped it open. Stunned, she found an order recalling John to Washington, "whither he was directed to return and explain why he had armed his party with a howitzer; saying that it was a scientific, not a military expedition, and should not have been so armed." Abert wrote that he was sending another officer to St. Louis to take control of Frémont's men. "Now Sir what authority had you to make any such requisition and what use can such a piece be in the execution of your duties . . . The object of the Department was a peaceable expedition . . . to gather scientific knowledge. If there is reason to believe that the condition of the country will not admit to the safe management of such an expedition . . . you will immediately desist and report to this office." Naturally, Jessie envisioned the worst, assuming that the predictable and long-standing envy of John's army rivals were behind the maneuver. "I suspected some obscure intrigue, such as had recalled the young traveler Ledyard when he had already crossed Russia into Siberia in carrying out the design of Mr. Jefferson, then minister of France, for opening up the Columbia River." Further, she believed Abert hoped to replace John with his own relative James W. Abert, whose ambitions were well known. "The report had given immediate fame to Mr [sic] Frémont," she wrote, "then why not the same to another officer?"

Abert had in fact been called on the carpet by the secretary of war, who had received Captain Bell's letter along with copies of Frémont's requisition list and Kearny's order. The outraged secretary had reprimanded Kearny and demanded an explanation from Abert, who assured the secretary that he had authorized pistols, rifles, and shotguns, but certainly not a cannon.

Jessie, fearless and determined that the mission proceed, and assuming that a duplicate order was en route to Kaw's Landing, rushed into action. Benton had left on a trip around Missouri, so she took matters into her own hands. "I felt the whole situation in a flash, and met it—as I saw right," she later wrote in one of several sometimes conflicting explanations. "I had been too much a part of the whole plan for the expeditions to put them in peril now—and I alone could act. Fortunately my father was off in the state attending to his political affairs. I did what I have always since been glad to remember. First I told no one. I knew that one of the men engaged, a French Canadian named de Rosier [Derosier] had been permitted to remain in St. Louis on account of his wife's health, gaining for her the month the party were at Kaw Landing with Mr. Frémont. Now I sent for de Rosier and told him an important letter had come for the 'Captain' and I wanted it delivered to him without loss of time."

She asked her messenger how long it would take him to get ready. "The time to get my horse, but two horses travel better," he responded. "If I take my brother, he will bring back a letter from the Lieutenant." While Derosier prepared, Jessie penned a letter to John, knowing better than to send Abert's original. "It was in the blessed day before telegraphs and character counted for something then, and I was only eighteen, an age when one takes risks willingly. It was about four hundred miles to Kaw Landing north of St. Louis as the crow flies. So I wrote urging him not to lose a day but start at once on my letter. That I could not give him the reason but he must GO. That I knew it would be bad for his animals, who would have only the scant early grass, but they could stop at Bent's Fort and fatten up. *Only trust me and go.*"

She gave the letter to Derosier with a warning. "Say nothing of this," she told him, though she apparently did not reveal to him the contents of the letter.

Within a week Derosier's brother returned with Frémont's brief message. "Goodbye. I trust and GO." If she harbored any doubts before, she now knew that John considered her a peer, as he had promised when they married. Surely he recognized that Jessie would not have sent two men on horseback on a four-hundred-mile journey without justification. "I never knew where the order originated," he wrote many years later. "It came through Colonel Abert. He was a quiet man, not likely to disturb an expedition gotten up, apparently, under his own direction and, so far as he knew, originating with himself. It was not probable that I would have been recalled from the Missouri frontier to Washington, fifteen hundred miles of water and stage-coach traveling, to explain why I had taken an arm that simply served to increase the means of defence [sic] for a small party very certain to encounter Indian hostility, and which involved trifling expense."

Receiving John's reply, and feeling certain the expedition had not been jeopardized, she wrote to Abert, explaining that the men would find the howitzer useful as they crossed through territory inhabited by Sioux, Apache, and Blackfoot Indians. These Indians, she claimed, would not know the difference between a scientific and a military expedition, and would not hesitate to attack a party that appeared defenseless. She then admitted to Abert that she had blocked his dispatch and that her husband remained unaware of the order.

Once the letter was sent, she began to consider the ramifications. She had acted solely in furtherance of the expedition, and only now did she realize that she had actually defied the U.S. government. She agonized in the days and nights ahead, anticipating her father's reaction. She had always seen herself as integrally tied to the triumvirate's larger purpose, but for the first time feared that her impetuous and daring insubordination could backfire on her husband's career. "She had longed not to be a man, but simply to act as a man could, freely and fully," wrote Pamela Herr. "But it was an era when the slightest blurring of roles could create a scandal."

To her surprise, Benton fully supported her, joining her in the means-justify-the-ends argument of America on the March. "He entirely approved of my wrong-doing, and wrote to the Secretary of War that he would be responsible for my act, and that he would call for a court martial on the point charged against Mr. Frémont." Still, she faltered briefly, wondering at the wisdom of disobeying the War Department.

Abert apparently never responded to either Jessie or her father, but her impetuous act would never be forgotten. Those in Washington whose designs had been thwarted would plot to avenge the audacity of a teenage girl acting far outside her female purview. The episode also gave potency to the characterization of Frémont as a reckless and disobedient rebel who egotistically disregarded the rigid formalities of the military's chain of command. "It placed a blemish of insubordination upon his conduct," wrote biographer Nevins. Indeed, he would never fully escape the condemnation, nor would Jessie. To John's credit, he never blamed his wife.

★ ★ ★

Frémont's second expedition "may have been conceived in a political conspiracy, born in controversy and nurtured by the majestic mountains and plains of the frontier, but it achieved greatness through the courage and stamina of its leaders and voyageurs," wrote historian Ernest Allen Lewis. "Only occasionally in the course of events does history combine a few bold and talented people, the best available equipment, and a noble purpose."

Though his orders were clear—to expand on his earlier survey of the Rockies and proceed to the Columbia River, where he was to connect with the navy's "Wilkes Expedition," which was returning from a five-year exploratory cruise to the South Seas—Frémont's actual route would once again deviate drastically. Having gotten a premature start, the party moved slowly, its pace further slowed by the unwieldy howitzer. Hoping to find a new road to the coast through milder terrain and more moderate climate, he intended to follow the Kansas River instead of the previously charted Platte, to the head of the Arkansas River in central Colorado. But they soon found themselves in arid country at the northern fork of the Kansas River, with little fresh water and the only stream a putrid trickle filled with buffalo excrement. Once they began traveling along the Republican River they found the "country beautifully watered with numerous streams."

On the Fourth of July they reached St. Vrain's Fort, where they celebrated the holiday feasting with fur traders and obtained some provisions, but not nearly as much as they needed. "We could not proceed without animals, and our own were not capable of prosecuting the journey beyond the mountains without relief." Frémont decided to vary their route again, "on account of the low state of our provisions and the scarcity of game . . . in the hope of falling in with the buffalo." When that proved fruitless, they headed toward the settlement of Pueblo, in what is now Colorado. Kit Carson, who was at Bent's Fort when he heard that Frémont had arrived at Pueblo, hurriedly rode seventy miles to meet up with his friend. Thrilled to see his old scout, Frémont quickly hired Carson at his previous salary, and sent him back to Bent's Fort to procure some mules, having heard that Ute Indians had impeded Maxwell's journey to Taos. Carson convinced Frémont that the expedition should retrace its steps back to St. Vrain's, to await the new mules and adequately provision before setting out to find a new pass over the Rockies.

On July 26, well stocked with ample food and fresh mules, the party set out along the South Platte River and made its way to present-day Fort Collins, sometimes forced to cross the river nine times in a day. By early August Frémont had abandoned all hope of finding an adequate southern route, as Abert had instructed him to do, pushing north to the Sweetwater River in Wyoming. On August 13 they crossed the Continental Divide at the southern extremity of South Pass, now treading ground they had explored in the previous expedition. Having failed in the first mission, he set his sights on Oregon and California, leaving American soil and crossing into Mexican territory. Neither he nor his men noted the venture into a foreign land. As taught by Nicollet, "Frémont remained far more preoccupied with physiographic boundaries— watersheds, mountain ranges, and the like—than with borders defined by treaties."

From there, Frémont began to improvise, moving his men first to the Great Salt Lake, he and Carson exploring the saltwater body in their rubber boat. Determined to conduct the first scientific examination of the vast lake that earlier explorers once thought was the Pacific Ocean, he concluded that the northern reaches of it could serve as a strategically placed military post and settlement. In fact, it would be Frémont's description of the area that convinced Mormon leader Brigham Young to pronounce it the new Zion. By September 12 the party had reached Fort Hall on the Snake River; they were now so overtaken with hunger that Frémont, in desperation, reluctantly allowed his men to kill a fat young horse. Though the meat restored the men, Frémont refused to partake, preferring to eat seagulls shot by Carson, and "feeling as much saddened as if a crime had been committed."

A week later it snowed all day and night, an early indication of the harsh winter ahead, and by September 21 the rivers were frozen. The men began to bicker, many disgruntled at having to transport the cumbersome howitzer, and Frémont made it clear that this was the time for any dissenters to return east, as he had every intention of moving forward despite the weather. Basil Lajeunesse agreed to lead ten men back to St. Louis, carrying letters home from Frémont. On September 23, Frémont's detachment began their journey toward Oregon, following the Snake River Valley toward the Pacific.

As Jessie waited for John, hundreds of migrants poured into St. Louis, beginning their trek to Oregon and California on the trail her husband was mapping. Benton had returned to Washington, and Jessie spent her days reading to Elizabeth, playing with Lily, and meeting with the many trappers, politicians, and adventurers who came to call—all eager for information from the expedition. Every evening she wrote a letter to her father, and as weeks passed into months with no word from John, she found herself unsuited for her task of waiting, and began a slow descent into gloominess.

"This was one of mother's good days," she wrote her father in early autumn. "After reading Thanatopsis aloud, I left her and Lily both asleep and took a long walk by the river. In a plot of meadow an emigrant wagon rested. I was attracted by 'Delaware' painted in bright blue on the canvas. No men were about, but seated on an overturned tub near the wagon was a young woman my age, nursing her baby. Her laughing blue eyes peeped up at me from a pink ruffled sunbonnet. A strand of wavy yellow hair, loosed from its coil, lay shimmering on the shoulder of her brown linsey dress. We talked for some time while the baby, 'John, named for his father,' lay asleep at her breast. I didn't tell her who I was. Finally she rewarded my interest with, 'Wouldn't you and your folks like to come along? There are three wagons of us. Did you know you can get a whole section of good land to yourselves and save your children from a life of wages?' I said, 'I can't go because of my sick mother, but how I wish I might.' Then I walked away quickly, for I was crying. If it weren't for mother, I would take Lily and go with them. I am strong and not afraid, and waiting grows harder every day."

Benton wrote Jessie back, telling her of the deaths of Nicollet, Hassler, and Senator Linn, the sad news plunging her further into her own grief. In early September Jessie received a letter from John, written three months earlier, and delivered by two Indians. He described the rains that had stalled their movements on the Plains, but said they had reached buffalo country and that all was well. They would be home by New Year's.

As winter approached, with no more news from the frontier, Jessie was distraught. When the eleven defectors returned to St. Louis, they brought the disappointing news that all of John's letters to her had been washed away during a river crossing. The man entrusted with the letters provided her with a personal account of the expedition, leaving out the more disturbing details of the grim adventure, not telling her that during the detour to Salt Lake they were near starvation and had killed a horse for food. Little did she know that her husband's spontaneous detours would keep him from her for several more months.

By early November the men were marching west, along the southern bank of the Columbia River, their mission complete and Frémont clearly disregarding his orders to return home along the Oregon Trail. Apparently he had determined to explore the West's interior. "The latest plan now is to turn south from Fort Vancouver through Mexican territory. There we shall have to find the route from Monterey to Santa Fé and follow it," Preuss wrote in his journal. Christmas Day found them in northern Nevada, where they fired the cannon to mark the holiday. By New Year's they were wandering what Frémont would name the Great Basin, and unable to find a safe way east across Nevada's vast wasteland, he decided to turn back toward California.

In January 1844, Frémont and his men were camped on what he named the Carson River. "We had now entirely left the desert country, and were on the verge of a region which, extending westward to the shores of the Pacific, abounds in large game, and is covered with a singular luxuriance of vegetable life." When he announced his plan to traverse the Sierra Nevada—no winter crossing had ever been recorded of the rugged mountain range, where twenty feet of snow regularly fell and where two years later members of the Donner Party would resort to cannibalism and suffer a terrible tragedy—his men cheered with joy. This decision led future historians to speculate that Frémont was indeed acting on secret orders from Washington, to conduct a spy mission into California. Their destination, he told his men, was seventy miles west, into the rich fields of the Sacramento River valley, where forty-one-year-old Johann (John) August Sutter had a magnificent ranch and where they would find a land of plenty. The poet John Greenleaf Whittier would immortalize their journey in "The Pass of the Sierra":

> *All night above their rocky bed*
> *They saw the stars march slow;*
> *The wild Sierra overhead,*
> *The desert's death below.*

The sheer physical endeavor was staggering, the fourteen-thousand-foot peaks stark and frozen, "as bleak, empty, and bitter as the Himalayas themselves," with few navigable passes, virtually unknown and unmapped. The Washoe Indians did all they could to dissuade him, and some of his men remained "unusually silent," yet Frémont pushed resolutely forward.

Unknown to Jessie during those agonizing months was that the expedition had met with devastating severity, their crossing of the Sierra Nevada a monthlong ordeal that left them starving, forced to abandon the howitzer, and even eat their camp dog and packmules. John pushed his men forward with what later critics would call an irresponsible dalliance with risk and disaster and what champions called a courageous and valiant act of leadership—exhorting them "like Napoleon before the Pyramids."

Five weeks later, on March 8, 1844, the ragged caravan reached Sutter's Fort. Only thirty-three of the sixty-three horses and mules had survived, and the ten men were emaciated and exhausted. "When we arrived at the fort we were naked and in as a poor condition as men possibly could be," Carson recalled. They rested and recovered for two weeks, Frémont absorbing the activity around Sacramento. The valley was the site of an extensive American settlement the Mexican authorities viewed with suspicion. Frémont quickly assessed that the situation was ripe for rebellion, with many settlers plotting an uprising to break free of Mexican rule. Sutter managed to stay neutral, assuming the appearance of allegiance to Mexico while making clear to the Americans that he would support them if the timing was right. Frémont met with many settlers and native Californians, who affirmed his conclusions that revolt was imminent. While hoping to explore as much land as possible during his homeward journey, he was also taken with an urgency to report his political findings to the "circle of friends" back in Washington.

"Life would possibly have flowed more smoothly for Frémont had he been more of a routine officer, and he would have been spared resentment and humiliation," wrote E. L. Sabin in his *Kit Carson Days*. "But, he would have been less of a man. For political ends he was styled the Pathfinder. The paths that he actually found were of scant public utility and were bettered by other paths. He was however a Pathseeker."

Every night for the last eight months of his absence, Jessie set a place at the table for her husband, made a bed ready for him, and lit a lamp in the window to burn until dawn. "From the moment I open my eyes in the morning until I am asleep again I look for him," she wrote a friend. "I hurry home from a visit and from church & the first question is, 'Has he come?'" By March her vigil intensified as she actively prepared for John's return. "So through the winter, through the spring, the lamp burned on until the sun rose, burned vain through the night, as for Lochiel." She had never felt such loneliness and despair, traumatized by reports making their way back to St. Louis that some of his men had died, and others had resorted to cannibalism. Her mother's ailments worsened, Lily battled a severe case of whooping cough, and Jessie began suffering the psychosomatic headaches that would plague her in times of stress for the rest of her life, caused as they were by what she called "sickness of the heart." Her mother had little compassion for her agony, perhaps competing for the role of victim, and even John's mother, with whom Jessie corresponded, seemed to belittle her distress. "She says '[John] Charles is all that the grave has left me—and should anything happen to him how utterly desolate must she be,'" Jessie wrote a friend. As she attempted to bolster the spirits of the two long-suffering women in her life, her own health began to weaken. She lost so much weight her clothes fell from her diminutive frame, and her physical energy plummeted.

The people of St. Louis were kind and deferential toward her. "I was taken into their most friendly sympathy when month was added to month, and another year of silence began without any news from the party. The old whaling days of Nantucket have these experiences as legends among them, where absence and silence lasted for years, but that was the sea. Here, on land, was then the same unbroken silence with its fears and anxieties, and its useless hopes."

That month, too, her father was injured while on the navy warship *Princeton* during a ceremonial cruise down the Potomac. With a demonstration firing of a new cannon, "The Peacemaker," the weapon exploded, killing several on board, including the secretaries of state and the navy. President Tyler escaped without injury, but Benton suffered permanent deafness in one ear, and Elizabeth, though an invalid herself, left for Washington to be at his side.

As Jessie waited in St. Louis, John and a party of twenty-one men were slowly making their way home. They left Sutter's Fort on March 24, marching south and paralleling the ocean to the west and the rugged Sierra Nevada to the east, following the San Joaquin River. Three weeks later they reached the southern end of the Central Valley, and turned east to cross the Tehachapi Mountains. Originally intending to travel northward to the Great Salt Lake, Frémont followed an Indian trail south instead, to the point where it merged with the Spanish Trail connecting Los Angeles with Santa Fe—perhaps, as later observers speculated, seeking possible routes Mexican soldiers would use if they headed north.

For weeks they would traverse the Mojave Desert, finally reaching in early May the oasis of spring-fed meadows the Spanish called Las Vegas. From there they headed northeast, across what is now south-central Utah, meeting the flamboyant and ruthless Indian chief Wa-kara, or Chief Walker, as the white men called "The Hawk of the Mountains." Fluent in Spanish and capable in English, Wa-kara and his warriors rode the finest horseflesh in the West, stolen from Mexican ranchos, their saddles embellished with silver. "They were robbers of a higher order than those of the desert," Frémont wrote. "They conducted their depredations with form, and under the colour of trade and toll for passing through their country." Fortunately, Walker was "quite civil" to Frémont, whom he knew by reputation, and the two men exchanged blankets.

They remained in Ute territory for several weeks, exploring and mapping this "Great Basin," which Frémont found endlessly fascinating— a region he felt would dramatically alter America's view of itself. "The whole idea of such a desert, and such a people, is a novelty in our country," he wrote, "and excites Asiatic, not American ideas. Interior basins, with their own systems of lakes and rivers, and often sterile, are common enough in Asia; people still in the elementary state of families, living in deserts, with no other occupation than the mere animal search for food, may still be seen in that ancient quarter of the globe, but in America such things are new and strange, unknown and unsuspected, and discredited when related. But I flatter myself that what is discovered, though not enough to satisfy curiosity, is sufficient to excite it, and that subsequent explorations will complete what has been commenced."

In the early morning of August 7, 1844, fifteen months after John's departure, Jessie was staying at the home of her cousin Anne Potts, whose husband was on his deathbed. Jessie was awakened by a messenger who said John had been seen in town the night before. That news was followed quickly by a report from Gabriel, the Benton family coachman, who "insisted he had been waked by a lot of gravel thrown into his room through the open window; that in the moonlight he saw the Captain 'in his uniform and thin as a shadow,' who asked him if everybody was well, and could he let him into the house without making a noise?" The coachman, answered that Jessie had gone to her cousin's home to help care for the dying man. "And then the Captain went off, quick, downtown." Gabriel thought it was an apparition, and with his reputation as a heavy drinker, Jessie worried that indeed he had seen a "ghost."

Just as she abandoned her hopes, John walked through the door, rushing toward Jessie, whom he carried to an easy chair. Holding her close, he recounted that he had come to the Potts home the night before, but decided not to rouse the family by ringing the bell. He then left to wait for daybreak. "The only green spot with trees was the open ground in front of Barnum's hotel, and there he sat on a bench watching for the slow stars to grow pale," Jessie later recalled. "One of the hotel people seeing the uniform came out and hospitably offered a room, when he recognized Mr. Frémont, who explained his waiting there." He gratefully accepted, and slept in a bed for the first time in more than a year.

Before breakfast was served, the house filled with friends and relatives who had heard the "ghost" story and rushed to see if the explorer had indeed returned. Jessie and John were amiable and gracious to the impromptu gathering, but eager to be alone. John briefly greeted the throng before lifting Jessie into his arms and carrying her to bed.

When John finally returned to St. Louis in August 1844, he was gaunt and exhausted. But the appearance of his young wife worried him most. "I am alarmed over Jessie's delicate and fragile appearance," he wrote to Benton. "While she is vivacious and winsome and touchingly concerned about me, I realize that her anxieties have cruelly robbed her of strength and color. She has little rest or privacy here, and I can but hope that when we are again in Washington, she will be quickly restored."

By the end of the month they were happily back in their room at the Bentons' Washington residence. "Our welcome was a joyous one," Jessie wrote to a cousin, "father laughing and crying together as he carried mother up the stairs. We had an early home dinner, even Lily at table. As I looked upon our united family group, the picture was all the more beautiful for those background shadows of anxious waiting."

As became a pattern in their marriage, each of his returns was greeted by a hero's welcome and a round of public festivities. What followed then were a few weeks of private, romantic, and leisurely intimacy, Jessie and John reconnecting emotionally with each other as they geared up for their next literary collaboration and started envisioning the next expedition. Upon his return this time Jessie knew she needed to broach the subject: did he feel she had overstepped her bounds by intercepting Abert's communiqué? John assured her of the heroic and historic role she had played in the exploration of the West, and implored her to disregard any criticism, all of which, he believed, was fomented by the West

Point clique jealous of his accomplishments. Thrilled to have her husband home, determined to nurture and sustain him back to his normal
state of fitness and health, the twenty-year-old Jessie had no idea that she
was about to enter what she would later call "a new and painful epoch"
in her life.

4

BEAR FLAG 1845–1848

. . . like gazing at a Flemish tapestry with the wrong side out; even though the figures are visible, they are full of threads that obscure the view and are not bright and smooth as when seen from the other side.

—Cervantes, *Don Quixote*

NOW FOLLOWED A time of work so delightful in itself, so use-ful, so undiluted by any drawbacks," Jessie wrote of the winter of 1844, "that it stands in my memory as 'the happy winter.'" John was quick to report to General Winfield Scott and the secretary of war, William Wilkins, who were impressed by Frémont's span of knowledge yet stunned by his youth—though Frémont admitted that "in my case it was a good failing, as young men never saw the obstacles." General Scott promoted him, giving him a double brevet as first lieutenant and captain. His immediate obligations acquitted, John immersed himself for a time in the congenial circumstances of family life, giddy at the reunion with Jessie and Lily. He traveled to South Carolina to fetch his mother, whom he brought to Washington to spend the autumn months.

John was a celebrity—the capital alive with talk of his adventures in California and Oregon, the Rockies and the Great Basin, the Sierra Nevada, and the Great Salt Lake—and invitations, letters, and requests for information besieged the attractive young couple. They coveted time for themselves and with their family, dining sometimes alone but more often than not with the Bentons and innumerable guests. They had their sights set on California, John's tales of the golden landscape enticing Jessie and everyone else with whom he engaged. "His account [was] enough almost to make you think that the Garden of Eden was the other side of the mountains," the scholar-historian George Bancroft wrote to his wife after an evening with the couple. "I had no idea that there [was] so beautifully picturesque and inviting a region: destined you may be sure to be filled with Yankees." Frémont's cartographer, Charles Preuss, confirmed John's animated, almost unbelievable account. "It is true," Preuss wrote of the Sacramento Valley, "this valley is a paradise. Grass, flowers, trees, beautiful clear rivers, thousands of deer, elk, wild horses, wonderful salmon . . . [the Indians] all go naked because it is eternal spring . . . At a dance with which the Indians entertained us one had painted his penis with the Prussian national colors."

By October, John and Jessie were once again focused on writing a report, but the C Street residence was so constantly filled with visitors, they found little opportunity for sustained work. Jessie suggested they rent a cottage a block away, where they could write uninterrupted, and soon they were installed in the two-story abode, along with a young Yale-trained astronomer. Joseph Hubbard, who would create the map, set up his work space on the first floor and served as sentry for unwanted interrupters. Jessie and John organized their office on the second floor. "Only my father had the privilege of coming up," Jessie said.

As before, they settled into a routine. At dawn, John and Jessie arose and breakfasted together on coffee and pastries. John then left for their workshop, and Jessie stayed at home to get Lily up and fed. At nine A.M. she joined him and they worked undisturbed until one P.M., when a black servant, Nancy, arrived with two-year-old Lily and a basket lunch of chicken, biscuits, and fruit. Following Benton's regimen of concentrated work followed by exercise and frivolity, they played with their daughter for an hour before returning her to Nancy. The couple then took a long, brisk walk along the banks of the Potomac. They spent the late afternoon relaxing and reading at the C Street home. Every evening, John met with Hubbard to discuss his mathematical and astronomical notes. Dinners were grand affairs, presided over by Benton—"Washington watch-dog of the Pacific coast," one writer called him—the mahogany table groaning with soups, salads, meats, desserts, wines, ports, and liqueurs, the discussion filled with talk of Oregon, California, and Texas.

Frémont's second report was three times longer and even more readable than the first, a literary adventure story filled with scientific data, frontier gossip, descriptions of natural beauty, tales of hardship and strife, and riveting human interest anecdotes. On March 1, 1845, Frémont officially presented it to the War Department, and two days later the Senate passed a resolution calling for the printing of five thousand extra copies. Senator James Buchanan—soon to become secretary of state under newly elected president James Knox Polk—moved to have the amount doubled. Newspapers around the country began excerpting the book before it was published, and the narrative received rave reviews though it would not be available to the general public until the end of the year. Destined to become a best seller, the book brought international attention to Frémont, whom admirers dubbed the "Pathfinder"— a name he "neither sought nor used" but would carry for the rest of his life. "Handsome Frémont and beautiful Jessie were acclaimed by the American public," wrote a twentieth-century historian. "They were everything a growing nation needed for a symbol of success, and the country was not to see this combination of youth and daring again until the later cults of hero worship for George and Elizabeth Custer, Charles and Anne Lindbergh, or John and Jacqueline Kennedy."

Frémont had proved that the continent could be traveled and then populated from sea to sea. The timing was propitious, for the very day Frémont submitted his report to the War Department, Congress passed a joint resolution admitting Texas as a new state, and rumors filled Washington of impending war with Mexico as a result. The main concern of the expansionists, as always, was not Texas, but Oregon. They feared the British would either use America's preoccupation with Mexico to seize Oregon and California, or join Mexico in a war against the United States, taking Oregon and California as prizes. The rivalry with Great Britain had sparked a storm of national chauvinism, and Polk's campaign promise of "fifty-four-forty or fight"—the slogan for American expansion beyond the forty-ninth parallel—had been crucial to his election. In his inaugural address the new president had said: "Our title to Oregon is in question, and our people are preparing to perfect it by occupancy." Finally, "the circle of friends" had a like-minded president. A Tennessean, a slaveowner, and a stubborn defender of Jackson's views, Polk even carried the nickname "Young Hickory," and had won the Democratic nomination in 1844 in part with Jackson's support.

The stage was set for Polk to take action, and Frémont would be a crucial instrument, agreeing with Senator Daniel Webster of Massachusetts, who had been expansion-minded as secretary of state despite belonging to the Whig Party, which Benton considered the enemy. Webster believed that San Francisco Bay and other Pacific ports were "twenty times as valuable to us as all of Texas."

Senator Benton rabidly opposed a war with Mexico, "unjust in itself—upon a peaceable neighbor—in violation of treaties and of pledged neutrality—unconstitutionally made." His many years representing Spanish families in Florida and Louisiana, his knowledge of their laws and language, led to a long-standing interest in Mexico and sympathy for its people. "He had always held that toward Mexico our relation should be that of the Great Republic aiding a neighboring state in its early struggles," his son-in-law would write of Benton's strong feelings, "and he belonged with those who preferred the acquiring of Texas by treaty and purchase, not by war. This he opposed and denounced. He came now to hold the same views concerning California."

While Benton believed Texas should eventually become a state, he saw the current machinations as a scheme for slavery extension, to which he had become increasingly opposed. Representing the antislavery wing of the Democratic Party, Benton supported former president Martin Van Buren in his bid for the candidacy. When his party turned instead to Tennessee governor James Polk—a clever and small man with bold, expansionist ideas—Benton, ever the Democrat, swallowed his pride and campaigned loyally for Polk in Missouri. As residents of a slave state, Missouri's constituents were losing their devotion to their increasingly radical senior senator. Polk carried the state handily, while Benton was narrowly elected to his fifth term—a stark warning for his own political future as well as for that of the nation.

Despite their differences, Polk and Benton established a close working relationship with regard to Texas, Oregon, and California, Benton one of the president's closest advisers. Within weeks of Polk's inauguration the president invited Frémont and Benton to the White House to discuss what was being called the "Western Problem." Frémont would later express to Jessie his disappointment in the meeting, claiming the president was refracted and inattentive when Frémont stressed the importance of the compilation of accurate maps, Polk apparently preferring the "ancient chaos" of western geography as it existed on old maps. "The President seemed for the moment skeptical about the exactness of my information and disposed to be conservative," Frémont wrote of the meeting. "Like the Secretary [Wilkins] he found me 'young,' and said something of the 'impulsiveness of young men.'" But within weeks,

Frémont found himself in frequent meetings with two of Polk's cabinet members who would be instrumental in dispatching Frémont back to California—Secretary of State Buchanan and Secretary of the Navy George Bancroft. "President Polk entered on his office with a fixed determination to acquire California, if he could acquire it in an honorable and just manner," Frémont later wrote of the administration's designs.

Meanwhile, Buchanan, an enthusiastic proponent for obtaining California, had come to distrust the only Spanish-speaking member of his staff. "The librarian and translator at the State Department, Mr. [Robert] Greenhow of course knew Spanish," Jessie later wrote of the situation. "But his wife [Rose] was in the pay of the English legation as a spy, and our private information reached them through her," just as she would later be a spy during the Civil War. Buchanan summoned Jessie—who had been his escort to the Bodisco wedding—and asked her to translate a document written in Spanish pertaining to the Mexican situation in California. From that point forward, she translated for Buchanan all correspondence for the department, including the incendiary articles appearing in the Mexican press, and would eventually act as personal interpreter as well for conferences between Buchanan, Polk, and Mexican government officials—her role of a secret and confidential nature. Through her position she learned early and firsthand of the positioning of Mexican troops, and of the foreign policy the president was formulating. Everyone seemed to want to go to war: Mexico was agitated over Texas; Great Britain wanted Oregon; and the United States wanted California.

Polk and his cabinet were hoping to negotiate a settlement with Mexico on the Texas boundary issues, while also maneuvering to acquire New Mexico and California—from El Paso west to the Pacific and to include San Francisco Bay, as Polk noted in his diary. "The President and Mr. Bancroft held it impossible for Mexico, situated as things then were, to retain possession of California," Frémont assessed the situation, "and therefore it was right to negotiate with Mexico for the acquisition of that which to her could be of no use. This it was hoped to accomplish by peaceful negotiation; but if Mexico in resenting our acceptance of the offer of Texas to join us, should begin a war with us, then, by taking possession of the province." Polk had sent an emissary to Mexico City to bargain with Mexican officials—prepared to offer as much as $40 million for the land in question—but the confidential agent, William S. Parrott, "was received abusively by the Mexican press and accomplished nothing." A second envoy, John Slidell of Louisiana, would fail equally in his mission.

Meanwhile, rumors persisted—later shown to be unfounded—that Great Britain intended to seize California. Indeed, Polk had ascended to the presidency partly on the national fears of a British invasion of the Pacific Northwest, and made the supposed threat the cornerstone of his foreign policy. He surrounded himself with like-minded advisers, Benton himself intensely wary and suspicious of Great Britain since the War of 1812. Benton had the fixed belief that England "in her secret counsels" regarded California as her own, dating back more than two centuries, when Sir Francis Drake claimed it for Queen Elizabeth and named it New Albion. Secretary of the Navy Bancroft urgently warned the president of the British warships patrolling the Pacific Coast. "All informed men knew that California was a derelict craft," wrote Allan Nevins, "ready to be picked up by any captain who would take it into the port of a strong and stable government."

By the end of 1844 it was clear that something had to be done. Frémont was the man for the moment, his orders for a third expedition created through secret meetings among Polk, Benton, Buchanan, and Bancroft. "As affairs resolved themselves, California stood out as the chief subject in the impending war," Frémont wrote much later, ". . . and with Mr. Benton and other governing men at Washington it became a firm resolve to hold it for the United States . . . This was talked over fully during the time of preparation for the third expedition, and the contingencies anticipated and weighed."

The origin of Frémont's orders, the actual details of his instructions, the covert nature of his mission, the chain of command he was expected to follow—whether army, navy, or the office of the presidency—would be murky and contradictory, controversial and mysterious throughout history. Because of the controversial and imperialistic nature of the operation, many of the participants carried their singular knowledge to their graves. A private conversation about the expedition between Benton and President Polk would be frustratingly vague in the diaries and recollections of both men. "Suffice it to say that the meeting and Frémont's subsequent actions in California probably yielded as many conspiracy theories as any other conversation in U.S. history," wrote Frémont biographer Tom Chaffin.

Frémont later claimed that the true nature of his orders could not be committed to writing, so delicate and potentially explosive was the situation with Mexico and Great Britain. "The relations between the three countries made a chief subject of interest about which our thoughts settled as the probability of war grew into certainty. For me, no distinct course of definite instruction could be laid down, but the probabilities were made known to me as well as what to do when they became facts. The distance was too great for timely communication; but failing this I was given discretion to act. The instructions early sent, and repeatedly insisted upon, to the officer commanding our Pacific squadron, gave specific orders to be followed in the event of war. But these frequent discussions among the men who controlled the action of the Government, gave to me the advantage of knowing more thoroughly what were its present wishes, and its intentions in the event of war."

Then and later, Frémont was unwavering in his commitment to what he thought were the government's "present wishes." From the start and throughout the expedition, he recognized the navy officer "commanding our Pacific squadron"—Commodore John Drake Sloat—as his superior officer, notwithstanding Frémont's position with the army and his actual orders from the Topographical Corps.

By the end of 1844, Bancroft had asked Polk to "lay aside fifty thousand dollars for Frémont's next venture"—a request the president passed along to the War Department. In a secret conference—which Jessie would always contend was known to Polk—Benton and Bancroft mapped the course for Frémont to survey the Sierra Nevada in California and the Cascades in Oregon for migrating American settlers. If he received word that war had begun, he was to continue into California and thwart any British designs on San Francisco Bay.

The official orders from Abert, issued in February 1845, made no mention of California and contained no instructions of a military nature. "He will strike the Arkansas as soon as practicable, survey that river, and if practicable survey the Red River without our boundary line, noting particularly the navigable properties of each, and will determine as near as practicable the points at which the boundary line of the U.S. the 100th degree of longitude west of Greenwich strikes the Arkansas, and the Red River. It is also important that the Head waters of the Arkansas should be accurately determined. Long journies [sic] to determine isolated geographical points are scarcely worth the time and the expense which they occasion; the efforts of Captain Frémont will therefore be more particularly directed to the geography of localities within reasonable distance of Bents Fort, and of the streams which run east from the Rocky Mountains, and he will so time his operations, that his party will come in during the present year."

Polk's earlier warning to Frémont against the "impulsiveness of young men" would later be publicized as evidence of the president's disavowal of Frémont's later activities, though the president strongly supported the mission behind the scenes. Abert's overt orders aside, Frémont believed his instructions from the navy were clear: he was to seize California when the opportune moment arose. If he proved unsuccessful, both the navy and the administration would deny the plan had been condoned. It was clear that the man who started the war with Mexico in California— the most unpopular war in the history of the United States—would be dismissed as a renegade operating without government authorization. He had sensed, though not yet fully, that he could be the scapegoat for powerful and ambitious men. Still, he and Jessie did not hesitate for a moment. Their vision of America was at stake, and here was their chance to make history.

Jessie had planned to travel with him as usual to St. Louis, to assist in the preparations, but her mother's illness kept her at home. Still, she would be an active participant from Washington, translating for Buchanan and staying apprised of the sensitive political developments. On one of their last evenings together, as she finished sewing a water-proof leather pocket for him to carry important documents, both of them suddenly broke down, her tears dropping onto the pouch. "There," she said, regaining her composure. "That's properly dedicated, and I must be willing to dedicate you to this service which fits you. You leave us to execute plans my father has worked for all his life. You both are part of me. My work is to let you go cheerfully. Besides, you would soon tire of a repining wife, and surely you wouldn't have me a Mrs. Preuss," she said, referring to the cartographer's wife, who insisted that her husband choose between his marriage and his life of wandering. In-deed, Preuss had elected to stay home, his place in the upcoming expedi-tion taken by a young Philadelphia artist, Edward Kern, a far more congenial figure than Preuss and a man who would describe Frémont as the "beau ideal of all that was chivalrous and noble."

John, once again, promised he would write to Jessie whenever he had the opportunity, and he steeled himself for another farewell—Jessie's fi-nal kiss, Lily's tiny wave, Benton's embrace—the "intangible supplies, the morale boosters for lonely moments in wild and desolate places."

"Captain Frémont has gone upon his third expedition, determined upon a complete military and scientific exploration of all the vast unknown region between the Rocky Mountains and the Pacific Ocean, and between the Oregon River and the Gulf of California," the *Union* newspaper reported in May. "This expedition is expected to continue near two years, and its successful result is looked to with the highest degree of interest by all the friends of science in America and Europe."

On May 15, 1845, Frémont left for St. Louis, where he found a strong contingent of army and navy men assigned to his "survey." His fame was so great that his arrival in the frontier city caused a stir. As he began recruiting men—first hiring the best of the group from his previous expeditions, including Kit Carson, who came out of retirement after swearing off his nomadic lifestyle—hundreds of volunteers came forward, clamoring to be chosen. He agreed to address all aspirants at the Planter's Warehouse, but the space was so crowded he was forced to move outdoors, where he was nearly trampled by the shouting men, eager to sign on. In the end, he chose sixty-two, including nine Delaware Indians—a diverse and tough combination of frontiersmen, scientists, soldiers, sharpshooters, and hunters. "It was a wild mixture, a free and easy lot," wrote one historian. "It was young America on the move." He held a contest and rewarded the best marksmen with the finest rifles of the day. Each volunteer received a Hawken rifle, two pistols, a knife, a saddle, a bridle, two blankets, and a horse or a mule.

In early August, the party reached Bent's Fort, where they learned that Colonel Stephen Watts Kearny and five army companies of dragoons had been three days earlier. Kearny's troops were conducting maneuvers in the hinterland to determine how well the cavalry could operate in distant locales.

In late August, the party left Bent's Fort with two hundred horses and a dozen cattle to be slaughtered for food; the men were heavily armed, well provisioned, and energetic. Frémont was the revered commander of what amounted to a small army. Unbeknownst to him, the president had received an alarming dispatch two weeks earlier from Thomas Oliver Larkin, a shrewd entrepreneur whom Polk had recently appointed as American consul at Monterey, California. Larkin, usually understated and always credible, warned Polk that Mexican troops, financed by Great Britain, were on their way to California. "There is no doubt in this Country but the Troops now expected here in September are sent on by the instigation of the English Government under the plea, that the American settlers in California want to revolutionize the Country."

Larkin's ominous letter prompted the president to dispatch Marine Corps lieutenant Archibald H. Gillespie on a secret mission to California, through Mexico, to carry a response to Larkin, orders to Frémont, and a sealed envelope from Jessie to John with encoded instructions from Secretary of the Navy Bancroft. "As we had a squadron in the North Pacific, but no army, the measures for carrying out this design fell to the Navy Department," Bancroft wrote forty years later of his dispatch to Frémont. "The Secretary of the Navy, who had good means of gaining news as to the intention of Mexico, and had reason to believe that its government intended to make war on us, directed timely preparation for it . . . Captain Frémont having been sent originally on a peaceful mission to the west by way of the Rocky Mountains, it had become necessary to give him warning of the new state of affairs and the designs of the President . . . Being absolved from any duty as an explorer, Captain Frémont was left to his duty as an officer in the service of the United States, with the further authoritative knowledge that the government intended to take possession of California."

Disguised as an ailing businessman seeking health in moderate climes, and chosen because he was a Spanish scholar, Gillespie was ordered to memorize and destroy the official documents before he reached Mexico. He also carried a letter from Buchanan to Larkin, appointing him as a "confidential agent" and requesting that Larkin use "the greatest vigilance in discovering and defeating any attempt" by foreign invaders to seize California, while encouraging the Californians to peacefully secede from Mexico and join the United States. So sensitive in nature, Buchanan's letter would remain classified by the U.S. government for forty years.

At the same time, Secretary Bancroft wrote to Commodore Sloat, commander of the navy's Pacific Squadron, with orders that if he should "ascertain with certainty, that Mexico had declared war against the United States," that his fleet should seize San Francisco. The War Department ordered General Zachary Taylor, in command of the Army of the Southwest, to proceed deep within Mexican territory, to make sure Mexican troops were not attempting to cross the Rio Grande. By October, after Polk's emissary to Mexico, William Parrott, reported excitedly that Great Britain intended to transport Irish immigrants to California to advance Catholicism while establishing a British colony, Bancroft sent new orders to Sloat stating that the U.S. Navy need not wait for an official declaration of war before acting.

Camped at the Great Salt Lake, Frémont knew nothing of the latest developments, determined to drive his men quickly to avoid the deep snows of the Sierra Nevada that had plagued his previous journey. They traversed the Great Basin, moving steadily across what is now northern Nevada, following St. Mary's River, which he renamed the Humboldt, for the Prussian scientist he so admired, and pushing across the desert toward Elko. On November 11 they crossed the magnificent Ruby Mountains and dropped southwest to the eastern slope of the Toiyabe Mountains. On November 24, Frémont divided his men into two groups with the plan to rendezvous at Sutter's Fort. The smaller party, led by Frémont and Carson, would follow the Truckee River north to find a pass over the Sierra; the larger party would continue south, crossing over into the San Joaquin Valley at Tulare Lake.

Jessie, meeting regularly with Bancroft, Benton, and Buchanan, kept abreast of the foreign intrigues. August brought a letter from John, who reported that the expedition was going very well and all were in good health. His mother, Anne, sent Jessie a daguerreotype of John, which she placed in her bedroom. "It hangs over the head of my bed and is my guardian angel, for I could not waste time or do anything you did not like with that beloved face looking so kindly and earnestly at me," she wrote to him. In September she traveled to Richmond, where she met an artist who asked if she would model for him. She agreed, as long as he would paint her looking serious and substantive rather than youthful and capricious, and he reluctantly agreed. "I found it difficult that in order to please my sitter, I had to ignore her most characteristic expression. Though her remarks are sensible, her animation, her flashing eye and smile give her the air of being about to say something charmingly frivolous." She would present the miniature to John upon his return, and he would carry it with him until his death.

The fall of 1845 found Jessie spending much of her time at home, caring for her mother and Lily, and hosting intimate dinner parties, which she found more agreeable in her current anxious if not somber mood than the large affairs of the past. A celebrity in her own right, she came to cherish her privacy. She entertained Samuel F. B. Morse, for whom Benton was instrumental in obtaining his first government funding for thirty miles of telegraph line between Washington and Baltimore. Her uncle James McDowell, now a congressman from Virginia, and a new senator, Sam Houston, who had served under her father in the War of 1812, were included in her coveted social circle. After visiting the C Street home, John Lloyd Stephens, whose books about Europe, the Middle East, and Central America were favorites in the Benton household, wrote: "I carried away with me that day an unforgettable picture of happy family life, the dining room at high tea, candle light playing over the silver service, a blazing wood fire, Mrs. Benton quiet as a shadow, swathed in a blue dressing gown, lying on a sofa, smiling up at the Senator, who had just carried her in from her bedroom and who now stood over her arranging her shawl before seating himself nearby to serve her. Pretty Jessie Frémont, in a wide-skirted dress of silk that made her look like a petunia blossom, sat at the tea urn."

Jessie frequently met with Elizabeth Blair Lee, their friendship maturing from childhood playmates into a deep and mutual relationship between two adult women. The daughter of Benton's closest personal friend, Francis Preston Blair, Lizzie had known Jessie all of Jessie's life, and the two were in fact distant cousins. Six years older, the educated and refined Lizzie found Jessie's spontaneity and candor, humor and openness to be refreshing among the staid Washington wives. Though different in temperament—Lizzie was far more conventional, a woman who would never have dreamed of defying her father and eloping with the man she loved and of whom her parents disapproved—their relationship was grounded in genuine affection and admiration. Blair had been Benton's political ally since Jackson's presidency, the two men now representing the antislavery wing of the Democratic Party. The Blairs' lavish Silver Spring, Maryland, estate was a second home to Jessie, where she retreated often to an upstairs bedroom they kept ready for her.

On a cold November evening, Lieutenant Gillespie came to the Benton home to retrieve messages from the senator and Jessie to be delivered to John. Gillespie announced that he would be making his way, via Vera Cruz, Mexico City, and Mazatlán to Monterey, carrying confidential dispatches from the president, secretary of state, and secretary of the navy to Sloat, Larkin, and Frémont. Jessie penned a letter, in what she later described as a family code, providing John with all the news she could reveal about the imminence of war, the president's decision to use force against the Californios, and a signal to take action. She took care to write the details in such a way that if the letter fell into enemy hands the government's strategy would not be jeopardized. Benton, too, wrote a letter, apparently veiled in a cipher previously agreed to among he, Jessie, and John. "These threw their own light upon the communication from Mr. Gillespie, and made the expected signal." Frémont would later describe the family letters. "In substance, their effect was: The time has come. England must not get a foothold. We must be first. Act; discreetly, but positively." How much was implied, inferred, and instructed would be a matter of speculation for more than a century. The Benton family letters were destroyed or classified, Gillespie's orders from Washington to Frémont were verbal, and official documents were vague, excised, or nonexistent. In the end, Frémont's subsequent actions would be seen as lacking official authorization, with few besides Frémont willing to take responsibility.

As John made his way toward California, Jessie began her anxious vigil. She knew it would be months before Gillespie reached California; months more before Frémont could safely send a letter without worry of interception; and, with the new state of affairs, more than a year before her husband would return. As the clouds of war gathered, she retreated once again to the unsatisfying role of the waiting wife.

"In the hands of an enterprising people, what a country this might be!" proclaimed author Richard Henry Dana in his 1840 *Two Years before the Mast*. The Harvard student did more than anyone else to popularize California for a national audience, extolling its beauty, resources, and endless opportunity. A desired prize for America, the golden shore, fertile land, and mild climate enticed a generation. Until Dana's book, California was considered a no-man's-land—six months' journey around Cape Horn at the southern tip of South America and overland travel blocked by what one historian described as "Cyclopean walls of the Sierra Nevada."

"It is a fundamental mistake to think of Mexico, in this period, or for many years before, as a republic or even as a government," wrote Bernard De Voto. "It must be understood as a late stage in the breakdown of the Spanish Empire." The Republic of Mexico had been established in 1821 following a revolt against Spain during the international climate of revolution. California was little more to either Spain or Mexico than a far-flung, unpopulated outpost. Though distinctively tranquil and sociable, the native Californios managed to stage nine rebellions in fifteen years against the notoriously inept governors sent to the colonial capital of Monterey by Mexico City. Twenty-one immense Spanish missions existed between San Diego and San Francisco at the time of Mexican

independence—"each an agricultural empire with a handful of Francis-
cans in command, an army of Indian neophytes to do the work, well-
tilled cattle, 60,000 horses, and 300,000 sheep and swine, in addition to
hundreds of acres of vineyards and irrigated farmland," as two
twentieth-century historians described the realm, which had fallen into
private hands by the 1830s.

The Mexican Colonization Act of 1824 allowed citizens of influence
and means to acquire land grants ranging from 4,000 to 48,000 acres.
The ranchos were supervised by indolent "rancheros," who used Indians
as virtual slaves to operate their vast domains. The terrain was scarcely
inhabited. One traveler through the territory reported that in 1844, approximately 100 people lived in San Diego, 250 in Los Angeles, 100 in
Santa Barbara, and 200 in Monterey—many of the residents American
or British. There was one lawyer and one physician, no hotels, no
schools, no newspapers, no theaters, and very few stores. "Why, they
asked, should we train lawyers when there is no litigation, teachers when
ignorance is bliss?" The only vehicle in all of California was a rude,
squeaking, ox-drawn cart with solid oak wheels—neither spoked nor
tire-covered—its axle lubricated with soap. Other population figures
for 1845 estimated 100,000 Indians, 14,000 European Spaniards and
people of mixed blood, and about 680 mostly American-born foreigners
throughout the province, with another 500 American migrants currently
following the Oregon Trail to California.

The charm and hospitality of the rancheros were legendary; the Californios "had a custom of never charging for anything." They routinely
gave visitors food from gardens laden with grapes, olives, figs, pomegran-
ates, and vegetables, freshly butchered beef, cheese, and wine. "The native
Californians valued and treated their favorite horses, in much the same
way as the Arabs and Persians did," Jessie later wrote, "—and not only
trained in the usual acceptance of the word but rendered them docile
by petting and kindness." Punctuating their life of leisure was raucous
entertainment—horse racing, gambling, and dancing—their lives so
thoroughly enjoyable and peaceable that any serious contemplation of
revolt was passively dismissed. Neither patriotic nor nationalistic toward
Mexico or the United States, the Californios had no inspiration or in-
centive for revolution, which posed a dilemma for the Polk administration. "California's separation from Mexico could be achieved in two
ways," wrote a distinguished historian of the state, Robert Glass Cleland,
"—by a revolt of the native Californians, aided by American residents; or

by an uprising of the American residents against the native Californians." Frémont would follow the second option, apparently convinced that that was the express desire of his president.

By the time Frémont arrived in California in December 1845, the Mexican governor, Manuel Micheltorena, had recently been ousted in an insurrection led by a native *politico*, José Castro, and former governor Juan B. Alvarado. Intelligent and evenhanded, Micheltorena was considered by the insurgents to be too friendly toward foreigners, dispensing broad land grants to John Sutter and the American "Dr." John Marsh— "each of whom aspired to be the Sam Houston of California." Castro and Alvarado exploited anti-American sentiment in order to launch a coup that would leave them in control of the vast revenues of the territory. Castro was installed in Monterey, where he became military *comandante* of the treasury, and Pio Pico became civil governor, ruling from the new capital of Los Angeles. Soon, perhaps inevitably, Castro and Pico were vying for power, their rivalry dividing California into northern and southern provinces, further weakening official ties to Mexico and threatening civil war. Sutter and Marsh observed the situation with alarm, fearing that either Castro or Pico would invite Great Britain to intervene at any moment. "The British were watching, the Americans were watching, and into this natural tinderbox rode Captain Frémont and his men."

On December 9, 1845, Frémont's party camped within sight of the adobe walls of Sutter's Fort. Frémont intended to be well rested and properly dressed in his army uniform before entering the fort the next day. When he and Carson rode down the following morning to greet Sutter and request much-needed supplies, they found his twenty-six-year-old majordomo in charge of the fort. The proprietor was not around, and the formal and arrogant New Yorker, John Bidwell, gave the men a cool reception. Frémont requested sixteen packmules, six saddles, and other supplies, which Bidwell refused to furnish, stating that the fort was short on provisions. Frémont turned on his heel, muttered something derogatory about Sutter to Carson, and the men mounted their horses and rode off "without saying good-day," as Bidwell remembered the unpleasant moment.

Bidwell followed the men to their camp, where he apologized and explained that tensions were mounting in California, and that unfortunately Sutter had been on the losing side of the Micheltorena ousting, so he was now preoccupied with mending fences with Castro and Pico.

Frémont begrudgingly accepted Bidwell's offer of fourteen mules, saddles, food, horses, cattle, and use of the fort's blacksmith. Still, the enmity engendered from the first meeting of the two men would not diminish over time, Bidwell thinking the captain haughty and rude, and Frémont thinking Bidwell a by-the-books stuffed shirt.

When Sutter returned three days later and learned of Frémont's appearance in California, the notoriously clever Swiss landowner—hoping to curry favor with all sides in the hostility-ridden territory—promptly reported Frémont's arrival to both General Mariano Vallejo and U.S. consul Thomas Larkin. Meanwhile, Frémont rode south, driving his cattle and horses, in search of the main body of his expedition that he had left more than two weeks earlier in the foothills of the Sierra Nevada. Traveling in a party of merely sixteen men, through a highly agitated political climate, Frémont was anxious to rendezvous with his men, to strengthen his little band to a heavily armed, well-mounted group of sixty. On their journey through the San Joaquin Valley, they had a clash with what Frémont called "Horse-thief Indians" in which one of his men shot and killed one Indian. The tribesmen pursued the Frémont party as it made its way to camp, and the next day another confrontation erupted, with Taos frontiersman Lucien B. Maxwell and one of the Indians dueling, Maxwell with a pistol, the Indian with arrows. Maxwell killed the Indian before Frémont could intervene. Frémont thought these "Christian Indians"—previously herdsmen, or vaqueros, to the Franciscan missions—to be the "scourge to the settlements." When the missions broke up after the Mexican Revolution, many of the Indian vaqueros banded together and terrorized the settlers. "Deprived of their regular food, the Indians took to the mountains and began to drive off horses," Frémont wrote of them. "In their early condition they had learned to eat wild horse-meat and liked it. Familiarity with the whites and the success of their predatory excursions made the Horse-thief Indians far more daring and braver than those who remained in fixed villages." Still, Frémont thought Maxwell should have spared the man's life. "I would have taken him prisoner . . . but was too late."

They had searched the entire San Joaquin Valley and failed to find their party. Frémont decided to head north again, turning his men back toward Sutter's Fort. There, after all, was the designated rendezvous location for the two parties, and despite his apprehension, he felt certain the other group was too well-armed and -provisioned to have met with disaster. "They were too strong to have met with any serious accident and my conclusion was that they had traveled slowly in order to give me time to make my round and procure supplies."

He arrived back at Sutter's Fort on January 15, 1846, where Sutter greeted him with gracious hospitality, the two men feasting together, sharing wine and gossip. He initially intended to wait for Kern and the rest of his party, but only four days later, he and eight of his men were once again heading off. They sailed on Sutter's schooner, *Sacramento*, to explore Yerba Buena, present-day San Francisco, and to visit William Alexander Leidesdorff, the U.S. vice consul. From there, Frémont decided, they would travel a hundred miles south to Monterey, where he would present to Mexican officials a passport authorizing passage given him by Sutter.

Frémont wrote Jessie a cheerful and optimistic letter dated January 24 from Yerba Buena, expressing his intention to continue the survey of Oregon before "we turn our faces homeward" once the winter had passed. "All our people are well, and we have had no sickness of any kind among us; so that I hope to be able to bring back with me all that I carried out. Many months of hardships, close trials, and anxieties have tried me severely, and my hair is turning gray before its time. But all this passes, *et le bon temps viendra* [and the good times return]."

He gazed at the striking setting, where the San Francisco Bay meets the Pacific Ocean. With an unrecognized prescience—for gold had not yet been discovered in California—and "on the same principle that the harbor of Byzantium was called Chrysopylae [Golden Horn]," he christened the break "the Golden Gate Strait."

Much would be made of Frémont's movements from this point forward, historians over the next century and a half debating his motives, his instructions, and his activities. He spent a few days at the home of Leidesdorff—a jovial American trader who had adopted Mexican citizenship and lived with his attractive Russian wife in "a low bungalow sort of adobe house with a long piazza facing the bay for the sunny mornings, and a cheerful fire within against the fog and chill of the afternoons." Leidesdorff's graceful and cultivated lifestyle, his voluptuous garden and dramatic ocean view, persuaded Frémont that he would bring Jessie, Lily, and his mother to California to make their home.

On January 24, Frémont's party, accompanied by Leidesdorff, began the journey to the coastal town of Monterey, stopping at the ranchos of Don Francisco Sánchez in what is now San Mateo, and Don Antonio

Suñol, in San José. The rancheros greeted them with the characteristic welcome—"the cordial hospitality which in those days assured a good bed and a savory supper to every traveler, and if his horse happened to be tired or hurt by any accident a good one to replace it for the journey." Three days later they reached Monterey, the strategic center of California where General José Castro presided over the serenely beautiful community from his customhouse headquarters. The Mexican flag waved from atop the fort overlooking the town, and the architecture and atmosphere were entirely Spanish, bringing to Frémont's mind what he imagined of the towns of Italy and elsewhere in the Mediterranean. Three curving streets, paved with sea sand, wound through the village, dotted with solid adobe homes, their flower gardens enclosed behind courtyard walls.

The first visit Frémont made was to Larkin, the consul who was "well on his way to being the first California millionaire," and who was married to the first American bride in California, a delicate blonde, Rachel Holmes. One of the earliest American settlers in Monterey, Larkin never rejected his Protestant faith or became a naturalized Mexican citizen. Still, he was much liked and honored by his Mexican neighbors. Though Larkin had not yet received the Gillespie dispatch appointing him "confidential agent" of the U.S. government, the forty-four-year-old Massachusetts native was keenly aware of the percolating political intrigues. He advanced Frémont $1,800 on behalf of the U.S. government to purchase supplies. The expedition force was immediately conspicuous in Monterey, prompting a letter to Larkin from a Mexican official demanding information about the American troops lodged at Larkin's residence. Larkin responded that Frémont was leading a scientific expedition to Oregon, and had stopped in Monterey to purchase animals and provisions.

For two days, Larkin accompanied Frémont on several visits to officials, including a personal call on Castro. Deferential and courteous, Frémont did his best to allay Castro's fears. "I informed the general and the other officers that I was engaged in surveying the nearest route from the United States to the Pacific Ocean. I informed them farther that the object of the survey was geographical, being under the direction of the Bureau of Topographical Engineers, to which corps I belonged; and that it was made in the interests of science and of commerce, and that the men composing the party were citizens and not soldiers." In truth, except for himself and two others, the entire expedition had been selected for its marksmanship and frontier capabilities.

Though suspicious, the Mexican officials granted Frémont permission to obtain supplies and travel unharassed throughout the territory. Frémont led his men sixty miles north to a vacated ranch near the Santa Clara Valley, between San Francisco (Yerba Buena) and Monterey, where they planned to rest and await the rest of their party.

By early February, Frémont had learned the whereabouts of his missing men, who had become lost in the Tulare Mountains before eventually finding their way to Sutter's Fort. He sent Kit Carson to find them, and by midmonth the entire expedition was reunited. On February 22 Frémont led his "troops"—not in the direction of Oregon but in a steady march southwest, in direct violation of his pledge to the Mexicans. On February 27 they pitched camp twenty miles from Monterey.

The group's enlarged number and their movements south alarmed Mexican officials. A week later, a "rude and abrupt" cavalryman, Lieutenant José Antonio Chavez, brought a letter from Castro ordering the men to leave California immediately. Refusing to dignify the letter with a written reply, Frémont responded verbally to Chavez, telling him to convey to his superiors that he would not obey an order that was insulting to both him and his country.

He then moved his group eight miles north, to the crest of Gavilán Peak—a tactically defensive position that provided plenty of water and grass for the livestock and, most important, a commanding view for miles around. They quickly constructed a log fort in the heavily timbered area. "While this was being built a tall sapling was prepared, and on it, when all was ready, the American flag was raised amidst the cheers of the men."

Any goodwill with the Mexican officials was now eroded—as was the cover story of a scientific expedition—and on March 8, General Castro began recruiting volunteers for an attack on Frémont. "In the name of our native country I invite you to place yourselves under my immediate orders at headquarters, where we will prepare to lance the ulcer which (should it not be done) would destroy our liberties & independence for which you ought always to sacrifice yourselves," read Castro's proclamation. Unknown to both sides, that very day General Zachary Taylor's first troops crossed the Nueces River into disputed territory, marking the unofficial beginning of the Mexican War.

For three days, Frémont and his men watched through their eyepieces as Castro gathered his troops and three large cannons. Frémont had cultivated many informants among the vaqueros and Californios who sneaked information to him, and received further details from Larkin's messengers and other couriers that Castro had collected some three hundred men, including Indians—"(*Mansos*) . . . kept excited by drink."

Larkin worked frantically as a mediator, urging Frémont to retreat. With drama and bravado, Frémont scrawled a note to Larkin. "I am making myself as strong as possible in the intention that if we are unjustly attacked we will fight to extremity . . . trusting to our country to avenge our death . . . We have in no wise done wrong to the people or the authorities of the country, and if we are hemmed in and assaulted, we will die every man of us, under the Flag of our country."

The American settlers were nervous, the Californios agitated, and Larkin desperate to prevent a clash that would spark war before the U.S. government was fully prepared. Still, Larkin was unaware of Frémont's orders from Washington, and could not help wondering if indeed the explorer was fulfilling a secret mission. "It is not for me to point out to you your line of conduct. You have your Government Instructions," Larkin wrote him in a dispatch that warned Frémont to be watchful of spies and traitors. "I therefore only wish you to suppose yourself in a situation where you must take every measure to prevent a supprise [sic], from those you may consider partially friends."

Just as an attack seemed about to begin, Frémont's flag fell down, which he took as a sign. "Thinking I had remained as long as the occasion required, I took advantage of the accident to say to the men that this was an indication for us to move camp, and accordingly I gave the order to prepare to move . . . I kept always in mind the object of the Government to obtain possession of California and would not let a proceeding which was mostly personal put obstacles in the way."

Though humiliating and humbling, as Frémont later described the incident to his father-in-law, Benton, he did not make a hasty retreat but rather a leisurely and deliberate removal. On the night of March 9, they set off slowly and defiantly, dropping down into the San Joaquin Valley toward Sutter's Fort. While Castro boasted about his victory, Frémont's men left with dignity, their heads held high from the standoff against a force five times their size. "Of course I did not dare to compromise the United States," Frémont wrote in a letter to Jessie, "against which appearances would have been strong; but, although it was in my power to increase my party by many Americans, I refrained from committing a solitary act of hostility or impropriety."

Frémont received a message from a prominent American settler in the

Napa Valley offering to raise a company of frontiersmen at a moment's notice, and the captain of an American merchant ship anchored in Monterey Bay sent word that he would establish a stronghold on the coast if Frémont desired his assistance. He declined both offers. "Captain Frémont received verbal applications from English and Americans to join his party," Larkin reported to Secretary of State Buchanan, "and could have mustered as many men as the natives." The very day that Frémont abandoned his makeshift fort, Larkin sent an open letter to "the commander of any American Ship of War" asking that a sloop be sent immediately to Monterey.

Even Castro was apparently impressed by Frémont's courage in the face of seemingly disastrous consequences. "He has conducted himself as a worthy gentleman and an honorable officer," Castro confided to his officers. Both men had managed to save face in the bloodless affair. But the episode presaged the coming conflict, when these two proud commanders would once again collide.

Excited and jubilant settlers had greeted Frémont at Sutter's Fort after the Gavilán Peak incident, where he remained a short time before heading up the Sacramento Valley toward Oregon. By the end of March 1846, he was camped two hundred miles north, at Lassen's Ranch, "but marching and counter-marching every day instead of proceeding on his way—as though he were waiting for something," one historian depicted his movements. He broke camp on the day of the first skirmish between General Taylor's troops and Mexican soldiers on the Rio Grande that signaled the official beginning of war. But Frémont could not have known of the events playing out. He journeyed to the foothills of the Cascade Mountains in Oregon, where he intended to wait for "the message he felt sure must come."

On the evening of May 8, while standing in front of his campfire, Frémont heard "the faint sound of horses' feet." He greeted two men, exhausted from galloping a hundred miles in two days, who said they were advance couriers of Marine lieutenant Archibald Gillespie. Gillespie had just arrived in California, they told him, and carried a confidential message for him from Washington. Gillespie had come up the Sacramento River in a small boat, inquired about Frémont at Sutter's Fort, and then proceeded on horseback to the upper Sacramento Valley. There, at the Neal Ranch, Gillespie was told the country was riddled with hostile Klamath Indians. Neal and a ranch hand agreed to overtake Frémont's party and bring him back to meet Gillespie, who would make his way slowly toward Frémont, and who was in danger of being cut off by the Indians.

They had followed Frémont's trail, and were now prepared to lead him to where Gillespie was camped. Frémont decided they should all get a full night's rest and leave the next morning with the men and animals refreshed. He chose Carson and ten of his best men, and set out at dawn. They rode sixty miles at full speed over steep and rugged terrain, sometimes nearly impassable, to a campground at the southern end of Klamath Lake. "A quick eye and a good horse mean life to a man in an Indian country," Frémont wrote. "Neal had both. He was a lover of horses and knew a good one; and those he had with him were the best on his rancho." There, they found the ground beaten down and feared momentarily the Gillespie party had been attacked by Indians. But before sundown, Gillespie and his escort approached. Frémont and his men could barely contain their exhilaration, as it had been eleven months "since any tidings had reached me."

"The meeting, with its physical background of wild forest and water in the virgin Northwest, its political background of territorial ambition and war, was one of the most dramatic in the history of the Pacific Coast," wrote Nevins.

What Gillespie told Frémont that night, what the letters he carried said, what verbal instructions from Secretary of the Navy Bancroft were conveyed, have all been left to historical speculation. The letters from Jessie and her father have never surfaced, and Frémont's account of what Gillespie told him and showed him—written thirty years later—was deemed accurate and credible by his supporters, obfuscating and self-justifying by his critics. Perhaps most revealing of the official surviving documents is the handwritten letter from Buchanan, articulating the president's intention, dated October 17, 1845, and directed to Thomas Larkin. "The interests of our commerce and our whale fisheries on the Pacific Ocean demand that you should exert the greatest vigilance in discovering and defeating any attempt which may be made by foreign governments to acquire a control over that country," it read. "In the contest between Mexico and California (which was at times acute) we can take no part, unless the former should commence hostilities against the United States; but should California assert and maintain her independence, we shall render her all the kind offices in our power, as a sister republic. This government has no ambitious aspirations to gratify and no desire to extend our Federal system over more territory than we already possess, unless by the free and spontaneous wish of the independent people of adjoining territories."

If the actual letter was less than specific—not least in the event that it fell into the hands of Mexican authorities—its encrypted intent was unmistakable to those representatives of the U.S. government operating thousands of miles from Washington. Singularly informed as Frémont was from his preparatory meetings with Benton, Polk, Buchanan, and Bancroft before undertaking his expedition, he found the subtext to be obvious. A "spontaneous" revolt was to be fomented without the appearance of U.S. government participation or sanction.

Gillespie, who had traveled to California through Vera Cruz and Mexico City, and then on the U.S. warship *Cyane*, knew that war had broken out between the United States and Mexico. While he might not have known about the battle on the Rio Grande, he would have had knowledge that the president's negotiations to purchase California had failed—all of which he conveyed to Frémont. "Now it was officially made known to me that my country was at war, and it was so made known expressly to guide my conduct."

In any case, Frémont read between the lines and inferred his orders. The president and the secretary of state would not have sent Gillespie on a six-month journey, in disguise, at large expense and with great haste, by warship and horseback, through enemy territory, to convey a vague political notion, he reasoned. "Through him I now became acquainted with the actual state of affairs and the purposes of the Government," Frémont wrote in his memoirs. "The information through Gillespie had absolved me from my duty as an explorer, and I was left to my duty as an officer of the American Army with the further authoritative knowledge that the Government intended to take California. I was warned by my Government of the new danger against which I was bound to defend myself; and it had been made known to me now on the authority of the Secretary of the Navy that to obtain possession of California was the chief object of the President."

John C. Frémont, then, was fated to become among the earliest of American undercover operatives to be directed to act by a calculating president who had meticulously protected himself with "plausible deniability"—a machination institutionalized a century later in American presidential politics. Layered as they were through a bureaucracy and a murky chain of command, Frémont's orders would forever be subject to partisan interpretation.

He was the only U.S. Army officer present in California—and would remain so for the next nine months. While his citizen army of sixty men could form a strong "nucleus for frontier warfare," he would have to muster a larger force for the invasion at hand.

"I saw the way opening clear before me," he recalled his thoughts on that momentous evening. "I resolved to move forward on the opportunity and return forthwith to the Sacramento valley in order to bring to bear all the influences I could command."

That night, in a portent for Frémont's changing fortune, they were awakened by the sound of an "axe being driven into the head" of Basil Lajeunesse. The bloody attack by the Klamath Indians left Lajeunesse, a Delaware named Crane, and a Métis Indian named Denny dead, and prompted Frémont's party to take gruesome revenge. "With our knives we dug a shallow grave, and wrapping their blankets round them, left them among the laurels. There are men above whom the laurels bloom who did not better deserve them than my brave Delaware and Basil. I left Denny's name on the creek where he died." Frémont and his men then circled the lake, killing all Klamath Indians they encountered. The retaliatory massacre left Frémont uncharacteristically smug with the satisfaction of spilling blood. "I had now kept the promise I made to myself and had punished these people well for their treachery; and now I turned my thoughts to the work which they had delayed."

Thirty-three years old, Gillespie was excitable and inexperienced. "By Heaven, this is rough work," he exclaimed emotionally to Frémont. "I'll take care to let them know in Washington about it."

"Heaven don't come in for much about here just now," Frémont replied, "and as for Washington, it will be long enough before we see it again; time enough to forget about this."

Jessie was desperate for news of John's well-being, after learning of the volatile Gavilán Peak affair from Larkin's dispatches to Washington. On June 11, the *Union* newspaper published letters from Larkin to President Polk concerning the confrontation, quoting Frémont's melodramatic remark "if we are hemmed in and assaulted, we will die." Praising Frémont's "courage and discretion," the newspaper's editorial brought further fame to the explorer, as well as prompting President Polk, always eager to please and appease Benton, to promote the explorer to lieutenant colonel.

That week, as Benton and Polk conferred regularly, Benton encouraged the president to name Colonel Stephen Watts Kearny commander of a brigade that would march to Santa Fe, while simultaneously sending Santa Fe trader James Magoffin on an advance mission to negotiate with the New Mexico governor. "Benton was clearly a major architect of Polk's highly successful and relatively bloodless military policies in both New Mexico and California" according to historian Elbert B. Smith. Benton maneuvered in Congress to obtain $30,000 for Magoffin's "secret services"—money to be used for bribing Mexican officials. On June 17, Jessie and her father gathered the reports and documents for Magoffin to carry to Bent's Fort, where Frémont could retrieve them while en route back to Washington. When the business tasks were completed, she sequestered herself in her room to write a personal letter:

My dearest husband . . . I had received the Mexican account of your being besieged by General Castro, and I was much relieved by what Mr. Larkin says: that you could present yourself at Monterey, alone if you wished, and not be harmed. But I hope that as I write you are rapidly nearing home and that early in September there will be an end to our anxieties. In your dear letter you tell me that *le bon temps viendra*, and my faith in you is such that I believe it will come! And it will come to all you love, for during your long absence, God has been good to us and kept in health your mother and all you love best.

. . . You must let me make you my heartiest congratulations. I am sorry that I could not be the first to call you Colonel. It will please you the more as it was entirely a free-will offering of the President's.

So your merit has advanced you in eight years from an unknown second lieutenant, to the most talked of and admired lieutenant-colonel in the army. Almost all of the old officers called to congratulate me upon it, the Aberts among them, and I have heard of no envy except from some of the lower order of Whig papers who only see you as Colonel Benton's son-in-law.

. . . I remembered so well what you once wrote to me . . . Do you remember, darling? It was soon after we were married, and you wrote me: "Fear not for our happiness. If the hope for it is not something wilder than the Spaniard's search for the fountain in Florida, we will find it yet" . . . Dear, Dear husband, you do know how proud and grateful I am that you love me. We have found the fountain of perpetual youth for love, and I believe there are few others who can say so. I try very hard to be worthy of your love.

. . . Editors have written to me for your biography and likeness, but I have no orders from you and then you know it would look odd to leave out your age, and you never told me how old you were yet. How old are you? You might tell me now I am a colonel's wife—won't you, old papa? Poor papa, it made tears come to find you had begun to turn gray. You must have suffered much and been very anxious . . .

Mr. Magoffin has come for the letter and I must stop. I have not had so much pleasure in a very great while as today. The thought that you may hear from me and know that all are well and that I can tell you again how dearly I love you makes me as happy as I can be while you are away . . . Farewell, dear, dear husband. In a few months we shall not know what sorrow means.

Jessie was disappointed to learn that Secretary of State Buchanan did not view Frémont's actions in California in as heroic a light as she and others did. That Buchanan thought her husband had acted in an impulsive, rash, and thoughtless manner—outside his official purview and embarrassing to the State Department—was attributable, she believed, to Buchanan's opposition to war with Mexico. Even her father, like herself, long opposed to war, had finally been persuaded that it was inevitable, if not justified. "While Benton opposed forcible acquisition of California," as historian Frederick S. Dellenbaugh described the senator's persuasions, "he did not intend to let it slip when opportunity came." Buchanan preferred diplomacy to combat, and had just negotiated the treaty with Great Britain partitioning the Northwest—owing his success to Benton's famous and rousing May 1846 speech urging Congress to abandon the battle for the fifty-fourth parallel, settling finally on the forty-ninth. The Oregon question, to which Jessie's father had devoted much of his political career, was finally resolved, and on June 15, present-day Oregon, Washington, and Idaho were added to the United States.

Throughout the humid Washington, D.C., summer, Jessie continued her translating for Buchanan and Bancroft, assisted her father in drafting legislation, and avidly sought news of John's movements in California. Finally, in early September, official word arrived in Washington: the American flag had been raised at Monterey on July 7, claiming California for the United States.

The first report that something had gone terribly amiss with the California conquest came to Jessie nearly a year later, in March 1847. "This will in all likelihood result in the removal of Colonel Frémont's as *Coman-dante*," she read in a dispatch from Monterey detailing a clash between navy commodore Robert Stockton and army general Stephen Watts Kearny.

A page from the State Department had brought her a packet of letters and papers, and she sat down at her desk to start decoding them. She read the distressing news in what seemed a benign document relating to land grants. Astonished, assuming it was a mistake, she methodically wrote out two copies of the letter and waited for her father to return from the Capitol. When he arrived, at four P.M., she rushed to show him the letter, certain he would be as baffled and outraged as she. But one look at his flushed face and she instantly knew not only that it was true, but also that Benton had been keeping it from her. Seating himself next to her, he admitted that he had known of the dispute between Kearny and Stockton over who should have the chief command in California, and that he had indeed been aware of it for several weeks. He had hoped, he told her, that the squabble between the army and the navy would be resolved and that she need not be bothered with it.

Though an army topographer, Frémont felt his orders to operate in a military rather than a scientific capacity had come from the secretary of the navy, the secretary of state, and the president—not from the army—and therefore believed his chain of command in California clearly rested with Stockton. The arrival in California of Kearny—now an army brigadier general and still heated over the howitzer requisition—signaled a power struggle between Kearny and Stockton, with the thirty-three-year-old Frémont in the middle. "I was but a pawn, and like a pawn, I had been pushed forward to the front at the opening of the game," Frémont later described his predicament. "Frémont was never to drink the cup of triumph or prosperity long," wrote Nevins, "and his life was to prove a dizzy alternation of successes and humiliations."

Until that fateful spring day in Washington, Jessie felt she had been uniquely informed about the unfolding events in California. She reviewed the dispatches to the State Department; clipped American news articles; read Mexican newspapers; received letters from John; communicated with family members of John's expedition force; and was privy to information her father, as chairman of the Senate Military Affairs Committee, gleaned from various parties. She had had every reason to believe that the conquest had been a grand success, and that her husband was widely honored as a hero by the American military commanders in California.

Jessie knew the essentials of the revolt. In May 1846, Frémont had swiftly moved from Klamath Lake to the Marysville Buttes, an isolated series of bluffs along the Bear and Feather rivers and sixty miles north of Sutter's Fort. There he met a group of settlers—"rough, leather-jacketed frontiersmen"—ready to join his militia and clamoring to lead a raid on Castro and the Californios. As they moved south, the band was joined by more dissident American settlers. The number of Americans in California had swelled to more than eight hundred in the previous two years, nearly all of them solid, resourceful men—ranchers, trappers, hunters, merchants, and farmers, though inevitably interspersed with rugged backwoodsmen and crude sailors and voyageurs.

On June 10, with Frémont's behind-the-scenes instigation, a group of the settlers captured two hundred horses being driven from the Santa Clara Valley to Castro and brought them to Frémont. Four days later, a group of thirty rebels seized Sonoma, the largest settlement in northern California, and took four prominent citizens prisoner. On June 15, amid brandy drinking and wild celebration, they hoisted a primitive flag—a strip of linen with a California grizzly bear painted by Mary Todd Lincoln's nephew—and declared themselves commanders of the Bear Flag Republic. Emboldened by that victory, several hundred more men joined the rebellion.

At this point, Frémont put Edward Kern in charge of supplies kept at Sutter's Fort. Characteristically, Sutter had been courting all sides, assuring the Americans he supported them while keeping Castro abreast of Frémont's activities. Frémont ultimately threatened to eject Sutter, a Mexican citizen, from his fort if he did not stop his double dealing.

The Bears captured more than a hundred saddle horses from Castro's army, and soon Frémont learned that Castro and several hundred mounted Mexicans were on the march up the Sacramento River, intending to burn American settlers' homes and crops. Still, Frémont and his men sat on the sidelines, not fully supporting the Bears but not dissuading them either—following Buchanan's orders, he believed, to tacitly and discreetly support a "spontaneous" revolt by the California settlers. "Frémont was willing to help all he could, provided it could be done under the pretext of defending American residents here in California against pretended threats of expulsion by the Mexican authorities," as one of his soldiers put it. "Frémont was playing a waiting game," wrote Nevins, ". . . what else could he do? He knew that the settlers were almost ready to act, he gave them encouragement, and he bided his time."

Later critics would charge him with being overly aggressive, while the settlers at the time, fearing an attack on their homes and families, accused him of hesitancy.

By late June, holding Sutter's Fort and Sonoma, the rebels effectively controlled northern California, though they feared they were on the verge of being overtaken by Castro's forces. Once Captain John B. Montgomery entered the port at San Francisco on the American warship *Portsmouth*, Frémont openly joined the rebellion. On June 23, Frémont and a hundred men rushed to Sonoma after hearing reports that Castro was on his way to retake the garrison. Finding no Mexican soldiers in the area, they marched to San Francisco and back, meeting no Mexican troops along the way. "We tried to find an enemy but could not," wrote one of his soldiers. They celebrated the Fourth of July in Sonoma, complete with a public reading of the Declaration of Independence, and Frémont took official control of the rebels. Three days later, under orders from Washington to occupy San Francisco and all other California ports, Commodore Sloat and the Pacific Squadron, consisting of three frigates, two transport ships, and three sloops, each with forty-four guns, were poised off the California coast. On July 7, a total of 250 sailors rushed into Monterey and raised the American flag in the central plaza. Sloat immediately sent orders to Montgomery to seize San Francisco, and dispatched a courier to Frémont to inform him of the American occupation. "Frémont had so played his hand," wrote Allan Nevins, "that when the vacillating Sloat came upon the scene, all California beyond San Francisco Bay was in American hands and a large and well-equipped land force was ready to cooperate with the navy."

The elderly Sloat, wishing to relinquish his command but awaiting official retirement orders from Washington, gave Robert Stockton, his heir apparent newly arrived on the USS *Congress*, command over Frémont's forces. Stockton formed the Naval Battalion of Mounted Volunteer Riflemen, putting Frémont in charge and designating him a lieutenant colonel under the control of the U.S. Navy. Frémont then recruited 428 men around Sonoma and Sutter's Fort, and 50 Walla Walla Indians from Oregon Territory, paying them the liberal salary of $25 per month. He planned to take his troops south to Los Angeles—"gathering recruits and seizing towns along the way." But on July 26, Commodore Stockton ordered him and 150 men to board the *Cyane* for San Diego, where, three days later, Stockton and Frémont raised the flag. They then marched north to Ciudad de Los Angeles, the City of the Angels, and took control there on August 13. Convinced the conquest was complete, Stockton sailed north, while Frémont took his troops overland, to Monterey. They left marine officer Archibald Gillespie in charge of Los Angeles. But insurgents plagued Gillespie, prompting Stockton to order Frémont and his battalion to return to Los Angeles. On January 13, 1847, after a few brief skirmishes, Frémont received the surrender of the remaining Mexican forces at Cahuenga Pass outside Los Angeles, the two sides signing a charitable peace treaty with Don Andres Pico, commander in chief of the Californios.

The generous treaty, drafted by Frémont, guaranteed protection of the Californios—their lives and property—and gave them permission to return to Mexico if they desired, or remain in California and receive the same rights and privileges as American citizens. Once they turned over their arms, they were free to return to their homes, and they would not be required to take an oath of allegiance to the United States until the two countries signed a final treaty. "His conciliatory course drew them rapidly to him," wrote John Bigelow in his 1856 campaign biography of Frémont. "The Picos who were the leading men of the revolt (Don Pio, Don Andres, and Don Jesus) became his friends. California became independent of Mexico by the revolt of the Picos, and independent of them by the revolt of the American settlers." In one of the more peaceable conquests in history, the conquered joined the conquerors. Frémont's success was unparalleled, and he won the undying devotion of the Mexican-speaking Californians, Andres Pico christening him "The Young Eagle of the West."

Amid cheers and fireworks, Frémont rode proudly at the head of his troops into Los Angeles—"like a Greek hero just in from the plains of Troy." On January 16, Commodore Stockton named him civilian governor of California. "The territory of California is again tranquil," Stockton wrote Secretary of the Navy Bancroft, "and the civil government formed by me, is again in operation in the places where it was interrupted by the insurgents. Colonel Frémont has five hundred men in his battalion, which will be quite sufficient to preserve the peace of the territory."

That was the state of affairs as known to Jessie—her husband was a hero who had been rewarded for his valiant service—so the March 1847 dispatch regarding his removal came as a devastating shock.

"But what is the President doing about this?" Jessie asked her father, barely able to contain her emotions. "Have you talked to him? Is Colonel

Frémont to be made the victim in a quarrel between the Army and the Navy?" Benton assured her that he had spoken to Polk, and that the president, like himself, hoped "the disputants will themselves settle the matter."

Temporarily mollified, Jessie was optimistic that the situation would indeed resolve itself—these were reasonable men, after all. Kearny, whom Jessie had known all of her life, owed much of his career to Benton. Indeed, Benton was responsible for Kearny's promotion to brigadier general and for persuading Polk to send him west as head of a twelve-hundred-man army. Certainly, Kearny would do nothing to jeopardize the friendship the two families had shared for three decades. She took comfort in that, and in the knowledge that John, who had been gone nearly two years, would be returning to her soon or she would join him in California. But several weeks later she received a letter from a cousin in Kentucky requesting elaboration on a newspaper article about Frémont's disgrace in California, followed by a similar inquiry from a St. Louis relative who had read an account of Frémont's dishonorable conduct and willful insubordination during the conquest of California. If the clash was still the subject of press accounts, she reasoned, its resolution was far from over.

Her fears were confirmed in June, when Kit Carson appeared one afternoon at the C Street residence. Delighted to see her husband's loyal comrade, impatient for an account of events in California, she ushered him quickly into the drawing room. Pouring each of them a brandy, she settled in, eager to hear the news, however alarming, knowing that if she were fully informed she could take the appropriate action to rectify the situation. Carson lit a pipe and began.

The conflict apparently erupted when Frémont effected the dramatic surrender of Mexican troops, rather than deferring the honor to General Kearny, who had recently arrived in California. The previous fall, Kearny and his Army of the West had begun its march from Santa Fe—which it had captured without firing a shot, thanks to Magoffin's efforts with the New Mexico governor—to California. He had been ambushed at San Pasqual, near San Diego, where his dragoons were crushed at the hands of well-armed and skilled Californios. Kearny was lanced twice in one arm, lost a great deal of blood from a deep wound in the buttocks, and suffered casualties of a third of his command before Stockton's relief forces rescued him. When Kearny arrived in San Diego in December 1846, he was in no mood to suffer the antics of an irregular junior army officer who had caused him embarrassment in the past. While Kearny and Stockton were coordinating their joint efforts for the conquest of Los Angeles, Frémont preempted them both—obtaining not only a full surrender from the Californios but also reclaiming two howitzers the insurgents had confiscated from Kearny during his ignominious defeat at San Pasqual.

As soon as the treaty was signed, Frémont had two copies drawn up, and dispatched a courier on one of Frémont's fastest horses to report the news to Kearny and Stockton. The courier, expecting to find two ecstatic officers, was greeted instead by two extremely angry men. Kearny refused to accept the treaty and claimed that Stockton, not he, was commander of all American forces in California. Stockton accepted the treaty but was angered by its lenient terms. There followed a series of exchanges almost laughable in their pettiness, the egos of two military giants irreparably bruised by an upstart explorer. Still, Stockton thought it prudent, given Frémont's overwhelming public support from both Americans and Californios, to appoint him "Governor and Commander-in-Chief of California until the President should otherwise direct." Kearny then suddenly proclaimed himself commander of all forces and demanded that Stockton and Frémont relinquish their positions. Both men refused to accept Kearny's authority.

Frémont wrote a letter to Kearny, copied and delivered by Carson, stating that he had received his commission from Stockton, who had been commander in chief in California. Therefore, Frémont would continue to take orders from the commodore until the two men resolved their dispute over rank. "I found Commodore Stockton in possession of the country, exercising the functions of military commandant and civil governor, as early as July of last year; and shortly thereafter I received from him the commission of military commandant, the duties of which I immediately entered upon, and have continued to exercise to the present moment. . . . I feel, therefore, with great deference to your professional and personal character, constrained to say that, until you and Commodore Stockton adjust between yourselves, the question of rank . . . I shall have to report and receive orders, as heretofore, from the commodore." Kearny ordered Frémont to withdraw the letter—gratuitously citing his deep affection for Senator Benton and Jessie—and when Frémont refused, Kearny vowed to ruin him. The two were sworn enemies from that point forward.

Kearny moved his forces to Monterey and installed himself as commander in chief of the province. For the next three months, south-ern Californians recognized Frémont as governor, while northern Cali-fornians recognized Kearny. In the south, hoping to mitigate opposition, Frémont took to wearing a sombrero and invited several prominent Cali-fornios into his administration—a move that further antagonized Kearny. Stockton was soon succeeded by Commodore William Shubrick, who sided with Kearny, and Frémont's fate was precarious. He had dispatched Carson to Washington to recount Frémont's version of events to Benton and Jessie, knowing that they would be able to enlist the president's inter-vention in the explosive imbroglio.

Carson then gave her a letter from Frémont directed to her father, who was in Missouri at the time, and which contained a cover letter asking that the information be immediately transmitted to the president. Fré-mont wrote to Benton,

> When I entered Los Angeles, I was ignorant of the relations exist-ing between these gentlemen, having received from neither any or-der which might serve as a guide. I therefore waited upon the Commander-in-Chief, Commodore Stockton, and after called upon General Kearny. I soon found them occupying a hostile attitude, each denying the right of the other to assume direction of this country . . .
>
> The country has been conquered since September last, and General Kearny had been instructed to "conquer the country." Upon its threshold his command had been nearly cut to pieces and but for the relief of Commodore Stockton would have been destroyed . . . As to his instructions, how could he organize a government without proceeding to disorganize the present one? . . .
>
> You are aware that I had contracted relations with Commodore Stockton, and I thought it neither right nor politically honorable to withdraw my support. No reason of interest shall ever compel me to act toward any man in such a way that I should afterward be ashamed to meet him.

Jessie thanked Carson for his fulsome report and asked if he would be willing to accompany her to see the president the following day. Carson replied that he was happy to "meet Mr. Polk under her protection." She invited Carson to dine with her and her mother, and had a servant pre-pare a guest room for the famous scout.

The next morning, Carson watched Jessie with awe as she moved evenly and efficiently through the routine of eating breakfast, playing with Lily, and attending to her mother. Following her father's dictum of maintaining calm during crisis, she braced herself for the meeting with Polk, who regularly opened his office to visitors at one o'clock. Dressed in a green cashmere gown, her long brown hair swept neatly under a green corded hat, she emerged from her room at noon. "Mr. Carson and Mrs. Frémont will now have a glass of sherry before going into battle," she announced to an astonished Carson, who had always admired her pluck.

President Polk greeted her warmly and expressed genuine interest in the short, blue-eyed frontiersman dressed in black broadcloth and about whom he had heard so much. Carson handed Frémont's letter to the president, and offered to carry dispatches back to California. When Polk finished reading the letter, Jessie said forcefully: "Doesn't Colonel Frémont's course seem reasonable in this case?" Polk avoided her eyes and was silent, and she knew instantly that they did not have his support. "The misunderstandings may by now be settled, and recriminations ended." With that, the president dismissed them.

"Mrs. Frémont seemed anxious to elicit from me some expression of approbation of her husband's conduct," Polk noted in his diary, "but I evaded. In truth I consider that Col. Frémont was greatly in the wrong when he refused to obey the orders issued to him by Gen'l. Kearny. I think Gen'l. Kearny was right also in his controversy with Com. Stockton. It was unnecessary, however, that I should say so to Col. Frémont's wife."

Jessie was appalled at his equivocation. "So President Polk got his republic, but something had gone wrong with it," wrote historian James A. B. Scherer. "It was not set up by the native sons, as Buchanan had suggested, but by American settlers . . . which, many observers thought, had been instigated by foreign plotters. But the President had his 'alibi' handy."

Americans, Europeans, and Mexicans roundly decried the Polk administration's imperialism, and the president needed a scapegoat. "To antislavery Whigs and Radical Democrats, Polk's spread-eagle nationalism looked increasingly like an apology for the South," wrote historian Wilentz, "and for those proslavery southern Democrats who saw the war as a means to extend the slaveholders' democracy." The United States was not involved in empire-building, Polk would maintain, but merely in establishing peace and order in a conflict instigated by, conveniently for Polk, a rogue explorer. "The Mexican War had progressed to a phase of serious reality," as Jessie later put it. "At first it had been all excitement of going into a foreign and romantic land and to the pleasure of fighting for fight's sake, which seems to address itself naturally to young men . . . But the gayety of the advance was changed for the realities all war brings and the home friends who had cheered forth the outgoing regiments now gathered hushed and sad to receive back their dead heroes."

A second meeting with Polk, a week later, was slightly more satisfying. Jessie implored the president to keep Frémont on duty in California. In response, Polk gave Carson orders for Frémont, giving him the option of remaining on duty in California or joining his regiment of the Mounted Rifles in Mexico—in any case, making clear that he was in the army, not the navy.

The night before Carson's departure, Jessie penned a letter to John:

My dear husband: Kit Carson is waiting to take a letter to you. Nothing I can say will express in the littlest degree the love and yearning in my heart—the grief that I cannot be with you. It hurts too much even to write. Besides, I would not make you unhappy by my repining. Kit will tell you everything. I am sending you myself— in miniature. I lay with it over my heart last night. I pray you wear it over yours until *le bon temps viendra*. Your devoted wife, Jessie.

She placed the miniature painting in the packet, sealed it, and wished Carson Godspeed.

Benton returned to Washington shortly after Carson's departure, and during a long walk with Jessie along the Potomac finally revealed all he knew. Benton was particularly outraged that Kearny had never furnished Frémont a copy of the orders—written in November 1846 and received by Kearny in February 1847—making Kearny governor and commander in chief, thus allowing the staid army veteran to lure Frémont into a trap of insubordination. A more honorable and gentlemanly officer would have informed Frémont of the new orders immediately rather than use the information to "plunge him deeper in seeming disobedience."

Benton had pieced together the details through various sources, but by the summer of 1847 Frémont's "mutiny" was the subject of much public and private attention. Benton was convinced that the press reports were generated by a carefully orchestrated defamation campaign, led by a coalition of Kearny's army friends and jealous West Pointers bent on maligning Frémont.

How such a dispute could arise between the navy and army commanders was an embarrassment to all sides—"a comic-opera quarrel," as Nevins put it—and could not have occurred "but for the vagueness and confusion of the orders sent to Stockton and Kearny from Washington." Further complicating matters were the distance and time required for official dispatches to arrive in California, all orders conveyed by messengers on horseback or boat in an era before the telegraph. "It was the misfortune of Frémont to be caught in the collision between these two officers; it was his further misfortune to choose the side which subsequent orders from Washington failed to sustain."

Kearny, a hot-tempered martinet—"the strictest sort of a disciplinarian," as William Tecumseh Sherman called him—had summoned Frémont to the territorial capital of Monterey in early March, ordering him to bring all archives and government documents from Los Angeles. Frémont, leaving the documents behind and accompanied by his faithful friend Don Jesús Pico and Dodson, his black servant, set out on a wild 420-mile journey north, each taking three horses so there was a ready supply of fresh mounts.

Frémont arrived in Monterey four days later and met with Kearny, who insisted that Colonel Richard Barnes Mason witness the confrontation. When Kearny learned that Frémont had refused to bring the requested documents, a heated argument ensued. Kearny's plan to entrap Frémont into willful defiance of authority was now complete. Frémont had no way of knowing that Kearny was operating under instructions from President Polk, that it had already been determined that Frémont be arrested and tried for mutiny, and that Kearny and Mason were merely seeking evidence for additional charges against him.

While in Monterey, Frémont learned from Thomas Larkin about the November 1846 orders placing Kearny in charge of California, and suddenly realized the seriousness of his situation. He went immediately to Kearny and offered his resignation, which Kearny refused to accept. Kearny instead ordered Frémont to return to Los Angeles, retrieve the archives as originally ordered, and surrender them to Colonel Mason, who would follow him south.

Mason, a grim tyrant, proceeded to make Frémont's life miserable, and a series of arguments inevitably broke out between the two men. Mason began harassing Frémont, regularly grilling him about his activities in California—"sending for him at inconvenient times, when there was no necessity for haste, several times a day, demanding and receiving various papers." Inevitably, Frémont lost his temper with the "man who was endeavoring to find some evidence against him that would justify harsh measures," as Jessie later put it.

The rancor between the two men culminated when, in response to Mason's insulting examination of Frémont about his role in the Bear Flag Revolt, Frémont requested that Mason "confine himself to the business at hand." With that, Mason exploded. "None of your insolence, or I will put you in irons!"

"You cannot make an official matter of a personal one, sir," Frémont responded. "As a man, do you hold yourself personally responsible for what you have just said?"

When Mason replied, "I do," Frémont left the room.

Following frontier protocol, Frémont immediately penned two letters to Mason: the first, a formal demand for retraction and apology for the "injurious language"; and the second, to be delivered in the expectation that the apology would not be forthcoming, was a challenge to a duel.

Though dueling in the military was officially prohibited, it was tacitly tolerated. Frémont was pleased to have "the satisfaction of having the challenge accepted." Their seconds arranged the preliminaries for the "meeting," and Frémont was shocked to learn that Mason's weapon of choice for the duel was a double-barreled shotgun loaded with buckshot. Frémont had never used such a gun, but his second procured one with the proper ammunition. On the appointed morning, April 15, 1847, as Frémont waited for Mason, a messenger rode quickly to the scene with a letter. "With a view to the adjustment of my *private affairs,* it is necessary that I return to Monterey, before I afford you the meeting you desire."

Fortunately, Kearny intervened a few weeks later, presenting orders to both men that the duel was to be stopped. (Frémont later concluded that Mason had intended to provoke a challenge and by selecting a weapon with which he, and not Frémont, was expert, he would easily kill Frémont. Three years later Frémont received a letter from Mason, who was then living in St. Louis, asking Frémont to travel to Missouri for the long-delayed duel. "Naturally Colonel Frémont paid no attention to the man or the note," Jessie wrote.)

★　★　★

In character, Kearny and Frémont could not have been more different. The thirty-four-year-old explorer was shy and modest, reserved to the point of aloofness, self-deprecating, and gentle in spirit. Kearny, fifty-seven, was gruff and menacing, a spit-and-polish army man known as the "Father of the U.S. Cavalry"—"a fighter without any mild or ingratiating qualities," as one historian described him.

General Winfield Scott had ordered Frémont to bring 60 men and 120 horses to Veracruz, Mexico, but Kearny refused to let Frémont join his regiment. Kearny was equally dismissive when Frémont asked that he be allowed to return to St. Louis, at his own expense, with his original exploring party. Secretary of War William L. Marcy ordered Kearny to employ Frémont "in such a manner as will render his services most available to the public interest, having reference to his extensive acquaintance with the inhabitants of California, and his knowledge of their language, qualifications . . . which it is supposed may be very useful in the present and prospective state of our affairs in that country." But Kearny, who had already determined to place the young officer under arrest, had no intention of honoring him in the way Marcy suggested. "It has become known here that he bore a conspicuous part in the conquest of California," Marcy wrote of Frémont, "that his services have been very valuable in that country, and doubtless will continue to be so should he remain there."

Instead, Kearny blazed with animosity and determination against Frémont. On May 29, Kearny sent for Frémont and his men from the Topographical Corps. All would proceed with him to the United States in two days, Kearny's orders read, and Colonel Mason would remain, as governor of California. Kearny further refused to allow Frémont to gather his scientific equipment, botanical and geological specimens, and refused payment to the members of the California battalion for their services in the conquest. As if to make sure Frémont could not redeem himself with yet another best-selling report, Kearny would not allow him to bring the sketches and maps created by Kern, the expedition artist, nor would he allow Kern to join them.

Frémont was able to attend to one final piece of business that would have far-reaching personal consequences. In February 1847 he had given Thomas Larkin $3,000 to purchase an old mission farm in the Sierra foothills behind San Francisco with an ocean view. The shrewd, profiteering Larkin—"through some combination of accident and shady dealing," as one historian described his machinations—bought the land for himself, purchasing for Frémont instead a remote 44,000-acre Mexican grant of mountain land 120 miles east of San Francisco, near Yosemite Valley. Operating through former governor Juan Alvarado, who owned the property, and taking a 7 percent commission for his services, Larkin bought Las Mariposas, or "The Butterflies," as the apparently useless land was known. Furious at Larkin and demanding a refund, Frémont gave power of attorney to Pierson B. Reading and asked him to buy "*Las Pulgas* on the [western shore of San Francisco] bay . . . I wanted Larkin to get it for me but for some reason he did not." Frémont had determined that the bay property would be the future home for his family. The wild tract at Las Mariposas was occupied by roving bands of hostile Indians and virtually uninhabitable by migrants.

The parties set out from Sacramento in early June, Kearny instructing Frémont to keep his men at a distance, far to the rear of Kearny's group. They stopped at Sutter's Fort, where Sutter gave the general a cannon salute and invited him and his men to attend a feast that did not include Frémont.

In yet another humiliating gesture, Kearny hired a tenderfoot guide for the Sierra Nevada crossing rather than draw on Frémont's vast knowledge of the mountains, the Great Basin, and South Pass. "Now commenced the journey across the continent, over which Colonel Frémont had, in three dangerous explorations, won the title of 'Pathfinder' over the paths he had shown to others," wrote Jessie, "he now most of the time, by Kearny's order, followed in the dust of the Mormon escort; camping at night in places designated, and, in a virtual state of imprisonment."

He was marched from California to Washington under the custody and surveillance of his nemesis Kearny, who made him trail behind Kearny's men across the Sierras and Rockies. Degrading Frémont's position and rank in the presence of his men, Kearny acted toward Frémont with contempt and disrespect, treating him, as Frémont claimed, "as a prisoner and a criminal."

Still, Frémont was not unduly worried; he felt certain that once he arrived in Washington, the debasing and belligerent behavior by Kearny would come to an end, that Jessie and her father would help him set things right. He by now also knew that he had neither the temperament nor the inclination to be a career army officer, and began dreaming of a life in California with Jessie, Lily, and his mother.

By late August they had traveled 1,905 miles, to Fort Leavenworth.

When the soldiers at the fort shunned Frémont and his men, they set up their camp outside the walls. Before Frémont had had a chance to rest or bathe, Kearny summoned him to the office of Lieutenant Colonel Clifton Wharton. Once inside, Kearny ordered Frémont to be seated. Frémont then, finally, learned Kearny's true intent. The general stood formally before Frémont and read his orders in the presence of Colonel Wharton:

Lieutenant Colonel Frémont, of the regiment of mounted riflemen, will turn over to the officers of the different departments, at this post, the horses, mules, and other public property in the use of the topographical party now under his charge, for which receipts will be given. He will arrange the accounts of these men (nineteen in number,) so that they can be paid at the earliest possible date.

Lieutenant Colonel Frémont, having performed the above duty, will consider himself under arrest, and will then repair to Washington City, and report himself to the adjutant general of the army.

Stunned, furious, and coldly silent, Frémont rose slowly and saluted both officers. He returned to his camp to report the news to his men, who were all as surprised and disturbed as Frémont. When they brought their animals and arms to the fort, as ordered, they were kept waiting for five hours in the hot sun. Finally free of Kearny's control and indignities, he and his men set out for Kansas Landing, as Kansas City, Missouri, was now called, where the sad little band would catch a steamboat for St. Louis. From there, Frémont planned to go on to Washington to stand trial in a military court. The once-proud explorer, his shoulders now rounded, must return to his beloved family not as a hero but as a disgrace. He had no idea what he would find. Would his father-in-law spurn him? Could Jessie bear the shame? Would Lily, an infant when he left, even know who he was? Could his mother survive the disappointment? Could he endure the humiliation? An outcast by birth, he had reached lofty heights, only to be wrenched back to his innate station in life.

In the end, all that mattered to him was what Jessie thought and felt. A broken man, he would look to her for his cues and be forever surprised and grateful for her strength and resolve. The man who arrived at Kansas Landing was bent and dejected, gray-haired and lined, remote and phlegmatic—a far cry from the dashing, vibrant man who had left two years earlier.

His had been "an unrestrained life in open air, and the faces which I had to look upon were those of nature's own, unchanging and true," he wrote. "Now this was to end. I was to begin anew . . . my path of life led out from among the grand and lovely features of nature, and its pure and wholesome air, into the poisoned atmosphere and jarring circumstances of conflict among men, made subtle and malignant by clashing interests."

"She looks thin & is sad," Lizzie Blair wrote of Jessie during the long, hot summer of 1847. "She seems tired of her courage & is now really pining for her husband." Serene by day, Jessie found herself weeping uncontrollably at night, stifling her sobs with a pillow. She became "convulsed and frantic," Benton described his daughter during this time of waiting, unsure whether John had joined his troops in Mexico or was a prisoner of Kearny's, as many of the nation's newspapers were reporting. "The heart bursting, the brain burning, the body shivering; and I, her father, often called, not to witness, but to calm this terrible agitation." Benton soothed her with hot milk and brandy.

She insisted on accompanying Benton to St. Louis, to be there in case John arrived, and after several weeks of anxiety, and amid fresh reports that John had been arrested, she decided to travel to Kansas Landing to await his return. "I went up the river alone to what is now Kansas City . . . a cluster of frame and log buildings on the bluff." She spent her nights in a log cabin, and every morning found her at the wharf staring out at the water, reminded yet again of the wives of Nantucket. At sundown one day, "the rapid trampling of many horses announced the long waiting was over." She rushed to the gangplank and saw him, dressed not in his uniform but in the revolutionary Spanish riding dress of the Californios—a wide-brimmed sombrero, gaucho pants, and red sash. Far more unusual than his clothing was what she called his "stern set look of endurance and self control . . . a silent repressed storm of feeling which entirely dominated his own light hearted courtesy and thought for others."

To her, he was still the larger-than-life hero, the warrior fresh from battle. That he was gaunt and crestfallen only made her more determined to return to him his dignity, his strength, his valor. Jessie cried out and he turned in her direction, never expecting to see her at Kansas Landing. The *New York Herald* reported the emotional reunion, how Jessie ran into his arms amid the crowd of roustabouts and migrants. Villagers came cheering, waving an American flag above his head and shouting, "Fré-

mont! Frémont!" The newspaper correspondent, witnessing the outpouring, predicted the court-martial would make him "ten times more
popular than ever."

Frémont was speechless. "He had not thought to meet me up there
and could not recover himself instantly from the long indignation of the
return journey and the crowning insult that morning at Fort Leavenworth." Alexis Godey, his longtime associate from the Nicollet expeditions and one of his most faithful men, spoke to Jessie when Frémont
was out of earshot, attending to his horse. "Now we have seen the Colonel safe home," Godey told her. "We would not trust him with Kearny.
We were not under Kearny's orders—the prairies were free and we came
along to watch over the Colonel—he's safe now."

Jessie, John, and the eighteen men—"true companions who had
learned not to trust a General of the Army any more than they would
have trusted a revengeful Apache"—boarded the *Martha* and headed
downriver to St. Louis. Well-wishers lined the banks of the river, cheering him along the way, in stark contrast to the cool reception Kearny
would receive in the same locales. The leading citizens of St. Louis, "after a complimentary address congratulating him on his safe return," invited him to a grand public celebratory dinner. Under the circumstances
he felt it only prudent to decline, though he gave an impromptu speech
to a gathering on the levee in which he defended his "political course in
North California."

Crowds continued to greet them as they traveled on to Kentucky,
where Jessie's parents were staying at their Woodford County farm in the
lush Bluegrass Country. If Frémont had any fears of how Benton would
receive him, they were quickly put to rest. "I have a full view of the
whole case—Kearny's as well as yours," Benton told him, greeting him
warmly, "and am perfectly at ease. You will be justified, and exalted; your
persecutors will be covered with shame & confusion." The support and
love from Jessie and her father were overwhelming to the man who had
never known the resilience of family devotion. "To Benton . . . the
Pathfinder was young Galahad with the pure heart being persecuted by
jealous West Pointers resenting his achievements," as one historian described Benton's intense family loyalty, "and the old man sprang to the
rescue with all the fury of a mother bear defending a cub."

On September 10, 1847, Benton wrote President Polk from Kentucky,
making it clear he thought the arrest of Frémont nothing less than an
outrage. Benton implored the president to endorse a court of inquiry

to determine if a court-martial was in order, and, indeed, with an eye toward the court-martial of Kearny and his toadies. Benton swore vengeance against Kearny, and many observers thought Benton's thundering outbursts made the court-martial of Frémont inescapable. Once ambivalent toward his defiant son-in-law, Benton now invested his great personal and political power in defending him like a son. "Thus, like Columbus," wrote a historian, "Colonel Frémont returned from the discovery and conquest of a new world . . . a prisoner and a disgrace. Like Columbus, his achievements have aroused sordid minds to jealousy, and like Columbus, instead of being permitted to continue his researches in that region which he first opened to science, he is compelled to return and defend himself against base attack."

Jessie and John returned to Washington to begin preparations for the trial. On September 17, Frémont wrote to Adjutant General Roger Jones reporting his arrest and requesting a thirty-day postponement until Commodore Stockton arrived in Washington. While he assured Jones he had no interest in delaying the trial while awaiting "far distant witnesses," he begged for time in which he could conduct a careful review of news stories that had smeared him and Stockton. "It is my intention to meet these charges in all their extent . . . Being a military subordinate, I can make no report, not even of my own operations. But my trial may become a report, and bring to the knowledge of the government, what it ought to know, not only with respect to the conduct of its officers, but also in regard to the policy observed, or necessary to be observed, with regard to the three-fold population (Spanish-Americans, Anglo-Americans, and Aboriginal Americans), which that remote province contains."

That day, Frémont received word that his mother was seriously ill at her home in Aiken, South Carolina, and was not expected to live much longer. "The news of his returning home in arrest, and the vicious newspaper attacks, proved too much for an invalid, whose only tenure of existence lay in the maintenance of undisturbed calm," wrote Jessie, "and these publications, appearing before her son's letters giving the truth had had time to arrive, broke the feeble hold on life."

Frémont rushed to South Carolina, arriving just hours after her death—"the still face, left, at her last request, turned toward the open door" in anticipation of her only son's return. He took her remains to Charleston for burial. There, on September 21, the *Mercury* reported the sad event in a lengthy profile of Frémont. Pronouncing him innocent of all charges, the newspaper revealed that the city had voted to present him with an honorary sword—purchased by individual contributions of one dollar—and that the ladies of Charleston had bought a gold belt to hold the sword and its scabbard.

He returned to Washington to ready himself for the event that had replaced the war as front-page news and was the primary topic of gossip in the nation's capital. President Polk, in pushing for the court-martial, had gravely misjudged the public sympathy for the best-selling author and national hero. The celebrated trial would bring Polk's blunders to the forefront of national attention. "All of this was coming just as the unpopular war with Mexico was ending," wrote historian Ferol Egan, "just as the casualty lists were a daily reminder that the military had carried out an invasion of a smaller nation even though a great portion of the public protested such an action."

Jessie felt certain that the court-martial would vindicate Frémont and solidify his good reputation, and threw herself headlong into organizing material for the trial. She identified and located witnesses, collected newspaper articles, gathered documents from the Navy, Army, War, and State departments, researched transcripts of previous court-martials, developed strategy, and served as secretary to her father and new brother-in-law, lawyer William Carey Jones, who were officially preparing the defense. "I shall be with you to the end," Benton wrote her and John, "if it takes up the whole session of Congress."

While Frémont was in South Carolina, twenty-three-year-old Jessie audaciously wrote to the president about two of her husband's accusers from Kearny's California staff who had been ordered to Mexico, and addressing the rumors that Kearny also might be absent from the trial. "You will see the manifest injustice to Mr. Frémont of letting his accusers escape from the investigation of the charges they have made against him. You have the power to do justice & I ask it of you that Mr. Frémont be permitted to make his accusers stand the trial as well as himself. Do not suppose Sir, that I lightly interfere in a matter properly belonging to men, but in the absence of Mr. Frémont I attend to his affairs at his request."

No longer just a teenage bride, Jessie had evolved into a woman of strength and power, her formidable courage remarked upon in Washington circles. Still, her feminine instincts were honed as she fiercely protected her fragile husband from the painful barbs, ever nurturing him back to emotional and physical health. She took seriously her role as supportive wife, and knew that regardless of the evidence amassed and the legal brilliance of her father, John's own stability and comportment in the trial would be paramount. The insecurities fostered by his illegitimacy always surfaced in times of stress, making him turn inward. Now the grief of his mother's death, the remorse at being unavailable to attend to her in her final days, only added to his despondency. Jessie's job, as she saw it, was to return him to a position of balance and fortitude. He must meet his accusers with dignity and resolve, with poise and firmness. Time was of the essence, and only she could rekindle the spirit that had been demolished. When Benton left for Norfolk to interview witnesses, Jessie determined to have a second honeymoon with John. "We are going to mutiny until father returns to whip us back into line," she confided in her newly married sister Eliza. "He doesn't realize that though this trial is important, it isn't everything in life."

She sequestered John from the outside world, not wanting anyone to see his weakened state. "For a week we lived alone together on a happy island surrounded by a sea of troubles," she later wrote of their idyll before the storm. "We arose late and had breakfast in our room before the fire. After the mail came, we went for a walk or a visit with friends. We even drove in the moonlight out to the school in Georgetown and looked up at the back window where the Colonel's first love letter had come up hidden in a basket of laundry."

As steadfastly as Benton and Frémont pushed for a speedy trial, Kearny began scheming for a delay. Press accounts made clear the popular verdict was in favor of the accused, and even Kearny, despite his animosity toward Frémont, held Benton in high regard and had a fatherly tenderness for Jessie. Kearny maneuvered to have the case tried quietly two hundred miles from Washington, at Fort Monroe in Virginia—far from the pro-Frémont newspapers of Washington and New York. Frémont requested that it be moved to Washington, claiming that the isolated and distant location would make it difficult for his attorneys to be present. "If . . . the War Dept. perseveres in sending you to a fortress in the Atlantic Ocean to be tried, for acts done on the Pacific, it will be sending you to be tried without counsel," Benton wrote Frémont with characteristic indignation. Adjutant General Jones denied Frémont's plea. But Benton quickly called in a flood of political debts, and soon, at the direction of President Polk, the case was moved to the capital and slated to begin November 2, 1847.

One newspaper called it "the most dramatic army trial since General Wilkinson's thirty years before," and it was widely compared to the prosecution of Aaron Burr for treason. Still, behind the testimony was another story the public never knew, and historians discovered only afterward—a chronicle of intrigue and empire, ambition and idealism, sacrifice and glory, politics and passion. Frémont's third expedition culminating with raising the Bear Flag in California had begun with a covert political scheme sanctioned by the highest levels of government. At its heart, as throughout their lives, was the extraordinary woman who was Frémont's wife and alter ego.

The day was clear and warm; the startling Indian summer had been lingering for weeks. A special omnibus carried the thirteen trial officers to the courtroom at the run-down Washington Arsenal, where they would act as judge and jury. Private carriages brought the spectators—an eclectic collection of congressmen, army officers, socialites, and tourists. Jessie chose a maroon gown rather than the black one Eliza suggested—"this isn't a mourning occasion!"—and fixed her hair beneath a burgundy velvet bonnet.

The charges were grave: multiple counts of mutiny, disobedience of a superior officer, and conduct prejudicial to order and discipline. From November 2 until January 31, 1848, the court met for five hours daily except Sundays. The most devastating testimony against Frémont came, predictably, from Kearny, who portrayed the young officer as a lone wolf who resisted authority, a self-centered, self-aggrandizing misfit who baldly maneuvered for the governorship. "He asked me if I would appoint him governor," Kearny testified against Frémont. "I told him . . . that as soon as the country was quieted I should, most probably, organize a civil government and that I, at that time, knew of no objections to my appointing him governor. He then stated to me that he would see Commodore Stockton, and that, unless he appointed him governor at once, he would not obey his orders."

Jessie was livid. "Had the case been tried before a Civil Court, it is safe to say that General Kearny would have left the Court room under bail for trial for perjury," she wrote.

As the weeks dragged on, Jessie became increasingly worried about the case. Despite her father's forceful efforts—attempting to show the charges against Frémont traced wholly to the dispute between Kearny and Stockton—the recalcitrance of the court, combined with what she called Kearny's perjury, seemed insurmountable. By Christmas and now in the first trimester of pregnancy, Jessie was fighting pneumonia, her mother had suffered another paralytic stroke, and Jessie struggled to maintain her optimism.

As the New Year began, the press seemed to lose interest. "The case ought never to have been brought to trial," opined the *New York Herald*. "Frémont ought to have apologized to Gen. Kearny, and the whole matter ought to have been settled, instead of being blazed about the world as it is now."

The testimony was dry and tiresome, broken only by a ludicrous incident in which Kearny accused Benton of "making mouths and grimaces at me . . . to offend, to insult, and to overawe me." Benton boasted of staring down the general. "When General Kearny fixed his eyes on Colonel Frémont, I determined if he should attempt again to look down a prisoner, I would look at him," Benton admitted. "I did to-day look at General Kearny when he looked at Colonel Frémont, and I looked at him till his eyes fell—till they fell upon the floor." Kearny took umbrage at Benton's claims that he had outstared the general, and observers feared there would be a duel between the two men who were "quarreling . . . like an infant school."

On January 11, 1848, the court recessed for thirteen days. When it reconvened on January 24, the room was crowded with spectators. The defense had decided that Frémont would deliver his own closing argument, since he had not had the opportunity, under military rules, to testify on his own behalf during the proceedings. Boldly accusing Kearny of perjury and false testimony, Frémont held his distinguished audience spellbound. With no hint of weakness or ambivalence, of regret or contrition, Frémont lambasted his accuser and defended his actions:

My acts in California have all been with high motives, and a desire for the public service. My scientific labors did something to open California to the knowledge of my countrymen; its geography had been a sealed book. My military operations were conquests without bloodshed; my civil administration was for the public good. I offer California, during my administration, for comparison with the most tranquil portion of the United States; I offer it in contrast to the condition of New Mexico at the same time. I prevented civil war against Governor Stockton, by refusing to join General Kearny against him; I arrested civil war against myself, by consenting to be deposed—offering at the same time to resign my place of lieutenant colonel in the army.

I have been brought as a prisoner and a criminal from that country. I could return to [California], after this trial is over, without rank or guards, and without molestation from the people, except to be importuned for the money which the government owes them.

I am now ready to receive the sentence of this court.

On January 31, 1848, after deliberating for three days, the jury found Colonel John C. Frémont, one of the U.S. Army's most celebrated and popular figures, guilty on all three charges. He was sentenced to dismissal from the army. But in supplemental "Remarks by the Court," seven of the thirteen jurors—citing his distinguished service—recommended Frémont be granted clemency by the president. "Under the circumstances in which Lieutenant Colonel Frémont was placed between two officers of superior rank, each claiming to command-in-chief in California—circumstances in their nature calculated to embarrass the mind and excite the doubts of officers of greater experience than the accused—and in consideration of the important professional services rendered by him previous to the occurrence of those acts for which he has been tried, the undersigned members of the court, respectfully commend Lieutenant Colonel Frémont to the lenient consideration of the President of the United States."

It was a confusing and indecisive verdict, prompting newspapers to cry foul, charging the case had been rigged. "A Dreyfus case to the end," Jessie called it. "A reprimand would have been proper," wrote painter, mapmaker, and Frémont biographer Frederick S. Dellenbaugh. "Frémont had not refused to act, but simply declined to acknowledge that a General had authority over the Commodore to whom he had pledged himself long before the General appeared on the scene . . . Was it a deliberate attempt to break the success of Frémont by the West Point element as so often charged by Senator Benton? Regretfully, I admit, it looks uncomfortably that way." Benton, of course, was outraged, attributing the entire affair to insidious jealousy. "He had not only entered the army intrusively . . . without passing through West Point, but he had done worse: he had become distinguished."

President Polk—a somber, stubborn, narrow-minded Scotchman with a colorless personality—sought the counsel of his cabinet, and a series of heated arguments ensued. Buchanan was vehement in his support of Frémont—though he failed to honor him publicly—arguing with Polk in favor of commuting the sentence. In the end, Polk dismissed the charge of mutiny and upheld the other two charges. "I am not satisfied that the facts proved in this case constitute the military crime of 'mutiny,' " he wrote on February 16. "Lieutenant Colonel Frémont will accordingly be released from arrest, will resume his sword, and report for duty."

Jessie and John were furious. Both felt betrayed by the government, to which they had been exceedingly loyal at great personal cost. They had been forewarned that the administration might, by necessity, disavow any sanction of Frémont in the event his activities in California were unsuccessful or proved detrimental to U.S. interests. He knew the risks when he agreed to undertake the covert assignment, and he would have been more willing to take the fall had he failed. But to the contrary, the conquest of California under Frémont's command had been a stupendous, bloodless victory. Throughout the trial—and to his death—Frémont honored the confidentiality of his assignment, stoically refusing to implicate Polk, Buchanan, or Bancroft. He naïvely believed that the men to whom he gave his loyalty were honorable men who, in the end, would never allow such a miscarriage of justice. And yet this was his reward for swiftly and peacefully obtaining California for the United States—a sustaining of the verdict against him. His bitterness, toward them and his country, would never be fully mitigated.

Public sentiment was firmly in their camp, bolstering them with a small measure of satisfaction. They saw themselves as victims of lesser men scheming for their own purposes, and would be forever changed by the incident. Proud and defiant, Frémont announced his intention to resign. "I want justice, not official clemency," he declared hotly, surprising even Jessie. "There is but one honorable course to pursue in face of this dishonorable verdict." Benton urged him to accept the president's leniency, arguing that he would be most effective and productive by remaining in the service. It was the first conflict Jessie witnessed between her father and her husband, and though she felt she must support her husband, she partially agreed with her father. Short of having the conviction overturned, John vowed to have nothing to do with the army ever again. He would prove himself without the largesse of the U.S. government.

"I hereby send in my resignation of Lieut. Colonel of the Army of the United States," Frémont wrote on February 19, 1848. "In doing this I take the occasion to say, that my reason for resigning is, that I do not feel conscious of having done anything to merit the finding of the court; and this being the case I cannot, by accepting the clemency of the President, admit the justice of the decision against me." The president, Benton, and Buchanan all implored him to reconsider, but he remained steadfast.

It seemed the end of one of the more promising military careers in the history of the young republic. No officer had risen so far, so fast, from such humble beginnings. None had fallen so far, so fast, from such heights. An adoring and outraged public greeted the humiliated officer, but no amount of outpouring or admiration could offset the profound sense of betrayal, the swift and brutal reminder that he was indeed, and always would be, an "outsider"—the bastard son of a runaway southern belle.

Little did John or Jessie know that the arrest and trial were but a pre-monitory brush with real politics and the cutthroat world of nineteenth-century American power as the nation advanced across the country. Neither seemed fully cognizant of the array of forces against them, as the stakes of Manifest Destiny escalated, with careers and ambitions hanging in the balance. Somehow they held fast to their confidence and common dream, underestimating how deep-seated and evolutionary these forces and machinations were. While Jessie had been raised at her father's knee, and had seen her share of political and bureaucratic squabbling and power struggles, she was strangely naïve when it came to her husband's career. Benton had managed to shelter his daughter from the more ruth-less behind-the-scenes maneuvering of political life. For his part, John, as the bastard son who rose quickly in the ranks with the incomparable support of Benton, was almost childlike in his idealism.

A private citizen now, John turned his attention back to California, the golden land of opportunity where Jessie could raise a family and he could pursue his dream of a transcontinental railroad, linking the At-lantic and Pacific, and perhaps a political career. "In turning away so abruptly from his profession and chief means of support, he had to at once consider the next step," Jessie wrote. "Although only thirty four years of age, he felt that he was better adapted to carve a future in new lands and conditions, rather than enter into competition with men who were more experienced in the ways of the settled part of our country."

While Jessie understood his desire to leave Washington, she was torn by the prospect. They had really spent very little time together during their seven-year marriage, and her emotional bonds were deeply rooted in Washington with her father, her sister, and her close friends. Still, she was a wife first and foremost, and she wistfully recalled her "whither thou goest" pronouncement to her father. "From the intolerable injustice and oppression of this military experience, Mr. Frémont's mind reverted longingly to the free life he had led and to the beautiful land of California," Jessie wrote. "There his life had been full and splendidly successful and he had found combined a perfect climate and a manly people and there 'on the shore of the sea' he had planned to make a new home . . . the only delay in starting off at once came from the necessity of making some money." He was offered a $5,000-a-year salary to become president of a railroad company that ran trains from Charleston to Cincinnati, and the College of Charleston recruited him for a professorship. But he was determined to move west.

That spring, they forged ahead with a "Geographical Memoir upon Upper California," obtaining government funding for the report through the efforts of Benton, called "one of the kindest and best fathers who ever lived" by the *New York Herald*. Gone were the days of cheerful and stimulating collaboration. They faced the task without enthusiasm, the writing process drudgery and tedium. John called it "the cursed memoir." Even so, the final report was a valuable document, presenting, for the first time, a defined picture of the Great Basin, the Sierra Nevada, and the Pacific Coast Range, and including the most accurate map ever made of the region.

One evening in April, while working with John, Jessie fainted. When she regained consciousness, she found the family doctor at her side. Clearly, the stress of the previous six months had taken its toll, and she was now severely ill. The doctor ordered complete bed rest until her baby was born, and for weeks she fought a "battle with a violent bilious fever," as she wrote a friend, "which like Bunyan's fight with Apollyon was the dreadfullest fight I ever had."

John blamed Jessie's illness and precarious pregnancy on Kearny, and a bitterness and caustic attitude overtook his once lighthearted manner. Jessie, too, had lost her innocence, and felt a cynicism invading her characteristically sunny disposition. During the months of confinement she struggled with her new worldview, her charmed upbringing suddenly dashed by events outside her control. "All the teachings, the examples of my twenty-three years, had been so in contrast with this experience that I really tried to believe the worst—not the best—of the human race."

She grappled with the concepts of good and evil, endlessly discussing the matter with her friends, and in her disillusionment found that most everyone with whom she pursued the subject considered the world a sordid place. Only her father, eternal optimist, indefatigable fighter, unfalteringly told her the world was good.

On July 24, 1848, Jessie gave birth to a sickly baby boy—the weakhearted infant suffering from what Benton called "the 'Court-Martial,' a family disease." She named him Benton for her father, and feared for his life from the moment he was born. Weeks later, President Polk nominated Kearny to a brevet major generalship, prompting Benton to filibuster the appointment before Congress for thirteen straight days. He was unsuccessful in stopping Kearny's promotion, and Benton never spoke to Polk again. The two men saw each other in church every Sunday, but the president privately bemoaned the fact that Benton "never speaks to me as he was in the habit of doing . . . [he] has been exceedingly hostile to me."

Benton—obsessed with the idea of a railroad from St. Louis to California—managed to obtain private financing from three St. Louis merchants for an expedition headed by Frémont. The men wanted Frémont to find a route along the thirty-eighth parallel. The Senate had appropriated $30,000 for the venture, but the House of Representatives voted against it. The couple decided that she, Lily, and baby Benton would accompany him to Westport on the Missouri in September, where he would outfit his expedition. They agreed that the following spring she and the children would board the new government steamer to Chagres in Panama, cross the isthmus by mule, and take another steamer from Panama City to San Francisco. There he would be awaiting her arrival and they would establish their new home on the sea. Her family and friends thought the plan preposterous, and Jessie herself had misgivings about being the first white woman to cross the Panama jungle. Secretary Buchanan—"who had known me very well and always liked me"—begged her to abandon the "cruel experiment," as he called it. "You have two children, you have been very ill this past year. Do you think you would be a help or a burden for your husband?"

"Mr. Frémont left it altogether with me to decide," she told the avuncular Buchanan, who felt personally responsible for much of the hardship the couple had suffered at the hands of the U.S. government. "I saw only the proud lonely man making a new start in life," she explained, "but for me quite alone. He must make the journey in the old difficult dangerous way but I would go by sea and together we would make it home."

In late September, his eyes filled with tears, Benton saw the small family off. "Promise me on your honor not to let Jessie Ann[e] keep on going westward when you reach Missouri," were the senator's parting words to his son-in-law. Frémont assured the old man that his beloved daughter would return to Washington by November to prepare for her later journey.

To observers, they seemed a classic migrant family—John in a civilian broadcloth suit, six-year-old Lily holding his hand, his young wife carrying a dark-haired infant. "He went now at his own expense and not at the expense of the government," wrote John Bigelow, "as an emigrant in quest of a home in the new State which he had emancipated, and not as an officer under orders." They kept to themselves, and when drawn into conversation said only that they were on their way to California. Like their fellow migrants, they were poor, relying entirely on Frémont's paltry savings from his army salary. "It was very pleasant," wrote a steamboat passenger who conversed with them, "to see how he was cheered on and encouraged by the vast prospect of doing good which was opened to them in that new territory. Neither had any other thought or expectation than to obtain an honorable and respected position by their own industry and economy."

They reached St. Louis on October 3 and boarded the *Martha* for the journey to Westport. As they moved upriver, ten-week-old Benton became ill and died suddenly. Jessie was hysterical, refusing to relinquish the small corpse to her husband. "Grief was new to me then and I could not bear to give him up," she later wrote to the child's godfather, Kit Carson. Finally, John pried his dead son from Jessie's arms. When they reached Westport she was forced to entrust the tiny body to a cousin who had accompanied them, who would take him back to St. Louis for burial. Jessie was devastated. She wondered where she would find the reserve to sustain her. "When one has had to meet death, and treachery, the sense of security never returns."

She, John, and Lily continued a few miles to Boone Creek, where the Delaware Indian agent gave them a room in his large log house. During the day, as John immersed himself in the expedition's preparation, Jessie and Lily observed from the shade of a massive cottonwood tree. "I sat watching all the many preparations for the long winter journey, I the

only idle one: weak from undermining illness and heavy at heart for all
that had come and what might yet come to us both." Grief-stricken, she
passed her days in quiet reflection. The men, moved by her sorrow, were
attentive to her every need, grilling quail for her lunch, erecting a Sibley
tent for her so she could view the daily activity, and playing games with
Lily. One man, an artist, presented her with a water-color of her tent
under the trees "already browned and growing bare with the coming
winter winds." She cherished the painting—"my résumé of that time of
severance from all I held indispensable to happiness." She dreaded the
parting more than any separation before, having lost her resiliency and
hopefulness.

She watched as her husband went through the motions, his own sadness reflected in his now-aged face and faraway eyes. She knew this expedition was one of necessity rather than pleasure, that he brought no
joy or enthusiasm to the endeavor, that it was underfunded, under-
manned. The crossing would be filled with the usual hardship and privation, danger and loneliness, without the excitement and glory of the
previous days. "We were pretty much in the conditions of shipwrecked
people," she later described their troubled state.

On October 20, 1848, Frémont and his thirty-three men departed,
leaving the once-lively camp desolate "though the ashes of the camp
fires were still warm." Major Richard Cummins, the Indian agent, led
her gently away from the deserted site toward his home. "There was
nothing left but to turn to what lay before me and hope for the meeting
of next year"—le bon temps viendra.

Along the way, Cummins showed her the den of a wolf that had been
preying on his sheep. The night before, Cummins told her, the men had
found her den and killed her entire litter of puppies. "I was sorry for
even a wolf's destroyed home and young ones, and the night closed in so
wet and windy I was thankful for early sleep. But the wolf was hunting
her cubs and her long mournful howls came nearer and nearer until they
were close up to the cabin . . . and the prairie wind seemed a shrieking
voice as it tore around the lonely cabin."

Finally returning to sleep, she was "again waked into renewed fright to
see a large dark object" coming toward her. Startled, she looked up to
find that it was John, who had ridden back through the night for one last
embrace. They held each other for an hour, Jessie likening the feeling to
the child who begs for "just five minutes more" before bedtime. He comforted her as best he could, telling her not to worry about him, urging her

to be careful crossing the isthmus, and assuring her they would have no more long separations. Then, inevitably, he was off again "into the night and the rain."

She returned to St. Louis, where she collapsed for several days at the lavish home of her cousin Sarah—Thomas Hart Benton's niece who had been raised like a sister to Jessie. Alarmed at Jessie's condition, Sarah had summoned the family physician. Dr. William Beaumont, a longtime Benton family friend and eminent army surgeon, was equally distressed by her appearance, knowing as he did her customary "fine health and inherited vitality."

Beaumont had a secondary concern. One of his other patients, also a dear friend, was General Kearny. Kearny was in St. Louis, recently returned from Mexico, where he had contracted yellow fever and dysentery, and lay dying just blocks away from where Jessie suffered her own infirmity. Kearny's deathbed wish was for Jessie to visit him so he could "make his peace before dying" and seek her forgiveness. Kearny had enlisted Beaumont as his messenger.

But Jessie could not forget the pain inflicted on her family by Kearny's actions, convinced that her pregnancy had been jeopardized by the strain of the court-martial. She held Kearny personally accountable for her baby's death, and refused to honor his wish.

"There was a little grave between us I could not cross."

5

GOLD 1849–1855

*Never, since the Roman legionary shadowed the earth with their eagles,
in search of spoil—not even when Spain ravished the wealth of a
world, or England devastated the Indies for its treasures—never has
such a gorgeous treasury been opened to the astonished world.*

—James Mason Hutchings

As FRÉMONT MADE his way toward a disastrously ill-fated expedition, Jessie returned to Washington to prepare for what would be her own wretched crossing the following spring. She commissioned seamstresses to sew light cotton dresses for her and Lily in anticipation of the steamy tropics. "Not only had none of us ever been to sea, but we knew but very few people who had made a real sea voyage," she later wrote, likening the trip to "the old journeys to India." She consulted with a friend who had recently traveled to China, and, along with the guidance of an outdated book called *The Lady of the Manor,* managed to compile a list of provisions. She spent her time "refreshing" her Spanish, and reconciling herself "to the fact that in a few months I should be cut loose from everything that had made my previous life."

The fall and winter of 1848 were dark and dolorous days at the C Street residence. Elizabeth was frail and despondent; Jessie was bereft; and Benton, agitated over the looming national crisis, was preoccupied with the debate on slavery extension into the newly acquired territories. "Overnight the question of slavery in the Southwest was lifted from the realm of the academic to the point where a solution was imperative," according to one historical account. That November, Whig candidate Zachary Taylor was elected the country's twelfth president. A disheveled

Southern slaveholder, Taylor was still a Whiggish nationalist first and foremost, and was determined to hold the Union together by force if necessary. A popular hero as an Indian fighter in the West, his characteristic unkempt appearance earned him the nickname "Old Rough and Ready." During the new administration Benton and his colleagues in Congress would face rising obstacles, from slavery to the immediate need for territorial governments in California and New Mexico.

At the same time, word reached Washington from California consul Thomas Larkin that John Sutter and his partner, James Marshall, had discovered gold while building a sawmill near Sutter's Fort in the Sacramento Valley—a fact that both Sutter and Marshall had tried in vain to keep secret. Outgoing president Polk was initially skeptical upon hearing of the discovery, dismissing reports as an attempt by Californians to spark migration and land speculation. It was not until late November 1848 that a special courier arrived in Washington with a dispatch from twenty-seven-year-old army lieutenant William Tecumseh Sherman—a West Point officer on assignment with the American military occupation of California. Sherman's courier, Lieutenant Lucien Loeser, carried physical evidence—a square metal tea caddy containing more than two hundred ounces of gold dust that Sherman had purchased for $4,000.

Loeser's arrival in the capital is widely regarded as the opening shot of the California Gold Rush, though in truth there were already thousands of men working in the gold fields, and thousands more making their way "across the greatest of the world's oceans," as historian H. W. Brands wrote in *The Age of Gold*. Almost all able-bodied men had poured out of San Francisco en route to the strike, leaving the small city a virtual ghost town, and the U.S. Army in California was plagued by mass defections. "The discovery of these vast deposits of gold has entirely changed the character of Upper California," Sherman wrote. "Its people, before engaged in cultivating their small patches of ground and guarding their herds of cattle and horses, have all gone to the mines, or are on their way thither; laborers of every trade have left their work benches, and tradesmen their shops; sailors desert their ships as fast as they arrive on the coast."

When President Polk addressed Congress in December 1848 and revealed the fantastic news, "the whole country—the whole world—went mad," as one account put it. Within months, American migrants were pushing en masse toward California, and the frenzy absorbed the national dialogue. "The Eldorado of the old Spaniards is discovered at last," proclaimed the *New York Herald*. "We now have the highest official authority for believing in the discovery of vast gold mines in California, and that the discovery is the greatest and most startling, not to say miraculous, that the history of the last five centuries can produce."

Still, the full significance of what the *New York Tribune*'s Horace Greeley had called "the Age of Gold" seemed lost on Jessie and John. They were seeking a new home in a beautifully serene environment, a refuge from the pain and anguish official Washington had come to represent for them, a fresh start for their marriage and their small, grieving family. Though California represented to them new political and economic possibilities, they could not have grasped the immeasurable potential about to unfold before them.

That spring of 1849, while encamped in Santa Fe, Frémont had heard the rumor of gold. But it was not until his party later encountered a group of several hundred Mexican miners and their families on their way to California that the reality took hold in his mind. "Why California?" he asked them. Only then did he learn of the gold strike in the Sierra Nevada foothills. He listened to their stories and studied their maps. Stunned by the proximity of the massive gold mine to his Las Mariposas tract—what he had thought was a useless expanse of uninhabitable land for which he had intended to demand a refund from Thomas Larkin—his months-long despair gave way to optimism. He made a deal with twenty-eight of the Mexican men: if they would accompany him to Las Mariposas and mine the property, he would split the riches with them. He gave each man a pack animal and provided them with food and supplies. Now his impending rendezvous with Jessie took on an urgency. Desperate to share with her his newfound faith and hopefulness, he pushed his men hurriedly from New Mexico to California. Life could indeed begin anew.

Benton had intended to accompany Jessie and Lily to California—"to know personally the newly acquired country, its people, and its needs," as Jessie described her father's enthusiasm for the westward expansion to which he had devoted his political life. He, "as a Senator from Missouri, had the neighbor's right to look out for its interests; and from many causes, personal, political, and geographical, this friendly representation would have been for him, as a queen of Spain said of something akin to this, *mi privilegio, prerogativa, y derecho*—my privilege, my prerogative, and my right."

But as Jessie's departure date drew closer, Benton realized he could leave neither Elizabeth nor the pressing matters before Congress. Still, he insisted that a male member of the family accompany Jessie, and enlisted his son-in-law Richard Taylor Jacob for the task. Married to Jessie's younger sister Sarah, Jacob had been with Frémont in California and felt confident that he could deliver Jessie safely to her husband. Benton also demanded that Jessie select a female attendant from the household. Jessie chose Harriet, a young black woman who had been with the family for many years, and with whom Jessie felt a warm affinity—"each of us . . . considered a victim selected for a sacrifice." One of the "upper class educated free colored people of the District," as Jessie depicted her, Harriet was quickly overtaken by "hysterical indecision" that reached a climax when her fiancé reported to a group of New York abolitionists that the Bentons were spiriting a "free negress out of the country against her will." Jessie found the charges appalling. "It seems incredible that a colored mob should have assembled against my father and myself on such a hue and cry," she later wrote of the group's ignorant and "vague ideas of a new land of slavery."

On March 14, 1849, Benton traveled with Jessie to New York City, where she was scheduled to board a steamer. There he hired a middle-aged New England woman to replace Harriet. "I barely looked at her, and saw she was a hard, unpleasing person to my mind; but the steamer sailed the next day, and there was no time for any choice. She was only an item in the many griefs that seemed to accumulate on me at this time. My father's going with me would have made it a delightful voyage for both of us; without him, it was in all its dreary blankness, my first separation from home."

Benton watched tearfully with a combination of pride, anxiety, and sorrow as his beloved daughter—a seven-year-old child in tow—set off for a faraway and unknown land. "It's like leaving her in her grave," Jessie heard someone whisper to her father. She would be one of the first white women to make the journey famously fraught with peril, the eastern coast of Panama teeming with deadly diseases, from cholera to a debilitating syndrome called Chagres fever. "I was much in the position of a nun carried into the world for the last time before taking the veil," she wrote of her feelings at the time, "all the pros and cons, old fears renewed, old griefs opened up, the starting made harder than ever." She could only wonder what life might hold for her, what opportunities California might present. What she *did* know, what she stoically and courageously abandoned, was a world of privilege, familial security, and deep historical and emotional ties. Only twenty-four years old, she was already world-weary.

On the morning of March 15, in a gray dawn, Jessie and Lily boarded the *Crescent City* Pacific Mail steamship bound from New York to Panama, where she planned to cross the isthmus by packmule and continue by boat up to San Francisco to meet John. Benton had paid the $500 fare for her and each member of her entourage, which guaranteed the highest class of accommodations. But if she had been expecting a relaxing journey, she found instead what one historian called "mobs of Argonauts (as they styled themselves, after Jason and his fleece-seeking shipmates) clamoring for space on the vessels heading down the Atlantic coast." Gold fever was rampant, and the boat, in addition to Jessie, Lily, the maid, and one Irish woman, carried 346 male passengers—the majority of whom were seeking their fortune in California.

"There comes a dulled edge to sorrow which makes one accept new griefs without feeling," Jessie wrote of her sad departure. The first night, she and Lily crawled into bed together, avoiding any conversation with the disagreeable maid. "My little girl was as sorry as a young heart can bear and we were comforting each other silently." Lying there in the darkness, weeping softly, Jessie heard the maid enter the berth. Pretending to be asleep, Jessie listened as the maid rifled through Jessie's trunk and began stacking objects in a small pile. She watched in disbelief as the woman removed a dark wig and shook out her long blonde hair. She "stood there, not the dark-haired middle-aged woman who was to be so much better for me than my Harriet, but a light-haired woman under thirty, with an expression of hardness that puzzled me then, and frightened me too, so that I kept as much asleep as possible, and let her help herself to all she wanted from the trunk." As soon as the thieving impostor left, Jessie rushed from the bed and barricaded the door, refusing to answer the woman's repeated knocks throughout the night. The next morning she reported the incident to the captain, and the maid was held under guard for the rest of the journey.

Jessie fell in love with the sea, beginning a lifelong attachment to its soothing and healing qualities—"the silent teaching of sky and sea lifted me from morbid dwelling on what was now ended"—and as the ocean restored her health and morale she vowed to always live near it in the future. Preferring solitude and introspection—what she called her "gentle state of mental convalescence"—she made no attempt to converse with the other passengers. Instead, she sought personal meaning in the tragedies that had befallen her and John, marveled at the capacity for renewal found within the human spirit, the ability of a broken heart to mend, the resilience of a soul. "Perhaps the sharpest lesson of life is that we outlast so much—even ourselves," she wrote of this period in her life, "so that one, looking back, might say, 'when I died the first time.'"

Nine days later, on March 24, having encountered one storm after another in the Caribbean, they reached the chaotic port of Chagres. Crowds of gold seekers had poured into the historically rowdy city, its streets teeming with armed men, other men sleeping in doorways or under awnings, many suffering from yellow fever or malaria. "Thousands, then tens of thousands, of Argonauts descended upon Chagres, overwhelming the town's ecological, economical, and political carrying capacity," wrote Brands. "Housing had never been plentiful; now it was nonexistent for most of the travelers." Untold numbers poured in from the Atlantic Ocean, only to be stranded in the heat awaiting boats from the Pacific that failed to arrive. Raw sewage and rotting garbage lay exposed, the stench inescapable. "So notorious was the Chagres fever," according to Brands, ". . . that the life insurance policies purchased by many emigrants carried a Chagres-exclusion clause: if they slept ashore at Chagres, they voided their policies."

Dozens of "naked, shrieking, gesticulating Indians," as Jessie described them, maneuvering dugout canoes, approached the steamer to unload the passengers. Observing the horrendous situation, the ship's captain angrily implored Jessie to return to New York—a recommendation heartily endorsed by Jacob, who had been seasick for the entire journey and was now homesick as well. Panama was not a safe place for a woman and a child, they argued, neither wanting to be accountable to Thomas Hart Benton for entrusting Jessie and Lily to such a treacherous environment. Jessie faltered briefly. "If it had not been for pure shame and unwillingness that my father should think badly of me, I would have returned to New York on the steamer, as the captain begged, putting before me such a list of dangers to health, and discomforts and risks of every kind, as to kill my courage." Further, as if weighing her allegiance between her father and her husband, she thought of her promise to John to meet him in California. She steeled herself to continue—her decision, she reasoned, would satisfy both men. But what of her? What did *she* want?

Over the captain's forceful objections, Jessie handed Lily down from the *Crescent City* to a man on board a whaleboat. Then she and her reticent brother-in-law clambered down as well. Despite the privations and rugged conditions, Jessie's journey would prove positively luxurious in contrast to that of most travelers of the day, thanks to letters of introduction Jessie carried to William Aspinwall, an associate of her father's who was heavily invested in the mail steamers and the projected Panama Railroad. "This was a difference which I learned to appreciate more thoroughly on hearing afterwards of the murder of passengers by their crews." She invited the other two females who had been on the steamer— the Irish woman and, reluctantly, the thieving maid—to join her party. Under the special care of one of Aspinwall's trusted employees in the mahogany trade, Jessie and her comparatively pampered entourage traveled up the Rio Chagres on the boat. A palm-leaf canopy their only shade, they listened to the eerie sounds of the tropical rain forest— screeching monkeys and high-pitched parrots—and watched the ravenous alligators that circled their boat. A few miles upriver they switched to a smaller craft for the three-day, fifty-mile journey to Gorgona, on the Pacific coast, where they would mount mules to cross the mountains. Each night they stayed at camps set up for railroad surveyors. While Jessie welcomed the clean cots and linen sheets, the rapacious mosquitoes and oppressive heat took their toll. Blacks and Indians rowed the boat upstream against a strong current, the crew spending more time in the water pulling the vessel than they did on board. Jessie, like her husband on his many expeditions, found special beauty in the "fragrant and brilliant" passion flowers and noted them in the pages of her "well worn prayer book."

On the last day, as they approached Gorgona, Jacob became gravely ill. "His eyes rolled back in his head and he fell prostrate from sunstroke." A physician with the engineering corps examined him and predicted imminent death if he did not return immediately to New York. Not surprisingly, Jacob begged Jessie to return as well, as did everyone she encountered in Gorgona, and she actually considered a retreat—"the officers of the engineering corps all begging me to return to the United States, telling me that I had no idea of what I was to go through." The demoralization and despair around her might have been enough. "There were hundreds of people camped out on the hill slopes at Gorgona in apologies for tents, waiting for a certainty of leaving Panama, from which as yet there was no transportation. There were many women, some with babies, among these; they were in a hot, unhealthy climate, and the uncertainty of everything was making them ill: loss of hope brings loss of strength; they were living on salt provisions brought from home with them, which were not fit for such a climate, and already many had died." But in the end, her characteristic fortitude prevailed yet again, and she bade her brother-in-law farewell.

Daughter of a powerful senator, wife of a famous explorer, Jessie had cachet, prompting the village *alcalde* to invite her to a celebratory feast. She stifled her revulsion at the menu—"a baked monkey, which looked like a little child that had been burned to death"—and roasted iguana. After a few days in Gorgona, she and Lily began the twenty-mile over-land journey by mule to the walled Panama City. The rugged path— "the same trail that had been followed since the early days of Spanish conquest"—was strewn with dead mules being devoured by vultures. Jessie struggled against the defiles, terrified of the dangerous river cross-ings. Her sanguine demeanor charmed and surprised her male escorts, who marveled at her courage and lack of tears or complaints. But Jessie was in private agony, thinking it all a nightmare. "The nights were odi-ous with their dank mists and noises; but there was compensation in the sunrise, when from a mountain top you look down into an undulating sea of magnificent unknown blooms, sending up clouds of perfume into the freshness of the morning; and thus from the last of the peaks we saw, as Balboa had seen before us, the Pacific at our feet."

They descended into Panama—a city of about eight thousand people overrun, like Chagres, with stranded forty-niners—and took up resi-dence at a small, rustic hotel. Only days later, Señora Arcé z Zimena, the wealthy aunt of the Panamanian ambassador whom Jessie had known in Washington, visited Jessie and insisted that she and Lily move into her el-egant home. Installed in a high-ceilinged, second-story room with "a blue damask lounge, a grass hammock and several crystal chandeliers with wax lights," Jessie found her first real comfort in the soothing sur-roundings. Still, the respite was disconcerting as day after day brought no ships to transport the thousands pouring into the city. It was April 1849, and only one ship, the *California*, had left Panama for San Francisco, weeks earlier. It had been scheduled to return to pick up more passen-gers, including Jessie, but rumors abounded that the crew had deserted to go to the mines and the company was unable to recruit replacements.

The days turned into weeks as hundreds of migrants died of disease while waiting. As the rainy season began, Jessie became seriously ill from

Chagres fever. The more she struggled to recuperate, the more her spirits sagged. She became fearful that she would die, that Lily would be orphaned in this godforsaken land. Always intuitive, especially where John was concerned, she had a sixth sense that his expedition had met with disaster. "I became possessed with the conviction that he was starving." No amount of assurances from her generous hostess could pacify her, so firmly did she trust her instincts.

Her trepidation was only enhanced by newspaper reports that reached Panama indicating that John's expedition had ended tragically in the Rocky Mountains, beset by starvation and cannibalism. Her fears were confirmed upon receiving, finally, a letter from John—sent to Washington and forwarded by mail steamer to Jessie in Panama.

Taos, New Mexico, January 27, 1849

I write you from the house of our good friend Carson. This morning a cup of chocolate was brought to me while yet in bed. To an overworn, overworked, much-fatigued, and starving traveler these little luxuries of the world offer an interest which in your comfortable home it is not possible for you to conceive. While in the enjoyment of this luxury, then, I pleased myself in imagining how gratified you would be in picturing me here in Kit's care, whom you will fancy constantly occupied and constantly uneasy in endeavoring to make me comfortable. How little could you have dreamed of this while he was enjoying the pleasant hospitality of your father's house! The furthest thing then from your mind was that he would ever repay it to me here.

But I have now the unpleasant task of telling you how I came here. I had much rather write you some rambling letters in unison with the repose in which I feel inclined to indulge, and talk to you about the future, with which I am already busily occupied; about my arrangements for getting speedily down into the more pleasant climate of the lower Del Norte and rapidly through into California, and my plans when I get there. I have an almost invincible repugnance to going back among scenes where I have endured much suffering, and for all the incidents and circumstances of which I feel a strong aversion. But as clear information is absolutely necessary to you, and to your father more particularly still, I will give you the story now instead of waiting to tell it to you in California. But I write in the great hope that you will not receive this letter. When it reaches Washington you may be on your way to California.

Frémont then described, in horrifying detail, the dreadful journey. His party had left Bent's Fort for Pueblo on November 24, 1848, with one hundred mules and plenty of provisions. By early December, heavy snows had barricaded the San Juan Mountain passes in the southern Colorado Rockies, and he sought a guide. Disappointed that Kit Carson was unavailable, Frémont enlisted the services of the legendary "Old" Bill Williams, "who had spent some twenty-five years of his life in trapping various parts of the Rocky Mountains," as Frémont described his credentials. Known, too, for his keen survival instincts—prompting Kit Carson to once remark, "In starving times, no man who knew him ever walked in front of Bill Williams"—the hatchet-faced, sixty-two-year-old frontiersman was a character of the roughest sort.

"We occupied more than half a month in making the journey of a few days, blundering a tortuous way through deep snow, which already began to choke up the passes, for which we were obliged to waste time in searching," John wrote Jessie. By mid-December they had reached the Rio Grande near present-day Monte Vista, Colorado, where the main chain of the Rockies rose before them—"one of the highest, most rugged, and impracticable of all the Rocky Mountain ranges, inaccessible to trappers and hunters even in the summertime," as John described them. At this point, Frémont and Williams quarreled over how best to proceed. The exact nature of their disagreement is not known. By some accounts, Williams urged that the party turn south and skirt the San Juans, going west along a moderate and well-known trail traversing what is now the Colorado–New Mexico boundary. But Frémont thought to turn south would have defeated the object of the expedition—to prove the thirty-eighth parallel crossing of the Rockies was practicable for a railroad route that could be traversed in winter as well as summer. "Having still great confidence in his [Williams's] knowledge, we pressed onward with fatal resolution." (Frémont would forever blame Williams for leading the party to the impossible Wagon-Wheel Gap instead of the navigable Cochetopa Pass.)

"We pressed up towards the summit, the snow deepening, and in four or five days reached the naked ridges which lie above the timbered country, and which form the dividing grounds between the waters of the Atlantic and Pacific oceans. Along these naked ridges it storms nearly all winter, and the winds sweep across them with remorseless fury. On our first attempt to cross we encountered a poudrerie [blizzard], and were driven back, having some ten or twelve men variously frozen—face, hands, or feet. The guide became nigh being frozen to death here, and dead mules were already lying about the fires. Meantime it snowed steadily."

Now it was impossible to either advance or retreat. With Williams finally admitting that he was lost, the party camped in blizzard conditions at twelve thousand feet altitude. "We were overtaken by sudden and inevitable ruin . . . it was instantly apparent that we should lose every animal . . . They generally kept huddled together, and as they froze, one would be seen to tumble down, and the snow would cover him . . . The courage of the men failed fast; in fact, I have never seen men so soon discouraged by misfortune as we were on this occasion; but, as you know, the party was not constituted like the former ones. But among those who deserve to be honorably mentioned, and who behaved like what they were—men of the old exploring party—[was] Godey," he wrote of the brave French-Canadian scout who had been with him since the earliest expeditions.

By Christmas Day they were snowbound, their animals were all dead, and they suffered from nosebleeds and altitude sickness. They built pine fires and subsisted on the roasted carcasses of their frozen mules. With their provisions of sugar and macaroni nearing an end, Frémont decided their only hope was to be rescued, and to that end he dispatched four men, including Williams, to travel to the settlements of northern New Mexico to acquire fresh provisions and mules. "Like many a Christmas for years back, mine was spent on the summit of a wintry mountain, my heart filled with gloomy and anxious thoughts, with home of the merry faces and pleasant luxuries that belong to that happy time." He read volumes of Blackstone that he had borrowed from Benton's library—"they made my Christmas amusements"—and waited as the snow continued for days.

His men became downcast. One of them, during a moment of actual sunshine, threw his blanket down on the trail "and lay there till he froze to death." After sixteen days, with no word from the retreating party, whom Frémont feared had been ambushed by Indians or become lost, he decided to take a small party to the Red River settlement north of Taos to seek provisions, instructing his men to follow if he did not return within a stated time. On the sixth day after leaving his men, Frémont's party came upon the four men who had left twenty-two days earlier. One had starved to death a few days before, his remains left behind, and the other three were barely recognizable to Frémont in their skeletal state—"the most miserable objects I have ever seen." (Only later did Frémont learn that the three men had eaten the dead body of their fourth companion.) "I look upon the anxiety which induced me to set out from the camp as an inspiration," he wrote Jessie. "Had I remained there waiting the party which had been sent in, every man of us would probably have perished."

They managed to obtain horses from friendly Utah Indians, and when they finally arrived in Taos, Frémont and his party were near death from starvation, exhaustion, and, in Frémont's case, a frostbitten leg that had turned gangrenous. Unable to continue, he sent the trustworthy Godey back to rescue the main contingent. The American commanding officer of northern New Mexico provided Godey with thirty animals, provisions, and four Mexican frontiersmen. But the rescue party was too late, and the tragedy they encountered was overwhelming. When Frémont's party had not returned within the designated time frame, the twenty-two men who had been left behind had begun following the trail into northern New Mexico.

Frémont was stunningly graphic in the details he conveyed to his wife. "Manuel—you will remember Manuel, the Cosumne Indian—gave way to a feeling of despair after they had traveled about two miles, begged Haler to shoot him, and then turned and made his way back to the camp, intending to die there." Another man threw himself into a snowdrift to die, and two of his companions rolled him up in a blanket and buried him on the riverbank. A few days later another man wandered off from the party and was presumed dead. Two more refused to continue. Several of the men built them a fire and left them there, snow-blind and starving, to meet their fate.

"Things were desperate, and brought Haler to the determination of breaking up the party in order to prevent them from living upon each other. He told them 'that he had done all he could for them, that they had no other hope remaining than the expected relief, and that their best plan was to scatter and make the best of their way in small parties down the river. That, for his part, if he was to be eaten, he would, at all events, be found traveling when he did die.' "

In the end, ten of Frémont's party of thirty-three were dead—the catastrophe made all the more painful and revolting by the undeniable evidence that many of them had resorted to cannibalism. What Frémont felt about the heart-wrenching disaster that had befallen men under his command, the feelings of personal responsibility and guilt that must have coursed through him are starkly missing from his letter to Jessie. Perhaps they were too agonizing to convey; perhaps too excruciating to fully grasp; perhaps he didn't want to diminish himself in Jessie's eyes. "When Godey arrives, I shall know from him all the circumstances sufficiently in detail to enable me to understand clearly everything. But it will not be necessary to tell you anything further. It has been sufficient pain for you to read what I have already written."

For now, he wrote her, he would look forward, not behind, to the moment when he would meet her in California. "When I think of you all, I feel a warm glow at my heart, which renovates it like a good medicine, and I forget painful feelings in a strong hope for the future. We shall yet enjoy quiet and happiness together—these are nearly one and the same to me now. I make frequently pleasant pictures of the happy home we are to have, and oftenest and among the pleasantest of all I see our library, with its bright fire in the rainy, stormy days, and the large windows looking out upon the sea in the bright weather. I have it all planned in my own mind."

John's letter was more than Jessie could bear.

"Alone. Panama, May, 1849," she wrote inside her Book of Common Prayer. "On a narrow strip of land, 'Twixt two unbounded seas, I stand."

A few days later an acquaintance brought her a newspaper that carried an account of the expedition written by her father. The messenger returned the same day at sundown with another report. "He found me where he had left me in the morning—sitting upon the sofa, with the unopened paper clasped in my hand, my eyes closed, and my forehead purple from congestion of the brain, and entirely unable to understand anything said to me. All the long train of troubled feeling and uncertainties and discomforts, aided by the climate had culminated in brain fever."

Jessie was relieved to be certifiably ill, to suffer from something the doctors could diagnose as an actual physical malady. Now she had an excuse to abandon the ineffable emotional pain and relentless mental trauma and succumb to the sheer exhaustion that had overcome her. The kind Señora Arcé summoned both an American and a Spanish doctor, whose recommended courses of treatment canceled each other out. The American prescribed iced drinks, cool compresses to the head, and fresh air. The Spanish physician favored bleeding, hot drinks, and heating pads. "These two, with their contradictory ideas and their inability to understand each other fully, only added to the confusion of my mind, and became part of my delirium. My lungs were congested, and it was needed to apply a blister all over the chest. No leeches could be had, and croton-oil, which would have answered the purpose without leaving disfiguring marks, was not to be found anywhere." She was coughing blood and disoriented by the constant fever.

In the middle of the night on May 6, two steamers entered the harbor, a cannon blast signaling their arrival. Throngs of people rushed to greet the *Oregon* and the *Panama*, shouting to be among those selected for passage to California. Jessie made her way to the ships in the moonlight. "A full-scale riot threatened as it became clear that even the two ships together couldn't transport anywhere near the number clamoring to leave," according to one account. "Bribes were offered, blows exchanged. The situation was resolved by the only method able to command a consensus: a lottery." Standing on the dock, she heard a man call her name. She turned to see a familiar face. The naval officer was on his way to Washington carrying official documents and gold specimens, and bore an urgent message for Jessie—she was to return to Washington at once. He told her of John's leg injury and said that it would be necessary for John to seek medical treatment in Washington. San Francisco was a wildly lawless place, he told her, and without John there to meet her she would face the most dangerous conditions.

"This time I was not advised but ordered to go home, and everything short of force was used to make me return under their care. I had only a few hours to decide, for at the earliest light they had to leave to connect with the returning steamer. In the chronicle of the conquest of Mexico there is one night of disaster and massacre which Bernal Díaz del Castillo records under the head *tristísima noche*; I had had many sad nights since leaving home, but after my old friends left I think I could name this my saddest. After this I did no more deciding, but let myself go with the current."

Twelve days later she and Lily boarded the *Panama* bound for San Francisco, her social and political status having earned for her a waiver from the lottery system. Jessie paid the hotel expenses in Panama for the "maid" from New York, as well as for her passage on to San Francisco "on condition that she never came in my sight." (Jessie would learn later that, in revenge against a landlord, the same woman started one of the

great San Francisco fires of 1851.) The ship, built to hold eighty, over-
flowed with four hundred people. Food was scarce, and their cabin was
hot and airless, which aggravated Jessie's lungs. "The gentleman in the
next stateroom became alarmed by the peculiar sound of the cough
which he understood better than I did, and getting no answer to his
knock opened the door and found me, as he feared, with a broken blood
vessel." Fellow passengers built her a makeshift tent on deck so that she
could inhale the fresh sea air—what she called à la belle étoile.

When the ship dropped its anchor at San Diego a few days later, Jessie refused to disembark, afraid that she would learn the dreaded news that John
was not in California. But a short time later a group of passengers who
had gone on shore returned excitedly to her. "The Colonel was in the Angeles three weeks ago," they shouted. "The Colonel is safe!" He was on his
way from Los Angeles to San Francisco, where he would meet her. He had
not lost a leg after all, she was told, but had been badly frostbitten.

Jessie was elated. Deeply touched by the affection and concern her fellow passengers obviously felt for her, relieved beyond belief that John
had arrived safely in California, brimming with anticipation at their rendezvous, Jessie put the hardships of the past behind her. For the first time
since leaving New York more than two months earlier, a sense of optimism returned to her. She felt the ocean had healed her lungs and her
soul. Like her father had as a young soldier in the War of 1812, she had
cured herself of a life-threatening lung disease. Now, approaching her
twenty-fifth birthday in a few days, the world suddenly, finally, looked
very different—"life seemed very bright and full of happy possibilities."

On June 4 in a foggy dawn—seventeen days after leaving Panama
City—the steamship entered the channel John had named the Golden
Gate. The beach was teeming with men, and a dozen boats approached
the steamer. Jessie searched in vain for John, but he was not among the
crowd. Instead, William Howard, a prosperous gold miner and friend of
John's, greeted her, explaining that John had not yet reached San Francisco. Howard took her and Lily to a private gentlemen's club that had
once been the home of the recently deceased William Leidesdorff—the
same abode where John had stayed three years earlier during the Bear
Flag Revolt, its view of the sea convincing him that he should bring his
family to California.

San Francisco was bedlam—"a bleak and meager frontispiece to our
Book of Fate," as Jessie put it. Canvas and blanket tents dotted the treeless

hills, deserted ships rocked in the harbor, swarms of men milled about in the mud streets of the town inhabited by only sixteen women. More reminiscent of Chagres and Panama City than the Eden John had promised, the uncivilized atmosphere disappointed Jessie. Four houses existed, including a two-story structure belonging to a young New Yorker who had it shipped from the East at a cost of $90,000. The Leidesdorff residence—rented by a group of businessmen for $60,000 per year—was the best-appointed. Furnished with Oriental carpets, French fixtures, and a Broadwood piano, surrounded by a veranda and a garden, the house was drafty and cold to the still-recuperating Jessie. "The June winds were blowing, and I felt them the more from recent illness, which had left the lungs very sensitive." The fireplace was useless as a heat source. "There was no fuel," she wrote, ". . . and little fagots of brushwood, broken up goods boxes and sodden ends of old ship timber were all that could be had."

Jessie grew increasingly anxious while waiting for John. "I was already getting ill again with morbid imaginings that I had been deceived, and that he had not arrived in the country at all." Finally, on her tenth day in San Francisco, while sitting in her gloomy room, she heard a voice in the yard. "Your wife's inside the house, Colonel." She rushed to him, and as they embraced, both wept for a long while, each too overcome with emotion to speak. They had been apart for six months, and each looked severely changed to the other. His limp and bony frame made him seem much older than his thirty-six years. His tanned face was weathered and deeply lined, his blue eyes devoid of their characteristic sparkle. Still, it was Jessie whose infirmity was most pronounced. He carried her to a chair and knelt beside her. Then both began speaking at once, "each wanting the other to begin at the moment we had parted over a stirrup-cup of tea that morning on the Missouri," as Jessie recalled the scene.

"You have been ill, you are ill now, my darling," he said, alarmed by her appearance. Jessie began to deny it when Lily entered the room, the petulant child blaming her father for her mother's suffering. "You didn't come. Mother almost died," Lily said as John lifted her to his knee. "A lady downstairs says she will die." Stricken, John turned to his wife as if hoping for a refutation.

"In her innocence she is partly right," Jessie said. "Being away from you is a kind of death. Only with you am I fully alive and well."

That night in bed they talked for hours. She told him every detail of her trip from New York to Panama to San Francisco, playing down the hardship and fear that had marked the entire journey. He, too, glossed over the tragedy that had befallen his expedition—"reference to the preceding horrors was shunned by both," as one biographer put it—focusing instead on the glorious news of the potential of gold at Las Mariposas. He knew the geology, he *knew* it must be true. By morning Jessie's lungs were hemorrhaging again, and it was obvious that they needed to relocate immediately to a warmer, drier climate.

Before leaving for his last expedition, John had ordered in New Jersey a six-seated surrey to be built for Jessie and shipped around Cape Horn to California. The carriage was warehoused nearby, and John made arrangements to retrieve it. Complete with seats that converted into a bed, leather upholstery, and large storage compartments, the carriage was the first of its kind in California. He presented it to Jessie, appearing with a friend to implore her to embark on an outing he thought would renew her spirits and health. "Madame, we have come to entreat you to make a long leisurely journey overland in your carriage with Lieutenant Beale and myself as outriders and with a few minions and scullions for making camp," he said with dramatic flourish. "My friend Beale makes excellent *pot au feu* when it hasn't too much pepper in it, while I can make a bed of your surrey cushions that will tempt you to sweet slumber."

"Gentlemen, your offer intrigues me," Jessie responded with the same affected manner. "Pray, let us be off at once." But her feigned enthusiasm belied her true feelings. Years later she recalled the anxiety of the moment and the severity of her illness. "I preferred to stay quietly here, as by now all movements had become an effort, but I knew this journey was a desperate remedial measure, and I wanted so much to live."

"The little camping party that moved along the rough but well-traveled road toward the pueblo of San José resembled a gypsy caravan from an Italian opera rather than the sanitarium that it was," wrote one observer. The large black carriage was drawn by two mules—named Job and Picayune by Jessie—and caused excitement wherever they traveled. "Its rolled-up curtains revealed red-leather cushioned seats occupied by a pale dark-eyed young woman closely enveloped in a blue Army cape. Beside her sat a red-cheeked little girl of seven." Frémont, Beale, and several Mexican men Frémont had hired rode horses alongside the carriage. Strangers, recognizing John from the Bear Flag Revolt, saluted him and called him "Don Frémont." They stopped for relaxed noontime meals, and camped every night near a stream. Every evening they built a large campfire and drank "excellent claret" while the men told hunting stories—each "had a large experience of a kind only known to me through books: from Indians, from wild animals, and from war; while I gave the element of society," Jessie recalled. "About nine o'clock all would be still; only the sounds of the logs and boughs as they crackled and burned, and the steady munching of the animals over their feed, with occasionally a disturbance from a coyote that would come and try to steal his supper." Jessie and Lily slept in the carriage, its seats folded down into a bed, while the men slept in grass hammocks stretched between two trees. They would not allow Jessie to participate in any task, the men meeting her every need. For two months they traveled this way, Frémont and Beale nervously watching Jessie for signs of recovery.

For Jessie, it was a blissful time in her life—a glorious excursion up and down the coast, into the interior, and up into the mountains. She felt, for the first time, she gained a glimpse into John's years of exploration that had taken him away from her. John's knowledge of the plants and birds, the geological formations and the astronomical constellations, the wildlife and rivers, enthralled her. Following ancient horse trails, camping under the stars, cooking over a fire, John brought all of his explorer skills to bear, for his part eager to show her who he was, what this life in the wilderness was about, beyond the stories he had told her. Here was a man who knew the difference between the savory chanterelle mushrooms and their poisonous impostors, who could build a hot fire with aromatic wood, who could take her safely to the brink of splendorous chasms, who could teach her the difference between the call of the bluebird and the love song of the jay, how to listen for the bellowing of the elk and find the serenade in the coyote's lament. Both loved the wilderness and found regeneration in themselves and each other.

They visited the ranches of the native Californians, and Jessie was struck by "their genuine hospitality and their good housekeeping, their immense families—fourteen, twenty, even twenty-six children among whom sickness was unknown, and the wonderful grandmothers—all were proofs of the fine climate." One of these "grandmothers" particularly affected Jessie, the elderly Señora Castro symbolizing "a type of this patriarchal and contented people as they were until we brought among them our American unrest and turmoil. She wished to thank me in person for 'Don Flémon's' protection of all women during the military movements in taking the country."

But the idyll ended when Jessie's hacking cough returned with the arrival of the rainy season. Fearing that the damp San Francisco weather would exacerbate her condition, they decided to move permanently a hundred miles south, to Monterey. Though just a village, the old capital seemed a paradise to Jessie, its noble adobe villas scattered among the hillsides overlooking the bay. Sunny and warm, with massive pine trees that swayed in the breeze and filled the town with their fresh scent, Monterey was inhabited almost entirely by women and children. "There was a small garrison of married officers with their families," she later wrote, "but no man of any degree voluntarily kept away from the mines or San Francisco; it was their great opportunity for sudden money-making." There, ensconced, ironically, in a wing of the regal home of Señora Castro—the wife of José Castro, Frémont's onetime nemesis in the Gavilán Peak incident, and who was now in exile in Mexico—Jessie would embark on frontier domestic life while John would turn his attention to developing the gold veins on the Mariposa property.

It was during this time that Jessie experienced one of several vivid telepathic incidents that would occur throughout her life. It was June 1849.

I was in Monterey, California, ill from Panama fever—two severe hemorrhages from the lungs, and depressed by homesickness and illness. Mr. Frémont had gone up to the Mariposas to ascertain its value. So I was alone too. I had cried myself to sleep when this dream came to me:

I, at my present age—25—was back in the old home of my Aunt Edmonia. But as a strange visitor. I had been taken into the large front parlor and some way understood I was not to go into the bright sunny room where we used to sit, and have the music. I tried to talk with my Aunt, but only fell on my knees and buried my head in her lap—"I can't stand this being from home—I want to die."

"You must live," said my Aunt—"when we die to ourselves, *then* we begin to live for others. You have a great work to do." Then laying her hands on my head and lifting it as she smiled on me, "*You will help free the slave,*" and she vanished. Only calling back "write this down. *Now.*"

Jessie awakened from the dream, lit candles in the three A.M. darkness, and promptly and exactly recorded the entire dream—a contemporaneous copy of which she would send to her father. Only later would Jessie learn that her Aunt Edmonia's son was Stonewall Jackson's "right-hand-man,"

and only later would Jessie come to believe that, by virtue of her proximity, Edmonia "foresaw the effort to plant a slave state in California"
and was telepathically warning Jessie.

Benton, who always took Jessie seriously, placed her letter between the
pages of a favorite book for safekeeping. There it would remain for the
next forty years.

In Monterey, the coddled days of Jessie's youth and young adulthood
seemed an increasingly distant memory. As she set up housekeeping in
primitive circumstances, neither her wealth nor her breeding sheltered
her from the hardships of life that existed for all pioneer women of her
era. She created a home environment with the few provisions available.
"It was barely a year since the gold had been discovered," she wrote of
this period, "but in that time every eatable thing had been eaten off the
face of the country, and nothing raised. I suppose there was not a fowl
left in the northern part of the state, consequently not an egg; all the
beef cattle left had been bought up . . . There were no cows, consequently no milk. Housekeeping, deprived of milk, eggs, vegetables, and
fresh meat, becomes a puzzle."

Still, she brought her legendary resourcefulness to bear, serving canned
goods and rice on Canton china, and set about to decorate the rustic
house with Oriental fabrics, teak, cane, and bamboo furniture John
found for her in San Francisco, bear and buffalo rugs from John's outings, and baskets and other Indian artifacts. The wives of American soldiers immediately embraced her, but the native California women of
Spanish descent—"to whom my name represented only invasion and
defeat"—were standoffish. She found them dignified and gracious, "erect
and of free firm movement. You could see that neither in mind or body
had they known depressing influences," she wrote of them. "I do not
like to remember how we changed all that. A carefully drawn treaty had
guarded their rights, but this proved of no avail."

But before long, her fluent Spanish made her a favorite among them,
and she developed close friendships with many of the women, whom
she found charming. She was struck by their sense of fashion—their full
petticoats "of scarlet broadcloth with points of green silk, stitched beautifully . . . over this a gown of the dulltoned damasked Chinese satin."
They reminded her of the women of her genteel Southern past, their
homes neat and orderly, their children busy and content, their needs attended to by sweet and loyal "domesticated Indian girls," as the women

continually planned the next grand ball. They had an obsession with satin dresses, which they kept stored in brightly painted Chinese trunks, had what Jessie called a "passion" for household linen, and most of them smoked hand-rolled cigarettes. Their homes were decorated with French clocks and ornate chandeliers. "Pictures of church subjects and hunting scenes were to be met everywhere."

The tragedies of their past firmly behind them, Jessie moved gracefully and logically into the larger role in life she had been bred and reared to fulfill. "Now, commencing a new life in California, she would begin to assert an independence and display a self-confidence commensurate with her long-standing intellectual and social precocity," wrote historian Tom Chaffin. She began hosting the salons that would bring her recognition and renown throughout the territory, bringing together the most progressive minds in frontier California—both American migrants and native Californians—and soon, inevitably, both she and John became enmeshed in the lively and raucous politics of the new territory. Within months they struck gold at Las Mariposas, and with such overwhelming financial success the anguish and fatigue disappeared completely from John's face. "Up to a certain point everything seemed to be against us," she wrote. "Then the tide turned, and it was indeed a flood of good fortune."

Frémont traveled regularly between Monterey and Las Mariposas, where his twenty-eight Sonoran workers mined $25,000 worth of gold a month. In accordance with his original deal, Frémont took 50 percent and the Mexican men shared the rest. The Frémonts could barely accommodate the piles of hundred-pound buckskin sacks of gold that filled their Monterey home. "There were no banks nor places of deposit of any kind," wrote Jessie. "You had had to trust some man that you knew, or keep guard yourself." The placer mine was so vast that it became necessary for Frémont to hire more men. He paid $5 a day to his workers, and still the profits were exorbitant. Then, in the fall of 1849, a vein five miles long was discovered on his land—a strike so rich it could be expected to bring more than $16 million a year. "We were in the most delightful season of the year," Jessie wrote, "no rains, no heavy dews; the wild oats were ripe, and gave the soft look of ripe wheat fields to the hillsides; the wild cattle were feeding about or resting under the evergreen oaks, which looked so like orchard trees that one was disappointed not to find the apples on the ground beneath them; the sky was a deep blue, without a cloud. We were young and full of health, and in all the exhilaration of sudden wealth which could enable us to realize our greatest wishes." Finally, they thought, they could be free of meddle-some bureaucrats, jealous colleagues, and sinister machinations.

Jessie and Lily joined John frequently in his travels to the ranch, located high in the Sierra Nevada on land Jessie found breathtaking—"resembling in beauty the grandeur of Chamonix in France—even Grindelwald in Switzerland," as one account described the terrain. Lodgepole pines and salmon-filled rivers, clover-covered ground and quaking aspen marked the forty-three-thousand-acre estate. They named a prominent peak on the land Mount Bullion in honor of her father, "old Bullion Benton." Wearing a sombrero and native-style clothing made by locals, Frémont oversaw the enterprise from a two-story frame house he had had built in Bear Valley, and now, as a man of great wealth, became ever more famous as Easterners—ravenous for news of Gold Rush California—read his ex-pedition reports with a new passion. "I have seen in no other man the qualities of lightness, activity, strength, and physical endurance in so per-fect an equilibrium," wrote a *New York Tribune* correspondent who vis-ited Frémont during this time. The Frémonts also established a home in San Francisco—a prefabricated Chinese structure fitted together with grooves instead of nails and for which they paid $90,000—on the site of what later became the Palace Hotel. There, Jessie entertained the many adventurers and writers pouring into the city, and the family lived what Lily later described as a nomadic and fun-filled existence among Mon-terey, Las Mariposas, and San Francisco.

But soon, inevitably, problems arose as word spread of the incredible Mariposa Lode. Not "a mere mining enterprise," as Frémont's biogra-pher Allan Nevins described Las Mariposas, "but . . . one of the great controlling influences upon Frémont's career . . . a perfect Pandora's box of complications . . . a will-of-the-wisp, beckoning him forward with promises of stupendous wealth, sometimes placing small gifts within his grasp, and yet always cheating him." Frémont had neither the financial wherewithal nor the physical ability to extract the gold from such a rich vein, and set out to find investors and laborers. Proslavery agitators pressed him to solve his problems with slave labor, and his strong anti-slavery stance brought him attention throughout the territory and, even-tually, the nation. "With slave labor there would be no delay in opening up the mineral wealth of the country, and to the fabulous profits of the owners," Jessie wrote of the heated political debate. "Slave holders and speculators in slaves only waited the decision to bring them overland in great droves." John and Jessie resisted all proslavery arguments. "With slaves in the mines, as our Southern friends constantly urged upon us, we would have certain and immediate wealth by millions," Jessie wrote. "Our decision was made on the side of free labor. It was not only the question of injustice to the blacks, but of justice to the white men crowding into the country."

Instead, Frémont sought a solution abroad. Believing that English capitalists would be the key to his success, in June 1850 he engaged an American businessman living in London to seek partners in that country. David Hoffman, a former law professor, began organizing mining companies in London on the basis of leases. A month later Frémont had signed leases with seventeen parties, even though he had no clear proof of title to the land or its mineral content. Racial tensions also mounted, as native Latino Californians saw lands their families had held for generations appropriated by *yanquis*, and violence increasingly riddled the mining camps.

Frémont found it impossible to manage his property—"small armies of Argonauts were invading the Mariposa," wrote one historian, "stripping the richest placers of their gold." He and his Sonoran miners were no match for the squatters, many of them sent by French companies attracted to the mine by Frémont's celebrity status in France. The situation was utter chaos, matters further complicated by the murky boundary, a disputed land grant, and a challenge to mineral rights that would mire Frémont for years in extensive and expensive litigation, inspiring his critics to accuse him of greed and corruption. Ultimately proving himself, at the least, an inept businessman, he collateralized the property and oversold shares in the enterprise. Frémont would struggle for years to maintain control of, and further exploit, Las Mariposas. It would not be until six years, and millions of dollars in expenses later—after hiring his brother-in-law, William Carey Jones; his personal attorney, Montgomery Blair; and former senator and U.S. attorney general John Crittenden—that Frémont would receive clear title to the land. Years later, after a terrible, unrelated breach, Blair would complain that Frémont had never paid him for his services. Whether Frémont was bungling or venal, or a dangerous combination, the property would be his Achilles heel for most of the rest of his life.

Still, despite the hurdles and controversies surrounding the mine, Frémont's prosperity and hero status would launch him effortlessly into California politics, and just as naturally onto the national stage. "It was widely said that John Charles Frémont—California conqueror, senator's son-in-law, and gold-rush millionaire—could have his pick of offices," wrote one historian. He accepted President Zachary Taylor's appointment to survey the new U.S.–Mexico boundary—an offer the Frémonts and Benton regarded as a magnanimous and public apology for the harsh treatment of Frémont during his Washington court-martial—but he resigned the position almost immediately. "The commission sent in such a way had to be accepted for a time at least," wrote Jessie. "But as it would have involved some years of stay out there, there was no hesitation about not holding it. Our new independence was too complete and too sweet to be given up for any cause. That long white envelope, with its official stamp in the corner, which brings such terror into officers' families, and sounds the note of separation to so many, was not again to come to us; henceforth we were to direct our own movements." In any event, they now had political ambitions.

In September 1849 forty-eight delegates came to Monterey for a constitutional convention to create a civilian territorial government as California made its way toward statehood. The territory was near anarchy, the U.S. military regime incapable of keeping order while vigilantes and ad hoc courts dispensed crude frontier justice. "Mingling together were Missouri farmers, Yankee sailors, Georgia crackers, English shopkeepers, French peasants, Australian sheepherders, Mexican peons, 'heathen Chinee,' and a liberal sprinkling of 'assassins manufactured in Hell,'" as two historians described the milieu, "all drawn to California by the magnet of gold." When it became clear to Californians that Congress was hopelessly mired in the slavery and statehood debate—arguing the question of congressional power over territories and obviously incapable of quickly establishing a working government—President Taylor urged Californians to create a constitution and apply for admission to the Union. That year alone, more than eighty thousand migrants had settled in California, and the necessity for civil order had reached a crisis.

The flood of migrants West was unprecedented, due to what a Chicago newspaper attributed to "the universal desire of free laborers to possess land." The South, alarmed at the potential threat to its power in Congress, lobbied relentlessly for the newly conquered territories to be admitted as slave states. Though the House had a Northern majority and the Senate was technically balanced, Democratic Party loyalty and seniority provided the South with a tacit superior edge. "What it all came down to was whether the western social order would resemble that of the South or of the North," wrote historian Eric Foner. ". . . To northerners who were moving west, or hoped to, the question of slavery in the territories had a direct personal impact."

Jessie always saw slavery as the pivotal issue in California statehood, and became actively involved in fighting the institution. "The government had its special agents to support the slavery side," she wrote, "and southern planters had their throngs of negroes waiting at the frontier . . . they were sure of getting slavery in." When a wealthy Texan attempted to sell her a slave she refused, stating publicly that "for no reason would I consent to own or use a slave." Jessie had been fervently antislavery since childhood, when her mother, as an active member of the colonization society, taught family slaves to read, and then freed all the slaves she had inherited from her father's Cherry Grove estate—"because of her conscientious feeling on the subject"—financing some of them in their own businesses and sending the rest to their desired destinations of Canada or Liberia. Both John and Jessie were struck by the paradox that John's exploration of the West had energized the very proslavery forces they so abhorred.

"Mr. Frémont has called this the Italy of America," Jessie told a group of proslavery leaders. "It is an ideal place for small homes and well-tended acreage. If we keep slave labor out, we will have the wealthy and comfortable middle class, but no poor," perhaps echoing the opinion of her father and other Jacksonian Democrats who were more concerned with protecting the rights of free white labor than with providing real equality for blacks. Benton, according to historian Sean Wilentz, "wanted to halt the expansion of slavery and to keep the West, as far as possible, lily-white."

One of the men challenged Jessie: "Fine sentiment, Mrs. Frémont, but the aristocracy will always have slaves."

"But why not an aristocracy of emancipators?" Jessie asked. "We Bentons could qualify for that. We freed our slaves long ago at voluntary sacrifice of money. Mr. Frémont and I have refused two legacies of slaves."

Undaunted and indefatigable, Jessie actively engaged the proslavery delegates. "It isn't a pretty sight in a free country for a child to see and hear chain gangs clanking through the streets or to watch officers chasing a fugitive slave and putting him in irons," she told one adversary. "Nor does such an advertisement as I recall make good juvenile reading: 'Sale of twenty-six valuable negroes, tobacco, and provender from the

Mendell estate,' or 'Fifty dollars' reward for the return of a black girl Nancy, five feet tall, thick built, and strong.' "

Whether John was as passionately antislavery as Jessie—at least at the beginning of the 1850s—is debatable. A confessed Democrat who belonged to the Free-Soil wing of the party, Frémont was not overtly political. He was widely seen as a creature of Jessie's own aspirations—ambition she could fulfill only through her husband, constrained as she was by the societal and cultural limitations for women. She "was the better man of the two, far more intelligent and more comprehensive," an acquaintance described her. But in the ensuing years, though always remote and contemplative, John's actions on behalf not only of the antislavery forces, but the more radical pro–civil rights factions as well, would be unimpeachable.

Their Monterey home became the headquarters of the antislavery delegates of the constitutional convention, with Jessie the unmistakable leader of what were called "star-chamber meetings." At these gatherings she prided herself in setting a fine table. "Every one knows the important part of a good dinner in diplomacy," she reasoned. "The great Napoleon knew and acted on this." The peripatetic John was often at Las Mariposas, but Jessie held court in Monterey and furthered their cause with commitment and determination. When one visitor expressed regret at Frémont's unavailability, another reassured him: "If you want the real Washington situation with well-thought-out opinions on it, ask Miss Jessie." One of the wealthiest women in America—"and growing wealthier by the week," as one historian put it—Jessie, as daughter of Benton and wife of Frémont, was also one of the more famous and powerful women in the country.

In November, a constitution—including a clause barring slavery—was unanimously accepted and referred to the voters of California for ratification. Only thirteen thousand came to the polls, and the new charter was accepted by a margin of fifteen to one. By December, John C. Frémont was the Democratic candidate for the U.S. Senate. "Mr. Frémont could have been either Governor or first Senator from the state," Jessie wrote. "As Governor he could have overlooked his private interests to the greatest advantage—in certain ways have been of most use to the state; but, on the other hand, as Senator he could defend the interests of the state in Congress." Running on a platform that opposed slavery and favored a transcontinental railroad, he defended his actions both as territorial governor in 1847 and in his acquisition of Las Mariposas. "I am strongly in favor of a central, national railroad from the Mississippi River to the Pacific Ocean," he wrote in the first political letter he had ever penned, responding to a constituent who publicly questioned his political and philosophical beliefs. "Recent events have converted the vague desire for that work into an organized movement, throughout the great body of our fellow citizens in the United States, and in common with them, I am warmly in favor of its immediate location and speediest possible construction. Its stupendous magnitude—the immense benefit which it will confer upon our whole country—the changes which it will operate throughout the Pacific Ocean and eastern Asia—commingling together the European, American, and Asiatic races—spreading indefinitely religious, social and political improvement—characterize it as the greatest enterprise of the age, and a great question proposed for the solution of the American people." As for Las Mariposas, Frémont described how Larkin had acquired the tract of land for him. "I regard the claim to the Mariposa in the same light as any other vested right. It was a purchase fairly made, and I have always supposed that at some future time the validity of the claim would be settled by the proper courts. I am satisfied to await that decision, whether it be favorable or otherwise, and in the meantime to leave the gold, as it is now, free to all who have the industry to collect it."

The legislature convened in San José on December 17 for its inaugural session and, in a compromise between the two factions, selected physician William Gwin as the proslavery advocate and Frémont the antislavery. As was customary in new states entering the Union, the two candidates drew straws to see who would serve a short term and who a longer term until a statewide election could be held to elect senators for a full six-year term.

Jessie waited in Monterey, housebound for several days due to uncharacteristically violent storms. On a dark, dreary evening just before Christmas, she sat before the fire with Lily, the two poring over copies of illustrated London newspapers. Suddenly Jessie heard hoofbeats in the rain and was startled when John burst through the door. "I couldn't wait," he told her, laughing. "I've ridden from San José to be first to greet Jessie Frémont, Senator's lady from the state of California."

"Mr. Frémont came in upon us, dripping wet, as well he might be, for he had come . . . seventy miles on horseback through heavy rain," Jessie recalled the moment. While she had enjoyed her time in California, she was homesick for her family and friends. "He was so wet that we could hardly make him cross the pretty room; but 'beautiful are the feet of him that beareth glad tidings,' and the footmarks were all welcome, for they pointed home." At daybreak he mounted his favorite sorrel horse to return to San José—"one hundred and forty miles within thirty-six hours, without fatigue to either."

Still, Frémont's new position as U.S. senator would not be official until Congress accepted California as the thirty-first state—and in the winter of 1849 such congressional action was far from guaranteed.

Opposition to California statehood had been fierce since the beginning of the Mexican-American War, when, in 1846, a Democratic congressman, David Wilmot, introduced an amendment to an appropriations bill stipulating that none of the territory acquired from Mexico would be open to slavery. Though the bill passed the House of Representatives, the Senate adjourned without voting on it. During the next session of Congress, Wilmot again introduced an antislavery measure, and the House passed it again. But the Senate created its own bill, excluding the Wilmot Proviso, as it had come to be known, and the proviso became emblematic of the conflict between the North and the South over the extension of slavery.

The episode captured what Northerners saw as a stark and dangerous reality. Though the North held the power in the population-apportioned House, influence was equally distributed in the Senate between fifteen Northern states and fifteen Southern states. "The voting on the Wilmot Proviso reminded northerners of the imperfectly democratic character of Congress," wrote historian Brands, "in which southerners wielded more power per person than northerners, and it inspired many northerners to try to break the southern hold by admitting more free states." Mythologized by later historians as a bold and humanitarian gesture, the proviso was in fact a pragmatic attempt to protect the rights of white laborers—not to endorse equality for blacks. Wilmot himself admitted he had "no morbid sympathy for the slave."

In December 1849, President Taylor made his recommendations to Congress: statehood for California, and New Mexico and Utah organized as territories. Led by the intrepid South Carolina senator John C. Calhoun, every Southern senator denounced the president. "I trust we shall persist in our resistance until the restoration of our rights, or disunion, one or the other, is the consequence," Calhoun charged. "We have borne the wrongs and insults of the North long enough." Though old and weakened by tuberculosis, too week even to deliver his own speech on the Senate floor, his voice barely a whisper, the former vice president, an intellectual giant and a legendary senator once called the "Cast-Iron Man" for his inflexibility, Calhoun still wielded enormous power. Northern extremists responded with equal passion and vitriol, while Henry Clay of Kentucky and Daniel Webster of Massachusetts advocated a compromise supported by many moderates of both sides. The issue of California statehood had triggered a national crisis, and the country seemed poised for disunion.

It was into this tempest of controversy and heated political debate that John and Jessie would rush headlong. If they had truly believed their past days of strife were over, they were sorely naïve and mistaken. For America was entering its darkest night, and the young California couple would find themselves in the middle of the most divisive sectional struggle in the nation's history.

On New Year's night of 1850, Jessie heard the steamer's gun as it entered the harbor at Monterey. The rain had not let up for weeks, and the streets were rushing streams. "Mr. Frémont carried me down, warmly wrapped up, to the wharf, where we got into a little boat and rowed out." The family embarked on the *Oregon* bound for New York through Panama. Carrying the two new California senators, as well as $3 million in gold dust belonging to Frémont, the vessel was saluted in Mazatlán by an English man-of-war anchored off the Mexican coast.

"We had planned to stay in California about seven years," Jessie wrote, ". . . our first object to live our lives in independence, and with the animating motive and object, to me, that in about seven years I should return to my people." But the discovery of gold had changed all that and now, a mere nine months later, they were returning to Washington not as downcast exiles but as victorious emissaries from a new world. It was with a mixture of excitement and sadness that they turned their backs on California, the invigorating outdoor life and unhindered freedom they had sought and embraced. They were nervous as well about leaving Las Mariposas in the hands of California friends, but they resolutely turned their sights to the future, each ecstatic at the opportunities before them.

"Frémont would have been more than human had he not felt a certain exultation in the changed circumstances of his return East," Allan Nevins wrote of him during this time. "A year and a half earlier he had been traveling west on the Great Lakes, an impoverished young man of bleak prospects, just resigned under attack from the army. Now he was coming back a Senator-elect, his trunk full of buckskin bags of gold dust, with the title to one of the richest tracts on the Coast in his possession."

For her part, Jessie was elated to be returning to her father's home, especially under such triumphant circumstances. She missed her invalid mother, her siblings and friends, and though she had thoroughly enjoyed California—playing hostess in a lively political atmosphere, touring in her carriage through spectacular landscapes, fraternizing with native Californians and American adventurers—Washington was still her home. She had left a frightened and insecure young woman, and was returning with a newfound confidence. "Her California experience brought forth her latent courage and independence," wrote biographer Pamela Herr. "What at first seemed banishment had become an escape from Victorian America, a release that put her in touch with her own buried powers. But there was danger lurking in Jessie's new strength, for she would now find it far harder to resume the narrow life she had once so reluctantly left behind."

By the time they reached Panama, twenty days later, Jessie, Lily, and John were extremely ill—Jessie with malaria, Lily with Chagres fever, and John with rheumatism in the leg that had been frostbitten. John and Jessie were dangerously near death, and found it necessary to stay a month in Panama City, where Señora Arcé nursed them in her home. John recovered first, while Jessie, racked with fever and drugged with opium, was carried by a makeshift stretcher onto the New York–bound steamer. The sea voyage was stormy, and Jessie awoke once to find herself lashed to a sofa on deck so she wouldn't fall overboard as the ship rolled and pitched.

She and John, recounting all the hardships they had suffered in the past year, determined the health risks were too great to ever contemplate a return crossing to California. "Having just gone through the experience that all our 'best laid plans had gone agley,' and that it was of no use for man to propose when the whole chapter of accidents lay open to dispose of you otherwise, I would lie contentedly making plans for the long peaceful time ahead of me in Washington." She had no way of knowing, of course, that eight months later she would again be at sea, and would again become ill at the isthmus, in one of many journeys to California throughout her life. "But it is only the Immortals who read the Book of Destiny," she would write many years later. "Fortunately for us, we live our lives only as we see the days."

They arrived in New York City in March, dragging themselves from the harbor to a luxurious hotel. "We were a sorry-looking lot," Jessie recalled. Lily's long, silken hair had been shaved during her feverish illness, and a faded bandanna covered her bare head. Jessie was bone-thin, her dark blue, once stylish riding habit "hanging straight and shapeless about my ankles as the clothes on the women in a Noah's ark." Generously doling out gold, they took a lavish suite at the uptown Irving House—rooms that had been specially decorated for the Swedish soprano Jenny Lind, who was touring the United States with P. T. Barnum. Filled with white roses and violets, the warmly carpeted suite was a vivid reminder to Jessie of her indulged childhood. They took long, hot baths and rested for two days before venturing out to spend more gold on new wardrobes. Once they felt rejuvenated and presentable, they made their way to Washington—the dashing first senator from California and his glamorous wife.

"No person living understands better than I the term 'speechless with joy,'" Jessie wrote of her reunion with the Benton family. "Father, mother, all the others in the old home greeting us, our old rooms with their heavenly smells of geraniums, old friends greeting us, the whole city greeting us! I took sedate little walks down Pennsylvania Avenue and across the Common in the spring twilight, but I wanted to run and shout, to hug the tree trunks, to drop down on the ground and lay my cheek against the new grass, to kiss the crocuses and wild violets, and to float away upon that misty gray-green cloud of young leaves above me."

Feted at balls and private dinners, the couple moved seamlessly back into Washington society. Socializing with Daniel Webster and Harriet Bodisco—"heavy now, a mountain of lace and jewels," as one account described Jessie's longtime friend, whose Russian husband had recently died—Washington mayor William Winston Seaton, Henry Wadsworth Longfellow, the Blairs, and a host of New York abolitionists and Washington political figures, Jessie and John were once again the talk of the town. "He listened with grave deference to whoever was speaking," Seaton wrote of Frémont's reticent demeanor during the early days of their return to the capital, "but under cover of general conversation he lapsed into frequent silences, his glance resting with scarcely veiled admiration on his wife as she spoke and laughed with the sparkle of a carefree school girl. When Jessie caught his glance upon her, there was an exchange which I can only describe as a mental wink, a flash of eye, a fleeting smile, discreet flirtation throughout the long dinner."

The discussion at all events centered on slavery and sectionalism, and while the debate about possible disunion was grave and politically charged, social civility still reigned during the spring of 1850 as Frémont waited to take his seat in the U.S. Senate. Unable to assume their positions until California was formally admitted to the Union, Frémont and his newly elected colleague, Gwin, lobbied Congress. "The Government of the United States has been three years indebted to the people of California for property taken and services rendered," Frémont wrote in a letter published in the *National Intelligencer*, "and during this time they have been without representation, and without protection." What had effectively been a largely academic debate centering on the Wilmot Proviso became actuality when Frémont and Gwin appeared in Washington. The arrival of the two duly elected California senators forced Congress to immediately accept or reject California statehood—and with that, a decision on the fate of American slavery.

Southern extremists and Northern abolitionists galvanized their positions, and by summer the political climate had become hostile and polarized. Kentucky's elder statesman Henry Clay—known as "The Great Compromiser" for his role in the Missouri Compromise of 1820 that divided the Louisiana Territory between slave and free states, and again in the Nullification Crisis when South Carolina threatened disunion—rose once again to the helm. But the revered Whig was ultimately ineffectual, the mythology surrounding his machinations notwithstanding. It would be a young Democratic senator from Illinois, Stephen A. Douglas, who brilliantly engineered the passage of what would become known as the Compromise of 1850, though even the moniker is deceptive. In his magisterial *The Impending Crisis*, David M. Potter called it "a truce perhaps, an armistice, certainly a settlement, but not a true compromise."

"[T]he very idea that the bargain was a compromise is misleading," Sean Wilentz wrote in his 2005 book *The Rise of American Democracy*. "A genuine compromise involves each side conceding something in order to reach an accord . . . The phrase 'Compromise of 1850' . . . has been so routinely repeated by generations of historians and schoolteachers that it is unlikely ever to be replaced. But the bargain was actually more of a balancing act, a truce that delayed, but could not prevent, even greater crises over slavery."

Clay's compromise contained eight resolutions that proposed admitting California as a free state, organizing Utah and New Mexico as territories with no restrictions on slavery, adjudicating in favor of New

Mexico in its boundary dispute with Texas, assuming Texas's $10 million debt, abolishing the slave trade in the District of Columbia while allowing slavery to continue in the nation's capital, stiffening the Fugitive Slave Law, and denying congressional authority over the slave trade in or between slave states. On February 5, 1850, Clay launched one of the most historic debates in U.S. history, speaking before Congress for two full days in support of his bill. The border state moderate, determined to hold his beloved Union together, railed at his colleagues. "It is passion, passion—party, party—and intemperance; that is all I dread in the adjustment of the great questions which unhappily at this time divide our distracted country. At this moment, we have in the legislative bodies of this Capitol, and in the States, twenty-odd furnaces in full blast in generating heat and passion and intemperance, and diffusing them throughout the whole extent of this broad land. Two months ago, all was calm in comparison with the present moment. All now is uproar, confusion, menace to the existence of the Union and to the happiness and safety of this people." He would have spoken for a third day had a colleague not interrupted him. He brought his speech to an end with a stirring plea. "And, finally, Mr. President, I implore, as the best blessing which Heaven can bestow upon me upon earth, that if the direful and sad event of the dissolution of the Union shall happen, I may not survive to behold the sad and heart-rending spectacle." Indeed, he would be dead in two years.

The legendary Calhoun answered Clay—the dying senator's last great speech read for him by his friend Senator James Mason of Virginia. Exhibiting what historian Richard Hofstadter called Calhoun's long-standing obsession "with the North's tendency to 'monopolize' the territories for free labor," Calhoun contended the current crisis had been spurred by a Northern conspiracy to admit California. Speaking on behalf of the Southern extremists, Calhoun warned that the South would accept nothing less than a constitutional amendment protecting its institutions and equal access to the Mexican territories. He closed with a wearied resignation. "I have exerted myself . . . with the intention of saving the Union, if it could be done; and, if it could not, to save the section where it has pleased Providence to cast my lot, and which I sincerely believe has justice and the Constitution on its side. Having faithfully done my duty to the best of my ability, both to the Union and my section, throughout this agitation, I shall have the consolation, let what will come, that I am free from all responsibility." Two months later, Calhoun would be dead.

Daniel Webster spoke next, as hundreds of observers filled the Senate chambers to hear the famously handsome and accomplished orator. The Massachusetts senator spoke on behalf of moderate Northerners, advocating a compromise. "I speak today for the preservation of the Union," Webster began. Holding his audience spellbound, Webster's measured thoughtfulness—what some saw as ambiguity—"stirred up a groundswell of sentiment for compromise," as one account put it—and cost him the admiration of many Northern Free-Soilers.

William Seward of New York addressed members on behalf of the antislavery Northerners. An uncompromising foe of slavery, Seward attacked Clay's proposal as "radically wrong and essentially vicious." While contending that Congress had the constitutional authority to ban slavery, he appealed to the "higher law" of God—or perhaps to the idea that the land itself was not conducive to slavery, making the issue moot. For the extremists he represented—like those represented by Calhoun—there could be no compromise. The three-hour speech elevated the freshman senator to hero status in the antislavery districts of the North—setting the stage for his eventual presidential candidacy—while it spawned vitriol from the South.

The debate continued into the sweltering summer, but Clay's "omnibus" bill languished, with the once-powerful statesman barely able to rally a third of the members to his cause. Thomas Hart Benton—who robustly opposed Clay's compromise not only because he despised Clay, but also because he was against the extension of slavery and impatient for California statehood—addressed the Senate on June 10, attacking Southern slaveholders for making California the "scape-goat of all the sins of slavery in the United States." His outspoken stance would run counter to the views of his Missouri Democratic constituency, marking him as a Northern sympathizer and dealing a fatal blow to his bid for reelection to a sixth term. "[M]y father, a veteran leader who never felt his full power except in opposition, put forth all his strength and was true to the Missouri Compromise under which he had been admitted to the Senate thirty years before," Jessie wrote. "A new election was impending in Missouri and he realized the consequences to himself of this position against the South. The word went forth: 'Slay him.' And slay him they did."

What seemed a deadlock for the "Compromise" changed with the sudden death of President Taylor, who was stricken with what was thought to be food poisoning on July 4 and succumbed five days later. Vice President Millard Fillmore ascended to the presidency and threw his support behind Clay. "A pragmatic second-rater to whom compromise was second nature," as one account portrayed the conservative New Yorker, who was Seward's opponent in New York's Whig Party, Fillmore pressured Congress to no avail. At the end of July, Clay's bill was defeated and its demoralized architect retreated to Rhode Island for a much-needed rest. His younger colleagues remained behind in Washington, led by the diminutive Stephen Douglas, who was determined to break apart the "omnibus bill" and usher its individual resolutions through Congress. By September the bills had been passed one by one. California entered the Union as a free state. Utah and New Mexico could become slave or free depending upon their state constitutions. The Texas–New Mexico boundary was fixed, and the United States assumed Texas's debt. Slavery would continue in the District of Columbia, but the slave trade in the capital was abolished, and fugitive slave laws were strengthened.

The nation's capital erupted in celebration. Clay, Webster, and Douglas were serenaded at their residences with revelers singing "The Star-Spangled Banner," and a one-hundred-gun salute sounded through the city. The Union, for now, had been preserved.

On September 11, 1850, John C. Frémont was sworn into the U.S. Senate for what would be a mere twenty-one days before the first session of the Thirty-first Congress ended. He launched into his Senate career with energy and focus—though still suffering from recurring bouts of painful rheumatism in his leg—and during his brief tenure distinguished himself as an uncompromising abolitionist, severing ties with his native Southern roots and forging coalitions with Northern antislavery men such as Seward and Ohio Free-Soiler Salmon P. Chase. "His votes on the question of Slavery were with the Northern side," Jessie later wrote, "and it was here that his alienation from the Democratic party commenced." Joining what one author called "a club of gentlemen in stiff collars, with beards and whiskers askew, who argued every procedural point that divided South from North," he was roundly regarded as a surrogate of the redoubtable Benton. Predictably, he inherited his father-in-law's enemies in the Senate, and after only a few days he encountered Benton's hotheaded rival Henry Stuart Foote. The diminutive, bald Mississippi legislator had recently drawn a pistol on Benton and now transferred his hostility to Frémont, whom he accused of "corrupt private motives," relating to Frémont's proposed legislation that Foote alleged would benefit Las Mariposas. Challenging him to a duel, Frémont backed down when Foote withdrew his offensive remarks—"Mr. Foote went out of his way . . . to deliver a deliberately considered insult and defiance to me."

Frémont refused to let the Foote fracas distract him, and in a few short weeks introduced eighteen bills relating to California—which Jessie helped him pen—including legislation to provide for the appointment of an Indian agent and the establishment of postal routes and expedition of the confirmation of land titles, gold-mining regulations that secured "to the miner the entire product of his labor," and appropriations for the construction of public universities, an insane asylum, and a transcontinental wagon road. What became known as his "Indian Bill" was based upon what Frémont described as the "general policy of Spain, in her Indian relations," providing that the "Indian right of occupation was respected, but the ultimate dominion remained in the Crown. Wherever the policy of Spain differed from that of the other European nations, it was always in favor of the Indians . . . The policy of Spain in regard to the Indians, differed somewhat from that of the United States, and particularly in this: that, instead of removing the Indians from amidst the Spanish population, it kept them there, and protected them in the possession of their lands among their civilized neighbors." In California, Frémont informed his Senate colleagues, there existed converted Christian Indians and the "wild Indians of the mountains, who were never reduced to subjection." Still, all California natives, according to Frémont, disputed the Americans' right to be there. "Our occupation is in conflict with theirs," he argued in support of his proposed legislation, "and it is to render this occupation legal and equitable, and to preserve the peace, that I have introduced this bill."

Even South Carolina senator Robert W. Barnwell, a staunch proslavery advocate, was impressed with the urgency Frémont brought to the issues facing California. "I must admit that the Colonel showed statesmanlike qualities in so prompt and clear a presentation of bills covering the immediate needs of his infant charge," Barnwell remarked at a Washington dinner party. His colleagues quickly saw Frémont as the authority on all matters relating to California, and though he gave numerous speeches, they "were always brief and in their structure almost exclusively expository," according to one account. "[He] never rose without having something to say, and always sat down when he had said it. He displayed great clearness and precision of statement in the few forensic efforts which are reported, and established a character for modesty, good sense and integrity among his associates." Frémont's beloved Charleston mentor Dr. Roberton wrote with pride about his "favorite pupil" after Frémont had joined the ranks of the U.S. Senate. "My prayer is that he may ever be opposed to war, injustice, and oppression of every kind, a blessing to his country and an example of every noble virtue to the whole world."

Jessie loved being back in the rough-and-tumble political milieu that was second nature to her, but the bitter divisions between North and South had infected the C Street residence in more personal ways. Her uncle James McDowell Jr. was now a proslavery Virginia congressman, despite his antislavery stance twenty years earlier in the Virginia legislature, and domestic tensions escalated as the Bentons and the Frémonts became increasingly estranged from Virginia and Missouri relatives. If the Compromise of 1850 was expected to ease sectional disputes, it had the opposite effect: both sides felt defeat. Northerners considered the Fugitive Slave Law, compelling free states to return escaped slaves to their owners, immoral and untenable. Southerners were equally appalled at the admission of California as a free state and felt they had been outmaneuvered by sinister forces. Still, both sides, for the moment, were committed to preserving the Union, and Southern secessionists remained in the minority.

Correspondence to Frémont from his California constituents suggested strong public support for his views, but alarming reports also arrived indicating that the proslavery faction that supported Gwin was gaining strength and actively planning to unseat Frémont. Meanwhile, squatters had overrun Las Mariposas, and its management was falling apart in Frémont's absence.

Deliriously happy in Washington, and exhibiting the first signs of pregnancy, Jessie was stunned when John decided to return to California without completing his term in the second session to challenge Gwin before the state legislature—which would once again select the senators—and seek the longer term. Convinced that both his reelection and his financial solvency hung in the balance, Frémont abruptly announced his intentions to Jessie. "I had five days notice only," Jessie later wrote. Her baby was due the following April, and she was tormented with fears of crossing Panama again, of succumbing to the dreaded Chagres fever, of leaving her sixty-eight-year-old father, whose health was declining and who was facing certain defeat for reelection, of subjecting her unborn baby and Lily to the rigors of travel, of immersion in a bitter campaign in California.

Characteristically, John left the decision to her, and predictably, her devotion to her husband guided her choice. "Of course I decided to go with him," she wrote; "in his condition of health I could not let him cross the Isthmus alone." Benton and other family members halfheartedly attempted to dissuade Jessie, but they had learned from experience that their entreaties would be futile. The "Colonel's chief-of-staff," as they called her, would always seek her own counsel.

By early October, the family was bound for California, and once again Jessie would become gravely ill in Chagres. But all in all, the journey, by now almost routine to them, was made in relative comfort, and they arrived in San Francisco on November 21.

They found the city much changed—"for the bad," as Jessie put it— with a gauche and greedy lust for wealth pervading the atmosphere. The pioneer adventure spirit of the past had been overtaken by ruffians and thugs, while the nouveau riche "lived in a splendor of gold ornaments and red plush upholstery, crystal chandeliers, and costly French furniture," as one account described the vulgar display. The seaport was crowded with ships from around the world, filled with roughnecks with a get-rich-quick mentality. "From France was deliberately shipped by its Government a large body of the *Garde Mobile*," Jessie observed, "a turbulent element used in preparing the second Empire, but which had now become too troublesome to be retained in Paris." That element, combined with Australia's wholesale shipments of criminals from the penal colonies—supposed "escapees," but in fact government-sponsored evacuees—made the city a dangerous and harrowing place.

The Frémonts bought an unfashionable but sturdy house on Stockton Street, where John left Jessie to set up housekeeping as he set off for the state legislature in San José to begin politicking. Popular among the native Californians and early migrants, his antislavery stance had irrevocably eroded his support among the moderate and conservative Democrats of his party. The proslavery wing of the party had grown in strength, and the forces arrayed against him were formidable. As in the rest of the country, the debate over the Compromise of 1850 had polarized California politics, and an "outspoken free-soiler like Frémont could no longer pass muster with the predominantly Democratic and South-leaning California legislature," as historian H. W. Brands depicted the volatile moment. Frémont became seriously ill in December—confined to bed "by sciatica, rheumatism, neuralgia," as Benton reported to his Senate colleagues. Had he been stronger physically, he might have waged a more successful campaign with the legislators who would choose the next senator. As it was, he faced an uphill battle, and when it became clear that the forces arrayed against him were insurmountable, he turned his attention to Las Mariposas and other business ventures. His instincts were correct, and in February 1851 he was decisively defeated after 140 ballots.

"Frémont would have liked nothing better than to continue in the area of state and national politics," wrote his biographer Allan Nevins, "but the situation was unfavorable to a man of his temperament." For her part, Jessie seemed eager to put politics behind them for the moment. "Mr. Frémont . . . says I must tell you to prepare yourself for a Whig Senator in his place," she wrote to her father's old and dear friend Francis Preston Blair, "politics being too costly an amusement in this country just now, but that he will come to it with renewed vigor by the next election. The state is decidedly Whig—partly I suppose from the great commercial interests involved, but more from the misrule of those who have had the state government in their hands and who but used it for private ends. As they were nominally Democrats we the genuines must suffer for their sins."

On April 19, 1851, Jessie gave birth to a robust baby she named John Charles. "He is as strong as a native son should be, and as a son of Colonel Frémont is already well traveled," she proudly announced to her attending physician.

Jessie was still bedridden two weeks after childbirth, regaining her strength after a long pregnancy and difficult delivery, when San Francisco became engulfed in flames—the fifth major fire deliberately started by disaffected migrants. Throughout an entire night she watched the fire approach their Stockton Street home. John told her to lie still, to keep Lily and the baby they called "Charley" near her, while John and neighbors hung water-soaked carpets and blankets on the outside walls of their house. The city's men fought the fire, but the winds fanned it out of control as it burned a quarter of the city, including the downtown business district, destroying $7 million worth of property. It was finally contained just before it reached the Frémont residence, but the incident left Jessie badly shaken.

Immersed in her own personal domestic tranquillity, enjoying the magical days with her newborn, the depth of despair and rage rocking the city had caught her unaware. A shortage of jobs, housing, and food had left hundreds of men homeless, starving, and bitterly resentful of the city's monied residents. But Jessie had been protected from the mount-ing insurrection. Her days had "revolved about a very young life newly added to ours," as she described her peaceful cocoon. "Into this hushed atmosphere harsh topics did not penetrate, so I knew nothing of the im-mediate causes which were trying the endurance of good citizens to the point where patience ceases to be a public virtue . . . against the passions of an evil class."

Vigilantes banded together, "to remove that class from their midst," and to bring order to the increasingly violent city, and on June 11 a thief was hanged in the city center amid shouts from an angry crowd calling for more justice. Jessie, no longer removed from outside events, came upon one of the many handbills blanketing the city, threatening its resi-dents. "While you are persecuting our people we will make your wives and families suffer for your acts," it read. Terrified, Jessie was unable to sleep through the long nights, fearing another fire. But it was in the "holy calm of a summer Sunday morning"—on June 22—that the next fire was set, the city's warning bells masked by the ringing of church bells. Jessie was home alone with the children—John had gone to Las Mariposas—when she saw the flames heading for their house. She grabbed her naked baby, fresh from his bath, and wrapped him in the skirt of her dressing gown. Holding the hand of a shrieking Lily, she climbed up the hill behind her to an isolated house. There she joined hundreds of other women and children "who did not know where to go next." From the upstairs window, Jessie watched her home burn to the ground. This, the most devastating of the fires, had burned the city hos-pital, the newspaper offices of the *Alta California*, the Jenny Lind Theater, and dozens of residences.

By evening she had relocated to a makeshift shelter prepared by the city's businessmen and soldiers. Distraught, she found that her breast milk stopped flowing. "[T]he shock was too much for even my youth and health—I did not have a break-down of illness, but blinding distress-ing headaches, and trembling nerves made me wretched and useless to that much disturbed, troubled baby who however throve steadily through all the unusual conditions." With help, she found a new "nurse" for the baby—a "silky white goat" who would be "an admirable substi-tute in having the great advantage of no mind or nerves." Fortunately, tenants who rented part of the Frémonts large home managed to save nearly everything from the abandoned house—the china, crystal, silver, books, furniture, and clothing.

With no mail service into the mountains, Jessie could only wait for John to hear of the devastation. When he learned of the fire, he returned by riverboat from Stockton, finding only a chimney where their home once stood. Searching for his family, he learned that they had relocated to a house "near Grace Church." Wandering the streets near the church, he saw white muslin curtains, the pink ribbons that tied them blowing in the breeze, and knew he had found Jessie—her "love of frippery and fresh air" an unmistakable guidepost.

Alarmed at Jessie's physical and emotional fragility—their home destroyed and the couple now in dire need of outside capital to extract the ore from Las Mariposas—John surprised her that winter with tickets to Europe. "How would you like a trip to Paris as a New Year's gift?" he asked her in December. Before she could answer, he removed steamer tickets from "San Francisco to Chagres, thence direct to France." He had planned to travel to Europe to seek funding for machinery and mining equipment to construct ore mills, and now thought a family holiday would be restorative for them all. "It will be your first vacation and rest," Jessie responded ecstatically. "And yours—well earned," he replied. "The first since you spoke those fateful words, 'Whither thou goest, I will go.' "

In the months since returning to California, John had invested heavily in various financial ventures, including real estate and cattle. "Always restless, always inclined to speculation, he did not confine himself, as common sense dictated, to his estate," as biographer Nevins put it. Perhaps his most impulsive scheme involved supplying beef to the Indians as part of a government contract designed to mitigate Indian depredations against white cattle-raising settlers. "Frémont happened to have cattle interests," according to one account, "and he offered to furnish some $180,000 worth of beef at the usual rates; an offer which the commissioners accepted as 'the lowest and best yet made by any responsible man.' " Critics charged that his prices were inflated, and his Washington enemies spread rumors that he fraudulently overpriced the beef he supplied the government. Meanwhile, in addition to mining at Las Mariposas, he developed part of the tract for agriculture and cattle ranching, while purchasing an additional Mexican land grant in San Joaquin County. Heavily leveraged and incurring enormous fees in the numerous legal tangles relating to the land titles, he fell further and further behind in his financial obligations. "[T]he original archives of the old Mexican administration had been

nailed up in boxes at Benicia," wrote one historian of the chaos surrounding the boundary issues, ". . . and could not be utilized by either
the owners, claimants, or the government officials."

When a dispute arose between his agents, David Hoffman and Thomas
Denny Sargent, a mustachioed American promoter who had turned up
in London selling leases he had purchased from Frémont, Frémont decided to suspend all sales transactions regarding Las Mariposas until the
court ruled on the titles. "I am certainly disposed to rid myself of the
trouble of managing the property," he wrote to Hoffman when Hoffman
objected to being supplanted by Sargent. Profits were dwindling while
lawsuits were swelling, prompting Benton—to whom Frémont had
given his power of attorney—to agree to sell the entire property to Sargent for $1 million. His son-in-law, Benton confided to Hoffman, was
"not adapted to such business and it interferes with his attention to other
business to which he is adapted." But Frémont, realizing that he could
not sell Las Mariposas without clear title, and resenting what he saw as
Benton's interference, reneged on the offer to Sargent, causing the first
serious rift between Frémont and his father-in-law since Frémont had
eloped with Benton's underage daughter ten years earlier. "When Benton learned that John would not sell, he was furious," according to one
account. "Not only did he believe that his impatient, impulsive, sometimes gullible son-in-law was temperamentally unsuited to business, but
he viewed Las Mariposas as a tainted pursuit, far less worthy than politics, writing, or exploration." The split between her father and husband
would place Jessie, for as long as the three of them were alive, in the awkward middle between the two men she loved. "I know both my people
too well ever to look for concession from either side. And with Father
this is only the expression of years of distrust of Mr. Frémont's judgment," Jessie later wrote to her friend Lizzie Blair—daughter of Francis
Preston Blair, distant cousin of Jessie's, and Jessie's closest friend.

Under the strained personal circumstances, the Frémonts' international
sojourn was a welcome respite. "Now came a year of absolute rest,"
Jessie wrote, "the only prolonged interval of intentional rest and enjoyment that ever came into that life of continuous purposeful work." Taking a steamer in late February 1852 to Chagres, they continued to New
York, where they stayed once again at the Irving House before boarding
Cunard's side-wheeler *Africa* for England. Accompanied by Lily, Charley,
and John's niece Frances "Nina" Cornelia, they arrived in Liverpool on
March 22. They took up residence at the Clarendon House in a suite

prepared for them by Jessie's childhood friend the Marchioness of Wellesley. "It was the luxury of Do-nothing," Jessie described their situation. "A beautiful stately suite of rooms . . . cheerful with fires and lights and plants and cut flowers and we had only 'To be.' "

In London Jessie was a much-sought-after American belle, introduced into the Court of St. James's, hosted by society doyennes, and presented to Queen Victoria wearing a pink satin gown trimmed with ivory lace. "Because I was thinned and almost pale from constant travel—four crossings of the Isthmus in as many years—I had to abandon my favorite color, violet, and avoid blues and greens," she wrote of her court dress. "When I beheld the Queen and the Prince Consort, Albert Edward, at her side the picture of devotion, I lost all nervousness," Jessie recalled. "I felt myself not a Democrat bowing the knee to royalty but an American paying homage to a figure of womanly goodness and power." John was an equally coveted guest of the titled class—a millionaire fresh from California, a celebrity famed for his American explorations who was known as "the American Humboldt," and a recent inductee into Britain's prestigious Royal Geographical Society. He met the Duke of Wellington and was invited to inspect vessels at Woolrich that were soon to depart in search of the missing explorer Sir John Franklin, who had been lost in the Canadian wilderness since 1846.

Still, the quagmire of California dogged them, and on April 7, Frémont was suddenly and very publicly arrested by four constables in front of the Clarendon House. Told only that he was being charged with $50,000 in debts incurred while he was acting governor of California, he was jailed overnight in Sloman's Lock-up on Chancery Lane. The allegations stemmed from drafts that he, as governor, had drawn in Los Angeles that were later sold to English holders. When Congress failed to appropriate funds to cover them, the Englishmen held Frémont responsible. Frantic and furious, Jessie scrambled during the night to find someone to post bail for her husband. "I spent one night in a 'Sponging House' (ante room to the jail)," Frémont wrote Benton after his release, "being arrested at night, and was bailed out the next day, by George Peabody, the eminent American merchant here . . . If I was a great patriot as you," he continued with thinly veiled sarcasm and cynicism, "I would go to jail and stay there until Congress paid these demands, now over a million, but my patriotism has been oozing out for the last five years. As my detention here promises to be long, you will greatly contribute to our comfort by getting me appointed chargé to some neighboring power, to protect me from further arrests and help to pay expenses." Despite their recent disagreements, Benton, ever the family patriarch, forwarded Frémont's letter to the president and Secretary of State Daniel Webster. The U.S. government eventually paid the fine imposed by a London court against Frémont, but the entire incident left Frémont embittered and disaffected against his country, his anger reminiscent of the rage he felt during the court-martial proceedings against him.

Embarrassed and outraged, Jessie feared that to remain in England would subject John to further harassment by creditors, including disenchanted investors in Las Mariposas. As they prepared to relocate to Paris, Jessie received word that her twenty-two-year-old brother, Randolph, had died unexpectedly of a malarial infection. Dissolute and alcoholic, hot-tempered and irreverent, Benton's only son had never measured up to his father's larger-than-life character and reputation. Still, Jessie loved her only brother and empathized with his futile lifelong struggle to conform, and was deeply affected by the sudden loss. Beseeching her "not to wear that grief-reminder black" during the time when each was desperately seeking happiness, John sought to console his grieving young wife. In Paris he bought her a brougham and two chestnut carriage horses, and hired an Irish coachman. They moved into a graceful mansion furnished by Count d'Orsay on the Champs Élysées. The abundant garden, enclosed by ivy-covered walls, stretched to the banks of the Seine. They were both so taken with the property that Frémont attempted, unsuccessfully, to purchase it. Filled with velvet draperies and original paintings, Persian rugs and Hungarian crystal, their new home was in stark contrast to their makeshift California dwellings. "This twenty-eight-year-old girl who three years earlier had bathed from a barber's basin in a blanket dressing tent now saw her bath water flow from the beaks of gilded swans into a marble tub," wrote one of her biographers. "She dried her skin with satin-damask towels and made her leisurely toilet in a mirror-lined dressing room. She who had transformed adobe quarters into a salon now received her callers in a tapestry-hung drawing room."

Typically, Jessie was ever solicitous of her husband's peace of mind. "After the many years of sleeping on the ground and a 'wet saddle for a pillow' it was delightful to Mr. Frémont to have the silk hangings, the down pillows of his warm room, where a sevres bowl of roses near his head replaced the weapons so long needed. He had a boyish satisfaction at times in taking a long walk in the teeth of sleety wind and rain for the content of 'coming back into camp' to such a contrast."

Both of them fluent in French, they traveled freely in elite society, Jessie indulging in the latest couture—from satin boots to fine lace bonnets. They were invited to receptions for Louis Napoleon, and attended the wedding of Eugénie de Montijo to Napoleon III at Notre Dame Cathedral. Jessie envied the power and status wielded by Parisian women, contrasting it with the stifled role of women in her native land. "In France she might have ruled openly in the councils of the nation," wrote a nineteenth-century memoirist; "in America she merely gave suggestions and advice to those who controlled the people's destiny." John took long horseback rides, practiced fencing every day, and avidly sought European investors for Las Mariposas, returning often to London to meet with his lawyers. In Paris, the scientific world opened to him through Benton's longtime friendship with an American expatriate once associated with the U.S. Mint in Philadelphia. This "Dr. Farnham" taught Frémont the most advanced methods for mining and treating gold, and a coveted introduction to France's most famous physicist and astronomer, Dominique François Arago, "revived" her husband's "astronomical research," as Jessie put it. One evening, at a ball at the Tuileries, John had a chance encounter with an English army officer who had been with him on the ill-fated expedition in the San Juan Mountains. They had not seen each other "since the two came back from the gates of death," Jessie said of the reunion. "Now they met face to face, one leaving, the other ascending the splendid stairway lined with flowers, their feet on velvet carpets and the perfumed air full of music. Different this, from the shrieking winter storms, the scant mouthful of mule meat, the dead and dying comrades."

While a governess cared for the children, Jessie and John explored the countryside, driving their carriage through the "old Royal forests" to Versailles, visiting galleries and gardens, and by June Jessie was pregnant again. In January 1853 Jessie hosted a lavish fortieth-birthday party for John, filling their Italianate estate with bouquets of his favorite flowers— heliotrope and white roses. A wonderfully blissful time for both of them, neither could entirely turn their attention from events back home. Debts were mounting at Las Mariposas, and reports reached them that Frémont was being passed over in favor of West Point topographers to lead a wildly popular and well-financed railroad survey expedition to California. Those exigencies—along with the death of her brother and her growing homesickness—convinced Jessie that they must bring their European residency to an end. While awaiting her confinement, she began preparations for the family's return to Washington.

On February 1, 1853, after a long and difficult labor, Jessie gave birth to a tiny girl they named Anne Beverley, after Frémont's mother. Our *petite Parisienne*, as John affectionately called her, the infant was pale and placid. Bedridden for several weeks, Jessie gradually regained her strength while her father maneuvered, calling in favors from old political cronies, to have John appointed to lead an expedition. In March, Congress voted for five expeditions to explore five possible midcontinental routes between the thirty-second and forty-seventh parallels. Frémont fully expected a choice assignment, but "there were men in position to prevent his being connected," as Jessie put it. Indeed, many factions in the debate opposed Frémont, recalling his disastrous expedition in the winter of 1848–1849, when he lost so many of his men to starvation, hypothermia, and even cannibalism. Those supporting West Point's rising star Captain John Williams Gunnison—including Gunnison's longtime family friend and patron newly elected president Franklin Pierce—recalled Frémont's court-martial and controversial antislavery stance. They sought to limit Frémont's role and discredit the validity of the much-ballyhooed "central route"—between the thirty-seventh and thirty-eighth parallels—that Frémont had long advocated.

The dream of a transcontinental railroad had consumed the second session of the Thirty-second Congress, with all sides agreeing only on the need for immediate surveys. There was what historian David Haward Bain called "a quality of madness abroad in the land . . . the nation's 'manifest destiny' had prevailed over barriers both natural and political." Predictably, the factions divided along partisan lines—the Southern slave owners favoring a southern route to the Pacific, the Northerners lobbying for a central or northern route. While legislators and journalists debated the issue, Congress suddenly passed an appropriations bill authorizing the new secretary of war, Jefferson Davis, to establish the Bureau of Explorations and Surveys and dispatch his army topographical corps to find a suitable route. Naturally, the former West Point cadet and Mississippi senator—and future president of the Confederacy—allied himself with Southern slaveholders. "His expansionist views, which the Pierce administration pushed with great vigor and greater clumsiness," William and Bruce Catton wrote about Davis, "were aimed at Mexico and the Caribbean and above all Cuba, areas of benefit to slavery; his diligent labors in behalf of a Pacific railway pointed strongly to the cotton states."

Though he had growing uncertainties about his son-in-law, Benton's passionate commitment to the viability of his beloved central "Road to India," his alarm at Davis's unabashed attempt to use the railroad to expand slavery into the new territories, along with his belief that John was still the most accomplished explorer in America, outweighed any personal reservations. Benton was convinced that Southern interests were conniving and conspiring to build a "Cotton Kingdom" line from Texas to California. "The Southern line, in the interest of the cotton growing regions, was to be favored at the expense of the more Northern routes," Jessie wrote of the administration's view, "and . . . Mr. Jefferson Davis allowed no interference with his idea. Of this, and all its inner meanings and future policy, my Father wrote to Mr. Frémont fully, and it was at once decided he would make, at his own expense, a survey of the line he thought the best for all . . . the 'Santa Fe' route."

Benton promptly organized an independent survey, with Frémont at its helm, financing it with his own money and contributions from his political cronies. Under the circumstances, with an astronomical $150,000 congressional appropriation earmarked for five surveys, Benton's private expedition appeared superfluous, self-promoting, and grandiose. Critics accused him of trying to control the political and financial spoils of the enterprise, pointing to the Frémonts' vast California real-estate investments. Even railroad visionary Asa Whitney accused Benton of turning the venture from an altruistic government project into a "gambling, stock-jobbing Wall Street and Threadneedle street concern." In fact, the charge was gratuitous. Benton had devoted much of his political life to proving that the thirty-eighth parallel was not too far north to be traversed in winter, and when it became clear to him that that route would not get Davis's backing, he saw no choice but to proceed on his own. "No one had worked harder than [Frémont] and Senator Benton to keep the idea of a Pacific railroad alive," wrote one historian, and neither man had any inclination to be deprived of participation in the historic moment. Despite the calamity of the fourth expedition, Frémont had remained convinced that the route he had taken through the San Juan Mountains was by far the best possible path for a transcontinental railroad. He had eloquently documented his preference for the route in a lengthy letter to the Philadelphia railroad convention in 1850, citing the advantages: it was direct, abundant with wood and water, more moderate in climate than the northern passes through the Rockies and the Sierra Nevada, and well suited for habitation by migrants. "Many lines of explorations through the wilderness country, from our inhabited frontier to the Pacific Ocean, have conclusively satisfied me that the region or belt of country, lying between the 38th and 39th parallels of latitude, offer singular facilities and extraordinary comparative advantages for the construction of the proposed road," he wrote in what one author called "one of the most explicit and instructive documents which, up to that time, had appeared upon the subject, from any quarter."

Still, Jefferson Davis assigned Captain George B. McClellan to survey through the Dakotas and Montana; Lieutenant E. J. Beckwith to survey from Great Salt Lake City through the Humboldt Valley in present-day Nevada; Gunnison to follow between the thirty-eighth and thirty-ninth parallels; Lieutenant A.W. Whipple to survey a line following due west from Fort Smith, Arkansas; and Captain John Pope to survey the southernmost route from El Paso through Yuma. To be so publicly snubbed was a monumental affront to both Frémont and Benton. "Senator Benton had been the foremost advocate in America of the transcontinental railway," wrote Allan Nevins. "No officer of the army possessed so much practical experience of western exploration and surveying as Frémont; the name of none would carry so much weight in any official recommendation. But Jefferson Davis . . . felt that regular army officers were entitled to preference."

Benton summoned John and Jessie home. With time of the essence, "Arago himself aided Mr. Frémont" in selecting his instruments. John made plans to depart immediately for Washington, where he would begin outfitting for the expedition. Jessie was deeply moved by her husband's willingness to subject himself to the rigor and danger of yet another expedition. "I told him what I truly thought—that he had never done so fine a thing as to renew voluntarily this wearing old life, after the year of beautiful rest had made him see its painful aspects. But to him it was a question of honor as well as of national advantage. 'Fame's couriers, Death and Honor, call us to the field again.'"

Jessie was far less sanguine than she appeared on the surface, reluctant to once again begin what she called "the waiting, and hoping, and fearing." She followed John to the United States a few weeks later, her entourage now including her three children—Lily, Charley, and Anne—as well as John's difficult niece Nina, and two French maids who served as governess and tutor to the children. Nina, the beautiful teenage daughter of John's dead brother, was a constant burden and worry to Jessie. Flighty and flirtatious, Nina was rude and unmanageable. All was not paradise for the millionairess Jessie. Her vacation over, she was returning to a sharply divided and unfriendly capital, her husband and father estranged if civil, and John once again seeking that amorphous notion of glory. "We had long since subsided into a lotus-like oblivion of any other life than this of exquisite rest and unfolding in a congenial atmosphere, when the cloud arose—no larger than a man's hand, but destined to cover our land with gloom and strife," she wrote later.

The Frémonts set up housekeeping in a modest home near the Benton residence on Capitol Hill, and John found himself cloistered frequently with Benton, the two men hurriedly making arrangements for the expedition. Competing with the five government teams, Frémont and Benton scrambled to hire their share of qualified experts. "Not since Napoleon had taken his company of savants into Egypt had the world seen such an assemblage of scientists and technicians marshaled under one banner," historian William H. Goetzmann wrote of Secretary Davis's historic gathering of explorers, engineers, geographers, geologists, artists, botanists, and cartographers. Still, it was Frémont—"the most romantically heroic western explorer in the United States," as a twenty-first-century account described him—who was fresh back from Europe with the finest French and English instruments money could buy. As a further triumph in his rivalry with the Army, Frémont persuaded a talented artist and daguerreotypist, a devout Sephardic Jew named Solomon Nuñes Carvalho, to join as the first official photographer ever attached to an exploring expedition.

As spring moved into summer, both Frémonts turned their attention to the newborn Anne, who had become suddenly listless and pale—a change Jessie attributed to the stifling Washington heat and humidity. Jessie refused to believe that Anne could be suffering from the fatal digestive illness that had become epidemic in the capital, and took the baby to the Blair estate in nearby Silver Spring, where the evenings were cooler. There, Lizzie Blair helped care for the five-month-old infant, deepening the childhood friendship between the two young women. At dawn on July 11, even as the physician was assuring Jessie that Anne would survive, the baby died in her arms. The childless Lizzie had remained with Jessie throughout the night—a devotion Jessie would later remember with sadness as life took both women down antagonistic trails. "Care and sorrow and childbirth pain," Jessie wrote somewhat matter-of-factly in her family Bible next to the list of four children, two of whom were now dead. When John reached her, he buried his face in the folds of her skirt and wept like a child, so aggrieved was he at the loss of his little Parisienne, his beloved mother's namesake. And just as John had held Jessie at the time of baby Benton's death, Jessie now consoled her heartbroken husband. "It was she who remained dry-eyed to comfort me," John told Benton of Jessie's strength, "for I was unmanned over the cruelty of this bereavement. Her calm stoicism, so superior to mere resignation, soon shamed me into control."

In September, John left for St. Louis to begin his fifth and final expedition—a treacherous, life-threatening journey for which he had little enthusiasm and none of the old spark that had propelled him forward in the past. "I would rather have Mr. Frémont at the fireside taking care of himself . . . than getting all the stupid laurels that ever grew," Jessie wrote to Lizzie. Driven wholly by ego and honor, John was once again manifesting Benton's aging dream as well as his own, and embarked on the expedition with only halfhearted passion.

He recruited twenty-two men, including ten Delaware braves "under charge of Captain Wolf, '*a big Indian*,' " as Carvalho wrote in his journal, and on September 20, 1853, the party left Westport. The men had all been armed with Colt six-shooters, rifles, knives, and sheaths, and their horses and mules had been branded with an "F" for Frémont. Only a month later, Jessie received a telegraph that John had returned to St. Louis, too ill from inflammatory rheumatism to continue the expedition. "I find a wet saddle no longer makes a good pillow," he wrote Jessie, "but I think with care I will get through as always, and this shall be the very last time I winter in the mountains. But I want you to promise me that if I do not get back, you will help your Father to get payment from the government for its debt to me for keeping the Indians fed and quiet—I prevented an Indian War, but they are waiting too long to repay what I spent in doing so . . . promise me you will do this, and it will take a heavy anxiety from me." Jessie rushed by train to join him in Missouri. There she found him racked with headaches and chest pains, but under the competent care of a homeopathic physician who had been in the Russo-Turkish War of 1828. "Dr. Ebers has soothed the pain, uprooted the inflammation & Mr. Frémont though greatly shaken is again literally 'on his legs,' " Jessie wrote to Lizzie. Jessie begged her husband to abandon the expedition, but he was determined to continue. "All I could say, however, met with gentle but fixed resolve to go on, but he so far yielded as to take with him a good physician, the first medical or surgical attendance in any of his journeys, for the government had never provided that care." She accompanied John to Independence. Once again they parted, Jessie dreading the winter ordeal John faced, once again feeling abandoned and increasingly resentful as well. "In my position as wife I am denied the utterance of such sentiments," Jessie wrote to a friend of John's, "but when I saw him rise from his suffering and resolutely abandon the care and comfort so grateful to him, to follow out his work at every risk, I honored him more than words." As Jessie returned to Washington, John caught up with his men fifty miles away; they were thrilled at his return. "No father who had been absent from his children, could have been received with more enthusiasm and more real joy," Carvalho described Frémont's rendezvous with his party.

The group left Bent's Fort on November 25, and by early December had reached the floor of the San Luis Valley in southern Colorado. Carvalho made what would become a famous daguerreotype from the crest of Mosca Pass that clearly indicated the winter navigability of the route. Approaching the pass, Frémont shared an intimate and melancholy moment with his artist. "On the opposite side [of the San Luis Valley] forty miles across are the 'San Juan Mountains,' the scene of Col. Fremont's terrible disaster on a former expedition," Carvalho wrote in his journal. "He pointed out to me the direction of the spot and with a voice tremulous with emotion, related some of the distressing incidents of that awful night."

On December 14 they easily surmounted the 10,160-foot Cochetopa Pass, or Buffalo Gate, and Frémont was delighted with the ease of passage of what had been "the failed objective of his fourth expedition," as one account put it. "He repeatedly emphasized the small amount of snow so far encountered, a crucial point to make in the argument for a central route for the transcontinental railroad." From this point the party ascended into the mountains, encountering, like Frémont's disastrous previous expedition, waist-high snow, freezing temperatures, hostile Ute Indians, dying animals, and dwindling provisions. "Every time a thin, starving horse died, the cooks saved the blood in their camp kettle, boiling the entrails and roasting the bones," wrote one historian. "Even the hide of a horse or mule, fried in tallow from melted candles, was preferable to eating porcupines with their quills singed off. For fifty days, when there was no meat available, the men lived on broiled cacti, wild rosebuds, and water bugs." When they were lucky they had beaver or coyote.

Carvalho was deeply impressed by Frémont's leadership—his vigilance and courage. His "lodge was sacred from all and everything that was immodest, light or trivial," Carvalho wrote; "each and all of us entertained the highest regard for him. The greatest etiquette and deference were always paid to him, although he never ostensibly required it. Yet his reserved and unexceptionable deportment demanded from us the same respect with which we were always treated, and which we ever took pleasure in reciprocating." The more hardships they encountered, the more resourceful and calm Frémont became, and the more he encouraged his men. "No matter how much he was suffering for want of food, no matter how intense the cold or stormy the weather, he kept up his astronomical observations, sometimes standing for hours in the deep snow taking his bearings," wrote his biographer Nevins. "He never lost his temper; he never dropped his dignity or acted with excitement. Not once, amid vicissitudes which tried everybody's patience, and in the face of stupidly irritating mistakes by his men, did Frémont forget that he was a gentleman; not once was there an oath or a display of uncontrolled anger. He gave his orders calmly, and they were always obeyed . . . So devoted were the Delaware Indians that they would have gone to certain death for him. He never asked an officer or man to undertake duties which he was not willing to share."

During their worst days of starvation, Frémont insisted upon eating alone in his tent—an act Carvalho and others thought was meant to provide his men with the freedom to openly voice their fears and complaints during their scant meals. When the first horse was slaughtered to feed the starving men, Frémont called them all together and emotionally addressed each one of them. He told them of his previous expedition and how some of the men had resorted to eating each other. Standing together on a snowy mountain under a star-filled sky, twenty-one white, Native American, and Mexican men huddled together, bowed their heads, and took a solemn oath. He "begged us to swear that in no extremity of hunger would any of his men lift his hand to prey upon a comrade," recalled Carvalho. "If we are to die, let us die together like men," he told them.

Frémont struggled to keep up the spirits and morale of the party, yet he found for the first time in all his travels that he was incapable of proceeding. "Going up a long mountain slope, I was breaking my way through the snow a little way ahead of my party, when suddenly my strength gave out. All power of motion left me. I could not move a foot; the mountain slope was naked, but it just happened that near by was a good thick grove of aspens, and across a neighboring ravine, the yellow grass showed above the snow on the south hill side . . . I sat down in the snow and waited." Feeling disembodied—a "curious sense of vacancy came over him"—his life was unmistakably slipping away. "And this is Death," he said to himself, slipping to the ground. His mind filled with speculation as to what would happen to the weaker members of the party, for there was no one else "who could make the astronomical observations necessary to their safety." After a few minutes, his strength returned—"the strong heart beat again." No one noticed what had happened, nor did he "tell how near he had felt to the end." His intrepid friend and associate Alexis Godey marveled at Frémont's stamina and determination, praising his "indomitable perseverance" to the *New York Evening Post*. "He ever partook of the same fare; underwent like hardships; rode when they rode—walked when they walked; and unhesitatingly exposed himself to every danger and privation. In his private character he is a model; singularly temperate and abstemious in his habits, he never uses spirituous liquors; profane language is a stranger to his lips . . . disturbances were a stranger to his camp."

Frémont's bedraggled and emaciated party had gone forty-eight hours without food. "It was to Frémont's assiduity and skill that the expedition, when on its last legs, owed its final extrication," according to Nevins. "Here was no chance work—no guessing," wrote Carvalho, "for a deviation of one mile, either way, from the true course, would have plunged the whole party into certain destruction." In early February 1854, following Frémont's astronomical calculations, they dragged themselves into the Mormon settlement of Parowan, at the base of the imposing Hurricane Cliffs in southwestern Utah Territory. Once in sight of the village, the men "became like children," according to one account. "They were entirely overcome. Some fell to the earth, unconscious, like dead men." Exhausted and frostbitten, most were barefoot, having eaten the soles of their moccasins. Four hundred hospitable Mormons greeted them, taking each man into a private home. Here, perhaps for the first time, Frémont and his men would have learned of the "Indian" massacre four months earlier of Captain John Williams Gunnison and his expedition party on the Sevier River in central Utah. Not until three years later—when President Buchanan ordered one-sixth of the U.S. Army to march to Utah as a *posse comitatus* to replace Mormon leader Brigham Young—was Mormon involvement in the massacre exposed. In May 1857, following a dramatic correspondence between Gunnison's widow and a federal judge from Utah Territory that was printed in the *New York Times*, Buchanan declared Utah Territory in a state of insurrection. "Not least in moving Congress to approve the military force," according to one account of the massacre, was the judge's allegation that Gunnison and his men had been murdered "under the orders, advice, and direction of the Mormons."

Still, Frémont would forever be grateful to Brigham Young and the controversial sect—and loyalty was among the explorer's most admirable traits. "The Mormons saved me and mine from death by starvation," Frémont would say many years later, refusing, at the behest of political allies, to condemn them and their peculiar institution of polygamy.

In the depths of the Washington winter, Jessie's anxiety took on a foreboding as she became convinced that John and his men were dying of starvation. There had been no word from him since November, and she was possessed with the fear that he was freezing—an obsession her family attributed to the heightened and unusual sensitivity and intimacy she shared with John. She chastised her family for "the criminal abundance of food and drink here, while her husband and his companions were starving." Sleepless, she would sit shivering for hours in the fire-heated library; frail and faint, she lost her appetite in empathy with her husband. Convinced that Jessie's intuition frequently bordered on telepathy, Benton indulged his daughter's strange behavior. "It fairly haunted me for two weeks," Jessie wrote, "until, young and absolutely healthy as I was, it made a physical effect on me. Sleep and appetite were broken up, and in spite of my father's and my own efforts to dissipate it by reasoning, by added open-air life, nothing dulled my sense of increasing suffering from hunger to Mr. Frémont and his party."

Then, just as abruptly, Jessie emerged from her cocoon of hysterical dread and was overtaken with a calm serenity, the "weight of fear" lifted as suddenly as it had come. "Mrs. Frémont and her family always believed that she had a strange psychic revelation, precise to the day and hour, of her husband's emergence from the jaws of death," wrote biographer Nevins. On the very evening that Frémont reached Parowan, Jessie's sister Susan and a young cousin had come to spend the night with

A young Jessie Benton Frémont in a portrait by T. Buchanan Read.
(Author's personal collection.)

John Charles Frémont, the first U.S. senator from California, in 1850.
(Author's personal collection.)

Artist Charles Preuss depicted the Frémont party's march along the western slope of the glacier-capped Wind River Range in what is now Wyoming. "Though these snow-mountains are not the Alps, they have their own character of grandeur and magnificence, and will doubtless find pens and pencils to do them justice," Frémont wrote of the stunning peaks. (Author's personal collection.)

Kit Carson was John C. Frémont's indomitable guide, lifelong devoted friend, and loyal supporter. Internationally celebrated as a fearless and competent scout, Carson led Frémont through territory previously known only to Indians, trappers, and traders. (Author's personal collection.)

A twenty-one-year-old Jessie Benton Frémont was painted in miniature by a Richmond, Virginia, artist. John C. Frémont carried the image with him from 1845 until his death in 1890. (Courtesy of the Buffalo Bill Historical Center.)

John C. Frémont ascending an overhanging buttress at what he mistakenly believed to be the highest peak in the Rocky Mountains. Nearly falling off the three-foot-wide precipice into an immense snowfield, he regained his balance and planted a unique American flag he had commissioned for the event. He then measured the altitude at 13,500 feet, and the men in his exploring party fired guns and broke open a bottle of brandy. (Author's personal collection.)

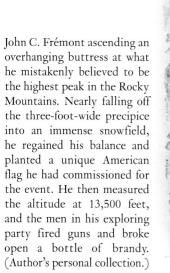

John C. Frémont's flag that he planted August 15, 1842, on a peak in the Wind River Range, a sub-range of the Rockies. He had commissioned the flag, with twenty-six stars and an eagle whose talons held an Indian peace pipe along with arrows, to claim the western territory for the United States. Three months later he presented the unusual flag to his wife, Jessie, upon the birth of their first child. (Author's personal collection.)

A U.S. senator for thirty years, Thomas Hart Benton was an erudite and intellectual leader whom future president Theodore Roosevelt would describe as the most "enlightened . . . of his class." He was considered the father of Manifest Destiny, but his antislavery sentiments would signal his political demise. Benton's complicated and tormented relationship with his favorite daughter, Jessie, and her husband, John C. Frémont, would have tragic consequences for all three of them. (Author's personal collection.)

The artist Edward Kern captured the drama of packing up and moving camp during John C. Frémont's third expedition. (Author's personal collection.)

In search of a passable route to Oregon and California, John C. Frémont explored the Rocky Mountains during his second expedition in the late winter of 1843. The party traveled with the controversial twelve-pound howitzer provided to Frémont by U.S. Army colonel Stephen Watts Kearny. (Author's personal collection.)

John C. Frémont's ill-fated fourth expedition found his party camped at twelve thousand feet in blizzard conditions in the San Juan Mountains. Unable to advance or retreat, with many of their mules dead or dying, Frémont spent Christmas Day 1848 reading Blackstone to his men. When it was over, ten of his thirty-three men had died of exposure, and some had resorted to cannibalism. (Author's personal collection.)

Five feet, nine inches in height with a slight but muscular build, John C. Frémont wore a neatly trimmed beard throughout his life. In 1861 President Lincoln appointed him a Civil War major general to head the newly created Western Department, headquartered in St. Louis. In that capacity, Frémont struggled with an impractical and chaotic situation. (Author's personal collection.)

The Frémont exploring party reached Sutter's Fort in the Sacramento Valley in the spring of 1844. Missourian John Sutter had established the massive adobe fort five years earlier. With twelve pieces of mounted artillery and a walled enclosure capable of housing a garrison of a thousand men, Sutter's Fort established an American presence in what was then Mexican territory. (Author's personal collection.)

In the summer of 1846 the Pacific Squadron, under the command of U.S. Navy commodore John Drake Sloat, were poised with an English line of battle ships off the California coast. On July 7, 250 American sailors rushed into Monterey and raised the American flag. At the time, John C. Frémont was the only U.S. Army officer present in California. (Author's personal collection.)

The Frémont cottage in Bear Valley, where the family retreated after the devastating 1856 presidential race. Jessie Benton Frémont, with a sense of irony and humor, christened the modest structure "the White House." *New York Tribune* editor Horace Greeley visited the Frémonts in 1858 and was impressed by the elegance of Jessie's primitive home, later writing of their French chef and manicured lawns. (Author's personal collection.)

Jessie Benton Frémont as she appeared in 1861 at Black Point, just before joining her husband in St. Louis at the beginning of the Civil War. Called "General Jessie" by her detractors, she played a fateful role in her husband's military career. (Courtesy of the Buffalo Bill Historical Center.)

General John C. Frémont and his elite handpicked Hungarian soldiers drew the ire of his long-standing West Point rivals. Establishing their headquarters in a sumptuous St. Louis mansion rented from one of Jessie Benton Frémont's relatives, the "Frémont Bodyguard" inspired widespread suspicion and criticism. (Author's personal collection.)

As a Civil War major general, John C. Frémont was controversial and independent. After consulting only his wife, Jessie, and a couple of trusted advisers, Frémont declared martial law and issued the first emancipation proclamation in American history, freeing the slaves belonging to all slaveholders who were aiding the rebel cause. For that bold move, he incurred the wrath of President Lincoln. (Author's personal collection.)

Jessie Benton Frémont in 1868. Forty-four-year-old Jessie posed for the
famous portrait artist Giuseppe Fagnani at the family's Pocaho estate.
(Courtesy of the Buffalo Bill Historical Center.)

With their devastating downturn in fortune, Jessie Benton Frémont made no effort to hide her poverty. Once multimillionaires, the couple was destitute by the mid-1870s. Still, Jessie remained dignified and imposing as they moved to increasingly shabby abodes. "She wore her made-over garments with as little self-consciousness as she had worn the tasteful and elegant costumes of earlier days," wrote one observer. (Author's personal collection.)

A life-size bronze monument of Thomas Hart Benton sculpted by Harriet Hosmer and erected in St. Louis's Lafayette Park in 1868. Inscribed on the pedestal were the words that shaped the lives of Benton; his daughter Jessie Benton Frémont; and her explorer husband, John C. Frémont. "There is the East, There is the road to India." (Author's personal collection.)

In 1888, near the end of his life, John C. Frémont, along with his wife, Jessie Benton Frémont, and their daughter Lily, were photographed in front of California's oldest tree. Located in what is now the Henry Cowell Redwoods State Park, where Frémont headquartered in 1846, the massive tree had been named for him. (Courtesy of Paul Hutton.)

The last photograph taken of John C. Frémont. Engraved from a photograph by Doremus, the illustration appeared on the cover of *Harper's Weekly* shortly after Frémont's death in 1890. (Author's personal collection.)

Jessie Benton Frémont's "retreat"—a comfortable two-story, four-bedroom redwood home in a grove of orange trees at the corner of Hoover and Twenty-eighth streets in Los Angeles. The home was built for her in 1891 with money raised by a group of wealthy California abolitionist and suffragist women—"aware of their good fortune in having Jessie Frémont among them." She lived there for the remainder of her life, where she hosted literary figures, famous artists, and political dignitaries. (Author's personal collection.)

Jessie Benton Frémont aged gracefully into an elegant woman whose avid mind and generous spirit kept her engaged in the most pressing issues of her era. (Author's personal collection.)

her after attending a wedding ball. "As girls do, they took off their ball dresses and made themselves comfortable with loose woolen gowns and letting down their hair, while I, only too pleased just then to have an excuse for staying up with others, made them tea as we talked over the evening and the bride." The fire had gotten low and Jessie went to an adjoining room for some kindling where, as she stooped to gather the wood, she felt a touch on her left shoulder and heard John whisper "Jessie." In that moment, she instinctively knew "that whatever he had had to bear was over; that he was now safe and light of heart; and that in some way he himself had told me so." The clock chimed three A.M., and Jessie fell into a deep and dreamless sleep until ten the next morning.

When she awakened, her father and the family physician, who had been summoned by Jessie's sister, were sitting at her bedside. "Child, you have seen a vision?" Benton asked her, and then proceeded to interrogate her about the evening before. "This vision, as he named it, interested him deeply. He knew me to be soundly healthy; he had seen the sudden genuine fear holding and altering me as an illness would, and now, as suddenly and completely as a northwest wind clears the air and leaves it fresh, cool and lifegiving, this 'vision' had swept away all clouds of fear and brought me new life." It would not be until John returned to Washington in May that the couple would compare notes, ultimately calculating that Jessie experienced John's well-being at exactly the moment he had made a notation in his journal that he wished Jessie would know him to be safe—an entry made as soon as he was ensconced in a warm bed in Parowan, after having checked on the safety and comfort of each of his men. "When my father returned home we learned that it was at the time the party was starving that my mother had the premonition of evil having befallen them," Lily later wrote of her parents' supernatural connection, "and the entry in the journal showed that exactly at the moment he had written it at Parowan my mother had felt his presence and in that wireless message from heart to heart knew that my father was safe and free from harm. The hour exactly tallied with the entry in his book, allowing for the difference in longitude." For his part, John would always credit Jessie's clairvoyance as a natural extension of their intimacy. "It doesn't seem strange to me," he remarked. "With each so much a part of the other's thoughts and feelings at all times, a crisis with either might cause these thoughts to materialize into a sense of actual physical presence."

Throughout John's absence, Jessie had thrown herself into helping

Benton with the memoirs he had begun writing in 1851—*Thirty Years' View, or A History of the Working of the American Government for Thirty Years, from 1820 to 1850*—the first volume of which would be published in the spring of 1854. Though it pained her to feel Benton's decided coolness toward her husband, she remained devoted to her father, taking dictation for the book, transcribing notes, and researching congressional files. "Benton seemed aloof, almost unfeeling, more concerned by what he evidently considered another bungled mission than by the suffering John had undergone," as one account put it. He was strangely dismissive of Jessie's sensitivity. "Father shocked back & chilled all my feelings when I looked to him for sympathy [that] winter," Jessie told Lizzie Blair. Jessie attributed much of his harshness to his own world-weary despair, the old lion diminished in stature and influence and now even his "Road to India" ridiculed and disparaged.

After more than thirty years in the U.S. Senate, Benton had been defeated in Missouri in 1851 due to his opposition to slavery extension. The Whigs were all but disappearing from Missouri politics, the Democrats were under Southern proslavery domination, and "the Know-Nothings were running through their short and crooked lease of life," as future president Theodore Roosevelt referred to the emerging anti-Catholic, anti-immigrant political party that had formed in response to the flood of Irish and German immigrants during the 1840s. Anti-Benton Democrats united against him to elect the Whig candidate. "Taught to admire the founders of our government in my early youth, I reverence them now," Benton roared in a widely circulated speech that brought national and local opposition; "taught to value their work then, I worship it now. A Senator for thirty years, I cannot degrade the Senate by engaging in slavery and disunion discussions." Though encouraged by Blair and other former Jacksonian leaders to run for president—"the old Jacksonian most clearly in the apostolic succession," according to Arthur M. Schlesinger Jr.—Benton had no enthusiasm or desire for such a candidacy, determined instead to turn his attention to his memoirs. Forty years earlier he had told Andrew Jackson that "every young man should plan either to do something worth being written or write something worth doing." His "doing" had in effect now come to a halt, and it was time to write. Still, in 1852, he was returned to Congress as a representative from a St. Louis district, owing much of his victory to the support of his friend Francis Preston Blair's sons, Montgomery and Frank, who had both become lawyers under Benton's patronage. Stripped now of seniority and power, the distinguished Missourian, "though one of the greatest, most patriotic men of his time, outranking, in some respects, even Webster and Clay, was made to feel the blighting power of the proslavery element," as one historian put it.

Jessie watched with compassion as he continued his lifelong habits, rising with dawn and building his own wood fire, dry-scrubbing his skin with horsehair brushes and icy water (as the gladiators did) before dressing in cotton flannel underclothes, breakfasting on tea and fruit, and then beginning his day of writing, wearing an open collar and shirtsleeves. "I became more than ever part of my Father's life," Jessie wrote, "for my Mother's increasing ill health made both my parents need and value the freshness of my children's lives and the youthful strength of mine." Every day, Elizabeth Benton sat silently near her husband—"scarcely able to rise from her chair without falling"—as Benton labored "most strenuously . . . from dawn till dusk" on his tome. The touching scene was heartbreaking to observers, prompting Francis Preston Blair to marvel at the "conjugal tenderness" and Benton's indefatigable ability to proceed with his writing under such gloomy circumstances. As Elizabeth slid further into speechless catatonia, Benton became progressively disheartened, admitting to "spells of depression which instead of being removed by time only seem to fall more heavily upon me," while also turning his memoir into a nearly unmanageable trove of research material. Planning originally to rely upon the papers of Andrew Jackson, historical notes, and his own previous speeches with the hope of presenting a true insider's view of national politics—the book a "means of purifying the Democratic tradition and restoring party unity in face of latter-day corruptions"—the volume had expanded in scope as Benton harangued old friends and colleagues such as Martin Van Buren, Francis Preston Blair, Benjamin Butler, and others, eliciting their recollections. "Thucydides says his work was not written to be recited and applauded in theatres," Benton wrote a friend, "but for a 'perpetual possession,' and mine is written with the same view, but without any expectation that it will last so long." The 739-page book— "the story of the 'Working of the American Government' (as Benton saw it) from the 'agitating question' of Missouri admission in 1820 to the end of Andrew Jackson's administration"—was greeted by respectable critical reviews and sold an astonishing sixty-five thousand copies. Written, as Benton saw it, for the masses, "at best, the book showed insight, intensity, and eloquence," according to one account, "—at worst, distortion, dullness, and pomposity." Announcing that his book was "intended to show the capacity of the people for self-government, and the advantage of extending—instead of restricting—the privilege of the direct vote," *Thirty Years' View* was a powerful, often redundant summary of the Jeffersonian and Jacksonian doctrines Benton had advocated since the 1830s.

Many later historians dismissed the book as utter hyperbole, but Roosevelt, in his biography of Benton, contended that his life and passions could not be overstated. "Many of his expressions, when talking of the greatness of our country and of the magnitude of the interests which were being decided, not only were grandiloquent in manner, but also seem exaggerated and overwrought even as regards matter. But when we think of the interests for which he contended, as they were to become, and not as they at the moment were, the appearance of exaggeration is lost, and the intense feeling of his speeches no longer seems out of place or disproportionate to the importance of the subject with which he dealt."

Meanwhile, Frémont had left the Mormons at the end of February, and by April 16 had arrived in San Francisco, where the *Alta California* reported him healthy and robust. He "is as fat as a buck—so much so that his clothes seem too tight for him," wrote Montgomery Blair, who was then practicing law in California. "He has traveled great distances afoot eating horses & mules that had given out & grown fat on them & makes no account of his hardships." Eager to return to Washington, John declined public appearances in San Francisco, and by late May had returned east.

Their summer was frenetic as Elizabeth's health declined, Benton promoted his book, Jessie helped her father with the second volume of his memoirs, and John made a halfhearted attempt at writing a report of the expedition. John published a long letter in the *National Intelligencer* "setting forth the advantages of his easy central route to the Pacific," though it was neither easy nor central—a fact not lost on the national audience. "Frémont pronounced his pathetic little expedition a success," wrote twentieth-century biographer and harsh Frémont critic Andrew Rolle. Carvalho's daguerreotypes were printed in the Washington studio of photographer Mathew Brady, though they would later be destroyed in a warehouse fire, and Carvalho's memoir would become the unofficial account of the survey. In the end, the only real purpose of the expedition was to promote the general idea and physical viability of a transcontinental railroad. "It seems treason against mankind and the spirit of progress which marks the age to refuse to put this one completing link to our national prosperity and the civilization of the world," Frémont wrote in his letter to the national press. "Europe still lies between Asia and America; build this railroad and things will have revolved about; America will lie between Asia and Europe—the golden vein which runs through the history of the world will follow the iron track to San Francisco."

The fifth expedition terminated John C. Frémont's career as Pathfinder and marked the only time in American history when an explorer had undertaken a major expedition without government funding. Knowledge obtained in Frémont's five expeditions would be crucial in the development of a transcontinental railroad, but no rail line would ever be built along the thirty-eighth parallel that Benton and Frémont had so long and passionately promoted. In the summer of 1854 Frémont "permanently turned his back on those western campfires in whose embers his personal glory was once reflected so brightly."

By fall 1854, Jessie's world began to crumble. John had returned to California alone in August. "[T]he affairs of his mining property required his own supervision, but for once I failed to go with him," Jessie wrote. "It was one of the conflicting decisions women have sometimes to make, between their old life and the newer; but we were both in full strength and early life, and I could not turn from my failing patient Mother, and my Father's reliance on my cheerful companionship."

As John left for Las Mariposas, Benton returned to Missouri to campaign for reelection. Elizabeth had just turned sixty years old, and her health had seemed to take a turn for the better, so he felt he could leave her alone with Jessie and his other daughters. Suffering from chronic, often debilitating, headaches, Benton traveled first to Virginia to seek a cure at a hot springs. On the afternoon of Sunday, September 10, Elizabeth—who had been mute and immobile for months—suddenly asked Jessie to walk with her into Benton's library. In the book-filled study, Elizabeth reached out to touch her husband's chair and then ran her hand along his desk. "Good child—take care," she uttered to Jessie, holding her least favorite daughter while bursting into tears. Jessie led her mother back to bed, where Elizabeth died quietly in her sleep that night.

Though just a few years earlier Jessie might have felt ambivalent or worse upon her mother's death—their competition for Benton's attention once seething just below the surface, masked only by polite gentility—she had come to pity rather than resent the woman who had lived a life of utter disappointment. Elizabeth had hated the world of politics her husband inhabited, always looking back wistfully to Cherry Grove, wondering how her life would have been if she had married a Virginia blueblood and lived in simple opulence. Still, she had adroitly fulfilled her role as a senator's wife, entertaining the divorcée Rachel Jackson when official Washington snubbed the future president's wife, regularly hosting the capital's elite, and creating a rich domestic environment for the Benton family that made it possible for them all to thrive even as she withered in her martyrdom. Unable to cope with the mental depression that had not yet been identified by the medical community as a mood disorder, she did what thousands of educated upper-class women did—she took to her bed. Invalidism in her economic and social strata was epidemic, where a direct correlation could be drawn between a woman's intelligence and her physical fragility. "Various nervous afflictions & morbid habits of thought" infected many of the women of her milieu, observed a peer. Exploring the subject in an unpublished essay, Frances Seward, wife of a future secretary of state, questioned whether these ubiquitous psychosomatic illnesses were related to the frustration of educated women. Perhaps they suffered because they were "exempted from Labour," as Mrs. Seward put it. Like many women of her generation, Elizabeth McDowell Benton turned her bitterness and hostility not on her husband but on her energetic, accomplished, beautiful, and brilliant daughter. Elizabeth had made the undermining of Jessie her life's work for the past three decades, and now the rivalry had come to an end, its finality marked not by bitterness but by love and mutual empathy.

For his part, Benton was bereft at having missed his wife's final parting, as well as her funeral two days later. "That I should have been absent at that moment!" he said, sobbing. "I who had always been with her, and striving to keep every sorrow from her heart." The following month, one of Frémont's creditors obtained a court judgment against him, and a California sheriff seized nearly all of Las Mariposas. Jessie, now suffering from the morning sickness of early-stage pregnancy, was deeply disappointed to learn the news, bringing as it did the necessity for John to remain in California for several more months. Then, in a dreadful blow, her father lost his bid for reelection to Congress.

The previous spring, Senator Stephen Douglas of Illinois had placed his Kansas-Nebraska bill before Congress—one designed to repeal the

Missouri Compromise and open the new territory of Kansas to slavery. A blatant subversion of the 1820 compact banning slavery in all of the land acquired from France in the Louisiana Purchase, including the territory out of which Kansas and Nebraska were carved, Douglas's bill stirred fierce Northern opposition. The intensity of the debate—opening "a wound destined never to heal"—surprised the Northerner Douglas as much as anyone, who saw the issue as one of popular sovereignty and self-rule, whereby frontier democracies would settle their own slave controversies. Instead, the measure would signal the end of the Whig Party, create a schism in the Democratic Party that never entirely mended, and set in motion the inevitable creation of a new political party dedicated to the exclusion of slavery from all the territories. An abolitionist newspaper, the *National Era*, published an "Appeal" written by Salmon P. Chase, Charles Sumner, Joshua Giddings, and three other Democrats in opposition to the bill—a manifesto warning that the nation would become "a dreary region of despotism, inhabited by masters and slaves." The *New York Tribune's* Horace Greeley contended that Douglas and President Pierce together had "made more abolitionists in three months than Wendell Phillips and William Lloyd Garrison could have made in half a century," as a historian paraphrased Greeley.

At the center of the controversy was Senator Benton—attacking the proposal as a thinly veiled attempt to smuggle slavery into the West and north, to the Canadian border. He made what was widely regarded as his greatest speech—"the one in opposition to the Kansas-Nebraska bill, which was being pushed through Congress by the fire-eaters and their Northern proslavery followers," as Theodore Roosevelt described it.

At midnight on March 4, Douglas—dubbed by his followers the "Little Giant" or "Steam Engine in Britches"—had begun his four-hour speech in support of the bill organizing Nebraska into two territories that would effectively make Nebraska free and Kansas slave. "Midnight passed and the cock crew, and daylight broke before the vote was taken," the *New York Tribune* reported the scene. At five A.M. the Senate majority had voted in support of the bill, the single act destroying "seven decades of political handiwork by which Congress, to allay sectional tensions, had tried to balance the number of slave and free states brought into the Union," according to historian Tom Chaffin. Northern and Southern Whigs divided along sectional lines, while the Democratic

Party maintained discipline, with a majority of Northern Democrats voting with their Southern counterparts.

Benton promptly vented his disgust and pronounced the Senate "emasculated." Fearing the nation was now indisputably heading toward dissolution, Benton had fought tenaciously to hold on to his own seat in Congress. But his antislavery sentiments ran counter to the proslavery Democrats ascendant in Missouri, and he was crushed in the fall election of 1854, Missouri voters convinced he had betrayed them and his own Southern roots. He turned his attention to the lecture circuit, taking to the road to warn Americans of the peril of the Kansas-Nebraska Act, which he thought would lead to bloodshed and which should be opposed by all Americans, by all constitutional means available to them. Benton was the most educated man in Congress, and his written speeches had always been incomparable—their erudition far surpassing his oral deliveries. But in recent years he had come to speak with such "passion and trenchancy" that his public appearances were regularly greeted with packed galleries and auditoriums. "I will be a new Peter the Hermit," he declared, "and though you now call me mad, later you will admit I was inspired." The trade in human beings must come to an end, he argued, or the clash between North and South would lead inevitably to war and ruin. "While the proslavery South rejoiced in an entirely unexpected triumph, handed to it by a Western senator eager for its votes, gloom and wrath overspread the entire North," historian James A. B. Scherer depicted the national mood.

When Benton returned to Washington after his defeat, he was inconsolable. Jessie tried within her power to comfort him, perhaps recognizing for the first time that it had been her mother—not herself—who had indeed been Benton's most staunch devotee and lifeline. In fact, Jessie had abandoned her father long ago, first for Frémont, then for California and Europe. She had married someone whom her father had at first rejected then reluctantly embraced, and now had rejected again with what seemed to her a more palpable and sustained depth.

Lonely and grieving, Benton immersed himself in writing the second volume of his memoirs, and Jessie did her best to provide him with emotional and intellectual support. Each day, Jessie walked from her nearby residence to her father's C Street home, took her place in Benton's study, and transcribed his musings. Then, in February 1855, tragedy struck again when a spark from a defective fireplace ignited a rapidly spreading fire in the Benton family home. Benton was at the Capitol attending his last congressional session when word came that the house was in flames. Jessie was at a reception at the home of her cousin when the French cook "in white cap and apron" appeared at the door of the drawing room, waving his hands toward the street and shouting: "The house of Senator Benton BURN!" Jessie's sisters and the servants were barely able to escape, and both passersby and firemen nearly smothered as they attempted to retrieve items from the residence. Jessie's sister Eliza tried to save the completed manuscript of Benton's memoir, risking her own life in the process. The upstairs floor fell into the library, crushing and burning the thousands of books and papers. Eliza first sent her small children to safety, then turned off the gas at the meter to prevent an explosion before heading in to save the manuscript she knew was sitting on the library table. She "fell suffocated and would have been lost but for a young Irish groom who ran into the burning room after her and carried her into the air."

Jessie rushed to the home to find thick smoke filling the late afternoon sky and a large crowd gathered. Her father was standing outside in the icy street, hat in hand, watching helplessly as the fire consumed his personal and public papers and all his beloved books. "What little water was to be had was frozen, and the house was doomed," Jessie wrote. "Both houses of Congress had instantly adjourned, and they, and nearly all Washington, gathered in sympathy around my father," silently nodding and baring their heads to the elder statesman. Only his portrait, rescued by Frank Key, a neighbor and son of the author of "The Star-Spangled Banner," survived the inferno. Everything else was destroyed. His library, the library of his father, the folios of English state trials he had read with his mother, were gone. "Like a proud ship full-freighted, the dear hospitable noble home went down all standing," Jessie described the catastrophe. Benton's material loss was not covered by insurance, but it was the obliteration of the irreplaceable items that haunted him—"the bed on which my wife died, on which I sleep; her clothes, which were in a trunk setting at the head of it; the articles which she prized most, around it—the last things I saw at night, and the first in the morning."

That night, he went to Jessie's home, and the two of them talked until dawn "as only those who love one another can talk after a calamity." He gave her the portrait—the only thing saved from the burning residence—which made her cry uncontrollably. "All is gone that made my life," he said. "This makes it easy to die." Still, with characteristic fortitude and inexorability, Benton determined to rebuild his home and rewrite his book. "Not one book from his valuable library . . . was saved," Jessie recalled, "and he had to write over again, without much of the needed data . . . It required all his will, all his magnificent courage, but the writing and the rebuilding of his house prevented the dwelling on the grief of losing my mother." Though any man might have been broken by this "year of sorrows," Benton somehow mustered the inner strength to begin anew. Friends, colleagues, and mere acquaintances poured out their sympathy to the seventy-three-year-old political figure, offering hospitality and financial assistance. President Franklin Pierce came to Jessie's house the night of the fire, "too moved to be able to speak at first," grasping Benton's hands and choking back his emotion. An adversary with whom Benton "refused personal intercourse . . . from some political offense," Pierce invited Benton to move into the Executive Mansion. "He told my father he had been off riding when the news met him, and he had hurried to him stopping only at the White House to give the necessary order—'and you will find everything ready for you—the library and the bedroom next it, and you must stay there until you rebuild your house.'" The president's compassion moved Benton from his "stern endurance," as Jessie put it. "[I]t is Pierce's head that is wrong—his heart is always right," Benton said. Indeed, Pierce's only child, a twelve-year-old son, had recently died a gruesome death— "shockingly mutilated in a railroad accident"—so the president was keenly empathetic to another's grief. But the senator, proud and resolute, graciously declined all proposals, and moved into the Frémont home with Jessie and the children. He accepted an offer to join a lecture circuit through New England and the West to speak about the looming national crisis—issuing "Old Testament warnings . . . as though he were an ancient prophet who had come forth from the wilderness with a terrible vision."

In March, he made the sad journey to St. Louis for Elizabeth's final interment. The pallbearers, headed by Montgomery Blair, carried the casket while mourners sang Elizabeth's favorite song—"Jesus, Lover of My Soul." All eyes were on Benton, who was "convulsed with emotion," his head bowed, his hat covering his face. The funeral procession made its way to Bellefontaine Cemetery, on the banks of the Mississippi River, where Thomas Hart Benton laid the love of his youth to rest alongside his mother. The life he so cherished had come to an end, just as the nation he so revered seemed stumbling toward extermination. And yet the once-towering giant found he could only stand by in uncharacteristic helplessness.

6

FREE SPEECH, FREE SOIL, FREE MEN, FRÉMONT 1855–1857

Republics exist only on the tenure of being constantly agitated.
The antislavery agitation is an important, nay, an essential part
of the machinery of the state . . . Every government is always
growing corrupt. Every Secretary of State . . . is an enemy to the
people of necessity, because the moment he joins the government, he
gravitates against that popular agitation which is the life of a republic.
A republic is nothing but a constant overflow of lava . . . The republic
which sinks to sleep, trusting to constitutions and machinery, to
politicians and statesmen, for the safety of its liberties,
never will have any.

—Wendell Phillips

"[I]T WAS IN the person of John Charles Frémont that the nation's enthusiasm for the poetry of Lord Byron found a career," wrote Bernard de Voto. A literary man with a literary wife, as de Voto described him. "If his father's romance was out of Alexandre Dumas, his own was out of Italian opera. It rose in a fine cadenza when, secretly married to Jessie, the beautiful, bluestocking daughter of Thomas Hart Benton, he stood before the Senator to announce defiance of his will. Benton's rage had been known continentally ever since he had shot it out with Andrew Jackson in a community brawl. It now turned on Frémont but to violins Jessie stepped forward and sang her aria, 'Whither thou goest I will go, and where thou lodgest I will lodge.'"

By the spring of 1855, Jessie and John had been married for thirteen years, though they had spent only a fraction of that time together. She had borne four children and buried two, and was pregnant with her fifth.

They had traveled across the continent numerous times—alone and together—and experienced what one biographer called the "peaks of glory" and "valleys of despair." Still, for all the drama and adventure, it was as nothing compared to what would follow in the couple's future. Sectional tension was at a fevered pitch, and when John finally returned to Washington—just days before their last child, Francis Preston, named for Francis Preston Blair, was born on May 17—it was to a deeply pessimistic wife. Still grieving the loss of her mother and baby girl, the thirty-year-old Jessie was weakened by the birth of "Frank," who was "well but not strong." She had found the political atmosphere in the capital harsh and depressing, and had missed having her husband there to support her during the dark and sorrowful days. Too fragile to breast-feed, Jessie hired a wet nurse for the baby and began taking opiates to relieve the pain of what she called "neuralgia"—a bizarre, perhaps psychosomatic affliction that would plague her for years to come.

The coolness between her father and her husband was unbearable to Jessie, and the strife with friends and relatives was distressing. Her McDowell cousins, expressing rabid secessionist feelings, asked her to choose between the North and the South. "Are you and Colonel Frémont with *us*, or are you following your father's views, so strange for a Southerner?"

Debates in Congress over the Fugitive Slave Law, and then the Kansas-Nebraska Act, had raged out of control and beyond any sense of civil propriety, the issue of slavery cutting across all bounds of class, religion, and ideology. Long-standing friendships and family ties were strained to the breaking point, and the discourse was vicious and intensely personal. On the heels of the Compromise of 1850, Georgia slave-catchers had traveled to Boston to apprehend William and Ellen Craft, two fugitive slaves who had escaped to that city—the case becoming "the most famous runaway saga since Frederick Douglass's." They were forced to return South without their captives after being harassed by a vigilance committee headed by a minister, Theodore Parker, that hid the Crafts along with several other slavery escapees. President Fillmore had threatened to send in federal troops to capture the couple, but the committee put them on board a ship to Great Britain. "I would rather lie all my life in jail, and starve there, than refuse to protect one of these parishioners of mine," Parker wrote the president. That incident and other high-profile cases of slaves being returned in chains to their owners galvanized Northern abolitionists and those who once had dismissed them as fanatics, exposing as it did the brutal character of the institution and deflating "the slaveholders' argument that the slaves were content."

Then, the publication of two antislavery novels further stirred Northern sentiment into coalescence around the creation of a new political party. The first, Herman Melville's *Moby-Dick*—an allegorical tale of good and evil in which an albino sperm whale epitomizes evil—had appeared in 1851. Dedicated to Melville's hero Nathaniel Hawthorne, the book was too dense to be widely digested, but the Northern intellectual elite considered it brilliant and revolutionary. "It is in the general ambience and pile-up of references that his prophecy of America's destruction, propelled by the politics of 1850–51, acquires its force," as Sean Wilentz put it.

But it was a second book, published in March 1852, that swept the country by storm and provided the rallying cry for antislavery advocates. Harriet Beecher Stowe's *Uncle Tom's Cabin* sold more than three hundred thousand copies within a year, and unlike the opaque *Moby-Dick*, was a straightforward and literal plea for the end of slavery. Moved by the passage of the Fugitive Slave Law to write the book, the Cincinnati mother of seven, daughter of Reverend Lyman Beecher, and sister of famous reformer Henry Ward Beecher, "broke through the racism of white America as no one . . . had done."

As the last straw in a series of pivotal events—a sequence that ran from the Compromise of 1850 through the Kansas-Nebraska Act—*Uncle Tom's Cabin* ushered in the final dissolution of party allegiances begun with the creation in 1848 of the Free-Soil Party, whose motto was "Free Soil, Free Speech, Free Labor, Free Men" and the discriminatory and nativist Know-Nothing Party in the early 1850s. The Whigs had all but disappeared after being trounced by the Democrats in the 1852 elections, though a few diehards, including Abraham Lincoln in Illinois, maintained their party loyalties during the political upheaval. While a relative few antislavery Democratic leaders, such as Thomas Hart Benton, remained steadfast, most deserted, leaving the Democratic Party under the domination of Southern slaveholders. The defectors— even faithful old Jacksonians such as Francis Preston Blair—were looking for a new home, and political coalitions and fusion parties sprang up throughout the free Northern states. "All democracy left the democratic party, and every true democrat that was too intelligent to be cheated by a name deserted its ranks," wrote Massachusetts radical

Frederick Robinson. Blair, splitting with his closest personal and political friend, Benton, "set forth the radical case" in a piece called *A Voice from the Grave of Jackson!* "Against this spurious Democracy which has thus perfected its system in the Kansas act, and made it their test, I as a Democrat of the Jefferson, Jackson, and Van Buren school, enter my protest."

The Republican Party was christened in Ripon, Wisconsin, in 1854 when antislavery Democrats, Whigs, and Free Democrats united and named themselves after Thomas Jefferson's original party. Eventually Blair and other compatible dissidents, such as *New York Tribune* editor Horace Greeley, Ohio's Salmon P. Chase, and New York's William Seward, would join them.

In the spring of 1855, Jessie and John seemed strangely removed from the reality that their lives would be inextricably enmeshed with the birth of this new and radically progressive political party. As early as March, Democrats, desperate to find a more palatable candidate than Franklin Pierce, were mentioning Frémont as a presidential contender. Yet, as if oblivious to the events in which they would soon become entrenched, Jessie and John made travel plans for the summer and fall, giving little attention to the national political revolution taking place around them. Though Montgomery Blair and other high-priced lawyers had been able to clear the title to Las Mariposas—paving the way for lucrative gold mining profits—a squatter crisis was brewing, and it would be necessary for them to return to California in the autumn, when Jessie and the baby were stronger. But even as the Frémonts planned their return to the West Coast, the Democrats, Know-Nothings, and Republicans all turned to John as a presidential hopeful.

For all her years in Washington, Jessie had never fully appreciated how "Southern" the city was. As outspoken advocates against the extension of slavery, she and John could not escape the vituperative climate. Many of her own family members now shunned her, and old friendships disintegrated. "Before my baby was a month old, the bitterness of the coming strife invaded even my guarded room," Jessie wrote. "I felt the ground-swell—I felt I was no longer in my place." John encouraged her to move "North," where she had numerous like-minded and supportive friends. Wishing to distance herself from her father, whose aloofness was a daily discomfort to her, she decided to take the children to a beachfront cottage at Siasconset on Nantucket Island for the summer while

John traveled among Washington, Philadelphia, and New York attending to their financial, legal, and now, suddenly, political affairs.

The first approach to Frémont came from Edward Carrington, a Benton family relative who was a nephew of Democratic Virginia governor John B. Floyd. Carrington had joined the Native Americans—the rabidly anti-immigrant, anti-Catholic party that "bore the aspects of a secret fraternity" and became known as the Know-Nothings because members, instructed by leaders to vote only for native-born Protestant candidates, were told to respond "I know nothing" when asked about the party's activities. During Frémont's months in Washington over the spring and summer of 1855, Carrington lured him into discussions with fusionist leaders who were forming an alliance of the Native Americans and Democrats and actively seeking a viable fusion candidate. "The explorer-hero with an antiestablishment attitude," as one historian described Frémont, seemed perfect—a handsome, charismatic, and popular leader unidentified with the Democrats' corruption.

"At this time Colonel Frémont had given but little thought to political affairs," Jessie later wrote. "He was a Democrat, but chiefly because his sympathies were with the people at large." Though he was neither prejudiced nor anti-Catholic, Frémont saw burgeoning immigration as a threat to America, prompting the Nativists—"led by wealthy and middle-class evangelicals and by old-school Whigs"—to mistakenly consider him simpatico. In the decade between 1845 and 1855, almost three million mostly poverty-stricken immigrants had poured into the United States. Nearly half had escaped the potato famine of Ireland, while the other half came primarily from the economically depressed Catholic regions of Germany. Bloody riots between Protestant and Catholic workers beleaguered urban areas, especially Philadelphia, prompting the Nativists to blame the Catholic immigrants for the decay of American society.

"In the main features of their political faith Colonel Frémont agreed with them," Jessie wrote. "Looking at the actual happy conditions of the country and the broad fields it had to offer for labor, and foreseeing in the rapidly increasing immigration that the country would soon attain some of the conditions shown by the overcrowded nations of the Old World, Colonel Frémont felt that the time had come to close the United States against indiscriminate emigration; he believed that the true policy was to hold the great landed estate which belonged to the people of this Continent, strictly to the use of the people, and that new adult owners should not be added year by year." Frémont was convinced that the disenfranchised citizenry of the "Old World" brought their cynicism with them, the expatriates failing to assimilate into American society with what he saw as the optimistic vitality necessary for an "instructed, homogeneous people, educated and faithful to the institutions of the country, and with a comprehension and devotion to it." He believed that only American residents of twenty-one years or more should have the right to vote.

Frémont humored the Know-Nothing leaders, paying them minimal deference while enjoying the philosophical banter. Though he found them narrow-minded and racist, he was sympathetic to their "restrictionist aims," as one historian put it, agreeing "that America might be happier and better-governed if it granted citizenship less easily to a mass of ill-assimilated immigrants." He was initially unaware, naïvely so, that they were sounding him out as a possible fusion presidential candidate in an alliance between the Democrats and the Nativists. The discussions culminated in a three-day conference at the St. Nicholas Hotel in New York, where Southern agents led by Governor Floyd offered him the Democratic nomination, with two strings attached that would pacify the Southern wing of the party—that he endorse both the Kansas-Nebraska Act and Fugitive Slave Law. He was seen as a compromise candidate who could pull together the unity of the party. Not only was he young and vital, he also was a national hero, the dashing "Pathfinder" who had conquered California with only sixty-two men, a man of the people beholden to no one. That Benton's name was also being bandied about by political power brokers further pitted the two men against each other, though Benton roundly declared that he would not seek the presidency.

Frémont took Nathaniel Banks with him to the New York conference. A longtime friend and admirer, Banks was Frémont's political kindred spirit. A former Democrat, he had become a Know-Nothing congressman from Massachusetts and would soon be elected Speaker of the House. A passionate Free-Soiler, Banks was uncompromising when it came to the extension of slavery, and made his position clear to both Frémont and the Democrats, expressing "himself so strongly to Governor Floyd . . . as to nearly terminate the meeting." Banks denounced the

Fugitive Slave Law in "prophetic terms," as Jessie later described it, "telling Governor Floyd that it was the entering wedge which would divide the North and South, place them in arms against one another, and become the lever by which the institution of slavery would be overthrown." Banks's outburst dampened the mood of the conference. Though Frémont's mind was in fact made up, he declined to reveal his decision, telling the agents that he must first discuss the matter with his wife. Confident that the Democrats would win the election, and convinced that "no woman could refuse the Presidency," as Carrington put it, the Democratic leaders felt certain that Jessie would support their designs. But they sorely misjudged the independent character of Jessie Benton Frémont.

Even as the Democrats' negotiations with Frémont were in progress, his name was being bandied about by Republican Party founders, nearly unanimous in agreement that Frémont was the ideal nominee. While Jessie relaxed on a Nantucket beach, recuperating from childbirth, she made a conscious effort to dismiss the confusing and antagonistic political battlefield from her mind. "I longed for the peace and beauty and secluded dignity of such a home as we had had in Paris," she wrote. "When I was well enough to be taken to the life giving air of Nantucket, I was not told of any further political moves but was left untroubled to regain my strength." She focused her attention on her children and waited, as usual, for John to join the family. She wrote regularly to her dear friend Lizzie Blair, their correspondence increasing in frequency and intimacy as Jessie spoke of the mundane and profound, confiding her anxieties and seeking advice. "I think opiates are so sickening I want to be done with them," she wrote Lizzie, expressing her desire to obtain the "Black berry root medicine your mother makes." She delighted in the "fat and contented" baby Frank, was charmed by four-year-old barefooted Charley playing in "the thick of it" with his rolled-up pants, and expressed her pleasant surprise at the well-educated and well-traveled grandchildren of the celebrated suffragette Lucretia Mott, with whom thirteen-year-old Lily was enamored. "Badly as she thinks of southern people," Jessie wrote of Mott, the controversial and outspoken Quaker abolitionist and cofounder of the American women's rights movement who would eventually become Jessie's friend, "I always thought worse of a 'strong minded' speech making woman." Apparently ignorant of John's deepening discussions with the Democrats and the Know-Nothings, she wrote of her intentions to return to Washington for a week in the fall before sailing to California.

One summer day, Solomon Nuñes Carvalho arrived with his notebooks, eager to discuss with Jessie a book he was writing about his experiences on Frémont's fifth expedition. Beginning what would become a lifelong patronage of the arts, she offered to find space in New York for Carvalho, the photographer Mathew Brady, who was developing Carvalho's daguerreotypes, and a Philadelphia artist who was painting scenes from the expedition. Carvalho's manuscript was highly personal and would be the first book to include daguerreotypes of the American West. He announced his intention to dedicate the book to Jessie, and read her a passage about her husband. "To me Colonel Frémont is a hero in the highest sense," he had written. "I want to tell clearly and candidly the incidents in our experience where in that long gamut of hardship and suffering his heroic quality sang above the minor jangle of despair. I know why his old followers and the scouts, Carson and Godey, rally to him as their hero. Personal courage and skill he showed at all times, and his high qualities of fairness to subordinates. Through every vicissitude his self-control, his endurance of spirit against obstacles won from us a kind of worshipful loyalty. The Colonel's worst enemies grant him personal courage. We can prove all our claims from actual suffering with him."

Such fawning adulation of her husband was in stark contrast to the increasing disdain that her father exhibited. In August, Benton visited Jessie at the seaside retreat on a stopover between lectures in New York City and Boston. Benton was white-haired and stooped, the once-looming figure a mere shadow of his former self, his innate and legendary optimism overtaken by depression and gloom. "I am satisfied slavery will not go down until it goes down in blood," he quoted John Quincy Adams from 1843. For thirty years Benton had played a dominant role in the Democratic Party, and now he railed against the defectors, fellow Jacksonians, revered and respected colleagues, close personal friends, and political allies of three decades. The inveterate old nationalist held a special contempt for the nascent Republican Party, which he saw as spinning the nation into an inevitable spiral toward disunion and civil war. "With this nullification treason among us, we Union Democrats have become the victims of our loyalties," he declared. "If the Democrats don't unite, they will have plenty to fear from those rag-tags now trying to form new parties."

Jessie was puzzled over her father's obsession with the Republicans, considering the virtual obsolescence of the Whigs. The gravest threat to the nation, in Jessie's opinion, was slavery, not an infant, opposition party. Wasn't a strong two-party system a Bentonian ideal after all?

When John arrived at Siasconset in late August 1855, he stood for a while in the distance observing Jessie, dressed in the palest blue, her hair tied in a ribbon, serving tea on the terrace to their children. "As I watched that family picture, I longed for the power to make it the symbol of my Jessie's future," he later recalled. "But already I had come to impart disturbing knowledge." Lily was holding baby Frank in her lap, while Charley listened raptly to a story his mother was telling. As John approached the house, the family erupted in excitement. It was not until dusk, after the children had been fed and the baby settled, that he took Jessie for a long, private walk to Lighthouse Hill. "It was nearing sunset," she recalled. ". . . The struggling moon was often hidden by fog, which the revolving light pierced with flashes to leave in greater darkness—like my troubled mind there seemed no continuing in one stay."

When they were seated on a rocky outcrop in the moonlight, he turned to her, reaching for her hand. "Jessie, I've been offered the nomination for the presidency." She couldn't help thinking of the years as a child, visiting the White House, sitting on President Jackson's lap, dining with Van Buren's sons, the candlelight dancing off the walls of the stately rooms. Her initial elation subsided when she learned the conditions set forth by the Democrats: Frémont must endorse the Fugitive Slave Law, which would return slaves in chains back to their owners, and support the Kansas-Nebraska Act, which would extend slavery into western territories. Though both were untenable in Jessie's opinion, she considered the possibility—espoused by her father—that only a compromise candidate could save the country from civil war. Neither John nor Jessie had seriously harbored such grandiose personal aspirations. And yet now, suddenly, she wanted it desperately for them both. If he could rise to the presidency, the wounds of his illegitimacy and the humiliation of his court-martial would be mitigated once and for all. She was also frank to admit her intense desire to be first lady—the highest position to which a woman could aspire in America—believing that together they could change the course of history. But in the end, after hours of discussion and a well-considered attempt to justify the compromise in pursuit of the larger goal, the choice was clear. They could not go against their principles—*especially* with regard to slavery. Though staved off and contained for decades, the long-simmering sectional tensions between the North and South were now detonating. The western expansionism in which John, at the behest of Benton, had played such a large part had provoked the crisis—an irony keenly felt by these two, who had devoted their lives to Jefferson's agrarian idealism of what he had called "a peaceable and agricultural nation."

Jessie sensed a sudden and terrible apprehension, for she knew their course was clear. He was being courted as well by the gradually forming Republican Party that was being created by dissident Whigs and Democrats opposed to the extension of slavery, and old Free-Soilers who had abandoned the two parties. She knew her husband was the first choice of many of the new party's founders, and in an instant the recognition of all that entailed was clear to her. "There was no shadow of doubt in our minds," she described the moment. "At the foot of the bluff on which the lighthouse stood were the remains of a ship embedded in the sands, the seas washing her ribs. Above, steady and brilliant, flashed out the recurring light. Here was the symbol of a choice between a wreck of dishonor or a kindly light on its mission of good. With clasped hands we made our decision and turned homeward with the kindly beacon at our back."

On some internal level she knew that John would be the Republican candidate and that her family ties would be shattered—above all the bond with her already distant father. It would mean "excommunication by the South," she recalled her feelings, "the absolute ending of all that had made my deep rooted pleasant life." Still, there was but "one decision possible," and when they entered the Nantucket cottage long after midnight she knew "the past lay behind" her.

When Frémont officially rejected the offer from the Democrat and Know-Nothing coalition—issuing "several public letters on slavery in which he refused to reconcile his compassion over Negro rights with the racism of the Know Nothings," as biographer Andrew Rolle described his admirable stance—the Republicans moved swiftly, with Nathaniel Banks, now the "titular head of the Know Something detachment," leading the way. It was a bold and principled decision, for Frémont probably would have easily entered the White House as the Democratic nominee had he been willing to abandon his opposition to slavery extension. The Democrats, spurned by Frémont, turned their attention to

James Buchanan, while the Know-Nothings reorganized as the American Party and became embroiled in deep divisions over slavery. Meanwhile, Banks convinced other Republican leaders that Frémont was their best candidate, and they quickly organized a movement to nominate the famous explorer. Still, "little was known of Colonel Frémont politically," Jessie wrote of the early days in the campaign, "except his attitude on the question of Slavery and its extension. The stand he had taken regarding California at the time of its admission to the Union, and his votes on the Slavery question while he was in the Senate, left no doubt in the minds of the people, as to which side he would be found upon, and the question was pushed to a division."

From the moment their choice was made, Jessie deserted her sickbed and began working vigorously behind the scenes to secure the nomination for her shy and reserved husband. It was Jessie, not John, whose keen political instincts went into high gear. "My dear Mr. Blair," Jessie penned a pivotal and strategic letter on August 27 to her father's closest friend and political ally, hoping not only to elicit Blair's crucial support for Frémont, but also candidly entreating Blair to persuade Benton to join the Republican Party and support her husband. "Mr. Frémont has under consideration so important a step, that before taking it he wishes for the advice and friendly counsel which have heretofore proved so full of sagacity and led to such success." Tactful if not cunning, Jessie brilliantly guided Blair, whom she knew to be deeply disaffected with the Democrats and leaning toward the antislavery Republicans, to think favorably of John's nomination. "It is not alone for your great experience and insight that Mr. Frémont refers to you, but for the exquisite good taste that is so grateful to his own nature, and assures him from the shocks that Father with his different organization is dangerously apt to give."

Jessie's most primal, most ominous fear was that her father would forsake her at this critical moment in her life. While she wished to believe his love and support for her trumped all else, her child's instincts—the part of her that had competed unsuccessfully with her mother for her father's ultimate devotion, the little girl who watched as her father chose Miss English's academy despite Jessie's heartfelt pleas—warned her that dark days of emotional pain were on the horizon. "I never spoke of this subject with my Father," she wrote years later. "Our minds were in too intimate comprehension for me to doubt his course, or to let any discordant element come to mar the wonderfully beautiful friendship between us. I knew that no earthly gratification could be so great to him as to have me near him in Washington, in the highest position possible for any woman in our country; and I knew that he, of all men, had the best knowledge of the tried and proved high qualities Mr. Fremont would bring to its highest office. But I knew also his unswerving fidelity to 'party.'"

Now sixty-six, Francis Preston Blair had risen in Kentucky politics during the rough-and-tumble antibank wars, had been a Democrat most of his life, and had been summoned to Washington during Andrew Jackson's first term to serve in the president's "Kitchen Cabinet." Jackson relied heavily on him as an adviser and confidant, and the Blair Mansion across from the White House had been Jackson's second home. As longtime editor of the *Globe*—the Jackson administration newspaper—Blair broke with the Polk wing of the Democratic Party over the Mexican War, became an ardent supporter of Van Buren on the "Free Soil band-wagon in 1848," and supported Franklin Pierce until the "Kansas-Nebraska Act was too much for [his] free soil inclinations."

One of Washington's most powerful political figures for decades, though Blair never held elected office, he was widely considered a "mover and shaker" on the national stage. "In private life he was the meekest and mildest of men," wrote his biographer, "but four presidents—Jackson, Van Buren, Lincoln, and Johnson—had all been accused of submitting to his domination." As the Democratic Party's official voice, he developed a deep and abiding friendship with Thomas Hart Benton, and their families became enmeshed, with Jessie referring to the Blair family patriarch as "Father Blair." Daughter Lizzie was Jessie's best friend, and sons Montgomery and Francis Jr. (Frank) were surrogate brothers. Blair Sr. and Benton had once entertained the idea of an arranged marriage between Jessie and Frank—a dream match that had been thwarted by Jessie's elopement with Frémont. Blair once said that he and Benton would "be blended together when we have left the stage of life in history."

With his opposition to the annexation of Texas and expansion of slavery, Blair, like Benton, had been marginalized by the Democratic Party he and Benton had helped to create. Although a Southern slaveholder, Blair passionately opposed slavery's extension beyond where it already existed, and became what Doris Kearns Goodwin described as "one of the first important political figures to call for the founding of the Republican Party."

So Jessie's quest to enlist Blair's aid was both vividly calculating and thoroughly predictable—a continuation of her pattern of writing powerful men on behalf of her husband—and Blair's favorable response was a decisive endorsement at a vital moment. Within days of receiving Jessie's letter Blair drafted a political platform for Frémont based on the restoration of the Missouri Compromise, and led the movement within the new antislavery party to nominate him, though credit would later be given to Nathaniel Banks. It would be a yearlong run-up to the nomination, a complicated process that involved some of the most powerful men in American political life—figures such as Salmon P. Chase and William Seward, who themselves were jockeying for position in the fluid state of affairs. While Seward and Chase were the favorites of Republicans from the East, each "bore the scars of long warfare against slavery," as one historian put it. "I think of Frémont *as a new man,*" Blair wrote to a skeptical Van Buren. "He is brave, firm, has a history of romantic heroism . . . & has no bad political connections—never had— no tail of hungry, corrupt hangers on like Buchanan who will I think be the [Democratic] candidate." While Jessie stayed at Nantucket to recuperate and gather strength for the upcoming onslaught, John traveled to Washington, where Blair and Banks, later called "the discoverer of Frémont," rallied support for the candidacy among national political figures and prominent newspapermen. The enthusiasm was infectious, with Horace Greeley of the *New York Tribune,* John Bigelow and William Cullen Bryant, coeditors of the *New York Evening Post,* the poet John Greenleaf Whittier, and even New York power broker Thurlow Weed moving toward Frémont. His principled rejection of the Democratic nomination elevated him to hero status among Northern abolitionists. His romantic past and millionaire status, his relative youth and famous courage brought a dark-horse hope to a struggling new party. Not least, his forceful and dynamic young wife brought a celebrity aura to what was widely seen as an underdog effort to wrest control from a co-opted party comprised of yesterday's men. "Jessie Benton's heritage added just the right touch of establishment respectability to her husband's outsider appeal," wrote H. W. Brands. That John was a Georgia native and Jessie a descendant of Virginia slaveholders was further regarded as an advantage in the Southern states.

By fall, the viability of the candidacy seemed so promising that Jessie

and John altered their plans to return to California, taking up residence
at the Clarendon House in New York City before renting a town
house at 176 Second Avenue there John relocated first while Jessie
oversaw the packing at Nantucket. He immediately set out to purchase
a masculine wardrobe befitting a president, ordering an overcoat "of
rough coarse material and loose make, without any velvet about it,"
and by October Jessie and the children had joined him. From the comfortable hotel suite Jessie began a shrewd and tactical correspondence
with various potential backers, often writing in cryptic code lest President Pierce's Democratic postal officials penetrated the mail. "Mr.
Frémont wants me to tell you that the result of Mr. B's [Banks's] in-
tervening was all that could be wished and more than he had looked
for," Jessie wrote to Blair on October 21, 1855. "The turkey is getting
restless," she wrote Blair two weeks later, referring to John, who was
dubbed "wild turkey" in the Frémont/Blair cipher, "and will make his
next flight to the pines of Silver Spring—where he will be found the
middle of next week." The first week in November they moved into
their town house, between Tenth and Eleventh streets across from St.
Mark's Church in the Bowery. "Hamilton Fish [New York senator] has
quite a palace just by us—and the new Historical society raises its grey
stone towers next door but one," she wrote Blair. The apartment was
large and comfortable for the family and would serve as the de facto
headquarters for a fresh and progressive political party. Though Jessie
was slightly embarrassed by the ostentatious neighborhood, she was
pleased to find accommodations large enough to provide office space
for both her and John. From there, as if launching a new expedition,
the couple would explore "the wilds of the political world," as one
historian described it.

John traveled frequently to Washington, while Jessie covertly strategized, ever sensitive to the potential backlash of operating beyond her
womanly sphere. She turned childrearing over to the two maids she had
brought to the United States from France and gave her full attention
to the political matters at hand. She eschewed social engagements—"I
make no visits and don't intend to go into that weary round, except of
course in some few cases where there have been previous reasons," she
wrote Blair, and when she did venture out into New York society she
found the "women were dressed within an inch of their lives and stupid
as sheep."

But as Frémont's candidacy gained momentum, as the couple became ubiquitous in New York newspaper articles, they were among the most highly sought-after invitees. Jessie viewed it all with a healthy nonchalance, accustomed as she had long been to the sycophantic whirlwind that attended social and political celebrities. "Just here & just now I am quite the fashion—5th Avenue asks itself, 'Have we a Presidentess among us'—and as I wear fine lace and purple I am in their eyes capable of filling the place. So I go out nightly—sometimes to dinner & a party both the same night and three times a week to the opera where I hold a levee in my box."

The more visible and potent Frémont became, the more hostile and antagonistic his father-in-law grew. Twice that November Blair broached the subject of Frémont's candidacy with his old and dear friend, hoping to persuade Benton to endorse Frémont. But Jessie's worst fears prevailed as her father obstinately rebuffed all overtures, citing the forty-two-year-old Frémont's lack of experience and what he saw as the Republican Party's presumptuous and disruptive overreaching. Benton, who had played such a large part in the Democratic Party for thirty years, found the idea of a Republican Party, and of his son-in-law's candidacy, appalling. Though Benton considered himself antislavery, he fiercely opposed the creation of a new party focused on only one discordant issue that could tear the country apart—calling it a "motley mixture of malcontents with no real desire in any of them to save the Union."

Jessie was heartbroken. The rejection was as publicly embarrassing as it was personally painful. "Since the revoked sale of the Mariposas nearly five years ago, Father has put great constraints on his temper," Jessie wrote Lizzie, "and now he has what he considers a fair occasion for an opposition." At first she sought to blame others, believing her father was unduly influenced by her brother-in-law William Carey Jones, who had long been jealous of John and had evolved into a maudlin and vindictive drunk intent on driving a wedge between Benton and Jessie. "The dropping of water wears away stone," Jessie wrote of Jones's undermining, "and I think the constant dropping of insinuations by Mr. Jones has worn away much of Father's remaining regard for Mr. Frémont."

"The Frémont children found it very confusing because they still adored Grandpa," wrote Blair's biographer. "They were finally persuaded to blame all the trouble on Jones." Jessie loved her father dearly and was overcome with compassion for the embittered elder statesman.

She made excuses for him, alluding to his life of utter isolation. He had lost his wife, his home, his career, and now his favorite daughter. But all intellectual rationalizations aside, the break was a devastating emotional blow to her. In December she sent the teenaged Lily to Washington to visit "that lonely old man." She confided her agony to Lizzie Blair. "And if you should see in him at any time a need for me, you will let me know." An impromptu trip to see her father at Christmas did nothing to assuage the ill feelings that had grown between them, and when she returned to New York the breach was nearly complete. The father-daughter relationship that had once been the envy of Washington was now reduced to common gossip fodder. The man who once would have given his life to see his little Jessie become first lady of the United States would now seek to destroy that possibility for her. To him it was a matter of principle. Now at the end of his life, the proud and stubborn Benton cared more about preserving the Union than about any youthful idealism embodied by Jessie, John, or their upstart political party. He could not end his life knowing he had contributed in any way to bringing on civil war.

Benton refused to attend Blair's "legendary Christmas conclave," held at the Silver Spring estate just days after Jessie left Washington. Salmon P. Chase and Nathaniel Banks both attended the gathering of Republican leaders, along with the rabidly antislavery senator Charles Sumner of Massachusetts; Gamaliel Bailey, the abolitionist editor of *The National Era* who had first published *Uncle Tom's Cabin;* and Congressman Preston King of New York. William Seward had been invited but declined, preferring to watch from the sidelines as events unfolded. His longtime adviser political kingmaker Thurlow Weed, felt that the party had no chance of victory in 1856 and that Seward should avoid being tainted by failure and instead begin posturing for the 1860 campaign, when the party would be nationally organized.

The topic of the meeting—the lavish dinner paradoxically cooked and served by Blair's slaves—was the selection of the party's presidential candidate. Blair was single-minded in his support of the explorer, though his "sudden enthusiasm for Frémont was not without self-interest," as Blair's biographer pointed out. Frémont was "not only an excellent practical choice. If elected, he would be likely to follow Blair's counsel in important matters." At least one newspaper reported that Blair, Banks, King, Chase, and Sumner all agreed that Frémont was the most desirable candidate, though Chase held out hope that he would ultimately be chosen as the nominee at the upcoming Republican national convention.

The choice was solidified at a follow-up meeting in New York hosted by John Bigelow of the *New York Evening Post* and attended by Blair, New York governor Edwin D. Morgan, and other powerful political figures. By January 1856, a strong organization had been created, a machine capable of challenging the Democrats in a national election. "Thurlow Weed says he is contented with Frémont," Bigelow reported to the group, "and, if so, of course Seward is." Since Seward was the obvious favorite among influential Republicans, his withdrawal from consideration removed the only real stumbling block to a Frémont candidacy. With Banks's election as Speaker of the House in February and Blair's selection as president of the Republican planning convention, Frémont became the undeniable front-runner. The power brokers decided to hold a conference in Pittsburgh the following month to bring together the organizers of the party to plan their nominating convention and informally settle on the man. Attended by antislavery moderates and radicals alike from the North as well as from five border states, and comprised of Democrats, Free-Soilers, and Whigs, the new party's leaders were united in opposition to the extension of slavery. "They would submerge their differences in favor of Frémont," wrote one historian. "No other prospect could match the popularity of a candidate who already had seventeen towns and counties named for him."

By spring, newspapers in New York, St. Louis, Boston, and Cleveland were endorsing Frémont. The Chicago correspondent of the *New York Tribune* reported that a "sort of intrusive feeling pervades the people that he will be nominated and elected. The same sentiment is extending over Iowa and spreading into Wisconsin. He seems to combine more elements of strength than any man who has yet been named."

The Know-Nothings, recently reorganized under the more palatable name of the American Party, nominated former president Millard Fillmore and vice presidential running mate Andrew Jackson Donelson of Tennessee, hoping the choice of Jackson's nephew would help the inchoate party make inroads with the Democrats and the Republicans. The Democrats settled on Buchanan and John C. Breckinridge of Kentucky. "As all these men were identified with the slave interests of the country, their election was opposed by those who hoped to limit the spread of slave power," Jessie later wrote. "To this end, a meeting was called in New York in April 1856, for the purpose of obtaining a full expression of opinion from the moneyed centre of the country, against the policy which the administration was following." Frémont was unable to attend the meeting, held at the Broadway Tabernacle, but conveyed his views in a strongly worded statement: "I heartily concur in all movements which have for their object to repair the mischiefs arising from the violation of good faith in the repeal of the Missouri Compromise. I am opposed to slavery in the abstract and upon principle, sustained and made habitual by long settled convictions. While I feel inflexible in the belief that it ought not to be interfered with where it exists, under the shield of State sovereignty, I am as inflexibly opposed to its extension on this continent beyond its present limits."

Antislavery sentiment was further incited when Charles Sumner was beaten nearly to death on the Senate floor in May in retaliation for an incendiary speech attacking slavery in which he singled out South Carolina as a state racked by "its shameful imbecility from slavery," and included a personal attack on one of that state's senators. Two days after the speech, while sitting at his desk, Sumner was attacked by a South Carolina congressman wielding a gold-headed cane. The assailant, Preston Brooks, beat him across the head and back with more than twenty blows, stopping only when the senator was lying motionless in a pool of blood. Blinded and suffering severe injuries to his brain and spinal cord, Sumner would become emblematic of the sharp divisions within the country and would inspire untold numbers of moderates and conservatives to join the Republican Party. While Southerners saw the caning as the proper treatment of someone who had dishonored one of their number, the cold-blooded brutality was shocking to Northerners who had previously been unmoved by the slavery debate. The "knocking-down and beating to bloody blindness and unconsciousness of an American Senator while writing at his desk in the Senate Chamber is a novel illustration of the ferocious Southern Spirit," observed the *New York Tribune*. William Cullen Bryant expressed shock and alarm in his *New York Evening Post*. "Has it come to this, that we must speak with bated breath in the presence of our Southern masters? . . . Are we too, slaves, slaves for life, a target for their brutal blows, when we do not comport ourselves to please them?"

Northern sentiment was galvanized when Southern editors lionized the assailant, who was inundated with requests for fragments of the legendary staff, presented with a silver goblet by the governor of South Carolina, and fined a paltry $300 by a local court, though he was never arrested. "We consider the act good in conception, better in execution, and best of all in consequences," the *Richmond Enquirer* editorialized. "The vulgar Abolitionists in the Senate are getting above themselves . . . They must be lashed into submission." The venerated *Richmond Whig*, known for its objectivity and professionalism, was both most disturbing and most revealing of the deep schism in American society. "The only regret we feel is, that Mr. Brooks did not employ a horsewhip or a cowhide upon his slanderous back, instead of a cane. *We trust the ball may be kept in motion. Seward and others should catch it next.*"

By May it seemed stunningly possible that Frémont could actually win. Conventional wisdom had initially held that the first presidential candidate for the infant party would be a sacrificial lamb in preparation for the election four years later. The party's main threat was the insurgence of the American Party, with Fillmore as its candidate, making the contest a three-man race in which the Democrats secretly financed Fillmore. The Republicans feared that disaffected Whigs, Democrats, Free-Soilers, and Know-Nothings who might have been inclined to join the Republicans would drift to the American Party instead, siphoning off crucial votes in what was shaping up to be an extremely close general election.

Jessie continued to reach out to her father, believing that as John's star rose, her father's heart would soften. "Success, if it comes, gives a more graceful position to be friendly from and if it should be so I think Father cannot resist the influence of it." But throughout the winter and spring of 1856 her overtures to Benton went unanswered. "I have written constantly to Father. I always tell him whatever I think may interest him—never saying politics—but for four months I have not had a line from him . . . ," she wrote Lizzie. "So I am put into Coventry," she continued, referring to the Benton family term used when a child was banished from the dinner table for raising "any vexatious topic." Jessie bristled at the shunning, despising the powerless position in which she found herself, caught between her father and her husband. She implored both Lizzie Blair and Lizzie's father, Francis Preston Blair, to intervene as peacemakers. Bemoaning the fact that her father had not written her since she had visited him the previous Christmas, she revealed a poignant lack of surprise, suggesting a pattern of behavior. "He always drops me that way when he is offended with Mr. Frémont." Still, the devoted daughter was unflagging in her advances. "I wrote about a month ago, saying I would go on to make him a visit when Mr. Frémont returned, but as he made no answer I feel like asking again before going even into what used to be my home. One outlives many things. The burning of our old house was the funeral pyre of home bonds and old ties. However nothing shall make me fail in my respect and duty to Father and if he will ever have it my affection too. I think if he had softer natures about him it would greatly add to his own comfort."

Finally, Benton invited Jessie to "come on and bring the whole." But by the time she made the arrangements to travel to Washington in late May, she arrived only to find that her father had left for St. Louis in what seemed to her an obvious attempt to avoid the meeting. Instead of a much-anticipated reconciliation, she was snubbed rudely by Jones and her sister Eliza. "That was a very bad visit I had to Washington," she wrote Lizzie. "The disappointment of missing Father, the want of hospitality in the house and the fatigue were altogether too much." Upon her return to New York she was seized by a "violent attack of neuralgia—beginning . . . in cramping at the heart" and took to her sickbed. "This time my head shared the attack & I write now with one eye blackened & nearly closed by the stagnated blood which will have to be leeched off."

To add insult to injury, Benton attended the rowdy Democratic convention in Cincinnati, where he was vocal and passionate in his support for the shady Buchanan. Jessie saw it as another humiliating betrayal, made all the more painful by its public display, which was reported by national newspapers. That her father, famous for roaring his views, chose to support over her husband a lackluster man who had spent most of his political career as a party regular seeking to offend no one, was embarrassing. Jessie had begun to feel that her own physical well-being depended upon finally resigning herself to their estrangement. She made a "fixed resolve—not to be hurt at heart any oftener than it is forced upon me—to go deliberately into agitation and pain is almost suicide." There seemed nothing she could do to remedy the relationship. Now it became for her a matter of life and death to turn her back on one of the men she loved.

At eleven o'clock on the morning of June 17, 1856, the Republicans gathered at the Musical Fund Hall in Philadelphia, where the Declaration of Independence had first been read, for their inaugural nominating convention. Signaling the official birth of the Republican Party, the historic event had a "camp meeting fervor, a crusading enthusiasm such as was hardly known again in American politics till the Progressive Convention of 1912 in Chicago." More than a thousand delegates attended, representing all the free states, as well as Kansas, Nebraska, and Minnesota territories. The slave states of Delaware, Maryland, Virginia, Kentucky, and the District of Columbia even sent a smattering of delegates. The air was suffused with revolutionary, revivalistic excitement, as if all gathered believed they were participating in an uprising against oppression— "the slaveocrats and stockjobbers were at last to be vanquished," as one writer put it.

Eighty news reporters covered the event, observing the "Frémont Fever" that swept through the crowd. Even Horace Greeley, whose support for either Seward or Chase was well known, was forced to admit the strength of Frémont's candidacy, though he privately believed that Frémont was ill prepared for national politics and that Jessie, rather than the candidate himself, drove the ambition for his success. "All would be well if F[rémont] were not the merest baby in politics," Greeley wrote to Indiana congressman Schuyler Colfax "He don't know the ABCs." Still, Greeley could not ignore the reality. "Though young and born poor, he has done more service, braved more peril, and achieved more reputation, than any man of his years now living. That must be a very dark and squat log cabin into which the fame of Colonel Frémont has not penetrated ere this," he wrote on June 6. Less than a week later, Greeley had moved from lukewarm observer to outright endorser. "There is no name which can find such favor with the masses," he wrote, describing Frémont as a "man of the People, sprung from the working class." Though he found the candidate woefully inexperienced, Greeley contrasted the explorer's "patriotic and perilous achievement" with the nation's savvier political creatures. "We have had enough of third-rate lawyers and God knows what rate generals." Frémont was a military hero, albeit of a different stripe than Washington, Jackson, Harrison, Taylor, or the failed 1852 Whig nominee, Winfield Scott. Still, the Republican selection reflected the old Whig tendency to nominate someone known for exploits outside of politics and without knowing where the candidate stood on most major issues.

Neither Jessie nor John attended. "All the proprieties forbid it," Jessie wrote to Lizzie, referring to the standard nineteenth-century custom that precluded presidential hopefuls from appearing at national conventions. Edwin D. Morgan presided over the convention, and David Wilmot read the party platform that upheld the Missouri Compromise, opposed the extension of slavery, called for the admission of Kansas as a free state, linked Mormon polygamy and slavery as "twin relics of barbarism," and endorsed the transcontinental railroad.

For two days, the supporters of various contenders—from Seward, to Chase, to Supreme Court justice John McLean—gradually moved to the Frémont camp. Francis Preston Blair, accompanied by his daughter Lizzie, carried with him in his pocket a letter from Frémont authorizing Blair to do anything necessary short of allowing his nomination for vice president. "As respects the nomination to the Presidency," he wrote Blair, "you can, of course introduce or withdraw my name as may judge expedient, taking always the ground that I am a soldier in the ranks, and while I would feel honored, as every foot soldier should, in being promoted, I am sincerely determined to apply time and energy in laboring for the common cause, should the convention determine to entrust its leadership to other hands." On June 18 the vote was taken, and the forty-three-year-old Frémont was overwhelmingly nominated as the Republican candidate to become the fifteenth president.

The crowd burst into cheers, the hall filled with tossing hats and waving handkerchiefs, and a band broke into a rousing rendition of patriotic music. The ovation could be heard from blocks away as banners poured out of the hall's windows. "The enthusiasm is tremendous," Greeley wired his office about the crowds pouring into the streets from nearby homes, joining the delegates in citywide jubilation. An American flag bearing Frémont's name was unfurled onstage, and an enormous pennant inscribed with *John C. Frémont for President* lined the hall. Immediately, the slogan "Free Speech, Free Soil, Free Men, Frémont" was christened.

"The Path-Finder of the Rocky Mountains, the chivalric John C. Frémont, the type and embodiment of the spirit of Young America, was yesterday afternoon nominated on the first ballot, by the Republican Convention in Philadelphia, as their candidate for the Presidency," declared the *New York Times* on June 19. "At the first trial he received nearly two thirds of the whole vote of the convention, and was then nominated by unanimous consent. Such a degree of unanimity and enthusiasm as this has had no example in the political history of the country."

What followed was what John and Jessie both considered the greatest mistake of the convention—the nomination of conservative New Jersey ex-Whig William L. Dayton as Frémont's running mate. Both Abraham Lincoln and Simon Cameron, a Pennsylvania senator and former adjutant general who had been a Democrat and then a Know-Nothing, had been front-runners. Frémont strongly favored Cameron, whom he thought would be crucial for the ticket to carry Buchanan's home state of Pennsylvania, although the contrast between the two would-be vice presidents was striking: Lincoln had enjoyed little political success and would become known as "Honest Abe," while Cameron had risen in Pennsylvania politics but had earned a reputation for corruption. Frémont blamed Blair, who had personal animus against Cameron, for what would prove to be a grave miscalculation. Thurlow Weed agreed with Frémont. "The first, and as I still think fatal error, was in not taking a Vice-President in whose nomination the North Americans would have concurred cordially," Weed later wrote to Cameron. Jessie, too, would always see the choice as a destructive misstep, and, long after a brutal falling-out between the Frémonts and the Blairs, attributed it to Blair's posturing as the power behind the throne. "As Colonel Frémont had never had the early political training, then considered essential to the formation of a clear judgment of the political situation, the question of the Vice-Presidency had been determined contrary to his wishes and judgment," she later wrote.

Francis and Lizzie Blair traveled from Philadelphia to New York to report firsthand to the Frémonts, who had just purchased a commodious residence at 56 West Ninth Street. For two weeks the Blairs would stay with the Frémonts, Blair holding court, despite a debilitating cold, with the dozens of well-wishers congratulating him on the "immense good he is doing by being the medium for bringing into a common action & movement very discordant and opposing elements," as Lizzie described it. "This house has people pouring in from all quarters from 6 oclk in the mng until late at night."

Speaking in Missouri just two days after Frémont's nomination, Benton dismissed his son-in-law and the Republicans with a swipe. "It is unnecessary for me to speak of these [other] parties: I adhere to my own, and support it, and that to the exclusion of all the rest. One only I allude to—one with which the name of a member of my family is connected, and in reference to which some persons who judge me by themselves . . . attribute to me a sinister connection . . . I am above family and above self, when the good of the Union is concerned."

Eventually Benton softened slightly toward Frémont, telling a group of Buchanan supporters in St. Louis of his affection for his son-in-law. "There was nothing which a father could do for a son which I have not done to carry him through his undertakings, and to uphold him in the severe trials to which he has been subjected." But he was also quick to point out that he had attempted to persuade Frémont of the grave dangers the Republican Party posed to the nation. Upon first learning of Frémont's decision to join the Republicans, Benton had made clear his opposition. "I told him at once that I not only could not support him, but that I would oppose him."

The Frémont campaign marked the first time in American history when women were drawn into the political process, the zeal for Jessie unparalleled. The "Frémont and Jessie" campaign, as it immediately became known, inspired thousands of women to take to the streets. Widely seen as a full-fledged partner in her husband's pursuits, Jessie became an overnight heroine to women who had been disenfranchised in America since the nation's inception. She straddled the boundaries of Victorian society—outspoken but polite, irreverent but tactful, opinionated but respectful—a woman so far ahead of her time that other women flocked to her. That she was young, beautiful, well-bred, intelligent, refined, educated, and rich further enhanced her aura. A devoted wife, a dutiful daughter, an engaged mother, and a clear-minded intellectual, the thirty-two-year-old Jessie was the embodiment of womanly virtue and feminine power. "She had seen much of the world, and knew men, cities, politics, and literature," a Frémont biographer described her. "Vivacious, keenly interested in life, quick to measure others, strong in her dislikes, stronger in her likes, with a delightful combination of poise and animation."

Jessie, more than anyone else, recognized her abilities and the limitations imposed upon her by society and culture. "I can say as Portia did to Brutus," she wrote in 1856, " 'Should I not be stronger than my sex, Being so Fathered and so Husbanded?' " Still, she was self-deprecating and deferential to both her father and her husband, who she felt were heroes of mythic proportions.

The adulation of Jessie began within a week of John's nomination, when a massive crowd gathered at the New York Tabernacle to welcome him back from Philadelphia. A speaker introduced the candidate, extolling his qualifications as the conqueror of California, the explorer of America's frontier. "He also won the heart and hand of Thomas H. Benton's daughter!" the speaker continued. With that, someone from the crowd yelled, "Three cheers for Jessie, Mrs. Frémont!" There followed the prerequisite speeches and applause, and when the grandstanding was over the throng marched half a mile up Broadway, in a torchlight procession, followed by Dodworth's Band, to the Frémont residence. Once there they yelled for the candidate, and when Frémont appeared on the balcony, they cheered riotously. The candidate's words were drowned out by the enthusiastic shouting, which soon turned to a call for Jessie. "Mrs. Frémont! Jessie! Jessie! Give us Jessie!" A man appeared at Frémont's side and tried to disperse the crowd, but the chanting continued, and it became clear to everyone at the Ninth Street home that the fans would not leave until they saw Jessie. "Give us Mrs. Frémont and we'll go!"

Never before had a candidate's wife been called to appear in public. Nineteenth-century protocol dictated that candidates remain distant from their campaign, a showy display or overt personal interest considered grasping and unseemly. In such a climate, the demands for Jessie were incomparable. Surrounded by male dignitaries, Jessie finally came onto the balcony. Her appearance drove them wild, "as though all their previous cheering were a mere practice to train their voices for this occasion," one observer described the scene. Whether disconcerted or emboldened, Jessie never wrote of her reaction to that evening. Having professed her disdain for "speech giving women" and having been reared in the shadow of a powerful man and under the guidance of a passive woman, she had no female role models to emulate. Still, the historic precedent must have struck her deeply, as it marked a major step in the growth of widespread American feminist activism.

The Frémont candidacy—"waged almost exclusively on the slavery issue," as historian Eric Foner put it—exuded celebrity status from the start. Throughout the nation during the summer of 1856, processions miles long cheered for Jessie and John. Bands played inspiring songs to accompany the lyrics written by nationally renowned poets. White-clad glee singers led the parades, chanting:

> *The choice made by Jessie is ours;*
> *We want the brave man she did wed.*
> *He crowned her with gay bridal flowers,*
> *And she is a crown to his head.*
> *She shall be our Liberty's queen,*
> *And he shall rule over the state*
> *From mountains of granite and green*
> *To the land of the Golden Gate.*

Sixty thousand people accompanied by fifty bands marched in Indianapolis alone. A cannon thundered throughout the day, and twenty-five marshals were needed to keep order. The float that led the parade carried thirty-two young women wearing white, representing each state, and one girl dressed in black symbolized "bleeding Kansas." As day turned into night, the torches from the procession could be seen throughout the city. Frémont demonstrations drew twenty-five thousand people in Ohio, another thirty thousand in Michigan, and in Wisconsin a procession reached six miles in length. At a Cleveland demonstration, a speaker referred to Jessie as "the gallant wife of a gallant man," telling the immense crowd of how an eighteen-year-old Jessie thwarted the War Department's efforts to stop Frémont's second expedition. Women poured into the streets, unlike anything in the history of the country, wearing violet-colored muslins or pinning a violet to their white dresses in honor of Jessie's favorite flower and color. One prominent New York minister and orator reported that half of the women in his congregation were copying her hairstyle and mannerisms and that new mothers were naming their babies "Jessie Ann."

At the heart of the groundswell was the abolitionist fervor, what feminist Eliza W. Farnham called "a moral earthquake." Women across the land rallied to the cause with an evangelical devotion, feeling, as one twentieth-century scholar put it, "an obligation to fight an institution that broke up families and subjected young women to sexual molestation." This breakup of families, so devastatingly portrayed in *Uncle Tom's Cabin* for a massive national audience, resonated deeply with middle-class women who in recent decades had become increasingly enlightened in the realm of family structure—choosing to have fewer children and treasuring those they had. Though the abolitionist movement had been gaining in strength over the previous ten years, its female activists were now drawn further into mainstream politics, finding a voice that had previously eluded them.

Maria Weston Chapman, the wife of a wealthy Boston businessman, wrote somewhat playfully of her sex's liberation:

> *The women have leaped from "their spheres,"*
> *And instead of fixed stars, shoot as comets along,*
> *And are setting the world by the ears!*
>
> *They've taken the notion to speak for themselves,*
> *And are wielding the tongue and the pen;*

They've mounted the rostrum, the termagent elves!
And—oh horrid!—are talking to men!

Equal rights for women remained a far-off ideal, but activists in both the suffragist and antislavery movements pinned their hopes for the future on the new and progressive Republican Party. Suffragette leaders embraced the candidacy, bringing attention to what seemed to many in the country a dangerous precedent for the involvement of what were contemptuously called "unsexed women" in the male world of the electoral process. "What a shame women can't vote!" the New England abolitionist Lydia Maria Child wrote at the time. "We'd carry 'our Jessie' into the White House on our shoulders." Elizabeth Cady Stanton, the famous feminist reformer who, along with Lucretia Mott, had radically proclaimed in 1848 at Seneca Falls, New York, that "all men and women are created equal," now bemoaned that she was imprisoned by the obligations of raising six children while her husband was out campaigning for Frémont. "I would almost lay down my life to have him elected," Child wrote a friend.

"This is election day and my brother is twenty-one years old," a Wisconsin woman would write in her journal the following November. "How proud he seemed as he dressed up in his best Sunday clothes and drove off in the big wagon with father and the hired men to vote for John C. Frémont, like the sensible 'Free-Soiler' that he is. My sister and I stood at the window and looked out after them. I said, 'Wouldn't you like to vote as well as Oliver? Don't you and I love the country just as well as he does, and doesn't the country need our ballots?' She looked scared, but answered in a minute, ''Course we do, and 'course we ought—but don't you go ahead and say so, for then we would be called strong-minded.'"

In truth, the women activists sought far less than their adversaries feared, for even the most visionary among them were comfortably entrenched in their cult of domesticity. "Equal partnership between husbands and wives would have been quite satisfactory," as one historian described their modest dream. To that end, Jessie and John Frémont symbolized what would be called a century and a half later a power couple— "symbols of a national identity that no longer had to look back toward Europe for its cultural heroes." Their individual political philosophies had evolved into a joint, acutely held ideology, their pragmatic intellectual symbiosis matched only by their profound emotional bond. Their romantic love was legendary among the masses, while palpable to intimate friends. As if thinking the same thought, they could finish one another's sentences. Many years earlier, John had called her his "second mind." So synchronistic had they become, it seemed now that they shared one mind. They were "as *one*," their oldest son would later write, "but each was of such caliber as to permit of independent action correctly, when necessity arose, and had the ability to recognize conditions sufficiently in advance, to time such action correctly."

In one of the stormiest campaigns in American history to that point, Jessie was the behind-the-scenes manager every step of the way. Opponent Buchanan and the Democratic Party exploited the role of Jessie and the mass participation of women to alarm the populace. Though she was brilliant and calculating in maintaining a proper public image, confining herself to the Ninth Street residence that was the campaign's headquarters, she oversaw all correspondence, worked surreptitiously with two writers who were rushing Frémont biographies into print, met regularly with John's closest advisers, vetted those wishing an audience with the candidate, sheltered John from the increasingly vitriolic attacks flung their way, and was a party to all crucial decisions. Posters and signs declaring "Jessie Bent-on Being Free" and "John and Jessie" added fuel to the Buchanan camp, which used every opportunity to imply that the expressive Jessie wore the pants in the family, while the diffident Frémont had surrendered his manly status.

Frémont was a Renaissance man with European manners—soft-spoken, laconic, and contemplative—readily caricatured by his critics as an effete, self-absorbed dilettante. Jessie, in contrast, had the attributes of mental acuity, emotional toughness, and political confidence more commonly associated with the "stronger sex." What his detractors saw as weak, his admirers glorified. "Moving in a material age, among practical matter-of-fact men, he exhaled, as it were, an atmosphere of bygone chivalry," wrote Alonzo Rothschild, a later biographer of Abraham Lincoln. "The slender, well-knit frame, with its alertness of action and grace of bearing, could have belonged only to one who had spent many of his adult years in the saddle, close to nature . . . The handsome weather-browned face, with its high forehead, deep blue eyes, and aquiline nose, gave index of mental vigor."

On July 9, Frémont's formal acceptance of the nomination was published. It gained widespread approval for how eloquently he expressed the antislavery Republican platform and strongly opposed aggression against foreign nations. As for the issue of slavery, his position was plain:

> Nothing is clearer in the history of our institutions than the design of the nation, in asserting its own independence and freedom, to avoid giving countenance to the extension of slavery. The influence of the small but compact and powerful class of men interested in slavery, who command one section of the country and wield a vast political control as a consequence in the other, is now directed to turn back the impulse of the Revolution and reverse its principles. The extension of slavery across the continent is the object of the power which now rules the government; and from this spirit have sprung those kindred wrongs of Kansas so truly portrayed in one of your resolutions, which prove that the elements of the most arbitrary governments have not been vanquished by the just theory of our own.
>
> It would be out of place here to pledge myself to any particular policy that has been suggested to determine the sectional controversy engendered by political animosities, operating on a powerful class banded together by common interest. A practical remedy is the admission of Kansas into the Union as a free state. The South should, in my judgment, earnestly desire such a consummation. It would vindicate its good faith. It would correct the mistake of the repeal; and the North, having practically the benefit of the agreement between the two sections, would be satisfied and good feeling be restored.

The possibility of a Republican victory emerged from the beginning, the antislavery enthusiasm catching the country by storm. "Fife and drum corps shrilled and rattled," according to one account. "Frémont glee clubs shook the village lyceum halls and opera houses. Long lines of gigs and wagons raised the dust on prairie roads as farming people streamed to Frémont picnics and rallies." Party leaders campaigned vigorously, with such luminaries as Banks, Chase, Sumner, Greeley, and Lincoln stumping throughout the country. Lincoln gave ninety speeches in support of Frémont, calling him "our young gallant, and world commander" and "the man for the day," and drawing a crowd of thirty-five thousand people in Alton, Illinois.

Greeley's *Tribune* offices became the center of operations for Republican propaganda, where 150,000 copies of a pamphlet biography of the candidate written by William F. Bartlett were produced. Greeley even published campaign speeches in German and Welsh for distribution in the Pennsylvania coal fields, and wrote a handbook to be used by Republican workers and speakers titled *A History of the Struggle for Slavery Extension or Restriction in the United States*, arguing that the Founding Fathers, even the southern Revolutionary leaders, opposed the extension of slavery.

Poets and other men of letters, including Ralph Waldo Emerson, John Greenleaf Whittier, Robert Lowell, Henry Wadsworth Longfellow, William Cullen Bryant, Bayard Taylor, and Washington Irving committed their support to the Republican ticket, many of them writing impassioned lyrics about the explorer who had been christened the "Pathfinder" by campaign advisers, though it was never a term with which Frémont was comfortable. Northern university chancellors and professors unanimously supported Frémont, the religious press followed the lead of Henry Ward Beecher, and clergymen from the Midwest to New England prayed for a Republican victory—all of the North's cultural and intellectual leaders "united in what seemed to them a great moral crusade."

Throughout the campaign, Frémont stayed in the background. "His bearing was very well so far as he appeared before the public," Gideon Welles wrote in his diary. "I saw that he was anxious to be elected but not offensively so; he was not obtrusive, but, on the contrary, reserved and retiring." The candidate's introverted demeanor, allowing others to speak on his behalf, soon began to alarm the members of his inner circle who feared that voters would be reluctant to choose a man so thoroughly inexperienced in, and uncomfortable with, political life.

The necessary strategy of the Frémont campaign was simple: The Democrats were assured 108 electoral votes from the South and border states. Republicans could count on the 114 electoral votes from the North and the West. The potential swing states were Pennsylvania, Indiana, Illinois, Maryland, New Jersey, and California—totaling 70 electoral votes altogether. Republicans needed to carry Pennsylvania and either Indiana or Illinois to be successful. But with three candidates in the field—Buchanan, Fillmore, and Frémont—the fear was that Fillmore would draw the necessary margin of disaffected Democrats and Whigs who would otherwise vote for Frémont. The battleground was obviously Pennsylvania, whose 27 electoral votes looked to be equally divided between Frémont in the western half of the state and Buchanan in the eastern section.

It was a brutal campaign, filled with invective and innuendo as the Democrats offensively sought evidence with which to tarnish Frémont. As if unprepared for the onslaught, the Republicans responded with a lackluster counteroffense. They launched no ad hominem attacks against Buchanan except for vague references to his bachelorhood. But even those implications served only to question whether a president would be better qualified were he a married man, and stopped far short of suggesting homosexuality. "Old Public Functionary," as Buchanan was called, was portrayed by Democrats as a safer bet than Frémont, if only because of all the public offices Buchanan had held over the decades—congressman, senator, secretary of state, diplomatic minister to Russia and to Britain. In Buchanan's home state of Pennsylvania the anti-Frémont vitriol was a portent of the looming civil war. Frémont was called "a shallow, vainglorious, wooly horse, mule-eating, free love, nigger-embracing, black Republican—a financial spendthrift and a political mountebank."

Inevitably, the Democrats unearthed Frémont's allegedly sordid past as a Frenchman's bastard, prompting Jessie to work feverishly with John Bigelow on a campaign biography focused on dispelling the rumors of the candidate's illegitimacy. In early July, Jessie began locating relatives of John's mother, Anne Beverley Whiting, and made arrangements to visit them in Virginia with the hope of obtaining evidence that Frémont's parents were married at the time of his birth. "I think no time is to be lost in seeing into all that can be collected in regard to Mr. Frémont's Mother," she wrote Lizzie as she prepared to travel to Old Point Comfort to interview Anne Frémon's sister, Catherine Whiting Lowry.

Jessie was able to construct a poignant love story from her discussions with Lowry, though apparently she was unable to find evidence that Anne and Fremon were married at the time of John's birth. "One of the most beautiful women of her day in the State of Virginia," as Catherine Lowry described her sister to Jessie, Anne had been forced to marry Pryor, who was "in every respect repulsive to the young creature who was sacrificed to him." Whiting conveyed to Jessie the facts surrounding

Anne's extramarital affair with Fremon, the dashing French fresco painter, according to historian Pamela Herr, which Jessie conveniently failed
to pass on to Bigelow. "[In] her account for Bigelow," wrote Herr in her
1987 biography of Jessie, "Jessie said nothing of Anne's desperate elopement with Charles Fremon, though Catherine Whiting had confided it
to her in gripping detail. In Jessie's truncated version, the childless Pry-
ors, after 'twelve long years of wedded misery,' simply agreed to separate
and were promptly granted a divorce by the state legislature. 'Not long
after,' Jessie neatly concluded her story, 'both married again, Mrs. Pryor
to Mr. Frémont and Major Pryor, in the 76th year of his age, to his
housekeeper.' "

Jessie made a note to herself at the time that the "power to re-marry
must be looked into." Opponents later charged that no evidence existed
that the Virginia legislature had granted Pryor's divorce petition. But
Pryor's remarriage almost immediately after Anne's departure—and
long before John was born in 1813—indicated to Jessie, and others, that
he was free to do so, and therefore so was Anne. It had been Jessie's
"task," as authors Herr and Mary Lee Spence described it, ". . . to transform the scandal in the Republican nominee's past into sentimental romance." Divorce and illegitimacy in the Victorian era were volatile and
sensitive subjects, the scorn resting always on the woman and her out-
of-wedlock children, regardless of the extenuating circumstances. Jessie's
unenviable role, as one author saw it, was to steer "her dangerous course
between the Scylla of censure-evoking factual incident and the Charyb-
dis of censure-evoking evasion."

Bigelow's *New York Evening Post* excerpted the biography in conjunc-
tion with the forty thousand books published that sold for one dollar
each. The response was predictably partisan, Republicans embracing the
book that glorified their candidate, Frémont's opponents North and
South dismissing it as novelistic and seizing on the Pryor gossip as evidence of Frémont's foreign background and illegitimacy. "Tell me," Virginia governor Henry Wise said in a widely disseminated speech, "if the
hoisting of the Black Republican flag . . . over you by a Frenchman's
bastard . . . is not to be deemed an overt act and declaration of war." Privately, Wise confided to a friend that if "Frémont is elected there will be
a revolution." He then put his state militia on alert.

Still, just as the parentage question receded as a serious issue, the
Democrats leveled even more serious accusations against Frémont that
would have the most far-reaching and ultimately fatal impact: that he was

secretly a Catholic. In an era of heightened religious bigotry, the charge irrevocably alienated the rabidly anti-Catholic Know-Nothings and signaled the death knell to Frémont's campaign.

Though untrue, hyperbolic, and easily refutable, the charges of Catholicism dealt an insurmountable blow to the Republicans. John had been an Episcopalian since early childhood and baptized and raised all his children in the Protestant faith, but he refused to refute the allegation in the anti-Catholic fervor of the moment. He reasoned that America was founded on religious tolerance, that a man's religion was between him and his God, and he refused to make a public statement on the matter. His determined silence was widely considered an irrevocable mistake, his supporters rightfully fearing the charges were losing him votes.

"Proof" of Frémont's Catholicism put forth by the Democrats included a ludicrous list of evidence: That he had carved a crucifix on Independence Rock during his first expedition; that he had been seen crossing himself in a Catholic cathedral in Washington; that he had sent his niece Nina to a Catholic school; that his father was a French Catholic; that he and Jessie had been married by a Catholic priest; that he had told a West Point professor that he was Catholic; and that he had confessed his belief in transubstantiation. "We have linked together the names of Bishop Hughes, Wm. H. Seward, and John C. Frémont," charged a publication disseminated by the Democrats, "and charge upon this trio the most foul combination."

Numerous Protestant clergymen provided evidence of his and Jessie's long-standing membership at Grace Episcopal Church, but the fact that they had been married by a Catholic priest, along with the French heritage of Frémont's father, kept the charges alive. He became the victim of a defamation campaign, and inflammatory pamphlets were circulated throughout the country with such titles as *Frémont's Romanism Established*, *Frémont's Principles Exposed*, and *Black Republican an Imposter*. One such publication promised "Proof of His Romanism, Proof of His Proslavery Acts, Proof of His Conviction of Mutiny, Proof That He is a Duelist, Proof That He is a Bully, Proof of His Swindling the Government, and Proof of His Complicity With the Swindling Operations." Despite the absurdity of the allegations, the anti-Catholic sentiment was too entrenched and too explosive to be overcome. Though Frémont had publicly espoused his support of immigrant restriction, "he could not quiet the uneasiness of persons who believed that a

Roman Pope might run the country if a Catholic were ever elected president."

Throughout it all, Frémont remained silent—"contrary to the advice of most of his political friends and which they maintained would lose him the election if he did not clearly state his opinion upon it," as Jessie later wrote about his position. By the end of August his inner circle of advisers had become panicked by the overwhelming political damage that was occurring. "He was a Protestant, and had never been anything else, but took the position that the main issue of the canvass was freedom, and that it embraced freedom of mind as well as freedom of body;" Jessie wrote, "that the Constitution declared for absolute freedom in religion, and, if it was recognized, that belonging to any lawful sect or religion was disqualification in the eyes of the voters of the United States, then the principles of the Constitution were violated, and he would not appeal for the vote of a single man, if for that vote he appealed to the religious fanaticism that had caused untold miseries in the nations of the Old World."

Forty Republican leaders called Frémont to a meeting at the Astor House in New York where, led by Thurlow Weed, they implored the candidate to publicly deny the charges. He refused again, and after the meeting sought counsel from the powerful newspaper proprietor James Gordon Bennett. "What are your convictions?" the *Herald* publisher asked him. When Frémont explained his fervent adherence to the separation of church and state and belief that a candidate's religion had no place in American politics, Bennett replied: "Follow those convictions, Colonel, and I will sustain you to the end."

While Jessie agreed with her husband's decision, the political strategist within her undertook an avid letter-writing crusade to friends, supporters, and newspaper editors, countering the charges as John stood stubbornly mute. "Three years spent with Mr. Nicollet brought him into acquaintance and friendship with many Catholic gentlemen—clergymen and laymen," she wrote in one letter. "As to any one's speaking by authority for Mr. Frémont's religion, it is impossible for them to say he is or was a Catholic," she wrote in another. "He says himself that he never was one—not once has he ever gone into a Catholic Church for service— only to weddings & some shows in Paris where it was like an opera box & we were all talking as in a theater."

Coming to their defense for being married by a priest, the Reverend Henry Ward Beecher recalled the obstacles surrounding the elopement of the lovestruck young couple. "Had we been in Col. Frémont's place we would have been married if it had required us to walk through a row of priests and bishops as long as from Washington to Rome, winding up with the Pope himself." Ironically, it had been Benton himself who had refused, despite his wife's request, to allow a Protestant clergyman to perform a second marriage for John and Jessie, fearing it would cause a scandal.

Jessie felt that the proslavery power structure was so vehemently lined up against them that it would stop at nothing to destroy the Republican candidacy and John in the process. The main issue of the campaign— "the preservation of freedom and the non-extension of slavery, was intolerable to the Slavery party which intended and was determined to extend its territory and power," she wrote. "The Southerners admitted no division of feeling, and expressed their will as follows: 'If there be Frémont men among us, let them be silenced or required to leave. The expression of black Republican opinions in our midst is incompatible with our honor and safety as a people.' Such was the public sentiment." Under these deeply polarized conditions, Jessie realized that the smearing of her husband would continue unabated. "He considers himself as belonging to the greatest cause ever at stake since the Revolution," she wrote Lizzie in August 1856, "& his whole life shows that he 'throws away his body' for his duty. In this case he 'throws away his heart' & lets them slander & attack, in silence—knowing how injurious violence would be & how inadequate anything but death would be as punishment to such slanderers. The best answer will be in the triumph of our party."

Indeed, the attacks had only begun. Legendarily abstemious, Frémont was accused of being an alcoholic. Though both he and Jessie had repeatedly refused to accept slaves from their Southern relatives, rumors circulated that he had secretly owned seventy-five slaves. His financial problems with Las Mariposas were exaggerated, with Democratic newspapers alleging fraud if not outright theft, calling him a "landshark" and a "master monopolist." The *Los Angeles Star* claimed he was culpable in the murders of three native California prisoners during the Bear Flag conquest. Published stories "revealed" that Frémont had been born in Montreal and was therefore ineligible for the presidency. He was accused of overcharging the government in his Indian beef contract, of partaking in cannibalism during the 1848–1849 expedition, and of conspiring with Palmer, Cook, & Co., financial agents for the state of California, to swindle the public.

"Dear Lizzie," Jessie wrote, "it is easy to say 'possess your soul in patience' but not so easy to do it & far harder for me than for you for I have a bad rebellious nature that is always escaping even when I watch it . . . Could you possess your soul in patience if your Father and brothers were openly aiding . . . to break down Mr. Lee [Lizzie's husband]—discrediting his capacity, impeaching his character and outraging his mother's memory?"

Most painful to Jessie, in what she called "a trial by mud," were the stories of John's extramarital sexual affairs. They ranged from the far-fetched—that he had kept a harem of sisters, mothers, and daughters in Los Angeles while acting governor—to the more disturbing, that he had impregnated a French chambermaid. This "French mistress," according to the reports, was threatening to expose her relationship with Frémont unless the Republican National Committee paid for her silence.

The second main strategy of the Democrats, in addition to discrediting Frémont as a man, was to instill the fear of secession and civil war that would send the nation into anarchy. The Republican Party was depicted as a dangerous and reckless sectional party that intended to "turn loose," as an Ohio Democratic newspaper declared, ". . . millions of negroes, to elbow you in the workshops, and compete with you in the fields of honest labor." Democrats in Pittsburgh blatantly pronounced the campaign to be a battle between the white and black races, and in an Indiana parade white girls wearing white dresses carried banners that read: "Fathers, save us from nigger husbands." The election "of Frémont would be the end of the Union," declared a Georgia senator. Even Benton, with his unabashed hostility to his son-in-law, fueled the terror. "We are treading upon a volcano that is liable at any moment to burst forth and overwhelm the nation."

Frémont's daughter Lily later wrote that her "father's nature was such that he could not have withstood [the campaign's] bitterness. He was used to life in the open and wanted a square fight, not one filled with petty innuendoes and unfounded recriminations." In deference to her husband's sensitivity, Jessie censored all newspapers and mail, protecting him as much as possible from the distressing allegations. As Jessie had intuited when they made the choice to run, close family ties and friendships were irrevocably shattered. "Those sacred ties were severed and hearts were broken, thick and fast, during the dark days that followed," Lily wrote, "there being no compromise between North and South."

Jessie was immersed in a balancing act between campaign director and mother, all the while protector of the thin-skinned, increasingly aloof John. She consulted regularly with Francis Preston Blair, John Bigelow, and Isaac Sherman, managed the political correspondence, and entertained a steady stream of visitors. Every morning she brought fruit and coffee into the dining room to meet with her "private committee," carrying a market basket brimming with letters. "The personal and friendly letters were allotted to me to answer. The public and political to Mr. Bigelow, and Mr. Sherman took the matters specially belonging to the State of New York." She also supervised the household of her three children and John's problematic teenage niece. "Both ambitious and maternal," according to one observer, "she found herself pulled from an exhausting night with a teething baby to a long day at campaign headquarters." For the first time in American history, the wife of a presidential candidate took an active role in a national campaign.

"I am horribly tired," she confided to Lizzie, while John lived in an isolated cocoon, "gay as a boy." The candidate practiced his fencing every morning, read books and wrote letters during the day, greeted the many well-wishers who made their way past Jessie's guard, gave impromptu speeches to mostly adoring crowds, and took long walks every evening. "We let him read no papers (unless you write them)," she wrote to Francis Preston Blair, "and he has the pleasure of doing daily good work in the cause." As John greeted each day with confidence and optimism, Jessie's own despair increased. Inevitably, the rumors, though moderated, reached John. The smears were difficult to bear, made worse by her father's escalating attacks and the vitriol flung by her Southern friends and relatives.

In July the family retreated to a "breezy hill-top farm-house" on Staten Island, but even that respite proved no escape. She and John commuted to New York by boat, and the campaign venom continued unabated. Before long the burden took a physical toll on Jessie as she suffered in silence, unable to share her despair with her husband, who was also her best friend. "All this has made me ill," she wrote to Francis Preston Blair from Staten Island. "The pain in the heart lasted longer than usual & a general inflammation has followed making me tired & feverish & still after five days quiet and care, in pain if I do not keep perfectly hushed & quiet. Dr. Van Buren says 'no newspapers, no ideas, no excitement of any kind' & by way of forgetfulness I am to get well enough to go to town next week when the opera re-commences & lead a life steadily devoted to amusements disconnected with politics."

The Democrats made great hay of the schism between Benton and the Frémonts. "But you know this is an old wound for the opening of which politics are only an excuse," she wrote Blair. "Father has absolutely disliked Mr. Frémont since the refusal to sell the Mariposas." Running as an antislavery Democrat for governor of Missouri, Benton stumped the state for himself and Buchanan, and every report of Benton's anti-Frémont remarks struck Jessie like "a Brutus stab." The coup de grâce came for both John and Jessie when Senator William Bigler of Pennsylvania, a Buchanan and Benton ally, launched a Senate investigation into John's financial transactions during his first California expedition. Implying malfeasance or worse, Bigler sought to reopen for a national audience Frémont's controversial role in the Bear Flag Revolt and his ensuing court-martial. Jessie was livid. "I am blazing with fever from the sudden anger I felt last night on reading Mr. Bigler's motion in the Senate," she wrote to Lizzie Blair. "Mr. Frémont says if Father takes no notice of that & continues to work with them he will never speak to him nor shall any of his children." It was one thing for Benton to have disagreed politically with his son-in-law, but to stand aside and countenance slander was beyond the pale for Jessie.

Apparently for the first time Jessie, who for months had been maneuvering the dangerous minefield between father and husband, realized the breach was insurmountable and final. "This shuts off all future relations between Mr. Frémont & himself. Mr. Frémont says he would not willingly see his children go where he has been so injured—so you see why it hurts me for Mr. Frémont is right. A Father-in-law has not the right to the forbearance and duty of a child unless he gives the protection & love of a parent. I mean to the forbearance of a 'law child'—his own born child cannot but feel one way and Mr. Frémont is good enough to leave me to do as I feel for myself." Unflagging, and against all odds, Jessie continued to seek a rapprochement with her father, begging Francis Preston Blair to intervene yet again. She knew that her father "could by one line set right this Bigler movement" and she was staggered by his willful impotence. "Father's silence when he has always been so prompt to do battle for the right hurts me literally to the heart."

Lizzie took it upon herself to approach Benton on the Frémonts' behalf, and reported happily back to Jessie that the "Old Roman" spoke "lovingly of you in his way." There followed a letter from Benton to Jessie inviting the entire family to visit Washington. "He only wrote of family matters but it was enclosed in a very kind note to Mr. Frémont (family altogether) which Mr. Frémont answered immediately." Jessie took Charley and Lily to Washington in September to spend a week with her father, leaving the baby and John behind, and had a pleasant but strained visit. She was stunned to see the Old Bull, who was losing his bid in Missouri, looking so thin and weary. It "seems as if sadness and silence were so fixed upon him that he could not shake them off."

Jessie's mood was further dampened by reports from Pennsylvania that the Democrats had poured nearly $500,000 into both the Democratic and Native American coffers in that state to assure a Democratic victory—money raised by Wall Street merchants, bankers, and brokers. Allegations of fraud involving the illegal naturalization of thousands of immigrants in Philadelphia in exchange for their Democratic votes were widespread as well, and Pennsylvania, which was crucial if the Republicans were going to stand a chance, began to look hopeless. Colonel John W. Forney, a Democrat running for the Senate in Pennsylvania, had traveled to New York and "issued a confidential call to those New York merchants who were interested principally in trade with the Southern States to meet at a certain bank . . . and confer with reference to means of preventing the success of the new Republican ticket and its candidates," Jessie later wrote. Forney presented the case as a "desperate one for Northern merchants interested in Southern trade."

Meanwhile, the Republican Party in Pennsylvania was impoverished, and the influx of critical Democratic money arrived just before the election, which was held in mid-October—a full three weeks before other states. While Thurlow Weed scrambled to raise money, nearly two hundred Republican speakers blanketed the state. Weed assured the Frémonts that machinations were under way to overthrow the voter fraud, but Jessie was less sanguine. "If it were not for the false notes in Philadelphia I should consider the state safe. As it is, wiser people say it is safe but 'je suis de l'école de St. Thomas,'" she wrote, referring to the biblical doubting Thomas.

On October 14, as voters in Pennsylvania went to the polls in a drizzling rain, Jessie waited with Francis Preston Blair and his wife, Eliza, at the Ninth Street residence while John was in Vermont meeting with advisers. Early that evening John Bigelow brought disturbing news from

Pennsylvania that the Republicans were trailing the Democrats. Jessie and Bigelow decided to withhold the information from the frail Blair until the following morning. "He was not a strong man, and mental disturbance hurt him physically." To distract Blair, they took him to a play at the Metropolitan Theater on Broadway, but they could not disguise their own somber mood, and Blair suspected the worst.

It would be two more days before they learned definitively that the Frémont ticket had lost Pennsylvania by less than three thousand votes—many of them fraudulent. The Indiana election had also gone to the Democrats. As the bellwether they expected, the Pennsylvania defeat demoralized the Frémont camp as it headed into November's election. "I heartily regret the defeat we have met and do not look for things to change for the better," Jessie wrote to Lizzie on October 20. "I wish the cause had triumphed. I do wish Mr. Frémont had been the one to administer the bitter dose of subjection to the South for he has the coolness & nerve to do it just as it needs to be done—without passion & without sympathy—as coldly as a surgeon over a hospital patient would he have cut off their right hand Kansas from the old unhealthy southern body."

Though deeply embittered, John handled the defeat with his characteristic grace and stoicism. Privately he blamed Blair for preempting his choice of Simon Cameron as vice presidential running mate, and to the end of his life Frémont believed Cameron would have possessed the political clout to thwart the fraud in his state. But Blair had opposed Cameron from the start—"almost as a condition of his support of the new party," as Jessie saw it. Convinced that the Pennsylvania election had effectively been stolen from them, many Republican leaders urged Frémont to contest the election—something that had never before been done in American national politics. But he refused to be the first to go down in history setting such a precedent, and instead he did all he could to rally his forces for the final election.

Then, in late October, their seventeen-month-old Frank became suddenly and life-threateningly ill with a fever and convulsions. Jessie turned her attention away from politics, recalling the torment of losing her beloved Benton and Anne as babies—"all the sorrowful images I had shut down in my heart until I thought them forgotten." Jessie abandoned all campaign duties and moved into the nursery with Frank. "I don't care for the election. Let it go." John managed, much to Jessie's surprise, to keep up his spirits and optimism, and actually believed they were going to win. But when Frank regained his health two days before the election, Jessie found that she did indeed care, and her own giddy buoyancy returned. "I don't dare say anything more than to tell you we may be successful. Telegraphs will do the rest," she wrote to Lizzie on November 2.

In the end, victory was not to be theirs, for the infant Republican Party had neither the money nor the political machine in place. The returns were encouraging at first—a stunning 83 percent of eligible voters turning out in the North—with New York, New England, Ohio, Michigan, Wisconsin, and Iowa solidly in the Frémont camp. But when Illinois, Indiana, and New Jersey joined Pennsylvania for Buchanan, the race was over. The final tally was 1,836,072 for Buchanan to 1,342,345 for Frémont. Of the country's electoral votes, Buchanan received 174 to Frémont's 114—the 114 that Republicans had known all along they could count on. Buchanan carried nineteen states, Frémont eleven, and Fillmore one.

The following morning, Blair joined the somber family for breakfast. Assuming her father had won his bid in Missouri, Jessie sardonically remarked: "Colonel Benton, I perceive, has the best of this family argument." Even Frémont could not suppress a smile, but an angry and emotional Blair broke down. "Tom Benton's stubborn stand cost us many a vote outside Missouri." Seeing a grown man cry was too much for Lily, who burst into tears. When the girl was unable to get control of herself, Jessie quietly left the room and returned with a hat, coat, mittens, and a veil. After wiping her daughter's tears away, Jessie cloaked her with the veil and nudged her forward. "Go take a walk, a long walk. First the wind and then the rain, Hoist your topsail up again."

Lily walked around New York until her tears subsided. When she returned to the family home, Jessie embraced her and sat her down. What Lily remembered for the rest of her life was her mother's talk of courage in the face of adversity and defeat—an attribute that Jessie herself was struggling to maintain. "I'm very glad that all my little Jessie Anns are too young to weep over the discovery that they are *not* the namesakes of a President's wife," she would remark during this most painful of times.

If the Frémonts were personally demolished, Republican leaders saw the showing as what came to be called a "victorious defeat" and immediately began looking forward to 1860. "We are beaten," remarked

Maine's senator William Pitt Fessenden, "but we have frightened the rascals awfully." The young party had made a valiant showing and irrevocably advanced the antislavery cause.

Most historians have argued that a Frémont presidency would have been disastrous for the nation, ushering in secession by the Southern states and prompting immediate civil war under the helm of an intractable abolitionist. The Frémonts, of course, saw it differently. "General Frémont always believed that had he been elected President, that through the influence of his own and Mrs. Frémont's large family connections through the Southern States, arrangements would have been entered into, preventing the resort to war which occurred later," as Jessie later portrayed their grand vision. "A plan which had been suggested, and the details of which had been outlined, was the gradual abolishment of slavery, and the payment by the Government of the property so taken from the owners; the sum necessary for this purpose would have been far less than that expended in prosecuting the war, and there would not have been the loss of life accompanying it; nor would the great mass of slaves have been turned adrift, to obtain at the same time their maintenance and education."

In the event, the Frémont defeat temporarily staved off civil war and laid the groundwork for a Republican victory with Abraham Lincoln four years later. Frémont's plan for gradual abolition with federal compensation—which he devised with the assistance of Jeremiah S. Black, who would become attorney general and then secretary of state under Buchanan—would later find an advocate in Lincoln.

Meanwhile, Jessie was cynical about her father's defeat, despite his thirty years of public service for the constituents of Missouri, the Democratic Party, and the nation at large, and saw it as further evidence of Democratic corruption. "[S]tates and republics are like any other business associations—they have neither memories nor sentiments only necessities and whoever serves those necessities best is the one preferred. The Democratic party has always shewn itself especially remorseless in that way. The Whigs kept on with Clay & Webster again & again but the Democrats follow Napoleon's example and divorce their oldest friend without flinching when they want a new heir."

In the weeks following the election, John and Jessie were adrift, each as unsure as the other on how to proceed. Jessie turned her energy and sorrow inward, retreating into motherhood and personal reflection while trying her best to assuage the pain of her crushed husband. John became refracted and withdrawn, the viciousness of the campaign deeply wounding him. He considered writing a book about his last two expeditions but decided instead to turn his attention to Las Mariposas, which had suffered financially from his absence. "Mr. Frémont . . . has already mounted his old hobby and is in full chase after his butterfly," Jessie wrote of his boundless but elusive search for riches from Las Mariposas. As John began plotting a return to California, Jessie became ever more desirous of creating a rooted family life. Washington, with the campaign hostilities fresh and piercing, held no appeal for her, and after their time in the sophisticated cities of Paris and New York, she felt no romantic yearning for the primitive California existence. "Mr. Frémont says I may live where I like & I like here," she wrote a week after the election, "California has no attraction for me."

Then, within a few weeks of the election, John Bigelow—the skilled coeditor of the *New York Evening Post* and, next to Lizzie and Francis Preston Blair, Jessie's closest personal friend—suddenly became estranged from the Frémonts. Bigelow had apparently become convinced that John had "debauched" a maid in the family household, and when Bigelow broke off contact, Jessie was beside herself. "As a candidate for President in 1856, he [Frémont] did everything pretty much that he could do to bring his party into contempt though it was only partially discovered until after the election," the longtime loyal friend and supporter wrote in his journal—an oblique passage later Frémont biographers pointed to as evidence of Frémont's infidelity. When the rumors had surfaced, Jessie fiercely defended John's honor, dismissing the allegations as malicious smears promulgated by the Buchanan camp.

Though she never wrote or spoke of the charges of John's unfaithfulness, an aura of sadness settled around her, and those closest to the couple thought their fifteen-year marriage was in crisis. Still, on the surface, she remained devoted to her husband. In a search for new purpose, he alternated between book ideas and railroad ventures, in addition to his focus on Las Mariposas. He implored her to come with him to California, to help him write while he oversaw Las Mariposas. But Jessie remembered California as an endless stream of cooking, laundry, and cleaning under archaic and adverse conditions. "Mr. Frémont thinks of the climate & the sunrise over the fine mountain scenery, the spring flowers & horseback rides that send him with a vigorous appetite to breakfast & a clear healthy mind to write. I am to be ready to do that writing but I am to know & provide the component parts of that breakfast first," she wrote somewhat disdainfully.

Instead, she sailed to France with Nina, Lily, Charley, and Frank.

7

WAR 1857–1862

Let us discard all this quibbling about this man and the other man, this race and that race and the other race being inferior, and therefore they must be placed in an inferior position. Let us discard all these things, and unite as one people throughout this land, until we shall once more stand up declaring that all men are created equal.

—Abraham Lincoln, Chicago,
July 10, 1858

I will say, then, that I am not, nor ever have been, in favor of bringing about in any way the social and political equality of the white and black races; that I am not, nor ever have been, in favor of making voters or jurors of negroes, nor of qualifying them to hold office, nor to intermarry with white people . . . And inasmuch as they cannot so live, while they do remain together there must be the position of superior and inferior, and I as much as any other man am in favor of having the superior position assigned to the white race.

—Abraham Lincoln, Charleston,
September 18, 1858

JOHN TRAVELED TO Las Mariposas for another futile attempt to salvage the enterprise, which suffered from neglect during the campaign. Though separation had become habitual for them, this was the first time Jessie had chosen it for herself. "I have had the blues desperately," she wrote a friend with what many thought was as much a reference to the allegations of John's infidelity as to the heartbreaking defeat. She recognized the early signs of pregnancy—"I have not had a sight of bloody mse [menses] since the fifteen of November"—and she futilely hoped that she was entering menopause. She apparently miscarried, and was suffering physically when she, the children, and her two French charges departed for France on the steamship *Vanderbilt* on June 20, 1857. "[T]his continued pain at the heart wears out strength of mind as well as body."

They settled in a villa near an old castle in St. Germain en Laye, five hundred feet above the Seine Valley and ten miles from Paris. Estranged from her father, siblings, and Virginia relatives, a new distance now between her and her husband, she sought solace in her dear friend Lizzie Blair and the newer friends from New York with whom she corresponded. She hired numerous household servants and a German governess for the children, and was once again courted by Parisian society. She devoted her energy to regaining health and strength, walking between seven and ten miles in the forest every day, often visiting the districts of Champagne and Burgundy to enjoy the year's "great wine crop," and immersing herself in reflections on the past and contemplation of the future. "Those long breaks in married life are dangerous," she wrote Francis Preston Blair in August, "—one must either be unhappy or indifferent & if one is bad the other is almost worse."

She worried incessantly about her father, who had been injured in a railway accident near Pittsburgh and whom her friend Lizzie had described as angry and abusive, a "lump of malignity" still railing against Jessie and John. "We have narrow channels for our love but terribly deep," Jessie described a Benton family trait. "If they cannot come to the surface they wear inward. Father has thrown himself violently into writing but work never yet filled the heart, it only uses up time. When I saw how he was embittered last summer it went to my heart that the injury, fancied as it was, should have come through me. I wanted success that I might put it at his feet and let him make use of it and feel his old power returned."

Though she was thoroughly enjoying the richly pleasant family life, she missed John terribly. Perhaps able to forgive and even understand the innate and often grasping need for acceptance that might have led him to stray from the marriage, she longed for him in a new way. "My sweetheart," she wrote him after only a month in Europe, "I spoil quantities of my pretty paper writing you things that begin well enough and then degenerate into the most selfish laments at not being with you . . . I love you with all my heart and trust you to give it health." Then, just days later, she wrote: "Love me in memory of the old times when I was so dear to you. I love you now much more than I did then." By September her yearning for him took on a new sense of urgency as she threw herself into diet and exercise for his benefit. "I am trying to make the sun go from west to east—that is trying to look young and pretty . . . I am becoming coquettish in my old age to please you." If she had initially considered a break with him, she now sought reconciliation with renewed ardor. "My darling I want to see you more than you can think. I am well but I am such a great fool I want to be still beside you with nothing to think or do but sit and wait for a little kind word from you— Sirius by the dear master . . . Most of all darling I love you and want you."

For his part, John was determined to win her back, wooing her with promises of building a home for them in San Francisco. His crossing through the isthmus had once again brought on illness, and though Las Mariposas under his guidance was reaping profits of $60,000 to $100,000 a month, the mining operations were in chaos. The mines were spread across a vast and isolated terrain, and he traveled among the sites that included the Princeton, Mount Ophir, Josephine, and Pine Tree mines, all the while missing Jessie and the children. The remote tract of land Frémont had purchased a decade earlier for $3,000 was now worth $10 million. Like all mine owners of that era, Frémont faced a steady onslaught of litigation. He had incorporated the mine and offered stock on exchanges in San Francisco, New York, and Paris. California law provided for the courts to determine the scope of the various lodes, so the legal challenges to Frémont's claim kept him embroiled in expensive lawsuits. His property was the only Mexican grant in the state that contained substantial amounts of gold, and debate swirled around the validity of the original grant—controversy aggravated in Frémont's case by the accusations that Senator Benton had favored the Mexican grantees to establish Frémont's title. Some alleged that indefinite boundary lines were manipulated to favor Frémont as well.

Even with his entreaties and her desire to see him, she rented an apartment on rue d'Angoulême in Paris and reserved a box at the opera for the coming season, apparently expecting John to join her there. Unbeknownst to her, her father was dying a slow and excruciating death from rectal cancer, which he went to lengths to hide from Jessie. She had learned from the Blairs of Benton's illness, which Benton dismissed as chronic constipation, and despite the Blairs' assurances that the infirmity was not life-threatening, Jessie was frantic with worry. When, by mid-October, she had received no further word about Benton's condition, she booked passage on the *Arago*, scheduled to depart on October 20 and due to arrive in New York thirteen days later. She would be reunited with her father on November 4—a year to the day after the election that had so divided them. "How things fade," she wrote of the irony. "I don't care two straws for the last fourth of November now—personally I mean . . . this year I only hope that day will give me the sight of Father, in health, & quite free from any bad thoughts about me. I would go farther to cure him of a heart ache than of a bodily pain." She left Nina, Lily, and Frank in the charge of friends, and took six-year-old Charley with her solely because it was unacceptable for a woman to travel alone.

John had left San Francisco on October 11 on the *Golden Age*, initially intending to continue to Paris but now planning instead to rendezvous with Jessie in New York. Despite a rough crossing that left Jessie seasick, she was too thrilled at the prospect of seeing her father and husband to let it dampen her spirits. The *New York Herald* reported her arrival on November 4, when John, who had arrived from Panama via Havana just one hour earlier, greeted her at the pier. As in earlier times, the couple retreated to a suite at the Astor House, where Jessie nursed John, who was suffering from a cold. Each was surprised by the further graying of each other's hair—his had "silvered over" and hers was "getting hard on to white."

Jessie rushed to Washington, where she found her father gravely ill though determinedly working on his final book—a compilation of congressional debates from 1789 through 1796 that he hoped would bring much-needed income. Indexed by speaker and subject, the tome, one historian predicted, would be "the monument of the age." Benton had risen from what his doctor considered "the bed of death" to continue writing. But his resiliency was waning, and he had recently written his final will and testament, leaving the rebuilt C Street residence and all its contents except his books to his daughter Eliza, his library to his son-in-law William Carey Jones, $10,000 to Eliza, and $5,000 to his youngest daughter, Susan Boilleau. Any remaining assets, after his debts were paid, were to be divided equally among his daughters Jessie, Sarah, and Susan.

Though she was stunned by his condition, Jessie felt he was recuperating and, finding Washington under the Buchanan presidency unwelcoming and humiliating, she returned to New York after several weeks, with plans to sail with John to France.

When she had arrived in New York that fall of 1857, she found John a changed man, less restless and more committed to family life. Though he had withheld from her the details of how precarious their financial situation was becoming, with the 1857 financial panic and looming economic depression, he now had no choice but to seek her counsel. "Frémont would never transact business without his wife being present, who had a much clearer head than he," an acquaintance wrote of the evolving marital business partnership during the upcoming months and years.

Now forty-five, he cherished her and was finally able to be the fully available and loving partner she had so long sought. He begged her to abandon the plans for Paris and to bring the entire family to California. The California Supreme Court—in a decision "aimed to injure Mr. Frémont," as Jessie saw it—ruled that anyone could seize and hold any "unworked" mine, setting loose lawlessness in the California minefields. "The construction as to what constituted an *unworked* mine was left to each one wishing to 'seize' it," Jessie wrote. "If a man left his small holding to get his dinner, his mine was 'jumped.'" Frémont's watchmen at his large mines were being threatened and bribed by leagues of jumpers, sometimes numbering as many as one hundred men who had banded together to grab control of Las Mariposas.

Jessie was initially adamant against the move to California, but she could not resist John's charming affection and newfound devotion to the family. "I refused so flatly to hear even of going to California that I suspected myself at the time & of course I am going," she wrote Lizzie in December 1857. "So is the whole caravan. We are only to stay six or eight months—to go immediately up to the Mariposas where Mr. Frémont will write as well as direct his work there. I held out a little about taking Lil and Nina but gave up to day—feeling a little convinced by Mr. Frémont's arguments but much more influenced by the wish he expressed to have them all around him . . . This is my last wail against my retreat to the mountains but since my country, my spouse & thy sire demand that this victim expire Strike—or rather take the passage and say no more about it."

She complained privately about the primitive conditions in the Sierra Nevada foothills, the fools and scoundrels with whom her husband had associated in business, the piles of laundry she would face without domestic help, the lack of "clever and intelligent young men" for Lily and Nina, and her own suspicions that John would leave her isolated and alone at their home in Bear Valley—"we will see if that comes to more than being in the same state with him." Still, she knew she would rather be with him on the frontier than alone in Paris, and by December was making arrangements for Lily, Nina, and Frank to join them in New York. "[A]s usual after a brief rebellion I am led in docile & already making the most of my coming position," she wrote Lizzie.

In January 1858 the children arrived in New York, and Jessie took them all to Washington to see Benton before preparing for their departure in March. Benton knew he was mortally ill, though he presented a cheerful façade made easier under the influence of opiates. Then he made a demand of her that would pit her once again between father and husband: he insisted that she leave Nina and Lily with him as veritable ransom for Jessie's return. "[U]pset again by having to displease him," Jessie sided with John that it was crucial at this stage in their marriage to keep the family together. "It is not easy to serve two masters and I would like so much to obey both of mine, but if I must choose it will be for the one that I think needs & wishes me the most."

She visited Benton one last time, on March 14, 1858. It was his seventy-sixth birthday, and both knew intuitively it would be their last meeting, though neither was able to speak of it. A few days later the Frémont family left New York for Panama, and on that day Benton retreated to his bed, never to rise again.

The isthmus crossing was much improved from their earlier passages—a swift train now replaced the packmules—and John and the children were deliriously happy and excited. Jessie succumbed to illness and depression, heartsick to have left her father, and apprehensive about their new life in California. "I broke down the second day, had fever & heart aches & afterwards seasickness." But as the *Golden Age* steamship glided through the Golden Gate at dusk on April 12, her health and good-natured optimism returned.

They spent several days purchasing household furnishings in San Francisco before heading to Las Mariposas. Traveling first by steamboat up the San Joaquin River to Stockton, the little entourage transferred to stagecoaches for the eighty-mile trip to Bear Valley in the Sierra

Nevada foothills. They moved into the rough-hewn two-story frame house on the hillside above the raucous mining camp, and Jessie set about making it a home. She hired a Pennsylvania carpenter to build a fireplace in the living room and a lean-to addition for the kitchen; retained a gardener to plant Madeira vines and scarlet runners on all four sides of the house and cultivate a sloping lawn dotted with honeysuckle and shrubs; hung French wallpaper and Chinese silk curtains, placed Indian rugs and bearskins on the floors; and after having the entire cottage whitewashed, christened it, with irony that was lost on the locals, the "White House."

Surrounded by thigh-high grass, wild geraniums and roses, lodge pole pines, and scrub oak, the rustic cabin was transformed into a jewel of domestic tranquillity and gentility. The children played on the landscaped grounds of the fenced twelve-acre parcel while John oversaw his operations from an office in Oso House, a hotel half a mile down the road, in Bear Valley. "In appearance, the Frémont estate departed from the generally ramshackle style that in those days characterized buildings and settlements in the Sierra gold country," a biographer said of the compound. "In the design of their house and grounds, it was as if the couple sought to architecturally underscore John's vision—articulated in his *Geographic Memoir Upon Upper California*—of California as a New World Mediterranean province." As they added a chain of connected outbuildings, the property took on what California historian Kevin Starr would later describe as a "villa-like style, bringing together smaller units in a way which respected the contours of the hills" that would come to define California architecture.

Jessie tutored Lily in history, German, arithmetic, and poetry, taught Charley to read, and wrote cheerful letters to Lizzie Blair filled with details of their happy and idyllic life. "We have a fine pair of carriage horses and Lil has a horse of her own," she wrote, describing how Charley and Frank were learning to ride bareback. "They are already browned with red cheeks & the baby Frank thrives on the fine milk & pure air." As in earlier days, gunny sacks of money were pouring in, with Frémont earning an estimated profit of $40,000 a month.

One day, only weeks after arriving in California, John's lawyer and his wife paid them a visit. Jessie greeted the woman, who remarked that she was happy to see Jessie so cheerful and wearing color instead of black. "Why not?" Jessie replied. "I am very well now."

"Oh, so soon after your father's death."

Before Jessie could respond, John had rushed to her side. "Is my father dead?" Jessie asked.

"For answer he gathered me in his arms, and as I asked, 'When?' I saw his tears."

On April 8, a week after completing his last book, Benton had written to Sam Houston of Texas asking that no formal notice of his death be mentioned in Congress, signing the letter "your old Tennessee friend." On April 9 he had uttered his final words in the presence of his daughter Eliza: "I am comfortable and content." He died at seven thirty A.M. on April 10. Two days later, Eliza's small son McDowell Jones, one of Benton's favorite grandchildren, fell suddenly ill and died. That day, April 12, Sam Houston led a cortege through a steady rain as two black caskets were transported to the railway station for a three o'clock train to St. Louis.

"As soon as the news reached Missouri, a great revulsion of feeling took place," Theodore Roosevelt wrote, "and all classes of people united to do honor to the memory of the dead statesman, realizing that they had lost a man who towered head and shoulders above friends and foes."

The public buildings in St. Louis were draped, all businesses closed, and the flags flew at half mast as thousands of people viewed his body lying in state at Mercantile Library Hall. Near the courthouse stood a lithograph of Benton with an engraved inscription:

> *Among the foremost men in all this land,*
> *The great Missourian stood pre-eminent;*
> *A man whom gold could neither buy nor bribe,*
> *Nor smooth-faced flattery, with soft tongues reduce,*
> *Nor domineering clans nor cliques control.*
> *"Old Bullion" was no disrespectful name;*
> *His words were gold, coined in the mint of mind;*
> *In council wise, in battle always brave—*
> *A statesman—scholar—gentleman!*

Though it had stormed for days, the sun broke through the dismal sky on the morning of his funeral. Forty thousand mourners lined the streets and stood on balconies as the solemn procession made its way to Bellefontaine Cemetery. There the "Magnificent Missourian" was laid to rest next to his beloved wife, Elizabeth McDowell Benton.

Jessie never forgave herself for not being present at her father's deathbed, and she was grief-stricken by the loss. She preferred her memories from childhood—at her little desk in his study serving as his devoted assistant as he taught her and shaped her lovingly into the woman she had become—rather than the strife and tension that had existed between them in recent years. She took solace in his last letter to her, urging her to go to California, telling her "it is not right for a family to be divided." Still, it had been a difficult choice and one that left "lasting regret."

On April 16, without knowing it was the day of her father's burial, Jessie and John were camped at Mount Bullion—the highest peak on their property they had named for Benton. They had built a raging bonfire on its summit, turning the mountain into a "blazing beacon." Knowing "how fond Father was of the classics & classical comparisons," Jessie wrote to Blair after learning of her father's death, "it seems to me he would have liked to hear me—his favorite scholar—tell him what thought links itself with that day. How as the old Greeks sculptured a jet of flame on the tomb to typify the soul purified & ascending, so that great flame rising from the mountain of gold rock is to me an image of his great heart & mind freed from the clay and rising to the great master."

John postponed a business trip to San Francisco, not wanting to leave his deeply saddened Jessie alone at their little White House. "I remained with Jessie until I had got her through the first & worst two weeks," he wrote Blair on June 4. "When I left she was in a more cheerful, or rather, less oppressed condition." She joined him in San Francisco at the end of June, where John, through legal means, hoped to stave off a confrontation with the Hornitas League—a band of squatters threatening bloodshed at his mines.

They returned to Las Mariposas in early July, Jessie wearing a black mourning hat and dress, and made preparations to fend off the "aggrieved miners and hired thugs" threatening to take possession by force of one of Frémont's richest veins in response to his "aggressive, rapacious aims." The expected violence broke out on the night of July 9, when a horseback messenger galloped to the White House to report that eighty members of the Hornitas League had seized Frémont's Black Drift mine three miles away and had then moved on to the nearby Pine Tree mine. Several of John's miners barricaded themselves inside the Pine Tree mine and threatened to ignite powder kegs if anyone entered.

John and his thirty men—outnumbered and underarmed—sent for help. On July 18, Jessie dictated a letter from John to Blair indicating that California Democratic governor John B. Weller had agreed to come to his aid. "The Governor sent me word . . . that he had telegraphed to the military companies at Columbia, Sonora, & Stockton, to hold themselves in readiness to start at a moment's notice to our protection. Friends in San Francisco have sent me up 100 muskets with bayonets & abundance of ammunition & 50 good men have volunteered to come & use them."

One evening a note was delivered to their home giving Jessie and the children twenty-four hours to leave or see their house burned down. Jessie was terrified and immediately sat down to write a forty-four-page will. But then she replaced her fear with fury. Along with Isaac, "a faithful part-Indian, part-negro man, a great hunter and long with Mr. Frémont," as she described him, she took a carriage to a saloon in Bear Valley to answer the threat. Facing down a crowd of ruffians, she began speaking. "You may come and kill us, we are but women and children, and it will be easy—but you cannot kill the Law," she told them, revealing that reinforcements were on the way from several nearby communities. When she turned and walked away she struggled to hide her trepidation, for she fully expected to be shot in the back.

Word of her courage spread throughout the region, and after the crisis had finally subsided a group of women from the area came to Bear Valley on horseback to thank her for staying during the clash when everyone knew she had the financial means to withdraw with her family to San Francisco. "Had you given up and left the cottage, our hills would have run blood," they told her.

John had underestimated the volatility of the situation, and once the crisis turned violent, he wished he had removed his family to safety. But when peace returned to Las Mariposas, he was glad to have had them with him. "Jessie as usual was my best ally," he wrote Francis Preston Blair.

By August, the temperatures in Bear Valley were soaring to 115 degrees—hot enough for the kids to fry eggs on flat rocks and making it necessary to sew leather shoes for their dogs. Jessie decided to move the entire family from their parched valley to Mount Bullion, where there were cool streams and high mountain breezes. Pitching a large tent, the family would refer to their new retreat as "Camp Jessie." Frémont rode his horse to Bear Valley every morning, and returned to Camp Jessie at five every evening bearing fresh vegetables, dairy, and meat from their estate below. "We have the most delightful open air dining room with a view that cannot be matched out of the Alps," Jessie described the setting. "We face an amphitheatre of mountains which rise from the river Merced—ourselves being on the steep descent to its banks. It is about thirty miles as the crow flies to the snow mountains but in this transparent, rarified air they look not ten. The cliffs & chasms of the Yosemite Valley are perfectly distinct."

In subtle and not so subtle ways, the death of Benton released Jessie to commit to John more fully, just as it enabled John to rise to the position of primary male figure in Jessie's life. "Mr. Frémont's nature demands to be met two thirds of the way," Jessie wrote that summer, and perhaps for the first time, with his rival now gone, John could expect Jessie's undivided attention and would respond in kind. John had always come and gone, dovetailing through the marriage like a long-distance lover, sending money and bearing gifts while restlessly seeking the next objective. And though Jessie could not have admitted it in nineteenth-century culture and society, a part of her no doubt relished the independence the unique marriage had provided her. While most of her peers were trapped in conventional domestic roles, Jessie had traveled the continent alone, resided in California, Washington, Paris, New York, and Nantucket, communed with some of the nation's most powerful male figures in politics and journalism, and raised her children without any interference. Now, for the first time, she had an actively involved partner.

"I have gone about like a stork with my young ones, building new nests summer & winter & rebuilding again & again as fast as they were abandoned or destroyed. All my energy—and I think I must have started with an unusual share for it to hold out yet—has gone to keeping a home & home feelings in our scattered little set. And of late I am getting a great reward. I am friend and adviser now."

John supervised the mining and milling operations from his Bear Valley office, presiding over sixteen thousand workers, overseeing the construction of canals and dams and a railroad connecting the mines, and importing equipment. "Mr. Frémont was his own engineer," Jessie wrote, "and he contracted for his large laboring force in San Francisco with a Chinese House—quite the first employment of Chinese in railroad building in California. Many hundreds of Chinese swarmed in their orderly busy way over that mountain face." He hired a Viennese baker and an Italian chef to cook for the unmarried workers at his

Benton Mills on the Merced River, where he prohibited alcohol and weapons. He returned home every evening, a full participant in family life, and developed a fresh bond with his children, who had once considered him an avuncular stranger. "When I knew I should never see Father again I turned my whole heart into this house and sometimes I think I magnetized Mr. Frémont into home life," Jessie wrote. "He takes part in & likes all the details of our household—the children's plays & witticisms and lessons—he looks after our comforts & is in fact head of the house. No 'wild turkey' left . . . I feel now as if we were a complete and compact family, and really Mr. Frémont used to be only a guest—dearly loved and honored but not counted on for worse as well as better. To him the palms. To us the shade. Now we share & share and he is far the happier for it."

Jessie handled the correspondence with associates, lawyers, lobbyists, and engineers, accompanied him on business trips to San Francisco, and hired assistants to manage the $10,000 monthly payroll. She also supervised the household servants, tutored the children, read, and wrote letters to her friends in Washington, New York, and London.

They had grown closer as a couple than they had ever been, the shared adversity of the past, the sheer work of the present deepening their bond. Having resisted such intimacy for seventeen years, John now openly embraced it, and both were solidly happy in the security of a mature marriage. He was the first to admit he could never have endured all of life's hardships without her.

In the spring of 1859, Horace Greeley visited them in Bear Valley during his first overland journey to the West. He wrote letters back to the *Tribune*, later published in a book, describing the scenic grandeur and marveling at the prosperity of the Frémonts' settlement, estate, and mining operation. "In the spirit of . . . determination, he [Frémont] has since lived and labored, rising with the lark and striving to obtain a complete knowledge and mastery of the entire business, taking more and more labor and responsibility upon his own shoulders as he felt able to bear them, until he is now manager, chief engineer, cashier, accountant, and at the head of every other department but law, for which he finds it necessary still to rely upon professional aid."

The sumptuousness of Jessie's household stunned Greeley, from the French cook to the freshly laundered clothing and manicured lawns. Learning of Greeley's visit with only three days notice, Jessie had quickly sewn a cashmere dress for herself after cutting up two out-of-style couture dresses from Paris, and made crisp white frocks for Lily and Nina and new linen shirts for Charley and Frank. "I was prepared for your enormous development here and seeing you in good health from successful work," Greeley told Jessie, "but I expected to see Jessie Anne [sic] a worn if not a resigned little recluse, living on bacon and greens. What I see is French frills and blue sash ribbons, and what I eat is good rolls and French made dishes." They "fitted him out with a quiet mule and good guide" to visit the nearby waterfalls at Yosemite, which he found unspectacular—a fact Jessie attributed to his leaving his spectacles on the guest room nightstand.

The purpose of his visit, as Jessie and John saw it, "was the shaping of the next convention for President" and, if John refused to consider another run for the presidency, then to solicit his endorsement of Lincoln over Seward. Both made it clear to Greeley that they had no intention of participating in the upcoming national presidential election. After experiencing Las Mariposas, Greeley "soon realized why Mr. Frémont would not reenter political life in a way which would again entail the abandonment of his property."

That year, too, they received a visit from Richard Henry Dana, the author of the best-selling *Two Years before the Mast*, which had first romanticized California for a national audience nineteen years before. The Harvard-trained explorer was back in California gathering material for a new edition of the book. "He and Mr. Frémont talked, as no two other men could, of the former California, and both realized its amazing future," Jessie wrote of his stopover. Dana was as charmed as Greeley by the Frémonts' Bear Valley existence, but was particularly entranced with Jessie, whom he called "a heroine equal to either fortune, the salons of Paris and the drawing-rooms of New York and Washington, or the roughest life of the remote and wild . . . Mariposa."

The Greeley and Dana visits underscored Jessie's utter isolation and hunger for intellectual contact—a fact she could not hide from John. He had known her since she was fifteen years old, intuited her every mood and longing, and recognized "the abstraction of her gaze when she thought herself unobserved," as Jessie's biographer Catherine Coffin Phillips put it. He secretly set out to purchase for her, subject to her approval, a large estate on a bluff directly across from the Golden Gate. "Without telling me, he bought it and gave it to me, as the realization of what he knew I had long wished to combine in a home. I was entranced when I went out and saw the unique place; a little headland running out into the Bay, opposite Alcatraz Island, having its name of Black Point from the laurels thickly covering it." The rambling house had views from all sides, of the Pacific Ocean, the San Francisco Bay, and the Contra Costa Mountains in the distance.

"Here are the three things we have always held as requirements for a home," John told Jessie when he brought her to the site for the first time. "The sound of the sea, a view, and a gentle climate. I can get the twelve acres from Mark Brumagim, the banker, for forty-two thousand dollars. It shall be in your name to have and to hold for your heirs forever."

Jessie was instantly smitten. "So swift moving is Fancy's brush that even as he spoke, I saw myself walking in the glassed-in corridor connecting the house Virginia fashion with the outside kitchen and the servants' quarters and glancing out at the La Marque roses already climbing its roof."

They stayed several days at the Union Hotel in San Francisco while John finalized the purchase, and when John returned to Bear Valley to oversee the family's move, Jessie remained at the hotel, where she made plans for renovating the house. "It was solitude by the sea," she later wrote of the enchanting property, "yet within city limits, and within touch of friends and all city life near. Near here, so many years before, Mr. Frémont had rowed across and spiked Spanish guns, and here he had named this the Golden Gate; now it was my home . . . At last, after many wanderings, many separations, and many strange experiences, we saw a home of congenial beauty and repose—a home which time would make a fortune to our children as holders of this little property; its . . . acres were more dear to me than the many miles and mines of the Mariposas."

Jessie was beside herself with excitement and immediately begged the Blairs to visit. "I have always gotten solid health in sea air & Mr. Frémont has found me here a 'house by the sea' that is more beautiful than any Sea Dream that Tennyson or any poet ever fancied." By June 1860 the family was ensconced at Black Point, though John necessarily commuted to Bear Valley. Still, he spent as much time as possible at the estate; they reserved a box at the opera house in San Francisco, a thriving metropolis of nearly sixty thousand; and the Frémonts became the city's most celebrated couple. During this time Jessie became enamored with the daughter of her neighbors, ten-year-old Nelly Haskell, with whom she formed an attachment the moment they met and who would go on to be a lifelong friend and correspondent. Astonished by Nelly's quick and curious mind—she "absorbs poetry, and her reading of it becomes a picture in sound"—Jessie added Nelly to the family "school," where Jessie taught the children for four hours each day.

Jessie rekindled the salon gatherings she had hosted years before in Monterey, and she entertained influential visitors such as Herman Melville and the noted Unitarian minister and orator Thomas Starr King, newly arrived from Boston. King and a young Bret Harte, whom Jessie discovered and nurtured as a writer, became her closest friends. She was impressed with the twenty-four-year-old Harte's poems and sketches in *Golden Era*, the city's literary journal where he worked as a typesetter making $16 a month, and invited him to Black Point. Harte would return to the estate for Sunday dinner every week for a year, bringing his manuscripts for Jessie to critique. "He was shy and proud and almost unhappy from want of success," Jessie described him. She thought him the most brilliant literary talent in the West and was determined to see him break into New York publishing circles. Tall and swarthy, ineffably handsome and painfully sensitive, he had bounced around California's gold fields as a teenager, writing sharply observant stories, and had landed in San Francisco at about the same time the Frémonts moved to Black Point. He lived in a small room above a restaurant, and his Sunday outings to Black Point became the center of his social life. Though she was lavish with her praise, Jessie was piercing with her criticism, pointing out that he possessed the dangerous gifts of grotesquerie and irony. "Don't ride them too hard. It will tell on your heart," she advised him.

Through her contacts, Jessie would help him publish his first *Atlantic Monthly* story, "The Legend of Monte del Diablo," which launched his national literary career. She further helped the impoverished writer by asking her old friend General Edward F. Beale, who would become California's surveyor-general, to give Harte a government appointment with a salary and light duties so he would have the luxury to write. Harte called Jessie his "fairy godmother" and would be devoted to her for the rest of his life. "I believe that if I were cast upon a desert island, a savage would come to me next morning and hand me a three-cornered note to say that I had been appointed governor at Mrs. Frémont's request, at $2,400 a year," Harte wrote to her, expressing his gratitude.

If her relationship with Harte was maternal and protective, her friendship with King was intellectual, spiritual, and delightfully playful—their time together marked by infectious laughter, in stark contrast to their reserved spouses.

They had first met when Jessie and John went to hear the Unitarian minister recently arrived from the Hollis Street Church in Boston. She was initially unimpressed with the slight man whose blond hair hung at shoulder length and whose frame rattled indistinguishably in the folds of his robe. But once he spoke, Jessie was mesmerized by his fiery passion and rich voice, his brilliant and earnest eloquence belied by his boyish face. "Though I weigh only 120 pounds, when I'm mad I weigh a ton," he had once said, and Jessie immediately grasped how this slender young man had become one of the nation's most powerful orators. The thirty-three-year-old abolitionist minister had just moved to San Francisco with his wife, Julia, and their eight-year-old daughter, and was already attracting worshipers from as far away as Stockton and Sacramento.

Born December 17, 1824, the son of a Unitarian minister, King at fifteen became the sole support of his family upon his father's sudden death. Inspired by Ralph Waldo Emerson and Henry Ward Beecher, he set out to educate himself for the ministry, reading the classics and mastering six languages. At age twenty he became pastor of his father's church in Charlestown, Massachusetts, and two years later was appointed to the Hollis Street Church in Boston. During his eleven-year tenure there he rescued it from bankruptcy and increased the congregation to five times its original size. One of the most famous preachers in New England, he was recruited by churches in Chicago and New York, but thought California more desperately in need of an effective voice against slavery. The country was obviously heading toward disunion and civil war, and King feared that California's governor and legislature would be sympathetic to the South.

"I thought it unfaithful to huddle so closely round the cozy stove of Blessed Boston," he had explained as his reason for coming to San Francisco, "and I wished to go out into the cold and see if I were good for anything. I do feel, however, that my size tells against me here in a land of big trees, big waterfalls, and big vegetables."

His pleas for a liberal, broad-minded, humanitarian Christianity resonated intensely with Jessie, and the lifelong Episcopalian immediately purchased a pew at King's church and invited him to Black Point. "I have none but a parlor acquaintance with him," Jessie wrote excitedly to Lizzie Blair in June 1860, "but he is new life in a literary way. He is so clever & charming in conversation." By August they were inseparable companions, made easier by John's absences and Julia's sullen disdain for San Francisco. "Before our friendship progresses farther," King asked Jessie one day at Black Point, "let me ask: Do you think it sacrilegious for a man constitutionally hilarious to become a minister?"

Soon Black Point had become a second home to the patriot preacher, with Jessie providing at the far end of the property studio space where he could write his lectures and newspaper articles undisturbed by his throngs of fans. At noon Jessie sent a household servant bearing lunch, and at tea time he would come to the main house and read Jessie what he had written. "I rode to Mrs. Frémont's, two miles off, & sat in her lovely cottage, hearing her talk & enjoying it hugely," he wrote a childhood friend. And in another letter to the same confidante he wrote enthusiastically about the glorious time he spent with Jessie. "Yesterday I dined with Mrs. Frémont & walked bareheaded among roses, geraniums, vines & fuchsias in profuse bloom." In October King reported to a friend that he had once again had a "fine time with Mrs. F. The Col. was at home. It is the 19th anniversary of her wedding—where all Washington was horrorstruck, as she said, because she had made 'such a foolish match.' Now that Frémont's mills turn out $16,000 a week in solid gold, I suppose Washington would pass a different judgment. She *is* a superb woman."

Though Jessie was always characteristically devoted to, and proud of, John, King considered John a predatory, gold-mining capitalist—an ironic view, given Frémont's Jeffersonian idealism and Republican presidential candidacy—who was far inferior to Jessie. When John was later being considered as ambassador to France, King confided to a friend that Jessie would be the better appointee to the position. As the close friendship blossomed between Jessie and King, Jessie always included Julia in her invitations to Black Point, though the unhappy wife rarely accompanied her husband.

For his part, John seemed genuinely pleased that Jessie was so blissfully cheerful and intellectually stimulated. He spoke of his pleasure in listening to Jessie and Bret Harte converse. "When we heard the two talking together, their low well-modulated voices rising and falling, it was beautiful. When to them was added the deep and vibrant tone of King's voice, it was a trio as good as music." John frequently participated in her gatherings, and though quiet and circumspect, his active mind and dignified courtesy impressed their guests. He visibly loved observing Jessie in her milieu, and when he contributed to the conversation it was with a plain and lucid insight that indicated a thoughtful and clear mind. "He is about forty-five years old, tall and slender, of modest demeanor, and of quiet, undemonstrative manner," wrote an acquaintance at about this time. "At first, he makes no strong impressions upon you, but in conversation, by degrees, you come to the conclusion that you are in the presence of no common man. There is a deep [intensity] of expression in his eye, which taken in connexion with his calm, measured words, forces upon you the conviction, that his extraordinary [career] is but a just reflection of his inherent character." He rarely drank, sometimes taking a glass of claret with dinner, and always retired early, to awaken at sunrise to enjoy nature, where he was far more comfortable than with people. "He was simple in all his private habits: he liked plain food, gave a plain hospitality," a biographer wrote, "and found his chief amusements in horseback riding and walking."

All the while, Jessie thrived on the social intercourse, the cerebral discussions of topics ranging from politics to economics to culture to creativity. Her salons became a gathering place for California's literary and political luminaries, Jessie the impenitent muse who by this stage in her life was resigned to her female position of channeling her abundant mental energies through influential men. Her visitors to Black Point would "walk about & admire until they are hungry & then have a delightful chatty luncheon from one to three hours at table," she reported to Lizzie. "You know the sea is my life and my love. I love the light—& the sound and the smell of its water & here on this point of land we have it on three sides while the slope down to the very water's edge is covered with wild holly & laurel & other native trees & good taste & money have been for seven years adding all sorts of planted flowers & vines & shrubs. The flapping of the sails as the schooners round this point & the noise of their paddles as the steamers pass are household sounds really that come to us through closed doors."

She absorbed San Francisco society as if she had been starved during her years in the mountains, attending lectures by noted feminists, Verdi operas, plays at the Lyceum, and a steady stream of private dinners and balls. As much as she loved the nightlife, the formal dinners, and the theatrical productions, John eschewed such social activity, preferring quiet evenings at Black Point surrounded by friends and family in lively conversation. Jessie honored this aspect of his personality, rarely insisting that he accompany her, and there developed between them a comfortable and mutually respectful understanding through which each allowed the other the independence necessary for personal fulfillment—a progressive marital arrangement that baffled their friends and fueled their detractors in an era of Victorian convention.

In personal taste and style they were vastly different as well. He dressed simply and preferred "a Spartan existence even when his wealth seemed greatest." As he once put it, he found the utmost joy in "old garments, old books, old friends." He loved horses, dogs, and children, and he focused his passion on the grandeur of the American West, finding singular pleasure in his long walks and horseback rides around Black Point or in the wild mountains surrounding his mines. He refused to hunt or fish, except out of necessity, and thought every living thing divine. "Out of doors was life to him," his son Frank described him. ". . . Stormy weather appealed to him as well as fair. Trees were to him sacred, and he would not let them be cut down on our property, unless dead or dying; then he would do the cutting himself. Flowers especially appealed to him . . . he would guide his horse so as to avoid crushing a flower or ant-hill; all life had a significance for him. Once we were climbing in the mountains . . . and I came across a snake. Boylike, I started to kill it, but he would not permit it. 'No, let it go! It has not harmed you and probably enjoys life,' he said, adding: 'Besides, any Indian knows that to kill a snake causelessly will bring rain and a wet camp.' "

He preferred action to contemplation, though his vision for a new America was grandiose and complex. While he would rather engage in a chess match or a fencing joust, he was courtly and amiable, a gracious host and convivial conversationalist when the situation demanded his attention. When he was "induced to take his seat in the circle indoors, his restlessness abruptly left him," wrote Allan Nevins, "and his dignified immobility, his perfect quiescence, with never an unnecessary gesture or motion, impressed all who saw him."

Jessie, by contrast, had an unabashed flair for the dramatic. She loved French fashion, dressed herself and her children in the finest fabrics and most up-to-date styles, and decorated her California home with a resplendency reminiscent of plantation Virginia; Regent Street, London; Champs Élysées, Paris; and Capitol Hill, Washington—damask duvets and chenille throws, satin sheets and silk bed canopies, Irish linens and Indian tapestries. She loved fine art, especially the grand paintings and daguerreotypes of the West, and valued Native American weavings and baskets as much as the products of the European masters. What John and Jessie loved equally besides each other and their children were books, and their library was the most extensive and imposing in all of northern California.

Their Black Point home was haven to all the misfits and loners, radicals and intellectuals, brilliant and alienated minds of mid-nineteenth-century California. It was the happiest of times for John and Jessie, but the idyll was soon to end. Once again, the raw, tumultuous world of politics, further complicated by war, would intervene in their lives, and Jessie would soon, of necessity, turn her back on Black Point, never to see it again.

Frémont had served his purpose for the nascent Republican Party, which sought to modify its platform and turn its attention to more serious politicians—men such as William Seward and Abraham Lincoln. Though nominally considered a possible candidate in 1860, Frémont had lost the backing of John Bigelow and Francis Preston Blair—both of whom had come to doubt his ability as a leader, as well as apparently to believe rumors of his womanizing. When Gideon Welles attempted to learn the reasons for the complete dismissal of Frémont by his onetime avid supporters, "he heard various gossipy explanations," as one historian put it. Indeed, Blair was actively speaking out against Frémont—something to which Jessie, despite her ongoing correspondence with both Blair and his daughter Lizzie, seemed oblivious, but which signaled the beginning of a breach that would have far-reaching consequences. That Frémont had avowed a lack of interest in the candidacy, both to Greeley during the journalist's visit to Bear Valley and in letters to Blair, as well as his decision to immerse himself in the business of Las Mariposas without making any effort to keep his hand in national politics, solidified his banishment. "Four years ago we went to Philadelphia to name our candidate and we made one of the most inexcusable blunders . . . We nominated a man who had no qualification for the position of Chief Magistrate," Thurlow Weed said, voicing the prevailing sentiment among Republican leaders.

After a nominating convention full of intrigue in Chicago in May 1860—following what Doris Kearns Goodwin called "a night of a thousand knives"—Lincoln had defeated Seward for the Republican nomination. The party's new platform, designed to broaden its political base, was as opposed to the extension of slavery as it had been in 1856, but also included a call for a Homestead Act that would fill up the West with northern antislavery settlers, and the construction of a transcontinental railroad to the Pacific that would provide employment, transport antislavery settlers west, and open the wealth of California to the rest of the country.

A month after the Republican convention, a House investigating committee published a massive report of malfeasance, fraud, and abuse of power by the Buchanan administration—conveniently released in time for Republican use as a campaign document. Though Buchanan was not running for reelection, the allegations of widespread corruption tainted the entire Democratic Party. The congressional report exposed graft in numerous government agencies, bid-rigging and kickbacks in government contracts, bribery by the administration of judges and congressmen for favorable decisions and votes, fraudulent loans from the Interior Department's Indian trust fund, and on and on. "Americans had always viewed malfeasance and abuse of power as the gravest dangers to republican liberty," wrote historian James McPherson, and now, with the most far-reaching corruption scandal in the history of the nation, the lumbering, inexperienced, plain-spoken Lincoln suddenly became the reassuring Honest Abe. With characteristic irreverence, Greeley penned the obvious contrast between "an honest administration on one side, and wholesale executive corruption, legislative bribery, and speculative jobbery on the other."

In November 1860, the Pony Express brought word to California that Lincoln had been elected president, and the Frémonts' political future seemed at an end. Later that month, Oregon's U.S. senator Edward D. Baker visited Black Point. Baker, an old and dear friend of Lincoln's, "had lately returned from the successful campaign which put Mr. Lincoln into power," Jessie wrote, "and was authorized to offer a Cabinet position or a first class foreign appointment to Mr. Frémont. The mission to France would have been tempting in time of peace, but we all saw war ahead and it was not a time to leave one's country." Baker, King, and the Frémonts held what Jessie described as "prophetic discussions on the near future, each feeling actual hostilities certain, each seeing the inevitable result."

Frémont made clear to Baker that he thought he could be of most service to the new administration if he were appointed secretary of war—a position for which Seward, soon to become secretary of state, was lobbying Lincoln on Frémont's behalf. But even that coveted position would be an impossibility for Frémont in the immediate future, since he had opened negotiations in Paris for the sale of half of Las Mariposas and planned a trip abroad. He asked Baker to convey to Lincoln that he was unavailable at the moment, but that if war broke out he would accept a commission to command an army in the field.

During November and December John made preparations for his journey to Paris. He amassed financial and technical documents about the Bear Valley mining operation to take to potential European investors, and collected a portfolio of breathtaking photographs of the landscape taken by Carleton Watkins. While the Mariposa mines were enormously productive, John was having difficulty paying back the massive construction loans he had taken out, and not until the fall of 1860 was he forced to admit to Jessie the severity of their fiscal situation. In fact, John had been under serious financial pressure since at least the previous spring, unable to meet his payroll obligations and the usurious 2-percent-per-month interest payments on his loans, and was now more than $1 million in debt. Jessie was shocked to learn of the sudden downturn in their circumstances, but at thirty-six was more optimistic than most about the fickleness of fortune.

John retained San Francisco attorney Frederick Billings to accompany him to Paris, and placed Las Mariposas under managers in the event the breakout of civil war would preclude him from returning in the near future. The group—which included George W. Wright, one of the founders of the Mariposa Mining Company, as well as a San Francisco woman named Margaret Corbett and her child—departed on January 1, 1861. Billings would later contend, though strongly contradicted by Wright, that Corbett was Frémont's paramour who, according to Frémont biographer Tom Chaffin, "traveled in her own stateroom paid for by Frémont," one of many "glancing references to extramarital dalliances [that] run through the paper trail of Frémont's life like some sotto voce leitmotif." If indeed Corbett was John's lover, Jessie seemed either unaware or unaffected, revealing no hint of displeasure with John in either her correspondence with close friends or her unpublished memoir.

Instead, Jessie was wholly preoccupied with the impending war, made more ominous with South Carolina's decision in late December 1860 to secede from the Union. Over the next six weeks, Mississippi, Louisiana, Florida, Alabama, Georgia, and Texas all followed suit, and within three months of Lincoln's election, the Confederate States of America had been organized, and Jefferson Davis elected president of the provisional Confederate government. "The fear of what may be in store for us all if this cloud of civil war takes shape, makes me restless," she wrote King.

In February, before departing New York for London, John met with Lincoln at the Astor House. "At this time Colonel Frémont and the President were in full sympathy in their views of the situation," Jessie later wrote. "The campaign of '56 in which Lincoln had done his best to assure the election of Colonel Frémont, the reverse of the situation in '60, when Colonel Frémont had enlisted the active aid of his friends to secure, as far as he was able, Mr. Lincoln's nomination, had given them a deeper bond of association than usually comes to men who had had but little personal intercourse." John reported to Jessie that he found the president "unwilling to believe in actual war," and while Frémont concurred in the president's hope that war could be averted, he thought it naïvely optimistic and again pledged his willingness to lead an army in the field. "With the inflammatory press and inflammatory conversation on every hand, I am convinced that actual war is not far off," he wrote Jessie. Upon receiving this letter, Jessie began preparing to leave Black Point, convinced that war was imminent and determined to join John wherever that "field" might be.

In April, Jessie was thrown from her carriage when her horses bolted down Russian Hill, and though her injuries were not serious, she suffered lingering headaches and back pain. King and Harte doted on her, bringing her books and flowers, but her convalescence only made her more agitated and eager to enter the national fray. "She saw herself as part of a great cause," wrote biographers Herr and Spence, "one that would permit her, as well as other women, to step beyond the boundaries of their separate sphere."

On March 4, 1861, President Lincoln gave an inaugural address intended to "cool passions and buy time," as historian James McPherson put it, with its theme of preserving an undivided union. He vowed to "hold, occupy, and possess" all federal property located in the secessionist states, though he was intentionally ambiguous about his willingness to use force.

The next day, the very first dispatch he received as president was a let-

ter from Major Robert Anderson at Fort Sumter. Anderson, a Kentuckian and former slaveowner, was entrenched with approximately eighty
U.S. Army soldiers at the garrison, four miles from downtown Charleston
His supplies would last but a few more weeks, Anderson reported. His
letter contained a recommendation from General Winfield Scott, suggesting that the Union surrender the fort to the South since a reinforcement would require twenty-five thousand soldiers and a large fleet to
blast its way to the mouth of Charleston Harbor—neither of which the
U.S. government had available. At that moment, the nation's army was
limited to sixteen thousand men "scattered over two thousand miles of
frontier" and its navy "fleet," if it could be called that, was "patrolling
distant waters or laid up for repair."

Determined to preserve peace for as long as possible, and afraid that an
armed reinforcement of Fort Sumter, the Union garrison in the harbor,
would be the spark of war that would drive the upper South states to
align with the Confederacy, the new president strategized over the deadlock. "On Sumter lay the issue of peace or war;" wrote William and
Bruce Catton, "on Davis and Lincoln lay the issue of Sumter. It was as
simple, and as complicated, as that." Then, in what McPherson called a
"stroke of genius" and "the first sign of the mastery that would mark
Lincoln's presidency," Lincoln conceived of a plan and set it in motion.
On April 6, Lincoln notified the governor of South Carolina that "an
attempt will be made to supply Fort-Sumter with provisions only; and
that, if such attempt be not resisted, no effort to throw in men, arms, or
ammunition, will be made, without further notice, [except] in case of an
attack on the Fort."

If the Southerners opened fire on unarmed boats carrying food for
starving soldiers, they would bear the onus of starting the war, Lincoln
reasoned. If they allowed the provisioning of Union troops, they would
"weaken the Confederate cause at home and sap its prestige abroad,
where diplomatic recognition was so precious," as historian Richard
Hofstadter portrayed the dilemma. Jefferson Davis, under intense pressure to preempt Lincoln's relief expedition, had little choice. "Border
southern States will never join us until we have indicated our power to
free ourselves—until we have proven that a garrison of seventy men cannot hold the portal of our commerce," the *Charleston Mercury* railed.
"Let us be ready for war . . . The fate of the Southern Confederacy
hangs by the ensign halliards of Fort Sumter."

At four thirty A.M. on April 12, Confederate forces opened fire on Fort

Sumter, assailing the fort for thirty-three hours and firing four thousand rounds of shells. On April 14, with the fort in flames and his men suffocating from the smoke, Major Anderson finally surrendered. Before departing, he and his men gave a fifty-round salute to the tattered Stars and Stripes. They then hauled down the flag, and in a poignant scene, Anderson handed it over to Confederate general Pierre G. T. Beauregard, who had been his teacher at West Point.

The next day, Lincoln issued a proclamation to the Northern states calling for seventy-five thousand volunteer soldiers to serve for ninety days to put down the insurrection—an appeal based on a 1795 law that provided for enlisting state militias into federal service. News that war had broken out in the United States reached Frémont in England within days of Fort Sumter, and he immediately turned his attention away from Las Mariposas business and back toward serving his country. "He wrote me from London, that he was returning immediately to take part in the war," Jessie noted, "and that if I could risk the rebel cruisers in the Gulf and was again well enough to move . . . he hoped I would join him—that he thought the war would last *years*, and he would be in it to the end."

Frémont was alarmed by the blatant and robust weapons trade between British arms dealers and Confederate agents "who were busy obtaining everything from ammunition to 'war steamers,'" as an observer described the frenzied moment. On his own initiative, and with his own money, he began purchasing arms and ammunition from European weapons merchants. Within a week he had spent $125,000 for ten thousand rifles from France, and another $75,000 on cannons and artillery shells from England. "I have succeeded in procuring the control of funds sufficient to purchase three or four batteries of guns . . . and perhaps 10,000 rifles," he wrote to Francis Preston Blair from his suite at the Athenaeum Club in London. "I trust that you have already offered my services to the President . . . My great desire is to serve my country in the most direct and effective way that I possibly can."

In May the president called for forty-two thousand three-year army volunteers and eighteen thousand sailors. That month, too, John received word that he had been commissioned as one of the four major generals created by an act of Congress. After learning of his appointment, he placed an order for two thousand French rifles, five hundred revolvers, eight cannons, and two million percussion caps, and pledged $60,000 in government funds as payment.

He arranged to have the weapons shipped to New York, placed his personal business in the hands of an English agent, sent word to Jessie to join him in the East, and made preparations to sail to the United States. "We go to join Mr. Frémont & I will be with him everywhere—I will," Jessie wrote excitedly to a friend. "Mr. Frémont has written to us to join him at once at New York," Jessie wrote to the manager of Las Mariposas; ". . . [he] was called to his old first love and duty, and I have not been so happy in years for him as now . . . An army of cares has been boring into our lives these few years past, and I thank heaven for this noble chance in a great cause . . . I am so glad I am going into an atmosphere where dollars and cents are not the first object. The noble and beautiful side of the nation is now apparent, and it will be a comfort to feel its influence."

Jessie dismissed her servants and rented the Black Point house to their old friend Edward Beale, who also bought the furniture, horses, and carriages. With one arm and a foot still in splints from her accident, she managed to pack for herself and her children, with only eight days' notice to leave on June 21. The last evening at Black Point she sat on her favorite bench overlooking the bay and watched the sunset on the Golden Gate, never dreaming it would be the last time she would be there.

The next day, King accompanied her on board the *North Star*—a well-built steamer that carried $1.2 million in gold. He was reluctant to leave her, standing at the door of her cabin holding an armful of long-stemmed English violets. Finally he released the flowers to her, pressing a volume of Emerson's *Essays* into her hands as well. "Smell, read, and rest," he said, and the two parted tearfully.

"Have you met Mrs. Frémont?" he wrote a few days later to a friend in New York. "I hope so. Her husband I am very little acquainted with, but she is sublime, and carries guns enough to be formidable to a whole Cabinet—a she-Merrimack, thoroughly sheathed, and carrying fire in the genuine Benton furnaces."

Confederate pirates preyed on merchant ships traveling in the Gulf of Mexico along the southern coast from Panama, and the *North Star*, laden with California treasure, was a prime target. The captain showed Jessie a small island on the map where he suspected an ambush was waiting. He altered the course to travel eighty miles south of Cape Hatteras. "The ship showed no lights whatever; we had early dinner, and silence and darkness were the rule after sundown." Still, with all the precautions, a notorious vessel, the swift *Jeff Davis*, chased them. "It was a sparkling cold and windy day, and we had the out-of-date sensations described in pirate stories as the wind now helped, now hindered our pursuer; but the wind of the North was our ally, and we outran her before night."

John had caught a fast ship to Boston, arriving on June 27, and proceeding immediately to Washington to meet with the president. He and Montgomery Blair, a West Point graduate who was now postmaster general, attended several conferences with Lincoln at the Blair estate in Silver Spring. Although the president and several of his military advisers were eager for Frémont to assume command of an eastern post, Blair pushed for the creation of a western department headquartered in St. Louis. The region, as the Blairs saw it, was being gravely overlooked by Lincoln's chief general, Winfield Scott, who seemed strangely uninterested in, surprisingly ignorant of, and grossly negligent of the critical situation in the West. Montgomery Blair was the only cabinet member to steadfastly advocate provisioning the men there.

Though Missouri was a slave state, it remained in the Union. But the hold was precarious, and the sympathy of St. Louis was with the South. Recruiting for the Confederate Army was blatant and thriving in the city of 160,000. Missouri congressman Frank P. Blair, Montgomery's brother, was the "brains and backbone of the Union element" in the state. Blair and the large German immigrant population had so far kept Missouri from seceding, but the political situation was fluid. Frank Blair's close friend, U.S. Army captain and soon to be general Nathaniel Lyon—a Connecticut native and a popular veteran of the Mexican-American War—had prevented the rebels from seizing the St. Louis arsenal, but both Blair and Lyon feared an attack on vitally located Cairo, Illinois, which could threaten southern Missouri and sweep Kentucky into the Confederacy. "Missouri had been saved from organized rebellion, but the smell and blackness of insurrectionary fire were strong upon her," observed the *Century Illustrated Quarterly*.

Of the approximately one million Missouri residents, a slight majority supported the Union, despite being "attached to the South by blood, tradition, a common history, and similar institutions," as Allan Nevins described the wavering state. A strong militant minority was increasingly difficult for Blair to counteract. Governor Claiborne Fox Jackson, along with the lieutenant governor, both U.S. senators, and most of the legislators, were secessionists. "Your requisition is illegal, unconstitutional, revolutionary, inhuman . . . Not one man will the State of Missouri furnish to carry on any such unholy crusade," Jackson had responded to the president's militia requisition. He had then boldly countered Lincoln's request with a proclamation of war, calling fifty thousand volunteer soldiers into service for the Confederacy.

Fighting was imminent throughout the state, from the capital of Jefferson City to Booneville on the Missouri River, from Springfield in southwestern Missouri to the border town of Cairo, at the confluence of the Ohio and Mississippi rivers. The Blairs lobbied Lincoln relentlessly to expand the war effort in the West.

Lincoln was fixated on keeping the upper South from seceding, especially Kentucky, and placed great stock in the Blair argument. "The President was anxiously concerned for the Border States, and since the Blairs were distinctly border-state-men in political thought and social inheritance, they found him attentive to their advice," according to Blair family biographer William E. Smith. While the Blairs would have preferred Captain Lyon to head the department, conservative Unionists such as Attorney General Edward Bates adamantly opposed Lyon, whom they considered a reckless Yankee, and whom the old Whig Bates particularly distrusted for his closeness to the longtime Democratic Blair family. Frémont was the Blairs' next best choice.

On July 3, Lincoln created the Western Department and tendered Frémont's commission to head the division, based in St. Louis and embracing Illinois, all the states west of Missouri to the Rocky Mountains including New Mexico, and eventually Kentucky once Frémont's forces had solidified Union support in Missouri. The appointment seemed inspired, for thousands of men responded with enthusiasm for a chance to serve under the famous Pathfinder. "His name is a tower of strength to his friends and a terror to his foes," the New York Times reported of his stunning ability to recruit volunteers. "He is just such a person as Western men will idolize and follow through every danger to death or victory," wrote John Hay, a young journalist turned presidential aide. "He is upright, brave, generous, enterprising, learned and eminently practical."

By all accounts, the president left the western war strategy to Frémont, though Frémont discussed in general terms with both Scott and Lincoln the scheme to descend the Mississippi to Memphis and New Orleans. "The President had gone carefully over with me the subject of my intended campaign," Frémont wrote of his orders, "and this with the single desire to find out what was best to do and how to do it.

This he did in the unpretentious and kindly manner which invited suggestion, and which with him was characteristic. When I took leave of him, he accompanied me down the stairs, coming out to the steps of the portico at the White House; I asked him then, if there was anything further in the way of instruction that he wished to say to me. 'No,' he replied, 'I have given you carte blanche; you must use your own judgment and do the best you can. I doubt if the States will ever come back.'"

On July 13, Jessie and the children arrived in New York, where they found John deeply absorbed in a multitude of tasks. He would later be criticized for spending three weeks in New York rather than proceeding immediately to St. Louis after receiving his assignment—hindsight criticism spawned by Montgomery Blair only after the two suffered a terminal breach, and which, in any case, was unfounded. In fact, John had initially planned on traveling to St. Louis on July 16, shortly after receiving his command, but had been told that Scott, his commanding officer, wanted to convey further instructions to him.

In New York he assembled his team of aides and set out on the task of procuring supplies for his desperately underequipped army. Though troops were being enlisted in record numbers throughout the western region, they had no shoes, weapons, uniforms, blankets, canteens, tents, horses, mules, or wagons, prompting the governor of Illinois to charge the Lincoln administration with a public scandal. Frémont had initially been promised seventeen thousand stands of arms from federal arsenals, but that number had been reduced to five thousand, leaving him to seek firearms from private owners. Having outfitted several expeditions through supply contacts in New York, and having staged a national presidential campaign from the city, Frémont naturally returned to that locale to meet his logistical demands.

He hired three celebrated Hungarian soldiers, all veterans of the Revolt of '48—General Alexander S. Asboth as his chief of staff, Colonel John Fiala as his chief topographical engineer, and Major Charles Zagonyi to head an elite bodyguard. Preferring foreigners to Americans—a preference that would antagonize his West Point critics—Frémont recruited German, Prussian, French, and Italian soldiers to accompany him to St. Louis, including a natural-born son of Lord Byron. In characteristic fashion, Jessie immersed herself in the tasks at hand, acting as John's partner. "Mr. Frémont has stacks and stacks not only of bayoneted muskets to examine but of work of all sorts," she wrote to King on July 20. "We have really had no chance to have a talk . . . I haunt around taking my chances of a word—sometimes it is only a look—but after the hungry yearning of that far off blank life at Black Point it is enough."

Like John, Jessie was extremely frustrated by the political ineptitude and military disorganization, thinking it was as if the administration was sleepwalking through the nation's greatest crisis. "There was great confusion and indecision in affairs at the time," she wrote. "Many of the people in power refused to believe that the Union had been as far as lay in the power of the Secessionists, disrupted, the actuality of war was doubted, and many tried to believe that it was only a local insurrection that would subside almost of itself." The army was led by aged officers, most of whom had first served in the War of 1812 and had never commanded so much as a brigade. The government possessed few if any accurate maps of the South, and its stockpile of weapons in the federal arsenals were mostly antique flintlocks. The seventy-four-year-old General Scott suffered from dropsy and narcolepsy and was overweight, inspiring little confidence among his men, and the president and his advisers seemed woefully oblivious to the scope of the coming conflict.

All of that changed on July 21, when federal forces suffered their first defeat of the war, thirty miles southwest of Washington at the Bull Run stream at Manassas, Virginia. That very day, the Frémont family left New York by train, bound for St. Louis.

"The position in which General Frémont now found himself differed from that of any other Union commander during the war," Jessie wrote. "Not only was he sent to his Department in his military capacity as a General charged with military administration of the affairs of his Department and the conduct of its army, but he was sent to raise, organize and equip that army; to provide its means of transportation, to buy everything from its shoes to its arms. This he had to do, not in a friendly country, not in a Union State, not with the support of the Civil Government of the State, not with the support of the majority of its citizens. St. Louis was a stronghold of Southern sympathizers and the State of Missouri was practically in the hands of the Secessionists."

Once the most gracious and hospitable community to anyone bearing the name Benton or Frémont, St. Louis was now "an unfriendly and vindictively triumphant rebel city." A somber mood overcame them all as their train entered the eerie and hostile environment at nine o'clock on the sultry morning of July 25. The streets were deserted, businesses shuttered, and empty steamboats rocked idly against their moorings. "Not a Union flag was flying," Jessie wrote, "in its place the Secession flag hung on the building in which recruits for the rebel forces were being enlisted. The United States army officers had been intimidated and terrorized, so that being few in number, they had found it best not to wear their uniforms, except at the Arsenal." The Frémonts made their way by carriage to Chouteau Avenue and the impressive three-story mansion they had arranged to rent from Jessie's cousin Sarah Benton Brant. Jessie found the stillness disquieting, "the wheels and the horses' hoofs echoed loud and harsh as when one drives through the silent streets late at night."

Jessie was momentarily relieved when the Brants' old black butler, whom she had known for most of her life as "Uncle Vincent," greeted them at the door. By noon, John was ensconced on the second floor of the residence, surrounded by maps and diagrams, secretaries and aides, advisers and bodyguards, when he called his first staff meeting. It was but the beginning of what would later be called "the hundred days in Missouri"—"the drama which tested Frémont's strength and weakness as never before," as historian Nevins described the period, "and which fixed in the popular mind a cruelly unjust impression of his character and capacities." For the next hundred days, Frémont would rise at five A.M. and retire at midnight as the situation in Missouri became increasingly chaotic and uncontrollable.

Jessie was eager to play a role in the war, ever passionate about slavery and union, and threw herself headlong into the enterprise, earning the unflattering sobriquet of "General Jessie." "The restraints of ordinary times do not apply now," she said of the historic moment that she considered liberating for women. Though the Blairs had implored her to stay in Washington rather than join John in St. Louis, she would hear nothing of it. "Few other women had stepped so conspicuously outside their proper boundaries," wrote one historian, "and she was dangerously vulnerable." Installing the command at a walled estate where the family would live as well, Jessie organized the headquarters, attended to John's correspondence, hired staff, met with emissaries, and served as his primary confidante and consultant. The family moved onto the third floor, the second floor was filled with tables and desks for Frémont and his officers, the first floor housed lower-level subordinates as well as printing and telegraph equipment, and the basement became a heavily guarded arsenal of arms and ammunition. Jessie, who had first devised the idea that the federal government lease the Brant home in order for the intimate staff to live and work in one place, thought the arrangement sensible and pragmatic. She considered the $6,000 annual rent extremely reasonable, given the property's size and location, but the fact that the payment went to one of Jessie's relatives would later fuel critics who charged the Frémonts with lavishness if not outright corruption.

By June 17, before Frémont had even arrived in St. Louis, Captain Lyon had saved the city's arsenal, engaged Confederate soldiers at Booneville and sent them into retreat, captured seven hundred Confederate militia soldiers at Camp Jackson, driven Confederate general Sterling Price's rebels out of the capital of Jefferson City, and was now occupying the town of Springfield, in the southwestern corner of Missouri. But the Union's hold remained tenuous, as Frémont faced the dual challenge of guerrilla warfare within the state and massive mobilized Confederate forces moving from outside the state toward key locales.

When Frémont assumed command on July 25, he inherited a two-pronged war at Cairo and Springfield, with outlying skirmishes multiplying as well. He took charge of 15,943 men—"scattered at nine points in Missouri, ill-equipped, ill-trained, and ill-organized"—of whom most were "three months' men" whose time had expired, and the vast majority of whom had not yet received compensation from the government. Still, as troop morale plummeted, he could expect no reinforcements despite a dangerous shortage of men and matériel.

Secessionists Jackson and Price had reportedly amassed an army of thirty thousand, which was poised for action in the southwestern corner of Missouri and included a large contingent of cavalry. Another twenty thousand Confederate forces were mustered in southeastern Missouri under the command of Gideon Pillow. Emboldened by Bull Run, Confederate leaders had ambitious designs for the West, and though they exaggerated the strength of their forces, claiming twenty-five thousand men under General Benjamin McCulloch, who were preparing to march against Lyon in Springfield, their strength was formidable.

Only three days after the Frémonts arrived in St. Louis, Jessie wrote a desperate letter to Montgomery Blair—the only West Point graduate in Lincoln's cabinet—on behalf of John, begging for money and arms. "Mr. Frémont asks you to take this from him, I write it from his telling—not absolutely from dictation," she penned on July 28, 1861.

"The enemy has already occupied, & in force, points which Mr. Frémont intended holding against them. For want of arms to arm new regiments & because not a cent of their pay has been given to the others
which disheartens & indisposes them to re-enlist, it is almost impossible
to make head against them. He is doing the best he can without money
without arms without moral aid. . . . Mr. Frémont says send anything in
the shape of arms—arms we must have. Send money, & both arms &
money by the most rapid conveyance." Then, scrawled across the letter
in John's bold handwriting, was: "Money & Arms without delay & by
the *quickest Conveyance*."

The urgency expressed in these early letters to the Blairs is telling.
Jessie obviously was alarmed at the unsustainable situation they immediately encountered in St. Louis—circumstances for which she held Frank
Blair, Montgomery Blair, and President Lincoln personally accountable.
"Is your brother Frank coming out here?" she asked Lizzie Blair sardonically. "Ask him if he brings his arms or is like the rest here to wait on
chance for them." Having grasped the local situation, she immediately
began contemplating a trip to Washington to meet personally with Lincoln. "It is not safe to say on paper all that should be said at Washington.
The President is a western man and not grown in red tape. If he knew
the true defenceless condition of the west it would not remain so. I have
begged Mr. Frémont to let me go on & tell him how things are here.
But he says I'm tired with the sea voyage—that I shan't expose my health
any more & that he can't do without me." In this July 27 letter to Lizzie,
the first intimation of fractured relations between the Frémonts and the
Blairs can be glimpsed. "Your letter reached me last night," Jessie wrote,
"and but for the genuine interest in the cause I should have taken it for a
sarcasm. You say all we need is 'Generals.' That is simply and literally the
whole provision made for this Dept. An arsenal without arms or
ammunition—troops on paper and a thoroughly prepared and united
enemy thick and unremitting as mosquitoes . . . It's making bricks without straw out here & mere human power can't draw order of chaos by
force of will alone."

Meanwhile, Frémont focused on blockading the Mississippi River, for-
tifying Cairo, Cape Girardeau, Ironton, Rolla, and Jefferson City, trans-
forming ferry boats into gunboats, training raw troops, reinforcing the
outposts, taking possession of the Iron Mountain and Pacific railroads,
policing St. Louis, reorganizing the Reserve Corps, stopping Confederate recruiting, personally guaranteeing the three-month soldiers' pay if

they would stay on for a fourth month, and establishing the first Union depot in the nation. "For a man whose genius could have risen to the requirements of the occasion," wrote a contemporary journalist, "it was a magnificent opportunity, an imperial theater."

Captain Nathaniel Lyon had been pleading for reinforcements since occupying Springfield on July 13—nearly two weeks before Frémont arrived—and even though thousands of men rushed to volunteer to serve under the famous explorer, Frémont could not possibly get them trained and equipped in time to assist Lyon. Though Lyon had five thousand troops from Missouri and Kansas, most had not been paid or clothed by the government, more than half were "ninety-day men" whose terms were expiring, and by mid-July they were 120 miles from the nearest railhead at Rolla and dangerously low on provisions. At the same time, a nervous general Benjamin M. Prentiss, the Union commander at Cairo, feared an imminent Confederate assault, as General Leonidas Polk was advancing with six thousand troops toward Bird's Point, just across the Mississippi River from Cairo, to join General Gideon Pillow's eleven-thousand-man army in the Mississippi Valley. "Have but eight regiments here," Prentiss wrote to Frémont on July 23. "Six of them are three-months men. Their time expires this week—are reorganizing now. I have neither tents nor wagons, and must hold Cairo and Bird's Point." Frémont agreed with Lincoln that Cairo was crucial for command of the Ohio and Mississippi rivers, while Springfield was of far less significance.

In addition to responding to Lyon and Prentiss, Frémont sought to stem the bloody guerrilla fighting that had broken out around the state, while also struggling to maintain peace and control in St. Louis, which was under the domination of rebel sympathizers. "All this had to be done by a man who had never commanded forces of more than a few hundred," wrote biographer Nevins, "who had for years been engrossed in civilian pursuits, and who was new to the city, the post, and the problems about him. It had to be done with the most inadequate resources, under a War Department indifferent to the West. The situation would have taxed the capacity of abler men than Frémont."

Having received nothing from Washington, the guns and equipment he had ordered in New York having been diverted to Virginia, and now desperate for money to pay troops and purchase supplies, Frémont seized treasury funds in St. Louis without waiting for government authorization. On

July 30, Frémont explained his action to the president and literally begged for Lincoln's help. "My Dear Sir: You were kind enough to say that as occasions of sufficient gravity arose, I might send you a private note . . . I have found this command in disorder, nearly every county in an insurrectionary condition, and the enemy advancing in force by different points of the southern frontier . . . Our troops have not been paid, and some regiments are in a state of mutiny. The Treasurer of the United States has here $300,000 entirely unappropriated, I applied to him yesterday . . . but was refused. We have not an hour for delay . . . This morning I . . . will send a force to the treasury to take the money, and will direct such payments as the exigency requires."

Such were the circumstances when Frémont organized a flotilla of eight steamboats and four thousand soldiers, artillery, and supplies to bolster the Union garrison at Cairo. Jessie disguised herself and hid in a stateroom on Frémont's flagship, the *City of Alton*, until "much to the General's surprise and apparent annoyance she made her appearance in the cabin," according to one account. Decorated with evergreens and flags, the steamers churned into the Cairo harbor, firing their signal guns, and were met by thousands of uniformed men yelling "Frémont! Frémont!" as the general descended the gangplank. The demonstration made by Frémont—"exaggerated as it was by rumor," as Jessie described it—sufficiently intimidated General Pillow, who was camped nearby, and spurred him and his substantial army to retreat.

So many of the troops suffered from fever and dysentery that John and Jessie turned the steamers into floating hospitals—an innovation they would continue throughout the months ahead. He wrote to Montgomery Blair of the dire situation. "I judge from all information, that the enemy is forming himself into bodies along the southern frontier. Appearances indicate that he designs a simultaneous movement from M[issou]ri to Washington, and I think he wants to get the same position in M[issou]ri that he has in Virginia. You may be sure he is vigorously organizing south of Memphis."

Unfortunately, Frémont's entreaties to Washington fell on deaf ears. "I find it impossible now to get any attention to Missouri or western matters from the authorities here," Montgomery Blair responded to him on July 26. "You will have to do the best you can and take all needful responsibility to defend and protect the people over whom you are specially set." Outraged, Jessie fired off a letter to Montgomery Blair. "This is a great scandal—this dept.," she wrote to him. "By dint of begging

and bullying some guns & money are being gotten in, but every useful
thing is being concentrated around Washington . . . War on paper & war
on the ground are two sides of the medal. Undisciplined & untrained
they are, but the volunteers are knights and crusaders of the best kind
and a little loving care such as the first Napoleon gave would make an
invincible army of them." Not only was Jessie boldly chastising a man
and a longtime friend—which perhaps signaled the beginning of ill feeling between her and Montgomery—but also she was also forcefully and
presumptuously lecturing a West Pointer on the fine art, and male domain, of war.

At the end of July, a Russian officer in the 5th Missouri Volunteers
brought Frémont the most distressing intelligence about the Confederates' designs. Charles D'Arnaud came highly recommended as a trustworthy gentleman who had infiltrated the rebel lines, and Frémont
listened with alarm at the plan of campaign he put forth. The Confederate Army was at that very moment planning an advance on Springfield
under Sterling Price and a simultaneous attack on Ironton under Pillow,
whose forces would be joined by troops led by McCulloch, with soldiers
and cavalry totaling nearly forty-six thousand men and with an object of
conquering not only Missouri, but Kansas and southern Illinois as well.
Engaging D'Arnaud as a spy, Frémont sent him immediately into enemy
territory to map strategic points on the Tennessee and Cumberland
rivers and to report back on any forward movement by Pillow. In response to what seemed a formidable array of forces against him, Frémont
made one of his most brilliant tactical decisions: he posted Ulysses S.
Grant, a West Pointer who had begun the Civil War signing in recruits,
first to Ironton, and then to Cairo, hoping that Grant's call for men,
arms, equipment, transportation, and clothing would resound in Washington. "As a regular army officer he [Grant] knew how much better the
morale of properly clothed and equipped men is," Jessie wrote, "than
those who feel that they represent a government too weak to properly
care for them or redeem its promises."

Within a week of arriving in Ironton, Grant, through drill and discipline rather than fortifications, had gained control of an unwieldy crisis.
"Frémont's selection of Grant to command the Union advance is a
benchmark in American history akin to FDR's selection of Eisenhower
to lead the Normandy invasion," according to Grant biographer Jean
Edward Smith. "It was the right choice at the right time." Though he
barely knew Grant, had only met him twice, Frémont admired the fact

that Grant had voluntarily freed his only slave and was drawn to Grant's unprepossessing manner. After a mere twenty-minute interview, over the objections of his staff officers, he passed over Prentiss and Pope, selecting Grant for what he saw as unusual qualities. "I believed him to be a man of great activity and promptness in obeying orders without question or hesitation. For that reason I gave General Grant this important command at this critical period. I did not consider him then a great general, for the qualities that led him to success had not had the opportunity for their development. I selected him for qualities I could not then find combined in any other officer, for General Grant was a man of unassuming character, not given to self-elation, or dogged persistence, and of iron will."

By early August, Frémont saw clearly that no significant reinforcements for Lyon were forthcoming from other departments, and even though men were pouring into St. Louis by the thousands, volunteering to serve with the legendary Frémont, it was useless to send untrained and unarmed men to Lyon. He realized he had no choice but to issue orders to Lyon to retreat, while giving him the option to fight as he saw fit under the circumstances. On August 4 he sent two regiments to meet Lyon—one from Booneville and the other from Leavenworth, Kansas, which he fully expected Lyon to retreat to meet. "If he fights, it will be upon his own responsibility," Frémont remarked to a messenger who conveyed to him Lyon's intention to fight whether or not he received more troops. Indeed, Lyon found his position untenable. If he remained in Springfield he faced certain capture; if he retreated while under pursuit by a powerful army, he risked an overwhelming defeat that would leave southwestern Missouri in rebel hands. "Knowing General Lyon's ability as an officer, his varied familiarity with the conditions in the State and of the rebel forces, General Frémont placed no restrictions upon his movements," Jessie described the unusual latitude he dispensed to Lyon. Frémont had given Lyon the authority to act as he deemed necessary, since he was beyond the reach of railroad and telegraphic communication, as well as any meaningful military assistance—authority that, later critics would charge, resulted in one of the fiercest battles of the war. "Under the critical conditions fully pointed out to him, he could at least have recalled Lyon and assisted his safe withdrawal to his railroad base at Rolla," as Lincoln's secretaries and biographers John G. Nicolay and John Hay later put it. "But he neither recalled him nor substantially reinforced him."

The feisty and obstinate Lyon had grown increasingly critical of the administration, and now, feeling abandoned by the government, took matters into his own hands. "If it is the intention to give up the West, let it be so; it can only be the victim of imbecility or malice," Lyon wrote to Colonel Chester Harding in St. Louis. "[Winfield] Scott will cripple us if he can. Cannot you stir up this matter and secure us relief? . . . The want of supplies has crippled me so that I cannot move, and I do not know when I can. Everything seems to combine against me at this point."

Indeed, Lyon's officers believed Frémont's orders for a retreat—sent on August 6 and received by Lyon on August 9—were not only reasonable and proper, but imperative as well. Lyon called together fifteen officers for a council of war and told them he had no hope of being reinforced and that he was unhampered by instructions. "Our retreat to Rolla was open and perfectly safe," his second in command, General John T. Schofield, later wrote, "even if begun as late as the night of the ninth. A few days or a few weeks at most would have made us amply strong to defeat the enemy and drive him out of Missouri, without serious loss to ourselves." The fifteen officers were unanimous in their support of a retreat, but Lyon, apparently underestimating the massive reinforcements bolstering the rebel forces, perhaps inflating the tactical significance of Springfield, or possibly motivated by personal glory, overruled them all.

In the muggy predawn of August 10, "disregarding the maxims of military textbooks," as Civil War historian James McPherson described the fatal miscalculation, Lyon divided his small army. Under the command of Franz Sigel, twelve hundred of his men marched ten miles south of Springfield to attack the right flank of the Confederate camp, while Lyon simultaneously drove thirty-seven hundred men into the center of the camp, on Wilson's Creek. As the firefight began at sunrise, the Federals had achieved surprise, and victory seemed possible even though they were outnumbered three to one. But McCulloch and Price rallied their troops and engaged in one of the most vicious encounters of the Civil War. The tide turned for the rebels when a Louisiana regiment dressed in militia uniforms resembling those of Lyon's men were mistaken for Union soldiers, and stealthily penetrated the Union lines with a brutal attack.

Lyon was famously gallant, suffering three wounds and having his horse shot out from under him but still refusing to retreat. Flamboyant and pugnacious, the redheaded general mounted another horse and waved his hat in the air, driving his men forward into the center of the Confederate column. As a contingent from the 2nd Kansas joined him at the line, a ball pierced Lyon's heart and he dropped dead instantly. Within minutes, at eleven thirty in the morning, Lyon's surviving officers held an impromptu council and ordered retreat. Demoralized by the defeat and distraught at having lost their beloved general, the exhausted Union soldiers withdrew from the battleground and slowly made their way, unpursued by equally shattered rebel soldiers, to Rolla, one hundred miles north of Springfield. With great drama and pageantry, Lyon's body was mourned from city to city as he was taken to his native New England for burial.

Each side had lost more than thirteen hundred men, and though it was not a decisive victory for the Confederates, public opinion held that Frémont was to blame for the death of the legendarily brave and enormously popular Lyon. The Battle of Wilson's Creek would signal the beginning of the end for Frémont, as he came under widespread criticism in Missouri and beyond. Unknown to his contemporary critics was that Lyon had disregarded Frémont's order to retreat, that Washington had failed to send either money or arms to Missouri, and that the president himself had indicated that Cairo be fortified at all costs—even at the expense of Springfield. Later, the joint congressional Committee on the Conduct of the War investigating the incident would absolve Frémont of any wrongdoing in the matter, reporting that "even if he failed to do all that one under the circumstances might have done, still your committee can discover no cause of censure against him."

In any event, Lyon had refused to retreat from Springfield, which had cost him his life and the lives of more than one quarter of his troops as well as, ultimately, the surrender of much of southern Missouri to Confederate forces. Frémont's friends blamed Lyon for disobedience, while Frémont's detractors charged that his failure to reinforce Lyon showed egregious incompetence. Among Lyon's closest friends was Frank Blair, who declared in Congress that he "never knew a man more devoted to the honor and integrity of the Union—so careful of its interests and so careless of himself" as Nathaniel Lyon. Lyon's death marked the beginning of the Blairs' distancing from the Frémonts, though it was but obfuscation for the real reason for their disaffection. The three men who had once been Frémont's most staunch promoters—Montgomery, Frank, and Francis Preston Blair—now began conspiring for his removal. They turned wholly and ruthlessly against Frémont, slandering him throughout the halls of Washington. The real source of the breach was a deep disagreement over the slavery issue, with Frémont squarely in the radical camp and the Blairs among the most conservative Republicans on the issue, as well as Frémont's refusal to award exorbitant no-questions-asked profiteering contracts to the Blairs' political cronies. Frémont had denied Frank Blair's numerous requests to dispense contracts for horses, beef, mules, and wagons to Blair's associates after one of Blair's friends "supplied such miserable steeds that Frémont was compelled to issue an order that no more Missouri stock should be bought," as one account described the situation—charges that a War Department investigation later confirmed.

Though Blair later pointed to Lyon's defeat as evidence of Frémont's incompetence, in fact it was not until Frémont declined to give Blair a high military appointment and lucrative war contracts that Blair set out with a vengeance to sabotage Frémont.

At the core of their dispute, however, was the Blairs'—and, at the time, Lincoln's—vehement opposition to expanding the war from saving the Union into one of freeing the slaves—an issue so passionately held by Jessie and John as to render the break inevitable.

Frank Blair could barely conceal his jealousy at being eclipsed in Missouri by the famous Pathfinder. The hard-drinking, hot-tempered, and grasping young Republican congressman who once had been Jessie's suitor harbored deep ambitions to become president, and he now began a concerted campaign to destroy his rival. "When the Blairs go in for a fight, they go in for a funeral," was the family credo, and never would it be more accurate than in their battle with the Frémonts. At the end of their feud, the reputations and political futures of both families would be ruined, and a decades-old friendship would be irreparably broken.

With their eye to Missouri as the national political base from which to launch Frank's presidential candidacy, the Blair family was alarmed by Frémont's rampant popularity with the citizenry. Suddenly the man they had recommended to Lincoln with the assumption that he would follow their direction had become a formidable adversary for power and prestige. Although he was courteous to Frank Blair and even acceded to many of the Blairs' demands, Frémont, with Jessie at his side, was exasperatingly independent, even prompting old Francis Preston Blair to audaciously order Frémont to share authority with his son Frank. "I shall expect you to exert your utmost influence to carry my points," the elder Blair wrote Frémont, "and now to begin, I want to have Frank made a militia major-general for the State of Missouri." Frémont refused the elder Blair's request, appointing Frank commander of a brigade instead. The Blairs "bitterly resented my Father's action in this respect," Francis P. Frémont wrote many years later, "but knowing Frank Blair as he did, he could not ask to have Pope or Halleck removed to place a man utterly ignorant of military affairs, in charge of disorganized conditions, unpaid, discontented regiments, and expect organization and action where the other two mentioned officers were not succeeding any too well."

"I am beginning to lose my confidence in Frémont's capacity," Frank wrote his brother Montgomery on August 29, knowing full well that Montgomery would share this sentiment with the president.

Once the character assassination of Frémont was launched, as in the 1856 presidential campaign, there was much at the Western Department headquarters to nourish and sustain the most outlandish rumors. Jessie made no attempt to conceal her active role in men's affairs, openly recruiting and selecting John's elite bodyguard of three hundred cavalry troops. The guard, led by the flashy Zagonyi, accompanied John in his travels around St. Louis in what a critic described as a "showy spectacle of galloping horses and flashing sabers." Reports soon began circulating in Washington that Frémont was vain and arrogant, aristocratic and inaccessible; that his headquarters in the elegant Brant mansion was an inappropriate extravagance; that his personal staff was comprised of a motley and dangerous mixture of European revolutionaries, abolitionists, shady California associates, and foreigners with fantastic titles; that he capriciously issued contracts; and that he surrounded himself with a "knot of flatterers." One far-fetched rumor, later promoted by Lincoln himself, even suggested that Frémont's secret purpose was to set up an independent dictatorship in the West, in imitation of Aaron Burr's plans in Louisiana more than half a century before.

The allegation that carried the most weight was Frémont's seeming lack of judgment in men, though in addition to selecting Grant he had made an equally inspired appointment in the person of a legendary West Pointer, Charles Ferguson Smith. Indeed, it would ultimately be the symbiotic relationship between Grant and Smith that would prove one of the "high points of the Union campaign on the Mississippi," as a twenty-first-century political scientist put it. Still, insulating himself with Jessie and a trio of politically radical advisers, he allowed several

unpopular regular army officers into his inner sanctum as well. Among
the least regarded was Major Justus McKinstry, whom Frémont inherited upon his arrival in St. Louis but to whom he unfortunately granted
great autonomy. Arresting and darkly handsome, McKinstry was disliked
by his peers and hated by the St. Louis citizenry for his tyrannical and ar-
bitrary dictums. He imposed a nine P.M. curfew and capriciously censored the press, especially the Blair mouthpiece, the *St. Louis Republican*,
which brought him the special ire of Frank Blair. Blair became increasingly agitated with McKinstry, who owed his command to Blair but
who then, like Frémont, took umbrage at Blair's transparent requests for
favoritism for his friends.

The behavior that perhaps stirred the most contempt among Frémont's rivals was his isolation. Reminiscent of the presidential campaign, Jessie and a handful of counselors and sentries controlled access to
the general in order for him to devote his full time and attention to the
crisis at hand. Politicians and merchants, all thinking Frémont "should
stop and give them a half hour's chat," were turned away curtly. If indeed Jessie contributed to or encouraged John's seclusion and inacces-
sibility, she was operating with less tact and brilliance than she has been
commonly credited.

Inevitably, Frémont's command brought inspection from Washington.
The Blairs widely expressed their doubts about Frémont's military competence, and sought to engage Lincoln in the controversy. Eventually
Lincoln gave credence to Frémont's critics, who branded the St. Louis
staff an unmanageable group of renegades operating with single-minded
devotion not to the Union but to Frémont himself. Lincoln had appointed Frémont as western commander at the insistence of the Blairs,
who had portrayed the explorer as their "pet and protégé." Their abrupt
and bitter breach would aggravate Lincoln for the next few years, and
though he never fully comprehended all of the underlying reasons for
the schism, he recognized the depth, complexity, and possible ramifications, and tried without success to appease everyone. By the fall of
1861, the stage was set for presidential intervention.

The first emissary from Washington to arrive in St. Louis was Lincoln's secretary John Hay, who spent several days in late August with the
Frémonts and who reported back favorably. Though offended by Jessie's
assertive nature and prominent position, feeling that she talked too much
and too loudly, Hay praised Frémont for his earnestness and industriousness. Hay wrote several articles for New York newspapers applauding

Frémont's efforts, but the criticism continued, and soon Lincoln, at the Blairs' behest, would send more spies to secretly observe Frémont's command of the Western Department.

The Frémonts' enemies were as forceful as ever—powerful slaveholders and their Washington representatives, conservative Northerners, jealous colleagues, competing politicians, and the ever-alienated West Point officers—but John and Jessie operated boldly and autonomously, attracting even more attention to themselves. "General Jessie," as she was snidely called, was the liaison between John and a controversial relief organization called the Western Sanitary Commission, which advocated bringing women nurses onto the battlefield—a highly divisive initiative that Northern women promoted and that men in the army deeply resented.

The Wilson's Creek battle brought hundreds of wounded soldiers to St. Louis, and Jessie was instrumental in organizing hospitals and recruiting nurses. She arranged for her friend Dorothea Dix to visit St. Louis, and accompanied the famous organizer of the army nursing corps and national hospitals to Jefferson Barracks, where they found mangled patients suffering from neglect. Both women were horrified at the conditions. "The men who had offered their lives for their country's cause were too ill with the fever to raise the crude food to their lips," her daughter Lily wrote of Jessie's observations. In one hospital "there were no shades on the windows, and the sun blazed in on the sick and dying men; there were no funds with which to purchase supplies, and my mother took it upon herself to see that the boys in blue had at least the comforts of civilization." Jessie personally went to St. Louis businesses soliciting food and clothing, undaunted by the overwhelmingly hostile reception with which the secessionist merchants greeted her. She was often grudgingly presented with donations because she was the daughter of Thomas Hart Benton—not because she was the wife of the despised Yankee general occupying their city. Jessie took it upon herself to organize knitting circles among St. Louis women to provide desperately needed socks for the soldiers. While most housewives were unwilling to participate, the city's large patriotic female German populace led the undertaking. The German Americans were the Frémonts' most loyal political base, then and later, and Jessie cultivated them with particular finesse.

Writing an article for the *St. Louis Democrat* on August 27, Jessie called

Dix "our American Florence Nightingale," referring to the aristocratic Englishwoman who had brought female nurses to the battlefields of the Crimean War in 1855. Nursing had always been the domain of men and lower-class women, but Nightingale's efforts in British hospitals reduced the death rate from 45 to 2 percent. Jessie had known Dix since 1848, when Thomas Hart Benton first began supporting her campaign for federal appropriations to care for the indigent insane.

An intimidating sixty-year-old spinster, Dix remained wary of placing attractive young women in contact with bedridden soldiers and initially accepted only plain-looking women who were more than thirty years old. She insisted that they dress in drab black or brown dresses without hoop skirts and wear no jewelry or bows, nor have curls in their hair. Jessie confronted Dix one day when the celebrated reformer had rejected a dozen attractive young girls who Jessie thought were all suitable candidates. "Would you have *no* moral standards, Mrs. Frémont?" Dix asked. "Standards, yes," Jessie replied, "but surely in this crisis strong hands and a desire to serve make up for a lack of experience. And as to morals, you and I have both observed that the hand of female virtue often has chilly fingertips." Eventually, as the war dragged on and the medical emergency grew, Dix would relax her standards.

Jessie knew that her involvement with Dix was but one more contentious stance to which Jessie's enemies could point, and she was keenly sensitive to the public resistance to the training of female nurses. She worked closely with William Greenleaf Eliot, a Unitarian minister, founder of Washington University, and close personal friend of Thomas Starr King, on her article for the St. Louis newspaper. A grandfather of T. S. Eliot, he was an outspoken abolitionist and revered community leader, and he collaborated adroitly with Jessie in shaping public opinion.

Jessie embodied the dangerous stereotype of the Northern woman who was using the war as an opportunity to break the rules of decorum, who seized the venue to escape the nineteenth-century chains of female oppression, who leaped at the chance to join their husbands on grisly battlefields far from home. "She had a man's power, a man's education, and she did a man's work in the world," her friend the writer Rebecca Harding Davis described Jessie during this period, "but her wonderful charm was purely feminine."

Though Jessie was emboldened by circumstances, her overt wielding of power would backfire. The nation, as it turned out, was not yet ready for emancipation—of slaves *or* of women—and Jessie and John were destined to be caught in a tragic purgatory between the past and the future.

Unionist Missouri was in anarchy in the weeks after Wilson's Creek as marauding bands of guerrillas burned bridges, cut telegraph lines, and tore up railroad tracks. Frémont's ragtag troops were spread throughout the West—in Missouri, Kansas, Kentucky, and Illinois—and while he intended to move toward Cairo, he was determined not to proceed until he was properly equipped and prepared. Taking a lesson from the disaster of Bull Run, he plotted meticulously while ignoring criticism of delayed action.

In addition to the civilian disaster that was driving thousands of Union loyalists to seek protection in neighboring states, the military situation was reaching an emergency. The crisis met its climax when some sixty-five thousand armed citizens were actively fighting for the South in Missouri. More than twenty thousand were soldiers from Arkansas and Tennessee who had poured across the borders, but the vast majority was comprised of Missourians who had joined the rebel cause. Roaming the countryside, stealing horses and grain, recruiting soldiers, and terrorizing the public, the insurgents posed a real threat to overtake Missouri. "The farmers would, when notified, join the camps of the rebel commanders in great numbers, suddenly augmenting their forces," Jessie wrote, "and then, if the projected raid or attack was deferred, would return again to their homes, reducing the force correspondingly. In this manner, however, it was impossible to foresee which point would be threatened next, and failing sufficient troops to control the State through force of arms, it became necessary to devise some means to prevent this guerrilla warfare. The credit of the Government was about used up, and had so lost prestige through non-payment of its debts to the soldiers, and those who furnished them the supplies, that it was regarded with contempt by the Secessionists, and many Unionists came to doubt its power to compel."

It was amid these turbulent conditions that John C. Frémont undertook the most courageous and momentous act of his public life. After consulting only Jessie and a couple of trusted advisers, John made the most fateful decision of his military career: he would declare martial law and issue an emancipation proclamation to free the slaves belonging to all slaveholders who were aiding the rebel cause.

On August 28, John called Jessie into a private meeting with him and two of his most trusted advisers—John A. Gurley and Owen Lovejoy. Gurley and Lovejoy were abolitionist congressmen from Ohio and Illinois, respectively, both of whom Frémont held in great esteem. Apparently for the first time, Frémont discussed a proposed proclamation that would impose martial law, placing the state of Missouri under his military authority and stripping the power of the conservative states' rights, proslavery provisional governor—a close ally of Frank Blair named Hamilton R. Gamble. "The South has seceded. The secessionist has forfeited his right to protection for his home or property," the radicals put forth their argument to Frémont. "The local secessionists are responsible for the wiping out of peaceful Union homes and the killing of peaceable Union citizens in guerrilla outbreaks. Only the stern measure, confiscation of the property of men in arms against the Union, will serve in this crisis."

Jessie wholeheartedly concurred with their argument. Innocent citizens were being killed and their homes destroyed. As a war measure, the federal government was within its power to seize property belonging to the men fighting against it, John reasoned, and first and foremost, that property included slaves. John conferred with the three about the proclamation he had in mind. Under martial law, he told them, armed secessionists would be arrested, their property confiscated and put to public use, and their slaves set free. John particularly wanted to make sure that his wife fully understood his reasoning and the potentially dangerous consequences—politically, militarily, and personally. When their conference concluded some hours later, "the conviction of us all [was] that no other course was possible in Missouri under existing conditions," Jessie later said.

At dawn two days later, John asked Jessie to meet him at his desk. There she also found Edward M. Davis, the famous Quaker abolitionist and son-in-law of Lucretia Mott, whom Frémont had summoned from Philadelphia. "I want you two but no others," the general said to them.

He then read aloud the first emancipation proclamation ever ordered in the history of the United States. "Circumstances, in my judgment, of sufficient urgency, render it necessary that the commanding general of this department should assume the administrative powers of the State," it began. "Its disorganized condition, the helplessness of the civil authority, the total insecurity of life, and the devastation of property by bands of murderers and marauders, who infest nearly every county of the State, and avail themselves of the public misfortunes and the vicinity of a hostile force to gratify private and neighborhood vengeance, and who find an enemy wherever they find plunder, finally demand the severest measures to repress the daily-increasing crimes and outrages which are driving off the inhabitants and ruining the State."

"Mr. Seward will never allow this," Davis warned Frémont of the likely response by the secretary of state, a response that reflected the incorrect attitude of many Republicans that Seward, not Lincoln, was the driving force in the administration. "He intends to wear down the South by steady pressure, not by blows, and then make himself the arbitrator."

"It is for the North to say what it will or will not allow, and whether it will arbitrate, or whether it will fight," Frémont replied. "The time has come for decisive action; this is a war measure, and as such I make it. I have been given full power to crush rebellion in this Department, and I will bring the penalties of rebellion home to every man found striving against the Union."

The proclamation was immediately printed at a small press housed in the adjutant general's office and was posted throughout the city. Frémont provided the press with copies of the order, and notified the president by messenger—a tactical political error by Frémont, as Lincoln would apparently first learn of it by reading it in the newspaper along with the rest of the nation. Declaring martial law, calling for the immediate confiscation of the property of Confederate sympathizers in Missouri, including freeing all of their slaves, and ordering the execution of all armed guerrillas captured behind Union lines and convicted by court-martial, Frémont's order would fall "upon the country like a thunderbolt."

At least for the moment, Frémont had single-handedly changed the issue before the country from union to emancipation, from a war to preserve the Union to a war to liberate the slaves. Overnight, the famed explorer of the West became the most popular man in the North. While greeted with untamed enthusiasm from antislavery advocates and even moderates in the North—Harriet Beecher Stowe voicing a common reaction that "the hour has come, and the man"—less radical Republicans and Democrats alike thought Frémont had destroyed all chances of restoring the Union.

A preempted Lincoln was livid, fearing that Frémont's action would jeopardize the loyalty of Kentucky and Missouri—two border states that Lincoln had been "so tactfully nursing." He supported gradual emancipation with voluntary colonization, stating in his inaugural ad-

dress with what historian Richard Hofstadter called a "pathetic vehemence" that "slavery would not be attacked in the states." Lincoln felt
that Frémont's firm convictions had undermined his policy and challenged his authority; above all, Lincoln believed that *any* such procla-
mations should be issued by the president and not by a general in the
field.

Frémont's action stunned Lincoln, and placed the president in a thorny
position between radical and conservative Northerners, and with the
border states. So far the war had been an effort to preserve the Union,
and neither the president nor anyone in his administration had indicated
any other purpose. While Frémont had acted solely in his military capacity to stem the guerrilla violence in northern Missouri, the proclamation had national implications far beyond the general's personal
calculations. He was unaware of the fierceness with which the members
of Lincoln's cabinet and other Northern leaders were debating the issue
of liberating the slaves.

Although the abolitionists had long been advocating emancipation, by
the fall of 1861 more Northerners were beginning to believe that man-
umission to the slaves was not only practical but also inevitable. "[W]hy
take a costly and weary way to put it [the rebellion] down when a cheap
short one is at hand?" Lovejoy said, articulating a sentiment that was
gaining ground in the North. "Why choose crushing burdens of debt
and immense human slaughter when both can be avoided? The liberation of the slaves has obviously become one of the necessities and therefore one of the rights of the country. Let the President, in his capacity as
commander of the army, proclaim such liberation and the war would
end in thirty days."

Many were beginning to see emancipation as what one historian
called the "master-key of victory," arguing that such action would im-
pel slaveholders to abandon their militias and return home to guard their
property.

By nearly all historical analyses, Frémont's action was spurred by re-
gional military concerns rather than national political calculations. "The
object of this declaration is to place in the hands of the military authorities the power to give instantaneous effect to existing laws, and to supply such deficiencies as the conditions of war demand," he wrote. "But
this is not intended to suspend ordinary tribunals of the country, where
the law will be administered by the civil officers in the usual manner, and

with their customary authority, while the same can be peaceably exercised."

Later history would pronounce Frémont's edict the first and most courageous Union challenge to slavery. But at the moment, Lincoln and his allies regarded it as impetuous, premature, and above all, presumptuous. Calculating as always on the slave issue, Lincoln was focused on saving the Union above all else, an impractical situation that historian T. Harry Williams described as conducting "the war for the preservation of the status quo which had produced the war." Frémont's audacious and decisive move underscored the president's own expedient conservative hesitancy—never an exposure Lincoln, a consummate politician, took lightly. The president envisioned a slow and compensated emancipation, ideally followed by the deportation and colonization of the freed Negroes, and feared that if Frémont's edict became public it might garner unbridled support from both radicals and moderates within his own party. Forced by events and the course of the war into a position he did not want to occupy, Lincoln was seen by many observers to be moving toward full emancipation only after his other policies had been bungled.

The Republican press almost unanimously commended Frémont, and his bold proclamation was greeted enthusiastically in Chicago, Boston, New York, and Washington. Once again, the Pathfinder was celebrated throughout the North, his name synonymous with freedom, and whether intended or not, he was maneuvering Lincoln toward emancipation. Rallies and torchlight parades erupted. One congressman wrote that "it stirred and united the people of the loyal States during the ten days of life allotted it by the Government far more than any other event of the war." Most in Lincoln's own party supported Frémont, and even his secretary of war, Simon Cameron, who tended to move with the political winds, telegraphed congratulations to Frémont, only to later claim to be surprised by Lincoln's animosity toward the general. Charles Sumner, now chairman of the Senate Foreign Relations Committee, heartily endorsed the action, having been vocally impatient with Lincoln's foot dragging.

Lincoln's dilemma was complicated. Any endorsement of Frémont's proclamation would jeopardize the support of loyal border state slaveholders and their Northern allies. The president feared that recasting the war into one for the extinction of slavery would send Kentucky and Maryland into the Confederacy. Perhaps even more unpalatable to the president was his own appearance of weakness if he allowed a general in the field to dictate federal policy of such national magnitude. Ever the pragmatist and conciliator, he sought a solution that saved face while serving his purpose. "The President could permit no subordinate to assume a responsibility which belonged only to himself," William Seward later wrote.

Still, as much as Lincoln needed to save the border states, he also depended on the loyalty of the radical Republicans, who overwhelmingly supported Frémont, and he could not be seen as riding roughshod over a wildly popular rival. Hoping to mitigate the controversy before it became public, Lincoln decided to ask Frémont to modify the martial law proclamation and to remove the slave property provision on his own accord. In a private letter to Frémont penned on September 2, he expressed his "anxiety" on two points:

First: Should you shoot a man, according to the proclamation, the Confederates would very certainly shoot our best men in their hands in retaliation; and so, man for man, indefinitely. It is, therefore, my order that you allow no man to be shot under the proclamation without first having my approbation or consent.

Second. I think there is great danger that the closing paragraph, in relation to the confiscation of property and the liberating slaves of traitorous owners, will alarm our Southern Union friends and turn them against us; perhaps ruin our rather fair prospect for Kentucky. Allow me, therefore, to ask that you will, as of your own motion, modify that paragraph so as to conform to the first and fourth sections of the act of Congress [relating to the confiscation of property].

This letter is written in a spirit of caution, and not of censure. I send it by special messenger, in order that it may certainly and speedily reach you.

Despite the haste with which Lincoln claimed to have sent the letter, Frémont did not receive his request to rescind the proclamation until six days later, on September 8, even though it was a comfortable fifty-hour journey between Washington and St. Louis. Frémont had "but a few hours in which to make the decision of a lifetime," as Jessie later described the moment, "and to do what General Frémont felt would lose him the support of the administration during the greatest war that would come to our country."

Apparently without consulting Jessie, John's response was firm, definitive, and explanatory. He wrote the president,

> Trusting to have your confidence, I have been leaving it to events
> themselves to show you whether or not I was shaping affairs here
> according to your ideas. The shortest communication between
> Washington and Saint Louis generally involves two-days, and the
> employment of two days in time of war goes largely towards success
> or disaster. I therefore went along according to my own judgment,
> leaving the result of my movements to justify me with you.
>
> And so in regard to my proclamation of the 30th. Between the
> rebel armies, the Provisional Government, and home traitors, I felt
> the position bad, and saw danger. In the night I decided upon the
> Proclamation and the form of it. I wrote it the next morning and
> printed it the same day. I did it without consultation or advice with
> any one, acting solely with my best judgment to serve the country
> and yourself, and perfectly willing to receive the amount of censure
> which should be thought due if I had made a false movement. This
> is as much a movement in the war as a battle, and in going into those
> I shall have to act according to my judgment of the ground before
> me, as I did on this occasion. If upon reflection your better judgment
> still decides that I am wrong in the article respecting the liberation of
> slaves, I have to ask that you will openly direct me to make the cor-
> rection. The implied censure will be received as a soldier always
> should the reprimand of his chief. If I were to retract of my own ac-
> cord it would imply that I myself thought it wrong, and that I had
> acted without the reflection which the gravity of the point de-
> manded. But I did not. I acted with full deliberation, and upon the
> certain conviction that it was a measure right and necessary, and I
> think so still.

Frémont's audacious refusal to rescind the proclamation has been
widely seen by historians to have been a tactless error with fatal consequences. After Jessie copied his words and presented the sealed envelope
to the messenger for its delivery to the president, the couple retreated to
discuss their situation. Jessie, even more than John, recognized the political jeopardy of their predicament, and felt the urgency of presenting
their case directly to the president without the buffer of biased interme-
diaries. Naïvely believing that she could convince Lincoln of the mili-

tary merit of the proclamation, idealistically supposing that the president would accept a woman if not as a peer then as a valid spokesperson—for her husband had always done so, and her father had deeply valued her judgment on many substantive matters until their split over the formation of the Republican Party—Jessie persuaded John that she should carry their message to the White House. She truly believed that she, the daughter of Thomas Hart Benton, could best articulate the strategic value of emancipation in deterring England, France, and Spain, who were on the verge of recognizing the South and were providing it with weapons, and she operated under the misguided assumption that Lincoln would value her insights. Jessie, who had been in "constant intimate friendship with . . . previous Presidents," fully expected Lincoln to accept her as qualified to speak on her husband's behalf.

They drafted a letter to Lincoln outlining Frémont's military plans—reinforcing Paducah, seizing the mouths of the Tennessee and Cumberland rivers, ordering Grant to occupy Cairo, and with a concluding advance toward Memphis on the Mississippi.

That evening Jessie and her English maid boarded the hot, overcrowded train bound for Washington. Jessie's meeting with Abraham Lincoln would be without precedent in nineteenth-century American history—the "only previous confrontation initiated by a woman against a president was Jessie's meeting with James K. Polk in 1847 over John's pending court-martial."

"When it is remembered . . . that Jessie Benton had inherited a son's full portion of her distinguished father's aggressive personality, we tremble for poor Mr. Lincoln," wrote one historian with the predictable chauvinism of the era.

It was September 10, 1861. She was exhausted from the two-day train ride from St. Louis to Washington, sitting upright the entire way in a hot and crowded car and subsisting on tea and biscuits. Her immaculate, stylishly arranged hair and white lawn gown were smudged from the soot of the locomotive.

Washington in early fall was stifling, and the 150,000 Union troops patrolling the streets and camped on the perimeter underscored that it was a city under siege. "The streets swarmed with soldiers, whores, runaway slaves, lobbyists, and contractors eager to profit from the war," as one account depicted the scene. Jessie proceeded directly to the Willard Hotel, where she met Judge Edward Coles, a close friend and ardent abolitionist, whom she had telegraphed in New York and asked that he accompany her to witness her meeting with Lincoln. She immediately sent a note to the president stating that she carried a letter from John and asking when she might be able to present it. She then intended to take a bath and go to bed, as she was disheveled and fatigued and in desperate need of rest. But before she could freshen up or retire, a messenger returned with a card on which was written: "A. Lincoln. Now."

Judge Coles implored her to wait until morning, insisting that she was too tired for such an important meeting. He looked at his watch and told her it was nine P.M. Her baggage had not yet been delivered, and she had no clean clothing in which to dress. Still, she felt she could not wait. The message she carried to the White House was too vital to the country— and to John—and the president had summoned her. She and Coles walked across Fourteenth Street to the White House. "All my life I had been at home in the President's House—as well received there as in the family circle, and with the old confidence of the past I went forward now."

It was near ten P.M. when she was ushered into the Red Parlor. She stood for what seemed an interminable period of time, given her fatigue from the journey. She surveyed the room, recently redecorated by the president's wife, Mary Todd Lincoln, in crimson and gold, but still familiar to her. She was as comfortable in this space as if it were her own home, having been welcomed there by nine previous presidents— beginning decades earlier with Andrew Jackson, who had tangled her child's locks with his fingers while discussing politics with her father. She had been a spy and a translator for two of Jackson's successors. But when the lanky, simple-mannered president entered, he neither spoke nor met her eyes, and she knew in that instant he was not the man she had hoped he would be. He nodded slightly in her direction but failed to offer her a seat in an insult they both understood. "I introduced Judge Coles as a member of the New York bar," and when the president still said nothing she handed him the sealed letter that had been penned by her husband, and told him that "General Frémont felt the subject to be of so much importance that he . . . sent me to answer any points on which the President might want more information." At this, Lincoln smirked. He then read the letter by the light of a candelabrum, as Coles paced at the doorway "like a sentinel." Another door to the room was ajar and Jessie detected someone there, observing the meeting.

Jessie, trembling from weakness, finally took a seat. After a theatrically long silence in which Lincoln read Frémont's explanation of why he thought his proclamation was a military necessity and outlining the Civil War's Western Theater, the president drew up a chair next to her. "I have written to the General and he knows what I want done," he told her. With that, Jessie launched into an eloquent amplification on the dispatch from the front lines, telling him "the General feels he is at the great disadvantage of being perhaps opposed by people in whom you have every confidence."

"Who do you mean?" he asked. "Persons of differing views?"

Now finding her voice, eager to dispel any nervousness, and to take full advantage of his attention, she set forth their case, speaking quickly and forthrightly.

"The General's conviction is that it will be a long and dreadful work to conquer by arms alone, that there must be other consideration to get us the support of foreign countries," she told him. She continued that Frémont "knew the English feeling for gradual emancipation and the strong wish to meet it on the part of important men in the South," and that England, France, and Spain were "anxious for a pretext" to enter the fray—"England on account of her cotton interests, and France because the Emperor dislikes us—"

The president frowned and cut her short. "You are quite a female politician," he said with a sneer.

While both recognized it as a rebuke, they also knew that she was indeed just that—a female politician—and he was demeaning her. This president, like most men of his time, was offended at a woman overtly acting as emissary and strategist, especially a woman so confidently displaying her own mind. This woman was as impressive and formidable a politician as any of the president's male colleagues or rivals, and he could not conceal his distaste for her. She was, as one historian put it, "simply a woman to be gotten rid of as quickly as possible"—a position in which Jessie had rarely found herself before. She was, after all, a woman accustomed to having her opinions and recommendations solicited and honored by the men in her life—from her husband and father and their colleagues, to the many admirers who sought her advice. Lincoln's gratuitous dismissal came as a rude awakening, even for her time and place. While the president was used to women expressing their interest in politics, he had no patience for overreaching wives or generals.

Lincoln then began speaking rapidly, launching into a tirade about how

Frémont should have consulted Frank Blair before taking any action. "Frank never would have let him do it. The General should never have dragged the Negro into the war," he said. "It is a war for a great national object and the Negro has nothing to do with it."

"Then there is no use to say more," Jessie answered, "except that we were not aware that Frank Blair represented you—he did not do so openly." It was the first evidence Jessie had that Blair had been actively undermining John, and the full impact of such a betrayal was staggering.

With that, she and Coles rose to leave. As they walked slowly through the darkness on the White House grounds, the reality of the situation set in. "Mrs. Frémont, the General has no further part in this war," Coles calmly expressed his assessment. "He will be deprived of all his part in the war; it is not the President alone, but there is a faction which plans the affairs of the North and they will triumph, and they are against the General . . . It will be thirty years before he is known and has justice. They will give reasons for keeping him down. But they hold the power and will keep him down."

As Congressman John Shanks of Indiana later described the situation, "the proclamation was the opening door at which [Frémont's] enemies entered and made common cause against him. The politician who fears his popularity; the friend to slavery; . . . the military bigot who sees West Point First, and after it, the country; and lastly, speculators at the public Treasury, who themselves guilty and suspected, point the finger of distrust at others—these are the classes in unholy combination against an honest and pure man, *whom they cannot control*, but hope to destroy."

By all accounts, Jessie's meeting with Lincoln was a historic disaster, though the record would become murky. Lincoln and some of his cronies would claim that she brandished her handkerchief and whipped it across his face, that she called him "Abe"—particularly far-fetched from a woman who had always referred to her own husband as Mr. Frémont—and even that she absurdly intimated that John would challenge him to a duel, or worse, become dictator of Missouri.

"Why, not an hour ago, a woman, a lady of high blood, came here," Lincoln is said to have told an Iowa congressman that evening, "opening her case with mild expostulation, but left in anger, flaunting her handkerchief before my face, and saying, 'Sir, the general will try titles with you. He is a man and I am his wife.' I will tell you before your guess. It was Jessie, the daughter of 'Old Bullion,' and how her eye flashed! Young man, forget your annoyances. They are as flea-bites to mine."

The story of what became known as "the slap" spread immediately, embellished by Lincoln's cronies and implied by Lincoln, who called her a beautiful "virago," while Jessie and her supporters denied and dismissed it as a vicious rumor meant to marginalize her. Lincoln and his witnesses reported her behavior as bullying. "That one of the so-called gentler sex should be sent on such a mission need not surprise us after we learn that during her stay at department headquarters she was described as the real chief of staff," wrote one of Lincoln's biographers. She and her witnesses mocked the president's unease. "Strange, isn't it," she would later remark, "that when a man expresses a conviction fearlessly, he is reported as having made a trenchant and forceful statement, but when a woman speaks thus earnestly, she is reported as a lady who has lost her temper."

Whether or not the slap was apocryphal, it took on legendary proportions for scholars, historians, and political observers for the next century and a half. In any case, the event became symbolic of a systematic, prolonged, and orchestrated distortion of her character. The more Jessie could be blamed for her husband's actions, the more Frémont's power could be diminished and his substantive accomplishments attributed to the personal ambitions of an overbearing wife.

"She sought an audience with me at midnight," Lincoln told John Hay two years later, exaggerating the hour and suggesting she had barged in rather than having been summoned by him, and "taxed me so violently with so many things that I had to exercise all the awkward tact I have to avoid quarreling with her . . . She more than once intimated that if General Frémont should decide to try conclusions with me, he could set up for himself."

The president had told Jessie that he would deliver to her the following day a response to be taken to Frémont, but in the end he even failed to validate her as a legitimate messenger. Early the next morning a furious Francis Preston Blair visited her at the hotel. Though he had been like a father to her, a loving and avuncular part of her life since early childhood, she had not seen him since leaving for California in 1858. But he exchanged no initial pleasantries, angrily chastising her the moment he entered her suite. "Well," the elder Blair huffed, "who would have expected you to do such a thing as this, to come here and find fault with the President!" Jessie laughed at first, thinking he must have been joking.

But his rage was unmistakable. "Look what Frémont has done: made the President his enemy!"

For nearly three hours the old friends argued, Blair patronizingly belittling her, reminding her of all the Blair family had done for John, implying that her father had been right to abandon his ingrate son-in-law. Blair blamed Jessie for going outside her sphere and getting mixed up in a man's world. "If you had stayed here in Washington and done what I wanted you to do—it is not fit for a woman to go with an army." For Jessie it was a painful reminder of how expendable a woman became in favor of a man's career—in this case, the presidential aspirations of Blair's son Frank.

Blair's anger had gotten the better of him, and he inadvertently said more to Jessie than he had planned, revealing the Blair family machinations that had resulted in John's sudden opprobrium with the Lincoln administration. He admitted that Frank had written Montgomery a letter that called John's competence into question—a letter that Montgomery had shown to the president. In response, Lincoln had dispatched Montgomery to St. Louis to investigate John. Now, finally and irreparably, Jessie fully understood the forces at play against them, and saw that her family's oldest and dearest friends had betrayed her and her husband. It was like being abandoned by her father all over again.

Challenging Frank to a duel on John's behalf, she heatedly dismissed the duplicitous and self-serving old patriarch, eager to end that "painful day of broken friendship."

The following day, on September 12, she wrote a note to Lincoln, telling him that the elder Blair had told her of Frank's derogatory letter and requesting a copy of the letter. Addressing her as "Mrs. Genl. Frémont," Lincoln refused her request. "I do not feel authorized to furnish you with copies of letters in my possession without the consent of the writers."

She knew she had to notify John immediately of the results of the meeting, to warn him that the Blairs had been conspiring against him with Lincoln and that Montgomery was at that very moment on his way to St. Louis with a mission to further undermine him. Distrusting the telegraph, she wrote John a letter in the family cipher they had used during the Bear Flag Revolt. "Things evidently prejudged. Collateral issues and compromises will be attempted but the true contest is on the proclamation . . . Listen but remember our Salem witch . . . Some true active friends here and the heart of the country with you everywhere." She folded it, sealed it, and dispatched her English maid to carry it to St. Louis.

"A formal quarrel fills me with a terror I can't articulate," Lizzie Blair wrote to her father upon learning of the incidents. Indeed, Jessie Benton Frémont would never forgive the Blairs for their subterfuge, and the "quarrel" would be to their deaths.

Disheartened and downcast, Jessie returned to St. Louis. "The result of what I have felt & seen is to make me more than willing that my children should die young," a profoundly saddened Jessie would write to her friend Frederick Billings in New York. "Such simple true patriotism as we both brought to the work—honestly we thought it was the country to be served."

Upon her arrival in St. Louis she found Montgomery Blair closeted with John, the postmaster general working to modify John's emancipation proclamation. Jessie ignored him—"I did not speak to him then, or ever again." Unbeknownst to Jessie and John, Blair carried with him a letter to General David Hunter, whom Lincoln was transferring to St. Louis to assist, and possibly replace, Frémont.

"General Frémont needs assistance which it is difficult to give him," the president's letter stated. "He is losing the confidence of men near him, whose support any man in his position must have to be successful. His cardinal mistake is that he isolates himself, and allows nobody to see him; and by which he does not know what is going on in the very matter he is dealing with."

The day Montgomery left for Washington, John had Frank arrested for "insidious and dishonorable efforts to bring my authority into contempt with the government." The Blairs saw the hand of General Jessie behind the embarrassing incident. "Frémont himself is too brave a man I believe to act in this way," Montgomery wrote to a friend. "Jessie threatened the old man [Blair Sr.] that Frémont should hold Frank personally responsible expecting that she could make the old father quail at the thought of losing the son of whom [he] is most proud in a duel with a skilled duelist . . . So we are to have a parcel of ridiculous lies trumped up to help out this woman's thirst for revenge. She is perfectly unscrupulous you know."

The Blairs accused Frémont of smoking opium and portrayed him as a bungling incompetent who was attempting to create a dictatorship for himself in Missouri. The Frémonts claimed Frank Blair was a drunkard and a conniving manipulator. By early fall 1861, the national press was teeming with the Blair-Frémont feud, and the North was in a quandary about who was to blame, with both men ultimately tainted by the unseemly scandal. In any case, Lincoln was losing patience with all of them. Montgomery telegraphed a request to John asking that Frank be released in deference to their, and the country's, mutual interests, and while John agreed, Frank stubbornly refused to leave his cell, demanding a trial. Then, as was inevitable, the war intervened.

Under orders from Frémont, General Grant seized Paducah, Kentucky, without firing a shot, in a move that would solidify Grant's forthcoming Civil War reputation. But even amid the applause for that grand success, a disaster was unfolding at Lexington, Missouri, where General Price's Confederate soldiers surrounded troops under Colonel James Mulligan's command. Reminiscent of the Wilson's Creek battle, the Union soldiers were desperately outnumbered, and Frémont had fewer than seven thousand untrained soldiers with whom to reinforce Mulligan, and even those had been requested by Simon Cameron and Winfield Scott, to be sent east to protect Washington from an expected assault. Asked by a colleague if he would consider refusing to send the troops to Washington, Frémont responded matter-of-factly. "No, that would be insubordination, with which I have already been unjustly charged. The capital must be in danger, and must be saved, even if Missouri fall and I sacrifice myself."

Though Frémont requested reinforcements for Mulligan from generals in neighboring states, none were provided, and on September 21, General Price captured thirty-five hundred Union soldiers and more than $100,000 worth of supplies. Frank Blair, whom John had released, rearrested, and released again, predictably blamed Frémont, and five days after Mulligan's defeat filed formal charges against his nemesis. Blair charged Frémont with violating presidential orders in his emancipation proclamation, with failing to reinforce Lyon and Mulligan, and half a dozen other allegations of misconduct and disobedience. "Every one who knew the situation in Missouri was aware that it grossly misrepresented Frémont's conduct there," as one historian put it, but the charges were laid before Lincoln, and the president was forced to take a stand. With Montgomery Blair in his cabinet and the Blair family wielding formidable power with the wavering border states, Lincoln's decision to remove Frémont was a foregone conclusion. Even so, with more patience and forbearance than might have been expected, Lincoln decided to send Cameron to make one final inquiry into the situation, and provided Cameron with the authority to displace or retain Frémont as Cameron judged expedient. Cameron had apparently intended to remove Frémont, but after interviewing the general and seeing his troops in desperate need of supplies, Cameron was sympathetic to Frémont's plight. He showed Frémont the order for his removal. "He is very much mortified, pained, and, I thought, humiliated," Cameron wrote to Lincoln on October 14. "He made an earnest appeal to me, saying that he had come to Missouri, at the request of the government, to assume a very responsible command, and that when he reached this state he found himself without troops and without any preparations for an army." Cameron felt that Frémont had comported himself to the best of his ability and had exhibited great energy and honorable intentions and that he should be given a chance to pursue the enemy that now seemed within reach. "In reply to this appeal, I told him that I would withhold the order until my return to Washington, giving him the interim to prove the reality of his hopes . . . giving him to understand that, should he fail, he must give place to some other officer. He assured me that, should he fail, he would resign at once."

Rightly suspecting that his days as a general were numbered, Frémont determined to personally take command in the field. Organizing all of his forty thousand troops into five new divisions, he moved his forces into southwestern Missouri toward the Ozarks. "My plan is New Orleans straight," he wrote Jessie after reaching Camp Lily at Jefferson City. "I think it can be done gloriously." With eighty-six pieces of artillery, three million rations, and thousands of supply wagons, Frémont's march was what one historian described as the "first deliberate Union offensive in the West."

At the end of September, Jessie and Lily, along with many other officers' wives and families, traveled on a heavily guarded army train to Camp Lily for a final good-bye to the troops before they headed inland. Though he dreaded receiving mail, certain that it would carry disappointing news, he was overcome with emotion upon opening an envelope from the abolitionist poet John Greenleaf Whittier. Standing before the campfire, Jessie read it aloud:

> Thy error, Frémont, simply was to act
> A brave man's part, without the statesman's tact,
> And, taking counsel but of common sense,

To strike at cause as well as consequence . . .
Still take thou courage! God has spoken through thee,
Irrevocable, the mighty words Be Free!

It was as if Frémont were suddenly reminded of all that had brought him to this place, as if he saw clearly for the first time that all of the pain, anguish, and strife that he and Jessie had endured had indeed been for a larger purpose. "I *knew* I was right," he said to Jessie, and then told her he was ready to die for their cause.

Desperately short of supplies, relying on bone-thin horses and rotted wagons, low on rations, and dressed in tatters, Frémont's army was energized by the emancipation proclamation and excited to be pushing Price's retreating column into the hinterland. "The army is in the best kind of spirits," he wrote Jessie from his camp near Tipton, "and before we get through I will show you a little California practice, that is, if we are not interrupted."

On October 25, Hungarian major Charles Zagonyi and his 150 "Frémont Bodyguard"—handpicked by Jessie—led a stunning attack against Price's men at Springfield. Shouting "Frémont and the Union!" the elite cavalry wrested control from two thousand Confederate soldiers. At the same time, Frémont's larger force pursued Price's main column. A week later, on November 2, Frémont massed all of his troops near Springfield with the anticipation of a battle the following day.

Spirits were high, his men eager to see battle, and Frémont was roundly serenaded by a force who felt their first major victory was at hand. Then, near midnight on November 2, a messenger from President Lincoln entered Frémont's tent. "I can never forget the appearance of the man as he sat there, with his piercing eye and his hair parted in the middle," the messenger later wrote. "I ripped from my coat lining the document, which had been sewn in there, and handed the same to him, which he nervously took and opened. He glanced at the superscription, and then at the signature at the bottom, not looking at the contents. A frown came over his brow, and he slammed the paper down on the table, and he said, 'Sir, how did you get admission into my lines?'" Later critics would point to this remark as evidence that Frémont intended to defy Lincoln's order at worst, or, at best, to thwart the messenger until the impending battle was over. Given Cameron's reprieve, it seems more likely that Frémont was rightly operating under the assumption that he had been given one more opportunity to prove himself, which superceded any order making its way with a courier from Washington.

In fact, Lincoln had specifically ordered that the messenger withhold delivery of Frémont's dismissal if the general was poised for battle—instructions that the messenger baldly violated. "On receipt of this . . . you will take safe, certain, and suitable measures to have the inclosure addressed to Major-General Frémont delivered to him with all reasonable dispatch," the president wrote to Brigadier General Samuel Ryan Curtis on October 24, 1861, "subject to these conditions only, that if, when General Frémont shall be reached by the messenger—yourself or any one sent by you—he shall then have, in personal command, fought and won a battle, or shall then be actually in a battle, or shall then be in the immediate presence of the enemy in expectation of a battle, it is not to be delivered, but held for further orders."

Word of Frémont's dismissal spread through the camps like wildfire, igniting what was called "one of the strangest scenes of the war." Whole companies threw down their arms in disgust, vowing to fight only for Frémont. Dozens of officers tendered their resignations. Impromptu meetings were called, and the German soldiers made a pact to resist Frémont's announced replacement—General David Hunter, who would issue his own emancipation proclamation the next year, only to have Lincoln revoke it. "It would be impossible to exaggerate the gloom which pervaded our camps," wrote a *New York Herald* correspondent, "and nothing but General Frémont's urgent endeavors prevented it from ripening into general mutiny."

Immediately upon receiving the dispatch, Frémont penned his one-line relinquishment of command. He then sat down and composed a sad farewell to his troops. "Agreeably to orders this day received I take leave of you. Although our army has been of sudden growth, we have grown up together, and I have become familiar with the brave and generous spirit which you bring to the defense of your country, and which makes me anticipate for you a brilliant career. Continue as you have begun, and give to my successor the same cordial and enthusiastic support with which you have encouraged me. Emulate the splendid example which you have already before you and let me remain, as I am, proud of the noble army which I had thus far labored to bring together. Soldiers, I regret to leave you. Most sincerely I thank you for the regard and confidence you have invariably shown to me. I deeply regret that I shall not have the honor to lead you to the victory which you are just about to win, but I shall claim to share with you in the joy of every triumph, and trust always to be fraternally remembered by my companions in arms."

By the next evening, Hunter had not yet arrived, and Frémont faced a mass of men champing at the bit for battle the next morning. Barely able to contain the zeal of his troops, he called a meeting of his officers and declared that if Hunter had not arrived by daybreak, Frémont would lead the attack against Price's army as planned. The camp exploded in cheers, and a dozen bands struck up in honor of their revered commander. But the soldiers' hopes were dashed when Hunter arrived at ten P.M.

The two men conferred in Frémont's tent, while the anxious troops awaited their orders for the morning. For two hours Frémont outlined his battle plan for the following day. But Lincoln had conveyed additional orders to Curtis to be delivered to the commanding general in the field—"I cannot now know whether Frémont or Hunter will then be in command"—ordering the federalists not to continue the pursuit of the Confederate army. "You are not likely to overtake Price," Lincoln wrote, "and are in danger of making too long a line from your own base of supplies and re-enforcements"—a further rebuke of Frémont's strategy.

When he emerged from the tent, a calm and dignified Frémont announced that the much-anticipated battle would not take place and beseeched his men to obey their new commander. It would mark the end of what would become known as Frémont's Hundred Days.

Six days later, on November 8, John arrived back in St. Louis to a hero's welcome. Twenty thousand residents turned out to greet him, bands marched in the streets, residents hung their flags at half mast, and rumors spread that Frank Blair would be lynched if he showed up in public. Chanting "Frémont and the Union!" the crowd organized into a torchlight parade. "Your—affectionate reception of me has moved my heart," he told the crowd. "It cheers me and strengthens my confidence—my confidence, already somewhat wavering—in our republican institutions."

"I could not stand it," Jessie wrote of her pain and anger. "I went far up to the top of the house, and, in the cold night air, tried to still [my] contending emotions."

John and Jessie remained in St. Louis for two weeks after his removal to gather the documents he would need for an impending congressional inquiry. While playing host to a stream of sympathetic and fawning political figures, he also reaped continued abuse and humiliation. Zagonyi's "Frémont Bodyguard" was unceremoniously dismissed without pay on the grounds of "disloyalty," and all of the contracts Frémont had issued were suspended. Jessie thought the government's treatment of John traitorous. "To leave him here without money, without moral aid of the govt. is treason to the people," she wrote to Ward Hill Lamon, a former law partner and close personal friend of Abraham Lincoln. "I cannot find smoother phrases for it is the death struggle of our nationality and no time for fair words."

"He was the life and the soul of his army, and it was cruelly wronged in his removal," wrote one of his soldiers who rose to become a prominent civic leader in New York. The groundswell of public support confirmed the Frémonts' stand on principle and demonstrated to them that John's emancipation proclamation, while perhaps politically inexpedient, was morally correct. John was confident that both his integrity and his devotion to his country had been intact throughout. For her part, Jessie, too, felt proud of their stance. She believed her destiny on earth was to "free the slaves"—a vision that had come to her years before, in a dream. At least a few slaves had actually been set free by their efforts, and that would have to be enough for the moment. She remained committed to the cause, even if Lincoln—whom she now viewed as having a "sly, slimy nature"—would be destined to eventually receive the credit she thought due John. From this point forward, both would be avowed enemies of the president and his administration.

The national outpouring in John's defense brought some small comfort to the beleaguered couple, who once again in their lives were suddenly thrust from the spotlight back into private civilian lives. The Northern press was uniformly supportive, one newspaper pronouncing that his proclamation "had stirred and united the loyal Northern States more than any event in the War so far"; and angry crowds in St. Louis trampled Lincoln's portrait and burned the president in effigy.

"Where are you that you let the hounds run down your friend Frémont?" an outraged Thaddeus Stevens demanded of his fellow radicals in Congress. The force against Frémont had "assumed form," as another congressman put it. "Slavery was its centre column; political knavery commanded on the right wing as the post of honor in this most unholy crusade, and on the left were semi-traitors in office and influence, disappointed contractors, and Treasury plunderers."

They moved the family to New York City, staying for a time at the Astor House while Frémont awaited further orders. "[T]here was nothing for him to do but wait the pleasure of the Government," Jessie wrote. "His military position obliged him to silence as well as this inaction." There they entertained a throng of well-wishers, the first and most avid among them the Reverend Henry Ward Beecher. Beecher, "who had become the recognized champion of the oppressed, whether white or black," as Jessie described him, brought Jessie a bouquet of violets and invited the couple to attend his Plymouth Church. "I have something to say and I want you to be there." When they arrived, ushers led them through the packed church to a pew set apart and decorated with flowers. The tall, powerful clergyman, brother of Harriet Beecher Stowe, gave a moving sermon about the higher calling for an immediate emancipation of slaves. He then turned to John and with drama and a booming voice, said: "Your name will live and be remembered by a nation of *Freemen!*"

Soon the family relocated to a more permanent residence, on Fourth Avenue, and John traveled frequently to Washington to aid in the congressional investigation of the Western Department. The extensive support they received from those they believed to be in the "right" kept them from becoming embittered, though Jessie had a more difficult time than John in maintaining her buoyancy.

By late fall of 1861 she had thrown herself into her first solitary book project, though she was self-deprecating and insecure about calling herself a "writer." Driven by her need to tell the heroic and unjust story of the "Frémont Bodyguard," she approached James Fields, the editor of the *Atlantic Monthly* and junior partner of the Boston publishing house Ticknor & Fields, and proposed writing a narrative about the plight of those brave men. "I am incapable of writing a book," she told Fields, "but I can tell what I know." The maimed survivors of the Springfield battle had received no government relief, prompting Jessie to financially support many of them herself. "I believe that those truly soldierly young men, worthy of a place in chronicles of knightly deeds, were misrepresented, slighted & finally insulted out of the service because of the name they bore," she wrote Fields. "It seems to me as much an obligation of feeling and honor to do them justice and heal the hurts to their national pride, as it would be to visit them in the Hospital had they been wounded bodily in the discharge of their duty near the General in the field."

Jessie saw the book as an opportunity to raise money for the families of the fallen guard, while also providing her a vehicle for dramatizing for a national audience John's experience in Missouri. Politically progressive and culturally erudite, Fields was immediately intrigued with the concept, recognizing Jessie's literary talent more than she did herself. "They were all young, many with younger members of their families looking to them for protection and assistance, some few married—some were sons of widows, and it was an additional sorrow to find that those killed at Springfield comprised the greater number of the married men & some of the most needed sons," Jessie wrote Fields of the poignant tale. "I cannot let those mothers & wives feel our name only the synonym of sorrow and loss to them."

Fields offered her a $600 advance, and little did Jessie know that it would be but the first of many writing contracts that would sustain her and John over the coming decades. She had never intended to enter that legion of nineteenth-century female writers whom Nathaniel Hawthorne had disdainfully called "a damned mob of scribbling women," yet before her life would end she would publish numerous books and more than fifty magazine articles. For now, though, she saw herself as a woman driven by one story to tell, and sought the publishing contract as a venue to expose a hidden truth. She wrote *The Story of the Guard* in a white heat, barely eating or sleeping, and delivered the finished manuscript to an astonished Fields within twelve days.

Publication would be delayed for nearly two years, apparently because the publisher, George Childs, found it too critical of the administration. When it was finally published in October 1863, it met with instant success, selling well in the United States and abroad.

In January 1862, Jessie and John relocated to Washington, to be available full-time to testify before the Joint Committee on the Conduct of the War. In early February, President and Mrs. Lincoln invited them to what would become a famous gala and ball at the White House. Scheduled for February 5, the social occasion prompted an outcry from the start, with many radical Republicans and other members of Washington society refusing to attend on the grounds that it was distasteful during a time of war. "Are the President and Mrs. Lincoln aware that there is a civil war?"

Senator Benjamin Wade, who chaired the joint committee, wrote in response to the invitation. "If they are not, Mr. and Mrs. Wade are, and for that reason decline to participate in feasting and dancing." The Wades were among more than eighty invitees who declined.

The Frémonts also declined. "It was a very serious time, sorrow and mourning had come into many homes, and the gloom and uncertainty as to the outcome of the struggle to preserve the Union cast its shadow everywhere," Jessie described the moment. "It was a surprise and something of a shock, to be invited at that time to a ball at the White House . . . We were in mourning for a near member of our family and would not have gone on that account; also I was in grief for several near relatives who had been killed on the rebel side." But in response to their regrets, Lincoln sent a household messenger expressing his personal desire that the couple attend. Under the circumstances, while John was still an army general awaiting another command, they considered the president's urging "almost an order."

On the morning of the ball, Dorothea Dix visited Jessie and related to her that Lincoln was despondent over the illness of his ten-year-old son Willie. Lincoln had begged Dix to move into the White House to care for Willie, but Dix, recognizing the child's imminent death from typhoid fever, refused, explaining that she was far too busy with her own work. The president apparently wanted to cancel the ball, but his wife, the extravagant Mary Todd Lincoln—whom Lydia Maria Child called a "vulgar doll"—insisted that the party proceed as planned. In deference to the illness in the household, if not to the war, the first lady hesitantly agreed to prohibit dancing.

In one of the more macabre events of the era, five hundred guests attended the lavish ball—what Jessie described as a "ghastly failure" and Mary Todd Lincoln pronounced a triumph—catered by New York's famous Maillards. The Marine Band played at the foot of the steps and "filled the house with music while the boy lay dying above," Jessie wrote. Mary wore a stunning, low-cut white satin gown trimmed in black and with a long train, while her husband donned his trademark wrinkled black suit. "A sadder face than that of the President I have rarely seen," Jessie wrote. Lincoln received guests at the door to the East Room, and he was so morose that the Frémonts' feelings of anger and contempt gave way to compassion.

They stayed but a short time, put off by the inappropriateness of the extravaganza, but before they could leave the premises, Charles Sumner approached them. Bearing a message from the president, Sumner asked that they return to the East Room in order for Frémont to meet General George McClellan. Jessie was shocked to see that Mrs. McClellan was dressed in the colors of the Confederacy. "A band of scarlet velvet crossed her white dress from shoulder to waist, and in her hair were three feathers of scarlet and white. If this was intentional, it was unpardonable in the wife of the commander-in-chief of the Union armies, and yet it seemed impossible to have been quite an accident." After an uncomfortable silence, with neither McClellan nor Frémont finding much of anything to say to each other, the Frémonts withdrew again.

Two weeks later, Willie was dead.

In the spring of 1862, after a lengthy investigation, the joint congressional committee exonerated Frémont. "Gen. Frémont, upon taking the command, was clothed with the most ample authority, and the exigencies of the Department were such that much should be pardoned in one compelled to act so promptly, and so little at his command," concluded the committee, whose members tended to share Frémont's emancipationist views. ". . . Our brilliant victories in the West will bear enduring testimony to the correctness of his judgment in that respect. But that feature of Gen. Frémont's administration which attracted the most attention at the time, and which will ever be most prominent among the many points of interest connected with the history of that Department, is his Proclamation of Emancipation. Whatever opinion may be entertained in reference to the time when the policy of Emancipation should have been inaugurated, or by whose authority it should have been promulgated, there can be no doubt that Gen. Frémont at that early day rightly judged in regard to the most effective means of subduing this Rebellion. In proof of that it is only necessary to refer to the fact that . . . the President as Commander-Chief of the army and Navy, has applied the same principle to all the rebellious States, and few will deny that it must be adhered to until the last vestige of treason and rebellion is destroyed."

As if to underscore Frémont's complete absolution, Senator Wade wrote a letter to the committee calling Frémont the innocent victim of a treacherous plot. "No public man since Admiral Byng . . . has suffered so unjustly as General Frémont."

The findings were too much for Frank Blair, who rose in anger before Congress to attack Frémont, and called the investigation "an apology for disaster and defeat; ingenious upon its face by the omission of important facts, and by the suggestion of others which never existed."

In hindsight, Frémont's successes in Missouri seemed to far outweigh his errors, which, in any case, seemed exaggerated by his many enemies. In a mere three months he had managed to retake control of St. Louis for the Union, had virtually banished rebel forces from Missouri, had built an armada of warships, tugboats, and gunboats that were patrolling the Mississippi River, and had found a most able commander in the then little-known Ulysses S. Grant. By putting Grant in command of the river operations, Frémont had "helped to create the materiel and leadership infrastructure by which Grant, in a stunning series of victories culminating in the July 1863 Union capture of Vicksburg, secured Union control over the river, thus fatally dividing the Confederacy into two isolated eastern and western sections," as historian Tom Chaffin drew the final analysis. Most significant of all, history would prove that Frémont—who was the first to free any slaves under the authority of the U.S. government—had laid the groundwork for Lincoln's later Emancipation Proclamation. Still, that history had not yet unfolded, and the public acquittal of 1862 was minor, if welcome, consolation to John and Jessie.

Meanwhile, Lincoln was inundated with letters from outraged citizens and public figures alike. "This offering is made at the altar of truth and patriotism," wrote one, "in behalf of a man who has suffered silently and nobly in a cause worthy of the highest admiration and respect. The history of revolutions of the world shows us that in nearly every case a great man has arisen who has been the leader, and through his influence the revolution has progressed. This revolution in many respects has no parallel." An editorial in the Cincinnati Gazette proclaimed that Frémont "is to the West what Napoleon was to France, while the President has lost the confidence of the people."

In the summer of 1862, Frémont's actions were further vindicated when Congress passed the Confiscation Act, legislation identical to that issued by Frémont, freeing all slaves of those supporting the rebellion. Weary from the dispute and eager to placate more radical factions—who believed, right or wrong, that Lincoln intentionally and methodically overlooked antislavery generals—the president sought a solution. He recognized that the abolition movement had gained national support, and he had come to question the credibility as well of Frémont's main detractors, particularly Francis Preston Blair and his sons. "I have had it on my mind for some time that Frémont should be given a chance to redeem himself," Lincoln said at the time. "The great hue and cry about him has been concerning his expenditure of the public money. I have looked into the matter a little, and I can't see as he has done any worse or any more, in that line, than our eastern commanders."

Lincoln then assigned him to command the newly created Mountain Department, headquartered in Wheeling, Virginia. Again, Jessie joined her husband, setting up headquarters at the McLure Hotel, and as before served as his intermediary with the outside world. John took his orders directly from the president—orders widely considered impracticable if not impossible—and faced a series of defeats in the Shenandoah Valley Campaign. Lincoln wanted him to march from western Virginia (the state of West Virginia was not admitted to the union until 1863) to Tennessee, but Frémont, who had twenty-five thousand men on paper and far fewer in reality—troops that were ill-trained and ill-equipped— thought the strategy flawed. Like other Union generals, Frémont was outmaneuvered by the unstoppable Stonewall Jackson, and Frémont's command was hopelessly chaotic and disjointed. When Lincoln created a new Army of Virginia that absorbed Frémont under the command of General John Pope, greatly diminishing Frémont's capacity, Frémont faced a dilemma. Frémont felt that Pope, an irascible Mexican-American War veteran, had been undermining him for more than a decade, dating back to when Pope competed with Frémont to lead one of the railway expeditions of 1852. Frémont "detested Pope only less than he detested Frank Blair," as one observer put it, and "could not bring himself to hold any intercourse with the man." Under the circumstances, he requested to be relieved of his command, which Lincoln readily granted. By the end of the summer, Pope's army was defeated at the Second Battle of Bull Run.

Frémont returned to New York, and the family settled at Little Neck, on Long Island. Still, the antislavery factions sought a role for their hero. Horace Greeley, William Cullen Bryant, and other prominent citizens carried a petition to Lincoln suggesting that he commission Frémont to organize and command an army of "Negro troops." Lincoln declined, stating it was "very objectionable, as a general rule, to have troops raised on any special terms."

While Lincoln continued to promise Frémont various commands, "the promises were never fulfilled," Jessie wrote.

"I have great respect for General Frémont," Lincoln would later tell a large delegation of citizens who had approached the president on Frémont's behalf. "But the fact is, that the pioneer in any movement is not generally the best man to carry that movement to a successful issue. It was so in olden times, was it not? Moses began the emancipation of the Jews, but did not take Israel to the promised land, after all. He had to make way for Joshua to complete the work."

Indeed, many years after her father's death, Lily Frémont agreed with Lincoln's assessment. Someone once said that "my father should have been called Moses, instead of John," Lily recalled, "for like the biblical character, he was led up to the hilltop and permitted to view the promised land below, though he never was permitted to enter."

For all intents and purposes, the war had ended for the Frémonts.

8

RETREAT 1862–1902

Fame is a vapor; popularity an accident.
Character is the only thing that endures.

—Horace Greeley

JOHN MAINTAINED A small staff in New York, awaiting a new assignment, but when it became clear that none would be forthcoming he reluctantly, and humiliatingly, relieved everyone of duty. The next year would be trying as John turned once again to the convoluted financial problems of Las Mariposas, which was awash in debt under the corrupt supervision of its manager. John took long horseback rides in Central Park with Zagonyi, who for a while anticipated another assignment as well, and the two fallow soldiers were usually accompanied by twenty-year-old Lily. Riding horses that had seen battle with the Guard—one having shed its pedigreed blood from a rebel's bayonet stab—Frémont and Zagonyi strived to keep physically fit. "Isn't it a shame that such men have no higher use of their time than to train a girl to ride?" Jessie lamented to her dear friend Thomas Starr King, who had replaced Lizzie Blair as her faithful correspondent.

During the winter of 1862, eleven-year-old Charley and seven-year-old Frank consumed much of Jessie's attention, while she was busy as well with final edits on *The Story of the Guard*, which James Fields was shepherding into production. "Please shape it slenderly," she wrote to Fields. "Dumpy books are so unsuggestive of elegance of thought or deep feeling. It's cruel enough to have lost my own slenderness without seeing that misfortune befall this child of my heart & memory . . . Don't hesitate to draw your critical pen through anything that seems sentimental or stilted."

Meanwhile, she immersed herself in an ambitious fund-raising effort, working with New York feminists and Unitarians, including King, to raise more than $1 million for the U.S. Sanitary Commission, and became an increasingly committed advocate for women's rights. Her anti-slavery activism deepened as well, and as casualties mounted she watched Lincoln—whom she derisively called "Honest Abe" or "the ass"—with disgust for what she saw as bungling incompetence, or worse, small-minded obfuscation. She kept a shrine in her study—a collection of anti-slavery books, including *Uncle Tom's Cabin* and Frederick Olmsted's *Slave States*—and placed a bronze sculpture titled *The Slave Auction* on a prominent shelf.

"I do a good deal of desultory work & in one way & another the General & the children fill the time," she wrote to King. "Charley was down for his Christmas & has returned—growing tall & behaving very well & learning very satisfactorily. Frank goes from ten to one daily to a French kinder-garten school, & has also drawing lessons as he has positive talent that way. Lily is deep in serious study of German & polishing off in French. That with skating & riding keeps her 'alive.' "

Jessie's book was published just before Christmas 1862, and within a few short weeks Fields announced that $500 in profits had already been forwarded to the families of the slain Guardsmen. Her publisher and numerous reviewers went to great lengths to dispel rumors that John had been the book's actual author, while also striving to downplay Jessie's unwomanly professionalism and to dismiss the ubiquitous charges that had plagued the couple since the first expedition reports that she was a more talented writer than John. It was a delicate and confusing balance. "Mrs. Frémont is a true woman and has written a true woman's book," the *Atlantic* declared. "Her style is full, free, vivid, with plenty of dashes and postscripts . . . We cannot be mistaken. The hand that penned the 'Story of the Guard' could not hold the pen of the [Emancipation] Proclamation or . . . the narrative of the Rocky-Mountain Expedition." Still, other reviewers perpetuated the notion that John was at the very least a full-fledged collaborator. "Instead of being a labored and exhaustive defence of General Frémont by the fair Jessie, while her Benton blood was up, it is as mild and gentle as the heart of a woman," pronounced San Francisco's *Hesperian* magazine.

"The parts . . . by Mrs. Frémont are exceedingly well done and make the reader regret that the whole is not in her neat, compact and forcible style."

Jessie was typically more outraged and embittered by the politics that had undercut her husband than John was. She confided to her intimates that John had been "betrayed by pretended radical and anti-Lincoln men who deserted him in time of greatest need, after encouraging him to stand in the breach." But with the issuance of Lincoln's Emancipation Proclamation on New Year's Day 1863, freeing the slaves behind rebel lines, Jessie felt compassion for the beleaguered president.

"Well, my dear Eliza," Jessie wrote in her last letter to her sister before Eliza suddenly died, "the Emancipation Proclamation has brought England to our side, and emancipation has proved a *pivotal* term after all. A few of us felt this in '61. War-politics—hyphenated heartache. My one hope is to see the end of both in *our* lives. At fifty the General is gray, worn, and in poor health. At thirty-nine my heart, played upon by joy and bereavement, pride and humiliation, longs only for the privacy of a real home again . . . I am no prophet, though the daughter of one, but I foresee the fall of the House of Blair. I still have filial affection for father Blair, but Frank and Montgomery will soon betray to the long-suffering President that the Blair *soul* is with the South. Mr. Greeley, Mr. Sumner, and Mr. Chase know that already. When I talked with Mr. Lincoln, what a pity he could not consider my analysis of the Blairs *à bon entendeur salut.*"

By the spring of 1863, Las Mariposas was more than $2 million in debt, and the monthly interest payments on the loans exceeded $13,000 dollars. The company faced legal expenses of more than $600,000, which, according to Jessie, John paid out of his personal assets. John and Jessie blamed much of the catastrophe on the washing away of the dam John had built on the Merced River—a disaster they attributed to a venal business associate who had intentionally failed to open the sluice gates during flood season. "This genius of a man once worth $10,000,000 and more," a New York judge once remarked of Frémont, testified that it had "all been stripped away from him, and he has but little left." The testimony to which the judge referred came when Frémont appeared as a witness in a sensational libel trial brought by former New York mayor George Opdyke against Thurlow Weed. Weed had published charges that Opdyke and others had bilked Frémont out of millions of dollars' worth of Las Mariposas stock while Frémont was preoccupied as a general in Missouri, in a swindle worthy of one of "Balzac's novels of business life," as one account described it.

Frémont finally sold his interest in the property—much to Jessie's relief—and received a profit of close to $4 million. He then invested all of his proceeds in what "had been the engrossing idea of his early life—a transcontinental railroad from the Atlantic to the Pacific," Jessie wrote later. Given his stunning lack of financial acumen, he would have been more prudent to have found a safer investment—or at least to have diversified his holdings. But true to his passion for western exploration and his romantic dream for a transcontinental railroad, he threw everything into the enterprise. Initially he purchased the franchise and property of the struggling young Kansas Pacific Railroad and paid for the construction of its lines. He then bought the Missouri Pacific and renamed it the Atlantic & Pacific. Soon he sold both and purchased a controlling interest in the Memphis & El Paso. "I procured from the Texas Legislature a large grant of lands, which was all in the interest of the Memphis & El Paso, which was planned to run from the harbour of Norfolk to San Diego and San Francisco," he wrote in his *Memoirs*, "and its extended name was the Transcontinental, and I had acquired for it franchises in South Carolina, Arizona, and Arkansas." It was a grandiose and ill-fated vision—one that would have given him the practical control of all western transportation that railroad magnate Collis P. Huntington eventually obtained. But for now Frémont was back in the maelstrom of exploration and entrepreneurship that he loved, which mitigated the rancor of politics and war.

In July 1863 the family left their brownstone at 21 West Nineteenth Street and retreated to a cottage they purchased from social reformer Wendell Phillips at Nahant on the Massachusetts coast north of Boston. There they spent a leisurely summer, where they socialized at the beach with like-minded neighbors such as the Whittiers and the Longfellows. "We have had so much to make us thankful & happy this summer and this little sea-side place is so unmarked with any care or grief," she wrote in a good-bye letter to Whittier just before leaving their haven in October to return to their New York mansion, which had been renovated in their absence. Expressing her fear of "tomorrow," Jessie hated breaking up yet another joyful family interlude. "The rule of our life—our lives even—has been struggle & unrest. This summer has been so peaceful, so full of every good home blessing, that I am nervous about what must follow this lull in our stormy lives." Still, she looked forward to the holidays, writing to King that she intended to "make a good Christmas this year." Frank would get a Shetland pony and Charley a big Newfoundland dog.

Indeed, their idyll was not to be. Jessie was devastated to learn that the government had seized her Black Point estate in California to build an army fort. In another ironic twist and cruel swipe, the fort would be named for John's rival Colonel R. B. Mason, Kearny's lackey whom Frémont had once challenged to a duel after the Bear Flag Revolt. Ostensibly necessary as a result of blustering by France, Black Point and Alcatraz were being fortified, and Jessie's flower gardens and favorite home were leveled for earthworks and a battery. John had purchased it for her and placed it in her name alone, and she had long envisioned a glorious family compound to be passed down to the Frémont children for generations to come. As a further affront, the government refused to reimburse her even the $42,000 purchase price. It was but one more blow from a country she and John had served with faithfulness and dedication, and she was at a perpetual loss to understand the depth of the ill feeling and animosity heaped on them both.

On the heels of that shocking news came the heartbreaking report that King, not yet forty years old, had contracted diphtheria and died abruptly. Jessie wept for days. "I've a certain conviction that when I have a garden again, I'll meet Mr. King walking there," she told John. King had been tirelessly touring California, raising money for the Sanitation Commission, which he sent by the thousands to New York. "His brave pure soul has gone through those golden gates," she wrote to Whittier, "and to him it is well earned rest. But to us it is a loss and loneliness that cannot be repaired."

Jessie arranged to have violets placed on the grave of "our dear dear friend who held California in the Union & whose efforts obtained the half million for the wounded." Bret Harte, newly married and the father of an infant, wrote Jessie of the details of King's funeral and the sorrow that had invaded all of their lives. Enclosed in the envelope was a copy of his poem "Relieving Guard," which he had written in honor of King.

Grieving now for King and Black Point, as well as for the recent death of her sister Eliza, Jessie began looking for a new home site in the Hudson River Valley. With Las Mariposas and Black Point gone forever, she turned away from the vision of returning to California and sought a final refuge in New York that would provide the Frémonts with the rich, stable, and lasting family home she had coveted for two decades. As it turned out, she would live that dream for ten blissful years before crueler fates intervened yet again.

As the war casualties mounted, and with the takeover of Congress by anti-administration radicals, discontent pervaded the country. By the spring of 1864, the war seemed to be a disaster for the Union and there seemed no victorious end in sight. The death toll was staggering, and except for Grant's proficient control of the Southwest, inept or slow generals were mismanaging every other theater in the East. The Confederates held Richmond, and even Grant—the president's new commanding general—had led nearly seventy thousand soldiers in a six-week period to their gruesome deaths.

Lincoln was widely regarded as diffident and dilatory—even his Emancipation Proclamation considered a reluctant concession to critics—and most major newspapers were calling for a new Republican candidate for president. Schuyler Colfax, an outspoken administration adversary, had defeated Lincoln's candidate for Speaker of the House, and as a long-standing and fervent supporter of Frémont was promoting the explorer's candidacy. Lincoln's own cabinet was divided and hostile, with Salmon P. Chase nursing presidential aspirations of his own and members of Congress showing little or no affection for Lincoln or his candidacy. "The principal cause of the Cabinet antagonisms was evident to every observer—the Blairs," wrote Allan Nevins. Montgomery, Frank, and Francis Sr. were Lincoln sycophants, obstinately opposing emancipation until the end and favoring the South in postwar reconstruction planning, inspiring the wrath of Seward and Bates. Montgomery was the author of Lincoln's colonization plan, which Frémont and other abolitionists considered racist, immoral, and un-American. Granting that, Lincoln had favored the colonization plan. But by late 1862 to early 1863, historians now generally agree, Lincoln was just bringing up the plan as a sop to the conservative wing, knowing it wouldn't work. "The whole Blair family was for treating the South mildly and kindly, and restoring its rights promptly."

Union opposition to Lincoln increasingly centered around Frémont, though he was decidedly uninterested, having turned his full energy to his railroad venture. Frémont was the bold martyr of the emancipationists, and his experiences in Missouri had further galvanized his antislavery sentiments, drawing the country's abolitionists firmly into his camp.

Frémont believed that free blacks should have all the rights of whites and that there should be no distinction between races within the nation's laws or Consitution. Meanwhile, Thaddeus Stevens was endorsing General Benjamin F. Butler, and Greeley was rallying for anyone but Lincoln, suggesting Chase, Butler, Grant, or Frémont. By May it had become clear that the Union Party, as the Republicans now fashioned themselves, would renominate Lincoln even though his election in November seemed unlikely, which encouraged the Democrats. "The Convention will not be regarded as a Union Convention, but simply as a Blair–Lincoln Convention," Salmon P. Chase complained to Ohio's governor.

Those seeking a third candidate gained momentum, judging that a third ticket could serve to either manipulate Lincoln's withdrawal from the race or split the vote, resulting in Lincoln's defeat. "Lincoln will be nominated and a copperhead will be elected," wrote James A. Garfield. "Not a dozen men in Congress think otherwise."

Despite Frémont's indifference, a "dissident convention" held in Cleveland nominated him by acclamation on May 31, 1864. Neither he nor Jessie held any illusions about the viability of his candidacy, though both recognized the pragmatic reality that millions of Americans supported him and he therefore had a role to play in the political process. He graciously accepted the nomination, writing of the "honorable" and "difficult" action undertaken—"Very honorable, because in offering it to me you act in the name of a great number of citizens who seek above all things the good of their country . . . Very difficult, because in accepting the candidacy you propose to me I am exposed to the reproach of creating a schism in the party with which I have been identified. Had Mr. Lincoln remained faithful to the principles he was elected to defend, no schism could have been created and no contest could have been possible."

Using the opportunity to blast his political nemesis, Frémont was unstinting in his harsh censure of the administration—a remarkable foreshadowing of the future criticism of a twenty-first-century American president and war. "To-day we have in the country the abuses of a military dictation, without its unity of action and vigor of execution. An Administration marked at home by disregard of constitutional rights, by its violation of personal liberty, and the liberty of the press . . . Its course has been characterized by a feebleness and want of principle which has misled European powers and driven them to a belief that only commercial interests and personal aims are concerned . . . Sympathies which should have been with us from the outset of the war were turned against us, and in this way the Administration has done the country a double wrong abroad. It created hostility, or at best indifference, among those who would have been its friends . . . Against this disastrous condition of affairs the Cleveland Convention was a protest."

At first Lincoln and his supporters regarded the Frémont nomination as irrelevant, if not ridiculous. The president, upon learning of the Cleveland convention, opened his Bible and read aloud from the Book of Samuel: "And everyone that was in distress, and everyone that was in debt, and everyone that was discontented gathered themselves unto him; and he became a captain over them: and there were with him about four hundred men."

But after the Democrats nominated the handsome and popular General George McClellan on August 29 as a "peace" candidate who vowed to end the war without abolishing slavery, the Lincoln forces viewed the Frémont candidacy as disastrous. When it seemed clear that Lincoln would almost certainly lose to McClellan if Frémont stayed in the race, Republican power brokers—especially senator Zachariah Chandler of Michigan, who had been trying to pacify Lincoln's harshest critics among his fellow radical Republicans—lobbied the general to withdraw for the welfare of the party.

In several meetings in early September in the New York office of Frémont's lawyer and political adviser David Dudley Field, Chandler presented a deal: If Frémont withdrew, the president would assign him to a high military command and would dismiss Montgomery Blair from his administration. Frémont found the offer insulting and the bargain dishonorable. "The latter part of the proposition General Frémont at once declined," Jessie described his immediate reaction. "The worst that his enemies could do had been done, and any affiliation with the Administration, which had through personal motives attempted to ruin his career and reputation, was an impossibility. But he took the question of withdrawing as a candidate, under consideration."

Some historical accounts suggest that Frémont was subsequently offered a cabinet position when Lincoln loyalists worried about his apparent reluctance and the time he was taking to make a decision. John and Jessie discussed the offer with several friends and supporters. Wendell Phillips strongly urged him to stay in the race, while Whittier just as forcefully encouraged him to withdraw. In a strangely prescient letter,

Nathaniel P. Sawyer of Pittsburgh recommended he withdraw. "If you have assurance of Mr. Blair's immediate removal and also Mr. Stanton's and the assurance that Mr. Seward will be not be reappointed, my advice is that you withdraw as soon as practicable in favor of Lincoln and [Andrew] Johnson. Something tells me that Lincoln will never fill a second term. If I am right, Johnson will be the President . . . I have no doubt he will do you and your friends justice."

Frémont finally decided to abandon his candidacy—"not in favor of Abraham Lincoln, but in order to preserve the Union, and keep the administration of its affairs in the hands of the party which had forced the emancipation of the slaves, and was slowly forcing the war to a termination," Jessie wrote. Characteristically indignant on behalf of her husband, Jessie thought it a rotten bargain. "That such a sacrifice should have been asked from the man whom the Administration had thwarted and oppressed to its utmost is an act which is in itself its own comment." Frank Frémont, writing years later to the historian Allan Nevins, would insist that Frémont refused all offers from the Lincoln administration. "One thing you may be sure of, and that is my Father never stooped to ask Lincoln for a consideration in return for his act of withdrawal. The fact that weighed with him was the necessity that the Republican Party dominate in the reconstruction of the South, and he fully realized that with both Lincoln and himself in the field, the Democratic ticket would be elected."

In his letter of withdrawal, published on September 22, Frémont's disrespect for the president was unconstrained—further evidence that he had rejected all offerings from Lincoln, for if he expected concessions he certainly would have been less adversarial. "In respect to Mr. Lincoln," Frémont wrote, "I continue to hold . . . his administration has been politically, militarily, and financially a failure, and that its necessary continuance is a cause of regret for the country." The following afternoon Lincoln dismissed Montgomery Blair. Suspecting Seward and Weed of maneuvering against him, Blair was unaware that Zachariah Chandler had been the culprit. The person most responsible for sabotaging Frémont's Western Department command had been emasculated.

Frémont's withdrawal was indeed unifying. Lincoln received a margin of more than four hundred thousand votes at the polls and the overwhelming majority of the presidential electors. "If my Father had been a politician instead of a patriot," Frémont's son Frank would later write, "he would have played the game with Lincoln, kept the influence of the

Blairs, soothed the fears of Lincoln in respect to the coming elections, and controlled the persons inimical to the 'Pathfinder' through the usual means. If he had thrown his influence to have Lincoln elected, he in turn would have had the support of all Lincoln people, later. But he was not that kind of a man."

Twenty-five years later Jessie wrote to Whittier, thanking him for guiding John during those crucial two weeks in September 1864. "Among the words I remember from you are: 'There is a time to do and a time to stand aside.' . . . It was a deciding word, coming from you."

On April 9, 1865, when Confederate general Robert E. Lee offered his sword to the victorious Union general Ulysses S. Grant at Appomattox Court House, John C. Frémont was far removed from the scene— destined now for a kind of anonymity that belied what a historic role he had played in this incredible resolution by arms that America had just endured. Still, like thousands of other ecstatic Americans, he and Jessie went to Washington to welcome the triumphant Union armies back into the capital. John watched the parade of waving flags and marching bands, saluting the long blue columns of soldiers. It was an affecting and ironic end for the man whose exploration had opened the West—an act that had exacerbated this conflict so sharply. Here was the man who had issued the first emancipation proclamation that lay the groundwork for Lincoln's later proclamation; the man who had run for president on a strong Republican ticket in 1856, helping to make possible Lincoln's victory four years later; the man who had commanded thousands of Union soldiers in the earliest days of the war. Yet at the end of this great struggle he stood defeated by political forces that he often did not see and could never overcome. No figure had been so important or promi-nent as Frémont in the tumultuous decades that were the prelude to war, and yet no figure of his stature was more obscure at the moment that peace was finally made.

"[I]t's a very risky thing to tell the whole truth," Jessie concluded of her own life thus far. "It was not natural to me or easy for me to bend my pride . . . I am sure if it was all written out in a book it would grieve any one to see how I got broken in."

Removed from politics once and for all, John pursued in earnest his ca-reer as a railroad speculator. Jessie yearned for a home in the countryside that was as magically picturesque as Black Point, and during the spring of 1864 took long drives along the Hudson River in search of such a sanctuary. "We must soon find something to cure this Black Point nostalgia," John told her, "for it can prove as destructive to your health as an organic disease." John, too, was bridling at urban life and eager to find a locale where he could pursue his favorite pastimes of horseback riding, hiking, and boating.

When they learned that the estate of newspaper publisher James Watson Webb was available for sale, they purchased the two-hundred-acre estate overlooking the Tappan Zee—a natural widening of the Hudson River—two miles north of Tarrytown, New York. The massive gray stone house provided stunning views of rugged mountains, thick woods, a scenic expanse of water below, acres of orchards, manicured lawns, flourishing flower gardens, and roomy stables for their spirited Kentucky Thoroughbreds. Jessie christened it with the Indian name "Pocaho," and she felt it incorporated all of the finest elements of her best-loved homes. "The sweetness of honey locust and elms combines St. Louis and Washington," she wrote a friend. "The bluebells and wild grapevine, the thickly wooded glens where the eye travels from the fern carpet at one's feet to the blue upland trails—that is Cherry Grove. And the fresh breeze off the water when Little Mountain wraps her fog ruff about her neck is our own beloved Black Point."

A twenty-by-thirty-foot room with floor-to-ceiling bookshelves was designated as John's study, where he could display his many maps and trophies, and vast collection of books. They filled the mansion with dozens of paintings by artists of the West, including Prussian-born Albert Bierstadt—a personal art collection that rivaled the best in the country. Their favorite was a landscape of the Golden Gate at sunset, which they purchased for $4,000 from their neighbor Bierstadt, who had just returned from a sketching tour of the Rocky Mountains. Upon the death of John's idol the great Prussian explorer Alexander von Humboldt, John purchased his library. The leather-bound collection rested near Jessie's own favorite books, including the colored Audubon volumes she had treasured as a child. Here at this idyllic retreat from the cruel world of politics they turned their attention to their children and each other.

"After we got the books arranged," wrote Nelly Haskell, the young woman whom they had first befriended at Black Point, and who lived with them for a time at Pocaho, "I watched the big room grow into a home under her direction. On the floor was spread a moss-green carpet with a rich border. The well-spaced windows were hung with green and cream fabric, the glass of the French doors to the terrace left clear for the view. On one side of the fireplace she set the General's easy chair; beside it, a stout oak table with a reading lamp. Opposite was her own chair and table with its now historic Martha Washington sewing basket . . . Next day we arranged the music room: piano, cabinet, guitars, and a violin. Here she had a couch placed in a quite dark corner . . . [explaining] 'I want one in shadow, for music is a tonic to be taken sometimes in repose and darkness.'"

They kept their Manhattan mansion primarily so Jessie could attend the theater and socialize with her many New York friends, and a well-trained staff of domestics maintained both homes. French chefs prepared all meals, and though the residences were large and prepossessing, John and Jessie both fought any semblance of ostentation. Every comfort existed, and the furnishings were the finest that could be found, but the overriding ambience was one of elegant simplicity. Both homes were hospitable, and the couple regularly hosted intimate dinners. John belonged to no clubs and had no interest in formal social engagements, preferring small gatherings with their close friends. His only indulgences were his wife, his children, his horses, and his books, and he rarely accompanied Jessie to her affairs in the city. After the years of brutal politics and family schisms, they were painstakingly discerning about whom they chose to include in their private circle.

"The general was often away in the West on his railroad business," Nelly wrote, "but when home he usually read quietly or took evening walks with Mrs. Frémont or long rides through the woods and along the postroads with the boys, Lil, and myself. He loved to listen to what he called home-made music. He went occasionally to the theater when Mrs. Frémont asked him, which was seldom, because she knew he preferred to play chess or chat with the neighbors, the Phelpses, Schuylers, Aspinwalls, or Beechers, who dropped in often. As to formal dinners, he attended them only when Mrs. Frémont said: 'You really must go this time.' She attended many such functions when he was West on business, going to Washington for dinners and musicales. She was present at Mrs. Grant's first White House reception . . . But when Mr. Frémont was at home, she tried to have only the sort of guests in the house agreeable to him."

They traveled frequently to Europe, alone and with the children, and at one point left Frank and Charley in Dresden at a private boarding academy. Like other spoilsmen of the Gilded Age, they associated with their aristocratic neighbors who shared John's entrepreneurial spirit, and at one point even purchased a small island off the coast of Maine.

In May 1868 they traveled to St. Louis, where Jessie had been invited to unveil a life-size bronze monument of her father sculpted by Harriet Hosmer. Holding an unrolled map and facing westward, the "Old Roman" statue was described as "grand and simple" by the *Cincinnati Commercial*. At the moment, President Johnson was facing impeachment, and the nation's newspapers were too crowded with that sensational story to devote much space to the celebration. It was a deeply emotional and trying time for Jessie. Forty thousand citizens poured into Lafayette Park to witness the unveiling. A band played while Jessie pulled the cord that revealed the colossal statue. As the drapery fell away, thousands of schoolchildren tossed roses onto the base. "At the same moment the outgoing train to San Francisco halted and saluted with whistles and flags," she depicted the poignant moment in a letter to a friend. A salute of thirty guns for each year that Benton had served in the Senate was fired under order of the secretary of war. The hardest of all for Jessie to endure, in a day filled with painful memories, was the eulogy to his old friend and benefactor delivered by Frank Blair. Written with the collaboration of his brother Montgomery and his father, Francis Sr., it was pronounced "the ablest effort" of Blair's public life.

It would be the last time she would see the man who had single-mindedly set out to sabotage John and to destroy the personal reputations of both John and Jessie. Five weeks later Blair would be nominated for the vice presidency at the Democrats' Tammany Hall convention.

Throughout the 1860s their prosperity was abundant, and Jessie devoted much of her time and energy to giving money to those in need. She supported nieces and nephews, friends and friends of friends, made introductions between struggling writers and New York publishers, and contributed to charities and progressive political causes. Though she was distinctively stylish and enjoyed fine clothing and shoes, she was markedly understated in her personal appearance. "In a day of excess in food and display in jewels and clothes, Jessie's personal habits were almost as Spartan as Frémont's own," wrote Catherine Coffin Phillips in her mid-twentieth-century biography of Jessie. "Her guests praised her hospitality, not in the abundance and variety of food, but in the taste and distinction of service. She bought no jewels, nor allowed Frémont to buy them for her. Her only indulgence lay in the quality of the fabrics and laces that went into the gowns suitable for the functions which as a social personage she must attend."

In the fall of 1868, Charley entered the Naval Academy at Annapolis, and John traveled to France where, through the Paris brokerage house of Paradis et Cie, he sold $8.4 million worth of his railroad company's bonds. By the following year, reminiscent of the Las Mariposas debacle, that transaction was clouded in scandal. Frémont's French agents—including Baron Gauldrée Boilleau, who was married to Jessie's sister Susan—were accused of claiming to French investors that the Memphis, El Paso, and Pacific railroad was already a transcontinental line and that the U.S. government had guaranteed a fixed rate of return on its bonds. In fact, the company's only land grants were in Texas, and though Frémont had been lobbying the government for guarantees, none had yet been granted.

Jessie, John, Lily, and Frank traveled to France in the summer of 1869 on the *Ville de Paris*, ensconced in the ship's lavish bridal suite with adjoining rooms. The scandal broke in French newspapers just as the family arrived in Paris, prompting the U.S. minister in Paris, Elihu B. Washburne, once the congressional patron of new president Ulysses S. Grant, to call for a congressional investigation of Frémont. Jessie and the children toured the continent while John remained in Paris, attempting to sort out the financial complications of his company.

In Paris John met Vinnie Ream—a staggeringly talented young sculptress who had become the first woman, and youngest artist, to receive a U.S. government commission for a statue of Abraham Lincoln. A teenage art prodigy, Ream had studied in Washington during the Civil War, and Lincoln had closeted himself with her for half an hour a day for five months as she sculpted his bust, despite Mary's strong objections to the arrangement. After Lincoln's assassination, the eighteen-year-old won a fierce competition for the lucrative government contract to sculpt the martyred president in Carrara marble for placement in the Capitol rotunda. Dauntingly beautiful, with long, dark curls, penetrating eyes, and a tiny figure, she faced the predictable chauvinistic slander instigated by her older male rivals who had sought the highly coveted commission. (She would also be the first to create a freestanding sculpture of a Native American, her Sequoyah, which would be placed in Statuary Hall in the Capitol.)

Ream was with her parents in Paris, where she was working on the

Lincoln sculpture, and John saw her frequently, having retained her to make a medallion of him. He was, like everyone, captivated by her proficiency and charming personality. When Jessie returned to Paris, John was eager for his wife and daughter to meet the gifted young woman, and hired Ream to create a bust of Jessie and to make casts of her hands.

Jessie and John returned to New York in November 1869, leaving Lily, Frank, and a household maid in Dresden for tutoring in German. That fall and winter ushered in the start of the demise of the Frémonts' good fortune. By the following year, Frémont's company was in financial crisis, and he and Boilleau faced criminal charges in France for selling worthless bonds. Convicted in absentia and sentenced to five years, Frémont escaped imprisonment by remaining in the United States, though his brother-in-law would serve three years in jail. Saturated by scandal and financial problems, the Memphis, El Paso, and Pacific fell into bankruptcy and was taken over by John A. C. Gray, a sharp operator who, in collusion with a New York judge, forced John out in order for another company in which Gray had an interest to acquire the railroad. "Only the wise counsel of my Mother prevented my Father from shooting Gray," Frank Frémont later remarked.

Frémont was said to have walked away with nearly $1 million, and initially it appeared that their economic health was intact, though Frémont's reputation as a businessman was sullied beyond repair. The Paris criminal trial received publicity in the United States, and Frémont's many enemies in Washington seized the opportunity to expose him. One senator reported investigative findings that placed Frémont in "suspicious proximity to foul and fraudulent transactions." As an entrepreneur, the explorer and scientist was hopelessly incapable. Inept at best and unethical at worst, his capitalist ventures were inevitably shrouded with poor judgment, shady associates, and the unrealistic optimism of a dreamer. Though difficult to reconcile that a man with such an acute sense of honor would be consciously involved in improper or corrupt practices, the proof of wrongdoing by his chosen associates was overwhelming. "It is evident that he had acted with entire honesty in the matter, but it is also certain that he had shown a lamentable lack of discretion and care," concluded his biographer Nevins. "His fault was of omission, not commission, but it was nevertheless real . . . Once more his precipitancy and lack of circumspection betrayed him." Other biographers were less forgiving. "Although he does not really belong in the company of such rascals as [Jay] Cooke or Jay Gould, Frémont was indeed morally careless . . ." wrote Andrew Rolle. "Yet when judged by the heady standards of the Gilded Age, from the end of the Civil War to the turn of the century, when fortunes were made and lost overnight, his speculative errors were common enough."

The sudden downturn took a physical toll on the family, and in the summer of 1870 John was bedridden with malaria, Lily had a recurrence of the eye trouble that had begun years earlier from an infection she contracted in Panama, Jessie's "neuralgia" returned from the stress and exhaustion, and the cold Frank caught in a freezing sleet in Washington turned to pneumonia. When lung hemorrhaging made Frank's illness life-threatening, the family removed to Maine with the hopes that the sea air would alleviate his suffering. Jessie, of course, feared that it was the tuberculosis that had long haunted the Benton family. She turned out to be right.

Meanwhile, the money was dwindling, and personal debt was strangling them. Jessie cut down their household staff, brought to a halt her philanthropic contributions, and seemed to sense that they were indeed on the verge of ruin. Still, proud and defensive of John, she hung on as long as there seemed the possibility that he would be vindicated and they would witness a reversal of luck. "It is an inextricable mass out of which I can glean only an impression of millions of dollars of railroad bonds floated abroad which brought profit only to the agent, advertisements published abroad that misrepresented the whole railroad picture, of which Mr. Frémont knew nothing." she wrote to Nelly Haskell, her primary confidante during these darkest years. "One thing, however, stands out perfectly clear: my husband was in Washington working for the rights of way for his road while his agents were selling bonds through misrepresentations. He has had no part in any dishonest transaction. Certain of that I am strong for whatever is to come."

When Jay Cooke's Wall Street banking firm collapsed on September 18, 1873, throwing the nation into financial panic and ushering in massive unemployment, whatever investments the Frémonts had managed to retain disappeared. "We had houses and lands and stocks and no money for unpremeditated uses," Jessie wrote a friend.

Sixty years old, nearly penniless, his business, political, and military careers in shambles, unemployable as a financier or explorer, and with a wife and three dependent children, Frémont had no viable options for the future. "All the courage that he had shown in facing the snow-choked Sierras and the storm of wartime obloquy in St. Louis was needed again; all of it and more," as one account put it. But he was unable to muster it, and once again, Jessie would rush in to fill the breach. "He is so solitary," Jessie described his sad condition to Nelly, "so lonely, my poor dear darling—you know how tender hearted he is & he has no one now."

It would be Jessie who approached their creditors, elicited help from old friends such as Jeremiah Black, and fought with all her ability to hold on to their assets. "I am like a deeply built ship," she had remarked years earlier. "I drive best under a stormy wind." Indeed, the situation would require all the resourcefulness that Jessie could summon, and she turned her attention to the one venue that had been lucrative for her in the past: writing. After the commercial and critical success of *The Story of the Guard*, *New York Ledger* editor Robert Bonner had frequently asked her to write for his weekly newspaper. Not wanting to draw attention to herself, and never having needed the income before, she had always declined. But now she arranged to write a series of reminiscences called "Distinguished Persons I Have Known," for which Bonner contracted to pay her $100 per column.

Whether Jessie recognized that she was embarking on a new career or merely responding to a temporary crisis was not clear, but readers enthusiastically greeted her first articles, on Andrew Jackson, Hans Christian Andersen, Kit Carson, Thomas Starr King, and Martin Van Buren, and these essays marked the beginning of a twenty-year literary occupation during which she would produce dozens of articles for various magazines and newspapers. Jessie wrote feverishly as their bills mounted and they were unable to make their many mortgage payments. "The Tax collector is here," she wrote to Nelly's husband, George Brown, in early 1875, "—he says he can levy on anything moveable, no matter who it belongs to, even if to one of the servants . . . the collector is at the stable now looking at the horses, carriages etc. with a view to moving them into the village, advertising them for six days &, if not redeemed, selling them."

For his part, John worked at attempting to get compensation from the government for the Black Point estate, which they hoped would be enough to pay the mortgage on Pocaho. Jessie oversaw the piecemeal sale of California land parcels, their horses, Charley's boat, the Humboldt book collection, the Manhattan brownstone, and the island in Maine.

Soon it became clear that they could not hold on to Pocaho. "The rooms are large," she told a prospective buyer. "They have held much happiness. The new owners will find few shadows on the walls." They sold it in late 1875 and moved into an unfashionable rental at Seventy-seventh Street and Madison Avenue. "The General has been so tired and hurt by the undeserved griefs of these two hard years that, to spare him, I have to do many things I hardly understand." Soon the art collection and personal belongings were auctioned off as well, and Jessie fought with all her might against mental depression and physical illness.

John had been one of the incorporators of the Texas Pacific, which had taken over the bankrupt Memphis, El Paso, and Pacific, and though it provided only minuscule compensation, it gave him an opportunity to travel to his beloved West. Journeying by train on the railroad that had been completed in 1869, across paths he had forged, he was melancholy as he made his way across the Continental Divide, astonished at the populated areas that had once been wild terrain, the Native Americans who had once inhabited it freely now removed to desolate and unproductive sites. "Some of the brave men, who, along with Frémont, had 'tamed the West' were reduced to riding alongside Indians in theatrical extravaganzas like that of Buffalo Bill Cody," one historian wrote of Frémont's peers who had become caricatures of themselves.

Capturing his unspeakable sorrow, he penned a poem that he sent home to Jessie:

Written on Recrossing the Rocky Mountains in Winter After Many Years

Long years ago I wandered here,
In the midsummer of the year,
Life's summer too.
A score of horsemen here we rode,
The mountain world its glories showed,
All fair to view

These scenes in glowing colors drest
Mirrored the life within my breast,
Its world of hope.
The whispering woods and fragrant breeze

That stirred the grass in verdant seas,
On billowy slope.

And glistening crag in sunlit sky,
Mid snowy clouds piled mountain high,
Were joys to me.
My path was o'er the prairie wide,
Or here on grander mountain side,
To choose all free.

The rose that waved in morning air,
And spread its dewy fragrance there
In careless bloom
Gave to my heart its hue
O'er my glad life its color threw
And sweet perfume

Now changed the scene and changed the eyes
That here once looked on glowing skies
When summer smiled.
These riven trees and windswept plain
Now shew the winter's dread domain
Its fury wild.

The rocks rise black from storm packed snow,
All checked the river's pleasant flow,
Vanished the bloom.
These dreary wastes of frozen plain
Reflect my bosom's life again
Now lonesome gloom.

The buoyant hopes and busy life
Have ended all in hateful strife
And baffled aim.

The world's rude contact killed the rose,
No more its shining radiance shows,
False roads to fame.

But here thick clouds the mountains hide
The dim horizon bleak and wide
No pathway shews.
And rising gusts and darkening sky
Tell of the night that draweth nigh
The brief day's close.

Where still some grand peaks mark the way
Touched by the light of parting day,
And memory's sun,
Backward amid the twilight glow
Some lingering spots yet brightly show
On roads hard won.

Jessie found the poem heartbreakingly poignant, and immediately sent it to *Littell's Living Age*, which published it anonymously. "The General knew nothing of this until I gave him the number with the lines in print," she wrote to Whittier years later, after Whittier had been incorrectly credited with authoring the poem. "He was very pleased," she told Whittier. "But his is the most reserved and shy nature I ever met. Not that nor any other beautiful evidence of his inner life would ever be known but to those of us who have been his inner life."

Sitting every day at a small desk in a dismal apartment, she wrote her finest stories. *Harper's* paid her $1,500 for a three-part series about her childhood in St. Louis, Cherry Grove, and Washington, her first journey to California, and her early experiences during the Gold Rush days. They were insightfully drawn and elegantly written, her style impressively matured from her earlier forays, and they were so warmly received that the magazine bought the copyrights for $100 and published them as a book titled *A Year of American Travel*. Like her previous book, it was an immediate sensation, though it evoked the predictable disdain and dismissal from the couple's many political enemies. Eschewing self-pity, she attended the many social functions to which she was invited, appearing with a dignity and a pride that belied their much-gossiped-about adversity. "She wore her made-over garments with as little self-consciousness as she had worn the tasteful and elegant costumes of earlier days," wrote one of her biographers.

Despite her successes and attending financial compensation, they were forced to sell more belongings. Auctions of the personal effects of the famous Frémonts brought huge crowds—throngs that Jessie welcomed for their money, though she was appalled by the parasitic frenzy. The *New York Times* reported one such sale at which a ravenous mass picked over Jessie's most beloved objects: a portrait of Jessie by the famous artist Giuseppe Fagnani; a marble bust of Benton; a painting of John by Thomas Buchanan Read; their Steinway piano. "When the time came for my Father with his old world ideals of honesty, to give up all his property for his creditors, my Mother, without a word, put in her property, and we children did the same, thousands of acres of the best land in California," Frank Frémont would say, remembering the total ruin.

"But I am only a ghost of the past," Jessie wrote a friend of her resignation to the current circumstances, "and my place now is not to work or help in great things, but to ask for my own and confine myself to 'putting money in my purse.'"

They moved to a series of shabby, progressively smaller, and less expensive apartments in New York City—"we went forth literally like picked chickens," Frank Frémont later wrote—until their luck seemed to turn for the better in 1877 with the inauguration of Rutherford B. Hayes. A longtime admirer of Frémont, Hayes had served under the general in the Western Department and his wife, Lucy, was an avid devotee of Jessie dating back to the 1856 election. Another enthusiast of John's from the Civil War days was Carl Schurz, who had become secretary of the interior, and Schurz had recommended to Hayes that Frémont be offered the governershop of Idaho. Frémont asked instead to be appointed to the territory of Arizona, needing a warmer, dryer climate for Frank, who still suffered from tuberculosis. The salary was a mere $2,600 a year, but it seemed like their deliverance, and Jessie set to work resolutely to lobby old political friends to help in the quest for Senate confirmation. Belatedly calling in the Republican Party's offer of a government appointment in exchange for John's withdrawal from the 1864 election, Jessie boldy interceded with Senator Zachariah Chandler of Michigan, who had been the intermediary between Lincoln and Frémont thirteen years earlier, and a party leader whose actions after the 1876 election did a great deal to help put Hayes in the White House despite Democrat Samuel Tilden's victory in the popular vote.

Chandler graciously upheld his end of the old bargain, and implored colleagues to help get Frémont confirmed. It was an uphill battle, with many old rivals in the Senate rising to oppose him. William Evarts, the secretary of state, lobbied for Frémont's appointment. "General Frémont was an explorer, a statesman, and a soldier. His appointment as Governor of Arizona would draw a hundred thousand men to the territory at once."

After a bitter Senate battle taking several months, where eleven Democrats and two Republicans initially voted against him, Frémont was confirmed, and John, Jessie, Lily, and Frank traveled by rail from New York to San Francisco. Charley had recently married a woman named Sally Anderson and had been appointed commander of the navy's *Pinta*, so stayed behind in the East. Before their departure, John's erstwhile rival and later friend John Sutter gave them a party at the Sturtevant Hotel. Jessie and John were elated at the reception they received along the way, the Pathfinder's name still golden in the West. "It is all good for the General," Jessie wrote to a friend. "He needs a little extra warming to thaw him back. Omaha claims the same privilege of welcome & godspeed and the Pioneer Society in New York and San Francisco ditto."

The owner of Chicago's Palmer House put the family up in his private suite, refusing to accept any payment, and Frémont was invited to address a group of local millionaires. "It would give you thorough pleasure to see how father is brightening and freshening up as we widen the distance between us and New York," the thirty-six-year-old Lily described John's renewal to a friend. "By the time we make Prescott, we think he will be quite himself again." At each train stop dozens, sometimes hundreds greeted them, and banquets were held in Omaha and San Francisco. Well-wishers provided Jessie with bouquets of violets and baskets of wine and whiskey. The train churned through a snowstorm in the Rockies and beneath a full moon in the Great Basin, each mile bringing new life to John. When they reached Sacramento William Gwin, the governor of California and Frémont's old Senate colleague, greeted them, and in San Francisco they were met by an enthusiastic group from the Society of California Pioneers. William Sharon, the owner of the extravagant new Palace Hotel, the operator of the Bank of California, and a magnate of Nevada's Comstock Lode, gave them a suite with four bedrooms, two parlors, and two bathrooms. The commanding general at the Presidio escorted them to their old Black Point property—among the most bittersweet moments in a stirring journey. Of all the uplifting experiences, the most touching was John's emotional reunion with longtime friend and unwavering defender Godey. "Happy as all the adulation made me, my greatest thrill was in watching the meeting between my Chief and his old scout Alexander Godey."

A marching band playing "Hail to the Hero" welcomed them to Los Angeles, which celebrated Frémont for his role in the Cahuenga Capitulation thirty-one years earlier. From Los Angeles they would travel to the end of the rail line at Fort Yuma, in Arizona Territory. Along the way they encountered William Tecumseh Sherman, the arrogant West Pointer with whom John had crossed swords for forty years. Mounted on a large stallion and smoking a cigar, Sherman gave them a hint of their new home, warning them of the dangerous 230-mile desert crossing from Yuma to Prescott. "Going over that road there are places where I shut my eyes and held my breath. You will cry and say your prayers." Sherman then provided them with three horse-drawn army ambulances from Fort Yuma to make the journey more comfortable for Jessie, Lily, and the other female attendants.

For eight days in the hundred-degree heat of Arizona's Indian summer, they traveled through hot blowing sand, occasionally passing a remote ranch or primitive adobe Indian settlement. They camped along the meager streams under star-filled skies, where Jessie fought to overcome her "loathing of crawling things." Jessie, fifty-four, and her sixty-five-year-old husband were exhausted and bedraggled upon reaching Prescott, the capital of Arizona Territory, but were enlivened upon being escorted through the plaza by a parade led by the outgoing governor. Four days later, the local elite of lawyers and mining entrepreneurs gave a dazzling gala dinner dance in their honor.

Nestled below the Sierra Prieta, the tiny town boasted a new theater, the biggest saloon in the West, a two-story schoolhouse, and a general store. Houses were hard to find, and a congenial local lawyer gave them temporary lodging until they were able to rent a six-room log cabin at the exorbitant fee of $90 per month. They hired a Chinese cook, and Jessie and Lily sewed curtains, cleaned the walls with lye, and decorated sparsely with Indian pots and wildflowers. Though she bemoaned the fact that they were four days' journey from a lemon, Jessie was grateful and relieved to be free of the stress of the past several years, and refused to utter any complaints. Even so, extreme poverty marked their lives, a fact underscored by the reality that though they were within easy travel of the wondrous Grand Canyon, which they were all fervent to see, it was financially impossible to make the trek.

After a brief few weeks of illness and exhaustion, John and Jessie recovered, and Frank soon saw a marked improvement in his condition. In
addition to his gubernatorial duties involving Indians and miners, John
dabbled in ventures that he hoped would bring additional personal income. They had arrived at the height of a gold, silver, and copper mining boom, and John partnered with Charles Silent, a Territorial
Supreme Court judge, and began scouting potential mining investments. Soon John diversified his interests into irrigation and railroad
projects as well. Ever the dreamer, John embodied the sentiment expressed by a nineteenth-century author and forty-niner who observed
firsthand the boom-and-bust mentality of the Gold Rush adventurers.
"It is no uncommon thing to see men who have been wealthy on three
or four different occasions and then poor again. 'A fire,' 'an unfortunate
speculation in merchandise,' 'a revulsion in real estate,' 'a crash among
the banks,' 'an unlucky investment in a flume,' these are the phrases used
every day to explain the fact that this or that man of your familiar acquaintance, though once rich, is now poor. When men fail they do not
despair . . . they hope to be rich again."

Frémont's particular passion that he believed would reverse his fortune
was a vision to turn the desert green by diverting the Colorado River
toward California's Salton Sink. John envisaged an agricultural paradise
in the deep Southwest and even proposed a partnership with his close
friend Mexico's president Porfirio Díaz, to acquire rights in Mexico to
irrigate the border land. He had "unqualified faith in the future of Arizona as an agricultural state," his son later wrote. He sought to raise $1
million in capital to build the diversionary canal that would create a
body of water that would "induce cool and tempering winds to blow
over and form clouds to moisten the parched and arid plains," as he described the potential he foresaw.

After the territorial legislature adjourned in early 1879, Frémont and
Silent headed to Washington to find investors for their ventures. Frank,
in desperate need of medical and dental care, accompanied them as far as
San Francisco, leaving Lily and Jessie alone in the remote and raucous
frontier boomtown.

John returned six months later, elated at having recruited several businessmen interested in investing in the mines he and Silent had recommended, and having hired two German-trained mining experts. Among
his investors was Colonel Charles King Rogers, private secretary to Pres-

ident Hayes, and suddenly the Frémonts' personal business interests seemed promising again. They decided that Jessie, who had been spending her time teaching history classes to the youth of Prescott, could best serve the family interests by returning to New York and creating a company to finance their Silver Prince mine.

By November 1879, Jessie was living at the Everett House and working to find investors. By the following spring, John had obtained a leave of absence to join Jessie in New York. He was back in Arizona in October to participate in the legislative session, and when it ended in March 1880 he helped Lily relocate to the more populated settlement of Tucson, then headed East again to promote his numerous speculative enterprises and to obtain weapons for Arizona militias to use in fighting the Apaches.

They had planned to return to Arizona and settle on a ranch near Tucson, with the hopes that twenty-nine-year-old Charley, a navy officer stationed in New York, and twenty-five-year-old Frank, now an army officer at Fort Missoula in Montana, would come and help John run it. But fate intervened again with the July 1881 assassination of President James Garfield, leaving a distinctly unfriendly Chester Arthur at the helm.

Having lost his patronage and Washington support, and under pressure from Arizona critics who thought Frémont had been absent from the territory an excessive amount of time, the explorer tendered his resignation on October 11, 1881. Jessie had settled into a small house on Staten Island, where she continued to write stories and wait for John and Lily to join her. "There is only one piece of news in the world today," Jessie wrote a friend when John arrived, "the General is here. He tells me I am beautiful, but I tell him the truth. He looks young, rested, and as handsome as that day in '41 when I saw him swinging down the avenue in his uniform."

Jessie engaged in a contract to write a series of stories for *Wide Awake*, a trendy magazine for children and young adults whose contributors included Harriet Beecher Stowe and John Greenleaf Whittier, while John traveled frequently to Washington to press their claim for compensation for Black Point. Though none of their mining, railroad, or agricultural speculations—including both the Salton Sea diversion and the irrigation of the Imperial Valley in California—were bearing any fruit, and Jessie's articles brought minimum income, Jessie managed to maintain her eternal optimism, writing to Nelly that she hoped they could soon move to "a pretty flat in town" when their financial situation improved.

Still, as if sensing that the earthly belongings she currently held would be the sum of her physical estate, she drafted an informal will in April 1882, dispensing the paltry total of fifty-eight years of living:

> I wish to make known as clearly and legally as I can, that such personal effects as remain to me after the uprooting of our home I desire to have belong to my only and dear and good daughter Elizabeth Benton Frémont. We two have many ideas connected with these things and they mean much to us. It is my daughter's wish that here brother Frank should have after her the silver tea set and all the table silver. The little coffee pot which I gave to the General when we were young together in Paris, and when our oldest (living) boy was a baby, I would like the General to leave to that son John Charles Frémont to be given through him, after, to "little Jack"—the General's namesake and my little darling grandson.
>
> My diamond-enamelled buttons and pin I wish to go to my three children. The pin to Lily, the buttons, one each to Charley and Frank. And I would like Charley to leave his to my little new namesake now five days old. I intend having attached to each piece on the reverse side a good miniature of myself with some of my hair between.
>
> My seal ring I give to my dear Frank. He has been daughter and son both to his Father and myself during many trying times.
>
> This is only putting into writing what the children and myself have agreed to verbally.

During these leanest of years they made no effort to hide their poverty, remaining dignified and imposing figures to the many reporters, old friends, and political acquaintances who visited them. Their cottage was decorated with the few things left to them—a handful of paintings; some cherished books; the swords John had received from the people of Charleston and St. Louis; the flag from Wind River Peak; campaign banners of 1856. "Their pride permitted not the slightest recognition, by word or gesture, that they had fallen in fortune," wrote one twentieth-century biographer, "or the slightest intimation of regret . . . Their devotion was, as always, beautiful to see. Observers who were much with them have said that they seemed never to need to discuss a question to reach the same conclusion; they intuitively knew each other's wishes and mental processes."

They had managed to see that their sons were educated at the Naval Academy and West Point, and though Lily would never marry, she would be a lifelong companion and dedicated assistant to both of her parents. Compensation for Black Point to which the Frémonts were unquestionably entitled was never forthcoming from the government. By the summer of 1883 they managed finally to move back into the city, to a furnished apartment at 218 West Fifty-ninth Street. Owning no furniture of their own, they were both saddened and relieved to find that among the furnishings in their new abode was a sofa that had once graced Pocaho.

In July, Lizzie Blair visited Jessie, and Jessie welcomed her old and dear friend, who had shunned her for twenty-two years, as if no ill feeling had passed between them. With typical grace, Jessie thanked her profusely for her visit. "It was so good of you to come and see me," Jessie wrote her immediately afterward. ". . . It was such a happy surprise to me that you must not let that tell against the good it did me and thank you again for coming—there is no need to put such feelings in words—not in written words which are so feeble after all. Life narrows and grows chill when one is as transplanted as I have been time after time—it was more to me than you who have 'lived among your own people' can realize, to have the earlier time of unbroken home and friends brought livingly to me."

In a particularly revealing and tender exchange, Jessie reminisced about how Lizzie had suffered with her the death of infant Anne so many years before at Silver Spring. "I never never forget that time and your pitying care for her. I knew it dimly, then—I know it surely now that for the death of a baby girl there should be no sorrow for life is hard on women."

Lizzie, too, reacted in keeping with her character, criticizing Jessie's marriage to John. She had apparently been inspired to visit Jessie upon learning from a mutual friend of Jessie's supreme poverty, fearing that Jessie might actually be in want of food. Blaming the couple's insolvency on John's financial irresponsibility and wandering nature, Lizzie contemptuously reported to a friend: "She belongs to him body & soul & he does with [her] as he pleases as much as he does with his own right hand."

By the end of the year they had moved yet again, to a cheaper furnished house on Staten Island, and while Jessie continued writing her *Wide Awake* stories, John began pressing Congress for a military pension for his many years as an explorer and Civil War general. Jessie traveled with him to Washington to personally visit various congressmen and senators and plead for their support. Harkening back to her tutelage at her father's knee, understanding patronage and partisan politics as well as any man in the capital, she unabashedly called due various political markers. "I called yesterday to make you the General's thanks—and mine—for the kind way in which you have interested yourself in the matter of putting him on the Retired List," she wrote to Senator John Sherman of Ohio. She wrote to Simon Cameron, asking that he intercede on Frémont's behalf with Cameron's son, who had recently been elected to the Senate from Pennsylvania. "Now that we need friends—I write to say that as your son is on the Military Committee of the Senate, and that Committee can by a favorable report insure the passage of the Bill now before it for placing the General on the Retired list—I so need the active good will of your son that I write to ask your influence with him."

Though many friends, associates, and admirers came to their aid, a government pension was stymied.

In December 1884, Jessie and John were interviewed by a researcher for Hubert Howe Bancroft, who was writing his self-described definitive history of California. Bancroft had harbored deep hostility for Frémont dating back to the 1856 presidential election, and eagerly passed his prejudices along to a retinue of young researchers he retained to gather information. A bigoted California Democrat, Bancroft viewed the early progressive Republicans as traitors, and held a special animosity for Frémont and the Californians who had fought in the Mexican-American War. Bancroft, a San Francisco bookseller with the largest collection in the country of western historiography, had initially planned, somewhat grandiosely, to write an encyclopedia. Instead he settled on what would become an equally pretentious thirty-nine-volume history called *The Works of Hubert Howe Bancroft*, though he hired more than a dozen assistants to research and write the tomes for which he would take credit.

To interview John and Jessie, both of whom Bancroft viewed with disdain, if not disgust, he selected an unpleasant, conniving twenty-nine-year-old Harvard scholar named Josiah Royce. Freckle-faced and sadly unattractive, Royce would ultimately be conflicted about his dual allegiance to Bancroft, who was paying him, and the Frémonts, who were unstinting in their cooperation with him. Royce, whose parents had migrated to California in 1849 under the guidance of Frémont's expedition reports, only to find that the golden California dream eluded them, was decidedly ambivalent about the U.S. government's role in the conquest of California and Frémont's role in the Bear Flag Revolt. Royce had seen a government document that Bancroft had convinced him contradicted claims that Frémont was acting under secret orders from President Polk and Secretary of State James Buchanan, and set out to entrap Frémont in a lie that would discredit him once and for all.

Reporting directly to Henry Lebbeus Oak, Bancroft's ghostwriter, Royce described his first meeting on December 9, 1884, with John and Jessie at their modest Staten Island home. "The General is well-preserved, a pleasing old gentleman, quiet, cool, self-possessed, patient, willing to bear with objections of all sorts, but of course not too communicative. Mrs. F. is, I grieve to say, none the better for old age—very enthusiastic, garrulous, naively boastful, grandly elevated above the level of the historical in most that either remembers or tells of the past. Both were very cordial to me, and I owe them quite a debt for their good will and patience."

Determined to prove that Frémont had overstepped his direction and authority because he preferred "personal glory to obedience," Royce would publish several venomous magazine articles about Frémont while also providing Bancroft with the negative portrayal the historian so avidly sought. "Royce's historical detective work was brilliant," wrote one historian, "but his concern with John was curiously obsessive." In any event, Royce's depiction of Frémont, embellished and disseminated through Bancroft's widely read history that glorified Thomas Larkin at the expense of Frémont, would serve as the definitive character study for the next century, and one perpetuated by later historians.

Ever determined to restore John's reputation to the grand hero she believed him to be, Jessie urged him to finally begin work on his memoirs, inspired and emboldened by the recent commercial success of Ulysses S. Grant's autobiography. Grant entered the 1880s penniless, having, like Frémont, lost all of his resources in speculative postwar business ventures. But in the summer of 1885, just as Grant died of throat cancer, his two-volume memoirs brought nearly $500,000 to his impoverished family.

By March 1886 John had received what Jessie called a "most liberal" contract from Belford, Clarke, & Company to publish the two-volume *Memoirs of My Life: A Retrospect of Fifty Years*, which would include a sketch of Thomas Hart Benton written by Jessie. "It will be a most beautiful book," Jessie wrote excitedly to a friend. "Over a hundred illustrations all original—all fine—and with *meaning*, and the publishers mean it to be, they say, '*the* American book of the 19ᵗʰ Century.' Paper, size, type, illustrations—all will be of the best order."

That summer they rented a comfortable house in Washington at 1310 Nineteenth Street near Dupont Circle so that John could cull government documents relating to the many affairs in which he had participated. They settled into a comfortable routine reminiscent of their early days of collaboration and were pleasantly surprised by the warm reception with which Washingtonians greeted them. It was a time of disciplined work, lively social interaction, and enjoyable surroundings, a time of optimism and faith in the future that had eluded them for the past several years. Now sixty-two years old, Jessie was alive with the happiness of writing about her father; thrilled with John's book, which she called a "labor of love"; cheered to be near her children, grandchildren, and other family members; and genuinely hopeful that the book would be their salvation.

In a large library overlooking the grounds of the British legation, Jessie and John worked nearly every day from eight thirty A.M. until five P.M., breaking at noon for lunch and a short rest. Their individual desks sat at either side of a large bay window, and another desk, for Lily, had been placed across the room. "The General dictates and Mrs. Frémont writes down each word of the story as it falls from his lips," wrote a newspaper reporter who visited them during this time. "In the alcove is placed a typewriter, and with it Miss Frémont transforms her mother's manuscript into neat, legible print . . . In the evening the copy is sent out, and in the morning the proof-sheets are received from the printer. Gen. Frémont is now seventy-four years old, but looks scarce sixty. His hair, short beard, and moustache are white, but his . . . eyes are clear and bright as stars, and his complexion has the ruddy, healthy glow of childhood."

The 650-page first volume was published in 1887 and covered only the expeditions and the conquest of California. The more dramatic years, including the court-martial, the rise of the Republican Party, and the Civil War intrigues, were to be published in the second volume. But the high price of the book—from $5.75 to $12.50, depending on the binding—coupled with the tedium of the narrative, which was for the most part an unimaginative rehashing of the previous expedition reports, resulted in a commercial failure.

Any hopes John and Jessie had to remain permanently in Washington were dashed when the publisher canceled the contract for the second volume and they could no longer afford the lease on the Nineteenth Street residence. By June 1887 they moved yet again—this time to a small cottage at Point Pleasant on the New Jersey coast. Jessie turned feverishly back to her *Wide Awake* stories, John resumed his attempts to secure a government pension and continued writing the second volume even though the chances of its publication were negligible. With characteristic bravado, Jessie found joy in the songbirds and wild laurel, writing to friends of the rejuvenating sea air and fresh eggs and produce, and gamely named their modest retreat "The Anchorage." But once again their safe haven would prove a mirage.

Thanksgiving found them at "The Anchorage," John and Lily ill with bronchitis and Jessie finally recovering from a respiratory infection that had kept her bedridden for months. In December, John was seized with a brutal hacking cough, his acute infection now dangerously close to pneumonia. When their family physician told them that John would not live unless he moved immediately to a warm, dry climate, Jessie became frantically determined to find a way to get them all out West.

There was no money for transportation, no realistic prospects for income, and no one from whom Jessie felt she could borrow funds. Yet she seized on an idea, and the very day that the doctor made his grim pronouncement, she traveled to New York to call on an old friend. She had long since abandoned her pride, and now she went forward with determination, visiting Collis P. Huntington, president of the Central and Southern Pacific railroads, and confided her desperation. Famous for his parsimoniousness, Huntington reacted swiftly with atypical generosity. Before she had even finished her tale of woe, he responded: "It must be California. You should have my private car, but it is already lent." He promised to find a solution and told her to go home, not to worry, and said he would visit them that evening.

Embarrassed and humiliated, John made no attempt to hide his anger toward Jessie when she told him of her meeting with Huntington. "Here we were, lovers for forty-seven years, having our first lovers' quarrel," she later recalled. "The General, thin and pale, sat frowning, staring out the window, answering my questions and protests with the exaggerated politeness I had often seen him use so effectively when angry with the boys. I prepared his favorite chicken broth; he barely touched it. The papers came; he didn't feel like listening to the news. I was perfectly miserable, but whenever I looked at his sunken cheeks, I determined to see this thing through unless the General refused to stir, and I thought this quite likely as I waited for Mr. Huntington to come."

When Huntington arrived, he, too, had anticipated Frémont's resistance to the charity, and he presented them with a fait accompli. He came bearing railroad tickets to Los Angeles for John, Jessie, Lily, and a maid named Mary, letters of introduction to various railroad officials that he said would guarantee their privacy and comfort, and a large check to cover their expenses on the journey and to help them get established in California. "His heartiness, his solicitude for his old friend's health quite overcame Mr. Frémont's protests," Jessie described the moment.

"You forget," Huntington told Frémont in a gracious attempt to salvage his friend's pride, "our road goes over your buried campfires and climbs many a grade you jogged over on a mule; I think we rather owe you this."

A day later they were in a Pullman, "outrunning the snow," as Jessie put it. As the train churned into Manassas, Jessie could not bear John's sullen silence any longer, and crossing the site of the famous Civil War battlefield unleashed her emotions. When the conductor announced their location, "the years rolled back to that ordeal of the nation, the time of partings, of unreturning feet, of great aims and great deeds, and in its mighty shadow, personal pain felt rebuked." As if feeling all the same painful sentiments, John finally relented. "The General's set unsmiling face had been a great trial to me, but toward night he beckoned me across to his section, and taking my hand, he said: 'You were right to come. I feel better already.'" It was then that Jessie burst into tears, overwhelmed with sorrow to be leaving their eastern home, overcome with relief that John was improving, swollen with gratitude toward Huntington, and ever hopeful for better days in their beloved Golden State.

They arrived in Los Angeles on a temperate Christmas Eve and settled at the Marlborough Hotel. "The General is 'perfectly well,'" she wrote to a friend in March 1888. "How can one fail to regain health here . . . Open windows, sunshine, orange blossoms, clover knee-deep, that makes an earthly Paradise." By then they were walking three to five miles every day, and seventy-five-year-old John seemed to have fully recovered.

They were greeted warmly wherever they went, in stark contrast to the years of chilly receptions they endured in the East, and each found a contentment that renewed their spirits. The *Los Angeles Times* noted their relocation to California, describing John's "firm, erect military bearing" and calling Jessie "a perfect woman, whose massive coils of snow-white hair are a veritable crown."

Jessie continued writing while John maneuvered, with his friend and former business partner Charles Silent, to capitalize on the current real-estate boom—the population of Los Angeles would burst from eleven thousand to fifty thousand between 1880 and 1890. Silent, with Frémont's help, had made a fortune in the Arizona mines and was now a successful California real-estate developer. Through Silent, John met a group of entrepreneurs who were developing Inglewood, California, and in exchange for Frémont's help in promoting the community, the group gave the couple a residential lot and built them a small house. But true to their luck, the boom went bust, the Inglewood development turned sour, and they moved back to a rented cottage on Oak Street in Los Angeles.

In the fall of 1888, John returned to Washington with high hopes that he could convince Congress to finally compensate them for Black Point, as well as to restore him to the army and provide him with a pension. Three prominent Californians—M. H. Sherman, Charles Lummis, and Jonathan Slauson—were lobbying California congressmen on Frémont's behalf for compensatory legislation for Black Point. Meanwhile, John had outlived most of his enemies, and the current political climate was more forgiving of the famous Pathfinder and his celebrated wife. Despite his travails he remained "hale and serene," according to a soldier who had served under his command and visited him in his old age. "He seemed like one who had never known trouble or disappointment."

Jessie and Lily stayed behind, and Jessie put the finishing touches on her group of stories about the early days at Las Mariposas that would be published as a book the following year. She cultivated an interesting social circle, and developed a particularly close friendship with a young artist named John Gutzon Borglum, whose work she had seen in a frame shop and whom she had commissioned to paint a portrait of John in full military dress. "Frémont always came in on the arm of his wife who seemed the person he wanted to please," a friend of Borglum's recalled. "She brought with her a military coat adorned with gold fringe and epaulets, a garment the great Indian fighter wore with dignity . . . day after day it assumed more life and grandeur." The painting was Borglum's first major success, and signaled a turning point in his life. "It is the most truthful portrait we have had," Jessie told him when the portrait was completed, "and I shall see that others know of your work."

As she had done years earlier with Bret Harte, she nurtured Borglum into a stunning career that culminated with his carving of the presidential heads at Mount Rushmore. She encouraged Borglum to travel to Europe to study painting and sculpture, and wrote letters of recommendation to her many wealthy New York friends urging them to buy paintings from him to pay for his trip. Taken with his western-theme paintings of horses and stagecoaches, Jessie recognized a talent in the self-taught Borglum that she felt would blossom with classical training in France. In addition to his oils, he also modeled in clay and chiseled in stone, and Jessie thought his true calling lay in sculpting.

Jessie sent dozens of art-collecting eastern friends to Borglum's studio, often writing him in advance and advising him about how much to charge for specific paintings, and through her introductions Borglum landed career-launching exhibits in Omaha and New York. He carried letters from Jessie to the editor of the *Omaha Bee*, which assured Borglum of publicity and success in that city, and to Huntington and the young Theodore Roosevelt, who both helped Borglum sell his art in New York.

She forged a close friendship with Caroline Severance, an early abolitionist and leader in the national women's movement, and through her Jessie met many reform-minded women. Severance enlisted Jessie's aid and support in a movement to introduce kindergartens into the public school system, and the two women hosted a steady stream of suffragist speakers and lecturers. All the while, Jessie was prolifically writing her stories, sending long letters to her friends, the envelopes invariably stuffed with dried specimens of her favorite flowers, and eagerly anticipating John's return.

He arrived back in Los Angeles during the summer of 1889, healthy, rested, and sanguine about both Black Point and his pension. By fall he was on his way back to New York and Washington, having been commissioned by *Century* magazine to write an account of the California conquest to rebut a series of vindictive articles that Royce would soon

publish. Apart from missing John and her sons and their families, Jessie
was solidly happy in California. "I have my daughter with me," she
wrote the poet Whittier in November 1889, "my other children and the
dear young grandchildren I have not seen for two years. It is much that
they are well and write me fully and often but your Angel of Patience is
more than ever part of my life. You may remember my telling you I
read it in a newspaper when I was young—only twenty four—and
pasted it in my prayer book of which it has all that time been part in its
teachings."

In April 1890, John sent Jessie a telegram that Congress—"in view of
the services to his country rendered by John C. Frémont now of New
York, as explorer, administrator, and soldier"—had approved a $6,000
annual pension. It was the first time in more than fifteen years that he
had a safe and secure income, and friends described his reaction as positively giddy and childlike. Typically irreverent, Jessie thought the pension "sadly belated" and "small payment on account," considering that
the government had owed them $42,000 plus twenty-seven years of in-
terest for Black Point. Still, she was delighted for John, who she knew
was grateful for the honor and saw it as much-needed vindication for
his years of patriotism and dedication to a country that seemed to always spurn him. That he had been incapable of being a provider for
Jessie had weighed heavily on him, and now he acted as if he had been
set free of a bondage he had been powerless to control. He had
been staying in Washington with the family of his son Charley, who was
away on shore duty, and he wrote to Jessie daily, expressing his profound
happiness and excitement at the thought of returning permanently to
Los Angeles.

Upon receiving confirmation of the pension, he set off for New
York, where he planned to complete the *Century* article and oversee a
business proposition he had entered into with a longtime family friend
and physician, William James Morton. In July, Jessie wrote him that she
wished they "could be together so there would be no need for tele-
grams . . . I like you—and it makes such a happy difference to see
you."

A family friend in Washington had asked John to visit a cemetery in
Brooklyn and place flowers on the grave of her son on his birthday. On
a blistering Tuesday in July, John road a streetcar to the cemetery and
placed a bouquet at the child's headstone. He returned to the Manhattan boardinghouse where he was staying, at 49 West Twenty-fifth Street

and sat down to write Jessie and the boy's mother. That night, the temperatures dropped unseasonably and there were no blankets in the apartment. Fatigued and overheated during the day, he was racked with chills during the night. By morning, the seventy-seven-year-old explorer was gravely ill.

On Wednesday, July 9, John felt dizzy and feverish. Still, he continued working on his article and followed through with meetings he had scheduled with some potential English investors for California real-estate he was representing. On Friday he wrote to Jessie, disappointed at the outcome of his meetings. "I have no confidence in anybody here. My love to home. Frémont." He did not mention that he was bedridden and in severe abdominal pain. By Saturday, his friend and doctor "Sandy" Morton was so alarmed at John's condition that he sent for Charley Frémont, who was then stationed at Ossining, New York.

By the time Charley reached his father's bedside at five P.M. on Saturday evening, July 12, Frémont's pulse was barely perceptible. Charley called for a nurse, and by midnight he seemed to be improving. Early the next morning, Frémont began vomiting, and Dr. Morton diagnosed peritonitis, probably caused by a burst appendix. Charley sat with him as the poison coursed through his body and he lapsed in and out of consciousness. "The three hours previous to the end he was completely out of his head," Charley later recalled, "and he was insensible for the last half hour."

Just before slipping into his final coma, John mentioned going home. "If I keep this free of pain I can go home next week," Charley quoted his father's final words.

"Home?" Dr. Morton asked. "What do you call home?"

Smiling his last smile, and with his eyes closed, he answered: "California, of course."

"And with the name which had been so long his guiding star, he spoke no more," Jessie would later write of John's final moments.

On Monday, July 14, 1890, Jessie received a letter from John, speaking of "living out our years together in a content most absolute." Within minutes of reading that letter, she received a telegram from Charley: "Father is seriously ill." Upon receipt of that, Lily rushed to the telegraph office to see if any additional information had arrived. By then the next dispatch had already been sent with a courier to the Oak Street house. "Father is dead. Charley."

Lily, in tears, returned home as fast as she could, hoping to be the one to break the news to her mother. But the telegraph had already been delivered. "Like a bolt from a clear sky the blow fell. It seemed to fairly shrivel up my arm. It is the last telegram I ever opened," Jessie later wrote.

On July 13, shortly after his father had died, Charley wrote a letter to his sister Lily. "My dear sister: It is impossible for me to write what I feel, and I can't write mother at all . . . The end came painlessly. It was blessedly quick and easy, and as I looked at him lying there so still and peaceful, I questioned whether I was not heartless, for I could find no sorrow or pity for him at all, but a feeling of relief that his life was over . . . Of what the effect is going to be on mother, I don't dare think, and when I do think, I doubt whether the cruelest result would not be the kindest. They lived in each other; so I don't think there is any life for the one left."

Jessie was so catatonic at hearing the news that Lily summoned a doctor, fearing paralysis. When she finally came out of her trance several hours later, Jessie became absorbed with one thought: that John should carry with him the miniature portrait of her he had carried since she had presented it to him in 1845. She wired Charley and asked that he place her telegram and the miniature in John's hand, where she would have put them if she were with him.

"Your message and your picture I put into his hand as it lies with the arm partially crossed over his breast," Charley wrote his mother on July 17. "I folded up the telegram and wrapped it and the miniature in the ribbons which were tied to it. And I want to tell you that he looks peaceful and so quiet . . . I did everything in the last arrangements as I thought you would have wished . . . Only the simple service in the church, and a few of us took him to where I had to leave him, the Trinity Receiving Vault at One Hundred Thirty-fifth Street. I gave him your message there, the last thing."

It was the end of one of the most classic American love stories, which had begun in 1840 and lasted fifty years.

Charley, honoring his mother's wishes, had insisted on a simple ceremony, "for he was not a man of parade and display." Charley had declined "grand army and society offers," thinking them a mockery of his father's life. Charley deposited his father's body in a Manhattan funeral home vault, where it could remain until Jessie decided on a permanent burial site in California. But in a final irony and heartbreak, there would not be enough money to bring his body "home."

Every day for more than a week, Jessie continued to receive letters John had written, many during the period when he was ill, though he made no reference to his illness. The abiding sentiment was happiness for his pension, love for his family, and a keen desire to return to Los Angeles—"the daily arrival of his letters, filled with his plans and hopes for the future and for our lives in Los Angeles," as Lily later described them.

The social reformer and renowned writer Rebecca Harding Davis predicted that Frémont would go down in history as one of the nation's greatest abolitionists. "When the true story of Emancipation shall be written, the colored people of this country will understand, as they never yet have done, what they owe to John C. Frémont and his wife."

When he was finally buried at Piermont-on-the-Hudson, overlooking the Tappan Zee near their beloved home of Pocaho, he was placed in a plain pine box and wearing an ordinary black suit, not his uniform, as he had requested.

When John died, his pension ceased. He had received only two months' pay since his restoration. The government had made no provision for a widow's pension, and now Jessie was returned to the most straitened of circumstances, forced to borrow money from Los Angeles friends.

Jessie fell into a despondency that lasted several months. Though their fifty-year marriage had been marked by many years of painful separation, their partnership an unconventional romance that friends, family, and acquaintances found difficult to penetrate but that made her wildly happy, the final parting seemed more than she could bear. "She was deeply in love with my father," Frank later wrote ". . . Always, before self, he came in all things."

Her children feared that she would die of grief. "It was," she wrote to her friend Borglum, "work to keep alive." Still, in characteristic fashion, Jessie embraced life once again, and set resolutely to the task of completing John's unfinished writings and overseeing his legacy. In the short term her hours and days—and nights, for Lily watched worriedly as Jessie refused to go to bed—were filled with the comforting rote and necessary details of ending a life. She clipped the many obituaries from newspapers throughout the nation and the world, receiving letters and articles from admirers as far away as China and Australia, organizing them as if the most mundane of tasks brought her solace. She sat at her desk for hours on end, responding to the outpouring of condolences, writing personal, heartfelt letters to all who sent their sympathy.

She endured numerous interviews and requests from the press. "Our friend Mr. Greeley said near the end of his career: 'Fame is a vapor; popularity, an accident. Character is the only thing that endures,'" she told one interviewer. "I know better than most the questionable value of contemporary judgments. Time will vindicate General Frémont. I am past sixty-six years old. I may not live to see his enemies sitting in homage at the unveiling of his statue, as in the case of my father, but John C. Frémont's name can never be erased from the most colorful chapters of American history. From the ashes of his campfires, cities have sprung."

Word of Jessie's poverty leaked to the national press, with San Francisco and New York newspapers reporting on her condition. "If Mrs. Frémont is without a dollar in the house it is a consuming reproach to the thousands of wealthy people of California," railed the *New York Times*. "The first intimation of such a condition should have brought prompt and generous relief from the many men who have become many time millionaires, while the founder of California died in abject poverty." Reacting to a California reporter, Charley was offended at the call for charity. "Neither my brother nor myself would permit her to suffer in that way, though I am free to confess she is poor."

On September 24, Congress, in response to the national press attention, passed a special bill granting Jessie an annual widow's pension of $2,000. At about the same time, Caroline Severance and a group of wealthy women—"aware of their good fortune in having Jessie Frémont among them"—raised enough money to build Jessie a two-story redwood house at the corner of Hoover and Twenty-eighth streets in Los Angeles.

Meanwhile, a movement arose to remove John's body from the New York vault and bring it to California for burial at Lone Mountain, overlooking Golden Gate. The plan "has taken hold of Mother's heart & its accomplishment would bring her sustaining strength," Lily wrote. ". . . We want Father in this state." The California legislature took up the matter, but when the issue became mired in controversy, in keeping with Frémont's life, Jessie indignantly settled on the gravesite at Rockland Cemetery near Pocaho—deciding it too undignified to have John subjected to further humiliation.

Jessie managed to complete John's article for *Century* magazine, called "The Conquest of California," and that year, too, her *Far West Sketches* were published. By October she was forcing herself to take the long walks she and John had always enjoyed, and would spend an hour or two every day aimlessly traveling the city by cable car. "[But] there are unexplored depths in us that only solitude of heart can find—a weary exploration but leading nearer to Divine strength."

By early 1891, the architect Sumner Hunt was overseeing the construction of her new home in accordance with her wishes that it be modern and simple, without any flourish or grandeur. In July, she and Lily moved into the pleasant four-bedroom house, situated in a large grove of orange trees. She decorated it with books, the few paintings she still possessed, and Indian baskets and weavings from their early California life. There she continued her writing; promoted other writers, such as Charles Lummis; relentlessly lobbied Congress for compensation for Black Point; entertained a retinue of authors and political activists; received a steady stream of visitors, including such dignitaries as President William McKinley, Secretary of State John Hay, and Susan B. Anthony; and corresponded with her many famous friends.

She had become a diminutive and elegantly delicate old woman, her face deeply lined but her eyes still sparkling. "Sunday is my seventy-second birthday," she wrote to Borglum in May 1896, "and it is not reasonable to be so thoroughly—unconsciously, well as I am, but it is so." The only remaining vestiges of her long and illustrious life were the three portraits she tenaciously held on to through the decades of poverty. They hung next to each other. One was of the handsome and powerful senator Thomas Hart Benton, another of an elderly, distinguished, and proud John C. Frémont. The third was a painting of herself—Jessie Ann Benton Frémont—a thirty-year-old beauty cloaked in white gauze and a pale blue scarf.

In June 1900 she fell and broke her hip, and was confined to bed and a wheelchair. Lily and a hired nurse took care of her, and Jessie used her enforced invalidism to turn inward. She began to write her memoirs. "I only hope that the youth of this country will learn to evaluate the past in the light of our heroes' dreams as well as their achievements," Jessie wrote near the end of her life, "and this for their own sakes, since by the largeness of our dreams do we truly live." Her friend Charles Lummis sought a publisher for her, but by 1901 her energy was waning and she set her work aside. "If Jessie Frémont had been born in '58 instead of '24," Lummis wrote, "she would be an Agnes Repplier with the bark on."

By autumn of 1902, the light had gone from her eyes. Visitors would find her wrapped in a white shawl, sitting outside in the sun among her violets and orange trees. When her health began a downward spiral she graciously accepted her fate, withdrawing to bed to patiently await death. "I always sleep well," she told a visitor during her final days. "For no matter where my thoughts sail by day, they sail safely home to the same harbor every night." All she asked of her caretakers was that her favorite photograph of John be placed within reach, "for my eyes to rest upon last."

On Christmas night 1902, she slipped into unconsciousness, and at seven P.M. on December 27, she drew her last breath. She was seventy-eight years old.

A violet-covered gray casket held her during a funeral service at Christ Episcopal Church, on the corner of Pico and Flower streets. Hundreds of mourners thronged the tiny church, as hundreds more lined the street outside. Charley and Frank were both stationed in the Philippines and could not attend, but Charley's son, John Charles, a midshipman on the *New York*, docked off the coast of Santa Barbara, represented his father and uncle as a pallbearer. When the organist played Chopin's "Funeral March," a distraught Lily leaned heavily on her nephew's arm. Jessie's sixty-year-old daughter had devoted her entire life to caring for her parents, and now she was bereft at her loss.

When the service ended, Jessie's body was taken to Rosedale Cemetery where, as was her wish, her body was cremated—the ashes of her favorite flowers mingling with her own. Seventy years earlier, as an eight-year-old child, she had said to her father: "When I die, don't bury me in a box. Lay me in a bed of violets, for I want the flowers to grow up through my bones." She was then transported to Rockland Cemetery at Piermont-on-the-Hudson, where she, with John, would overlook Pocaho.

A thousand miles away, in St. Louis's Lafayette Park, a bronze sculpture of Benton faced west toward Jessie and the Pacific. Inscribed on the pedestal were the words that had so compellingly drawn and shaped the lives so grandly and so tragically of all three of them:

There is the East
There is the road to India

AFTERWORD

Historiography has depicted John as a glory-seeking fraud and Jessie as a manipulative and overly ambitious shrew. In fact, both were complicated figures far ahead of their time. Political progressives are often marginalized, but even that reality fails to explain why so much energy has been invested—over more than a century—in discrediting his accomplishments and belittling her contribution to society.

There have been numerous biographies written, either ardently iconographic or viciously negative. Still, John has remained an enigma and Jessie dismissed as hysterical and overbearing. Not since George and Elizabeth Custer—and evocative of Bill and Hillary Clinton—has an American political couple so fascinated and baffled the public.

John has routinely been denigrated as an incompetent, a philanderer, and a scoundrel—the caricatured whipping boy of historians. The myths surrounding the Frémonts during the nineteenth and twentieth centuries that have been perpetuated are focused on the following: that John did not explore any territory that had been uncharted; that he was a bungler who owed his entire career to his powerful father-in-law; that Jessie was the true author of all of John's expedition reports; that John was driven by a pathological insecurity spawned by his illegitimate birth, which manifested in an egomaniacal striving for fame; that John was a womanizer; that Jessie was a hysterical female obsessed with promoting her husband's image.

I began my research of this remarkable couple with those stereotypes ingrained, and one by one I found a surprising lack of evidence for each of them, which begs the question: Why do the caricatures persist?

John the explorer: By 1833 he had been at the top of his class at a select Charleston academy, was considered brilliant by his instructors, and
had received a coveted assignment to teach navigational mathematics to
U.S. Navy midshipmen. He had "devoured" the classics, learned several
languages, and at twenty years old had come to the attention of the
French savant Joseph Nicolas Nicollet. By 1837, at twenty-four, Frémont had been personally selected by Secretary of War Joel Poinsett to
participate in a reconnaissance survey for the U.S. Army's Bureau of
Topographical Engineers, and at twenty-five he became a a second lieutenant in that elite corps of thirty-six officers. By the time he met Senator Thomas Hart Benton, and Jessie, John had already distinguished
himself as one of the brightest stars in America's rarefied world of exploration, capable of making the most sophisticated astronomical, botanical, and geographical observations. The favorable match with Benton's
daughter accelerated a career that was already destined for success, if not
greatness.

Indeed, he traveled over many trails that had been traversed before by
Native Americans, and his indomitable guide Kit Carson undeniably led
him into regions that other traders and trappers had explored. But John
was the first to bring scientific methodology to a region that most earlier
explorers had dismissed as uninhabitable, and was the first to map these
routes with a precision and conscientiousness previously unknown in
American exploration. "There is no chance that he was part charlatan,"
Richard H. Dillon concluded in 1985, ". . . he could not have fooled
the mountain men."

The expedition reports: Jessie and John had a true peer marriage—
unusual for the twenty-first century and unthinkable for the
nineteenth—and while Jessie doubtlessly contributed editorial and literary insight, as any educated and engaged spouse would do, a careful reading of their individual writings reveals a distinct difference in style and
tone. John's expedition reports and later memoirs—laden with scientific
data and often dense narrative—bear no resemblance whatsoever to
Jessie's fluid and dramatic voice.

John the glory-seeking, ambitious egomaniac: The evidence overwhelmingly indicates a painfully shy scientist, romantic by nature, introverted to the point of reclusiveness, sensitive to the point of melancholia,
trusting to the point of naïveté.

John the womanizer: Any fifty-year marriage, in any century, is destined to be challenged—especially one as unconventional, autonomous,

and marked by long separations amid celebrity social circles as theirs. John, like many other husbands, may have "strayed" during the marriage, just as Jessie, like many wives, may have engaged in a romantic entanglement with one or more of her many male admirers. But all of that is conjecture, for no convincing substantiation exists that either Jessie or John was unfaithful to the other. What the evidence *overwhelmingly* indicates is that regardless of the nuances of their marriage—their fidelity or lack of it—they were devoted to each other for fifty years; their devotion was based on mutual love and admiration, not weakness or dependency or sympathy; and their connection, a love affair envied and awed, was often threatening to observers living marital lives of quiet desperation and/or inequality.

Jessie, the hysterical "unsexed" woman promoting John as her vessel to power: Jessie was, unquestionably, a political animal. She was as tutored to be president as any man. "Being so fathered and husbanded, should I not be stronger than my sex?" she paraphrased Portia from Shakespeare's *Julius Caesar*. Yet as clever and ambitious, brilliant and idealistic as she was, her life and fortune were constrained, or dictated, by the Victorian era in which she lived. Viewed historically as the wife of a gifted adventurer and daughter of a shrewd politician, she was in fact an indomitable political force in her own right. Evolving from the role of privileged senator's daughter, to wife and mother, she eventually elevated herself into the position of military and political strategist and national bestselling author. These accomplishments were attained not *through* John as her surrogate, but *with* John as her partner—indeed, as an *equal* partner, which made them all the more unusual and even easier targets for their critics.

A witness and participant in the defining moments of American expansionism—from the exploration of the West to the Mexican War to the Gold Rush to the birth of the Republican Party to the Western Department of the Union Army, where she was called "General Jessie"— she was confidante and adviser to the inner circle of the highest political powers in the land. All the while she struggled to operate within the bounds of acceptable female behavior. "She could not trek across the wilderness with Indian scouts and Kit Carson, run for President, or command a Civil War department," wrote a twentieth-century scholar, but she "created opportunities for herself by acting as her husband's strategist and, later, as the chronicler of their history." In fact, she could not even vote.

Still, though hiding in plain sight, as it were, she has been grossly misunderstood and chauvinistically demeaned, her motives distrusted, her assertiveness ridiculed, and her candor called into question.

His is a poignant story of ostracism arising from a suspect background as the bastard son of a French Royalist émigré and a runaway Southern belle, the pall of "outcast" haunting him throughout his long and tumultuous career. In what would become a tireless pattern of glory and defeat, his worst crime, as Benton said in 1848, was daring to distinguish himself without graduating from West Point.

Casualties of one of the dirtiest smear campaigns in American politics, they were slandered and nearly destroyed for their progressive beliefs and broad-minded lifestyle. Their story cannot be separated from the anti-slavery movement—the forces at work in the singularly divisive and wrenching issue of a nation—and the Frémonts' radical, to many unthinkable, view that America should be a social and economic democracy in which African Americans enjoyed civil rights.

It is the story of a woman caught in the crossfire of men history has designated as "great," men whose competition and vanity, ambition and pride restricted her as she tried to influence the major events of her time. "For man is man and master of his fate," Jessie wistfully quoted Tennyson. "That is poetry," she added. "When one is not man but woman, you follow in the wake of both man and fate, and the prose of life proves one does not so easily be 'master' of fate."

At a moment when the nation was defining itself for the next century and a half, they shared a quixotic political and ideological vision of what America should be. Through all the disappointment and failure, some of their own making, some at the hands of fate, they remained steadfast in their commitment to one another and to their country.

ACKNOWLEDGMENTS

This book would not exist were it not for the early and unwavering dedication of my publisher, Karen Rinaldi at Bloomsbury USA, who recognized from the start that Jessie and John Frémont were not mere footnotes to history—where they had been relegated for more than a hundred years—but were the *embodiment* of American history during its most vital moments. Karen Rinaldi; Gloria Loomis, my incomparable agent and dearest friend; and Kathy Belden, my brilliant and energetic editor, came together in a perfect storm to shepherd this dream toward fruition. These three women not only grasped the significance of the story but also shared my passion for uncovering a history that had been intentionally obscured and distorted for reasons that go to the heart of the American experience.

I owe a seminal debt of gratitude to the John Simon Guggenheim Memorial Foundation, which honored me with a generous fellowship at a most crucial moment. I have never been so humbled and grateful as I was to be included in the ranks of this most esteemed community. That the foundation recognized an independent woman scholar, dealing with western Americana, is particularly gratifying.

Mark Adams at the New Mexico State Library made it possible for me to conduct a large part of my research from my home in Santa Fe. He graciously provided me unique access to the Interlibrary Loan System, resolutely tracked down rare and remote sources, and made it feasible for me to spend as much time as possible with my three teenage sons at a pivotal moment in their—our—lives.

Professor Michael Green, whose knowledge about the birth of the

Republican Party through Reconstruction is singular in its depth and insight, generously gave of his time and expertise in reading and editing the manuscript. Once again, Mike has worked his magic and saved me from myself.

Page Stegner, Paul Hutton, Virginia Scharff, and Dan Flores were most helpful to me as scholars and friends, and I don't want them to fall away exhausted, for I will be picking their brains again in the future.

I am continually thankful for the scholarship that has come before, without which this story would have been even more elusive than I found it. Pamela Herr's meticulous and poignant 1987 biography of Jessie Frémont, along with the collection of Jessie's letters edited by Herr and Mary Lee Spence, are remarkable bodies of work.

Anyone writing about John C. Frémont is standing on the shoulders of many historians and biographers with widely varying conclusions and analyses of his actions and character. I drew from the work of Tom Chaffin, H. W. Brands, Allan Nevins, Ferol Egan, Andrew Rolle, and Frederick S. Dellenbaugh, and found the papers of novelist Irving Stone—author of the 1944 *Immortal Wife*—to be particularly rich with historical research and detail. While I do not share many of their conclusions, I am grateful for their scholarship.

Many archivists and librarians throughout the country were generous with their time and assistance, particularly at the Library of Congress, the Bancroft Library, the New York Public Library, the Denver Public Library, the New-York Historical Society, the Nevada State Library, the Society of California Pioneers, and the New Mexico State Library.

Thank you to Forrest Fenn, Sharyn Udall, and Turkey Stremmel for the last minute mad search for the Bierstadt painting.

As always, there are many friends who have sustained me during this long process. I am especially thankful to Shaune Bazner, Nancy Cook, Felice Gonzales, Judy Illes, Dana Merrell, Ellen Reiben, and Gail Sawyer, who by now are accustomed to my disappearing for weeks on end, only to resurface and expect their undivided attention despite my neglect of our friendship. They are always there to cheer me on, to help with my kids and dogs, and to remind me of the true joys of life when the pressures sometimes seem overwhelming. I am bowled over by their loyalty, devotion, and generosity, and hope that I can someday repay them for their unbelievable support. The Martini Girls—Sandy Blakeslee, Lucy Moore, and Marla Painter—keep me laughing, while the Hardy Boys And Girls keep me fit. The original HBAGs—Sandy Blakeslee, Carl

Moore, Dan Flores, and Bill DeBuys—have pushed me to summits I thought insurmountable. Through a glorious spring and summer of 2006, we ascended breathtaking peaks in New Mexico's Sangre de Cristo, Pecos, Jemez, Ortiz, and Cerrillos mountain ranges, where I could only imagine the pristine and awe-inspiring landscape that Frémont encountered in the 1840s.

Thank you to Margaret Storey for teaching me that the truth does indeed set you free, and to John Tull and Lucinda Marker for showing me that one can indeed experience "the peaks of glory and valleys of despair" and come out the other side, as Jessie and John well knew.

Thank you from the utmost reaches of my heart to Bob Samuel—coparent extraordinaire. For keeping the daily air-traffic-control-like status of Ralph's diabetes bearable; for making Grant's trip to the AIDS orphanages in Uganda possible; for occupying Carson with trout fishing, electronic gadgetry, and pyromania; for making the New Mexico Academy for Mathematics and Sciences a reality for all of them; for our stunning family spring in Europe; and, especially, for navigating the uncharted wilderness of the college application process.

Once again, I owe everything to my remarkable parents, Ralph and Sara Denton, and my three staggeringly patient, loving, independent, self-sacrificing, and humorous sons. Ralph, Grant, and Carson have each vowed never to become writers. They are too young to realize that this book could not have been written without their contributions.

July 2006
Santa Fe, New Mexico

NOTES

ABBREVIATIONS:

JBF	Jessie Benton Frémont
JCF	John C. Frémont
THB	Thomas Hart Benton
EBL	Elizabeth Blair Lee
FPB	Francis Preston Blair Sr.
TSK	Thomas Starr King
NHB	Nelly Haskell Brown
JCF Jr.	John Charles Frémont Jr.
EBF	Elizabeth Benton Frémont, "Lily"
FPF	Francis Preston Frémont
Great Events	An unpublished memoir of JBF, Bancroft Library
JBF Memoirs	An unpublished manuscript, Bancroft Library

The research sources for the lives and times of the Frémonts are among the richest and most extensive in American history, though the primary sources have been little mined. I have drawn heavily on these primary documents, even though other scholars have dismissed them—particularly the Frémonts' memoirs—as self-serving. When the history is seen and written as the participants recorded it, it takes on a freshness and immediacy that no secondary source can give it, allowing the author to bring the characters and the events that they lived through alive in their own words. Such documents are, by nature, subjective. Because it has been my purpose to restore these two highly controversial figures to their rightful place in history, I have sought to give them their voices and allow them to express their often passionate points of view. Victims of one of the most vicious and sophisticated smears of their era, they were naturally defensive, angry, sad, and disappointed. I have placed the Frémonts in their historical context and leave it to the reader to determine their motives and credibility.

Waiting for this book, like the gold discovered at Las Mariposas, was a treasure trove of unassayed sources, including the letters of Jessie Benton Frémont, her numerous published books, and dozens of published magazine articles. Particularly revealing and insightful was the unpublished manuscript called "Great Events in the Life of General John C. Frémont . . . and of Jessie Benton Frémont" in the possession of the University of California's Bancroft Library. Also at the Bancroft Library is an unpublished manuscript I refer to as Jessie's "Memoirs," written in 1901 and 1902. Her literary legacy, in addition to her books and articles, includes a vast collection of correspondence with a varied group of contemporaries, including Horace Greeley, Bret Harte, John Gutzon Borglum, Elizabeth Cady Stanton, Henry Ward Beecher, Francis Preston Blair, Thomas Starr King, Henry Wadsworth Longfellow, John Greenleaf Whittier, Nathaniel Banks, Dorothea Dix, and Rebecca Harding Davis.

John's own *Memoirs* were published in 1887, and were reissued more than one hundred years later, in 2001, by Cooper Square Press in New York. He had begun writing a second volume, but after the first book met commercial failure, he abandonded the project. The narratives of his first two expeditions were published by the U.S. Senate.

In addition to the writings of Jessie and John, their daughter Lily published two books—her "recollections," and a diary of the family's sojourn in Arizona. Thomas Hart Benton's *Thirty Years' View* was also useful.

Unfortunately, there were three major fires during the lives of Jessie and John that destroyed numerous letters and documents—the San Francisco fire of 1851; the 1855 Washington, D.C., fire that destroyed the Benton family home; and the 1881 New York City fire that destroyed what Jessie mockingly called Morrell's "Fire-Proof" warehouse, in which Jessie and John had placed all of their most cherished pictures and papers, including the steel plates and woodblocks of Carvalho's daguerreotypes of the fourth expedition that had been photographed by the famous Civil War photographer Mathew Brady. In addition to those losses, Lily Benton Frémont burned nearly all of her parents' surviving letters out of fear that they would end up in the hands of their enemies. Many more Frémont family papers were lost or destroyed during the natural course of their many moves, as they crossed and recrossed the country throughout the decades.

Still, it is remarkable how many of the Frémonts' papers survived these many calamities. I conducted most of my research at the Bancroft Library, the Library of Congress, the New York Public Library, the National Archives, and the New-York Historical Society, where I found many of the extant Frémont papers.

Pamela Herr and Mary Lee Spence located more than eight hundred of Jessie's letters and selected nearly three hundred to be published in their masterfully annotated *The Letters of Jessie Benton Frémont* (Urbana: University of Illinois Press, 1993). Donald Jackson and Mary Lee Spence edited valuable documents relating to John's expeditions in three volumes (plus two supplements) *in The Expeditions of John C. Frémont* (Urbana: University of Illinois Press, 1970).

There have been several biographies of John, ranging from hero-worshipping to vilifying. Particularly insightful and useful are the works of Allan Nevins, Tom Chaffin, Ferol Egan, Andrew Rolle, and Frederick S. Dellenbaugh.

Pamela Herr's groundbreaking 1987 biography of Jessie is especially valuable. Catherine Coffin Phillips's 1935 biography of Jessie is lovely and revealing, and important because the author had an intimate acquaintanceship with Jessie during the last six years of her life, though frustratingly devoid of notes and supporting documentation.

PROLOGUE

xi "the square root of Tom Benton": Irving Stone Papers, Bancroft Library. Quoted in Stone's *Immortal Wife* (New York: Doubleday, 1944), 221.

xi "a Benton in petticoats": Phillips, xvi.

xi "Miss Jessie": Brands, 64.

xii "Gallic good looks": Chaffin, 23.

xii "girlish beauty, and perfect health": JCF, *Memoirs*, 66.

xii "gave shape and solidity to my own crude ideas": JCF, *Memoirs*, 63.

xiii "very perfect gentle knight": Duffus, 289.

xiii "rose of rare color": JCF, *Memoirs*, 66.

xiii "At last I've met a handsomer man": Phillips, 50.

xiii "I have fallen in love at first sight": Phillips, 51.

ONE: JOHN 1813–1840

1 "About [his] cradle": Nevins, 1.

1 For discussion of Frémont's possible Canadian heritage see Rolle, 2, and "Exploring an Explorer" (Rolle). Rolle asserts that Louis René was born December 18, 1768, which would place him at age forty-two at the time he began his affair with Anne Whiting Pryor. A genealogical pedigree chart produced by the Church of Jesus Christ of Latter-Day Saints identifies Frémont's father as Jean Louis Fremont, born 1768 in "Boucherville, Quebec, Canada," who was married in 1813 to Anne Beverley Whiting in Savannah, Georgia. See FamilySearch.com, Ancestral Files.

2 he apparently joined his brother Francis Fremon. Chaffin, 23.

2 "I will do as I please": Chaffin, 20.

2 "a fit person to give instructions": Rolle, 4.

2 "Richmond people do not care": Wood quoted in Nevins, 6.

3 For the relationship between the Whiting and Washington families, see Bigelow, 12ff. "This Colonel Whiting's father was the brother of Catherine Whiting, who was a grand aunt of George Washington."

3 "thirty negroes": Bigelow, 14.

3 "disagreeable from the vexations": Bigelow Papers, New York Public Library.

3 "the greatest of all calamities": Bigelow, 20.

3 "the negroes contained in lot No. 3": Herr and Spence, 117, n. 2.

4 "disabled, stiff-limbed": Richmond *Dispatch* clipping. Bigelow Papers, New York Public Library.

4 "I was married too young to be sensible": Anne Beverley Whiting Pryor letter to John Lowry, August 28, 1811, attachment to Pryor divorce petition, quoted in Herr and Spence, 117, n. 8.

4 "You may spare yourself the crime" . . . "I shall leave your house": Bigelow Papers, New York Public Library.

4 "I did not run away": Anne Beverley Whiting Pryor letter to John Lowry, August 28, 1811, attachment to Pryor divorce petition, quoted in Herr and Spence, 117, n. 4.

4 "totally alienated her affections": Pryor's divorce petition, published in the *Virginia Patriot*, July 11, 1811.

4 "a thriving hybrid": Winik, 43.

5 "gratify Fremon's wish": Nevins, 7.

5 "We are poor": Anne Pryor to John Lowry, August 28, 1811. Copy in Pryor divorce petition, Virginia State Library.

5 "the dual heritage": Egan, 2.

6 "A child of love": Egan, 2.

6 "The quarrel was an opera bouffe": Nevins, 10.

7 "a woman of most extraordinary grace": John Frémont quoted in an anonymously written campaign pamphlet, *Life of Col. Frémont*. See also Rolle, 6.

8 "Negroes abounded": Nevins, 11.

9 "He lived an inner life": JCF, *Memoirs*, 18.

9 "I could not help loving him": Roberton quoted in Upham, 13.

9 "the very seat of genius": Roberton quoted in Upham, 12.

9 "I entered upon the study of Greek": JCF, *Memoirs*, 19.

9 "as if he learned by mere intuition": Roberton quoted in Upham, 13.

9 "When I contemplated his bold, fearless disposition": Roberton quoted in Upham, 13.

10 "devoured myriad Greek and Latin texts": Chaffin, 23.

10 "They were all unusually handsome": JCF, *Memoirs*, 20.

10 "bit of sunshine . . . days of unreflecting life": JCF, *Memoirs*, 21.

10 "Taking counsel of his heart": Bigelow, 28.

10 "habitual irregularity": *Faculty Journal*, February 5, 1831. Quoted in Nevins, *Frémont*, 16.

10 "To me this came like summer wind": JCF, *Memoirs*, 19.

11 "by its aid I became well acquainted": JCF, *Memoirs*, 21.

11 "who had made themselves": JCF, *Memoirs*, 21.

12 "When General Jackson's course drew the line": JCF, *Memoirs*, 64.

12 "By his aid but not with his approval": JCF, *Memoirs*, 22.

12 "We were only two . . . Circumstances had more than usually endeared us to each other": JCF, *Memoirs*, 21–22.

13 "our little *ruse de guerre*" . . . "nobody hurt and nobody wiser": JCF, *Memoirs*, 23.

13 "All day long I was at my books": JCF, *Memoirs*, 23.

13 "one of the cruelest acts": Nevins, 27.

13 "For the good of the bordering States": JCF, *Memoirs*, 24.

13 "empire of liberty": Wilentz, 136.

13 "But the Cherokees": JCF, *Memoirs*, 24.

14 "he envisioned it as a conduit": Chaffin, 31.

14 "here I found the path": JCF, *Memoirs*, 24.

14 "Through many of the years to come . . . As it sometimes chanced": JCF, *Memoirs*, 24–25.

14 "Handsome as Lord Byron": Rolle, 9.

15 "flattened lonesomeness": JCF, *Memoirs*, 30.

15 "no attractive spot": JCF, *Memoirs*, 30.

15 "Shut in to narrow limits": JCF, *Memoirs*, 30.

15 "Parisian intellectual": Egan, 17.

15 "the Connecticut Marco Polo": Scherer, 7.

16 "blocked and forced to retrograde": Flores, *Southern Counterpart*, xi.

16 "an international incident": Flores, *Southern Counterpart*, 9.

16 "its last heroic acts": Flores, *Southern Counterpart,* xiv.

16 "both competing imperial powers": Flores, *Southern Counterpart,* xi.

16 "Their instructions from the President were detailed": Billington and Ridge, 85.

17 "In regard to this extensive section": Major Stephen Long quoted in Billington and Ridge, 92.

17 "absorbing the mounting tension": Flores, *The Natural West*, 80.

17 "in the circles": JCF, *Memoirs*, 31.

17 "personally feared for the ultimate destruction": Rolle, 15.

18 "who was ending his honorable days": JBF, "The Origin of the Frémont Explorations."

19 "filled with Irish wolfhounds": Nevins, 34.

19 "he belonged to the men": JCF, *Memoirs*, 33.

19 "former travels by early French explorers": JCF, *Memoirs*, 33.

20 "consideration, compassion, and tact": Egan, 24.

20 "It is necessary to make haste": Nicollet quoted in Chaffin, 53.

20 "Nicollet's passions": Chaffin, 53.

20 "In all the course of our campaign": Nicollet quoted in Chaffin, 53.

20 "with bright fires, where fat venison": JCF, *Memoirs*, 37.

21 "friendly to the United States": Nicollet to Poinsett, December 28, 1838. Nicollet, 227.

21 "considerable knowledge in such fields": Egan, 36.

21 "The experience which you have had": Abert to JCF, March 2, 1839, quoted in Chaffin, 61.

22 "taking its customary advantage" . . . "struggling against the currents": JCF, *Memoirs*, 38.

22 "The village covered some acres of ground": JCF, *Memoirs*, 39.

22 "I promptly replied": JCF, *Memoirs*, 40.

22 "toward the British line and the rising sun": Egan, 29.

23 "The only things visible to me in our flying course": JCF, *Memoirs*, 41.

23 "You wanted geography": Nicollet, *Report*, 45, quoted in Nevins, 40, n. 18.

23 "The fact that the ground": Nicollet, 166.

23 "Mosquitoes had infested the camp": JCF, *Memoirs*, 49.

23 "the wide-spread valley": JCF, *Memoirs*, 52.

23 "He had learned comradeship": Nevins, 45.

24 "I had time enough" . . . "to assist Mr. Nicollet": JCF, *Memoirs*, 54.

24 "Here, as in St. Louis": JCF, *Memoirs*, 55.

25 "bachelor quarters": JCF, *Memoirs*, 57.

25 "opposite in complexion of mind and in manner . . . the one flint and the other steel" . . . "Mr. Nicollet was urbane": JCF, *Memoirs*, 56.

25 "In this arrangement there was some disparity": JCF, *Memoirs*, 57.

25 "incomprehensible even to Mr. Nicollet": JCF, *Memoirs*, 57.

25 "made him master of the situation": JCF, *Memoirs*, 57.

26 "a condition of happy thoughtlessness": JCF, *Memoirs*, 56.

26 "was in demand for his vivacity": Nevins, 51.

26 "the wealth of linen": JCF, *Memoirs*, 55.

27 "It must be exact": JCF, *Memoirs*, 64.

27 "the one man who had foreseen": JBF's "Biographical Sketch of Senator Benton," JCF, *Memoirs*, 10.

27 "greater than that of Tyre and Sidon": THB quoted in JCF, *Memoirs*, 17.

28 "pregnant of results and decisive of my life": JCF, *Memoirs*, 65.

28 "Manifest Destiny": The term would not be coined until 1845 by John L. O'Sullivan, editor and columnist for the *Democratic Review*. O'Sullivan argued that the United States had a divine mandate to expand throughout North America . . . "the right of our manifest destiny to overspread and to possess the whole continent which Providence has given us for the development of the great experiment of liberty and federated self-government entrusted to us." *New York Morning News*, December 27, 1845.

28 "In this interview with Mr. Benton": JCF, *Memoirs*, 65.

Two: Jessie 1824–1840

29 "The plan of reading": Thomas Jefferson to François de Barbe-Marbois, December 5, 1783, quoted in Jenkinson, 47. See also McLaughlin, 188–191.

29 "Out of his element in the new Republic": JBF's "Biographical Sketch of Senator Benton," JCF, *Memoirs*, 2.

29 "man of high character": JCF, *Memoirs*, 3.

30 "the angry agitation": JCF, *Memoirs*, 3.

30 "When I came out": JBF's "Biographical Sketch of Senator Benton," JCF, *Memoirs*, 4.

31 "old-Whig intellectual passion': Chambers, 12.

31 "active sense of justice": JBF's Biographical Sketch of Senator Benton, JCF, *Memoirs*, 5.

31 "I am leaving here now": Chambers, 17.

31 "home to the family seat": Chambers, 17.

32 "You may have this land": THB quoted in Phillips, 5.

32 "a raw, pretentious place": Roosevelt, 24.

32 "Anne is still beautiful": Phillips, 4.

33 "one of the luckiest strokes": Wilentz, 109.

33 "a virtual second Declaration of Independence": Wilentz, 110.

33 "Give the people land": Chambers, 31.

33 "They were above all a people" . . . "They had narrow, bitter prejudices": Roosevelt, 17–18.

34 For Benton's skill as a lawyer, see Schlesinger, 61. "Horace Mann considered him the best constitutional lawyer in the country."

34 "He was the first person": JBF, "Senator Thomas H. Benton," *Independent*, January 29, 1903.

34 "enlightened . . . of his class": Roosevelt, 27.

34 "He could stand a little straighter": Chambers, 34.

35 "Who are we?" Jackson quoted in Wilentz, 171. See n.73, 836.

35 "on the same sad downward road" . . . "Constant fever, the hacking cough" . . . "the occasion to end his life" . . . "If it had been a battle": JBF's "Biographical Sketch of Senator Benton," JCF, *Memoirs*, 6.

35 "open air, night and day": JBF's "Biographical Sketch of Senator Benton," JCF, *Memoirs*, 6.

36 "a savage, unequal, unfair, and base manner": Chambers, 50.

36 "as many versions were reported": Phillips, 10.

36 "the report" . . . "with great formality": Greeley and McElrath, 1.

37 "I see no alternative": THB quoted in Herr, 15.

37 "I am literally in hell here": THB quoted in Chambers, 52.

38 "her dark beauty": Phillips, 22.

38 "not particularly good looking": Phillips, 22.

39 "pleasure and pride": Ellett, 430.

39 "No high-born Virginia maiden": Ellett, 430.

39 "Both parents fell under the spell": Phillips, 22.

40 "a reputation in some quarters": Chambers, 65.

40 "gently but with a firmness": THB quoted in Phillips, 24.

40 "No other woman except my mother": THB quoted in Phillips, 24.

41 "placed forever under the domination": THB quoted in Phillips, 13.

41 "equally opposed to slavery agitation": Roosevelt, 39.

42 "Neither he [Jefferson] nor most": Wilentz, 220.

42 "Papa and Mamma admire you": Phillips, 24.

42 "I cannot alter the color of my hair": Phillips, 24.

42 "one whom I find to be": Phillips, 24.

42 "It is indeed a great day": Phillips, 25.

43 "unfailing gentleness to all women" . . . "both in his mother and his wife": Jessie Benton Frémont's "Biographical Sketch of Senator Benton," JCF, *Memoirs*, 7.

43 "Army man, Westerner": Phillips, 27.

44 "Several Senators saw our situation": Phillips, 28.

44 "Two daughters are a crown": Phillips, 29.

44 "I think I came into my father's life": JBF, *Memoirs*, 5.

45 "go straight to the hidden spot": JBF, *Memoirs*, 3.

45 "his praise acted upon her": Phillips, 32.

46 "the *demos krateo*": Benton, Vol. 1, 47.

46 "the highest and most polished": Chambers, 156.

46 "the feud between the capitalist": George Bancroft quoted in Schlesinger, 163.

46 "bought by my father": JBF, *Souvenirs of My Time*, 57.

47 "any vexatious topic" . . . "high shaded lamp": JBF, "Washington in Past Days," *Wide Awake*, 53.

47 "Banishment, 'putting into Coventry' " . . . "In this way": JBF, "Senator Thomas H. Benton," *Independent*, January 29, 1903.

47 "slandered": JBF, *Souvenirs of My Time*, 90.

47 "Among my earliest memories": JBF, *Souvenirs of My Time*, 88.

48 "did the important part of appointing studies": JBF, "St. Louis," *Wide Awake*," 151.

48 "*First*, to look for every word": Smith, 138.

48 "good old Jeffersonian": Jackson to FPB, August 22, 1836, quoted in Wilentz, 4, n. 4, 799.

48 "When I die, don't bury me in a box": Phillips, 36.

49 "a broad macadamized turnpike": JBF, *Souvenirs of My Time*, 130.

49 "Although St. Louis was not more than a *petite ville*": JBF, "The Talent in the Napkin," *Wide Awake*, 135.

49 "Thither came buckskin-clad voyageurs": Duffus, 290.

49 "kind-faced young officer": JBF, *Souvenirs of My Time*, 136.

49 "The Potomac was a wide and beautifully blue river" . . . "her extensive reading" . . . "She was more English" . . . "It was a pleasure" . . . "She had been trained" . . . "of our near neighbor" . . . "beeswax heads" . . . "what might have been": JBF, "St. Louis," *Wide Awake*," 149ff.

51 "Their thick white caps" . . . "Sallow-faced, tawny-haired": JBF, "The Talent in the Napkin," *Wide Awake*, 135.

51 "go to mass to learn": Phillips, 41.

51 "provincial Paris": Ellet, 435.

52 "put through the ordeal of examination": JBF, "A Virginia Wedding," *Wide Awake*, 30.

52 "The oak floors": JBF, "William Rufus," *Wide Awake*, 161.

52 "double avenue of cherry-trees": JBF, "A Year of American Travel," *Harper's*, December 1877.

52 "little slippers laced to and fro" . . . "Pope and all his works": JBF, "Uncle Primus and Dog Turban," *Wide Awake*, 37.

52 "despised" white people: JBF, "Crazy Sally," *Wide Awake*, 356.

52 "I grew to connect": JBF, "Uncle Primus and Dog Turban," *Wide Awake*, 37.

53 "played battledoor and shuttlecock" . . . "shucklin' songs to Buryin' hymns" . . . "After the charming way" . . . "to be read in a respectful manner": JBF, "William Rufus," *Wide Awake*, 162.

54 "There was a large working force": JBF, "A Virginia Wedding," *Wide Awake*, 30.

54 "You should never waste your time": *Souvenirs of My Time*, 151.

54 "because they were not true": JBF, "William Rufus," *Wide Awake*, 162.

54 "She will not do so when she is older" . . . "no words could so hurt me": JBF, "Crazy Sally," *Wide Awake*, 359.

55 "He belongs in that group of men": Roosevelt, vii.

55 "mild contempt": JBF, *Great Events*, 81.

55 "covered with every good": JBF, *Souvenirs of My Time*, 95.

55 "always made a sort of royal progress": JBF, "The Bodisco Wedding," *Wide Awake*, 7.

56 "two members of the official family" . . . "You will find Eliza" . . . "And Miss Jessie?" . . . "I fear you will find her" . . . "a great misfortune": Phillips, 43.

56 "I won't need other groups of girls": Phillips, 44.

56 "Then I learned": JBF, *Memoirs*, 30. See also Herr, 50.

57 "It was a favorite place": JBF, *Memoirs*, 30.

57 "Naturally we were in sympathy with other idlers": JBF, "The Bodisco Wedding," *Wide Awake*, 7.

57 "more worthy of the honor": Phillips, 45.

57 "we, the commons": JBF, "The Bodisco Wedding," *Wide Awake*, 7.

57 "This decision is most unjust": Phillips, 45.

57 "to study and be his friend": JBF, *Memoirs*, 30. See also Herr, 49.

57 "Fancy the stir": JBF, "The Bodisco Wedding," *Wide Awake*, 7.

58 "first unaided appearance" . . . "I was in grownup finery" . . . "the fairest and tallest": JBF, "The Bodisco Wedding," *Wide Awake*, 10.

58 "could cite with equal facility": Elbert Smith, *Magnificent Missourian*, 77.

59 "chartered companies": *Washington Globe*, November 21, 1835.

59 "Democracy implies a government by the people": *Niles Register*, August 29, 1835.

59 "To whom is all this power granted?": THB quoted in Elbert Smith, *Magnificent Missourian*, 121–122.

59 "Unlike Jefferson's inward-looking": Chaffin, 85.

60 "course of empire": THB quoted in Chaffin, 80.

60 "resolve . . . to carry out" . . . "My father became possessed": JBF, "Biographical Sketch of Senator Benton," JCF, *Memoirs*, 10.

60 "This conduct is a shameless revulsion": JBF quoted in Phillips, 47.

61 "Miss Jessie": Brands, 64.

61 "Mr. Benton had expected to find": JCF, *Memoirs*, 64.

62 "The interview left on me": JCF, *Memoirs*, 65.

62 "From Poinsett, Frémont had acquired an ideology": Chaffin, 87.

THREE: THE PATHFINDER AND HIS WIFE 1840–1844

64 "slender, upright, elastic": JBF, *Souvenirs of My Time*, 37. See also Egan, 38.

64 "I'm so glad": Phillips, 50–51.

64 "in the bloom" . . . "perfect health" . . . "her beauty had come": JCF, *Memoirs*, 66.

65 "a highly superior young man": Phillips, 51.

65 "She has a delicacy": Phillips, 51.

66 "rip-roaring campaigns" . . . "silver spoon": *Columbia Encyclopedia*, 6th ed., 2005.

66 "We all admire Lieutenant Frémont": Phillips, 51.

66 "not only a passionate impulse": Herr, 60.

67 "red letter day": JCF, *Memoirs of My Life*, 68.

67 "It was for my grandmother's special pleasure": JBF, *Souvenirs of My Time*, 37.

67 "frankly stated the case" . . . "detaching him from his duty": JBF, *Memoirs*, 34.

68 "cure the special complaint": JCF, *Memoirs of My Life*, 68.

68 "I truly believe" . . . "I'm not grieving": Phillips, 55.

69 "The violet is": JBF quoted in Phillips, 55.

69 "real Paris dress": JBF, *Souvenirs of My Time*, 69.

70 "It was in a drawing room": JBF to EBL, July 23, 1856. Blair-Lee Papers, Princeton University. See also Herr, 63.

70 "The possibility of an accidental discovery": Herr, 63–64.

70 "Let me go to the Senator" . . . "Come to the house": Phillips, 58.

70 "looking at Frémont": Egan, 47.

70 "Get out of my house" . . . "Whither thou goest": Nevins, 71.

71 "Damn it, sir!" . . . "I am told": MacDowell Family Papers, University of Virginia. See also Herr, 65.

71 "To most Washingtonians": Herr, 70.

71 "It is a sad & distressing business": MacDowell Family Papers, University of Virginia. See also Herr, 65.

72 "Go collect your belongings": Egan, 48.

72 "The thought of my own endless courtship": Phillips, 59.

72 "We three understood": JBF introduction to JCF, *Memoirs*.

72 "Mr. Tyler threw the weight": JCF, *Memoirs*, 71.

73 "His piercing eyes": Herr, 72.

74 "Louisiana, Florida, Texas": JBF, *Souvenirs of My Time*, 171.

74 "I think it would be well for you to name" . . . "If you can do what he [Benton] desires": Chaffin, 99.

75 "The object of the expedition": JCF, *Memoirs*, 71.

75 "the product of the training": Nevins, 80–81.

76 "distance estimates, angles of elevation": Schlaer, 7.

76 "the first boat of the kind": JCF, *Memoirs*, 71.

76 The flag designed and commissioned by Frémont for the first expedition is in the possession of the Southwest Museum in Los Angeles.

77 "literal, indisputably accurate": Schlaer, 3.

77 "unimpeachable veracity": Schlaer, 11.

77 "for the development of mind": JCF, *Memoirs*, 75.

78 "The poor half-orphan": Nevins, 89.

78 "look exactly like his father": Phillips, 63.

78 "gone into the silence" . . . "you are too young": JBF, *Memoirs*, 38.

78 "Be not disturbed": Phillips, 64.

79 "My father gave me early": JBF quoted in Rolle, 29.

79 "She no more had a woman's mind": Charles Moody, "Here Was a Woman." *Out West*, 18 (January 1903): 173.

80 "then bolt to his own room" . . . "so good . . . so kind": JBF, *Memoirs*, 41ff.

81 "The friendship begun": Nevins, 101.

81 "clear steady blue eye": JCF, *Memoirs*, 74.

81 "I had been some time in the mountains": Chaffin, 102.

81 "Since the attention of the country": Dary, 81.

82 "A lofty snow-peak": JCF, *Memoirs*, 139.

82 "growing appetite": Chaffin, 119.

82 "nothing but our arms": JCF, *Memoirs*, 145.

82 "infested by Blackfeet": JCF, *Memoirs*, 142.

82 "the peak appeared so near": JCF, *Memoirs*, 145.

83 "We rolled ourselves up": JCF, *Memoirs*, 148.

83 "Hitherto I had worn" . . . "putting hands and feet" . . . "an immense snow-field": JCF, *Memoirs*, 149.

83 "Here, on the summit" . . . "As soon as I had gratified" . . . "unfurled the national flag": JCF, *Memoirs*, 150.

84 "This is the first hard blow": Phillips, 68.

84 "This flag which I raised": Egan, 118.

84 "Jessie is sitting up": Herr, 78.

84 "a series of maps": JCF, *Memoirs*, 162–163.

84 "I write more easily by dictation": JCF, *Memoirs*, 163.

85 "The horseback life": JBF, *Memoirs,* 41.

85 "amanuensis": JCF, *Memoirs*, 163.

85 "It was a true collaboration": Nevins, 119.

85 "It was both a keenly observed": Herr, 82.

86 "Frémont chasing buffalo": De Voto, 40.

86 "Events justified the wisdom": JBF, "The Origin of the Frémont Explorations," *Century Illustrated Monthly Magazine*, 768.

88 "gentlemen-travelers": Herr, 87.

88 "I shall be led into countries": Jackson and Spence, Vol. 1, 343. (JCF to Kearny, May 8, 1843.)

89 "In true bureaucratic fashion": Lewis, 23.

89 "his long cherished work" . . . "grand plan ripening and expanding from Jefferson's time": JBF, "The Origin of the Frémont Explorations," *Century Illustrated Monthly Magazine*, 766ff.

89 "I . . . had full knowledge of the large scope" . . . "a geographical survey[s]" . . . "Following out my duty" . . . "whither he was directed": JBF, "The Origin of the Frémont Explorations," *Century Illustrated Monthly Magazine*, 768ff.

90 "Now Sir what authority": Jackson and Spence, Vol. 1, 345-346. (Abert to JCF.)

90 "I suspected some obscure intrigue": JBF, "The Origin of the Frémont Explorations," *Century Illustrated Monthly Magazine*, 769.

90 "The report had given immediate fame": JBF, *Memoirs*, 43.

91 "I felt the whole situation": JBF, *Memoirs*, 43–44.

91 "The time to get my horse": Phillips, 78.

91 "It was in the blessed day": JBF, *Memoirs*, 44.

91 "Say nothing of this": JBF quoted in Herr, 90.

91 "Goodbye. I trust and GO." Phillips, 78.

91 "I never knew where the order originated": JCF, *Memoirs*, 168.

92 "She had longed not to be a man": Herr, 6.

92 "He entirely approved of my wrong-doing": JBF, "The Origin of the Frémont Explorations," *Century Illustrated Monthly Magazine*, 769.

92 "It placed a blemish of insubordination": Nevins, 134.

93 "may have been conceived": Lewis, 41.

93 "country beautifully watered": JCF, *Memoirs*, 171.

93 "We could not proceed": JCF, *Memoirs*, 175.

93 "on account of the low state": JCF, *Memoirs*, 178.

94 "Frémont remained far more preoccupied": Chaffin, 163–164.

94 "feeling as much saddened": JCF, *Memoirs*, 238.

95 "This was one of": JBF quoted in Phillips, 80.

96 "The latest plan now": Preuss, 93–94.

96 "We had now entirely left": JCF, *Memoirs*, 322.

96 "All night above": Whittier, "The Pass of the Sierra".

96 "as bleak, empty, and bitter": Nevins, 152.

96 "unusually silent": JCF, *Report, Second Expedition* (Derby ed.), 324.

97 "like Napoleon before the Pyramids": Nevins, 154.

97 "When we arrived at the fort": JCF, *Report, Second Expedition* (Derby ed.), 324.

97 "Life would possibly have flowed": Sabin, 361.

97 "From the moment I open my eyes": JBF to Adelaide Talbot, February 1, 1844. Talbot Papers, Library of Congress.

97 "So through the winter": JBF, *Souvenirs*, 162.

98 "sickness of the heart": JBF quoted in Herr, 96.

98 "She says '[John] Charles": Jackson and Spence, Vol. 1, 356–357.

98 "I was taken into their most friendly sympathy": JBF, *Souvenirs of My Time*, 162.

99 "They were robbers" . . . "quite civil": JCF, *Report*, 370.

99 "The whole idea": JCF, *Report*, 377–378.

99 "insisted he had been waked" . . . "ghost": JBF, *Souvenirs of My Time*, 163.

100 "The only green spot": JBF, *Souvenirs of My Time*, 164–165.

100 "I am alarmed": JCF quoted in Phillips, 83.

100 "Our welcome was a joyous one": JBF quoted in Phillips, 83–84.

101 "a new and painful epoch": JBF, *Memoirs*, 53.

FOUR: BEAR FLAG 1845–1848

102 "Now followed a time of work": JBF, *Memoirs*, 46.

102 "in my case it was a good failing": JCF, *Memoirs*, 412.

102 "His account [was] enough": Howe, Vol. 1, 259–260.

103 "It is true": Preuss, 120.

103 "Only my father had the privilege": JBF, *Memoirs*, 46.

103 "Washington watch-dog": Scherer, 11.

104 "neither sought nor used": Chaffin, 244.

104 "Handsome Frémont and beautiful Jessie": Egan, 273.

104 "Our title to Oregon": Phillips, 92.

105 "twenty times as valuable": JCF, *Memoirs*, 420.

105 "unjust in itself ": Chambers, 275.

105 "He had always held": JCF, *Memoirs*, 420.

105 "ancient chaos" . . . "The President seemed for the moment": JCF, *Memoirs*, 418.

106 "President Polk entered on his office": JCF, *Memoirs*, 420. (Forty years later,

Bancroft would admit that Polk had confided his intention to obtain California. See Wilentz, 577.)

106 "The librarian and translator": memorandum, n.d., written by JBF, Frémont Papers, Bancroft Library.

106 "The President and Mr. Bancroft": JCF, *Memoirs*, 420–421.

106 "was received abusively": Nevins, 201.

107 "in her secret counsels": Scherer, 78.

107 "All informed men knew": Nevins, 201.

107 "As affairs resolved themselves": JCF, *Memoirs*, 423.

107 "Suffice it to say": Chaffin, 273.

108 "The relations between the three countries"..."commanding our Pacific squadron": JCF, *Memoirs*, 423.

108 "lay aside fifty thousand dollars": Rolle, 66–67.

108 "He will strike the Arkansas": Jackson and Spence, Vol. 1, 396. (Abert to JCF, February 12, 1845.)

109 "There," she said: JBF quoted in Phillips, 94.

109 the "beau ideal": Carvalho, 18.

109 the "intangible supplies": Egan, 279.

110 "Captain Frémont has gone upon": Phillips, 94.

110 "It was a wild mixture": Egan, 283.

110 "There is no doubt": Larkin Papers, Bancroft Library.

111 "As we had a squadron": Bancroft quoted in Scherer, 81.

111 "the greatest vigilance": Larkin Papers, Bancroft Library.

111 "ascertain with certainty": Bancroft to Sloat, June 24, 1845, quoted in Chaffin, 273, and Chaffin, n. 517.

112 "It hangs over the head": JBF to JCF, June 18, 1846. Nevins Papers, Columbia University. See also Herr and Spence, 25.

112 "I found it difficult": Phillips, 96.

113 "I carried away with me that day": John L. Stephens quoted in Phillips, 100.

114 "These threw their own light": JCF, *Memoirs*, 489.

114 "In the hands of an enterprising people": Dana, 237.

114 "Cyclopean walls": Scherer, xii.

114 "It is a fundamental mistake": De Voto, 13.

115 "each an agricultural empire": Billington and Ridge, 193.

115 "Why, they asked, should we train lawyers": Billington and Ridge, 194.

115 For population figures in California in 1845, see Chaffin, 271, 517, n. 5.

115 "had a custom of never charging": Bidwell, 30.

115 "The native Californians": JBF, *Great Events*, 38.

115 "California's separation from Mexico": Cleland, 75.

116 "each of whom aspired": Scherer, 85.

116 "The British were watching": Egan, 311.

116 "without saying good-day": Bidwell, 57.

117 "Horse-thief Indians": JCF, *Memoirs*, 445.

117 "Deprived of their regular food": JCF, *Memoirs*, 446.

117 "I would have taken him prisoner": JCF, *Memoirs*, 447.

117 "They were too strong": JCF, *Memoirs*, 451.

118 "we turn our faces homeward" . . . "All our people": JCF, *Memoirs*, 453.

118 "on the same principle that the harbor": Chaffin, 281.

118 "a low bungalow": JCF, *Memoirs*, 453.

119 "the cordial hospitality": JCF, *Memoirs*, 454.

119 "well on his way to being the first": Nevins, 224.

119 "I informed the general and the other officers": JCF, *Memoirs*, 454.

120 "rude and abrupt": JCF, *Memoirs,* 459.

120 "While this was being built": JCF, *Memoirs*, 460.

120 "In the name of our native country": Castro quoted in JCF, *Memoirs*, 456ff.

121 "(*Mansos*) . . . kept excited by drink": JCF, *Memoirs*, 460.

121 "I am making myself as strong" . . . "if we are hemmed in": JCF, *Memoirs*, 463.

121 "It is not for me to point out": Larkin to JCF, March 8, 1846. Jackson and Spence, Vol. 2, 78–79.

121 "Thinking I had remained as long": JCF, *Memoirs*, 460.

121 "Of course I did not dare": JCF to JBF. JCF, *Memoirs*, 460–461.

122 "Captain Frémont received": Larkin dispatches, State Department, April 2, 1846. Quoted in Nevins, 233.

122 "the commander of any American Ship": Larkin to JCF, March 8, 1846. Jackson and Spence, Vol. 2. 78ff.

122 "He has conducted himself": Castro quoted in Nevins, 231.

122 "but marching and counter-marching": Scherer, 94.

122 "the message he felt sure must come": Scherer, 95.

122 "the faint sound of horses' feet": JCF, *Memoirs*, 486.

123 "A quick eye and a good horse": JCF, *Memoirs*, 487.

123 "since any tidings": JCF, *Memoirs*, 488.

123 "The meeting, with its physical background": Nevins, 238.

123 "The interests of our commerce": Letter sent by special messenger Lieutenant. Archibald Gillespie to American consul Thomas O. Larkin, October 17, 1845. Reprinted in Scherer, 326ff.

124 "Now it was officially made known to me": JCF, *Memoirs*, 489.

124 "Through him I now became acquainted": JCF, *Memoirs*, 488–489.

125 "nucleus for frontier warfare": JCF, *Memoirs*, 490.

125 "I saw the way opening clear before me": JCF, *Memoirs*, 490.

125 "With our knives": JCF, *Memoirs*, 492.

125 "I had now kept the promise" . . . "By Heaven, this is rough work" . . . "Heaven don't come in": JCF, *Memoirs*, 495.

125 "courage and discretion": June 11, 1846, *Washington Daily Union*. Quoted in Herr, 137.

126 "Benton was clearly a major architect": Smith, 214.

126 "My dearest husband": JBF to JCF, June 16, 1846. Phillips, 105ff.

127 "While Benton opposed": Dellenbaugh, 451.

128 "I was but a pawn": JCF, *Memoirs*, 536.

128 "Frémont was never to drink the cup": Nevins, 305.

129 "rough, leather-jacketed frontiersmen": Rolle, 78.

129 "Frémont was willing": Gillis and Magliari, 102.

129 "Frémont was playing a waiting game": Nevins, 265.

130 "We tried to find an enemy": Bidwell, "Frémont in the Conquest of California," 523.

130 "Frémont had so played his hand": Nevins, 280.

130 "gathering recruits and seizing towns": Chaffin, 344.

131 "His conciliatory course": Bigelow, 145.

131 "The Young Eagle of the West": Sherwood, xi.

131 "like a Greek hero": Egan, 405.

131 "The territory of California is again tranquil": Stockton to Bancroft, January 15, 1847. JCF, *Memoirs*, 754.

131 "But what is the President doing" . . . "the disputants will themselves settle the matter": Phillips, 112.

133 "Governor and Commander-in-Chief ": Phillips, 114.

133 "I found Commodore Stockton": JCF to General Kearny, Jan. 17, 1847. Bigelow, 192–193.

134 "When I entered Los Angeles": Phillips, 115.

134 "meet Mr. Polk": Phillips, 115.

135 "Mr. Carson and Mrs. Frémont": Phillips, 115.

135 "Doesn't Colonel Frémont's course" . . . "The misunderstandings may by now be settled": Phillips, 116.

135 "Mrs. Frémont seemed anxious": President Polk quoted in Nevins, 327.

135 "So President Polk got his republic": Scherer, 104.

135 "To antislavery Whigs": Wilentz, 586.

136 "The Mexican War had progressed": JBF, *Great Events*, 50.

136 "My dear husband": JBF quoted in Phillips, 116.

136 "plunge him deeper": Nevins, 316.

137 "a comic-opera quarrel": Nevins, 312.

137 "but for the vagueness" . . . "It was the misfortune": Nevins, 309–310.

137 "the strictest sort": Sherman, 52.

138 "sending for him at inconvenient times" . . . "man who was endeavoring" . . . "confine himself to the business at hand": JBF, *Great Events*, 41.

138 "None of your insolence" . . . "You cannot make an official matter" . . . "I do" . . . "the satisfaction of having": JBF, *Great Events*, 42.

138 "With a view to the adjustment": JBF, *Great Events*, 43.

138 "Naturally Colonel Frémont": JBF, *Great Events*, 47.

139 "a fighter without any mild": Kearny, 305.

139 "in such a manner" . . . "It has become known": Marcy to Kearny, June 11, 1847, quoted in Nevins, 323.

139 "through some combination": Brands, 68.

140 "*Las Pulgas* on the [western shore of San Francisco]:" Hague and Langum, 181.

140 "Now commenced the journey": JBF, *Great Events*, 49.

140 "as a prisoner and a criminal": Bigelow, 315.

141 "Lieutenant Colonel Frémont, having performed": Court-Martial Proceedings, 115. Quoted in Egan, 431, and 554, n. 51.

142 "an unrestrained life in open air": JCF, *Memoirs*, 602.

142 "She looks thin & is sad": EBL to S.P. Lee, May 24, 1847. Blair-Lee Papers, Princeton University.

142 "convulsed and frantic": THB speech in the Senate, quoted in Nevins, 330.

142 "I went up the river alone" . . . "the rapid trampling" . . . "stern set look of endurance": JBF, *Great Events*, 51.

143 "ten times more popular": *New York Herald*, September 11, 1847.

143 "He had not thought to meet me" . . . "Now we have seen the Colonel safe home" . . . "true companions": JBF, *Great Events*, 51–52.

143 "after a complimentary address" . . . "political course": JBF, *Great Events*, 53.

143 "I have a full view": Letter, n.d., from THB to JCF. Wheat, 153.

143 "To Benton . . . the Pathfinder": Smith, 226.

144 "Thus, like Columbus": Bigelow, 214.

144 "far distant witnesses" . . . "It is my intention": JBF, *Great Events*, 57–58.

144 "The news of his returning home" . . . "the still face": JBF, *Great Events*, 55.

145 "All of this was coming": Egan, 440.

145 "I shall be with you to the end": Jackson and Spence, Vol. 2, 404.

145 "You will see the manifest injustice": JBF to President Polk, September 21, 1847. Polk Papers, Library of Congress.

146 "We are going to mutiny" . . . "For a week we lived alone": Phillips, 120–121.

146 "If . . . the War Dept.": THB to JCF, n. d. Wheat, 153.

147 "the most dramatic army trial": Nevins, 333.

147 "This isn't a mourning occasion": Phillips, 121.

147 "He asked me if I would appoint him governor": Jackson and Spence, Vol. 2, 39. See supplement.

147 "Had the case been tried": JBF, *Great Events*, 60.

148 "The case ought never": *New York Herald*, November 19, 1847.

148 "making mouths and grimaces at me" . . . "When General Kearny fixed": Jackson and Spence, Vol. 2, supplement 326–327.

148 "quarreling . . . like an infant school": Herr, 171.

148 "My acts in California": Jackson and Spence, *Expeditions*, 2S:446. See also Chaffin, 381.

149 "Under the circumstances" . . . "I am not satisfied that the facts": Court-martial proceedings, quoted in Egan, 461.

149 "A Dreyfus case to the end": Rolle, 105.

149 "A reprimand would have been proper": Dellenbaugh, 382.

149 "He had not only entered": Benton, *Thirty Years' View*, Vol. 2, 716.

150 "I want justice": Phillips, 125.

150 "I hereby send in my resignation": JBF, *Great Events*, 74.

151 "In turning away so abruptly": JBF, *Great Events*, 75.

152 "From the intolerable injustice": JBF, *Great Events*, 77.

152 "one of the kindest": *New York Herald*, January 19, 1848.

152 "the cursed memoir": JBF, *Memoirs*, 59.

152 "battle with a violent bilious fever": JBF to John Torrey, May 29, 1848. Quoted in Herr and Spence, 37.

152 "All the teachings, the examples": JBF, *Memoirs*, 52.

153 "'the Court-Martial,' a family disease'": THB quoted in EBL to S. P. Lee, August 8, 1848. Blair-Lee Papers, Princeton University. See also Chaffin, 523, n. 4.

153 "never speaks to me": Chambers, 324.

153 "who had known me very well" . . . "Mr. Frémont left it" . . . "I saw only the proud lonely man": JBF, *Great Events*, 77–78.

154 "Promise me on your honor": Phillips, 127.

154 "He went now at his own expense": Bigelow, 357.

154 "It was very pleasant": Nevins, 343–344.

154 "Grief was new to me then": JBF quoted in Herr, 177.

154 "When one has had to meet death" . . . "I sat watching": JBF, *Great Events*, 78.

155 "already browned and growing bare" . . . "my *résumé*": JBF, *A Year of American Travel*, 7.

155 "We were pretty much": JBF, *Souvenirs of My Time*, 189.

155 "though the ashes of the camp fires" . . . "There was nothing left" . . . "I was sorry" . . . "again waked" . . . "just five minutes more" . . . "into the night and the rain" . . . "fine health and inherited vitality" . . . "make his peace before dying": JBF, *Great Events*, 79–80.

156 "There was a little grave between us": JBF *Memoirs*, 59.

FIVE: GOLD 1849–1855

157 "Not only had none of us" . . . "the old journeys" . . . "refreshing" . . . "to the fact": JBF, *A Year of American Travel*, 10.

157 "Overnight the question": Billington and Ridge, 232.

158 "across the greatest": Brands, 48.

158 "The discovery of these vast deposits": Sherman quoted in Brands, 46.

158 "the whole country—the whole world": Billington and Ridge, 232.

158 "The Eldorado of the old Spaniards": Browning, 45.

159 "the Age of Gold": Bancroft, Vol. 6, 119.

159 "Why California?" Chaffin, 405.

159 "to know personally" . . . "as a Senator from Missouri": JBF, *A Year of American Travel*, 6.

160 "each of us . . . considered a victim": JBF, *A Year of American Travel*, 10.

160 "upper class educated" . . . "hysterical indecision": JBF, *Great Events*, 102.

160 "free negress": Phillips, 134.

160 "It seems incredible": JBF, *A Year of American Travel*, 12.

160 "vague ideas": JBF, *Great Events*, 102.

160 "I barely looked at her": JBF, *A Year of American Travel*, 11.

160 "It's like leaving her in her grave": Gardiner, 18ff. JBF, *Great Events*, 102, *New York Herald*, March 15–16, 1849.

160 "I was much in the position": JBF, *A Year of American Travel*, 12.

161 "mobs of Argonauts": Brands, 72.

161 "There comes a dulled edge" . . . "My little girl": JBF, *Great Events*, 102.

161 "stood there, not the dark-haired": JBF, *A Year of American Travel*, 13.

161 "the silent teaching" . . . "gentle state" . . . "Perhaps the sharpest lesson": JBF, *A Year of American Travel*, 15.

162 "Thousands, then tens of thousands": Brands, 74.

162 "So notorious was the Chagres fever": Brands, 77.

162 "naked, shrieking, gesticulating": JBF, *Great Events*, 103.

162 "If it had not been for pure shame": JBF, *A Year of American Travel*, 26.

163 "This was a difference": JBF, *A Year of American Travel*, 27.

163 "fragrant and brilliant": JBF, *A Year of American Travel*, 29.

163 "well worn prayer book": JBF, *Great Events*, 104.

163 "His eyes rolled back in his head" . . . "the officers of the engineering corps" . . . "there were hundreds of people" . . . "a baked monkey": JBF, *A Year of American Travel*, 30–31.

164 "the same trail that had been followed": JBF, *A Year of American Travel*, 32.

164 "The nights were odious": JBF, *A Year of American Travel*, 34.

164 "a blue damask lounge": JBF, *Great Events*, 105.

165 "I became possessed": JBF, *Memoirs*, 82.

165 "Taos, New Mexico, January 27, 1849": JCF letter, reprinted in JBF, *A Year of American Travel*, 42–43. See also JCF account from the *National Intelligencer*, published in the *Daily Union* 4, no. 293 (April 15, 1849).

166 "who had spent": JCF letter, quoted in JBF, *A Year of American Travel*, 42.

166 "In starving times": Reid, Ed. *The Grim Reapers* (Chicago: Henry Regnery, 1969), 214.

166 "We occupied more than half a month" . . . "one of the highest": JCF letter, reprinted in JBF, *A Year of American Travel*, 43.

166 "Having still great confidence" . . . "We pressed up towards the summit" . . . "We were overtaken" . . . "Like many a Christmas" . . . "they made my Christmas amusements" . . . "lay there till he froze to death" . . . "the most miserable objects" . . . "had I remained there" . . . "Manuel—you will remember Manuel" . . . "things were desperate" . . . "When Godey arrives" . . . "When I think of you all": JCF letter, reprinted in JBF, *A Year of American Travel*, 44–54.

169 "Alone, Panama" . . . "He found me where he had left me" . . . "These two, with their contradictory ideas": JBF, *A Year of American Travel*, 55–56.

170 "A full-scale riot": Brands, 91.

170 "This time I was not advised" . . . "on condition that she never" . . . "The gentleman in the next stateroom": JBF, *A Year of American Travel*, 58–60.

171 "The Colonel was in the Angeles" . . . "life seemed very bright" . . . "a bleak and meager" . . . "The June winds were blowing" . . . "There was no fuel" . . . "I was already getting ill": JBF, *A Year of American Travel*, 63–68.

172 "Your wife's inside the house" . . . "each wanting the other" . . . "You have been ill" . . . "You didn't come" . . . "In her innocence": Phillips, 142.

173 "reference to the preceding horrors": Phillips, 144.

173 "Madame, we have come" . . . "Gentlemen, your offer" . . . "I preferred to stay quietly here" . . . "The little camping party" . . . "Its rolled-up curtains": Phillips, 146–147.

174 "excellent claret" . . . "had a large experience" . . . "About nine o'clock": JBF, *A Year of American Travel*, 85.

174 "their genuine hospitality" . . . "a type of this patriarchal": JBF, *Souvenirs of My Time*, 198.

175 "There was a small garrison": JBF, *A Year of American Travel*, 68–69.

175 "I was in Monterey" . . . "right-hand-man": JBF Letter, c. January 15, 1902, Bancroft Library, Box 3, "Telepathy."

176 "It was barely a year": JBF, *A Year of American Travel*, 68–69.

176 "to whom my name represented": JBF, *A Year of American Travel*, 71.

176 "erect and of free firm movement" . . . "of scarlet broadcloth": JBF, *Souvenirs of My Time*, 199.

176 "domesticated Indian girls" . . . a "passion" for household linen . . . "Pictures of church subjects": JBF, *A Year of American Travel*, 71.

177 "Now, commencing a new life": Chaffin, 411.

177 "Up to a certain point": JBF, *A Year of American Travel*, 75.

177 "There were no banks" . . . "We were in the most delightful season": JBF, *A Year of American Travel*, 81–82.

178 "resembling in beauty the grandeur": Rolle, 133.

178 "I have seen in no other man": Taylor, 53.

178 "a mere mining enterprise" . . . "a perfect Pandora's box" . . . "a will-of-the-wisp": Nevins, 394–395.

178 "With slave labor": JBF, *A Year of American Travel*, 93.

179 "With slaves in the mines": JBF, *A Year of American Travel*, 95.

179 "small armies of Argonauts": Brands, 206.

179 "It was widely said": Herr, 207.

180 "The commission sent in such a way": JBF, *A Year of American Travel*, 76.

180 "Mingling together were Missouri farmers": Billington and Ridge, 233–234.

180 "the universal desire of free laborers": *Chicago Domocratic Press*, June 11, 1856.

180 "What it all came down to": Foner, 56.

181 "The government had its special agents": JBF correspondence, Bancroft Library, Box 3.

181 "for no reason would I consent": JBF, *Great Events*, 60.

181 "because of her conscientious feeling": Herr and Spence, 65.

181 "Mr. Frémont has called this the Italy of America": JBF quoted in Phillips, 161–162.

181 "wanted to halt the expansion": Wilentz, 671.

181 "Fine sentiment, Mrs. Frémont" . . . "But why not an aristocracy" . . . "It isn't a pretty sight": JBF quoted in Phillips, 161–162.

182 "was the better man of the two": Elisha O. Crosby quoted in Brands, 290.

182 "star-chamber meetings": Chaffin, 413.

182 "Every one knows the important part": JBF, *A Year of American Travel*, 93.

182 "If you want the real Washington situation": Phillips, 157.

182 "and growing wealthier by the week": Brands, 291.

182 "Mr. Frémont could have been": JBF, *A Year of American Travel*, 98.

182 "I am strongly in favor" . . . "I regard the claim": JCF to Jacob R. Snyder, December 11, 1849. Bigelow, 390.

183 "I couldn't wait": Phillips, 166.

183 "Mr. Frémont came in upon us" . . . "one hundred and forty": JBF, *A Year of American Travel*, 103.

184 "The voting on the Wilmot Proviso": Brands, 292.

184 "no morbid sympathy": Wilentz, 598.

184 "I trust we shall persist": John C. Calhoun quoted in Billington and Ridge, 234.

185 "Mr. Frémont carried me down": JBF, *A Year of American Travel*, 103.

185 "We had planned to stay": JBF, *A Year of American Travel*, 97.

185 "Frémont would have been more than human": Nevins, 390.

186 "Her California experience": Herr, 211.

186 "Having just gone through the experience" . . . "But it is only the Immortals" . . . "We were a sorry-looking lot" . . . "hanging straight": JBF, *A Year of American Travel*, 120–122.

187 "No person living understands": JBF quoted in Phillips, 171.

187 "heavy now": Herr, 217.

187 "He listened with grave deference": Phillips, 171.

188 "The Government of the United States": See Brands, 301, n. 501.

188 "a truce perhaps": Potter, 113–114.

188 "[T]he very idea": Wilentz, 637.

189 "It is passion, passion" . . . "And, finally, Mr. President": *Congressional Globe* 31:1, app. 116–118, 127.

189 "with the North's tendency": Hofstadter, 111.

189 "I have exerted myself ": *Congressional Globe* 31:1, app. 451–455.

190 "I speak today" . . . "stirred up a groundswell": Billington and Ridge, 236.

190 "radically wrong and essentially vicious" . . . "higher law": Billington and Ridge, 235.

190 "scape-goat of all the sins": THB quoted in Herr, 216.

190 "[M]y father, a veteran leader": JBF, *Great Events*, 154.

191 "pragmatic second-rater": Billington and Ridge, 236.

191 "His votes on the question of Slavery": JBF, *Great Events*, 143.

191 "club of gentlemen" . . . "corrupt private motives" . . . "Mr. Foote went out of his way": Rolle, 135–136.

192 "to the miner": Upham, 314.

192 "general policy of Spain" . . . "Indian right of occupation": Upham, 310–311.

192 "wild Indians of the mountains": Upham, 313.

192 "Our occupation is in conflict": Upham, 314.

192 "I must admit": Phillips, 173.

192 "were always brief " . . . "[He] never rose": Bigelow, 418–419.

193 "favorite pupil" . . . "My prayer": Roberton quoted in Upham, 15.

193 "I had five days notice only" . . . "Of course I decided": JBF, *Great Events*, 154.

194 The "Colonel's chief-of-staff ": Phillips, 174.

194 "for the bad": JBF, *Great Events*, 155.

194 "lived in a splendor": Herr, 219.

194 "From France was deliberately shipped": JBF, *Great Events*, 155.

194 an "outspoken free-soiler": Brands, 363.

194 "by sciatica" . . . "Frémont would have liked": Nevins, 396.

195 "Mr. Frémont . . . says": JBF to FPB, August 14, 1851. Blair-Lee Papers, Princeton University. See also Herr and Spence, 46.

195 "He is as strong": Phillips, 175.

196 "revolved around a very young life" . . . "to remove that class" . . . "While you are persecuting" . . . "holy calm" . . . "who did not know where to go" . . . "[T]he shock was too much" . . . "silky white goat" . . . "an admirable substitute" . . . "near Grace Church": JBF, *Great Events*, 156–160.

197 "love of frippery": Herr, 223.

197 "How would you like a trip?" Nevins, 401.

197 "San Francisco to Chagres" . . . "It will be your first vacation" . . . "And yours": Phillips, 178.

197 "Always restless": Nevins, 397.

197 "Frémont happened to have" . . . "the lowest and best": Nevins, 398.

197 "[T]he original archives": Dellenbaugh, 426–427.

198 "I am certainly disposed to rid myself " . . . "not adapted to such business": Spence, "David Hoffman: Frémont's Mariposa Agent in London," 400, n. 23.

198 "When Benton learned": Herr, 224.

198 "I know both my people": JBF to E. B. Lee, April 18, 1856, Blair-Lee Papers, Princeton University.

198 "Now came a year" . . . "It was the luxury": JBF, *Great Events*, 165–166.

199 "Because I was thinned": JBF, "A Queen's Drawing Room." *Wide Awake,* 16.

199 "When I beheld the Queen": Phillips, 183.

199 "I spent one night": JCF to THB, April 13, 1852, Rolle, 145.

200 "not to wear that grief-reminder": Phillips, 186.

200 "This twenty-eight-year-old girl": Phillips, 187.

200 "After the many years of sleeping": JBF, *Great Events*, 173–174.

201 "In France she might have ruled" . . . "in America she merely gave": Ellet, 428.

201 "revived . . . astronomical research": JBF, *Great Events*, 174.

201 "since the two came back" . . . "there were men": JBF, *Great Events*, 178–179.

202 "a quality of madness": Bain, 35.

202 "His expansionist views": Catton and Catton, 90.

203 "The Southern line": JBF, *Great Events*, 179.

203 "gambling, stock-jobbing": Bain, 37.

203 "No one had worked harder": Rolle, 150.

204 "Many lines of explorations": JCF to Messrs. B. Gerhard and Others, Bigelow, 400.

204 "one of the most explicit": Bigelow, 399.

204 "Senator Benton had been the foremost": Nevins, 406.

204 "Arago himself " . . . "I told him what I truly thought" . . . "the waiting, and hoping": JBF, *Great Events*, 179.

205 "We had long since": JBF, *Great Events*, 178.

205 "Not since Napoleon": William H. Goetzmann, *Army Exploration in the American West*, 305.

205 "the most romantically heroic": Schlaer, vii.

206 "Care and sorrow": Nevins, 407.

206 "It was she who remained": Phillips, 191.

206 "I would rather have": JBF to EBL, October 14, 1853, Blair-Lee Papers, Princeton University. See also Herr and Spence, 54.

206 "under charge of Captain Wolf ": Bigelow, 430.

206 "I find a wet saddle': JBF, *Great Events*, 180.

206 "Dr. Ebers has soothed the pain": JBF to EBL, October 14, 1853, Blair-Lee Papers, Princeton University. See also Herr and Spence, 53.

207 "All I could say": JBF, *Great Events*, 180.

207 "In my position as wife": JBF to John Torrey, fall 1853. See Herr and Spence, 56.

207 "No father": Carvalho quoted in Bigelow, 433.

207 "On the opposite side": Schlaer, 93.

207 "the failed objective": Schlaer, 105.

207 "Every time a thin, starving horse": Rolle, 156.

208 "lodge was sacred": Carvalho, 133–134.

208 "No matter how much he was suffering": Nevins, 414–415.

208 "begged us to swear" . . . "If we are to die": Carvalho, 101.

209 "Going up a long mountain": JBF, *Great Events*, 185.

209 "curious sense of vacancy" . . . "And this is Death": JBF, *Great Events*, 180.

209 "who could make the astronomical": JBF, *Great Events*, 185.

209 "the strong heart beat again" . . . "tell how near": JBF, *Great Events*, 180.

209 "indomitable perseverance" . . . "He ever partook": *New York Evening Post*, October 30, 1856.

209 "It was to Frémont's assiduity": Nevins, 417.

209 "Here was no chance work": Carvalho, 129.

209 "became like children": Greeley and McElrath, 28.

210 "Not least in moving Congress": Denton, 90

210 "under the orders, advice": W.W. Drummond to Martha Delony Gunnison, April 27, 1857. Denton, 258, n. 90.

210 "The Mormons saved": Nevins, 418.

210 "the criminal abundance of food": Phillips, 192.

210 "It fairly haunted me" . . . "weight of fear": JBF, *Far West Sketches*, 30–31.

210 "Mrs. Frémont and her family": Nevins, 418.

211 "As girls do" . . . "that whatever": JBF, *Far West Sketches*, 31–33.

211 "Child, you have seen a vision?" . . . "This vision, as he named it": JBF, *Far West Sketches*, 34–35.

211 "When my father returned": Bashford, 357.

211 "It doesn't seem strange to me": Phillips, 193.

212 "Benton seemed aloof ': Herr, 235.

212 "Father shocked back": JBF to EBL, April 18, 1856, Blair-Lee Papers, Princeton University. See also Herr and Spence, 97.

212 "the Know-Nothings were running through": Roosevelt, 313.

212 "Taught to admire the founders": Elbert Smith, *Magnificent Missourian*, 249.

212 "the old Jacksonian": Schlesinger, 472.

212 "every young man": Elbert Smith, *Magnificent Missourian*, 284.

213 "though one of the greatest": Dellenbaugh, 451.

213 "I became more than ever": JBF, *Great Events*, 191.

213 "scarcely able" . . . "most strenuously" . . . "conjugal tenderness": Chambers, 393.

213 "means of purifying the Democratic": Schlesinger, 473.

213 "Thucydides says his work": Chambers, 393.

213 "at best, the book showed insight" . . . "intended to show the capacity": Chambers, 395.

214 "Many of his expressions": Roosevelt, 233.

214 "is as fat as a buck": Blair quoted in Herr, 236.

214 "setting forth the advantages": Nevins, 419.

214 "Frémont pronounced his pathetic little expedition": Rolle, 148.

214 "It seems treason against mankind": JCF quoted in Nevins, 420.

214 "permanently turned his back": Rolle, 160.

215 "[T]he affairs of his mining property" . . . "It was one of the conflicting": JBF, *Great Events*, 191.

216 "Various nervous afflictions" . . . "exempted from Labour": Unpublished essay by Frances Seward, quoted in Goodwin, 155.

216 "That I should have been absent": Chambers, 413.

217 "a wound destined never to heal": Elbert Smith, *Magnificent Missourian*, 298.

217 "a dreary region": *Appeal of the Independent Democrats in Congress, to the People of the United States. Shall Slavery be Permitted in Nebraska?* (Washington, D.C.: Towers Printers, 1854).

217 "made more abolitionists": Scherer, 229.

217 "the one in opposition": Roosevelt, 309.

217 "Midnight passed": *New York Tribune*, March 4, 1854.

217 "seven decades of political handiwork": Chaffin, 434.

218 "passion and trenchancy": Schlesinger, 472.

218 "I will be a new Peter": THB quoted in Scherer, 231.

218 "While the proslavery South": Scherer, 229.

219 "The house of Senator Benton" . . . "fell suffocated" . . . "What little water": JBF, *Souvenirs of My Time*, 104.

219 "Like a proud ship": JBF, *Souvenirs of My Time*, 104.

219 "the bed on which my wife died": Chambers, 414.

219 "as only those who love one another": JCF, *Memoirs*, xxi.

220 "All is gone" . . . "Not one book": JBF, *Great Events*, 191.

220 "year of sorrows": Scherer, 231.

220 "too moved to be able to speak" . . . "refused personal intercourse" . . . "He told my father" . . . "stern endurance": JBF, *Souvenirs of My Time*, 104.

220 "[I]t is Pierce's head" . . . "shockingly mutilated": JBF, *Souvenirs of My Time*, 104.

220 "Old Testament warnings": Egan, 506.

220 "convulsed with emotion": Chambers, 415.

Six: Free Speech, Free Soil, Free Men, Frémont 1855–1857

222 "[I]t was in the person of John Charles Frémont": De Voto, 38–39.

223 "peaks of glory" . . . "valleys of despair" Egan, 505.

223 "well but not strong": JBF to EBL, July 1855, Blair-Lee Papers, Princeton University.

223 "Are you and Colonel Frémont": Phillips, 194.

223 "the most famous runaway saga": Wilentz, 646.

223 "I would rather lie": Theodore Parker to Millard Fillmore, quoted in McPherson, 82.

224 "slaveholders' argument": Wilentz, 651.

224 "It is in the general ambience": Wilentz, 654.

224 "broke through the racism": Wilentz, 656.

224 "All democracy left": Frederick Robinson, Address to the Voters of the Fifth Congressional District, quoted in Wilentz, 675, and 927, n. 20.

225 "set forth the radical case" . . . "Against this spurious Democracy": Schlesinger, 478–479.

225 "Before my baby": JBF quoted in Nevins, 423.

225 "bore the aspects of a secret fraternity": Chaffin, 435.

226 "the explorer-hero": Egan, xxiii.

226 "At this time Colonel Frémont" . . . "was a Democrat": JBF, *Great Events*, 192.

226 "led by wealthy": Wilentz, 679.

226 "In the main features" . . . "instructed, homogeneous": JBF, *Great Events*, 192–193.

227 "restrictionist aims" . . . "that America might be happier": Nevins, 424.

227 "himself so strongly" . . . "prophetic terms" . . . "telling Governor Floyd": JBF, *Great Events*, 193–194.

228 "no woman could refuse the Presidency": A Democratic agent quoted in Nevins, 425.

228 "I longed for the peace and beauty": JBF, *Great Events*, 203.

228 "I think opiates are so sickening": JBF to EBL, unknown date, quoted in Herr and Spence, 59.

228 "fat and contented" . . . "the thick of it" . . . "Badly as she thinks": JBF to EBL, August 17, 1855, Blair-Lee Papers, Princeton University.

229 "To me Colonel Frémont": Phillips, 195.

229 "I am satisfied slavery": John Quincy Adams quoted in Nevins, 423.

229 "With this nullification treason": Phillips, 197.

230 "As I watched that family picture": Phillips, 198.

230 "It was nearing sunset": JBF, *Great Events*, 203.

231 "There was no shadow of doubt": JBF quoted in Phillips, 199.

231 "excommunication by the South": JBF, *Great Events*, 203.

231 "one decision possible" . . . "the past lay behind": JBF, *Great Events*, 204.

231 "several public letters": Rolle, 163.

231 "titular head": Isely, 161.

232 "little was known": JBF, *Great Events*, 195.

232 "My dear Mr. Blair": JBF to FPB, August 27, 1855, Blair-Lee Papers, Princeton University.

232 "I never spoke": JBF, *Great Events*, 204.

233 "Free Soil band-wagon" . . . "Kansas-Nebraska Act": William E. Smith, "The Blairs and Frémont," 215.

233 "mover and shaker" . . . "In private life": Elbert Smith, *Magnificent Missourian,* xii.

233 "be blended together": Elbert Smith, *Magnificent Missourian*, 186.

233 "one of the first important": Goodwin, 24.

234 "bore the scars": Nevins, 428.

234 "I think of Frémont": FPB to Martin Van Buren, January 25, 1856, Van Buren Papers, Library of Congress.

234 "the discoverer of Frémont": Nevins, 426.

234 "Jessie Benton's heritage": Brands, 365.

235 "of rough coarse material": Herr, 244.

235 "Mr. Frémont wants me to tell you": JBF to FPB, October 21, 1855, Blair-Lee Papers, Princeton University. See also Herr and Spence, 72.

235 "The turkey is getting restless" . . . "Hamilton Fish": JBF to FPB, November 3, 1855. Blair-Lee Papers, Princeton University. See also Herr and Spence, 73–74.

235 "the wilds of the political world": Egan, 507.

235 "I make no visits": JBF to FPB, Nov. 3, 1855, Blair-Lee Papers, Princeton University. See also Herr and Spence, 73–74.

235 "women were dressed": Letter, n.d., from JBF to EBL, quoted in Herr, 245.

236 "Just here & just now": JBF to EBL, April 18, 1856, Blair-Lee Papers, Princeton University. See also Herr and Spence, 97–98.

236 a "motley mixture of malcontents" Phillips, 200.

236 "Since the revoked sale": JBF to EBL, April 18, 1856, Blair-Lee Papers, Princeton University. See also Herr and Spence, 97.

236 "The dropping of water": Job 14:19.

236 "and I think": JBF to EBL, March 8, 1856, Herr and Spence, 94.

236 "The Frémont children": Elbert Smith, *Francis Preston Blair*, 219.

237 "that lonely old man": JBF to EBL, November 21, 1855, Blair-Lee Papers, Princeton University. See also Herr and Spence, 77.

237 "And if you should see": JBF to EBL, December 14, 1855, Blair-Lee Papers, Princeton University. See also Herr and Spence, 81.

237 "legendary Christmas conclave": Goodwin, 186.

237 "sudden enthusiasm": Smith, 219.

238 "Thurlow Weed says": Nevins, 427.

238 "They would submerge their differences": Rolle, 164.

238 "sort of intrusive feeling": Nevins, 429.

238 "As all these men" . . . "I heartily concur": JBF, *Great Events*, 196–197.

239 "its shameful": Wilentz, 690.

239 "the knocking-down and beating": *New York Tribune*, May 24, 1856.

239 "Has it come to this": *New York Evening Post*, May 23, 1856.

240 "We consider the act": *Richmond Enquirer*, June 2, 1856.

240 "The only regret": Quoted in *New York Times*, May 26, 1856.

240 "Success, if it comes" . . . "I have written constantly": JBL to EBL, April 18, 1856, Blair-Lee Papers, Princeton University. See also Herr and Spence, 97–98.

240 "He always drops me that way" . . . "I wrote about a month ago": JBF to EBL, April 25, 1856, Blair-Lee Papers, Princeton University. See also Herr and Spence, 100.

241 "come on and bring the whole": JBF to EBL, April 29, 1856, Blair-Lee Papers, Princeton University. See also Herr and Spence, 101.

241 "That was a very bad visit" . . . "violent attack" . . . "This time my head": JBF to EBL, June 9, 1856, Blair-Lee Papers, Princeton University. See also Herr and Spence, 105–106.

241 "fixed resolve": JBF to EBL, April 18, 1856, Blair-Lee Papers, Princeton University. See also Herr and Spence, 97.

241 "camp meeting fervor": Nevins, 432.

242 "the slaveocrats and stockjobbers": Elbert Smith, *Magnificent Missourian*, 229.

242 "All would be well": Isely, 164.

242 "Though young and born poor": *New York Tribune,* June 6, 1856.

242 "There is no name which can find such favor" . . . "patriotic and perilous" . . . "We have had enough": *New York Tribune,* June 11 and 12, 1856.

242 "All the proprieties forbid it": JBF to EBL, June 9, 1856, Blair-Lee Papers, Princeton University. See also Herr and Spence, 106.

243 "twin relics of barbarism": Nevins, 434.

243 "As respects the nomination": JCF to FPB, June 17, 1856, Manuscripts and Archives Division, New York Public Library.

243 "The enthusiasm is tremendous": Nevins, 435.

243 "The Path-Finder": *New York Times,* June 19, 1856.

244 "The first, and as I still think fatal error": Weed to Cameron, November 12, 1856, Cameron Papers, Library of Congress.

244 "As Colonel Frémont": JBF, *Great Events*, 198.

244 "immense good he is doing": Elbert Smith, *Magnificent Missourian*, 231.

244 "It is unnecessary for me to speak": From a speech at the Buchanan ratification meetings in St. Louis, June 21, 1856, reported in *New York Times*, June 27, 1856.

244 "There was nothing which a father could do": *St. Louis Leader*, November 4, 1856, quoted in Chaffin, 441–442.

245 "She had seen much of the world": Nevins, 67.

245 "I can say as Portia": JBF to Charles Upham, May 31, 1856. See Herr and Spence, 102.

245 "He also won": Herr, 254.

246 "as though all their previous cheering": Herr, 255.

246 "waged almost exclusively": Foner, 130.

247 "the gallant wife of a gallant man": *New York Tribune*, July 22, 1856. Herr, 260.

247 "a moral earthquake": *California Chronicle*, October 2, 1856.

247 "an obligation to fight . . . "*The women have leaped*": Collins, 165–166.

248 "What a shame": Lydia Maria Child, August 3, 1856, quoted in Herr, 251.

248 "I would almost lay down my life": Meltzer and Holland, 290.

248 "This is election day": Herr, 257.

248 "Equal partnership": Brands, 368.

248 "symbols of a national identity": Egan, xxiii.

249 "as *one*": FPF to Nevins, letter,n.d., Nevins Papers, Bancroft Library.

249 "Moving in a material age": Rothschild, 294.

250 "Nothing is clearer": Nevins, 437–438.

250 "Fife and drum": Nevins, 441.

250 "our young gallant" . . . "the man for the day": Rolle, 164.

250 "united in what seemed": Nevins, 452.

250 "His bearing was very well": Nevins, 439.

252 "a shallow, vainglorious": Bashford, 367.

252 "I think no time is to be lost": JBF to EBL, July 2, 1856, Blair-Lee Papers, Princeton University. See also Herr and Spence, 112.

252 "One of the most beautiful women": See Herr, 264.

253 "[In] her account for Bigelow": Herr, 264. See also Bigelow, 12ff.

253 "power to re-marry" . . . "task . . . to transform": JBF notes for Bigelow, regarding and parentage and birth of JCF. Bigelow Papers, New York Public Library.

253 "her dangerous course": Phillips, 209.

253 "Tell me": Wise quoted in *California Chronicle*, October 1, 1856.

253 if "Frémont is elected": Wise quoted in Roy F. Nichols, *The Disruption of American Democracy*, 44.

254 "We have linked together": *Frémont's Romanism Established*, campaign pamphlet, New York, 1856.

254 "Proof of His Romanism" . . . "he could not quiet the uneasiness: Rolle, 165.

255 "contrary to the advice" . . . "He was a Protestant": JBF, *Great Events*, 199.

255 "What are your convictions?": JBF, *Great Events*, 200.

255 "Three years spent": JBF to EBL, July 23, 1856, Blair-Lee Papers, Princeton University. See also Herr and Spence, 119.

255 "As to any one's speaking": JBF to EBL, August 14, 1856, Blair-Lee Papers, Princeton University. See also Herr and Spence, 129.

256 "Had we been": *New York Tribune*, July 4, 1856.

256 "the preservation of freedom": JBF, *Great Events*, 199.

256 "He considers himself as belonging": JBF to EBL, August 12, 1856. Blair-Lee Papers, Princeton University. See also Herr and Spence, 125.

256 "landshark" . . . "master monopolist" . . . complicity in the deaths of Francisco and Ramon de Haro and their uncle José de los Reyes Berreyesa . . . allegations of Las Mariposas misdeeds: *Los Angeles Star*, August 23, 27, 30, October 4, 1856.

257 "Dear Lizzie, it is easy" . . . "Could you possess": JBF to EBL, August 20, 1856, Blair-Lee Papers, Princeton University. See also Herr and Spence, 130–131.

257 "a trial by mud": Phillips, 213.

257 "turn loose" . . . "Fathers, save us": MacPherson, 159.

257 The election "of Frémont": Senator Robert Toombs quoted in Herr, 266.

257 "We are treading": *New York Tribune*, August 18, 1856.

257 "father's nature" . . . "Those sacred ties": EBF, *Recollections of Elizabeth Benton Frémont*, 77.

258 "private committee" . . . "The personal and friendly": JBF, *Great Events*, 205.

258 "Both ambitious and maternal": Herr and Spence, 68.

258 "I am horribly tired": JBF to EBL, July 2, 1857, Blair-Lee Papers, Princeton University. See also Herr and Spence, 113.

258 "gay as a boy" . . . "We let him read no papers": JBF to FPB, August 25, 1856, Blair Papers, Library of Congress. See also Herr and Spence, 133.

258 "breezy hill-top": JBF, *Great Events*, 205.

258 "All this has made me ill": JBF to FPB, August 25, 1856, Blair Papers, Library of Congress. See also Herr and Spence, 133.

259 "a Brutus stab": JBF to FPB, August 310, 1857, Blair-Lee Papers, Princeton University. See also Herr and Spence, 168.

259 "I am blazing with fever" . . . "This shuts off ": JBF to EBL, August 12, 1856, Blair-Lee Papers, Princeton University. See also Herr and Spence, 124.

259 "could by one line set right": JBF to EBL, August 20, 1856, Blair-Lee Papers.

259 "Father's silence": JBF to FPB, August 25, 1856, Blair-Lee Papers, Princeton University. See also Herr and Spence, 132.

259 "Old Roman" . . . "lovingly of you": EBL quoted in Herr, 270.

260 "He only wrote": JBF to EBL, August/September 1856, Blair-Lee Papers, Princeton University. See also Herr and Spence, 135.

260 "seems as if sadness": JBF to EBL, September 16, 1856, Blair-Lee Papers, Princeton University. See also Herr and Spence, 137.

260 "issued a confidential call" . . . "desperate one": JBF, *Great Events*, 201.

260 "If it were not for the false notes": JBF to EBL, October 9, 1856, Blair-Lee Papers, Princeton University. See also Herr and Spence, 138.

261 "He was not a strong man": JBF, *Great Events*, 206.

261 "I heartily regret": JBF to EBL, October 20, 1857, Blair-Lee Papers, Princeton University. See also Herr and Spence, 140.

261 "almost as a condition": JBF, *Great Events*, 204.

261 "all the sorrowful images" . . . "I don't care for the election": JBR to EBL, late October 1856, Blair-Lee Papers, Princeton University. See also Herr and Spence, 141.

262 "I don't dare say anything": JBF to EBL, November 2, 1856, Blair-Lee Papers, Princeton University. See also Herr and Spence, 142.

262 "Colonel Benton, I perceive": See Nevins, 456, and Phillips, 214.

262 "I'm very glad": Phillips, 215.

262 "We are beaten": Wilentz, 701.

263 "General Frémont always believed": JBF, *Great Events*, 202.

263 "[S]tates and republics": JBF to EBL, January 23, 1857, Blair-Lee Papers, Princeton University. See also Herr and Spence, 147.

264 "Mr. Frémont . . . has already" . . . "Mr. Frémont says I may live": JBF to EBL, November 18, 1856, Blair-Lee Papers, Princeton University. See also Herr and Spence, 144.

264 "California has no attraction for me": JBF to FPB, January 31, 1857. Blair-Lee Papers, Princeton University. See also Herr and Spence, 149.

264 For allegations of Frémont "debauching" a maid during the 1856 campaign, see Herr, 281; Chaffin, 447–448; Rolle, 167.

264 "As a candidate for President": Bigelow quoted in Chaffin, 447–448.

264 "Mr. Frémont thinks of the climate & the sunrise": JBF to EBL, January 11, 1858, Blair-Lee Papers, Princeton University. See also Herr and Spence, 183.

SEVEN: WAR 1857–1862

266 "I have had the blues desperately": JBF to FPB, June 1857, Blair-Lee Papers, Princeton University. See also Herr and Spence, 160.

266 "I have not had a sight": JBG to EBL, January 23, 1857, Blair-Lee Papers, Princeton University. See also Herr and Spence, 147.

267 "[T]his continued pain": JBF to EBL, May 4, 1857, Blair-Lee Papers, Princeton University. See also Herr and Spence, 155.

267 "great wine crop" . . . "Those long breaks": JBF to FPB, August 30, 1857, Blair-Lee Papers, Princeton University. See also Herr and Spence, 168–170.

267 "lump of malignity": EBL quoted in Herr, 283.

267 "We have narrow channels": JBF to FPB, August 30, 1857, Blair-Lee Papers, Princeton University. See also Herr and Spence, 168.

267 "My sweetheart": JBF to JCF, July 25, 1857, Frémont Papers, Bancroft Library.

268 "Love me in memory": JBF to JCF, July 29, 1857, Frémont Papers, Bancroft Library.

268 "I am trying to make the sun" . . . "My darling I want to see you": JBF to JCF, September 23, 1857, Frémont Papers, Bancroft Library.

269 "How things fade": JBF to EBL, October 13, 1857, Blair-Lee Papers, Princeton University. See also Herr and Spence, 173.

269 "silvered over" . . . "hard on to white": JBF to EBL, November 4, 1857, Blair-Lee Papers, Princeton University. See also Herr and Spence, 174.

269 "the monument of the age": Chambers, 425.

269 "the bed of death": Chambers, 434.

270 "Frémont would never transact business": Galen Clark *Reminiscences*, Bancroft Library.

270 "aimed to injure" . . . "The construction as to what": JBF, *Great Events*, 267.

270 "I refused so flatly": JBF to EBL, December 15, 1857, Blair-Lee Papers, Princeton University. See also Herr and Spence, 175.

271 "clever and intelligent young men" . . . "we will see": JBF to FPB, December 25, 1857, Blair-Lee Papers, Princeton University. See also Herr and Spence, 177.

271 "[A]s usual after a brief rebellion": JBF to EBL, December 15, 1857, Blair-Lee Papers, Princeton University. See also Herr and Spence, 175.

271 "[U]pset again" . . . "It is not easy to serve two masters": JBF to EBL, February 1, 1858, Blair-Lee Papers, Princeton University. See also Herr and Spence, 185.

271 "I broke down the second day": JBF to EBL, March 28, 1858, Blair-Lee Papers, Princeton University. See also Herr and Spence, 193.

272 "In appearance, the Frémont estate": Chaffin, 450.

272 "villa-like style": Starr, 369.

272 "We have a fine pair of carriage horses": JBF to EBL, April 24, 1858, Blair-Lee Papers, Princeton University. See also Herr and Spence, 195.

272 "Why not?" . . . "For answer he gathered me": Phillips, 223.

273 "your old Tennessee friend" . . . "I am comfortable and content": Chambers, 439.

273 "As soon as the news": Roosevelt, 315.

273 "Among the foremost men": Elbert Smith, *Magnificent Missourian*, 324.

274 "it is not right" . . . "lasting regret" . . . "blazing beacon" . . . "how fond Father was": JBF to FPB, May 1858, Blair-Lee Papers, Princeton University. See also Herr and Spence, 197–200.

274 "I remained with Jessie": JBF to FPB, June 4, 1858, Blair-Lee Papers, Princeton University.

274 "aggrieved miners and hired thugs": Nevins, 464.

274 "aggressive, rapacious aims": *San Francisco Herald*, January 28, 1857, quoted in Herr, 295.

275 "The Governor sent me word": JCF dictated to JBF, to FPB, July 18, 1858, Blair-Lee Papers, Princeton University. See also Herr and Spence, 209.

275 "a faithful part-Indian": JBF, *Great Events*, 210.

275 "You may come and kill us": JBF, *Memoirs,* 99ff. See also JBF, *Great Events*, 207ff.

275 "Had you given up": Herr, 300.

275 "Jessie as usual": JBF to FPB, July 16, 1858, Blair Papers, Library of Congress.

276 "We have the most delightful" . . . "We face an amphitheatre": JBF to FPB, July 2, 1859, Blair-Lee Papers, Princeton University. See also Herr and Spence, 214–217.

276 "Mr. Frémont's nature" . . . "I have gone about": JBF to EBL, August 17, 1858, Blair-Lee Papers, Princeton University. See also Herr and Spence, 211.

276 "Mr. Frémont was his own engineer": JBF, *Great Events*, 213.

277 "When I knew I should never": JBF to EBL, June 2, 1860, Blair-Lee Papers, Princeton University. See also Herr and Spence, 227.

277 "In the spirit": Greeley, *An Overland Journey from New York to San Francisco*, 316ff.

278 "I was prepared": Greeley quoted in Phillips, 226.

278 "fitted him out" . . . "was the shaping" . . . "soon realized": JBF, *Great Events*, 214.

278 "He and Mr. Frémont talked": JBF, *Great Events*, 215.

278 "a heroine equal": Dana, *Two Years before the Mast*, 453.

278 "the abstraction": Phillips, 228.

278 "Without telling me": JBF, *Great Events*, 215.

279 "Here are the three things": JCF quoted in Phillips, 228.

279 "So swift moving": JBF quoted in Phillips, 228.

279 "It was solitude by the sea": JBF, *Great Events*, 215–216.

279 "I have always gotten solid": JBF to EBL, June 2, 1860, Blair-Lee Papers, Princeton University. See also Herr and Spence, 227. "Sea Dream" is a reference to Alfred, Lord Tennyson's poem "Sea Dreams."

280 "absorbs poetry": JBF quoted in Phillips, 230.

280 "He was shy and proud": JBF, *Great Events*, 215.

280 "Don't ride them too hard": JBF quoted in Phillips, 231.

280 "fairy godmother" . . . "I believe": Merwin, 34ff.

281 "Though I weigh only": www.sksm.edu. Starr King School for the Ministry.

281 "I thought it unfaithful": King quoted in Phillips, 230.

281 "I have none but a parlor": JBF to EBL, June 14, 1860, Blair-Lee Papers, Princeton University. See also Herr and Spence, 230.

282 "Before our friendship progresses": King quoted in Phillips, 231.

282 "I rode to Mrs. Frémont's" . . . "Yesterday I dined" . . . "fine time": King Papers, Bancroft Library.

282 "When we heard the two talking": JCF quoted in Phillips, 231–232.

283 "He is about forty-five": Chaffin, 444.

283 "He was simple": Nevins, 613.

283 "walk about & admire": JBF to EBL, June 14, 1860, Blair-Lee Papers, Princeton University. See also Herr and Spence, 229ff.

284 "a Spartan existence" . . . "old garments, old books": Nevins, 592.

284 "Out of doors": Frank Frémont quoted in Nevins, 617.

284 "induced to take his seat": Nevins, 614.

285 "he heard various gossipy": Nevins, 470.

285 "Four years ago": Thurlow Weed quoted in Addison G. Procter, *Lincoln and the Convention of 1860: An Address before the Chicago Historical Society*, April 4, 1918, 6–7. Chicago: Chicago Historical Society, 1918.

285 "a night of a thousand knives": Goodwin, 243.

286 "Americans had always viewed": McPherson, 225.

286 between "an honest administration": Greeley quoted in McPherson, 227.

286 "had lately returned" . . . "prophetic discussions": JBF, *Great Events*, 216.

287 "traveled in her own stateroom" . . . "glancing references": Chaffin, 453–454. For references to the alleged affair between JCF and Corbett, see Herr and Spence, 233, n. 1; Chaffin, 453–454; and Rolle, 187–188, and 312, n. 28.

288 "The fear of what may be in store": JBF to Thomas Starr King, quoted in Herr, 317, and 476, n. 17.

288 "At this time Colonel Frémont": JBF, *Great Events*, 219.

288 "unwilling to believe": JBF, *Great Events*, 217.

288 "With the inflammatory press": JCF quoted in Phillips, 234; Nevins, 471.

288 "She saw herself ": Herr and Spence, 243.

288 "cool passions and buy time": McPherson, 264.

288 "hold, occupy, and possess": Lincoln's Inaugural Address. Basler, vol. 4, 249ff.

289 "scattered over two thousand" . . . "patrolling distant": McPherson, 250.

289 "On Sumter lay the issue": Catton and Catton, 269.

289 "stroke of genius" . . . "the first sign": McPherson, 272.

289 "at attempt will be made": Basler, vol. 4, 323.

289 "weaken the Confederate cause": Hofstadter, 157.

289 "Border southern States": *Charleston Mercury*, January, 24, 1861.

290 "He wrote me from London": JBF, *Great Events*, 217.

290 "who were busy obtaining": Rolle, 190.

290 "I have succeeded in procuring": JCF to FPB, May 24, 1861. Fields Collection, Huntington Library, San Marino, California.

291 "We go to join": JBF quoted in Herr, 319.

291 "Mr. Frémont has written to us": JBF to Hopper, quoted in Nevins, 472.

291 "Smell, read, and rest." Phillips, 235.

291 "Have you met Mrs. Frémont?": King to Henry Bellows, March 18, 1862. Photocopy at Bancroft Library.

291 "The ship showed no lights" . . . "It was a sparkling": JBF, *Great Events*, 218.

292 "brains and backbone": Nevins, 478.

292 "Missouri had been saved": Nicolay and Hay, "Abraham Lincoln," *Century Illustrated Quarterly*, 292.

292 "attached to the South": Nevins, 478.

292 "Your requisition is illegal": Jackson quoted in McPherson, 276.

293 "The President was anxiously concerned": Jackson quoted in McPherson, 218.

293 "His name is a tower of strength": *New York Times*, August 18, 1861.

293 "He is just such a person": Hay quoted in Doris Kearns Goodwin, 389.

293 "The President had gone carefully": JBF, *Memoirs,* 221–222.

294 "Mr. Frémont has stacks and stacks": JBF to TSK, July 20, 1861, King Papers, Society of California Pioneers, San Francisco.

295 "There was great confusion": JBF, *Great Events*, 220.

295 "The position in which": JBF, *Great Events*, 222.

295 "an unfriendly": JBF, *Great Events*, 218.

296 "Not a Union flag": JBF, *Great Events*, 224.

296 "the wheels and the horses' hoofs": JBF, *Souvenirs of My Time,* 166.

296 "the hundred days": *The Atlantic Monthly* compared Frémont's tenure in the Western Department in Missouri to Napoleon's Elba Island-to-Waterloo legend.

296 "the drama which tested": Nevins, 477.

296 "The restraints of ordinary times": JBF quoted in Herr and Spence, 243.

296 "Few other women": Herr, 327.

297 "scattered at nine points": Nevins, 481.

297 "Mr. Frémont asks you": JBF to Montgomery Blair, July 28, 1861, Blair Papers, Library of Congress.

298 "Is your brother Frank" . . . "It is not safe" . . . "Your letter reached me": JBF to EBL, July 27, 1861, Blair Papers, Library of Congress.

299 "For a man whose genius": Nicolay and Hay, "Abraham Lincoln," *Century Illustrated Quarterly*, 294.

299 "Have but eight regiments": Prentiss quoted in Nevins, 483.

299 "All this had to be done": Nevins, 484.

300 "My Dear Sir . . . Our troops have not been paid": *Official Records. The War of the Rebellion: A Compilation of the Official Records of the Union and Confederate Armies,* vol. 3, 416–417. Washington, D.C.: U.S. Government Printing Office, 1880–1902. See also JBF, *Great Events*, 231–232.

300 "much to the General's surprise": Herr and Spence, 251, n. 4.

300 "exaggerated as it was": JBF, *Great Events*, 236.

300 "I judge from all information": JCF (by JBF) to Montgomery Blair, July 31, 1861, Blair Papers, Library of Congress.

300 "I find it impossible": Montgomery Blair to JCF, July 26, 1861. See JBF, *Great Events*, 233.

300 "This is a great scandal": JBF to Montgomery Blair, August 5, 1861, Blair Papers, Library of Congress.

301 "As a regular army officer": JBF, *Great Events*, 242.

301 "Frémont's selection of Grant": Jean Edward Smith, 117.

302 "I believed him to be a man": Frémont manuscript memoirs, quoted in Jean Edward Smith, 117.

302 "If he fights": *Official Records. The War of the Rebellion: A Compilation of the Official Records of the Union and Confederate Armies*, vol. 3, 57ff. Washington, D.C.: U.S. Government Printing Office, 1880–1902. See also Nevins, 486.

302 "Knowing General Lyon's ability": JBF, *Great Events*, 238.

302 "Under the critical conditions": Nicolay and Hay, "Abraham Lincoln," *Century Illustrated Quarterly*, 296.

303 "If it is the intention": Lyon to Harding, quoted in Nicolay and Hay, "Abraham Lincoln," *Century Illustrated Quarterly*, 296.

303 "Our retreat to Rolla": John M. Schofield, *Forty-six Years in the Army* (New York: Century, 1887), 40.

303 "disregarding the maxims": McPherson, 351.

304 "even if he failed": Committee on the Conduct of the War, part 3, 5–6. Also quoted in Nevins, 489.

304 "never knew a man": *Congressional Globe*, December 11, 1861.

305 "supplied such miserable steeds": Nevins, 498.

305 "When the Blairs go in for a fight": Nevins, 513.

305 "I shall expect you": FPB to JCF, quoted in Nevins, 510.

306 "bitterly resented": FPF to Allan Nevins, letter, n.d., Nevins Papers, Bancroft Library.

306 "I am beginning to lose": Frank Blair to Montgomery Blair, quoted in Herr, 332.

306 "showy spectacle of galloping horses": Herr and Spence, 245.

306 "knot of flatterers": Nicolay and Hay, *Century Illustrated Quarterly*, 297.

306 "high points of the Union campaign": Jean Edward Smith, 121.

307 "should stop and give them": Nevins, 496.

307 "pet and protégé": Lincoln quoted in Nevins, 408.

308 "The men who had offered": EBF, *Recollections of Elizabeth Benton Frémont*, 127.

309 "our American Florence Nightingale": *St. Louis Democrat*, August 27, 1861.

309 "Would you have *no* moral standards": Phillips, 239–240.

309 "She had a man's power": Rebecca Harding Davis, 239.

310 "The farmers would": JBF, *Great Events*, 251.

311 "The South has seceded" . . . "the conviction of us" . . . "I want you two": Phillips, 244.

312 "Mr. Seward will never allow" . . . "It is for the North": JBF *Great Events*, 253ff.

312 Frémont's proclamation of August 30, 1861:

Circumstances, in my judgment, of sufficient urgency, render it necessary that the commanding general of this department should assume the administrative powers of the State. Its disorganized condition, the helplessness of the civil authority, the total insecurity of life, and the devastation of property by bands of murderers and marauders, who infest nearly every county of the State, and avail themselves of the public misfortunes and the vicinity of a hostile force to gratify private and neighborhood vengeance, and who find an enemy wherever they find plunder, finally demand the severest measures to repress the daily-increasing crimes and outrages which are driving off the inhabitants and ruining the State.

In this condition, the public safety and the success of our arms require unity of purpose, without let or hindrance to the prompt administration of affairs. In order, therefore, to suppress disorder, to maintain as far as now practicable the public peace, and to give security and protection to the person and property of loyal citizens, I do hereby extend and declare established, martial law, throughout the State of Missouri.

The lines of the army of occupation in this State are for the present declared to extend from Leavenworth, by way of the posts of Jefferson City, Rolla, and Ironton, to Cape Girardeau, on the Mississippi.

All persons who shall be taken with arms in their hands within these lines, shall be tried by court-martial, and if found guilty will be shot.

The property, real and personal, of all persons in the State of Missouri who shall take up arms against the United States, or who shall be directly proven to have taken an active part with their enemies in the field, is declared to be confiscated to the public use, and their slaves, if any they have, are hereby declared freemen.

All persons who shall be proven to have destroyed, after the publication of this order, railroad tracks, bridges, or telegraphs, shall suffer the extreme penalty of the law.

All persons engaged in treasonable correspondence, in giving or procuring aid to the enemies of the United States, in fomenting tumults, in disturbing the public tranquility by creating and circulating false reports or incendiary documents, are in their own interests warned that they are exposing themselves to sudden and severe punishment.

All persons who have been led away from their allegiance are required to return to their homes forthwith. Any such absence, without sufficient cause, will be held to be presumptive evidence against them.

The object of this declaration is to place in the hands of the military authorities the power to give instantaneous effect to existing laws, and to supply such deficiencies as the conditions of war demand. But this is not intended to suspend ordinary tribunals of the country, where the law will be administered by the civil officers in the usual manner, and with their customary authority, while the same can be peaceably exercised.

The commanding general will labor vigilantly for the public welfare, and in his efforts for their safety, hopes to obtain not only the acquiescence but the active support of the loyal people of the country!

J. C. Frémont,

Major-General, Commanding

312 "upon the country like a thunderbolt": Nevins, 502.

312 "the hour has come, and the man": Harriet Beecher Stowe, *Independent*, September 21, 1861.

312 "so tactfully nursing": Rothschild, 298.

313 "pathetic vehemence" . . . "slavery would not be attacked": Hofstadter, 162.

313 "[W]hy take a costly": Lovejoy quoted in Nevins, 501.

313 "master-key of victory": Nevins, 501.

313 "The object of this declaration": JCF quoted in Nevins, 504.

314 "the war for the preservation": T. Harry Williams quoted in Hofstadter, 165.

314 "it stirred and united": Indiana congressman George Julian quoted in Nevins, 504.

315 "The President could permit": William Seward quoted in Dons Keams Goodwin, 390.

315 "anxiety" . . . "First: Should you shoot a man": Nicolay and Hay, *Lincoln*, vol. 4, chap. 24. See also Nevins, 505, and JBF, *Great Events*, 259.

315 "but a few hours": JBF, *Great Events*, 268.

316 "Trusting to have your confidence": JBF, *Great Events*, 262–263.

317 "constant intimate friendship": JBF, *Great Events*, 269.

317 "only previous confrontation": Blue, 257–258.

317 "When it is remembered': Rothschild, 301.

317 "The streets swarmed": Herr, 337.

318 "All my life" . . . "I introduced" . . . "General Frémont felt" . . . "like a sentinel" . . . "I have written to the General" . . . "the General feels" . . . "Who do you mean?" . . . "The General's conviction" . . . "anxious for a pretext" . . . "England on account" . . . "You are quite a female politician": JBF, *Great Events*, 270–272.

319 "simply a woman": Herr, 340.

320 "Frank never would have let him" . . . "The General should never have dragged" . . . "Then there is no use" . . . "Mrs. Frémont, the General has no further part": JBF, *Great Events*, 272.

The only written record of the meeting between Jessie Frémont and Abraham Lincoln was made by Jessie immediately following the event, and committed to the family papers. (The original is at the Bancroft Library.) Two years later, Lincoln referred to it casually in a conversation with John Hay.

320 "the proclamation was the opening door": Speech by congressman John P. C. Shanks of Indiana before Congress, March 4, 1862.

320 "Why, not an hour ago": Rothschild, 479, n. 16.

321 beautiful "virago": Phillips, 251.

321 "That one of the so-called": Rothschild, 301.

321 "Strange, isn't it": Phillips, 253.

321 "She sought an audience": Nicolay and Hay, *Lincoln*, vol. 4, 415.

321 "Well, who would have expected" . . . "If you had stayed" . . . "painful day": JBF, *Great Events*, 272. For an account of the meetings between JBF and Lincoln, and JBF and FPBr, see also Herr and Spence, 264 ff, and Nicolay and Hay, "Abraham Lincoln." *Century Illustrated Quarterly*, 297ff.

322 "I do not feel authorized": Basler, vol. 4, 519; JBF, *Great Events*, 274.

322 "Things evidently prejudged": JBF to JCF, n.d., Chicago Historical Society. See also Herr, 341.

323 "A formal quarrel": LBL to FPB, September 15, 1861. Quoted in Herr, 341.

323 "The result of what I have felt": JBF to Frederick Billings, October 18, 1861, Herr and Spence, 282.

323 "I did not speak to him": JBF quoted in Herr, 8 and Nevins, 518.

323 "General Frémont needs assistance": Lincoln to Hunter, September 9, 1861, quoted in Chaffin, 466.

323 "insidious and dishonorable": Nevins, 520.

323 "Frémont himself is too brave": Montgomery Blair to W.O. Bartlett, September 26, 1861, quoted in Smith, "The Blairs and Frémont," 249–250.

324 "No, that would be insubordination": Testimony of Schuyler Colfax, March 7, 1862, in *Congressional Globe*, 1128, quoted in Chaffin, 469.

324 "Every one who knew the situation": Nevins, 527.

325 "He is very much mortified": Cameron to Lincoln, October 14, 1861. See Nicolay and Hay, *Lincoln*, vol. 4, 430.

325 "My plan is New Orleans": JBF, *Guard*, 50ff.

325 "first deliberate Union offensive": Jean Edward Smith, 122.

325 "Thy error, Frémont": Whittier, 222–223.

326 "I *knew* I was right": JCF quoted in Herr, 344.

326 "The army is in the best": JBF, *Guard*, 50ff.

326 "I can never forget": Tarbell, vol. 2, 67–68.

327 "On receipt of this": Lincoln to Curtis, October 24, 1861. Official Records 1-03, p. 553. *War of the Rebellion: A Compilation of the Official Records of the Union and Confederate Armies. Prepared under the direction of the Secretary of War, by Bvt. Lieut. Col. Robert N. Scott, Third U.S. Artillery and Published Pursuant to Act of Congress Approved June 16, 1880.*

327 "one of the strangest scenes of the war": Nevins, 541.

327 "It would be impossible to exaggerate": *New York Herald*, November 8, 1861.

327 "Agreeably to orders": Frémont to the Soldiers of the Mississippi Army, November 2, 1861. Official Records 1-03, p. 560. *War of the Rebellion: A Compilation of the Official Records of the Union and Confederate Armies. Prepared under the direction of the Secretary of War, by Bvt. Lieut. Col. Robert N. Scott, Third U.S. Artillery and Published Pursuant to Act of Congress Approved June 16, 1880.*

328 "I cannot now know": Lincoln to Curtis, October 24, 1861. Official Records 1-03, pp. 553–554. *War of the Rebellion: A Compilation of the Official Records of the Union and Confederate Armies. Prepared under the direction of the Secretary of War, by Bvt.*

Lieut. Col. Robert N. Scott, Third U.S. Artillery and Published Pursuant to Act of Congress Approved June 16, 1880.

328 "You are not likely": Lincoln to Hunter, October 24, 1861. Official Records 1-03, pp. 553–554. *War of the Rebellion: A Compilation of the Official Records of the Union and Confederate Armies. Prepared under the direction of the Secretary of War, by Bvt. Lieut. Col. Robert N. Scott, Third U.S. Artillery and Published Pursuant to Act of Congress Approved June 16, 1880.*

328 "Your—affectionate reception of me": *St. Louis Democrat,* November 9, 1861.

328 "I could not stand it": JBF, *Guard,* 202.

329 "To leave him here without money": JBF to Ward Hill Lamon, October 26, 1861, Herr and Spence, 284.

329 "He was the life and the soul": George W. Waring Jr. quoted in Nevins, 543.

329 "sly, slimy nature": JBF to Thomas Starr King, October 16, 1863, quoted in Herr and Spence, 356.

329 "had stirred and united": Eyre, 296.

329 "Where are you": Stevens quoted in Nevins, 547.

329 "assumed form": Speech by congressman John P. C. Shanks of Indiana before Congress, March 4, 1862.

330 "[T]here was nothing" . . . "who had become" . . . "I have something to say" . . . "Your name will live": JBF, *Great Events,* 325.

330 "I am incapable" . . . "I believe" . . . "It seems to me" . . . "They were all young": JBF to James T. Fields, December 14, 1861, Herr and Spence, 298-99.

331 "a damned mob": Nathaniel Hawthorne quoted in Collins, 95.

331 "Are the President and Mrs. Lincoln": Benjamin Wade quoted in Nevins, 552. See also JBF, *Great Events,* 327.

332 "It was a very serious time": JBF, *Great Events,* 327.

332 "vulgar doll": Child quoted in Herr, 357.

332 "ghastly failure" . . . "filled the house" . . . "A band of scarlet": JBF, *Great Events,* 328-29.

333 "Gen. Frémont, upon taking the command": Report of the Joint Committee on the Conduct of the War, *Senate Executive Documents,* 37th Cong., 3rd sess.

333 "No public man": Wade quoted in Nevins, 459.

333 "apology for disaster and defeat": Smith, "The Blairs and Frémont," 256.

334 "helped to create": Chaffin, 472.

334 "This offering is made at the altar": *General Frémont, and the Injustice Done Him by Politicians and Envious Men* (Philadelphia: W. Brotherhead, 1862).

334 "is to the West": Richard Smith of the *Cincinnati Gazette* quoted in Rothschild, 315.

334 "I have had it on my mind": Rothschild, 316.

335 "detested Pope only less": Nevins, 562.

335 "very objectionable": Rothschild, 322.

335 "the promises were never fulfilled": JBF, *Great Events,* 379.

335 "I have great respect": JBF, *Great Events,* 380.

336 "my father should have been called": EBF, *Recollections,* 76.

EIGHT: RETREAT 1862–1902

337 "Isn't it a shame": JBF to TSK, early 1863, King Papers, Society of California Pioneers, San Francisco.

337 "Please shape it slenderly": JBF to Fields, October 22 and 30, 1862. Quoted in Herr, 366.

338 "I do a good deal of desultory": JBF to TSK, early 1863, King Papers. Society of California Pioneers, San Francisco.

338 "Mrs. Frémont is a true woman": *Atlantic* 11 (1863): 143.

338 "Instead of being": *Hesperian* 9 (1863): 636.

339 "betrayed by pretended radical": Herr and Spence, 251.

339 "Well, my dear Eliza": Phillips, 259.

339 "This genius of a man": Judge Edward Pierrepont in the December 1864 libel trial of former New York mayor George Opdyke quoted in Nevins, 586. Also see *New York Supreme Court: The Great Libel Case of George Opdyke vs. Thurlow Weed*, a pamphlet published by the American News Company in 1865.

340 "Balzac's novels": Nevins, 584.

340 "had been the engrossing idea": JBF, *Great Events*, 382.

340 "I procured from the Texas Legislature": Nevins, 587–88

340 "We have had so much" . . . "tomorrow" . . . "The rule of our life": JBF to John Greenleaf Whittier, October 17, 1863, Harvard University. See Herr and Spence, 357–358.

341 "make a good Christmas": JBF to TSK, October 16, 1863, King Papers, Society of California Pioneers, San Francisco.

341 "I've a certain conviction": Phillips, 263.

341 "His brave pure soul": JBF to John Greenleaf Whittier, March 10, 1864, Harvard University. See Herr and Spence, 373.

341 "our dear dear friend": JBF to Elizabeth Palmer Peabody, March 20, 1864, Massachusetts Historical Society. See Herr and Spence, 375.

342 "The principal cause" . . . "The whole Blair family": Nevins, 566.

343 "The Convention will not be regarded": Chase quoted in Nevins, 573.

343 "Lincoln will be nominated": Garfield quoted in Nevins, 573.

343 "Very honorable" . . . "To-day we have in the country": JBF, *Great Events*, 385–387.

344 "The latter part": JBF, *Great Events*, 390.

345 "If you have assurance": Sawyer to Frémont, September 13, 1865, Andrew Johnson Papers, Library of Congress. See also Nevins, 579.

345 "not in favor of Abraham Lincoln" . . . "That such a sacrifice": JBF, *Great Events*, 391.

345 "One thing you may be sure of": FPF to Nevins, April 19, 1927. Nevins Papers, Bancroft Library.

345 "In respect to Mr. Lincoln": JCF quoted in Nevins, 580.

345 "If my Father had been a politician": FPF to Nevins, letter, n.d., Nevins Papers, Bancroft Library.

346 "Among the words I remember": JBF to Whittier quoted in Phillips, 272.

346 "[I]t's a very risky thing": JBF to NHB, November 1, 1864, Frémont Papers, Bancroft Library.

347 "We must soon find something": Phillips, 274.

347 "The sweetness of honey": JBF to NHB quoted in Phillips, 274.

347 "After we got the books arranged": NHB quoted in Phillips, 278.

348 "The general was often away": NHB quoted in Nevins, 593, and Phillips, 281.

349 "grand and simple": *Cincinnati Commercial*, May 28, 1868.

349 "At the same moment": JBF to NHB quoted in Phillips, 284.

349 "the ablest effort": Smith, "The Blairs and Frémont," 260.

349 "In a day of excess": Phillips, 285.

350 Re Vinnie Ream. Biographers Pamela Herr and Tom Chaffin contend there was a romantic relationship between Ream and Frémont, citing letters from Frémont to Ream. "Whether or not the two consummated their relationship remains unclear," writes Chaffin, "but John's letters to her strongly suggest a rapport that went beyond mere friendship. On the eve of a visit by Vinnie's parents to Paris, for instance, he wrote her, ostensibly to provide travel suggestions for a trip she and her family planned to make. 'This is my little bulletin of business for you this morning my darling,' he wrote, concluding the letter. 'If I should be happy enough to see you tonight I will make it clearer—otherwise tomorrow.'" (Chaffin, 483) Herr quotes another letter: "'What I have been at to you here looks like the letter of a business agent, but although you may not see it, it is a love letter.'" (Herr, 389)

Glenn V. Sherwood, a descendant of Ream's through both of his parents, has written a thorough and revealing biography about Ream, *Labor of Love*. During his many years of research on his famous ancestor, and having culled the extant papers, letters, and other documentation on Ream's private and professional life, he concluded that no such relationship existed. Ream, an attractive and talented woman, had many older male admirers, among them Frank Blair, General William T. Sherman, and even Lincoln himself. While there is no doubt that Frémont would have, like his peers, been impressed with the beauty and prodigious ability of Ream, the author concludes that the relationship was probably platonic. Frémont was romantic and courtly, Southern and of French descent, and his use of endearing terms such as "darling" was characteristic and in keeping with his era. He was nearly forty years Ream's senior, and a romantic entanglement seems unlikely. Further, Jessie was intuitively and passionately involved with John on the deepest emotional levels, and the likelihood that she would have endured several hours of posing with a paramour of John's is not plausible.

351 "Only the wise counsel": Letter, n.d., from FPF to Allan Nevins, Nevins Papers, Bancroft Library.

351 "suspicious proximity": James H. Howard quoted in Herr, 390.

351 "It is evident": Nevins, 599.

351 "Although he does not really belong": Rolle, 245.

352 "It is an inextricable mass": JBF to NHB quoted in Phillips, 290.

352 "We had houses": Herr, 392.

353 "All the courage": Nevins, 601.

353 "He is so solitary": JBF to NHB Brown, fall 1873, quoted in Herr, 393.

353 "I am like a deeply built ship": JBF quoted in Phillips, 292.

353 "The Tax collector is here": JBF to George Brown, 1874–1875, Frémont Papers, Bancroft Library.

354 "The rooms are large": JBF quoted in Phillips, 293.

354 "The General has been so tired": JBF to George W. Childs, January 24, 1875. Dreer Collection, Historical Society of Pennsylvania. See also Herr and Spence, 425.

354 "Some of the brave men": Rolle, 246.

354 The original of JCF's poem is in Folder 53 of the Frémont Collection, Southwest Museum, Los Angeles.

356 "The General knew nothing": JBF to Whittier, January 21–22, 1880, Harvard University. See also Herr and Spence, 480.

356 "She wore her made-over garments": Phillips, 296.

357 "When the time came": FPF to Nevins, March 4, 1927, Nevins Papers, Bancroft Library.

357 "But I am only a ghost": JBF to Nathaniel Banks, January 30, 1877, quoted in Herr and Spence, 391.

357 "we went forth literally": FPF to Nevins, April 19, 1927, Nevins Papers, Bancroft Library.

358 "General Frémont was an explorer": Evarts quoted in Rolle, 248.

358 "It is all good for the General": JBF to William J. Morton, June 27, 1878, Morton Papers, Bancroft Library.

358 "It would give you thorough": E. B. Frémont to W. J. Morton, September 1878, Bancroft Library.

359 "Happy as all the adulation": JBF quoted in Phillips, 298.

359 "Going over that road": Sherman quoted in Rolle, 250.

359 "loathing of crawling things": JBF quoted in Phillips, 300.

360 "It is no uncommon thing": John S. Hittell quoted in Brands, 441.

360 "unqualified faith": FPF to Nevins, April 19, 1927, Nevins Papers, Bancroft Library.

360 "induce cool and tempering": JCF quoted in Chaffin, 486.

361 "There is only one piece": JBF quoted in Phillips, 305.

361 "a pretty flat in town": JBF to NHB Brown, January 1882, quoted in Herr, 409.

362 "I wish to make known": JBF informal will, April 21, 1882, in the Frémont papers of the Bancroft Library.

362 "Their pride permitted": Nevins, 605.

363 "It was so good of you to come" . . . "I never never forget": JBF to EBL, July 29, 1883. Blair-Lee Papers, Princeton University. See also Herr and Spence, 498.

363 "She belongs to him": EBL to S. P. Lee, July 21, 1883, quoted in Herr, 416.

364 "I called yesterday": JBF to John Sherman, April 14, 1884, John Sherman Papers, Library of Congress.

364 "Now that we need friends": JBF to Simon Cameron, June 11, 1884, Cameron Papers, Library of Congress.

365 "The General is well-preserved": Royce to Oak, December 9, 1884. Henry Oak Papers, Bancroft Library.

365 "personal glory": See Royce, "Light on the Seizure of California" and "Frémont."

365 "Royce's historical detective work": Herr, 421.

365 "most liberal" . . . "It will be a most beautiful book": JBF to George Brown, March 18, 1886. Frémont Papers, Bancroft Library.

366 "labor of love": JBF to William A. Croffut, November 30, 1885. Miscellaneous Manuscript Collection, Library of Congress.

366 "The General dictates": *New York Evening Post*, September 7, 1886, quoting the Washington *Star*.

367 "It must be California": Huntington quoted in Nevins, 607. See also Herr, 428, Chaffin, 487, and Phillips, 310.

367 "Here we were, lovers" . . . "His heartiness": JBF quoted in Phillips, 310–311.

368 "You forget, our road": Huntington quoted in Nevins, 607.

368 "outrunning the snow": JBF to NHB, December, 1887, Frémont Papers, Bancroft Library.

368 "the years rolled back" . . . "The General's set unsmiling face": JBF quoted in Phillips, 311.

368 "The General is 'perfectly well' ": JBF to Joseph L. Budd, March 28, 1888, State Historical Society of Iowa.

369 "firm, erect military bearing" . . . "a perfect woman": *Los Angeles Times*, December 26, 1877.

369 "hale and serene": Grierson, 261

369 "Frémont always came in": Shaff and Shaff, 33–34.

370 "It is the most truthful portrait": JBF quoted in Price, 27–28.

371 "I have my daughter with me": JCF to Whittier, November 19, 1889, Miscellaneous Jessie Benton Frémont, New-York Historical Society.

371 "in view of the services": Nevins, 608.

371 "sadly belated": JBF quoted in Phillips, 316.

371 "could be together": JBF to JCF, July 7, 1890, Frémont Papers, Bancroft Library.

372 "I have no confidence": JCF to JBF, July 11, 1890, Frémont Papers, Bancroft Library.

372 "The three hours previous to the end": JCF Jr. to EBF, July 13, 1890, Frémont Papers, Bancroft Library.

372 "If I keep this free of pain" . . . "Home?" . . . "And with the name": JBF *Memoirs*, addendum. Frémont Papers, Bancroft Library.

372 "living out our years": JCF quoted in Phillips, 316.

373 "Like a bolt": JBF, *Memoirs*, addendum, Frémont Papers, Bancroft Library.

373 "My dear sister": JCF Jr. to EBF, July 13, 1890, Frémont Papers, Bancroft Library.

373 "Your message and your picture" . . . "for he was not a man": JCF Jr. to JBF, July 17, 1890, Frémont Papers, Bancroft Library.

374 "the daily arrival": EBF, *Recollections of Elizabeth Benton Frémont,* 182.

374 "When the true story of Emancipation": Davis, 239.

374 "She was deeply in love": FPF to Nevins, March 4, 1927, Nevins Papers, Bancroft Library.

374 "It was work": JBF to J. G. Borglum, January 3, 1891, Borglum Papers, Library of Congress.

375 "Our friend Mr. Greeley" . . . "I know better than most": JBF quoted in Phillips, 325.

375 "If Mrs. Frémont is without a dollar": *New York Times,* September 18, 1890.

375 "Neither my brother nor myself ": JCF Jr. quoted in *San Francisco Morning Call,* September 17, 1890.

375 "aware of their good fortune": Philip, 326.

375 "has taken hold": EBF quoted in Herr, 437.

376 "[But] there are unexplored": JBF to William Carey Jones, October 28, 1890, Jones Papers, Stanford University. See also Herr, 441.

376 "Sunday is my seventy-second birthday": JBF to J. G. Borglum, Mary 25, 1896, Borglum Papers, Library of Congress. See also Herr, 445.

377 "I only hope": Phillips, 344.

377 "If Jessie Frémont had been": Ibid., 328.

377 "I always sleep well" . . . "for my eyes to rest upon": Phillips, 341.

377 "When I die": Phillips, 36.

Afterword

380 "There is no chance": Dillon quoted in Egan, xiv.

381 "Being so fathered": JBF to Charles Upham, May 31, 1856. See Herr and Spence, 102.

381 "She could not trek": Petrulionis.

382 "for man is man": JBF to Dr. William J. Morton, Christmas 1881, Frémont Papers, Bancroft Library.

BIBLIOGRAPHY

BOOKS

Abbott, John S. C. *Kit Carson: The Pioneer of the West*. New York: Dodd, Mead, 1873.

Bain, David Haward. *Empire Express: Building the First Transcontinental Railroad*. New York: Viking, 1999.

Bancroft, Hubert Howe. *History of California*. 6 vols. San Francisco: History Co., 1884–90.

Bartlett, Ruhl J. *John C. Frémont and the Republican Party*. New York: Da Capo, 1970.

Basker, James G., ed. *Early American Abolitionists: A Collection of Antislavery Writings, 1760–1820*. New York: Gilder Lehrman Institute of American History, 2005.

Basler, Roy C., ed. *The Collected Works of Abraham Lincoln*. 9 vols. New Brunswick, N. J.: Rutgers University Press, 1953.

Bennett, Whitman. *Whittier: Bard of Freedom*. Chapel Hill: University of North Carolina Press, 1941.

Benton, Thomas Hart. *Thirty Years' View; or, a History of the Working of the American Government for Thirty Years, from 1820 to 1850*. 2 vols. New York: Greenwood Press, 1968.

Bidwell, John. *In California before the Gold Rush*. Los Angeles: Ward Ritchie, 1948.

Bigelow, John. *Memoir of the Life and Public Services of John Charles Frémont*. New York: Derby & Jackson, 1856.

Billington, Ray Allen, and Ridge, Martin. *Westward Expansion: A History of the American Frontier*. 6th ed. Albuquerque: University of New Mexico Press, 2001.

Blackwelder, Bernice. *Great Westerner: The Story of Kit Carson*. Caldwell, Idaho: Caxton Printers, 1962.

Blue, Frederick J. *No Taint of Compromise: Crusaders in Antislavery Politics*. Baton Rouge: Louisiana State University Press, 2005.

Brandon, William. *The Men and the Mountain: Frémont's Fourth Expedition*. Westport, Conn.: Greenwood Press, 1974.

Brands, H. W. *The Age of Gold: The California Gold Rush and the New American Dream*. New York: Doubleday, 2002.

Britton, Wiley. *The Civil War on the Border.* New York: G. P. Putnam's Sons, 1899.

Browning, Peter, ed. *To the Golden Shore: America Goes to California—1849.* Lafayette, Calif.: Great West Books, 1995.

Bryant, William Cullen. *Poetical Works of William Cullen Bryant.* New York: AMS Press, 1969.

Busch, Briton Cooper, ed. *Frémont's Private Navy: The 1846 Journal of Captain William Dane Phelps.* Glendale, Calif.: Arthur H. Clark, 1987.

Carter, Harvey Lewis. *Dear Old Kit: The Historical Christopher Carson.* Norman: University of Oklahoma Press, 1968.

Carter, Robin Borglum. *Gutzon Borglum: His Life and Work.* Austin, Tex.: Eakin Press, 1998.

Carvalho, Solomon Nuñes. *Incidents of Travel and Adventure in the Far West with Col. Frémont's Last Expedition.* Edited by Bertram Wallace Korn. 1857. Reprint, Philadelphia: Jewish Publication Society of America, 1954.

Casey, Robert J, and Mary Borglum. *Give the Man Room.* Indianapolis: Bobbs–Merrill, 1952.

Catton, William and Bruce. *Two Roads to Sumter: Abraham Lincoln, Jefferson Davis, and the March to the Civil War.* Edison, N.J.: Castle Books, 2004.

Chaffin, Tom. *Pathfinder: John Charles Frémont.* New York: Hill & Wang, 2002.

Chambers, William Nesbit. *Old Bullion Benton: Senator from the New West.* Boston: Little, Brown, 1956.

Clarke, Dwight L. *Stephen Watts Kearny: Soldier of the West:* Norman: University of Oklahoma Press, 1961.

Cleland, Robert Glass. *The Early Sentiment for the Annexation of California, 1835–1846.* Austin: Texas State Historical Association, 1914–1915.

Collins, Gail. *America's Women: 400 Years of Dolls, Drudges, Helpmates, and Heroines.* New York: Perennial, 2003.

Creel, George. *Sons of the Eagle: Soaring Figures from America's Past.* Indianapolis: Bobbs–Merrill, 1927.

Curtis, G. Ticknor. *The Life of James Buchanan.* Vols. 1 and 2. New York: Harper & Brothers, 1883.

Dana, Richard H. *Two Years before the Mast: A Personal Narrative of Life at Sea.* 1887. Reprint, New York: Viking Penguin, 1981.

Dary, David. *The Oregon Trail: An American Saga.* New York: Alfred A. Knopf, 2004.

Davies, A. Mervyn. *Solon H. Borglum: A Man Who Stands Alone.* Chester, Conn.: Pequot Press, 1974.

Dellenbaugh, Frederick S. *Frémont and '49.* New York: G. P. Putnam's Sons, 1914.

Denton, Sally. *American Massacre: The Tragedy at Mountain Meadows, September 1857.* New York: Alfred A. Knopf, 2003.

De Voto, Bernard. *The Year of Decision: 1846.* New York: St. Martin's Press, 2000.

Donald, David Herbert. *Lincoln.* New York: Random House, 1995.

Douglass, Frederick. *Life and Writings of Frederick Douglas.* 4 vols. New York: International Publishers, 1955.

Dunlay, Tom. *Kit Carson and the Indians.* Lincoln: University of Nebraska Press, 2000.

Egan, Ferol. *Frémont: Explorer for a Restless Nation.* Garden City, N.Y.: Doubleday, 1977.

Eisenhower, John S. *So Far from God: The U.S. War with Mexico, 1846–1848.* Norman: University of Oklahoma Press, 1989.

Ellet, Elizabeth Fries. *Queens of American Society: A Memoir of Mrs. Frémont.* New York: Charles Scribner's Sons, 1867.

Elliott, Charles Winslow. *Winfield Scott: The Soldier and the Man.* New York: Arno Press, 1979.

Emerson, Ralph Waldo. *Journals and Miscellaneous Notebooks of Ralph Waldo Emerson.* Edited by William H. Glman Cambridge, Mass.: Harvard University Press, 1960.

Eyre, Alice. *The Famous Frémonts and Their America.* New York: Fine Arts Press, 1948.

Ferri Pisani, Camille. *Prince Napoleon in America, 1861.* Bloomington: Indiana University Press, 1959.

————. *Southern Counterpart to Lewis & Clark: The Freeman & Custis Expedition of 1806.* Norman: University of Oklahoma Press, 2002.

Flores, Dan, ed. *The Natural West: Environmental History in the Great Plains and Rocky Mountains.* Norman: University of Oklahoma Press, 2001.

Foner, Eric. *Reconstruction: America's Unfinished Revolution, 1863–1877.* New York: HarperCollins, 1988.

Frémont, Elizabeth Benton. *Recollections of Elizabeth Benton Frémont: Daughter of the Pathfinder General John C. Frémont and Jessie Benton Frémont His Wife.* New York: Frederick H. Hitchcock, 1912.

————. *The Arizona Diary of Lily Frémont.* Edited by Mary Lee Spence. Tucson: University of Arizona Press, 1997.

Frémont, Jessie Benton. *The Story of the Guard: A Chronicle of the War.* Boston: Ticknor & Fields, 1863.

————. *How to Earn and Learn.* Boston: D. Lothrop, 1884.

————. *Souvenirs of My Time.* Boston: D. Lothrop, 1887.

————. *The Will and the Way Stories.* Boston: D. Lothrop, 1887.

————. *Far West Sketches.* Boston: D. Lothrop, 1890.

————. *The Animal Story Book.* Boston: D. Lothrop, 1898.

————. *A Year of American Travel.* San Francisco: Book Club of California, 1960

————. *Mother Lode Narratives.* Edited by Shirley Sargent. Ashland, Ore.: Lewis Osborne, 1970.

————. *Letters of Jessie Benton Frémont.* Edited by Pamela Herr and Mary Lee Spence. Urbana: University of Illinois Press, 1993.

Frémont, John. *Narrative of the Exploring Expedition to the Rocky Mountains in the Year 1842.* New York: D. Appleton, 1849.

————. *The Mariposa Estate.* London: Whittingham & Wilkins, 1861.

————. *Explorer of the American West: Memoirs of My Life.* New York: Cooper Square Press, 2001.

————. *Memoirs of My Life.* New York: Cooper Square Press, 2001.

————. *Report of the Exploring Expedition to the Rocky Mountains.* Santa Barbara, Calif.: Narrative Press, 2002.

Gardiner, Howard C. *In Pursuit of the Golden Dream.* Edited by Dale Morgan. Stoughton, Mass.: Western Hemisphere, 1970.

Gienapp, William E. *The Origins of the Republican Party, 1852–1856.* New York: Oxford University Press, 1987.

Gillis, Michael J., and Michael F. Magliari. *John Bidwell and California: The Life and Writings of Pioneer, 1841–1900.* Spokane: Arthur H. Clark, 2003.

Goetzmann, William H. *Exploration and Empire: The Explorer and the Scientist in the Winning of the American West.* New York: Alfred A. Knopf, 1966.

Goodwin, Cardinal. *John Charles Frémont: An Explanation of His Career.* Stanford, Calif.: Stanford University Press, 1930.

Goodwin, Doris Kearns. *Team of Rivals: The Political Genius of Abraham Lincoln.* New York: Simon & Schuster, 2005.

Grant, Ulysses S. *Memoirs and Selected Letters.* New York: Library of America, 1990.

Greeley, Horace. *An Overland Journey from New York to San Francisco.* New York: Saxton, Barker, 1860.

———. *The American Conflict.* Hartford: O. D. Case, 1864.

———. *The Autobiography of Horace Greeley.* New York: E. B. Treat, 1872.

Greeley and McElrath. *Life of Col. Frémont.* New York: Greeley and McElrath, 1856.

Grierson, Francis. *The Valley of Shadows.* New York: History Book Club, 1948.

Hague, Harlan, and David J. Langum. *Thomas O. Larkin: A Life of Patriotism and Profit in Old California.* Norman: University of Oklahoma Press, 1990.

Harlow, Alvin F.. *Bret Harte of the Old West.* New York: J. Messner, 1943.

Hay, John. *Lincoln and the Civil War in the Diaries and Letters of John Hay.* Edited by Tyler Dennett. New York: Dodd, Mead, 1939.

Herr, Pamela. *Jessie Benton Frémont.* Norman: University of Oklahoma Press, 1987.

Herr, Pamela, and Mary Lee Spence. *The Letters of Jessie Benton Frémont.* Urbana: University of Illinois Press, 1993.

Hoffman, David. *The Frémont Estate: An Address to the British Public.* London: Charles Richards, 1851.

Hofstadter, Richard. *The American Political Tradition and the Men Who Made It.* New York: Vintage Books, 1989.

Howard, John Raymond. *Remembrance of Things Past.* New York: Thomas Y. Crowell, 1925.

Howe, M. A. De Wolfe. *The Life and Letters of George Bancroft.* 2 vols. New York: Charles Scribner's Sons, 1908.

Hurtado, Albert L. *John Sutter: A Life on the America Frontier.* Norman: University of Oklahoma Press, 2006.

Irving, Washington. *Adventures of Captian Bonneville, USA in the Rocky Mountains and the Far West.* Norman: University of Oklahoma Press, 1961.

Isely, Jeter Allen. *Horace Greeley and the Republican Party, 1853–1861.* Princeton, N.J.: Princeton University Press, 1947.

Jackson, Donald, and Mary Lee Spence, eds. *The Expeditions of John Charles Frémont.* 3 vols. Urbana: University of Illinois Press, 1970–1980.

James, George Wharton. *Frémont in California.* Los Angeles: Out West, 1903.

Jenkinson, Clay S. *Becoming Jefferson's People: Reinventing the American Republic in the Twenty-first Century.* Reno, Nev.: Marmarth Press, 2004.

Johnson, Kenneth M. *The Frémont Court-Martial*. Los Angeles: Dawson's Book Shop, 1968.

Jones, William Carey. *First Phase of the Winning of California*. San Francisco: Bosqui, 1887.

Kearny, Thomas. *General Phillip Kearny*. New York: G. P. Putnam's Sons, 1937.

Larner, Jesse. *Mount Rushmore: An Icon Reconsidered*. New York: Thunder's Mouth Press, 2002.

Lewis, Ernest Allen. *The Frémont Cannon*. Glendale, Calif.: Arthur H. Clark, 1981.

Longfellow, Henry Wadsworth. *Life of Henry Wadsworth Longfellow*. Edited by Samuel Longfellow. Boston: Ticknor & Fields, 1886.

Mabee, Carleton. *The American Leonardo: The Life of Samuel F. B. Morse*. New York: Alfred A. Knopf, 1943.

Macartney, Clarence Edward. *Little Mac: The Life of General George B. McClellan*. Philadelphia: Dorrance, 1940.

———. *Lincoln and His Generals*. Freeport, New York: Books for Libraries Press, 1970.

Magoon, James. *Life of Major-General J. C. Frémont*. London: Beadle, 1863.

Marti, Werner H. *Messenger of Destiny: The California Adventures, 1846–1847 of Archibald H. Gillespie*. San Francisco: John Howell Books, 1960.

McLaughlin, Jack. *Jefferson and Monticello*. New York: Henry Holt, 1988.

McPherson, James. *Battle Cry of Freedom: The Civil War Era*. Oxford, UK: Oxford University Press, 1988.

———. *Abraham Lincoln and the Second American* Revolution. New York: Oxford University Press, 1991.

Meltzer, Milton, and Patricia G. Holland, eds. *Lydia Maria Child: Selected Letters, 1817–1880*. Amherst: University of Massachusetts Press, 1982.

Merck, Frederick. *Manifest Destiny and Mission in American History*. New York: Alfred A. Knopf, 1963.

Merwin, Henry C. *Life of Bret Harte*. Boston: Houghton Mifflin, 1911.

Monaghan, Jay. *Civil War on the Western Border, 1854–1865*. Boston: Little, Brown, 1955.

Nevins, Allan. *Frémont: Pathmarker of the West*. Lincoln: University of Nebraska Press, 1992.

———, ed. *Polk: The Diary of a President, 1845–1849. Covering the Mexican War, the Acquisition of Oregon, and the Conquest of California and the Southwest*. London: Longmans, Green, 1952.

Nichols, Roy Franklin. *Franklin Pierce*. Philadelphia: University of Pennsylvania Press, 1931.

———. *The Disruption of American Democracy*. New York: MacMillan Co., 1948.

Nicolay, John G., and John Hay. *Abraham Lincoln: A History*. 10 vols. New York: Century, 1890.

———, eds. *Complete Works of Abraham Lincoln*. New York: Century, 1894.

Nicollet, Joseph N. *Joseph N. Nicollet on the Plains and Prairies: The Expeditions of 1838–39*. Edited by Edmund C. Bray and Martha Coleman Bray. St. Paul, Minn.: Minnesota Historical Society Press, 1976.

Peacock, Virginia Tatnall. *Famous American Belles of the Nineteenth Century*. Philadelphia: J. P. Lippincott, 1901.

Perrett, Geoffrey. *Lincoln's War: The Untold Story of America's Greatest President as Commander in Chief*. New York: Random House, 2004.

———. *Ulysses S. Grant: Soldier & President*. New York: Random House, 1997.

Phillips, Catherine Coffin. *Jessie Benton Frémont: A Woman Who Made History*. San Francisco: J. H. Nash, 1935.

Polk, James K. *The Diary of James K. Polk during his Presidency, 1845–1849*. 4 vols. Edited by Milo Quaife. Chicago: A. C. McClurg, 1910.

Potter, David M. *The Impending Crisis: 1848–1861*. New York: Harper & Row, 1976.

Preuss, Charles. *Exploring with Frémont: The Private Diaries of Charles Preuss*. Translated and edited by Erwin G. and Elizabeth K. Gudde. Norman: University of Oklahoma Press, 1958.

Price, Willadene. *Gutzon Borglum: Artist and Patriot*. Chicago: Rand, 1961.

Rather, Lois. *Jessie Frémont at Black Point*. Oakland, Calif.: Rather Press, 1974.

Richmond, Patricia Joy. *Trail to Disaster*. Denver: Colorado Historical Society, 1989.

Rolle, Andrew. *John Charles Frémont: Character as Destiny*. Norman: University of Oklahoma Press, 1991.

Roosevelt, Theodore. *Thomas H. Benton*. Boston: Houghton Mifflin, 1889.

Rothschild, Alonzo. *Lincoln: Master of Men: A Study in Character*. Boston: Houghton Mifflin, 1906.

Ruddy, Ella Giles, ed. *The Mother of Clubs: Caroline M. Seymour Severance*. Los Angeles: Baumgardt, 1906.

Sandburg, Carl. *Abraham Lincoln: The War Years*. Vol. 1. New York: Harcourt, Brace, 1939.

Scherer, James A. B. *Thirty-first Star*. New York: G. P. Putnam's Sons, 1942.

Schlaer, Robert. *Sights Once Seen: Daguerreotyping Frémont's Last Expedition through the Rockies*. Santa Fe: Museum of New Mexico Press, 2000.

Schlesinger, Arthur M. Jr. *The Age of Jackson*. Boston: Little, Brown, 1845.

Seitz, Don Carlos. *Horace Greeley: Founder of the New York Tribune*. New York: AMS Press, 1970.

Seward, Frederick. *Seward at Washington . . . 1846–1861*. New York: Derby & Miller, 1891.

Shaff, Howard, and Audrey Karl Shaff. *Six Wars at a Time*. Sioux Falls: Center for Western Studies, 1985.

Sherman, William Tecumseh. *Memoirs of General W. T. Sherman*. New York: Library of America, 1990.

Sherwood, Glenn V. *Labor of Love: The Life and Art of Vinnie Ream*. Hygiene, Colo.: Sunshine Press Publications, 1997.

Sherwood, Midge. *Frémont: Eagle of the West*. North Hollywood, Calif.: Jackson Peak Publishers, 2002.

Smith, Elbert B. *Magnificent Missourian: The Life of Thomas Hart Benton*. Philadelphia: J. B. Lippincott, 1958.

———. *Francis Preston Blair*. New York: Free Press, 1980.

Smith, Jean Edward. *Grant*. New York: Simon & Schuster, 2001.

Smith, Rex Alan. *The Carving of Mount Rushmore*. New York: Abbeville Press, 1985.

Smucker, Samuel M. *The Life of J. C. Frémont.* New York: Muller, Orton, & Mulligan, 1856.

Starr, Kevin. *Americans and the California Dream: 1850–1915.* New York: Oxford University Press, 1973.

Stephenson, Nathaniel Wright. *Abraham Lincoln and the Union.* New Haven, Conn.: Yale University Press, 1920.

Stone, Irving. *Men to Match My Mountains: The Opening of the Far West, 1840–1900.* Garden City, N.Y.: Doubleday, 1956.

Talbot, Theodore. *Soldier in the West.* Norman: University of Oklahoma Press, 1972.

Taliaferro, John. *Great White Fathers.* New York: Perseus Books, 2002.

Tarbell, Ida M. *The Life of Abraham Lincoln.* 4 vols. New York: Lincoln History Society, 1900.

Taylor, Bayard. *Eldorado, or Adventures in the Path of Empire.* New York: Alfred A. Knopf, 1949.

Thoreau, Henry. *Writings of Henry D. Thoreau: Journal.* 2 vols. Princeton, N.J.: Princeton University Press, 1981.

Trafzer, Clifford E. *The Kit Carson Campaign: The Last Great Navajo War.* Norman: University of Oklahoma Press, 1982.

Underhill, Reuben L. *From Cowhides to Golden Fleece: A Narrative of California, 1832–1858, Based upon Unpublished Correspondence of Thomas Oliver Larkin of Monterey.* Stanford, Calif.: Stanford University Press, 1939.

Upham, Charles Wentworth. *Life, Explorations, and Public Services of John Charles Frémont.* Boston: Ticknor & Fields, 1861.

Vestal, Stanley. *Kit Carson: The Happy Warrior of the Old West.* Boston: Houghton Mifflin, 1928.

Wagoner, Jay J. *Arizona Territory, 1863–1912.* Tucson: University of Arizona Press, 1970.

Webster, Daniel. *Writings and Speeches of Daniel Webster.* 18 vols. Boston: Little, Brown, 1903.

Wendte, Charles W. *Thomas Starr King: Patriot and Preacher.* Boston: Beacon, 1921.

Whittier, John Greenleaf. *Antislavery Poems: Songs of Labor and Reform.* Boston: Houghton Mifflin, 1892.

Wilentz, Sean. *The Rise of American Democracy: Jefferson to Lincoln.* New York: W. W. Norton, 2005.

Wiltsee, Ernest A. *The Truth about Frémont: An Inquiry.* San Francisco: John Henry Nash, 1936.

Winik, Jay. *April 1865: The Month That Saved America.* New York: Perennial, 2002.

Wright, John S. *Lincoln and the Politics of Slavery.* Reno, Nev.: University of Nevada Press, 1970.

JESSIE BENTON FRÉMONT'S MAGAZINE ARTICLES

An article signed *Lisa* in answer to one signed *Vixen* in *Atlantic Monthly* (1868).

"Distinguished Persons I Have Known." *New York Ledger* (January 2, 9, 16, 23, 30, February 6, 13, 20, March 6, 27, April 3, 17, 1875).

"A Year of American Travel." *Harper's Magazine* 55–56 (1878); *Harper's New Monthly Magazine* (November and December 1877, January 1878).

"The Bodisco Wedding." *Wide Awake* 19 (1884).

"Crazy Sally: A Negro Story." *Wide Awake* 20 (1884).

"Family Life of the White House." *Wide Awake* 20 (1884).

"Mrs. Madison and Mrs. Hamilton." *Wide Awake* 20 (1884).

"My Arizona Class." *Wide Awake* 17 (1883).

"Souvenirs of My Time." *Wide Awake* 19 (1884).

"The Talent in the Napkin." *Wide Awake* 20 (1884).

"A Virginia Wedding." *Wide Awake* 19 (1884).

"Washington in Past Days." *Wide Awake* 20 (1884–1885).

"American Midshipmen at the Tomb of Napoleon." *Wide Awake* 22 (1885).

"The Big English Bull." *Wide Awake* 21 (1885).

"California." *Wide Awake* 21 (1885).

"General Grant." *Wide Awake* 21 (1885).

"Men, Women, and Things." *Wide Awake* 22 (1885).

"A Military Fete Day in Paris." *Wide Awake* 22 (1885).

"New Orleans, Panama, San Francisco." *Wide Awake* 21 (1885).

"A Nobleman of the Old Regime." *Wide Awake* 22 (1885).

"Paris." *Wide Awake* 22 (1885).

"Queen Marie Amelie." *Wide Awake* 21 (1885).

"The Queen and the Peasant." *Wide Awake* 22 (1885).

"A Queen's Drawing Room." *Wide Awake* 21 (1885).

"St. Louis." *Wide Awake* 21 (1885).

"Uncle Primas and Dog Turban." *Wide Awake* 21 (1885).

"William Rufus." *Wide Awake* 21 (1885).

"At Niblo's." *Wide Awake* 25 (1886).

"Baby's Shoe." *Wide Awake* 25 (1886).

"Hans Andersen at Home." *Wide Awake* 25 (1886).

"The Little Princess Thyra." *Wide Awake* 23 (1886).

"A Midsummer Night with Shakespeare." *Wide Awake* 23 (1885).

"A Morning Visit to the Queen of Denmark." *Wide Awake* 23 (1886).

"Salzburg." *Wide Awake* 23 (1886).

"Taffy and Buster." *Wide Awake* 25 (1886).

"Their Last Appearance." *Wide Awake* 25 (1886).

"Tied to a Christmas Tree." *Wide Awake* 25 (1886).

"Ways to Do Things." *Wide Awake* 25 (1886).

"Chist-a-Pah-ens, or Swordbreaker." *Wide Awake* 26 (1887).

"The Cruise of the *Coverlet*." *Wide Awake* 26 (1887).

"Farragut's Flagship, the *Hartford*." *Wide Awake* 26 (1887).

"Off Barnegat." *Wide Awake* 26 (1887).

"Besieged." *Wide Awake* 28 (1888).

"How the Good News Came out of the West." *Wide Awake* 28 (1888).

"My Grizzly Bear." *Wide Awake* 28 (1888).

"The Ball; and the Camp on Mt. Bullion." *Wide Awake* 29 (1889).

"Camping near the Giant Trees." *Wide Awake* 29 (1889).

"The Deck Hand." *Wide Awake* 29 (1889).

"The House That Jack Built." *Wide Awake* 29 (1889).

"Kit Carson." *Wide Awake* 29 (1889).

"A Long Horror." *Wide Awake* 29 (1889).

"A Picnic Near the Equator." *Wide Awake* 29 (1889).

"Play and Work." *Wide Awake* 29 (1889).

"Sierra Neighbors." *Wide Awake* 29 (1889).

"Snowshoe Thompson." *Wide Awake* 29 (1889).

"The Good Samaritan." *Wide Awake* 31 (1890).

"The Hat of the Postmaster." *Wide Awake* 31 (1890).

"Miss Miller." *Wide Awake* 31 (1890).

"The Two Wills." *Wide Awake* 31 (1890).

"The Origin of the Frémont Explorations." *Century Illustrated Monthly Magazine* 41: 766–771 (March 1891).

"A Home Lost and Found." *Home-Maker Magazine* (1892).

"Sterilized Milk as Food." *S. S. McClure Newspaper Syndicate* (1892).

"California and Frémont." *Land of Sunshine* 4 (December 1895): 3–14.

"Dolores." *Land of Sunshine* 7 (1897): 3–4.

"Senator Thomas H. Benton." *Independent* 55 (January 29, 1903): 240–244.

"Kit Carson." *Historical Society of Southern California Quarterly* 42 (1960): 331–334.

PERIODICALS

Benton, Thomas Hart. Selections of editorial articles from the St. Louis Enquirer on the subject of Oregon and Texas. St. Louis: Missourian Office, 1844.

———. Three speeches on the subject of the annexation of Texas. New York, 1844.

Bidwell, John. "Life in California before the Gold Discovery." *Century Illustrated Monthly Magazine* 41 (n.s.) (December 1890): 163–183.

———. "Frémont in the Conquest of California." *Century Illustrated Monthly Magazine* 41 (February 1891): 518–525.

Buchanan, James. "The Official Policy for the Acquisition of California." *Century Illustrated Monthly Magazine* 41 (April 1891): 928–929.

Calhoun, Robert Dabney. "The Taensa Indians: The French Explorers and Catholic Missionaries in the Taensa Country." *Louisiana Historical Quarterly* 17, part 3 (October 1934): 642–679.

Collier, L. T. "Recollections of Thomas H. Benton." *Missouri Historical Review* 8 (1914):136–141.

Colton, Kenneth E., ed. "With Frémont in Missouri in 1861: Letters to Samuel Ryan Curtis." *Annals of Iowa* 24, 3rd Series.

Cox, Isaac J. "The Louisiana-Texas Frontier during the Burr Conspiracy." *Mississippi Valley Historical Review* 10 (December 1923): 274–284.

Davis, Rebecca Harding. "In Remembrance." *The Independent* (January 29, 1903).

Drew, Thomas. "Senator Benton Lays His Plans." *California Historical Society* 13, no. 2.

Duffus, Robert L. "Frémont and Jessie." *American Mercury* (November 1925): 289–297.

Fireman, Bert M. "Frémont's Arizona Adventure." *American West* 1 (Winter 1964): 8–19.

Frémont, John. "The Conquest of California." *Century Illustrated Monthly Magazine* 41 (April 1891): 917–928.

Gates, Paul W. "The Frémont-Jones Scramble for California Land Claims." *Southern California Quarterly* 56 (1974): 13–44.

Gillespie, Archibald. "Further Letters." *California Historical Society Quarterly* 18, no. 3.

Harrington, F. H. "Frémont and the North Americans." *American Historical Review* 44 (1939).

Hubbell, Thelma Lee, and Gloria R. Lothrop. "The Friday Morning Club: A Los Angeles Legacy." *Southern California Quarterly* 50 (1968): 59–90.

Jackson, Donald. "The Myth of the Frémont Howitzer." *Bulletin of the Missouri Historical Society* 23 (1966–1967): 205–214.

James, E. M. "Some of the Romance of Frémont." *Overland* 89 (1931).

Jensen, Joan M. "After Slavery: Caroline Severance in Los Angeles." *Southern California Quarterly* 48 (1966): 175–186.

Margaret C. "Jessie Benton Frémont." Obituary in *Land of Sunshine* (January 1903).

Lummis, Charles E. "Borglum and His Work." *Land of Sunshine* 4.

McGehee, Micajah. "Rough Times in Rough Places: A Personal Narrative of the Terrible Experiences of Frémont's Fourth Expedition." *Century Illustrated Monthly Magazine* 41 (March 1891): 771–780.

Nicolay, John G., and John Hay. "Abraham Lincoln: A History. The Advance, Bull Run, Frémont. Military Emancipation." *Century Illustrated Quarterly* 36, issue 2 (June 1888): 292–305.

Oliphant, John A. "Recollections of Thomas H. Benton." *Missouri Historical Review* 14 (1920): 433–435.

Petrulionis, Sandra Harbert. "Jessie Ann Benton Frémont." *Legacy: A Journal of American Women Writers* (June 2001): Legacy Profile.

Rolle, Andrew. "Exploring an Explorer: Psychohistory and John Charles Frémont *Pacific Historical Review* 51 (1982): 135–163.

Royee, Josiah. "Frémont." *Atlantic Monthly* 66 (1890): 548–557.

———. "Light on the Seizure of California." *Century Illustrated Monthly Magazine* 40 (September 1890): 702–794.

———. "Montgomery and Frémont: New Documents on the Bear Flag Affair." *Century Illustrated Monthly Magazine* 41 (March 1891): 780–783.

Smith, William E. "The Blairs and Frémont." *Missouri Historical Review* 23, no. 2 (January 1923): 214–260.

Spence, Mary Lee. "The Frémonts and Utah." *Utah Historical Quarterly* 44 (Summer 1976): 286–302.

———. "David Hoffman: Frémont's Mariposa Agent in London." *Southern California Quarterly* 60 (1978): 379–403.

———. "Jessie Benton Frémont: First Lady of Arizona." *Journal of Arizona History* 24 (1983): 55–72.

Stenberg, Richard R. "Polk and Frémont, 1845–1846." *Pacific Historical Review* 7 (1938): 211–227.

Tays, George. "Frémont Had No Secret Instructions." *Pacific Historical Review* 9 (1940): 157–171.

Volpe, Vernon. "The Frémonts and Emancipation in Missouri." *Historian* 56, no. 2 (1994): 339–354.

Wheat, Francis M. "Senator Benton Lays His Plans: Some Newly Discovered Material on the Frémont Court-Martial. *California Historical Society Quarterly* 8 (June 1934): 150–154.

Manuscript Collections

Library of Congress

Francis Preston Blair Papers
Edward William Bok Papers
John Gutzon Borglum Papers
Simon Cameron Papers
Horace Greeley Papers
Vinnie Ream Hoxie Papers
Abraham Lincoln Papers
Miscellaneous Manuscript Collection
Joseph Nicollet Papers
Joel Poinsett Papers
James K. Polk Papers
Horace Sawyer Papers
Theodore Talbot Papers
Gideon Welles Papers

New-York Historical Society

John Frémont Files, Jessie Benton Frémont files, Thomas Hart Benton files in Miscellaneous Manuscripts, James Wright Brown Collection

New York Public Library

John Bigelow Papers, "U.S.S. Congress;" John Charles and Jessie Benton Frémont file in Personal Miscellaneous Manuscripts, Horace Greeley Papers, Ferdinand R. Hassler Papers, David Hoffman Papers, Lee Kohns Collection, Thomas F. Madigan Collection.

"Frémont's Hundred Days" by M. F. Hixon (copy of manuscript at New York Public Library).

Princeton University

Blair-Lee Papers

Southwest Museum (Los Angeles)

Frémont Collection

University of California, Berkeley (Bancroft Library)

Irving Stone Papers
Alfred Baldwin Recollections
Hubert Howe Bancroft miscellaneous manuscripts
Letters from Thomas Hart Benton to his daughters
Galen Clark "Reminiscences"
Elizabeth Benton Frémont's notebook
Letters and autobiographical writings of Jessie Benton Frémont
Jessie Frémont: unpublished "Memoirs" and "Additions to the Memoirs"
Jessie and John Frémont II: MS: "Great Events during the life of John C. Frémont."
  Bancroft Library. University of California, Berkeley.
Letters and memoranda, John C. Frémont
John Charles Frémont Papers
Frémont Family Papers
James Alexander Forbes Papers
William Gilpin dictation and biographical material
Senator William Gwin's manuscripts
John Hittell Papers
Thomas Starr King Papers
Official Correspondence, Thomas Larkin
Thomas Oliver Larkin Papers
Joseph William McKay Recollections
Jacques Antoine Moerenhout Papers
Letters from Dr. Morton and Charles Frémont re John Frémont's death
Allan Nevins collection of newspaper articles
Henry Lebbeus Oak Correspondence and Papers
Isaac Pettijohn Diary
Charles Preuss Diaries
George Stewart, "Frémont Anecdotes"
Johann Sutter "Personal Reminiscences"

U.S. Government Documents and Publications

James K. Polk. "Occupation of Mexican Territory." Message from the president to
  the two houses of Congress, 29th Cong., 2d Sess., (December 22, 1846). House
  Executive Document 19 (serial 499).
Republican John P. C. Shanks, speech in the U.S. House of Representatives, "Vin-
  dication of Major General John C. Frémont against the Attacks of the Slave
  Power and Its Allies." Washington, D.C.: Scammell & Co., 1862.
U.S. Congress Joint Committee on the Conduct of the War. "Department of the
  West." (1862).

"Charges and specifications and findings and sentence of a general court martial in the case of Lietuenant Colonel John C. Frémont." Washington, 1848.

"War of the Rebellion: A Compilation of the Official Records of the Union and Confederate Armies." Official Records Series 1, vol. 3.

DISSERTATION

Crampton, C. Gregory. "The Opening of the Mariposa Mining Region, 1849–1859, with Particular Reference to the Mexican Land Grant of John Charles Frémont." Ph.D. diss., University of California, Berkeley (1941).

NEWSPAPERS

Daily Union, Washington, D.C. (June 16, 17, 18, 19, 26, 1845; May 26, June 15, December 9, 1846; February 12, 1847).

Jefferson Enquirer. On the return of Frémont (September 9, 1847).

London Daily Telegraph. Obituary of Frémont. (July 16, 1890).

Los Angeles Times. Obituary of Jessie Frémont (December 28, 31, 1902).

New York Evening Post. Article by Josiah Royce in answer to Frémont. (January 20, 1890).

New York Independent. Obituary of Jessie Benton Frémont. (January 29, 1903).

Washington Post. "Half-forgotten Romances of History." (September 24, 1934).

INDEX

A NOTE ON THE AUTHOR

Sally Denton is the author of *Faith and Betrayal*, *American Massacre*, *The Bluegrass Conspiracy*, and, with Roger Morris, *The Money and the Power*. She has been the recipient of a Guggenheim Fellowship, two Western Heritage awards, a Lannan Literary Grant, and the Nevada Silver Pen Award. Her award-winning investigative reporting has appeared in the *New York Times*, the *Washington Post*, and *American Heritage*. She lives with her three sons in Santa Fe, New Mexico.